Earlham College

A History, 1847–1997

Thomas D. Hamm

<small>WITH THE ASSISTANCE OF</small>

Jason Alberts, Killian Barefoot, Mary Katherine Carey,

Erica Christianson, Gwendolyn Gosney, Jessica Hedrick,

William Henry, Robert Micheli, Aaron Parker,

Rebecca Sedam, Emily Smith, Ellen Swain,

Robert Winternitz, and

Amity Wood

<small>INDIANA UNIVERSITY PRESS</small>
<small>BLOOMINGTON & INDIANAPOLIS</small>

The paper used in this publication meets the minimum
requirements of American National Standard for Information
Sciences—Permanence of Paper for Printed Library Materials,
ANSI Z39.48-1984.

Manufactured in the United States of America

Library of Congress Cataloging-in-Publication Data

Hamm, Thomas D.
   Earlham College : a history, 1847–1997 / Thomas D. Hamm
with the assistance of Jason Alberts . . . [et al.].
         p.   cm.
   Includes bibliographical references and index.
   ISBN 0-253-33256-7 (alk. paper)
   1. Earlham College—History.   I. Title.
LD1741.E4H36   1997
378.772'63—dc20   96–46171
         1 2 3 4 5   02 01 00 99 98 97

In memory of

Jackson Bailey

(1925–1996)

PREFACE *xi*
ACKNOWLEDGMENTS *xv*

1

Friends Boarding School, near
Richmond, Indiana,
1832–1859

1

2

Earlham's Surrender to the
Larger Culture,
1859–1895

35

3

Quakerism, Modernism, Professionalism,
Professor Russell, and
President Kelly,
1895–1915

82

Contents

4

The Trials of Liberal Quakerism,
1915–1946
117

5

The Creation of Modern Earlham,
1946–1958
178

6

"The Sixties,"
1958–1973
233

7

Earlham and the Culture Wars,
1973–1996
290

NOTES *347*
BIBLIOGRAPHY *417*
INDEX *437*

Illustrations

1. *Friends Boarding School in 1855*   15
2. *Joseph Moore*   67
3. *Dougan Clark*   78
4. *Elbert Russell*   84
5. *Robert L. Kelly*   91
6. *David M. Edwards*   120
7. *Clarence Pickett and Alexander Purdy*   140
8. *William C. Dennis*   146
9. *Tom Jones*   184
10. *Landrum Bolling*   236

Preface

*Q*uaker history is full of paradoxes, and none are more striking than those of Quaker education. While Friends are generally perceived as sympathetic to intellectual life, Quakerism had at its roots a strong anti-intellectualism. Known for their schools, Friends waited two centuries after their rise in England in the 1640s before they founded colleges. When Quakers finally did establish institutions of higher education, it was in the face of constant fears that they would become theological seminaries producing the classically learned clergy that Friends eschewed. Ironically, a century later, Quaker colleges would find themselves criticized by Friends because they were not turning out pastors for what was in many places now known as the Friends Church.

Nowhere are the paradoxes of Quaker education more apparent than at Earlham College in Richmond, Indiana. Founded as Friends Boarding School in 1847, it became in 1859 the second Quaker college in the world. It was established to provide a "guarded religious education for the children of Friends," according to the Discipline of the Society of Friends. In the original vision of Friends, that meant going against the grain of the larger society, being consciously different from "the world," as we would say today, *countercultural*.

Since 1859, both Indiana Friends and the college they founded have come to terms with "the world." For Indiana Quakers, that has meant giving up nearly all of the peculiarities that once distinguished them, and becoming much like other Protestant denominations. For Earlham, that has meant becoming much more like other colleges. By 1900, a visitor to campus would have found students and a curriculum not much different from those in other colleges. Similarly, the faculty, increasingly specialized by graduate training, took their cues from the larger world. It was a process that would be repeated in hundreds of church-affiliated colleges across the United States. By the late twentieth century, many would be completely secularized. The process, one that is now the subject of consider-able scholarly interest, has been complex, a combination of intel-lectual change emphasizing a hard, scientific "objectivity" that saw religious doctrine as a barrier to the pursuit of truth, and social forces that focused many colleges increasingly on career prepara-tion. Those schools that retained strong religious identities, often conceiving themselves as "Christian" colleges, were more and more marginalized by the educational establishment and the larger society.[1]

Earlham's story has been different. Financially struggling for much of its life, it is now well-endowed. Once content to be a respectable midwestern church school, it is now a nationally ranked liberal arts college, drawing students from across the United States and around the world. Earlham is still in important ways at odds with "the world," but often now with neighboring Quakers as well. Through all of its changes, however, it has retained its sense of itself as a Quaker place. That sense has changed over time—it was different in 1900 from what it had been in 1847, and it is very different now from what it was a century or even half a century ago. The struggle to maintain that self-understanding and definition, and the changes in what it has meant for Earlham to be a Quaker college, are the themes of this work.

This focus has required me to be both expansive and narrow. It means that in order to understand what was happening at Earlham, one must have a sense of developments in the larger worlds of religion and higher education. It also has required sensitivity to the worlds of students, faculty, and the Quakers who appointed the trustees who governed the school. As will be seen, much of Earlham's history has been a struggle among these groups. At the same time, I have excluded elements of the college history that are not directly relevant to understanding the evolution of Earlham's understanding of itself as a Quaker place. That has meant, for example, not follow-ing the careers of numerous alumni who have distinguished them-selves in myriad fields. It has also meant limiting attention to athlet-ics, except as sports reflect student culture. Much of the story of Earlham's living history museum, Conner Prairie, also falls outside the scope of this history, with the hope that it will soon find the historian that it deserves. While no history of Earlham as a Quaker institution would be complete without attention to the Earlham School of Religion, its story for its first twenty-five years has already been well told by Wilmer Cooper, its founding dean, and I refer readers to his work for a more detailed account.[2]

To make sense of Earlham's history, one must have some understanding of the Society of Friends. Its history and peculiarities will be described in some detail throughout the work, but here follows a brief description of its organization.

1. The individual Quaker congregation was called a *meeting.* At the time Earlham was founded, most individual congregations were called *preparative meetings,* since they prepared business for the

2. *Monthly Meeting.* The monthly meeting was (and is) the basic Quaker organizational unit. It has the power to receive, transfer, and disown (the Quaker term for excommunicate) members, solemnize marriages, and hold property. Usually a monthly meeting was made up of several preparative meetings. Two or more monthly meetings, in turn, made up a

3. *Quarterly Meeting.* The quarterly meeting, as the name implies, met for business four times a year. It dealt with matters of doctrine and organization deemed too important to be left to monthly meetings. By the mid-nineteenth century, many quarterly meetings were establishing academies, schools that would be vital to Earlham's development. Several quarterly meetings made up a

4. *Yearly Meeting.* The yearly meeting was, until 1902, the highest level of authority for Friends who lived within its limits. It set basic doctrinal standards, and served as a court of final appeal in cases of disownment. No yearly meeting had power over another, but intricate ties of kinship, correspondence, and traveling ministers bound them together. It is important to keep in mind that yearly meeting names can be misleading. For example, when Friends Boarding School opened in 1847, there were two yearly meetings of Orthodox Friends west of the Appalachians, Ohio and Indiana. Ohio included Friends in western Pennsylvania and eastern Ohio. Indiana stretched from the Scioto River in central Ohio to west of the Mississippi.[3]

Acknowledgments

A few years ago, I told an old college friend that my current
project was a history of Earlham. He reminded me that writing
in-house institutional histories was not how one advanced a scholarly career. While not convinced of the truth of that admonition, I
have kept it in mind while writing this book, hopeful that it is in
keeping with the spirit of Earlham, where so many people for so
many years have had goals other than personal advancement.

When I interviewed for a position at Earlham in 1987, the possibility of writing such a work was put to me, and I received a more formal
commission from President Richard J. Wood and Provost Len Clark in
1990. They wanted a new history to mark Earlham's sesquicenten-
nial in 1997, but they also made it clear that it would be my own
interpretation for which I would seek my own publisher. They read a
draft of chapter 7 and offered some suggestions, but they have been
absolutely scrupulous in avoiding any attempt to limit what I chose to
write on and how I chose to deal with it. Earlham was also generous
providing funds from its Professional Development Fund that allowed me to travel, especially to do oral history interviews.

My greatest debt is to fourteen remarkable Earlham students with
whom I worked on aspects of this history. Earlham is fortunate to
have two funds, one provided by the Ford Foundation, the other by
the Knight Foundation, to make possible joint faculty-student research projects. In 1990, I worked with Erica Christianson, Jessica
Hedrick, Robert Micheli, Rebecca Sedam, and Ellen Swain on Earlham in the Tom Jones Era. In 1991, I worked with Killian Barefoot,
Mary Katherine Carey, William Henry, Aaron Parker, and Robert
Winternitz on Earlham as a Quaker institution. In 1993, in conjunc-
tion with my History Department colleague Alice Shrock, I studied
Earlham in the 1960s with Jason Alberts, Gwendolyn Gosney, Emily
Smith, and Amity Wood. Their research is cited at appropriate places.

Their observations and questions made my understanding of Earlham's history far deeper than it would be otherwise.

It is my good fortune to have a joint appointment at Earlham that makes me part of both the Library and History faculties. The two library directors, Evan Farber and Thomas Kirk, have been remarkably supportive of this work. They, with Associate Librarian Philip Shore, have also been a treasure of useful memories. The same should be said of my colleagues in the History Department, especially Randall and Alice Shrock, Peter Cline, Jackson Bailey, and Robert Southard, who not only introduced me to Earlham but also have given me a sense of the place over the past fifty years. My assistant in the Earlham Friends Collection, Ellen Stanley, is now in her third stint at Earlham. Her knowledge of the college goes back to 1940, and she has always been willing to put it to use.

I met with unfailing kindness at the hands of all those from whom I sought information or aid. The bibliography includes a list of the alumni and faculty who shared memories in letters or on tape. For kindnesses in my travels and other aid I am especially grateful to Ralph and Martha (Calvert) Slotten, Joe and Jean (Hamm) Balestrieri, Laurence and Ruth Strong, Harold and Ann Cope, and Mary L. Baldwin.

This work is better for the number of people who commented on drafts. My Earlham colleagues Paul Lacey, Evan Farber, Stephanie Crumley-Effinger, and Randall and Alice Shrock read the entire work, offering numerous suggestions, corrections, and helpful memories. They have saved me from a number of embarrassing mistakes. Those who read portions of the manuscript and offered reactions and comments include Franklin Wallin, Landrum Bolling, Jackson Bailey, William Fuson, Warren Staebler, Ellen Stanley, Hugh Barbour, Thomas D.S. Bassett, Josiah C. Russell, Yuan Tien, Roy Shuckman, Robert and Grace (Cunningham) McAllester, Martha (Burns) Rush, Lee Chalfant, David Brock, Don Garner, David W. Dennis, and Horace and Vera Smith. They are not to blame for any oversights or errors of fact; those failings are solely my own.

I must acknowledge my debt to someone I met only once, long before I came to Earlham, Opal Thornburg. As Earlham's archivist from 1958 to 1975, she was responsible for gathering and preserving much of the material that is the basis for this work. Earlhamites will know her as the author of the college's first history, *Earlham: The Story of the College, 1847–1962*, which appeared in 1963. My interpretation of a number of events is somewhat different from Thornburg's, but again and again, as I have worked with the same sources she examined, I have been impressed with her incisiveness and thoroughness. This book would be much weaker without hers.

Finally, I thank my gentlest and most supportive reader and critic, my wife, Mary Louise Reynolds. My long-delayed acquisition of word processing skills meant that this is my first book that she did not type, but she has nurtured it, and me, and we are both the better for it.

Friends Boarding School, near Richmond, Indiana

1832–1859

*A*ny historian faces the question of where to begin the story. Earlham College regards 1847 as its beginning, but its roots go much farther back. To understand how and why there came to be an Earlham College, one must understand the lives and experiences of the Quakers who es-tablished it, their spiritual and intellectual heritage, and especially the tortuous evolution of Quaker attitudes toward higher education. Earlham is the fruit of a dual Quaker concern for practicality and morality, that is seen again and again in Quaker, and Earlham, history.

It is not especially difficult to understand why the Friends Boarding School that became Earlham College was established in the vicinity of Richmond, Indiana. It was one of the fruits of the great migration of Friends into Indiana and Ohio in the first third of the nineteenth century.

This migration was mostly from the South, from Virginia, the Carolinas, Georgia, and Tennessee, particularly North Carolina. By 1830, the Quaker communities of South Carolina and Georgia had disappeared, while those in other southern states had been so weakened that they would not recover until the twentieth century. In turn, by 1860, Indiana would equal Pennsylvania in its Quaker population, and Richmond would rival Philadelphia as a spiritual and intellectual center of the Society of Friends.[1]

The impetus for this westward movement was both practical and moral. Friends were not immune to the same economic forces that drove their neighbors westward. Friends were overwhelmingly farmers, and by 1800 the lands they had worked, in some cases for four generations, were almost exhausted. They were also relatively high in price, so that only the wealthiest could hope to achieve the dream of all rural folk, to see their children settled on farms around them. Thus it was natural that the fertile, relatively cheap lands west of the mountains drew Quakers.[2]

When southern Friends moved over the mountains, however, they did not go due west or south, into Alabama or Kentucky. Instead, they came north, and here moral considerations were paramount, most vitally Quaker opposition to slavery.[3]

By the 1780s, all of the yearly meetings of Friends in America had determined that slavery was an intolerable wrong, that Friends who owned slaves must free them or lose their membership. (Not a few Quaker slaveholders chose the latter.) In the South, the large number of Quakers who did emancipate or attempt to emancipate slaves, however, created hostility in non-Quaker neighbors, who saw the sympathy of Friends for blacks as a threat to white hegemony. In several counties in North Carolina in the 1790s, grand juries vilified Friends. Typical was a presentment from Chowan County that argued "that the country is reduced to a situation of great peril and danger, in consequence of the society of people called Quakers." The grand jurors, doubtless slaveholders themselves, raged that "the idea of emancipation amongst slaves is publically held out to them, and encouraged by the conduct of the Quakers—that the minds of the slaves are not only greatly corrupted, and alienated from the minds of their masters, in consequence of said conduct, but runaways are protected, harboured, and encouraged by them." Given such hostility, it was not surprising that southern Friends began to look to lands where slavery could not exist, as in the Northwest Territory.[4]

Slavery was a more complex issue for Friends than simply abstaining from evil, however. Quakers were convinced that a world in which slaves were held was a threat to their own. It pitted sensuality, indulgence, and violence against morality, self-discipline, and peace. Thus Quakers leaving the South wrote of departing out of "Egyptian darkness." Some of their fears were apocalyptic. Friends almost *fled* South Carolina and Georgia in 1802 and 1803 after a visit from Zacharias Dicks, a minister who had a vision that slave rebellion and war, the righteous judgments of an angry God, would ravage those guilty places. Other Friends recorded their fears that if they remained in the South, their children might marry slaveowners and not only be lost to Quakerism, but become part of slaveowning society and embrace its abhorrent values. Thus many Friends came north with a sense of divine mission. One wrote that when she "croste [sic] the Ohio River" she "could not compare [her] feelings to nothing else but like one set free from bondage."[5]

So Friends moved west. Most of those leaving the South before 1812 found new homes in western Ohio, especially in Clinton, Warren, Preble, and Miami counties. It was not until 1806 that Friends came into the Indiana Territory, and their first settlement, at the site of what would become Richmond, formed at least partly because of Quaker conscience. One of the Friends who had come up from North Carolina, Andrew Hoover, was uneasy on his Ohio farm. The land was part of the Virginia Military District, set aside by that state for grants to its Revolutionary soldiers. In his son Henry's words, Andrew Hoover "did not approve of the mode by which these lands were obtained, giving poor soldiers land for killing the poor Indians."[6]

Instead, the Hoovers and the other Friends found a home on the Whitewater River. The prominence among Friends of Andrew Hoover and of Jeremiah Cox and John Smith, who accompanied him with their families into the new territory, in turn drew other Friends. By 1809, there were about three hundred, enough to compose a new monthly meeting called Whitewater. The War of 1812 halted the influx of Quakers into newly formed Wayne County, but after 1815 there was a flood out of North Carolina and Ohio into Indiana. By 1821, when Indiana Yearly Meeting was formed of Friends in Indiana and western Ohio, there were ten monthly meetings in the state of Indiana. By 1830 the number had doubled, and for the next three decades it continued to grow, as Friends moved into the northern part of the state.[7]

The Friends who formed Indiana Yearly Meeting and swelled its membership in the 1820s and 1830s shared a vision of the kinds of communities they would form. That vision found its most complete expression in the Discipline, the compendium of custom and regulation that bounded the lives of all Friends. The greatest good was to keep Friends separate from "the world," confined by a wall of peculiarities that helped Quakers live lives acceptable to God.[8]

Custom and the Discipline set Friends apart from their neighbors in a variety of ways. Some of the differences were theological. While Friends were firmly Christian, they were at odds with the dominant evangelical culture on certain vital points. Difficult for non-Friends to grasp was the Quaker understanding of the Inner Light, George Fox's "opening" that "every man was enlightened by the divine light of Christ . . . and they that believed in it came out of condemnation to the light of Christ . . . and became children of it." Friends believed that salvation came gradually, by growth into a state of holiness. This was very different, of course, from evangelical Christians, who saw salvation as coming through an instantaneous conversion experience, and who were increasingly speaking of a second instantaneous experience in which they attained sanctification, or holiness.[9]

Equally strange to the sensibilities of their neighbors were Quaker ways of worship. There was no pastor or minister in charge of the service. Instead, Friends gathered in a barn-like, utterly unornamented building that they called a meetinghouse. Men sat on one side, women on the other. Facing them at the front sat the "weighty" Friends, those distinguished by gifts of leadership and spiritual discernment. Friends would sit in silence in the belief that if it were the will of God, the Holy Spirit would lead someone to speak. In theory that might be anyone, but in practice only a few ever did so. Meetings recognized that certain people, both men and women, had a particular gift for speaking "in the ministry," and so Friends recognized that gift by "recording" it. Being a recorded minister gave one status in the society, but nothing resembling pastoral authority or control. Some meetings, especially large ones like Whitewater, had several ministers, while other meetings had none, and might go for years without breaking the silence, unless a minister from another meeting visited. As influential as recorded ministers, and charged with oversight of them, were the elders. Each monthly meeting had several.[10]

Most visible among Quaker peculiarities was the plain life, an amalgam of custom and practice going back to the seventeenth century. Friends were immediately distinguishable by their dress: the drab colors, the broad-brimmed, high-crowned hats of the men, the "plain bonnets," usually of "dove-colored" silk, of the women. There was also their speech, the distinctive "thee" and "thy," the use of numbers instead of the "pagan" names of the days of the week and the months of the year. (Sunday was thus "First Day," January "First Month," etc.) Friends eschewed most amusements. Like many other Protestants, they condemned dancing, games of chance, and drunkenness—by the 1830s American Friends were rapidly moving to endorse total abstinence. In this respect, Quakers were more exacting than almost any of their neighbors. They discouraged the reading of "plays, romances, and novels, which being written by persons of corrupt minds, have a tendency to awaken and invigorate . . . impure propensities." Music was also under the ban, in meeting or out, as a "sop to the senses," a distraction from the pursuit of holiness. One of the chief "hedges" around Friends was the requirement that they marry within the group. To marry a non-Friend, or to marry another Friend in a non-Quaker ceremony, "contrary to discipline," in Quaker parlance, brought the ultimate sanction, loss of membership by being "read out of meeting," or disownment. Peculiarity extended even into death, as Friends discouraged the erection of tombstones and required that markers in their burying grounds be small and unornamented.[11]

For many Friends, the ideal community was a closed one, set off from the rest of the world. "When I and other Friends came here to found this New Settlement," one Indiana Friend said, "we came with the fixed determination to keep ourselves and our homes unspotted from the world." In many cases they were successful; one ex-Quaker from Indiana wrote that "a community of Quakers is almost a world within itself. It is as nearly separated from the world without . . . as any circle of mortals well can be." The requirement that Friends marry within the group created closely knit groups bound by ties of kinship. In Spiceland Monthly Meeting in Indiana, for example, in 1842 over half of the adult members, 164 of 276 men and women, were members of just nine extended families.[12]

However closely knit Quaker communities might be, there was always rebellion, particularly among younger Friends. There is ample evidence that many, while they might be birthright members, members because they were born into Quaker families, were quite willing to flout the Discipline, often in dramatic ways. This took a toll in disownments. Revealing are statistics from Whitewater Monthly Meeting. Between 1809 and 1860 it disowned 716 members, most of them under age 30. Of these, over a third were disowned for "marriage contrary to discipline." Ministers and elders worried, and the yearly meeting mourned, how many younger members appeared light and giddy, apparently unconcerned about true religion.[13]

Unruly youths were not the only source of anxiety among Indiana Friends. In the 1820s, they found themselves badly split by doctrinal controversy. The spiritual battle began in the East. Its immediate focus was an elderly Quaker minister from Long Island, Elias Hicks, although the conflict also involved issues of power, leadership, authority, and economics. Hicks, in his preaching, exalted the Inner Light, minimizing, although by no means denying, the divinity of Christ and the authority of Scripture. In the eyes of Hicks and his supporters, who, naturally, became known as Hicksites, the great problem facing Friends was the influx of dangerously un-Quakerly ideas from contact with evangelical Protestants. The foremost need was thus a reformation that would return Friends to the first principles of George Fox.[14]

For a majority of American Quakers, including most in Indiana, however, Hicks's views were not primitive Quakerism revived, but dangerous infidelity, the fruit of the influence of Thomas Paine and Fanny Wright. Charles Osborn, one of Indiana Yearly Meeting's leading ministers, was typical in holding forth that the "spirit of separation, imbibed and held by the followers of Elias Hicks," was "Anti-Christ, and those who promulgated it, . . . evil men and seducers." Indiana Yearly Meeting helped polarize the two sides in the fall of 1827 by issuing a "Testimony and Epistle of Advice" that caustically condemned Hicksite views as "wholly repugnant to our religious profession and subversive of the principles of the Christian religion."[15]

These differences brought bitter separations in five of eight yearly meetings of Friends in North America, starting with Philadelphia in the spring of 1827, followed by New York, Baltimore, Ohio, and Indiana. In Ohio, the separation climaxed in a full-scale riot in which the clerk of the yearly meeting had a rib broken when his table was torn apart by the two parties trying to gain possession of it. In Indiana, the Hicksites were a distinct minority, about 3,000 out of 18,000 members concentrated in relatively few meetings. Even so, the separation bred hard feelings. In one meeting, a Hicksite left proclaiming that "Elias Hicks is as good a man as Jesus Christ and that a certain approved minister aught [*sic*] to be killed." The clerk of the Orthodox yearly meeting found his father a Hicksite, while his stepmother remained an Orthodox minister.[16]

The separation had lasting effects in the Orthodox yearly meeting, and one of the results was a new view of education and learning. Among Orthodox Friends, there was a widespread sense that the separation was the fruit, in part, of ignorance—ignorance of the Bible, ignorance of basic Christianity, ignorance of the historic doctrines of Friends. Thus for the next two decades Indiana Friends attempted to deal with these needs in various ways. They encouraged meetings to build up libraries, filled with "sound" books approved by the Meeting for Sufferings, the yearly meeting's equivalent of an executive committee. Many supported the work of the Bible Association of Friends, which tried to make sure that every Quaker family had a complete copy of the Scriptures. There was also a growing interest in Sunday Schools, or, as Friends referred to them, "First Day Schools for Scriptural Instruction," as a means of inculcating biblical learning and sound doctrine in the rising generation.[17]

Finally, Orthodox Friends looked to Quaker schools, "for the education of our children," as a bulwark against the encroachments of "the world" and its temptations and infidelities. Here they drew on a complicated and uncertain heritage.

The Problem of Quaker Education

The legacy of the first generation of Friends on educational matters was mixed. On one hand, early Quakers were inveterate enemies of ignorance and dedicated founders of schools. On the other, they were suspicious of much of the educational culture of their day, especially of classical learning as they saw it in the British universities.

Two dicta of George Fox are the key to understanding Friends. One was his view of the ministry, often repeated by Friends, that "being bred up at Oxford and Cambridge did not make a minister of Jesus Christ." Friends were intensely fearful of anything suggesting that "head learning" could be a substitute for knowledge gained through obedience to the Inner Light, or that secular education was comparable to being "scholars in the school of Christ." The fact that Friends utterly repudiated a clerical class meant that there would not be an emphasis on theological education, and in fact they were fearful of anything that suggested it.[18]

On the other hand, Fox also, in a famous 1668 statement, urged Friends to establish schools for boys and girls to instruct them "in whatever things were civil and useful in creation." By 1691, there were fifteen Quaker schools in England. In 1695 London Yearly Meeting urged each of its quarterly meetings to establish a school. By 1758, the number of Quaker schools in England had grown to twenty, with several more in Ireland. It was not until 1779, however, that the yearly meeting itself established a boarding school, in this case Ackworth in Yorkshire. The impetus for Ackworth was a perceived need to provide for "members of the Society not in affluence."[19]

Historians have advanced a variety of explanations for this Quaker interest in founding schools. Since a fair number of early converts to Quakerism had been schoolmasters, it was natural that they would want to carry on their livelihoods, yet as Friends opportunities would otherwise have been limited. Since Friends were generally of the "middling" classes, disproportionately involved in trade or business, they had practical needs for basic literacy and numeracy. And, as Quaker educator Leonard Kenworthy has argued, since Friends could not look to an educated clerical class for leadership, it was all the more important for them to have a generally educated membership.[20]

The beliefs of Friends would bound and define that education, and those bounds were often the subject of discussion and debate. Friends were not opposed to many of the elements of the traditional classical education. Latin and Greek, for example, were, in the words of one Friend, useful "for the management of Foreign Transactions and Negotiations and Correspondence with other nations." Similarly, they saw value in studying Hebrew, since it was profitable for Scriptural study. However, in acquiring these languages, Friends agreed "to lay aside the Heathenish books" and instead "set up the Scriptures of Truth, and Friends books given forth from the Spirit of Truth, and what may be savoury and wholesome good matter." Overall, Quaker education placed far greater emphasis on the vernacular than on the dead languages. The classics were never at the center of a "civil and useful" Quaker education. As William Penn urged for his children, learning should be "liberal," but it should also "be useful knowledge, such as is consistent with Truth and Godliness, not cherishing a vain conversation or idle mind." Thus Quaker education emphasized natural science and mathematics more than did most contemporary schools.[21]

Whatever the intellectual content of a Quaker education, Friends were united in seeing schools as a means of strengthening the sense of peculiarity and separateness of their rising generation. Fundamental was the desire to keep Quaker schools "select," with all teachers and students being Friends in good standing. The governing committees of Friends would see to it that Quaker ways of dress and speech were observed. In turn, the schools would, in their "guarded" atmosphere, turn out Friends who possessed the practical knowledge needed for life in "the world" without being contaminated by the corruptions of classical learning or association with non-Quakers.[22]

In America, Friends followed much the same pattern. Local meetings set up schools almost as soon as Friends came to new areas. Within a year of the founding of Philadelphia in 1682, for example, Friends had engaged a schoolmaster. Many of the outstanding Quaker leaders of the late seventeenth and eighteenth centuries, such as Francis Daniel Pastorius, Anthony Benezet, and John Woolman, had been teachers. A number of Friends wrote textbooks for use by Quaker children. The best known of these, Lindley Murray's *English Reader*, went through numerous editions and was widely used in non-Quaker schools. In almost all respects, the American Quaker schools followed the English model in their suspicion of classical "pagan" learning and emphasis on a "guarded" atmosphere.[23]

Interest in and emphasis on education ebbed and flowed among American Friends, but late in the eighteenth century the American yearly meetings gave it renewed attention. This was part of what historians have called a "reformation" of American Quakerism that emphasized a heightened sense of Quaker distinctiveness through rigorous enforcement of the Discipline. This reformation produced a flowering of Quaker philanthropic and charitable work, especially leadership in the fight against slavery, but at the cost of the loss of thousands of disowned members who fell victim to a newly tightened Discipline. A renewed emphasis on educational distinctiveness was thus natural. In 1778 Philadelphia Yearly Meeting, the center of the reformation and the most influential American yearly meeting, made a query about monthly and preparative meeting schools part of its Discipline. Other yearly meetings followed suit, and between 1780 and 1800 the number of Quaker schools increased considerably.[24]

Realizing this vision, however, caused problems. One was lack of money, especially with the disruptions and inflation of the Revolutionary period. In other areas, the "thin and dispersed situation" of Friends made the establishment of schools difficult. Then there was the lack of qualified teachers, which was especially felt in New England and the South.[25]

The solution of New England Friends, one that other yearly meetings later embraced, was to emulate Friends in England and found a yearly meeting boarding school. After several years of struggle, the school opened in Portsmouth, Rhode Island, in 1784, but soon closed, not to open again until 1819. Other yearly meetings followed suit, however, with New York establishing a boarding school at Nine Partners in 1792 and Philadelphia the most influential of all at Westtown in Chester County, Pennsylvania, in 1799. Friends southward lagged behind. It was not until 1837 that North Carolina Friends opened a yearly meeting school at New Garden near Greensboro.[26]

These efforts met with uncertain support from Friends. There was always a financial struggle, as many members were slow in coming forward with contributions. More fundamental were objections that even Quaker boarding schools were irreconcilable with the true principles of Friends. From time to time these sentiments found expression in protest. An Indiana minister traveling around Philadelphia in 1820 heard many criticisms of Westtown, especially that it served mainly the rich and produced few teachers. In 1828 a monthly meeting actually minuted its lack of unity with such undertakings. When Christ came to earth, it noted, he was not found in "the congregated seminaries of that day." When "boarding schools were set up," they were "the fruitful source of that pride and ambition which characterises an aspiring priesthood." Friends had been favored in the past to testify against such things. Now, Quaker youth were found "not always walking in the path of humble industry under the guarded care of Pious parents but too often at popular boarding schools preparing to be Lawyers, Doctors, Merchants, Speculators in Bank, Bridge, Railroad and Canal Stocks, Money Mongers, Land-Jobers [sic], Teachers of the Higher branches and fashionable learning, . . . a link in the chain of Antichristian foibles" that inevitably led to "music & dancing." The worst offenders were "those large boarding schools, the too fruitful source of pride and Idleness and the nursery of that spirit that made such devastation among the flock and family of God in the primitive Church, and of latter times has got into the society of friends like a wolf in sheep clothing." Thus it was that, in the first quarter of the nineteenth century, as other denominations raced to found colleges, Friends showed little interest in higher education.[27]

The Decision of 1832 and the Founding of Friends Boarding School

This was the very mixed history that Indiana Friends would draw on for their own ideas about Quaker education. From the first days of settlement, they had schools, but these monthly meeting schools usually imparted only the most rudimentary education. Friends faced the usual difficulties on the frontier—teachers were scarce, and children's labor was often needed on new farms. When Indiana Yearly Meeting was set up in 1821, one of its queries asked monthly meetings if "schools are encouraged under the tuition of Teachers in membership."[28]

The Hicksite Separation moved Orthodox Friends in Indiana to give more attention to their schools. Beginning in 1829, in addition to the old query, there was a report on education with new exhortations to monthly meetings to establish schools, employ only teachers in membership, and bring students to midweek meeting for worship, as well as requiring "conformity in all other respects to the wholesome regulation of our Society." That year the yearly meeting appointed a committee on education. Its report the next year reiterated the need for more Quaker schools, while warning Friends against "the public Seminaries in the State of Indiana, and the District Schools in the State of Ohio," which were supported in large part by fines collected from Friends who refused to drill with the militia, and which, of course, did not uphold the peculiarities of Friends. The yearly meeting approved the committee's recommendation that monthly and quarterly meetings form committees on education to facilitate the establishment of schools, and it instituted a requirement that statistics on the number of Quaker schools and students be submitted to the yearly meeting.[29]

Still, these schools imparted only elementary instruction. Only in a few long-settled Quaker neighborhoods in the yearly meeting, like Waynesville, Ohio, or Richmond, did the monthly meeting schools offer any advanced teaching, the demand for which apparently was growing. By the 1830s some Indiana Friends were sending children east to Westtown. Early in 1832, Whitewater Monthly Meeting noted that a number of Friends from outside Richmond wished to enroll their children in its school, but encountered considerable difficulty because of a lack of boarding places. Its solution was to recommend that the yearly meeting open a boarding house on the yearly meetinghouse grounds that would accommodate such students, an idea that Whitewater Quarterly Meeting subsequently endorsed. The Whitewater Monthly Meeting school would in effect become a yearly meeting boarding school, although with the yearly meeting in control only of the boarding arrangements. The institution would meet another need as well. Every autumn the yearly meeting sessions brought thousands of Friends to Richmond, and accommodations were scarce. The Meeting for Sufferings, the yearly meeting's equivalent of an executive committee, had had that matter under consideration for some time, and it seemed to the weighty Friends who composed it that the proposed boarding house could serve a dual purpose.[30]

On Monday, October 8, 1832, the yearly meeting took up a minute from Whitewater Quarterly Meeting on "the subject of a Boarding School at Whitewater." It appointed a large committee of men and women Friends to report later in the yearly meeting. On Friday, October 12, the committee brought in its recommendation. "We are united in the belief that the establishment of an institution to be under the direction of the yearly meeting, for the religious and guarded education of the youth of all classes of the Society, would have a happy effect on the state of society in regard to education throughout our borders," the Friends reported. The yearly meeting united with their recommendation, and appointed a committee to receive contributions "so that in the course of a very few years an institution so desirable may be brought into operation."[51]

Curiously, the Meeting for Sufferings, which was charged with purchasing land to accommodate the school, chose not to locate it near the yearly meetinghouse. The Whitewater school did not become a yearly meeting institution. Instead, the Meeting for Sufferings bought two farms about a mile and a half west of the yearly meetinghouse grounds on the west side of the Whitewater River, containing a total of 320 acres. It is not clear why they made this choice. They may have preferred a rural setting as healthier and presenting fewer temptations than the town, or they may have felt that rent from the farms would provide income for the school. The need for accommodations at yearly meeting time was probably also important. Many Friends camped in their wagons, and the farm offered ample space.[32]

The proposal for the boarding school met with a less than enthusiastic response from the yearly meeting as a whole. Between 1833 and 1836 contributions amounted to only $155.50, with $131 coming from Whitewater Quarter and the other $24 from Blue River in southern Indiana. Nevertheless, in 1836 the yearly meeting appointed a new committee of twelve Friends to propose definite plans for the new school. Of the twelve, seven lived in Wayne County, three were from Warren and Clinton counties in Ohio, both major Quaker centers, one was from Cincinnati, and one was from Spiceland, Indiana, a growing Quaker community about thirty miles west of Richmond.[33]

The 1837 yearly meeting was a critical one for Indiana Yearly Meeting in several ways. One was the presence of the English Quaker minister Joseph John Gurney, who was beginning a three-year visit to the United States. Gurney was the most influential member of London Yearly Meeting between 1800 and 1850, perhaps in all of the nineteenth century. His relationship to the boarding school, however, has often been misunderstood.[34]

Gurney is a critical figure in Quaker history for several reasons. One is doctrinal. In his extensive writings on Christian doctrine and Quaker belief, he interpreted Quakerism in ways that brought it closer to evangelical Protestantism on subjects like the authority of Scripture and the nature of justification and sanctification. Gurney, in fact, came very close to dismissing the very idea of the Inner Light. He also redefined Quaker peculiarity. While upholding Quaker distinctiveness in dress and speech, silent worship, the peace testimony, and the ministry of women, he urged Friends to be less fearful of forming ties with non-Quakers in good works, such as antislavery, temperance, and education. Not all Friends viewed Gurney's ideas with favor—they would in fact cause separations in several Orthodox yearly meetings in the 1840s and 1850s. On the other hand, they met with favor in Indiana Yearly Meeting, where virtually all Orthodox Friends were willing to accept the label of "Gurneyite."[35]

Just as critical, perhaps, was the force of Gurney's personality. Charles F. Coffin, the son of Elijah Coffin, the yearly meeting clerk, remembered many years later that Gurney "made an impression on my mind that has never been erased," with his articulateness, commanding presence, and eloquent preaching. Gurney thus became for many in the rising generation of Orthodox Friends the incarnation of much that they wanted to see among Friends—a definite, aggressive Christian faith, a commitment to benevolence, a firm sense of Quaker distinctiveness. This would be the vision of the young teachers who would guide the boarding school in its early, struggling years, a Quakerism that was unafraid of learning, that in fact affirmed and valued it. This would be Gurney's gift to Earlham College.[36]

Gurney's role otherwise was fairly limited. He did contribute $50 to the school, substantial for the day, but not the largest donation received. He may well have encouraged the yearly meeting to persevere in the undertaking, but if he did neither he nor any other Indiana Friend left a record of it. His legacy would be chiefly intellectual.[37]

Gurney was present as the yearly meeting decided to move ahead with the school. The committee reported that it had corresponded with Friends in New England, Philadelphia, and North Carolina, who all operated boarding schools. It affirmed that the school should be located on the yearly meeting's farm. More significantly, it affirmed that "the males and females may be both instructed in the same house." It concluded by proposing that the yearly meeting erect a building similar to that at Westtown.[38]

The decision for coeducation was apparently made without debate, and we have no way of knowing what it implied for Friends at the time. In embracing it, Indiana Quakers were running counter to the practices of most denominational schools, whether academies or colleges. The first coeducational college in the United States, Oberlin, was only just beginning in 1837, as were the first women's colleges. In Indiana, even the state university in Bloomington was restricted to men. And even some Friends rejected coeducation. The Haverford School outside Philadelphia, for example, founded in 1833 and then struggling for survival, took only male students. Although evidence is lacking, it appears likely that practical considerations were paramount. Friends employed both men and women as teachers in local schools, and if the school was being established in large part to train teachers for Quaker schools, then women would have to be included. And given the financial strains that the school faced, it was inconceivable that Friends would attempt to set up two schools, one for men and one for women.[39]

The boarding school committee introduced one other element, "in order to render the institution more extensively useful." It proposed that each monthly meeting be allowed to enroll one student without charge. This, the members argued, would help remedy the "great deficiency in the number of suitable teachers in the different neighborhoods." Once educated in the boarding school, they "might afterwards be enabled to be very useful in their respective neighborhoods, and . . . introduce and practise a more correct and uniform system of instruction than is now common within our limits."[40]

The yearly meeting, in endorsing the plan before it, called for Friends to subscribe $16,000 in the next year. Significantly, however, the yearly meeting did not require quarterly meetings to raise the sum through an assessment, as was done with other yearly meeting expenses. Instead, it was left to individuals to contribute, meaning that no Friends would be required to support the school involuntarily. A year later, the results reported were disappointing. Only a little more than half of the needed sum had been raised. Elijah Coffin, the yearly meeting clerk, and Thomas Evans, the clerk of the Meeting for Sufferings, speculated about the causes. "The idea . . . seems to have been extensively circulated, that contributions were expected only from the rich; whereas it is well known that there are very few within our limits who can with propriety be placed in that class," they wrote. Instead, the yearly meeting had to look to "the middle class, who could contribute five or ten or twenty dollars." Ironically, the proposal to take one student from each monthly meeting gratis had proved unpopular; many saw it as a financial drain, and so the yearly meeting dropped it. The worst problem, however, was probably the economic depression, one of the worst of the nineteenth century, that began in 1837 and from which the country did not begin to recover until 1841 or 1842. By 1840, only about $2,400 more was raised. That year, a group of young Friends took up the cause, and in the next year raised another $2,000, still leaving the yearly meeting about $4,000 short of what was needed.[41]

This was enough for the yearly meeting to proceed with building. The boarding school committee had appointed a building committee, which in turn delegated oversight of the construction to four Friends, especially Elijah Coffin. They, in turn, engaged Ezra Baily, a strict Friend from Cincinnati, to be the architect for the building and sent him East to visit Quaker schools in New England, Pennsylvania, and North Carolina. In the autumn of 1839 the basement was dug, and in 1841 Baily put up the walls of what would be the west wing of the building. There operations stopped for lack of money. They resumed in 1845 when the yearly meeting secured another $4,000. By this time, however, costs had so increased that another $15,000 was needed to finish the entire building. There was no hope of raising such a sum, so the yearly meeting decided to complete only the west wing. The building committee sold the brick that had been fired on the grounds for the rest of the building, leaving the cellar for the central and east wings open. Full of mud, water, and trash, it became known to scoffers as "the Quaker folly." Finally, by the spring of 1847, there was enough of the building finished to house students. After fifteen years of struggle, in a makeshift, compromised way, Friends Boarding School near Richmond, Indiana, opened.[42]

Teachers and Students

From the beginning, authorities appointed to oversee the school were determined to keep it as Quakerly as possible. The yearly meeting, for reasons that stagger the imagination, appointed a committee of 62 men and 47 women to govern the school. Not surprisingly, it in turn created an acting committee of 29 to oversee the operations of the school. In 1852, the number was reduced to twelve men and twelve women, and in 1857 to six of each.[43]

The committee realized that it would be critical to obtain steadfast Friends to staff the school. Elijah Coffin, who had as wide an acquaintance among Friends as anyone in Indiana Yearly Meeting, took responsibility for securing the teachers and the superintendent and matron. For the latter positions, the primary qualifications were not experience as educators, but managerial ability and unquestioned standing as a Friend. The superintendent would be both head of the school and overseer of its finances; the matron would be responsible for housekeeping and domestic affairs. The first choice of the managing committee was a couple from Wilmington, Ohio, Joseph and Eliza Doan, both of whom had been active in the yearly meeting. When Eliza fell ill, however, the Doans had to decline the appointment. The committee then solicited Eleazar Bales, a prominent minister from Hendricks County, Indiana, and his wife Elizabeth, but they did not see their way open to come. The ultimate choice was Cornelius Douglas and wife Phebe, Friends from Maine; he was a minister who had visited Indiana in 1844. Cornelius, however, had "no experience whatever in public institutions," and the Douglases resigned at the end of only one term.[44]

The Douglases' replacements were a very different couple, Barnabas C. and Rebecca Tatum Hobbs, who would have considerable influence on the school and on two generations of Indiana Quakers. Barnabas Coffin Hobbs was born in the Blue River community of Friends in Washington County, Indiana, in 1815. His father, William Hobbs, was a respected minister and one of the leaders of the Orthodox party in the yearly meeting. As a young man, Barnabas caught the attention of two

FRIENDS BOARDING SCHOOL IN 1855.
*This is the earliest
known image.*

non-Quakers in Salem, Indiana: John I. Morrison, a teacher who later
became one of the state's leading educators, and Federal Judge Benjamin Parke. They gave him free run of their own libraries and encouraged him to enroll in Cincinnati College, where he took classes for
several years. He also taught in several Quaker schools before marrying
Rebecca Tatum in 1843 and settling in Richmond. By 1847, he was
marked as one of the yearly meeting's young leaders. "He held his head
up with a conscious air of superiority and was very precise and methodi-
cal in all his movements," one young Friend remembered. "My heart
swelled with pride at the thought of being in the presence of such a
fountain of knowledge and storehouse of wisdom."[45]

The Hobbses remained only two years, after which they were succeeded by a procession of middle-aged and elderly Friends, mostly
couples, but occasionally a widower and widow, none of whom had their
abilities as teachers. Until 1856, these were members of the yearly
meeting selected for their ability to manage the business and housekeeping of the school. By the end of the decade, there was a move in a
new direction when the committee engaged Charles Atherton, the
former principal of the Friends Boarding School in Providence, Rhode
Island, as superintendent, and Elizabeth Hopkins, formerly the matron
at Haverford, to fill that station in the Indiana school.[46]

The academic side of the school required somewhat more care, since
Friends with the requisite religious and academic credentials were
scarce in Indiana. Like other, non-Quaker midwesterners, the boarding
school committee looked to New England for teachers. The committee
decided to start with two, a man and a woman. The man was Lewis Alden
Estes, a Friend from Maine who had been educated in non-Quaker
schools, including two years in Bowdoin College. He had left after his
sophomore year, however, when Friends persuaded him that Bowdoin
would lead him away from Quakerism. The committee engaged him
after hearing that Estes was "said to be a religious young man, and a good
scholar." He was by all accounts both effective and popular in the
school.[47]

We know more about the first woman teacher, Huldah C. Hoag, since
Elijah Coffin's letters to her have survived. They are revealing because
of what they tell us about the committee's priorities. They were clearly
more concerned about doctrinal soundness than about academic credentials. He did confirm that she was "capable of teaching all the
branches commonly taught in English schools, and of translating Latin
and Greek." Although she came from a prominent Vermont Quaker
family (her grandfather, Joseph Hoag, had been a leading minister),
Coffin still felt that he had to make certain that she sheltered no
"worldly" views. "One thing I can say we look to, that is, we desire as far

as may be practicable to employ teachers who are *Friends* at heart, and who will manifest it in their appearance, conduct, and conversation," he wrote to her father. Coffin wanted her "profession of conviction of the truth and excellence of the doctrines held by our Society, and thy willingness to be placed in circumstances where thou canst contribute to the promotion of our peculiar and precious testimonies." Apparently Huldah satisfied Coffin that she was "settled in the principles of our Society," since the committee hired her.[48]

(There was a sequel to the arrival of the first two teachers. Almost immediately they began a courtship, initially on the pretense of studying French together. They were married in a meeting held in the Boarding School in February 1848.)[49]

The school brought other teachers from New England. Mary Ann Buffum, another Quaker from Maine, followed Huldah Hoag in the girls' side of the school. Moses C. Stevens, still another veteran of the boarding school at Providence, came to the Indiana institution to teach mathematics. There was also one English Friend, William Haughton, an experienced teacher and recorded minister who had been a student at Ackworth. After the first years, however, the school depended increasingly on Indiana Friends who were alumni, like Joseph Moore, William B. Morgan, Zaccheus Test, and Clarkson Davis.[50]

The students in these years were, of course, all Friends. For admission, one had to present a certificate indicating membership in good standing. The overwhelming majority of students came from Indiana Yearly Meeting. In the first ten sessions, from 1847 to 1852, 398 different students were enrolled in the school. Of the 352 whose homes are known, only 7 came from other yearly meetings. By 1858, when enrollment had grown to 172, the students were still coming overwhelmingly from within the yearly meeting. Of the 169 for whom there is a record of residence, 153 were members of Indiana Yearly Meeting, 14 of Ohio Yearly Meeting, and 2 of North Carolina.[51]

Within the yearly meeting, however, patterns of interest and support were extremely uneven. In the first five years, 50 of the 352 students for whom we have a residence were members of Whitewater Monthly Meeting. Not surprisingly, Wayne County contributed a disproportionate number of students—155 came from meetings there. Henry County, the next county west, supplied 49. Beyond this, patterns are difficult to find. Generally, students did not come from a distance in these years. There were none from the Quaker settlements in Illinois or Iowa. The monthly meetings in Hamilton, Howard, and Grant counties in Indiana, all growing Quaker areas, sent but 5 students, while only 4 came from the large

Quaker community in Parke County. The presence of a flourishing Quaker academy in Parke County at Bloomingdale may have kept potential students close to home. This was not always the case; for instance, 24 students came from the vicinity of Waynesville, Ohio, which had a long-established Quaker school. The lack of a good Quaker school did not necessarily guarantee enrollment. Only one student came from Randolph County, Indiana, which adjoined Wayne County on the north and had a large Quaker population. By 1858, these patterns were still similar, although the students were somewhat more dispersed in origins. Still, over a third were coming from Wayne County, with Henry County still ranking second.[52]

We also know little about what drew students to the school before 1852, or how these Quakers were different from neighbors and relatives who remained at home. Sometimes students came in family groups—the first session, for example, had three Bailey sisters and two Bales sisters. Three of the six students who came from Chester in Wayne County were Hampton siblings. Seven of the twenty-eight from Milford Monthly Meeting were Wilsons, five brothers and sisters and two cousins. Of the twenty-six who came from Walnut Ridge Monthly Meeting near Carthage, Indiana, all but six were connected with the Hill, Henley, or Clark families. There is some indication that students from various communities decided to make the trip to Richmond together and enroll as a group. Of the thirty-eight students who came from Spiceland, for example, twelve came for one term in 1851. Of the six who came from Blue River in southern Indiana, four came for just one session together.[53]

A "Guarded and Religious Education"

Indiana Yearly Meeting envisioned its boarding school to be a place, in Elijah Coffin's words, where "the guarded and *religious* education of the children and youth may receive special attention." It was a place in which reminders of the Gurneyite Quaker vision of religion were constantly before the students. It is not clear, however, how much Quakerism affected what happened in the classroom or what was taught.[54]

Certainly the subjects offered in the school were not peculiar to Friends, nor does the curriculum indicate any survival of the older Quaker doubts about "pagan" learning. The circular for the opening session in June 1847 promised "instruction in the following and other branches of learning, viz: Spelling, Reading, Writing, Arithmetic, Geography, Ancient and Modern History, Grammar, Rhetoric, Composition, Algebra, Geometry, Mensuration, Surveying, Astronomy, Natural Philosophy, Chemistry, Physiology, Botany, Mineralogy, Geology, Natural

History, Mental and Moral Philosophy, Evidences of Christianity, and the Latin and Greek languages." As the college's first historian, Opal Thornburg, noted, in a school with only two teachers this was probably overly ambitious, but during the year the school added "political economy, political grammar, French, trigonometry, and Bible" to the curriculum. In fact many of these subjects were probably offered only on an individual basis when students were interested or when there were teachers in the school capable of offering them—for example, the committee probably added French during the first year because Huldah Hoag was competent in it. It is also unclear whether, in the first years, there was a standard course of study. It was not until 1858 that the school was divided into primary and intermediate departments. Since most students stayed for only one or two consecutive terms, it seems likely that the same courses were offered over and over again to a constantly changing stream of new students. One student wrote in 1851: "Of those that helped to constitute our family last winter there are but few here."[55]

It is also notable that the curriculum, as we have it, was not much different from that found in other schools: an emphasis on Greek and Latin, on composition and rhetoric, and on "moral and natural philosophy." If there was a distinctive education to be had in the school, it was not found in the subjects taught.[56]

The school struggled to provide the necessary accoutrements for educating its students. Here Friends in England and Philadelphia were helpful, providing money both for a library and for apparatus to be used in experiments in the science classes. Still, the equipment was limited. One of the attractions of Barnabas Hobbs was that he could furnish his own maps, along with a "cabinet of minerals and apparatus," but of course they left when he and Rebecca did. When Joseph Moore began his long teaching career in the school in 1853, he found that the "museum" consisted of "a peck basket of minerals and fossils." In 1856 Moore and William B. Morgan actually spent $670 of their own money on badly needed equipment, with the understanding that the school would reimburse them over several years.[57]

Quaker peculiarity and restraint were more apparent in the selection of books for the library. By September 1848, over seven hundred were available. Fiction was notably absent, the Boarding School Committee heeding the yearly meeting's injunction to avoid "pernicious" books, "among which may be named all novels, romances, etc." Elijah Coffin entrusted the selection of the books largely to Thomas Evans, a Philadelphia printer of unquestionable Quaker orthodoxy. The first accession to the new collection was a copy of George Fox's *Journal,* the gift of Samuel Bettle, Jr., a prominent Philadelphia Friend who sent along thirty other standard Quaker works. Evans's selections ran strongly to history and travel, although with some natural science and a smattering of classics, like Plutarch's *Lives.* The largest single group of books was religious. There were many Quaker works, but just as many non-Quaker ones, including evangelical classics like John Bunyan's *Pilgrim's Progress* and Bishop Joseph Butler's *Analogy of Religion* and numerous pious works from the American Tract Society. The only poetry allowed in was safely religious, volumes by George Crabbe and William Cowper. English Friends provided a priceless gift of four hundred Quaker books, many of them seventeenth and eighteenth-century works, to serve as a reference library for the yearly meeting. There is little indication that many students ever found occasion to peruse these bulky, leather-bound tomes.[58]

It was in its religious life that the school distinguished itself from others. Religion was omnipresent. Each day opened and closed with the superintendent reading a chapter from the Bible. Twice a week, on First Day, as Friends called Sunday, and Fourth Day, there were meetings for worship held in the manner of Friends, the students sitting in silence, the men on one side, the women on the other. Sometimes one of the teachers, especially Lewis Estes, might speak. Occasionally there would be a visiting minister, as in 1858, when students heard an "aged woman who it seems was drawn here on duty." In 1860 the governing committee noted that the school often received visits from "Friends in the station of ministers, and other Friends interested for the religious welfare of the students, and much doctrine and exhortation has been from time to time imparted." Twice a month, on the days that Whitewater preparative and monthly meetings were held, the students proceeded as a group the mile and a half to the meetinghouse on the north side of town. More than one citizen found the procession of broad-brimmed hats and plain bonnets rather striking, quite ceremonial for a sect that eschewed ceremony. Others, especially small non-Quaker boys, found the columns of Quakers a wonderful target for dirt clods and taunts of "Shaker, Shaker, Hickory Quaker!"[59]

One of the things that the school lacked was a meetinghouse. Late in 1848 the committee approved constructing one on the grounds, even before the building was completed. Bad weather and the illness of Margaret White, the wife of Aaron White, the Friend who was to oversee the construction, held up the start. English Friends had donated £50 toward the cost, but this was hardly enough to pay for it, and so in 1849 the committee put off construction. In fact, there would be no meetinghouse for a century. In 1857 the funds from England went instead into the construction of a badly needed house for the teachers.[60]

The school did not neglect religious education, apparently modeling itself on the practices at Ackworth. Every student who lacked one received a Bible, and each Sunday afternoon students met for an hour to recite and answer questions on a chapter that they were supposed to have memorized. On Saturday evenings the students gathered to hear one of the teachers read from a religious book, not necessarily a Quaker one. From time to time, Friends distributed books at the school. In 1856 a woman Friend in Philadelphia donated $100 for "a thorough course of instruction of the pupils in the principles and testimonies of Friends." The donor saw it as a way of strengthening the society: "Every young man and woman who can read, should be able to give to persons of other religious denominations, sound Scriptural reasons for their belief, instead of being baffled and puzzled as so many now are when inquiries are made of them." The Boarding School Committee agreed, minuting its conviction that if there had been such instruction for young Friends earlier, the Hicksite Separation would not have taken place. There is no record, however, of how the school used the money.[61]

One aspect of the school that did live up to Quaker ideals was the commitment to coeducation. "The girls in all cases [are] to have equal opportunity of the best instruction, and the other benefits of the school with the boys," the Boarding School Committee decided in 1859. In another decision with a contemporary ring, it ordered "the number and influence of the male and female faculty to be kept as nearly as equal in the school as possible." When early in 1857, the committee sensed that the quality of instruction in the girls' department was inferior to that of the boys, it ordered an investigation, since they believed that "justice to the girls demands that something should be done." When Sarah F. Smiley, one of the last Friends from New England to teach in the school, criticized coeducation in 1858, she found no support and resigned.[62]

Still, no one at the school saw coeducation challenging established gender roles. William Tallack, an English Friend who visited in 1860, found that women received the same instruction as men, but, he assured readers, "there is no need to apprehend that these studies may unfit the female students at Earlham for household duties. They are all well trained in those at their rural western homes, before and after their college studies." Indeed, Tallack thought an Earlham woman's course far superior to the "light accomplishments of their sisters in eastern cities." The men at the school agreed. Echoing non-Quakers, they argued that mothers needed a sound education to prepare their children for responsible citizenship. At the Boarding School, the men said, woman was educated "that she may act in her sphere and know what that sphere is." A female graduate would not be a "parlor ornament," but a woman who would find it "a pleasure to wait on her husband and engage in domestic labor."[63]

Thus the authorities of the Boarding School tried to strike a balance between a "worldly" curriculum that was not greatly different from those of non-Quaker schools and one that would help to preserve the distinctiveness of Friends. There is no evidence of conflict over the classes taught, or even much interest in making them more Quakerly. On the other hand, worship and Bible study were very much part of the life of the school, and they were apparently the center of little conflict. When conflict did come, the source was the school's attempt to guide and control student life outside the classroom.

"Quaker Prison"

Like all American schools in the nineteenth century, the Friends Boarding School attempted to oversee and regulate every aspect of student life. If this burden was not enough, the school assumed the additional one of enforcing the peculiarities that the Discipline enjoined for Friends. By the 1850s, even some Friends were questioning the traditional regulations of speech and dress. At the Boarding School, rebellion by some students against Quaker tradition, when combined with the usual rebelliousness of youth, made it a scene of conflict between teachers and superintendents on one hand, and students, especially the boys, on the other.

Like other schools of the period, the Boarding School saw evidence of good order in regulating every hour of the day. Students rose at 5:00 A.M., awakened by the school bell. The first class ran from 5:30 to 6:30, then students were dismissed to make their beds before breakfast at 6:45. Classes met again from 8:00 until noon. After the noon meal there was time for individual study until 2:00, with more classes before supper at 5:00. Students were "at liberty" until "candle light," when they were again called together for individual study. At 8:30 the superintendent read a chapter from the Bible to the school "family," after which the students went to bed.[64]

When students were "at liberty," however, their pastimes were severely circumscribed. Writing letters was permitted only on weekends. The school allowed no conversations in the classroom, nor could students go back into the dormitory during the day. Even reading was circumscribed. When the school opened, students were allowed to bring with them only books to use in their classes, although it appears that this rule did not last long. Newspapers and magazines were banned as well. The school forbade virtually all games as "worldly amusements," although the Boarding School Committee was apparently more tolerant of athletics; some form of football was being played as early as 1851, with broken limbs inevitably following. The authorities were especially anxious to preserve good order on Sunday, a sign of the growing evangelical sabbatarianism among Gurneyite Friends. Students could go into town only on alternating Saturdays, and then only in a group under the supervision of a teacher.[65]

While the school might be coeducational, the authorities took pains to keep the sexes apart as much as possible. For the first few years, there was a partition in the classroom so that men and women could be instructed separately. In the dining hall there were separate tables for men and women, even separate walks up to the National Road. Conversation was forbidden between the opposite sexes; the sole exception was short visits with relatives on Friday evenings. Even the Saturday trips into town were segregated, with men going one Saturday and women the next.[66]

The school soon found it impossible to keep up this degree of separation, especially in a relatively small building. This was a continuing source of worry for the governing committee. In 1852 it told the yearly meeting that "it will be right to discontinue the School for one of the sexes, believing that the best interest of the school, as well as the character of our Religious Society, will demand that this course be taken." Fortunately, as will be seen, the yearly meeting did not agree, and in fact the committee chose to relax a bit, authorizing the sexes to be instructed together in 1851. Meanwhile, students proved ingenious in finding ways to evade the prohibitions; as one old student remembered: "insubordination became the popular thing among both sexes." They quickly found ways to pass notes through cracks or holes in partitions. On at least one occasion, some of the girls knocked over the stove in their room so that some boys would have to come in to help set it upright. "As regards communication between the two sexes, it is worse and more of it," one student wrote in 1851. The superintendent and matron might repair the partitions and take other precautions, "but after all [they] have not made things so secure as they think they have," the conspirator chortled.[67]

Even more problematic were the unrelenting attempts of the school authorities to maintain the desired degree of plainness, especially in dress. "The scholars shall use the plain scripture language; and be clothed in plain dress, becoming the appearance of Friends; having respect to decency and usefulness, and avoiding imitation of the changing fashions of the world," the circular for the first session of the school dictated. Clothing was a constant source of uncertainty and dispute, in part because there was not always agreement among Friends about what "plain" clothing was. The boarding school defined it as consisting of "dark grave colors." For women, it meant "stiff-plait bonnets"; for boys, hats, not caps, and coats "made with plain collars, to stand up, and not with rolling or falling collars." The enforcement was direct. When students arrived at the beginning of each term, the superintendent or principal and matron awaited them at the door of the school to inspect their persons and the contents of their trunks. One student who came in 1851, Hiram Hadley, remembered that Lewis Estes himself cut the hair of the boys whose locks were judged too long, and shears were wielded with equal facility on clothes. "We could not be admitted until the collars were trimmed off the coats and vests, and the ruffles off the girls' dresses, or the offending garments were exchanged for others made according to rule," another student recalled. This was not a complaint that abated over time. In 1859 another student complained that they were "tucked and *pinned* and *wrinkled* and *rolled in* and *rolled up,* yes, any way *imaginable* to make a friendly appearance."[68]

Despite the best efforts of the authorities to preserve order and plainness, there were numerous acts of rebellion. It is difficult to determine how frequent and serious they were, since much of what we know of them comes from reminiscences that probably shared the universal tendency of alumni to embroider on their schoolday exploits. On the other hand, these accounts are important because they suggest that many students were not only questioning discipline with the usual rebelliousness of youth, but were also expressing doubts about some Quaker orthodoxies.

The student complaints that led to defiance of the rules would have been found in most schools of the period. Indeed, compared with other schools, where student rioting against rules and professors was the norm before 1850, the students in Friends Boarding School were relatively well behaved. There was nothing to compare with the physical violence, destruction of property, and even murder that schools like Yale, Union, and the University of North Carolina witnessed. A Quaker commitment to nonviolence doubtless played a part, as did a Quakerly absence of the exaggerated sense of honor that made many men in most antebellum colleges resentful of authority. Nonetheless Friends Boarding School students, especially the men, were open in expressing their dissatisfactions. Some centered on food, a perennial source of unrest. In 1851, students unhappy about rancid butter were told that their complaints were groundless. After making no progress, about twenty of the boys carried all one hundred pounds of it out of the cellar to the hog pen, but then decided to leave it at the gate to melt. In 1857 there was "considerable disturbance in school" when some pies disappeared from the larder. The teachers were so upset that they searched all of the students' trunks, but without success. Attempts to keep Sundays staid were of uncertain effectiveness. In 1851, one student wrote home that "though they are so strict here I believe there is more noise on First Day than any other." And, among the boys, there were sometimes actual outbreaks of physical violence. Some students thought fighting a "disgrace." But when one newly arrived student whipped a town bully who had made life miserable for many of the boys, he became the school hero.[69]

There was also resentment of and rebellion against the plainness regulations. Again and again there were complaints from the school committee that in dress the boys had "not subscribed to that conformity to the rules which we believe is called for." At times students were imaginative, as in one case in the early 1850s when a group of boys asked permission to watch a passing circus parade. The superintendent told them that they might go no farther than the school gate on National Road. The boys took the gate off its hinges and carried it in front of them behind the parade all the way into town. Music was a particular annoyance for the authorities. It was under the ban of the Discipline, yet it seemed to hold a peculiar attraction for many students. "Now sometimes we get to singing here with a *good deal of spirit*," a student essayist wrote in 1859. "If they hear us singing our *very* prettiest, they take the uncalled for pains to kindly inform us that it can kindly be very well dispensed with." At times, however, some of the staff could be more lenient. About 1856 Elizabeth Hopkins, the matron, startled a group of girls singing in one of the dormitory rooms. "If you girls are going to sing, you must be very good, for only the angels in heaven sing," she told them, then left them to ponder her words.[70]

Student discontents had a variety of sources. Some undoubtedly stemmed from the timeless rebelliousness of youth. Some may reflect attempts by students to form their own culture, a culture separate from that the faculty governed. Some came from the reality that the school was probably far more strict than most of the homes from which the students had come. Mordecai Morris White, who entered the school from Raysville, Indiana, in the autumn of 1847, remembered that students held "frequent secret meetings . . . when the officers, rules, table fare, etc., were freely discussed, and the conclusions reached were, that if we survived the term of twenty-three weeks, we would sacrifice the advantages of an education for greater liberty, as we were all unrestrained by conventional forms in our rural homes." This was not just a memory of male bravado. "I never was as tired of one place as I am of this," wrote Miriam Jane Hill, a student from Walnut Ridge Meeting, in 1850. "The thought of staying here another year is enough to make a christian swear and if I do not get better satisfied I am going to make one stupendous bound and burst from the bonds of oppression and return to my native land where I can tread free soil and have bounds unlimited for I have been at Quaker prison long enough."[71]

Certainly Friends both in and outside the school had a sense that all was not always as it should be. The governing committee gave advice liberally, Amos Mills, one of the teachers, noted in 1851, but he had "no doubt but that there was more given than remembered." Writing in his diary in 1859, Clarkson Fulghum, a student from Richmond whose father was a member of the Boarding School Committee, recorded gloomily that a fellow student had been expelled for "pernicious proceedings" and that there were others "who had better share the same fate unless they will reform." Enos Kendall, who enrolled from Chester in 1857, was sarcastically encouraged by his grandfather, who told him "to go, that that school was built by Friends for just such boys as me, as many thought it was a sort of reformatory." The superintendent, Charles Atherton, Kendall remembered, did seem to have it as his goal "to reform the western boys."[72]

Another source of the problems may have been the age of the students. When the school was founded, the expectation apparently was that most of the students would be in their early teens, as had been the case at Providence and Westtown. They would still be children in the eyes of Friends. In Indiana, they were wrong. Of the 284 students between 1847 and 1852 whose ages we know, only 54 were under 15. The largest group, 155, were between 16 and 20, while another 75 were over 21. Many had already taught or borne other adult responsibilities, so it was not surprising that many of the regulations chafed. By 1858, the aging of the student body was more pronounced. Of 142 students whose ages we know, only 6 were under 16, compared to 60 over 21. Rules intended to control 14-year-olds sat ill with older students, but the authorities were slow to make changes.[73]

Finally, one should not assume that rebellion against certain unpopular regulations indicated a general disenchantment with the school. There is ample evidence that many students were quite content. "Some think the rules rather tight but I can stand them very well," Lydia Thomas wrote home in 1856. Mary Russell agreed: "I think I never saw a set of schoolmates agree better than they do here," she wrote in 1854. A student from Logan County, Ohio, Elizabeth Ann Watkins, was even more emphatic: "Oh I do wish I were there at the Boarding School. I never regretted leaving there but once and that has been all the time." Even those like Mordecai White, who plotted to regain his liberty, returned for several sessions.[74]

There is also tentative evidence that attending the Boarding School strengthened commitment to Quakerism, or at least made students in the school less likely to be disowned. This was of considerable concern to many Friends in the 1840s and 1850s, who perceived a hemorrhage of membership. Statistics from Indiana monthly meetings in the 1850s show that nowhere was a majority of young people marrying in meeting; between 33 percent and 65 percent of those marrying were being disowned for "marriage contrary to discipline." In contrast, 53 percent of Boarding School students from the first five years married "according to the good order used among Friends." Indeed, of all of the 352 students of the first five years, there is definite evidence of only 16 percent being disowned by Friends before 1870; at least 60 percent remained Friends until their deaths. Although we have few comparative statistics, all indications are that this was a far higher persistence rate than for Friends in the yearly meeting generally. And of course it is impossible to isolate just how much influence the school had in each case. It is equally possible that it attracted students who would have been more likely to remain Friends regardless.[75]

Thus the school apparently compiled a mixed record. Despite the best efforts of those in charge, in many respects the behavior of the Quaker students was not that different from those in other schools. They rebelled against both the standard regulations of schools of the period and the peculiarities of a Quaker school. Still, because the school strengthened Quaker identity, or because it attracted students from families with a strong sense of Quakerism, those enrolled were more likely to remain Friends than Quaker youth who remained at home, away from its influence.

Change, however, was taking place among Friends in the 1850s; this would be a critical decade for Friends, especially Indiana Friends. Nothing would make that clearer than the movement to make Friends Boarding School Earlham College.

Toward Earlham College

In the school's first decade, its future often appeared uncertain. While the school building was planned for 300 to 400 students, enrollment never approached that level, often falling below 100. Thus the committee and the yearly meeting often found themselves debating how to secure the funds to keep the school operating.[76]

Financial problems were the rule rather than the exception for nineteenth-century colleges—in fact most of the schools founded before 1900 failed for that reason. Like most other schools, the Boarding School faced the fact that many, perhaps most, potential students lacked the money to attend. Costs were low—$35 per term for room, board, and tuition in 1847, rising gradually to $65 by 1858. Yet many students had to leave school regularly for a term or two to earn the money to return, or because they were needed on farms at home. As early as 1850 the yearly meeting considered a scholarship fund for "the children of such members of the Yearly Meeting as are not in circumstances to be well able to pay the expense." But when the school tried to keep fees low, there were still not enough students to meet the costs. "Unless the school shall be made more productive by an increase in scholars, or otherwise, or some other means be brought in to its support," the yearly meeting decided in 1851, "the terms of admission must materially decline, or a considerable debt be incurred to keep it up."[77]

By 1851, the financial and other problems were becoming critical. As has been seen, the Boarding School Committee was insistent that students of both sexes could not be housed much longer together in the west wing. Meanwhile, facilities and arrangements that were a make-shift in 1847 were becoming less and less tolerable. The numerous stoves and fireplaces used for heating and tended by the students were a continual worry because of the threat of fire—on at least one occasion a defective flue caused a blaze in the attic that was detected just in time. Facilities for washing and bathing were in the basement—unheated, and with a dirt floor.[78]

Ezra Baily in 1851 put the cost of completing the building at $16,000. It took two years to raise that through donations, but in 1853 construction of the central and east wings began. Meanwhile, the yearly meeting decided to spend another $7,000 to install steam heat and put a slate roof, more resistant to fire than the old wooden shingles, on the building. By the fall of 1855, the building was completed.[79]

The ambivalence of many Indiana Friends made raising the neces-sary money difficult. The old prejudice against anything that smacked of a "theological school" lingered, as did fears of the "pernicious effect" of the boarding school. William Tallack, an English Friend who visited in 1860, found that "some of the elder and more rustic Friends thought the educational tendency would lead to a 'departure from the simplicity of Friends'; others boldly hinted at its being aristocratic." Lemuel Baldwin, a Friend from Champaign County, Ohio, who had a number of relatives in the school, wrote scornfully in 1855 that "in erecting such a Mammoth Building I am of the opinion that the present amount subscribed will not be near enough if it could be had will not not in my opinion complete this great *Tower.*" Even if it was completed, Baldwin concluded, he thought it unlikely that it would be "appropriated to the purpose of a boarding school in a way that will pay its way and stand on its own foundation." Francis T. White, a student traveling back to school in 1848 and stopping with a Friend near Milton, Indiana, received "a great deal of advice in respect to the behaviour in our meetings." White knew of nothing amiss, "but I suppose that if it is so, it has passed through the ears of many and multiplied and squared itself a dozen times or more."[80]

In fact, the completion of the building found the school in worse financial shape than ever; one sympathetic Friend called it "crippled." At yearly meeting in the fall of 1855, "the Boarding School occupied a prominent place," with a special committee appointed to appraise the situation. It reported that, because of higher than anticipated costs for completing the building, lower than anticipated enrollment, and improvements like the steam heat and roof, there was now a debt of $18,000. The first target for the anger of many was the current superintendent, David Hunt, but he ultimately was recalled for another year. Instead, the yearly meeting decided on a concerted effort to put the Boarding School on a firmer financial footing.[81]

The course the yearly meeting took still rejected an assessment of monthly or quarterly meetings. It remained committed to keeping support voluntary. It did send out yet another call for donations. When that yielded insufficient money, the yearly meeting raised funds in another way. The yearly meetinghouse now found itself near the Richmond train depot. By selling lots from the yearly meeting grounds, the yearly meeting raised several thousand dollars. In 1857, the yearly meeting sold 120 acres from the Boarding School farm, reluctantly, since this would reduce the future income, but there seemed to be no choice. The proceeds were enough to take the school out of debt. Happily, the liquidation of the debt coincided with growth in enrollment. Never again would the school know the straits of the 1850s.[82]

Even as the school was struggling to survive, changes were taking place among Indiana Friends. By 1860, they had moved much closer to the dominant evangelical culture of the United States. The faculty and students in the Boarding School shared in this change and were very likely agents of it. That change, in turn, laid the groundwork for the transformation of the Boarding School into a college.

Elsewhere I have written of the acculturation of Gurneyite Friends in this period. William Tallack, the English Friend who visited in 1860, grasped well what was taking place. He found Friends in "the West" a generally prosperous and contented people, but experiencing rapid change in their lives. The great tendencies of the nineteenth century were, he wrote, assimilation and consolidation. "From this tendency the farthest west and the wildest backwoods cannot withhold compliance, even if they wished it," Tallack concluded. "We find that in their most secluded homes there is a growing fondness for the refinements of literature and science."[83]

The two great agents of this assimilation and consolidation were revolutions in transportation and communication. The railroad made it possible for people and goods to travel at speeds and with ease unimaginable half a century earlier. Bernhard Knollenberg has described what that meant for Richmond, which the railroad reached in 1854: "In 1850 it was an isolated backwoods settlement dominated by the Quakers in dress, manners, and concepts"; ten years later "it was relatively cosmopolitan and closely linked by rail to a thousand other similar communities." And the market economy that the railroad and other forms of improved transportation made possible created wealth that made more education possible for bright Quaker youths.[84]

The changes in the economy also made it possible for Friends to take advantage of the revolution in communication that was making books, newspapers, and magazines available in unprecedented quantity. There is ample evidence that Friends, especially young Friends, were reading and being influenced by this literature. Increasingly, Quaker schools used McGuffey readers, a staple of the larger educational world. Friends read not only the Quaker poet John Greenleaf Whittier, but also Henry Wadsworth Longfellow and William Cullen Bryant. Even the ancient Quaker prejudice against novels fell away as Friends embraced *Uncle Tom's Cabin*. By 1868, some of the Earlham faculty were noting that "the amount of reading done in our Society at the present time is very great compared with what was done fifty, or even twenty-five, years ago." The impact, they found, was "incalculable."[85]

In fact, the impact could be seen in many ways. By 1860, Gurneyite Friends were forming numerous ties with the larger American society. Virtually all were enthusiastic Republicans, many seeking local office. They had fervently embraced the cause of temperance and prohibition. They were committed to a variety of good works and moral uplift for the poor. In their First Day Schools, the teachings were becoming increasingly more like those of other denominations. In fact, by the end of the next decade, this acculturation would be producing a revolution among Friends.[86]

Friends Boarding School shared fully in these currents. One sign we have is the reading that students were doing. The prejudice against novel reading still endured for some students. "What is more calculated to lead the mind astray, to cause it to speculate on imaginary visions, and indulge in frivolous motives, than to apply the attention to novel reading?" asked one student in 1855. Yet by 1858 the Ionian, the men's literary society, had Washington Irving, Goethe, Schiller, and *Don Quixote* in its library, along with numerous works of current interest: collections of the speeches of Henry Clay and Republican presidential candidate John C. Fremont, Frederick Douglass's *My Bondage and My Freedom,* and a number of the essays of the Massachusetts educational reformer Horace Mann. Such works far outnumbered the Quaker books. By this time non-Quaker, evangelical works were entering the college library with the approval of the governing committee.[87]

Equally compelling evidence of the growth of a literary culture in the school can be found of the formation of literary societies. From the beginning, men and women usually had separate organizations. In their goals and conduct they were identical to groups at other schools. The first attempts, like the Literary League of the Female Department of Friends Boarding School, or the men's Hesperian Junto, were short-lived. In 1856, the women organized the Phoenix Society, and a year later the men set up the Ionian. Both lasted more than a century.[88]

The records left behind by these groups show that they were very much absorbed with preparation for life in the larger, secular world. The Hesperian Junto began with a conviction of "the inestimable importance of Literary and oratorical attainments and how essential they are to our happiness and prosperity." The Ionian formed "for the purpose of culti-vating language and mingling conversational pleasantry, with the stern-er truths of Philanthropy and Science." The Phoenix was devoted to promoting "general intelligence and intellectual training and to culti-vate especially the arts of Composition, Argumentation, and Oratory."[89]

There was little that was distinctively Quaker about these groups. The Hesperian, for example, elected a president, vice president, secretary, and "marshal." Members were elected by a two-thirds vote, and other decisions were made by voting as well, rather than by the Quaker method of seeking the "sense of the meeting." Debates, declamations, and orations were staples of the weekly sessions of all of the groups. The debates were on questions of contemporary issues, for example, in 1857, "That the treatment of the African slaves of America is more odious than that of the poorer classes in England." The literary journals, mostly handwritten, that they produced were similar. As Opal Thornburg noted, students and their elders, "who so conscientiously eschewed outward fashions, unconsciously were following the literary fashion of the times," with their stories on "the sorrows of the lone orphan; of awesome night, which should be used to prepare for the greater night that will engulf all; of the delusion of happiness; of the joys of solitude; of the lonely grandeur of the ocean . . . ; of the consolation of religion." On the other hand, it is significant that in the Boarding School life centered on the literary societies, rather than on efforts to organize fraternities, which were becoming arbiters of student life at many schools in this period. Here Quaker ties were probably critical, since Friends condemned membership in secret organizations.[90]

With these developments, the school was laying the foundations of what would, later in the century, become a full-fledged student culture. The next step, however, would be the creation of the college.

In 1859, Friends Boarding School became Earlham College. It was, in some respects, a momentous decision. Earlham was the second Quaker college in the world, only three years younger than Haverford. Yet it was a decision that apparently was made with little public discussion or debate, certainly none that left a record behind.[91]

The first public discussion of the idea of a Quaker college came in a series of articles in the Orthodox Philadelphia journal, *The Friend,* in 1830. The author, writing under the pseudonym "Ascham," argued that "unfounded prejudice" was responsible for the Quaker suspicion of higher education. Seventeenth-century Friends like Robert Barclay, he claimed, had objected only to the corrupt schooling of their day, presided over by "crowds of dogmatic and self-sufficient pedants" inculcating a medieval scholastic philosophy. And because Friends had made it impossible to obtain "what could with any propriety be called a liberal education, within the pale of our society," those young Friends who wished more education had been forced to go outside the society, and had often been drawn away from it. No longer, however, could Friends remain aloof from "keeping pace with the progress of knowledge." It was this impulse that was critical in the founding of Haverford in 1833 and its formal transformation into a college in 1856.[92]

That Indiana Friends followed suit shows that these new currents also affected them. "We live in an age of profession. The impress of improvement is stamped upon almost every invention of man," Sarah Ann Hampton, a student from Chester, Indiana, told fellow students in a speech in 1857. "We are impelled to higher degrees of intellectual and moral attainment by the continually advancing character of the world in which we live." Caught up in that spirit, some young Friends began to aspire to the advanced training that a college offered. As early as 1845, Allen Furnas, a Friend from Bridgeport, Indiana, was writing to Oberlin for information about enrolling. In the 1850s, several Indiana Friends actually did go to Amherst, Oberlin, or Antioch, taking degrees.[93]

We know little about the experiences of these students, save two—Eli and Mahalah (Pearson) Jay, who would later be popular and influential members of the Earlham faculty. In 1849, both in their twenties and having absorbed as much as any Quaker school could offer, they decided to attend Oberlin. To prepare themselves, they studied Latin with an Oberlin student who was teaching in their neighborhood near West Milton, Ohio. Just before they were to leave for Oberlin, they became the target of a sermon by a much-exercised minister in West Branch Quarterly Meeting. "Such scorching and lashing as we got was awful," Eli remembered fifty years later. "No names were given but all knew who were alluded to and piously inclined seemed horrified at the audacity of those, who would so act, as to call down the dreadful things that were glowingly portrayed as about to befall them." In fact the Jays' stay at Oberlin was temporary; because Mahalah was not allowed to read her own essays in public there, they moved to Antioch, which Horace Mann was making one of the best-known colleges in the country and where they took degrees.[94]

It is significant that many of the teachers in the Boarding School shared this interest. Zaccheus Test went east to Haverford for an A.B. and returned to teach in the Boarding School in 1851, the first member of the faculty with a degree. William B. Morgan followed in 1853, as did Matthew Charles soon afterwards, Morgan to Haverford, Charles to Amherst. In 1859, Joseph Moore took the unprecedented course of enrolling at Harvard, albeit pursued by admonitions from Elijah Coffin to beware of Unitarianism.[95]

What was developing in these years as well was a growing sense of professionalism among the faculty. Morgan, Test, and Moore saw them selves as professional teachers, following a calling to which they had devoted years of preparation, different from the nomadic country school-masters who had been teaching Quaker children. Their course was often rocky—early in 1857 Morgan and Test actually resigned, then backed down, when the Boarding School Committee reneged on a commitment to give faculty the right to expel unruly students without first gaining the committee's approval. Significantly, the students backed the teachers with a petition to retain them.[96]

It was the faculty, especially Test, Morgan, and Moore, who were determined to upgrade the school to collegiate standing. As Morgan put it, they were not content that the school "serve only as a preparatory school for the various colleges and universities in our own and adjoining states." They began to work with the members of the Boarding School Committee toward this end. They moved by degrees. In 1856 the committee recommended that, for the first time, the school grant degrees. Significantly, they spoke in traditional terms. Such a course, they argued, "would prevent many of our best students from looking to other institutions for privileges to which they feel themselves justly entitled." This was too much for the yearly meeting. The next year it did approve giving "certificates," but not degrees, to students, since it was "not satisfied on their propriety or usefulness." As Morgan remembered it, some Friends saw degrees as "a cunning device of the Wicked One to exalt and administer to the creaturely pride of their recipients."[97]

Meanwhile, the faculty continued its campaign to persuade the yearly meeting, aided by Elijah Coffin and Levi Jessup, a Richmond Friend who had been assistant clerk of the yearly meeting. In 1859, pointing out that the equivalent of a college course was already in place, the Boarding School Committee recommended the change to college status. "In order to enable the Institution to meet more fully the wants of many students, both young men and young women, who look to it for a complete

education, and desire to obtain college advantages without going to
institutions outside our society," the committee reported, it had "adopted
regulations establishing a Faculty and authorizing . . . the granting of
regular College Degrees," omitting "all unnecessary forms and ceremonies which we do not approve."[98]

The committee recommended that the new institution be called
Earlham College. Unfortunately, we have absolutely no definite evidence about who first proposed the name or why. (Tradition has it that it
was Zaccheus Test.) The origin, of course, was obvious—Earlham Hall
was the English estate of Joseph John Gurney. Whatever appealed to Test
about the name, it was appropriate that the institution be linked with
Gurney. Like Gurney, it would attempt to move Quakerism in a different,
new direction, one that would preserve Quakerism's distinctive essence
while at the same time opening itself to the best features of the larger
world. For the rest of the century, that would be the challenge that both
Earlham and Gurneyite Friends would face. And their responses would
ultimately move them in different directions.[99]

2

Earlham's Surrender to the Larger Culture

1859–1895

*E*arly in the autumn of 1858, a group of faculty and students at Friends Boarding School invited a bright young Quaker physician recently moved from North Carolina to Indiana to address them. Dougan Clark, Jr., would later join the staff of the institution that had invited him, but at this time he was known primarily as the son, grandson, and great-grandson of eminent Quaker ministers. It was about Quakerism that he spoke: "the *Society of Friends* in the *Mississippi Valley,* their past history, their future prospects and probable destiny, and especially their present position, their present duties, and their present responsibilities," particularly the role of young Friends like those at the school.[1]

Not surprisingly, Clark was confident as he surveyed Quaker prospects. "To George Fox, . . . were revealed clearer views of Gospel Truth, loftier visions of human destiny, nobler ideas of human perfectibility, and more accurate ideas of human duty, than had before been communicated to any of our race since the days of the Apostles," he told his audience. Quakerism was "the great precursor of political Republicanism, and the pioneer of religious liberty." In all great reform and humanitarian causes, Quakers had taken the lead. And the future was bright for Friends. Growing in numbers in the West, Friends had great potential. If they could preserve their basic doctrines of simplicity, unprogrammed worship, peace, and direct revelation, the Society of Friends would be a wonderful force for righteousness.[2]

Thirty years later, Clark gave another speech at the same school, now Earlham College. But it was a very different Clark addressing a different institution that was linked with a transformed Quakerism. His medical career long behind him, Clark, when not teaching Bible at Earlham, was a nationally renowned holiness revival preacher and writer. This time, he was not speaking on Quakerism or Friends. He was speaking to students in the Earlham Biblical Department, most of whom planned careers as Quaker pastors. Unlike thirty years before, moreover, Clark did not view the world around him, or the future, with confidence. He saw heresy on all sides, ranging from infidelity to unitarianism, from Sabellianism to Arianism, from restitution to theosophy. Only a firm commitment to biblical inerrancy, premillennialism, and uncompromising evangelicalism offered safety.[3]

Dougan Clark's journey was one that many American Friends made between 1860 and 1895. In 1860, Gurneyite Friends were still a sect, set apart from their neighbors by centuries-old tradition—the plain life, unprogrammed worship, the nonpastoral ministry, pacifism, the pervasive influence of the Discipline. The overwhelming majority of Friends were still farm folk, eschewing towns and cities as temptations away from plainness and good order. Earlham was still officially committed to carrying on this vision through a "guarded religious education."[4]

By 1895, this had passed away. In many places, the "Society of Friends" had become the "Friends Church." The plain life was seen on campus only in elderly visitors or older faculty who still called each other "thee" and "thou." Friends now had pastors and music in their meetings. Pacifism was fading. In many places, all of the techniques of full-blown evangelical revivalism were given full play. Quakers had moved closer to the world. And Earlham had followed them.

Quakerism Transformed

The roots of these changes were complex. Since the 1820s, most Quakers had been moving closer to the larger society. Some of this change, as the first chapter showed, was social. The growth of markets brought Friends into a network of books, journals, newspapers, lecturers, and general intellectual and cultural life. Social change coincided with and reinforced doctrinal shifts. Since the 1830s, Gurneyite Friends had seen their theological bases transformed. By the 1850s, the necessity of an instantaneous new birth was becoming a central theme of Quaker preaching and writing. A visitor to Indiana Yearly Meeting in 1867 was impressed with the preachers "earnestly pouring forth solemn warning or making urgent appeals to come to Christ," concluding that "the most careless observer can scarcely fail to notice that other and more important changes have taken place."[5]

By the early 1860s, an articulate, energetic group of young Gurneyite Friends had emerged to advocate this vision of Quakerism. These proponents of renewal among Friends wanted to pare away practices that they saw as anachronistic, such as the "sing-song" style of preaching or the emphasis on hat brims and the shapes of bonnets. They wanted to hold on to what they saw as the essential, distinctive doctrines of Quakerism: unprogrammed worship, nonpastoral ministry, the equality of women, the peace testimony, and social reform. While evangelical in their emphasis on the centrality of Christ and the authority of the Scriptures, and quite open to working with non-Quakers in certain causes, they were convinced that it was the duty of Friends to keep certain great truths before the world.[6]

This "renewal movement" involved a number of Friends with ties to Earlham. Allen Jay, Clarkson Davis, and Joseph Moore, three of its most important leaders in Indiana, had been students in the Boarding School. Probably more important were the renewal Friends who would serve as members of the school's board of managers in the 1850s and 1860s. The most influential were Friends like Charles and Rhoda Coffin and Timothy Nicholson of Richmond and Murray Shipley of Cincinnati, who were to be among the most articulate advocates of renewal among Friends. Equally important among the renewal Friends was Barnabas C. Hobbs, who had been an important figure in the founding of the school and, in 1867, would be the first person to hold the office of president.[7]

This vision of Quakerism was never fully realized. Instead, late in the 1800s, it found itself pushed aside and ultimately supplanted by the holiness revival among Friends. The first such outbreak among Indiana Friends came in the autumn of 1867 at Walnut Ridge in Rush County, and by 1873 they had become widespread among Gurneyite Friends. The driving force behind the revival was holiness, or second experience sanctification. Advocates of holiness taught that sanctification was an instantaneous second experience, subsequent to conversion, the product of faith, a "second blessing." It freed the believer from the desire or propensity to sin. This teaching drew hundreds of thousands of adherents in the 1860s and 1870s, particularly in groups with a Wesleyan heritage.[8]

Between 1867 and 1873 this movement drew in a number of young Quaker ministers. Among the most prominent were David B. Updegraff of Ohio Yearly Meeting, and Dougan Clark, Luke Woodard, Nathan and Esther Frame, and John Henry Douglas of Indiana Yearly Meeting. All experienced sanctification in these years, and that experience made them aggressive evangelists. They used that experience to work a fundamental transformation of Gurneyite Quakerism.[9]

Probably few sects have changed as radically as did Gurneyite Friends in these years. The holiness group successfully challenged the plain life—it passed away forever. Music, even organs and choirs, became part of Quaker worship. Revivals became an annual event in many meetings. Some even came to call themselves "churches." The culmination of the revival's impact came in the 1880s and 1890s, when most of the Gurneyite yearly meetings moved to adopt a pastoral system of ministry. By the 1880s, moreover, the Quaker revivalists were following the larger holiness movement on the first steps of the path that would take many of them toward fundamentalism. Some embraced faith healing. Many became confirmed premillennialists, convinced that the second coming of Christ was imminent, presaged by an inevitable moral and spiritual decline. By 1900, in the Quaker communities of the Midwest from whence Earlham drew most of its students, Friends had become almost indistinguishable from the larger evangelical Protestant culture, the "Friends Church" just another among the denominations.[10]

Probably more important for Earlham was the growing anti-intellectualism among many revivalists. Prominent in their writing and preaching after 1880 was a note of fear—fear that "higher criticism," the application of critical scholarly analysis to Scripture, was challenging the inspiration and authority of the Bible. David B. Updegraff often sounded this note. Quakerism and all evangelical faith generally suffered, he wrote, from the "fearless attacks of unsoundness in high places. . . . It seems sometimes that if a man can get 'Prof.'" or L.L.D. or D.D., or get to sit in a chair, people will gulp down anything that he offers, and think it good, no matter how tainted." Some at Earlham noticed these attacks. One graduate wrote of the "hostility on the part of some of our most active religious teachers to college work." The problem, he claimed, was that there were too many "very ignorant" preachers. Earlham's duty was to rescue them from their ignorance.[11]

Earlham, however, found support from a highly articulate and influential group of moderate Gurneyite Friends that coalesced in the 1870s. They were evangelical in personal faith, but skeptical about the revival and the direction in which it was taking American Quakerism. They were self-consciously in the middle, between the unyielding conservative group on one side and the holiness revival on the other. The vision of these Friends was very much that of the renewal group of the 1860s. They were open to ties with other denominations, but with Friends retaining their own identity. This led them to oppose, in varying degrees, most of the revivalists' program. Some of the moderates, such as Allen Jay and Charles F. and Rhoda M. Coffin, had originally been sympathetic to, even active in, some of the early revivals, but later came to have reservations.[12]

When they looked at the revival, most moderates saw a clear threat to Quakerism. Many traced it back to the doctrine of instantaneous sanctification, which they saw as a source of great evil. Timothy Nicholson, a power both at Earlham and in Indiana Yearly Meeting, saw it as the cause of "fearful havoc, resulting in spiritual deadness. . . . It engenders strife, distraction, and disreputable maneuvering . . . the dire effects of which it will require years to remove." Instead, moderates held to the older Quaker vision that sanctification, and even conversion, were gradual. The moderates also regarded with skepticism the new directions of the revival in the 1880s and 1890s, especially premillennialism. The moderates' views of Scripture were similar. They revered the Bible, and acknowledged its authority for all Christians. But they abhorred biblical literalism as detracting from the direct inspiration of the Holy Spirit, the genius of Quakerism.[13]

The moderates were never numerous, but they were exceedingly influential in many yearly meetings, especially Indiana, because of their articulateness and abilities. As Dougan Clark, who feared their power, wrote, they were "leaders of the people in nearly all the yearly meetings—ministers, elders, influential men, and writers for the periodicals." By their wits and influence they were able to keep alive an alternative to the revival among Gurneyite Friends. And their influence was great at Earlham.[14]

Earlham and the Revival

The response of Earlham to the "Great Revival" among Friends was ambiguous. On one hand, the impact of the changes taking place among Friends was clear. Earlham, like the Gurneyite branch of the Society of Friends, was very different, much closer to "the world" in 1895 than it had been in 1860. On the other hand, holiness never took hold on the campus as it did in some of the other Quaker colleges. Most Earlham faculty, and the dominant group in its board, were firmly in the moderate camp. Thus began a critical divergence between the college and many of its Quaker constituents.

Earlham was not wholly immune from the influence of the revival. There were outpourings of religious fervor on campus as early as 1865, when what several labeled an "awakening" swept through the men's side of the dormitory. It began in a prayer meeting that a small group of men held daily. By the time that the "awakening" had run its course, almost every male student had professed conversion. There is nothing to indicate that the faculty or the board of managers regarded the events with anything but favor, but they also apparently gave them little attention.[15]

By the 1870s, the college had ties with a number of the leading revivalists. Luke Woodard, one of the revival's most influential figures, had been a student in the boarding school in the early 1850s. So had a number of the revival's lesser leaders, including Elwood C. Siler, Caleb Johnson, Mary H. Rogers, and Calvin W. Pritchard. Such holiness stalwarts as Woodard, Nathan and Esther Frame, David B. Updegraff, and Robert W. Douglas sent their children to the school.[16]

It is not difficult to find signs that the spirituality of the revival affected the campus. Visits by leading revivalists were common. Students recalled professors, especially Dougan Clark, laboring with them and helping them to conversion. Some students held nightly prayer meetings in their rooms in 1870 and 1871. By 1875, these were down to twice a week, on Wednesday and Sunday, but, the *Earlhamite* observed, "many of the students take an active part in the exercises, so that the voice of song, prayer, and earnest exhortation is frequently heard." When one student, John Branson, died in Earlham Hall in 1884, classmates gathered around his bed singing "Safe in the Arms of Jesus."[17]

The faculty also shared in the enthusiasm to some extent. Several of the teachers were recorded ministers; the three presidents in this period—Hobbs, Joseph Moore, and Joseph John Mills—were among the best-known Quaker ministers of their time. The sole criticism that John Henry Douglas, one of the leading Quaker revivalists, had to offer of Earlham was "against placing five of our most eminent ministers in one institution of learning." The *Earlhamite* boasted in 1874 that "a vivid recollection of four years' experience at Earlham fails to recall a single expression upon religious subjects that would not bear the test of the most rigid orthodoxy," while, it continued, "we remember hundreds of warnings against the insidious approaches of unbelief and doubt." The editors did not deny that there was questioning, but concluded that at Earlham it led to "the already revealed faith."[18]

It is not clear how deeply these influences penetrated the classroom. The Bible "recitations," required twice a week, were not part of the regular curriculum. There was no regular academic course work in religion until Dougan Clark took over the Biblical Department in 1888. There was instruction in metaphysics; the texts included books by Williams College president Mark Hopkins and Princeton College head James McCosh, both classics of evangelical piety. From the 1860s onward the school followed the model of most colleges in requiring of seniors a class in "Evidences of Christianity" that the president taught. At Earlham the text was Joseph Butler's *Analogy of Religion,* another evangelical classic.[19]

Still, one should not overstate the impact of the revival on the college, since there is a mass of evidence to the contrary. It indicates that the faculty strongly identified with the moderate opposition to the revival, rather than with the holiness group. This was also the case with the Earlham board. There is also evidence that the religious influences among the students were somewhat less than pervasive, especially after 1875, and that in fact there was considerable rebellion against them. Finally, by the 1880s, campus religious life increasingly fell under the influence of the Young Men's Christian Association (YMCA), which was expanding its power on college campuses nationwide, and its counterpart, the Young Women's Christian Association (YWCA). While evangelical, the "Christian Associations," as they came to be known, were not holiness in sympathy, and provided new points of resistance to revivalism on campus.[20]

A look at the college's faculty in these years shows that almost none were holiness enthusiasts. The two notable exceptions were Dougan Clark, who, as will be seen, would ultimately be forced to leave Earlham, and William P. Pinkham, whose stay was not long. Of the rest of the long-time, most influential teachers and officers, none was a revival preacher in the holiness mode. As has been seen, Allen Jay, who became the superintendent in 1881 and remained connected with the college in some capacity until his death in 1910, was one of the few well-known Quaker evangelists of the time who was not committed to holiness. William B. Morgan, who had been one of the teachers when the collegiate department opened and remained many years, doubtless spoke for his colleagues when a holiness preacher asked him if he had had "the second blessing," another name for sanctification. "Yes, I've had the second, the twentieth & the two hundredth," Morgan replied. Botanist David W. Dennis "was devout but unconventional in his religious ideas." One student remembered him saying, "It is better to be a good neighbor than a great preacher." The editor of the *Phoenixian,* writing in 1894, described Joseph Moore's faith as "no dogmatic creed, but a broad catholic belief, based on a love for Christ and humanity." That was a far cry from Dougan Clark, who told his students to "be dogmatic, with a holy dogmatism." When Clark in 1882 demanded that no unconverted person be allowed to teach at Earlham, Barnabas C. Hobbs replied that one's religious experience did not necessarily determine one's ability to teach. Hobbs apparently prevailed—while an open skeptic would have been unthinkable on the faculty, the college had no formal doctrinal standards for employment.[21]

While resisting a thoroughgoing holiness vision, Moore and Mills and the trustees tried to keep alive a Quaker identity. They arranged for frequent visits from weighty Friends to expound the nature and distinctive views of Quakerism, something most revivalists thought a waste of time. By 1890, there was a course in Quaker history that included books

by William Sewel, George Fox, William Penn, Stephen Grellet, Robert
Barclay, and Elizabeth Fry. Mills added a classic Quaker work, Jonathan
Dymond's *Essays on the Principles of Christian Morality*, to his senior
course on evidences of Christianity.[22]

At least some students were pondering the meaning and future of
Quakerism in these years. None saw anything but good in it. Typical was
Ola Brown, who in her 1887 graduation essay praised Quaker simplicity
and urged her audience to be tolerant of the conservatism of older
Friends. The year before, another 1887 graduate, Wilson S. Doan, had
moved in a liberal direction. He urged Friends to hold to the Inner Light
as the basis of their faith: "Remove this," he cautioned, "and you leave
Quakerism an empty shell, and men little more than a beast. This is the
whole faith." Doan went on to expound an early variation on universalist
Quakerism. "Truth has not confined itself to some one narrow creed in
order to make itself a unit, but to a greater or less extent it is found in all
religions; and whether found in the Bible, the Koran, the Vedas, or
wrapped amid the myths of heathen mythology, it is Truth the same,
Divine the same, and the Word of God the same."[23]

When students expressed opinions about the changes taking place
among Friends, they were ambivalent. Prevalent opinion was critical of
the more conservative forms of Quaker faith. In 1884 the *Earlhamite*
published a letter from Morris P. Wright, an 1864 graduate, that bemoaned traditionalism. "From being a church without formality, filled
with spiritual life, there has been in some places a drifting into the most
severe formality, and a drifting away from spirituality," he charged.
Another student even opined that the writings of the early Friends
included "a larger admixture of 'twaddle' than is consistent with inspiration." On the other hand, a number of students were critical of revivals.
The *Earlhamite* praised Earlham services for their lack of "that demonstration that is often seen on such occasions." One of the editors in 1885
rebuked the *Christian Worker,* the leading Quaker holiness journal, as
being much too narrow. Earlham students, he claimed, were interested
in the "political, intellectual, moral, social and religious" progress of
humanity. "To them it is not so interesting to read the account of how
many souls have been saved by the effectual preaching of this or that
minister, as to read how nations have been saved by the guiding hand of
an overruling providence."[24]

The ultimate outcome was to make Earlham, by 1895, much less of a
sectarian institution than it had been in 1859. In that year, the managers
admitted the first non-Quaker students. In 1878 the tuition surcharge for
non-Quakers disappeared. In the 1880s, the board approved the hiring of
the first non-Quaker member of the faculty. Nothing epitomized this

direction better than the growing power of the "Christian associations," the YMCA and the YWCA, in the 1880s and 1890s. By 1894, the presidency of the YMCA was one of the two most prestigious student offices on campus.[25]

By 1890, the nondenominational spirit of the "Christian associations" was the dominant one. "Earlham is in no sense a sectarian college," the catalog told readers in 1887. "No proselytizing influences are exerted in the College. . . . The utmost catholicity prevails in regard to non-essentials in matters of faith. Students of nearly all Christian denomina tions and those having no church connections are associated in the classes, receiving equal advantages and eligible to the same honors." Mills struck the same note in one of his last speeches at the college: "Sectarianism in college education is a thing of the past." The editors of the *Earlhamite* agreed, telling readers that the *"primary* object of a Friends' college, . . . should be to make *men* rather than Quakers."[26]

While those in authority on campus were unanimous in praising its sound Christian atmosphere, there are hints that some rebellion was going on. The editorials in the *Earlhamite* on the evils of skipping chapel are one indication. Allen D. Hole, who would become both a respected minister and one of the college's most beloved professors after 1900, remembered one student in 1889 who came to study under Dougan Clark, but left "saying he could not endure Earlham College because of the dearth of spirituality there." When Elbert Russell entered the college a year later, he found religious influences at a "low ebb," with most of the student leaders "not professing Christians." Chalmers Hadley, an 1896 graduate, remembered that students "looked somewhat askance at the evangelical religious revivals of the day." His roommate spent time on his knees in prayer that he would *not* be called to China as a missionary.[27]

Thus the revival among Friends had an uncertain impact at Earlham. It removed many of the pressures that heretofore existed for the preser-vation of many of the traditional Quaker peculiarities and practices. At times, revival-like "awakenings" appeared on the campus, but they did not set its basic tone. The moderate opponents of the revival who dominated the faculty and board did that. They rejected holiness teach-ings, but they were not able to prevent the religious life of the campus from becoming a kind of generic, bookish evangelicalism, symbolized by the growing influence of the YMCA and the YWCA. And some students apparently escaped spiritual influences entirely. In this, Earlham's stu-dent religious life was much like that of other colleges across the country, losing a sectarian commitment but affirming a "Christian" identity. And in taking this course, Earlham was setting itself on one that was increasingly divergent from the outlook of most Indiana Quakers.[28]

Students and Faculty

Ultimately, Earlham's identity as a Quaker school stood or fell with students and faculty. If non-Quakers became dominant on the campus, that would move the school away from the yearly meetings. On the other hand, if most students and faculty continued to be Indiana Friends, and if a significant number of alumni continued to be active members of the two yearly meetings, ties would be strong. The latter was clearly the case. As was characteristic of denominational colleges, Earlham drew largely on its local constituency for teachers and students.

In this period, the school enrolled between 150 and 275 students. By the 1880s, enrollment stabilized at about 250, and remained there for the rest of the century. The most significant change was in the ratio of the college to the preparatory department. In 1862, when the college graduated its first class, there were 36 college and 127 preparatory students. The ratio fluctuated for the next two decades, but the percentage in the college tended to edge upward. It was not until 1887 that college students outnumbered those in the lower division. Thereafter the college increased steadily in enrollment as the preparatory department declined. By 1895, out of an enrollment of 236, the lower division accounted for but 15. This rapid decline is difficult to explain, save by the increasing quality and accessibility of public secondary schools and the Quaker academies like those at Fairmount, Spiceland, Plainfield, Bloomingdale, and Vermilion Grove. By 1890 these schools, often staffed with Earlham alumni, had become a kind of feeder system for the college.[29]

The overwhelming majority of students continued to come from Indiana. In 1858, of an enrollment of 174, 128 gave Indiana as home. Thirty-two came from Ohio, with 2 each from Michigan, North Carolina, and Pennsylvania, and 8 from Iowa. The situation had not changed much in 1893. Enrollment was 317, with 228 from Indiana, 38 from Ohio, 8 from Kansas, and 5 from New York, with the rest from 17 other states.[30]

These figures do not tell the whole story, however, since most of the Indiana students came from a few counties with significant concentrations of Quakers; the largest group always was from Wayne County. Indeed, in any given year, between a quarter and a third of all students came from the area around Richmond. Usually second was Henry County, the next county west with its large Quaker population. A handful of other Quaker counties— Hamilton, Hendricks, Rush, Morgan, and Parke—accounted for most of the rest. Marion County was a special case, its students about equally divided between Indianapolis and the old Quaker farming communities southwest of the city. By 1890, a correlation was also developing between the presence of a Quaker academy (Bloomingdale in Parke County, Plainfield in Hendricks, Spiceland in

Table 1:

Indiana Origins of Earlham Students, 1858–1895

County	1858	1865	1870	1875	1880	1885	1890	1895
Bartholomew	3	1	0	6	9	5	6	3
Boone	1	0	1	4	1	0	0	6
Grant	0	6	0	6	3	3	3	3
Hamilton	6	0	5	2	2	7	5	5
Hancock	1	0	0	2	1	1	4	3
Hendricks	5	3	5	8	4	3	7	7
Henry	10	7	10	5	8	7	5	9
Howard	0	0	0	1	1	0	2	5
Jennings	0	0	0	0	1	1	1	0
Marion	2	9	1	3	8	18	9	11
Miami	0	0	1	0	0	0	1	0
Montgomery	1	0	2	0	0	0	0	0
Morgan	9	6	11	7	1	3	4	3
Orange	3	0	0	0	0	0	0	4
Parke	6	1	3	1	5	2	4	15
Randolph	3	2	2	1	2	1	8	3
Rush	6	8	1	3	10	4	0	1
Tippecanoe	1	0	0	0	2	0	0	1
Union	0	4	0	2	0	0	0	0
Vermilion	0	0	0	0	1	0	0	0
Wabash	1	0	0	1	0	0	0	1
Washington	11	3	0	3	2	0	1	0
Wayne	54	50	61	62	83	73	54	39
Other	2	13	20	8	8	6	6	7

Henry, Sand Creek in Bartholomew, Union in Hamilton) and enrollment at Earlham.[31]

The students also remained overwhelmingly Quaker, although the proportion of non-Quakers slowly increased. In 1862, of the 153 students in the college and preparatory departments, 19 were not Friends, about 12 percent. In 1895, the number of Friends was down to 137 of 236, about 60 percent. Most were from Indiana or Western yearly meetings, with the rest scattered among the other Gurneyite yearly meetings. A look at the list of students in these years bespeaks continuity—most of the family names would have been familiar to any member of North Carolina Yearly Meeting in 1780.[32]

Still, some areas with large numbers of Quakers were underrepresented at the school. Randolph, the next county north of Richmond, had one of the largest Quaker populations in Indiana, yet it sent few students to Earlham. Grant and Howard counties also had large and growing Quaker populations, yet by 1890 they also had few students in the college. What may have been even more significant was the almost total absence of students from the new meetings that had grown out of the revivals in downstate Illinois, in Jay, Wells, and Adams counties in Indiana, and in western Ohio in the 1870s and 1880s. They were not patronizing Earlham.[33]

It is difficult to interpret the full meaning of these data, particularly the underrepresentation of many Friends meetings. As mentioned earlier, it may reflect the influence of the academies; attendance at Earlham was low from areas that lacked strong Quaker secondary schools. (Grant County did have the Fairmount Academy, but it was founded only in 1885.) It may reflect lack of wealth. In the case of newer Quaker communities, it may reflect a lesser commitment to higher education. Certainly alumni periodically mourned what they saw as the unacceptably low percentage of Friends from Indiana and Western yearly meeting who attended college, seeing it as evidence that Friends had little appreciation of higher education. The consequences would become clear later—in the twentieth century: Portland and Van Wert quarterly meetings in Indiana Yearly Meeting, whose connections with the college were tenuous, would become centers of criticism of and opposition to Earlham.[34]

It was also in these years that the student body showed its first signs of diversifying ethnically and racially. The first black and American Indian students arrived in 1880. The first foreign students came in 1890. Unfortunately, with one notable exception, we know little of their experiences. The first black to enroll was Osborn Taylor, a former slave from Arkansas who had been a student at Southland College in Helena, Arkansas. Indiana Friends had founded Southland as the first black college west of the Mississippi and a number of Earlham students were teachers there. Alida Clark, a Richmond Friend who devoted her life to Southland, encouraged Taylor to come to Earlham. His presence on campus attracted little attention or comment, and in 1884 he returned to Southland to graduate.[35]

Friends had a long history of work among Indians, albeit with uncertain results. The first Native American student at Earlham was Arizona Jackson, who came from the Indian Territory in 1880 and stayed to teach in Indiana. It was another Indian, however, who was to be Earlham's best known Native American student, and who would leave the most complete—and ambivalent—account of her experiences.[36]

Zitkala-Sa, or Gertrude Simmons, was a Sioux woman, born in the Dakota Territory in 1876. She had been a student at White's Institute, the school for Indians at Wabash, Indiana, which Indiana Yearly Meeting had established in 1850. Her experiences there had been bitter; indeed, the school officials' harsh treatment alienated her from Christianity for the rest of her life. Nonetheless she completed the course at White's, and then came to Earlham, defying her mother, who feared the influence of white culture and schooling.[37]

The campus saw Zitkala-Sa as an exotic creature. "Her relations with other students were pleasant but somewhat distant," one remembered. "She walked alone about the campus intent on avoiding the fluffy dandelion heads she did not wish to injure." There were also stories that she would not study in her room on warm spring and autumn evenings, since she feared that moths would be attracted in through the open window and be injured in the flame of the gas jet. Nonetheless, if the *Earlhamite* is a reliable indicator, she led an active social life, often present at student gatherings and usually singing.[38]

Zitkala-Sa's memories, however, were originally of loneliness and isolation. "As I hid myself in my little room in the college dormitory, away from the scornful and yet curious eyes of the students, I pined for sympathy," she later wrote. She was "among a cold race whose hearts were frozen hard with prejudice." Nevertheless, she determined to enter the college oratorical contest. To her astonishment, her oration, on women's suffrage, was cheered heartily, and students presented her with a large bouquet when she finished. She was even more astonished when she was awarded first place and the right to represent Earlham in the state contest in Indianapolis. In consternation, she refused to attend the reception for her, but went back to her room to reconsider the hard feelings she had borne the other students.[39]

The state contest in Indianapolis was a mixed experience. Zitkala-Sa rewrote her oration, "Side by Side," as a call for new understanding between Indians and whites. It was hardly a radical production; it praised the "successful system of Indian education" that a "beneficent government" had created. Now it was the turn of Native Americans to come among the whites, seeking "skill in industry and in art, seeking labor and honest independence," seeking "the treasures of knowledge and wisdom, seeking to comprehend the spirit of your laws and the genius of your noble institutions." All would "stand side by side . . . in ascribing royal honor" to the flag. "America, I love thee," she concluded. "Thy people shall be my people and thy God my God." Unfortunately, the state contests were always rowdy occasions, with insults and heckling common. Racial epithets were flung at her, and someone raised a banner mocking Earlham for being represented by a "squaw." There was bitter satisfaction for Zitkala-Sa in winning second place in the contest.[40]

Earlham treated the second-place finish as a victory. When word came late on Friday evening, the whole campus and the faculty within hearing were routed out of bed for a celebration. The campus was decorated with school colors, and a mounted escort conveyed Zitkala-Sa and the oratory coach, Edwin P. Trueblood, from the train station. There was a reception with numerous tributes to the victorious orator, with Zitkala-Sa responding "in a few well-chosen words."[41]

Zitkala-Sa remained at Earlham only two years. In 1897 she left to teach at the Carlisle Indian School for two years, then go on to study at the Boston Conservatory of Music. In 1901 she began the literary career that would make her a well-known and respected champion of Indian rights and culture. Her ambivalence about Earlham remained, however, as after 1900 she cut virtually all ties with the college.[42]

Earlham's faculty showed considerable consistency over the years. In 1859, when the college opened, the era of the New England Friends was past. For the rest of the nineteenth century, Earlham would depend largely on its own products for faculty. Until 1886, all would be Friends, and until the end of the century nearly all would be.

One sign of increasing stability was the lower rate of turnover in the superintendent's position. In 1858 Walter T. and Susan Mabie Carpenter arrived to be superintendent and matron. Between 1847 and 1858 there had been six couples in the position; the Carpenters, in contrast, would remain, with two short breaks, until 1873. Walter Carpenter, educated in Quaker schools in Ohio and New York, and a successful farmer and merchant, was ideally suited to handle the school's business affairs. Both Carpenters were gentle souls who won the respect of generations of often restive students.[43]

In 1867, when the board created the office of president, its choice was Barnabas C. Hobbs. In choosing him, and his successors, Joseph Moore in 1868 and Joseph John Mills in 1883, the board set a pattern that would prevail well into the twentieth century. The president would be a weighty Friend, a recorded minister, with ties to Earlham and to Indiana or Western yearly meetings. A respectable scholastic record was necessary, but experience in Quaker schools was more important than other credentials.[44]

The same tended to be true of the faculty. When Hobbs became president, there were four professors in the college—Joseph Moore, William B. Morgan, Dougan Clark, and Eli Jay. All were birthright Friends, and all had some higher education in non-Quaker schools.

Above all, the four came from old Quaker families. By 1890, the college faculty was much larger. There were now fifteen full-time professors, along with thirteen others with faculty rank—financial agent, music and art teachers, student assistants. Once again, however, the names—Mills, Moore, Morgan, Clark, Dennis, Hodgin, Bundy, Brown, Jay, Trueblood— would have been familiar to any member of North Carolina Yearly Meeting in the year 1800.[45]

It is difficult to reconstruct how Earlham hired its faculty. There was a clear preference for its own alumni. Of the fifteen full-time faculty in 1890, twelve were Earlham graduates. This inbreeding apparently never became the occasion for public discussion on campus. It may reflect parochialism—many colleges in the nineteenth century preferred their own graduates. It may also reflect Earlham's definite policy of preferring Quakers. In 1890, all but German professor Adolph Gerber were Friends. Probably an argument could have been made that the best and brightest of Orthodox Quaker college graduates, or at least those willing to live in Indiana, were mostly Earlham graduates.[46]

The college's attitude toward scholarly credentials was uncertain. Between 1870 and 1900 the "best" American colleges and universities placed increasing emphasis on recruiting faculty with earned doctorates, especially those from German universities. On one hand, Joseph Moore and William B. Morgan recognized the value of the Ph.D. They encouraged Calvin W. Pearson, after he graduated in 1866, to go to Germany to study for his doctorate. When Pearson returned, they immediately hired him, along with another graduate, Alpheus McTaggart, who received his Ph.D. a few years later. On the other hand, of the fifteen full-time faculty in 1890, only three had Ph.D.s. Three of the older faculty did not even have bachelor's degrees, including President Mills, and nine had only that.[47]

The one controversy over hiring practices in these years was gender-related. In 1881, the Gurneyite Friends held an educational conference at Earlham. Women's education was part of the program, and Mahalah Jay took advantage of the occasion to direct a blast at Earlham. The school, she said, had not done enough for women. It always relegated women teachers to the preparatory department, where she saw "the constant spectacle of the few female teachers employed in this school, always held to the position of *least* pay, *least* recognition, and *heaviest* work—a position above which no diligence or faithfulness or success could enable them to rise." Rhoda M. Coffin joined in, tracing the scarcity of women faculty to Earlham's failure to graduate enough women. Barnabas C. Hobbs, obviously sputtering, responded defensively that "if our friends will tell us where to find them, we will thank them very much." The college did keep its eye on promising female students, he claimed, but when they graduated, "somebody steals them and takes them away . . . [to] teach in kindergarten schools." Later Hobbs elaborated; "they had searched England and America, but failed to find a woman to take the professorship vacant" because "they had gone and got married." Apparently Jay and Coffin made an impression. In the spring of 1882, the board agreed that it needed more women faculty, in order to have "more of woman's influence," and in 1883, the board finally acted by promoting Mahalah Jay to an instructorship in the college. She and Eli retired at the end of the school year, but Joseph John Mills opened his presidency in the fall of 1884 with three women professors—Marianna Brown in Greek and Latin, Phebe Furnas in Mathematics, and Mattie Dennis, the wife of David W. Dennis, in English. Brown, a recent Earlham graduate and member of a leading Quaker family in Waynesville, Ohio, would remain on the faculty until 1902. Still, women were unusual on the faculty of coeducational schools, and Earlham was no exception. The faculty would remain overwhelmingly male. It was not until 1915 that the first woman Ph.D., Martha Doan, arrived.[48]

If Earlham's record of hiring women was uncertain, its attitude toward female students was more progressive. To be sure, there were doubts about anything that smacked of the feminism of a Susan B. Anthony or Elizabeth Cady Stanton. When, in 1873, Anna Dickinson, a Philadelphia Quaker and feminist reformer, gave a lecture in Richmond, the faculty voted to allow any student who wished to attend to do so. It was the governess, Charlotte Davis, who asked to record her opposition "on the ground that she did not in this manner wish to appear to sanction the sentiment of the class of persons represented by Anna Dickinson." Occasionally, some student, always a man, would argue for the inherent inequality of the sexes, especially opposing voting as unsuited to women.[49]

Such cases, however, were rare. From the beginning, Earlham prided itself on coeduation. The 1864 catalog set the tone: "In all departments of the Institution, both sexes have the same privileges of instruction and receive similar testimonials or degrees." William B. Morgan openly criticized eastern Friends, who opposed coeducation, for neglecting women's education. "It is strange that Friends, who have from their rise given to woman equal privileges in the most important affairs of the church, should have failed to appreciate the necessity of conferring on her equal opportunities of acquiring thorough education," he wrote in 1866. "In no long time it will seem equally strange that there should ever have appeared to be a propriety in excluding one sex from social intercourse with the other." Students apparently agreed. In 1874, the male editors of the *Earlhamite* noted that, although Earlham was coeducational, women had never made up more than 40 percent of the students, and accounted for only a quarter of the graduates. "We fear that the Society of Friends, although professing to know no sex in education, is practically behind the general spirit of the age in regard to the importance of female education," they wrote.[50]

When Earlham people did reflect on the status and future of women, they usually spoke in terms of what Mattie Dennis called "the inevitable, irresistible march of progress for women's equality." Barnabas C. Hobbs agreed; suffrage was inevitable, and women had to be educated to "that comprehensiveness of thought, and that power to analyze governments, institutions and laws which qualified Miriam to be a worthy associate of Aaron and Moses." Anna M. Moore, Joseph's daughter, held up woman's rights pioneer Lucy Stone as a model for Earlham women. Education, other students concluded, was fitting women for even wider spheres. And some Earlham women of this period were pioneers—Caroline Miles and Mary I. Hussey were the first women to do doctoral work at the universities of Michigan and Pennsylvania, respectively.[51]

Even the advocates of women's rights at Earlham, however, were far from radical. One student, Elvira Hester, concluded an article in 1884 defending education for women: "I . . . consider that the strong-minded type of women who would destroy all social differences between women and men is justly odious." Many echoed the note struck by Edith J. Hunt, another student, in 1891, that women would raise the general level of politics and society through their superior moral nature. But that would not change basic gender roles. Women would best be found "quietly fulfilling the high destiny of their sex at the head of happy, intelligent, christian homes." If anyone at Earlham dissented, it was not public. Instead, Josephine M. Hadley spoke for the campus: "Never in all ages was it grander to be a woman than now." There is thus little to suggest that Earlham's Quaker ties made its vision of women's roles much different from that which many other Americans shared.[52]

Another question that we can answer only tentatively is why students came to Earlham. Even those who left reminiscences of their student days, or kept diaries, or sent letters home seldom reflected on why they had come, or what they hoped to accomplish, or what the education they received meant for their lives. The few bits of evidence we have indicate that Earlham students were not much different from most college students of the period, another indication of the degree of acculturation among Friends after the Civil War.

It is vital to distinguish, in this respect, between the preparatory and the college departments. There was probably considerably less volition and student initiative in the case of the former than in the latter. William B. Morgan noted this in 1868: "Many men in official positions, and others having wayward sons, have been anxious to place them in an Institution where there are so strict police regulations as exist at Earlham," he wrote, a situation that he thought at best a mixed blessing. It brought in students, but it also subjected Quakers to bad influences.[53]

Perhaps the best evidence we have for the aspirations of students in the college is the information about their subsequent careers that the alumni association carefully collected, and which the college often published. In 1876, the college noted that since the first graduating class in 1862, there had been seventy-five graduates. Of these, thirty-nine were teachers. The category with the next highest number was farming with eight. Then followed five physicians, four manufacturers and four lawyers, two editors, and two merchants, with the rest scattered. The 1887 catalog published brief biographies of most alumni to that date, with the following results:

Occupation	Number
Attorney	10
Business	18
Editor	6
Engineer	2
Farmer	14
Housewife	19
Minister	6
Physician	13
Politician	3
Teacher	93

At least thirty of those following other occupations had been teachers at one time. Women were found only in three categories—physicians (one, Dr. Mary L. [Binford] Bruner of the class of 1877), housewives, and teachers. The relatively low number, six, of graduates who were ministers is striking, especially since one was a Presbyterian. Many other Quaker ministers, however, had attended Earlham without taking degrees, and there were probably many recorded ministers who did not indicate that as their occupation.[54]

These statistics, moreover, are biased because they reflect only those who graduated, which the overwhelming majority of Earlham students did not do. For these "old students," as they were known, we have only impressionistic evidence, like the observation of Morris P. Wright in 1884 that there were in Indianapolis about one hundred former students, of "all ages and conditions of life," or the estimate of Richard Warren Barrett in 1899 that "the ratio of businessmen and women" was "one to every four preachers and teachers."[55]

In these respects, Earlham followed national trends, although it bucked at least one. After the Civil War, historians note, numerous denominational colleges, founded in large part to provide clergy for the sponsoring churches, saw that role decline. Earlham, of course, because of traditional Quaker beliefs about the nature of ministry, had *not* been founded for that purpose, but had come to emphasize it more as Friends moved toward the pastoral system. But in other respects, Earlham was typical. The prestige of many colleges fell after the Civil War, as the rising business community came to see them as frivolous and unnecessary. That view did not change until the turn of the century. Colleges increasingly focused on the professions. Earlham probably produced more teachers and fewer lawyers and physicians than its counterparts.[56]

The influence of those teachers among Friends cannot be overstated. By the 1850s, they had begun a tradition of providing faculty and leadership for other Quaker schools that lasted well into the twentieth century. All over the Midwest, Quaker academies like Damascus, Ohio, Raisin Valley, Michigan, Vermilion Grove, Illinois, and Bloomingdale, Plainfield, Union, Blue River, Sand Creek, Fairmount, and Spiceland, Indiana, were staffed by generations of Earlham alumni. One alumnus remembered that when he became the principal at Damascus that he ran it "as a miniature Earlham College. . . . We were parroting Earlham College and I governed in like spirit and fashion." In turn the academies served as "feeders" for the college.[57]

Earlham's impact on the other Quaker colleges was as great if not greater. Between 1870 and 1900 Gurneyite Friends founded five new colleges: Guilford in North Carolina (1888), Wilmington in Ohio (1870), William Penn in Iowa (1873), Pacific (now George Fox) in Oregon (1891), and Friends University in Wichita (1897). At Guilford, the first president, Lewis L. Hobbs, who had no Earlham connection, served until 1916, but every president of Guilford since then has been an Earlham graduate or former faculty member. At Wilmington, all four presidents up to 1903 were Earlhamites. Three of Pacific's four presidents from 1891 to 1941 were Earlham alumni. William Penn had five presidents before 1910, four of whom had graduated from Earlham. Only Friends University fell outside the Earlham orbit, although its two presidents between 1918 and 1939 were former Earlham faculty. The pattern also held for Whittier in California, founded in 1901: six of its first eight presidents were Earlham graduates or former Earlham faculty. Invariably, often in the face of fierce criticism, these Earlham men were forces for the moderate vision of Quaker distinctiveness that Joseph Moore, Timothy Nicholson, and the other leaders of Earlham in their day had upheld.[58]

Thus in some respects Earlham was a distinctive place, but distinctive mostly in the sense that any sectarian college would be distinctive. Its student body and faculty remained overwhelmingly Quaker. By the 1890s, they tended to follow a definite path. Students came to Earlham from the Quaker counties of Indiana and Ohio by way of the Quaker academies. For faculty, the first step was an Earlham degree. There were always significant numbers of women on campus, and the school prided itself on coeducation. But there was little that was distinctive in this respect—the Quaker testimony of equality for women did not move Earlham's women in a direction significantly different from other college women. And the ideal of a "guarded religious education," to help preserve the "children of Friends" from the blandishments of "the world," had given way to a vision of education to help them flourish in that world. Even so, Earlham continued to serve Friends, in part through training ministers, but even more by providing the leadership of much of the Quaker educational system.[59]

The Creation of Student Culture

The second great change at the college after 1860 was in student life. Indeed, one could argue that in these years student culture began at Earlham. By 1895, the student body had sufficient space for its own culture with several bases. One was the decline and disappearance of the regulations that enjoined observance of the plain life. Another was the growth of student organizations, which through their activities came to dominate the campus. Also born in this period was intercollegiate athletics, which, especially after 1900, became central to student life. And despite exacting disciplinary regulations, there is considerable evidence of regular and sustained student resistance.

Probably the most visible change on the campus between 1860 and 1890 was in the regulations enjoining observance of Quaker peculiarities. By 1875 they were gone. In fact, there is considerable evidence that they had become a dead letter years earlier.

The first challenge to the plain life came with the Civil War. Its outbreak presented Friends with an awful dilemma. For a century they had opposed slavery. Now they were confronted with a war being fought to end slavery. All of the yearly meetings, including Indiana and Western, reaffirmed the peace testimony and condemned war as unfit for the participation of Christians. But in fact hundreds of Indiana Friends enlisted in the Union army. In some cases, their monthly meetings moved to deal with them as offenders against the Discipline. Many monthly meetings did not, however—an unprecedented situation. This appears to have been the stance that the college assumed. When conflict broke out in April 1861, there was a "good deal of excitement" in the school, so much so that some of the boys claimed that they could not study. Neither the managing committee nor the faculty felt compelled to take any official notice of the coming of the war. At least thirteen students left to enlist in the Union army. Of these, the best known was probably Cyrus W. Harvey, an eighteen-year-old from Back Creek Meeting in Grant County, Indiana, who joined in 1861. He served three years, emerging as a sergeant and as a confirmed pacifist who in later life was an unwavering advocate of the peace testimony. There is nothing to indicate that the school ever contemplated any kind of action against the enlistees. After the war, former soldiers enrolled, again apparently without question.[60]

Still, some of those with an interest in the school made efforts to inculcate peace principles among the students. In 1865 the board noted, but did not take action on, a recommendation from a visiting committee from Whitewater Quarterly Meeting that "the production and reading of essays eulogistic of wars or warriors, or which, in any way, tend to cultivate the spirit of war, be discouraged." More revealing was an incident in 1867, when a non-Quaker peace lecturer spoke at the school. He was quite warm in his oratory, "saying that war never did accomplish any good, . . . and asserted that 99% of all the officers were degraded villains, called the soldiers 'poor fools.'" He concluded by asserting that "there was not a Christian in the army." The speech brought "low subdued hisses" from the boys in the audience, and a hot reply from James Bain, a Union veteran who was a student in the college, who asked "if we [should have] meekly submitted to the outrages of the southern soldiers." His speech made "the house . . . resound with the cheers of the boys," and only Barnabas C. Hobbs's grim face prevented those present from breaking into boos and catcalls.[61]

This response to the Civil War set the pattern that Earlham would follow in future conflicts. The school would remain more or less officially committed to pacifism. Students would orate on it, the *Earlhamite* would be filled with essays in praise of peace. The college would give its blessing to those who refused, on grounds of conscience, to perform military duty. (No Earlham student would test the limits of this until World War II.) But it would also recognize the legitimacy of the conscientious leadings of students who felt free to engage in military service. And they would be the overwhelming majority of Earlham students in future wars, at least until Vietnam.

The growing tolerance for deviations from the peace testimony paralleled a decline in the injunctions to plainness. By 1880, plain dress had apparently disappeared from the campus, while the plain language lingered only among older faculty.

Officially, throughout the 1860s, the school was committed to having students in traditional Quaker garb. It was a rule, however, that authorities were at best uneven in enforcing after 1860. An 1862 photograph of the student body, for example, shows none in plain dress. In 1866 the board expressed its concern over "gaudy and frivolous articles of dress or ornament, worn by the students at Examinations and Exhibitions." The faculty, rather obliquely, responded that "the object sought may be at least partially attained without attempting to make restrictions of a formal and rigid kind." Two years later a student, Amy Sanders, reflected acidly that she could not wear her new bonnet because it had a sprig of artificial flowers on it. She had noted that the women of the board "all wear plain bonnets, but in other respects they most of them wear dresses more stylish than I do, with long trailing dresses of the richest material." That year the board fulminated against "earrings, finger rings, artificial flowers & all gaudy and unbecoming articles of dress," but even it had given up on "specific rules with reference to the color of clothing." By 1871, the college catalog contented itself with a more general sentiment: "Since the proper idea of dress has more respect to neatness, beauty, and health, than to fashion and show, students are desired not to bring gaudy clothing or other articles of vanity and display." Injunctions against jewelry lingered, but by 1878 the *Earlhamite* was reporting the "stylish" weddings of former students like any society page.[62]

The plain language—"thee" and "thy," using numbers instead of the pagan names of the days of the week and the months of the year—disappeared about the same time. Apparently there were deviations as early as 1865, when a visiting committee of Friends urged "a rule requiring the students to use the plain language without compliments in all their intercourse with members of the faculty." This may have been an injunction against the use of titles like "Professor." If it was, it soon passed away. The last reference to the use of plain language came in 1873, when the faculty ordered Alpheus McTaggart and Calvin W. Pearson "to present a report . . . with reference to the proper use of 'thee' and 'thou.'" By 1875, the editors of the *Earlhamite* were poking fun at the older Friends who tried to force students to use Quaker dates. In 1877, the journal began using the conventional names for the months. The faculty meeting followed suit in its minutes in the 1880s, although the board held out until the turn of the century. "Thee" and "thy" continued to be heard in Quaker faculty families well into the present century, but the college was no longer interested even in encouraging their use.[63]

The decline of the plain life on campus, and the disappearance of an official commitment to keep students separated from "the world," opened the way for the development of a student culture not greatly different from that of other colleges of the period. It was based on student organizations and athletics, and would grow in power until the end of the century.

Student organizations dated back to the 1850s. The two most important were the literary societies, the Ionian for men and the Phoenix for women. By the 1870s, they were the leading student groups on campus. In some ways, they operated like fraternities and sororities. Current members tightly controlled admission, with a single member able to veto the admission of an applicant. Faculty control over their activities was limited. Both groups, in the fashion of literary societies, held debates and discussions. Both operated according to strict parliamentary procedure, apparently out of the belief that this was more progressive than the hoary, undemocratic Quaker method. Their exhibitions and socials were the high points of campus social life.[64]

The most visible contributions of the literary societies were in publishing. From their founding, both groups turned out handwritten journals. In 1873, the Ionian began publishing the *Earlhamite* as a combination campus newspaper, literary journal, and alumni magazine. The Ionian had offered to cooperate with the Phoenix in publishing the new journal, but for unknown reasons the latter declined. The Ionian rebuffed subsequent attempts by the Phoenix to accept. From 1891 to 1894 the Phoenix put out its own journal, the *Phoenixian,* before the Ionian capitulated and gave women equal rights in the *Earlhamite.*[65]

A careful reading of the *Earlhamite* tells us much about the world of Earlham students, or at least about the world of the campus leaders who edited it. It was not particularly Quakerly, or even especially religious. The first issue, in December 1873, was both typical and revealing. The lead article was a long essay on the need for careful evaluation of facts when writing history, the longest poem a plea for Cuban independence; the book reviews dealt with only history and literature. The only mention of Quakerism was a boosterish lament that Friends did not sufficiently appreciate Earlham. The impression is clear of an institution whose students were more interested in academic respectability and campus standing than in aggressive soul saving work.[66]

By the 1870s, the two societies, particularly the Ionian, had acquired considerable power and autonomy. In September 1880, when the superintendent "endeavored to check" what he considered a disorderly Ionian society meeting, the group's response was to appoint a committee to inform the faculty that they "felt insulted by his act." In a remarkable article in 1895, biology professor David W. Dennis, himself an old Ionian member from the 1870s, recalled how in his student days the faculty had refused to give the Ionian a reading room of its own in Earlham Hall. In response, the group "roasted the faculty," and then it "vowed that if it took until our children's children arrived, we 'never would lay down our arms' until we had a hall." Ionian Hall was never built, but Dennis noted that faculty allowed the society complete autonomy in its affairs. It could abolish the Ionian, but it agreed "that any interference with its business was not to be thought of." The group, Dennis concluded, was "bound only to good behavior, as all bodies of gentlemen are bound."[67]

One of the most notable features of campus life before 1890 is how inward-looking it was. The college took pains to keep students not only away from the town, but also from other colleges. The reasons are obscure. It may reflect a lingering Quaker exclusivity on the board's part, a fear that such contacts would introduce bad influences, like Greek-letter fraternities, to Earlham. It is clear that the trustees were the main barrier. The focus of their fears after 1880 was athletic competition.

Sports were not an innovation on campus. As early as 1851, Allen Jay broke his leg playing an early form of football. The faculty was by 1860 encouraging regular exercise by the students. In 1890, students raised the money to build a small gymnasium that both men and women would use. The trustees gave their blessing to all of these projects. They were much more skeptical about competitive athletics. When boys on campus organized a baseball team early in the 1860s, the board imposed a variety of restrictions—no uniforms, no games with other clubs or off campus, no girls as spectators. The first three rules were eventually relaxed, but not the last.[68]

The arrival, in 1888, of two new faculty members, Edwin P. Trueblood and Augustus T. Murray, was the stimulus for change. An athletic club had formed the previous year, and in the spring of 1888 had held the school's first field day. The board regularly rejected requests to attend the state field day until the 1890s, when it finally approved a Trueblood proposal that "our students be allowed to enter the milder State Athletics such as tennis running and jumping." Still, the board kept a careful and skeptical eye on the campus field day. A delegation that attended it in 1891 reported it was "convinced that these sports needed careful guarding," since they might lead to an "acceptance of competitive unions in places distant as well as near are of as dangerous a tendency for inexperienced youth in bringing them into unprofitable association with men whose moral character is not high." Two years later it recorded its sentiment that the athletes, "especially before a mixed attendance, be required to have some kind of a covering for their limbs as well as bodies."[69]

When the college formed its first football team in 1889, the board viewed it with as much, if not more, skepticism and concern. In language that doubtless reflected its vision of the proper nature of intercollegiate athletics, it allowed "the students of Earlham to invite the students of Butler University to play an amicable game of football on our grounds." But pressure from the students was inexorable. In 1890, a majority of boys signed a petition to join the "Inter Collegiate Football Association." The board vetoed that, but in 1892 it allowed the college to join the state athletic association, and a year later, approved "away" football games. Thereafter athletic competition became a focus of student life. The *Earlhamite* gave considerable coverage to the teams and their members. Star athletes became the heroes of the campus. By 1892, the college had its first yell:

> Rah-rah-rah-ri-ro-rem
> E-A-R-L-H-A-M Thee Thou Rah![70]

Almost as much enthusiasm went into forensic competition. The college began oratorical contests in the 1885–1886 school year. The arrival of Edwin P. Trueblood as professor of oratory and elocution in 1888 gave forensics a major push. In 1892, the college was admitted to the Indiana State Oratorical Association, and thereafter its annual contest in Indianapolis became one of the high points of the year. Competition to be the Earlham representative was intense, and a large delegation of students usually accompanied the college entrant. The contest was open to both men and women, and several times a woman went as Earlham's champion orator. When Eleanor Wood won the state championship in 1895, the campus exploded in a three-day celebration that culminated in Wood coming back to campus in a decorated barouche pulled by thirty male students, preceded by two trumpeters on horseback. In 1897, when the college began intercollegiate debating, old Walter T. Carpenter, living across the National Road from campus, commented after one win that "Earlham behaves better under *defeat* than *Victory.*"[71]

Thus competition became a vital part of campus culture. And in other respects, too, Earlham was beginning to resemble other small colleges. There were charges that life for students was "one eternal grind." There were complaints that the dormitory was unfit for human habitation. There was an awareness that Earlham was different in, for example, its lack of fraternities, which gave Earlhamites "the significant brand of 'barb'" in the athletic and oratorical competitions.[72]

Most of all, students were becoming aware that they had their own world on the Earlham campus, and that it was a world that was largely separate from the classroom. "Earlham owes it to herself to be something more than an institution of 'Gadgrinds.' It is certain that there are other things to be done here besides discovering the exact nature of an irregular French verb, or determining the proper use and beauty of the mathematical sciences," the *Earlhamite* editorialized in 1893. The next year's editors agreed. "College and class spirit is what makes a live college. . . . Remove from a college, college and class spirit, . . . and you will throw over it a lethargy that will cause retrogression."[73]

The limits of this new student culture were obvious. The place of the

"Day Dodgers," the students from town who did not live on campus, was uncertain. The emphasis on intercollegiate athletics tended to make men participants and women spectators. At worst, it could be actively anti-intellectual. Looking back, one student of the 1890s thought that many of his fellows "seemed to think of their college years as a grand lark." But the college authorities accepted this advance. "Teachers, laboratories, libraries, lectures and liberal courses of study provide for the prescribed and more formal elements of a thorough case," President Joseph J. Mills wrote in 1895. "But these are hardly of more vital consequence to the future welfare and success of young men and women than are their college friendships, their participation in what may be fitly called college politics, social relations, contests in athletics and oratory, religious organizations, and many other elements of college life that lie wholly outside of the serious work assigned in the course of study."[74]

The student world we have examined this far has been one that the governing authorities of the college sanctioned. There was another world of students, however, one that we can glimpse only through a handful of unguarded student letters that have survived and by the records of disciplinary cases. They hint at the existence of a student world, largely male, that was at cross purposes to the "definitely Christian" college that the trustees tried to guard, and even with the emerging campus culture.

Throughout this period, Earlham's regulation of student life was strict, but no stricter than in other colleges of the period. The first step in guarding students from bad influences was to require of applicants proof of "satisfactory moral character." Evidently that was not effective, since by 1868 the college catalog unhappily noted that "unworthy applicants" had been given "testimonials of good characters." It included a warning that would stand for decades, that "Earlham is not designed for the reformation of juvenile offenders."[75]

In some respects, the disciplinary structure of the college became more strict over time. The 1863 catalog described it as "mild and liberal, but firm," and noted that "punishments and penalties are dispensed with as far as possible." By the next year, however, the latter sentiment was gone, replaced by a warning that no one should enroll in the college "who cannot cheerfully comply with all its requisitions." Catalogs increasingly dwelt on prohibited activities, and they were numerous—consuming "ardent spirits," of course, along with "fighting, profanity or other gross violations of order," "cards, chequers, chess, and other similar games, all improper or dangerous plays, fire arms and the use of tobacco in all its forms." Over the years, there were additions, such as an 1875 ban on "visiting billiard saloons." The faculty strictly regulated contact between the sexes. Their time together was always under supervision, whether in the classroom, in the dining hall, on the grounds, or in the parlors of Earlham Hall. Regulations applied fully as much to students boarding in town as those on the campus.[76]

There were always challenges to this order. At times they came formally and respectfully from students. In 1884 a writer in the *Earlhamite* charged that Earlham had the reputation of being impossibly strict, and that many of the regulations were "ludicrously absurd." He singled out the rules against courting, silly in view of the college's reputation "as a match maker." A more fundamental challenge came from John Bradley, a non-Quaker student in 1867, whom Barnabas C. Hobbs had punished because he would not share information about the misdeeds of some classmates. Bradley's father commended his son's course, telling him that "he must not act as a spy or informant on his associates . . . unless the welfare of the institution shall imperiously demand it." The elder Bradley would withdraw his son before he would have him be subjected to *"dishonor* among his associates." This was a conception of honor common to colleges of the time, but at odds with Earlham's conception of itself. Apparently Earlham prevailed, since John Bradley left.[77]

There were other students, however, who challenged the regulations imposed on them more directly. Some found themselves before the faculty for conduct that would now be considered harmless, like Sophia Newby, who was expelled in in 1866 for writing four letters to a boy in the school. As late as 1803, a group of eleven students had to submit a written apology for visiting a Richmond theater.[70]

Beginning about 1870, the challenges became more direct and open. The faculty found itself facing a series of visitors to Richmond's all-too-numerous saloons, or, even worse, those who brought alcohol onto the campus, along with the inevitably resultant "boisterous conduct." At times the students went in groups as large as twenty. And there is evidence that many went undetected. Charles Mather, a young Friend from Waynesville, Ohio, who enrolled in January 1890, wrote home to a brother that it was common for students to visit the saloons and theaters in town, and that a "good many of the student loose [*sic*] lots of money at gambling, its increasing [*sic*] all over the college." One student, he reported, had lost five dollars in one day.[79]

Thus by 1895 Earlham had created a student culture. It had left behind the strictures of plainness and Quaker peculiarity that Friends Boarding

School had been founded to uphold. The lives of Earlham students, with their clubs, publications, competitive athletics, and acts of rebellion, had become much like the lives of other college students.

Curriculum

The least distinctive thing about Earlham in these years was its curriculum. There was relatively little that was peculiarly Quaker about it. Earlham's faculty adhered to the patterns that American colleges generally followed in the nineteenth century. The one feature of Earlham's curriculum that did set the school apart—Joseph Moore's early and persistent championing of Charles Darwin's theory of evolution—was not at all distinctively Quaker. In curriculum, as in student life and governance, the school saw progress in large part in becoming less distinctive and becoming more like other, non-Quaker colleges.

When the college opened in 1859, its curriculum continued the patterns that the Boarding School had begun. There were two courses in each, the classical and the scientific. The preparatory department's curriculum was geography, American history, English grammar, physiology, arithmetic, algebra, "natural philosophy," and Latin for the classical course. Those in the preparatory scientific course did not study Latin, but completed algebra, geometry, and chemistry. In the college, the freshman class did history, algebra, geometry, chemistry, Virgil, and Cicero in the first year of the classical course. The sophomore class took up geology, analytical geometry, rhetoric, calculus, Livy, Horace, Cicero, and Tacitus. The study of Greek began in the junior year, along with "mental philosophy," mechanics, and astronomy. In the senior year, the classical course dropped all forms of natural science for political economy, philosophy, and more work in Greek. The scientific course was identical in the first two years. In the last two it was entirely scientific, a combination of chemistry, botany, astronomy, geology, and civil engineering. Only the scientific course allowed any electives, one each in the junior and senior years. Although the school claimed that its classical course was suited "more nearly to the wants of the West" by requiring less work in Greek and Latin, it did not differ greatly from most other colleges in Ohio and Indiana. Similarly, the textbooks were standard works that most American colleges employed.[80]

Gradually, over the years, the curriculum broadened and left behind its old bases. The college added new areas of study slowly—English in 1873 (Shakespeare was admitted to the library in 1865), American and European history in 1887, speech in 1888, modern languages earlier.

The possible routes to the bachelor's degree also doubled, to four, in 1884. The ancient classical course still focused on Greek and Latin, while the modern classical substituted foreign languages. There were two scientific courses, the Latin and regular, with the latter substituting French and German for the classical languages. More gradual change followed with the addition of elective courses, although it was the 1890s before the modern system of majors was established. By that time it was possible to graduate without Latin. These changes did not come without comment. In 1876, James B. Unthank, an 1874 graduate who went on to become the president of Wilmington College, worried about the proliferation of possible courses of study. "Indeed, so varied have come to be the subjects by which the student's attention is divided and distracted, . . . he can get but a smattering," Unthank complained. The modern student, he concluded, was beginning "to regard his education in many respects as a sham and a fraud."[81]

The most definite breaks with the past came with the introduction of art and music into the curriculum. Art was less controversial. Although many Quakers had always regarded it with skepticism as a concession to worldliness and vanity and as a waste of time, painting was never under the ban of the Discipline. Some Friends did sit for portraits or miniatures, and there were even a few Quaker artists, such as Marcus Mote. As early as 1860, Earlham employed a drawing teacher, and as early as 1863 students wrote essays on painters. In 1874, Marcus Mote himself gave a guest lecture on the "Fine Arts."[82]

In 1882, the college established a Department of Painting and Drawing, with a "skillful artist" in charge. The first two teachers were women, Florence Chandlee and Gertrude Baily, succeeded in 1888 by John Elwood Bundy, a Quaker from Monrovia, Indiana, just beginning his career as a painter. By 1888, the college waxed eloquent about the advantages that the study of art offered at Earlham, matched as it was with "advantages for advanced study in other departments." This in turn meant "not . . . the ability to paint a few indifferent pieces with which to decorate bare walls, but to place within the reach of the student the means of positive intellectual training and true aesthetic culture." That same year the *Earlhamite* hailed the department as "one of the most attractive features of the college." Yet it is unclear how much of an impact it had. In 1895 there were complaints that few students made use of the studio.[83]

Music proved a much more controversial innovation. The traditional Quaker position was clear—music, vocal or instrumental, was a sop to the senses, a distraction from the true business of the soul. To indulge in it was an offense against the Discipline that could bring disownment. In the 1860s and 1870s, the school tried to hold fast to this testimony. There were reports that authorities even attempted to stamp out whistling, but this may well be apocryphal. Musical instruments were definitely under the ban.[84]

The prohibition eroded gradually. As early as 1865, the Phoenix sang a hymn at one of their meetings. A year later, the board of managers gave its cautious approval to singing "on the same basis as other religious or devotional exercises"—it was acceptable if there were no "preconcerted arrangements for this object." Yet concerts and other forms of public singing were still forbidden, and students could not take music lessons even off campus. In the 1870s, however, vocal music expanded its toehold. At the 1874 commencement the graduating class, after receiving their diplomas, sang a hymn, much to the distress of traditionalist Friends. In 1878, however, the board approved singing in Ionian and Phoenix society meetings "in proper moderation." That fall a "double quartette" performed on campus, although it is unclear whether they were students or townspeople.[85]

The last barriers fell in the 1880s. In 1882, the *Earlhamite* began agitating for change, claiming that "music is ennobling, it is elevating." "It is natural for the soul to praise its maker by song and by testimony," it argued. "The time is not far distant when Earlham College will be considered deficient in its instruction, unless it has a professor of music." Indeed, it asked, "how many ladies leave our college every year, and how many never come, because they cannot pursue their music?" Emily Wanzer Mills, the wife of future president Joseph J. Mills, joined in, pointing out that "vocal music has found its place in almost every meeting and Bible School." In vain did Barnabas C. Hobbs express doubts about the intellectual value of most of the singing done on college campuses.[86]

With these pressures, and probably, more importantly, the changes among Friends, the board relented. The 1882 catalog dropped the prohibition on musical instruments. In the fall of 1883, the board rejected a request for music lessons to be offered on campus, but it did approve students taking instruction "in instrumental music or vocal culture" off campus. Two years later, the board relented and agreed to the formation of a Music Department. The one concession to tradition was a continuing ban on musical instruments in meetings for worship, including commencement, a prohibition that drew student wrath. By 1892 there was agitation on campus for a music building.[87]

Just as much a departure from Quaker tradition, and in the end far more controversial, was the establishment of the Biblical Institute in 1888. It was largely the work of Dougan Clark, and it was the most direct outgrowth of the holiness revival at Earlham.

Clark had begun his connection with Earlham in 1866, when he became professor of Greek and Latin. He resigned in 1869 to return to medical practice. About that time, however, his life took a radical new turn when he encountered David B. Updegraff. In 1871, under Updegraff's guidance, Clark experienced sanctification. By 1884, when he returned to Earlham, Clark had become not only a leading figure in the Quaker holiness revival, but also a respected presence in the larger interdenominational holiness movement. His book, *The Offices of the Holy Spirit*, went through several editions, and Clark was a frequent contributor to holiness and Quaker journals. He also became a luminary at holiness camp meetings like Ocean Grove, New Jersey, and Mountain Lake Park, Maryland.[88]

Clark resigned his classical languages post in the spring of 1888, but a donation from Elizabeth H. Farnum, a Philadelphia Friend and holiness enthusiast, came to open up a new field. Farnum's gift was earmarked for a Biblical Institute, not a regular collegiate course but an adjunct for the practical and Scriptural training of Quaker ministers and other "Christian workers." There had been such a department in existence on paper since 1884, but it had never been sufficiently staffed.[89]

Clark's prestige among holiness Friends was enough to draw students. In vital respects, however, the institute was apart from the college, a kind of poor cousin. It offered a two-year course. Its audience, although according to the catalog "ministers, Bible school teachers, and other Christian workers," in reality consisted almost entirely of pastors, or aspiring pastors and missionaries. Enrollment was usually small, averaging about fifteen up to 1894. The students self-consciously separated themselves from the student culture of the rest of the college, living off the campus, eschewing the organizations and athletics. Still, Indiana and Western yearly meetings perceived the department as meeting a need, and they gave it some support. By the 1890s, as Friends in the Midwest embraced the pastoral system, there was a terrible shortage of pastors, and this was Earlham's first direct contribution to a solution. Earlham depended on contributions from the yearly meeting to help subsidize the living expenses of the students. There was tension when some Friends in the yearly meetings contended that Earlham should allow ministers to attend without paying tuition. Still, the institute, during its life, attracted a number of Indiana and Ohio Friends who would be well-known ministers in future years.[90]

Clark's teaching was unabashed in its holiness commitment. He decorated his classroom with a banner that read: "Holiness to the Lord." His main text, other than the Bible, was a manual by an Australian Methodist holiness minister. Most of all, the class emphasized a literal, inerrantist approach to understanding the Bible. "We have decided once for all that God has made a revelation to man, and that what He has revealed is included in the books of the Old and New Testament," he told his class. "We believe them to be the truth of God from Genesis to Revelation, and we therefore bow to their authority, and consider every question decided when we have a 'Thus saith the Lord.'"[91]

It is difficult to gauge how much influence Clark had on campus. He did teach the general student population in the Bible courses. Students apparently liked and respected him for his gentle personality and thoughtful devoutness. But, as has already been seen, there is little to indicate that his holiness faith became widespread at Earlham. And when Clark departed in 1894, there were few, if any, student protests.[92]

If there was little about Earlham's religious teachings that was truly distinctive in this period, the same is not true of the natural sciences. Here a remarkable teacher was bringing Darwinian evolution not only to Earlham, but to Indiana and the Midwest, and laying the foundations for Earlham's long-standing strength in the natural sciences.

That teacher was Joseph Moore. Like several other of Earlham's most important early faculty, Moore was born in the Blue River settlement of Friends in Washington County, Indiana. Educated in the monthly meeting school, and teaching for a time, in 1853 Moore came to Richmond to enter Friends Boarding School. He made such a favorable impression that he soon became part of the faculty. Conscious of his own uneven education, in 1859 he took the advice of William B. Morgan and Zaccheus Test and went to Harvard for two years of study that brought him a B.S. degree in 1861.[93]

At Harvard, Moore studied botany, zoology, and geology at a time when Charles Darwin's *Origin of Species* was rocking the scientific world. Darwin argued for the evolution of "higher" forms of life from the lower orders of species. The three professors under whom Moore studied responded differently to Darwin. Louis Agassiz, to whom Moore was personally closest, was perhaps the leading American scientific critic of Darwin. In contrast, Moore's second professor, the botanist Asa Gray, was one of Darwin's first American converts. The greatest influence on Moore, however, was apparently Jeffries Wyman, who in his classes dispassionately presented the evidence for and against evolution.[94]

When he returned to Earlham to teach in 1861, Moore began, cautiously at first, more openly later, to bring evolution into his geology and biology courses. He certainly was the first college teacher in Indiana, most likely west of the Appalachians, to do so. The unquestionably devout Moore was able to resolve his uncertainties about the compatibility of science and Scripture by taking a course common to scientists in the 1860s and 1870s, adopting a theistic view of evolution. Moore saw evolution as the working out of the divine will, the process of creation

JOSEPH MOORE

that God had chosen to employ. It was not until 1876, however, that Moore finally spoke publicly on the subject.[95]

It is difficult to gauge the response to Moore's teaching. A colleague later asserted that "the poor man was hounded to death almost, by people that thought he was teaching unsound things because he was teaching the evolutionary theory." Certainly some students arrived as skeptics. David W. Dennis, Moore's student and later his colleague, remembered that he came to Earlham in 1870 with "armor all on. I had heard that Earlham said that the world was over 6,000 years old. My high resolve was to learn as much geology as anybody ever knew, and show that Earlham was mistaken." Instead, Dennis became one of Moore's most committed disciples.[96]

Whatever their attitudes about evolution when they arrived, Earlham students usually left as admirers of Moore and in agreement with his teachings. When a local Presbyterian minister came to campus to denounce the "scientific infidelity" of evolutionists in 1886, students were outraged. They responded that the Bible was "the will of God revealed to man to govern him in his moral relations toward his fellow man and his creator, and not as a book of science." There would be no conflict between religion and science, they argued, if we would "let those who deal with the material answer the questions pertaining to the material, and those who deal with the spiritual answer the questions pertaining to the spiritual." The real problem, Dennis asserted, was the irrational fears of some ministers. "Christianity has lost more by fearing the truth than by any other one thing," Dennis told the class of 1876, "when if it had fearlessly accepted and defended it it might have basked with renewed strength on a higher plane with fairer prospects."[97]

The public attacks were few. There were murmurs in Indiana Yearly Meeting about taking action against David W. Dennis, but they came to nothing. William L. Pearson, an 1875 graduate, did proclaim evolution "Anti-Christian" and claimed that it aimed to put humans on a level with God. Pearson, however, found few supporters on campus. Historians now agree that evolution was not a major source of conflict in American religion before 1900, as most churches adjusted to theistic evolution as scientists like Moore expounded it. Friends were not much different. A few holiness revivalists, like Clark and Updegraff, blasted evolutionists as enemies of faith, but they, on this question, attracted few followers. There is nothing to indicate that the yearly meetings ever took up the issue. Evolution was by 1895 firmly established at the heart of Earlham's scientific curriculum.[98]

Still, one cannot underestimate the importance of the fact that it was Joseph Moore who taught evolution. His standing as a Friend was unquestionable. Recorded a minister in 1865, he became a fixture at quarterly meetings and conferences. His simple preaching made a lasting impression on his hearers. "There was never an effort to present anything sensational or emotional; he did not enter into controversial subjects or use high sounding or unusual diction," one of his students remembered. "He simply interpreted the plain teachings of Jesus Christ in terms of daily living." One North Carolina Friend doubtless spoke for many when he said of the professor: "He ain't an educated person. I understood every word he said."[99]

This was not Moore's only contribution to Earlham. Almost equally important was his ceaseless effort to build a natural history museum on campus. These were the days when a "cabinet" of samples of flora, fauna, and minerals was a fixture of any college. When Moore came back to Earlham in 1861, he found two crates of rocks used for geology classes. Moore set out to right that. For four decades, he tirelessly gathered specimens of everything that might be useful for teaching zoology, botany, or geology. Farmers brought him bones they plowed up in their fields; thus Moore acquired the museum's most valuable possession, the fossil beaver. In 1874–1875 he set off on a collecting expedition to the Hawaiian Islands, varying his scientific endeavors by preaching through an interpreter. He came back with twenty barrels and boxes, all collected at his own expense. At least three times he and his students descended on circuses passing through the neighborhood on hearing that they had elephants *in extremis* whose skeletons Moore coveted. Finally, in 1877, he was able to dig out of a mound near Connersville the remains of Tippo Sahib, supposedly one of the three largest elephants ever seen in the United States. When Moore died in 1905, the museum had a permanent home in Lindley Hall and was regarded as one of the best in the Midwest.[100]

Governance

If Earlham's curriculum was not distinctively Quaker, neither was its system of governance. Under the direct control of a yearly meeting part of the time, and under the governance of a board that two yearly meetings appointed for the rest, the college did not work according to the business procedures of a Quaker meeting. Instead, it took its methods from the non-Quaker "world." Nevertheless, its relations with Friends, while sometimes strained, were close. Most Earlham students continued to come from Indiana and Western (Western was formed from Indiana in 1858, embracing southern and western Indiana and Illinois) yearly meetings, and many returned there to live. Earlham took most of its faculty from the same places. Most had been students at Earlham themselves, and many returned to teach for long tenures. Job security, however, was uncertain, as two crises over the dismissal of professors in 1884 and 1894 showed.

When the Friends Boarding School became Earlham College in 1859, its relationship with Indiana Yearly Meeting did not change. Power remained in the hands of a board of managers that the yearly meeting appointed. Its authority was unrestricted, and it exerted its control, at least in early days, over virtually every facet of the college. The managing committee still consisted of a dozen Friends, half men, half women, appointed annually by Indiana Yearly Meeting. Later in the 1860s, they moved to three-year terms. Usually, managers lived in the Richmond area, with a few as far away as Carthage or Spiceland, and an occasional Friend from Cincinnati or Waynesville, Ohio. They were invariably "weighty" Friends, active in other affairs of the yearly meeting. Elijah Coffin, the school's guiding spirit in its early years, died in 1862. His mantle fell to Timothy Nicholson, who became a manager in 1865 and remained on the board until 1914. Nicholson, a native of North Carolina, had been superintendent at Haverford before moving to Richmond in 1860, where he became a prosperous bookseller and stationer. For many he was the "Master Quaker"—an elder, clerk of the yearly meeting of ministers and elders, active in all good causes. Timothy was a formidable force, to be crossed only at considerable risk, in both the yearly meeting and in the college. No other Friend among the managers had half as much influence.[101]

The method of choosing the managers is unclear. Especially after 1865, the yearly meeting tended to favor Friends who had some connection with the college as former students or as parents of students, or who had clear intellectual interests. The yearly meeting often favored former members of the faculty. By the 1870s, affluence also apparently became a consideration, with the appointment of Cincinnati banker Mordecai Morris White, a son-in-law of Elijah Coffin and the college's greatest benefactor before 1910, and Mary Hough Goddard of Muncie, Indiana, the wife of a successful wholesale grocer.[102]

The board theoretically controlled every aspect of the school. Until 1862, it was directly involved in student disciplinary cases, finally ceding to the faculty that year the right to expel students for specified offenses. The board set the schedule, and as late as 1879 had to approve even a change in the textbooks used in specific courses. It also had oversight of even the smallest expenditures. Its Visiting Committee regularly attended classes and was free with advice and comment about the practices and methods of the teachers and the preparation and accomplishments of the students. In 1864, for example, one visitor pronounced a Latin class "very defective in elementary drill," while in 1870 the committee urged students to achieve "better posture and more eye contact."

Students were aware of its power—"the Committee still reigns supreme," one wrote to a friend in 1866.[103]

This arrangement might have continued indefinitely had it not been for financial problems. For the first decade of its existence, the college department of the school was a money loser. It required three or four instructors to offer the minimum of instruction to twenty or thirty students, while the same number of teachers taught one hundred preparatory students. Essentially, the preparatory department had to subsidize the college, but even then there were operating deficits. Since there was no endowment, and little in the way of reserves, shortfalls had to be made up by canvassing friends of the school.[104]

By 1868, this had led to some tension between the college and the yearly meeting. The yearly meeting did not provide any kind of subsidy, on the grounds that Earlham served mainly well-to-do Friends whose education poorer members of the yearly meeting should not have to support. It was a particularly sore point in 1867 when the yearly meeting refused $2,000 from its treasury for a badly needed new laundry and washhouse.[105]

Two solutions to these problems appeared possible. One, which some members of the yearly meeting advocated, called for "some radical changes," abolishing the money-losing collegiate department. Supporters of higher education, however, pointed out that Friends were developing their own local academies that competed with Earlham for secondary students, and that as a result a majority of the preparatory students were not Friends. To take this course would mean the loss, in a few years, of any Quaker identity.[106]

Instead, the yearly meeting decided on the alternative, endowing the college and broadening its base of support. Barnabas C. Hobbs argued for this, urging Ohio, Western, and Iowa yearly meetings to join with Indiana to make Earlham *the* Orthodox Quaker center of higher education in the West. As a first step, in 1870 the yearly meeting agreed to mount a campaign for an endowment. By 1872, the school had raised $50,000. In the next year, however, a severe economic depression struck the nation, lasting five years. Enrollment fell, and the board cut faculty salaries. Meanwhile, debts for necessary repairs, and for installing gas for lighting, had piled up.[107]

Against this background of financial difficulty, the alumni association was becoming increasingly restive. Formed in 1871 and composed only of graduates, it aimed both at improving the school and giving alumni some voice in its management. The *Earlhamite* expressed its attitude in its first issue: "People generally even within a limited distance do not know what Earlham College really is, nor realize the high standard of Earlham scholarship, and even in the Society of Friends the object and workings of Earlham are not understood, and some even regard it with suspicion." The solution was to bring the alumni into the governance of the college by allowing alumni to elect members of the board. In 1877 the association sent a formal proposal to the managers.[108]

It is unclear how much influence alumni unrest had on the board or on Indiana Yearly Meeting. But the board certainly was aware that there was little chance of more money coming from the yearly meeting. In 1874, when the depression was at its worst, Indiana Yearly Meeting had approved a $3,000 appropriation for a desperately needed laboratory building, only to strike it out at a later session. The yearly meeting always had kind words for Earlham, but little more. In 1878 the board's report to the yearly meeting was blunt in saying that Earlham was "not duly appreciated."[109]

Amidst these problems, the board submitted to Indiana Yearly Meeting a proposal that was largely the work of Joseph Moore. Based on the premise that there was "a great need of concentration of action among Friends on a few higher institutions of learning," it invited Ohio and Western yearly meetings "to join in the management and control of Earlham." The three yearly meetings would appoint members of the board in proportion to membership. Indiana Yearly Meeting would then lease the physical plant of the college to the board for a set period of time.[110]

Moore's proposal met with a mixed reaction. Ohio Yearly Meeting, for reasons that are unclear, declined the invitation. It sent few students to Earlham and probably felt only a slight connection. There was also opposition to other provisions. Western Yearly Meeting had reported favorably on the link with Earlham, but felt that the lease arrangement would be unjust to it, creating a situation in which Western would spend money to improve property that was Indiana Yearly Meeting's and would revert to it. Instead, it proposed that both yearly meetings join in the management of the institution. Indiana Yearly Meeting would convey the property to an independent corporation. The two yearly meetings would appoint its trustees and thus have indirect control of the college. Proposals for the alumni association and the board itself to appoint members fell by the wayside. In 1880, both yearly meetings approved the modified proposal, and in 1881 Indiana Yearly Meeting conveyed the college to the new corporation. Each yearly meeting appointed twelve trustees, with the president as the twenty-fifth.[111]

The two yearly meetings created a legal curiosity. They gave up all direct powers of governance and control to the new corporation, reserving only the right to appoint a committee to investigate and make recommendations about conditions at the school. Yet they continued to speak of their relationship as one of ownership and control. And so long as they appointed all of the trustees, that was the effect.[112]

The institution that the new board took over was not exactly flourishing. One of its first actions was to bring Allen Jay back from New England as superintendent and financial agent. Years later, Jay remembered his first impression of his new charge:

> I had just left an institution where the buildings were in good repair, with plenty of room, and with sufficient funds to run it in a creditable manner, with its enrollment between two hundred and three hundred students. Here was a college with one building for everything—cooking, living, sleeping, eating, laundry work, study, recitations, lectures, library, reading room, museum, laboratory, meeting room, society halls, etc. The treasurer's office and the president's office were both in the same room. The treasurer's office was used for selling books and stationery, keeping accounts, post-office, and everything connected with the superintendent's office. . . . What made it more disagreeable, this building was in very poor repair. The heating apparatus had given out, the cooking and laundry department had to be torn down and rebuilt, barns and stables had to be repaired. . . . I have never told anyone my feelings, and I will not try to do it now, yet they are very vivid.[113]

Faced with this situation, the board grappled with possible solutions. By any standard, it was a strong group. The addition of the Western trustees had brought Barnabas and Rebecca Hobbs to the board, along with Moses C. Stevens, a Purdue University professor who had formerly taught at Earlham, William L. Pyle, a wealthy Indianapolis Friend, and Absalom Rosenberger, an 1876 graduate who would become president of both Penn and Whittier colleges. A year later, Charles F. Coffin and Joseph R. Evans, a well-to-do Indianapolis Friend and son of Thomas Evans, the first clerk of the Boarding School committee, came on. They were Friends long interested in the college, and not ones to be deferential to anyone, in their yearly meetings or on the campus.[114]

The board moved decisively in 1884. The occasion was hiring a new president. Joseph Moore had, as a courtesy, submitted his resignation to the new board when it formed. The board rejected it, and in fact gave every indication that it wanted Moore to remain. In the spring of 1883, however, Moore, always in frail health, found himself with a heart ailment and was advised by his doctor to move to a warmer place. This time the board reluctantly accepted his departure. William P. Pinkham, who had come to Earlham to teach English in 1879, became acting president.[115]

The board settled on one of its own members as Moore's successor. Joseph John Mills had but a slight connection with Earlham, having been a student for only one year. That, and a year at the University of Michigan, were his only academic credentials. Mills was an effective administrator, however, at this time the superintendent of the Indianapolis city schools, and was a member of a large and important Quaker family. He was also a recorded minister, and relatively young, only thirty-seven when appointed. The choice of a leading member of Western Yearly Meeting doubtless strengthened its feeling of connection with the school.[116]

At the same meeting that called Mills to the presidency, however, the board outraged the students and faculty by asking for the resignation of the two most popular and influential members of the faculty, Alpheus McTaggart and Calvin W. Pearson. It gave no reason—in fact it never did. When one of the two sent a letter to a board committee asking why, there came only an unsigned reply: "For the best interests of Earlham." Consternation was almost universal. The *Earlhamite* reported that "in the excitement and surprise of the news, many harsh expressions found ready vent." But the board refused to relent, and Pearson and McTaggart left. The affair continued to reverberate the rest of the year; in October a local newspaper taunted Friends for their "Quaker college scandals."[117]

It is impossible now to know what was behind the action. The two, along with Joseph Moore, had incurred the displeasure of Charles F. Coffin, a member of the board who was also the clerk of Indiana Yearly Meeting. Coffin apparently used his position to move against them. Probably more important is the problem that college historian Opal Thornburg noted. Pearson and McTaggart were both powerful figures on campus, popular with students and leaders in the alumni association. Mills may well have feared that their influence would overshadow his own. Both, moreover, had earned Ph.D.s—the only two on the faculty— a striking contrast with the new president, who lacked even a bachelor's degree. Ironically, the board may have overestimated the influence of the two. Neither the faculty nor the alumni mounted a serious challenge to the board on their behalf.[118]

Nevertheless, Mills realized that he had to move quickly to heal some of these wounds. He did that by hiring new faculty of unquestionable stature. Mills and the board tried but failed to persuade William P. Pinkham to remain and Joseph Moore to return (although Moore did so later). They did, however, find replacements of considerable ability: David W. Dennis for Moore, William N. Trueblood for Pinkham, and Dougan Clark for McTaggart. Clark, of course, was well known among Friends. Trueblood was a popular alumnus, while Dennis had been president of Wilmington College. Mills also broke with tradition by appointing the first non-Quaker member of the faculty, Hans von Jagemann. This array of talent apparently quieted potential objectors. And in fact Mills's presidency would be the longest in Earlham's history, nineteen years.[119]

With this action, the board settled down to a less obtrusive oversight of the faculty. The only other major change in governance came in 1889, when the number of trustees was cut in half. It was Timothy Nicholson's idea; he argued that the board was too large and that it would be "economical" to reduce its size. Surprisingly, the board and the yearly meetings agreed, each reducing the number of its appointees to six.[120]

The new board was also willing to take risks in another way, improving the physical plant. Thirty-five years after it had opened, the college still housed virtually every activity in Earlham Hall. As enrollment gradually grew, the college had no choice but to allow some students to board in homes near the campus. While this was probably not all bad in student eyes, the board and faculty agreed that it was a deplorable situation for maintaining discipline. In 1886, the board agreed to the construction of two buildings, a small one to house the natural sciences and a larger one for other departments, the library, and the president's office. Earlham Hall would become a dormitory only.[121]

The fund-raising campaign for the two buildings, the first since the endowment campaign in 1871, showed how difficult Earlham's situation was. Earlier in the decade, Barnabas C. Hobbs had noted that the average annual donation of members of Indiana and Western yearly meetings was one third of one cent. In 1884 the *Earlhamite* agreed. "Who has not seen hundreds of dollars raised in a single sitting in Indiana Yearly Meeting for missions, when 25 cents could not have been raised for Earlham College?" it asked. The experience of finding money for the two buildings confirmed their fears. The two yearly meetings minuted their entire approval, but appropriated nothing from their treasuries. Indeed, the two largest gifts, $10,000 and $5,000, came respectively from Alfred H. Lindley and Mordecai Parry, two Minneapolis Friends. The board dispatched faithful Allen Jay to travel and raise funds. His abilities, again and again called on, would prove considerable over the next two decades, but they were insufficient to provide everything needed. The cost of the two new buildings, named Parry and Lindley halls, came to about $77,000, of which $17,000 had to be borrowed. Still, with these new buildings, plus various outbuildings, by 1888 Earlham, with its buildings scattered around what was now called the "Heart," for the first time looked like a campus.[122]

Thus far, this discussion of governance has focused on the board. That is proper, given its powers relative to those of the teaching faculty. The powers, and the security, of the faculty, as was almost universally the case in American higher education at the time, were extremely limited.[123]

The first formal organization of the faculty had come with the establishment of the college in 1859. There was no differentiation between the preparatory and college faculty. The superintendent presided at the meetings, which were held almost weekly. In 1867, with the approval of the board, the superintendent's title was changed to president, with business affairs placed in the hands of a treasurer, although the superintendent's office was soon revived and the duties of the treasurer were reduced.[124]

Significantly, from the beginning the faculty meeting apparently did not follow the traditional Quaker business method of seeking the sense of the meeting. In 1860, the faculty recorded its decision that "decisions of the majority shall be reported to the students as decisions of the Council, and that no member or members be allowed to get up a minority report . . . thereby tending to create dissensions among the Faculty." From this it is clear that from the beginning, the faculty meeting made decisions by voting. In 1877 it adopted *Roberts Rules of Order*, the standard that remained in place for seventy years.[125]

In the 1860s and 1870s, the managers kept a close eye on the business of the faculty. In the 1860s, a few managers often attended the faculty meeting. In 1866, Joseph Dickinson, a weighty Richmond Friend, and the redoubtable Timothy Nicholson were even made part of the faculty to aid in "enforcing certain regulations." The faculty apparently had little to do with hiring new instructors, although it is unclear how much oversight the board exercised over the president. The faculty's main duties were enforcing discipline and approving substitutions and other deviations from the standard course requirements. Indeed, by the 1880s, they occupied most of every faculty meeting.[126]

Tenure in the modern sense, of course, did not exist for faculty. We have no way of knowing how many of the frequent departures of professors were involuntary. Aside from the spectacular dismissal of Calvin W. Pearson and Alpheus McTaggart in 1884, however, there appear to have been only two cases that involved disparate expectations about how Earlham faculty should conduct themselves. Both cases involved faculty who broke publicly with time-honored Quaker traditions. The first led to relatively little controversy. The second was very public, and explosively divisive, although more off the campus than on it.[127]

The quiet case was that of Zaccheus Test, an old student who had returned in 1855 to teach modern foreign languages. Test was a man of prodigious intellect, fluent in Latin, Greek, Hebrew, German, and French, and a medical doctor besides. A member of a prominent Richmond Quaker family, in 1865 Test was, with William B. Morgan, the senior member of the faculty.[128]

In one significant respect, however, Test departed from Quaker tradition. He often preached in the college meeting for worship, but he insisted on using notes that he had prepared in advance. Even with the changes taking place among Friends in the 1860s, referring to notes was unprecedented. Some Friends would not even allow reading from the Bible in meetings for worship. All ministry was to be under the direct leading of the Holy Spirit—if God intended one to quote from the Scriptures, the Spirit would bring the appropriate passage to mind. The managers agreed to tolerate Test's deviation.[129]

The practice, however, soon attracted unwelcome attention. "I have been charged on several times about Dr. Test's essays by some Friends here," wrote one recent graduate on a trip to Ohio. Part of the problem was that Test, a tenacious soul, not only insisted on reading his sermons, but also insisted that Friends acknowledge that to be consistent with Quaker belief. "I have no doubt that the doctor is sincere in taking the position he has," wrote Eli Jay; but, Jay concluded, "it seems that he is more concerned to carry his own point, and have his own way, than to do something for the spiritual improvement of the world." The board would not go as far as Test demanded, and he resigned from Earlham in 1866. His departure was quiet and little noted. Eventually (and doubtless not to the surprise of some), he left Friends and became an Episcopal priest.[130]

It was ironic that Test's successor in 1866 was Dougan Clark. Clark would be at the center of a controversy thirty years later that rocked Earlham and American Quakerism.

As we have seen, Clark emerged in the 1870s as one of American Quakerism's leading holiness preachers, and as a leading theologian of sanctification. He was especially close to David B. Updegraff, the outspoken Quaker holiness preacher from Mount Pleasant, Ohio. That devotion to Updegraff led Clark into controversy when, late in the 1870s, Updegraff began to challenge traditional Quaker views, especially on baptism. In 1884, Updegraff himself was baptized by a Baptist minister in Philadelphia.[131]

Updegraff was forthright and articulate in defending his views in pamphlets, articles, and sermons, and soon the Gurneyite yearly meetings found themselves divided between those who, like Updegraff, wished Friends to tolerate the ordinances, and those Friends who held to the traditional position. Clark quickly identified himself with Updegraff. Indiana Yearly Meeting just as quickly condemned Updegraff and the "waterites," ruling that no recorded minister could undergo water baptism and remain in that station. There was some criticism of Earlham for having a pronounced "waterite" like Clark on the faculty, but the board allowed Clark to remain. There were rumors that it had required him to sign an agreement that he would not teach his views on the ordinances in his classes.[132]

In May 1894, Updegraff died unexpectedly. That August, Ohio Yearly

DOUGAN CLARK

Meeting invited Clark to conduct the memorial service at its annual sessions. At one of the devotional meetings John Pennington, an outspoken "waterite," confronted Clark: "Dr. Clark, the Holy Spirit wants thee to be baptized now and publicly and at once." One Friend present thought that Pennington had "tricked" and "cornered" the dazed, grief-stricken Clark, but whatever the reason, Clark let Pennington baptize him.[133]

Clark's baptism created a crisis in Indiana Yearly Meeting and a major problem for Earlham. The yearly meeting could hardly tolerate this act of defiance by a leading minister, and Earlham could hardly have that minister as its chief teacher of religion. Yet the gentle Clark still had many admirers, and Joseph J. Mills feared the reaction to a public dismissal. So he acted stealthily—he contacted the students who had planned to enroll in the Biblical Department and persuaded each not to come. Thus when Clark returned, he had no students. After waiting two weeks he resigned.[134]

That did not end the case. Before his resignation, there were demands that Earlham dismiss him. A campaign to depose him from the ministry developed. Whitewater Monthly Meeting offered Clark a chance to recant, but he resolutely refused. Timothy Nicholson quickly emerged as the leader of the anti-Clark forces, and rumors spread about his conduct. One said that Nicholson had threatened an Earlham professor with dismissal if he supported Clark. Whitewater Monthly Meeting was badly split. There were rumors of an impending separation; one member took to the newspaper to accuse Nicholson of being a tyrant, leading an "irregular and arbitrary faction . . . responsible for . . . volcanic eruptions. The case finally brought the meeting to a halt in 1895. The quarterly meeting of ministers and elders had deposed Clark from the ministry, but in a stormy session, the monthly meeting refused to approve. After the impasse in the monthly meeting, there was a delay of two months, when the monthly meeting accepted the deposition. Clark, however, had but little time left to live; he died in February 1896.[135]

Earlham had changed fundamentally in the thirty-six years between Dougan Clark's first appearance to envision the future of Quakerism and his departure in 1894. At the end of the 1850s the new Earlham College was still a sectarian institution, dedicated to preserving and inculcating the peculiarities of the Society of Friends. In 1895 it was still under the control of Friends, still with a Quaker majority among its students, and almost all of its faculty were still Quakers.

In most respects, however, the dominant note was one of change, as Earlham became less distinctive, more like other colleges. In part this was because Quakerism changed. After 1870, most Gurneyite Friends in

Indiana gave up nearly all of the peculiarities that had set them apart for two centuries: dress, speech, silent worship. Instead, Friends meetings called pastors, held revivals, and introduced choirs and music. For many Friends, theology became a holiness commitment that gradually led them toward fundamentalism. If Earlham was less distinctive, it was in part because Quakers had become less distinctive.

This dramatic change deeply affected Earlham, but within limits. While the campus knew outbreaks of religious enthusiasm, there were never full-bore revivals. While expressions of faith were evangelical, few on campus embraced holiness teachings. Most Earlham faculty and students were moderate critics of revivalism. And while Earlham did move to train ministers, that never became central to its understanding of itself. Instead, Earlham's Quakerism was beginning its divergence from the Quakers around it.

The revival's weakening of the plain life did open the way for Earlham to develop a student culture very much like that of other schools. Life outside the classroom became increasingly central to student self-understanding. And that life focused increasingly on campus groups like the literary societies and the YMCA. It also became more male-dominated, with Earlham's entry into competitive athletics.

The college's curriculum and governance also showed the impact of change, especially the decline of Quaker distinctiveness. The curriculum had never been that much different from that of other schools, and by 1895 there were few differences, usually involving applying a Quaker gloss or adding a Quaker text to history, religion, or philosophy courses. As at most other colleges, the ancient languages lost their central place. What probably made Earlham most distinctive after 1865 was not anything Quakerly, but the early and uncontroversial teaching of evolution by Joseph Moore, which laid the foundation for Earlham's tradition of strength in the natural sciences.

Governance still lay firmly in the hands of the board. The faculty was limited largely to matters of student discipline and course requirements. The change in composition of the board to bring in Western Yearly Meeting in 1881 had little immediate impact. Personal ties still bound the college to the yearly meetings—the fact that most Earlham faculty and students continued to come from them, and that a significant proportion returned to be active in them.

The relationship was not always easy. In these years, a college education was undoubtedly beyond the financial reach of most Indiana Friends. Thus they saw no reason to tax themselves to provide one for more affluent Friends. The two yearly meetings were penurious in financial support, seldom drawing directly on their treasuries, which was a source of considerable irritation for many at Earlham.

This irritation, however, only occasionally burst into open controversy. The worst, when Dougan Clark defied Indiana Yearly Meeting's position on the ordinances in 1894, forced Clark out of the college. Clark's departure, and the way in which Joseph John Mills decided to fill his position, would have consequences that no one could foresee, as the next chapter will show.

Quakerism, Modernism,
Professionalism, Professor Russell,
and President Kelly,

1895–1915

*I*n May 1895 Elbert Russell was definitely Earlham's bright young man. The year before, he had graduated at the head of his class, and President Joseph John Mills thought so highly of him that he had invited Russell to stay on as governor of the men's dormitory. Russell's plan was to remain for a year or two, and then with his savings go off to do graduate work in German as the foundation for the teaching career he envisioned.[1]

President Mills, however, had other plans for Russell, plans whose consequences for Russell and for Earlham he could not have realized. One afternoon that May, Mills called Russell to his Lindley Hall office and put forward an astounding offer. Mills wanted Russell to take over Earlham's biblical department, which had been in limbo since the departure of Dougan Clark the autumn before. Russell protested that he had had no training, other than a required course on the life of Christ, and no knowledge of Greek or Hebrew. Mills waved off his objections with the assurance that a little time at the Moody Bible Institute in Chicago and a summer Chautauqua course would fit him for his new responsibilities.[2]

Immensely flattered by Mills's confidence, and also attracted by the salary that was offered, Russell accepted the position. He would not be content with a summer's training, however—he would make scriptural scholarship his life's work, and would fit himself for it with graduate work at the University of Chicago. As the head of Earlham's biblical department from 1895, with one break, to 1915, Russell would exert enormous influence over a generation of Earlham students, and make religion a discipline as critical and scholarly as any on campus. Russell would also become an internationally known Friend, one of the most influential of the twentieth century. Simultaneously, Russell's commitment both to a strong Quaker identity for Earlham and to critical, modernist biblical scholarship, would put him at the center of controversy with Friends both on and off campus.

These themes—the struggle to preserve a distinctive Quaker identity, the struggle to introduce critical methods of studying and understanding the Bible, and the struggle to professionalize the faculty and the college—are the keys for understanding Earlham's history between 1895 and 1915. Russell was at the center of all three, probably more critical for the first two than was either of the presidents he served. His commitment to modernist scriptural scholarship brought to Earlham the battles that other institutions and denominations faced in these years. He would also become an articulate and outspoken proponent for a new understanding of Quakerism and a reassertion of its distinctiveness, especially at Earlham, and this brought him into conflict with Earlham's other president of the period, Robert L. Kelly, who replaced Mills in 1903. Both Russell and Kelly were committed to professionalizing the college—a faculty of Ph.D.s, aggressive fund-raising tied to great foundations, participation in scholarly organizations. For Kelly, however, professionalization involved a considerable degree of secularization, and especially deemphasizing certain Quaker aspects of the college. That brought him into conflict with Russell, a conflict that climaxed in 1915, when Russell attempted to force Kelly out of the presidency. That attempt failed, and Russell left Earlham. Yet echoes of the controversy remained for another generation, and it is not difficult to make the case that Russell's influence on Earlham was as great as that of Mills or Kelly. Thus some understanding of Russell's life and background is critical for understanding Earlham.

Professor Russell

Elbert Russell was born in Friendsville, Tennessee, in 1871. His parents were Quaker ministers from Indiana who had moved south after the Civil War. His father, William Russell, an 1866 Earlham graduate, had come south in the hope that through his teaching and ministry he might

Elbert Russell

help to revitalize the forlorn little Quaker communities of East Tennessee. In 1879, however, he and his wife died within a few months of each other, leaving Elbert Russell and his two sisters to be reared by their grandfather and grandmother Russell at West Newton, Indiana.[3]

West Newton was a largely Quaker community, and Russell grew up surrounded by Quaker relatives and neighbors. He was precocious both in school and church—an outstanding student in high school, he was chosen the clerk of the preparative meeting at West Newton at age eighteen. In 1890 he entered Earlham, graduating with a straight-A average four years later, and remaining, at President Mills's invitation, as a member of the staff and to work on a master's degree in German.[4]

Russell later described his early religion as a mixture of Quaker nonconformity and pietist commitment to biblical literalism. In Russell's first year in college, Walter Malone, a holiness Quaker minister from Cleveland (and an Earlham student in the 1870s) who would later be one of Russell's most persistent critics, held a revival that swept in most of the campus. Russell was among the converts, although the effects were to be less than lasting. By the time he graduated in 1894, he considered himself steady in basic Christian beliefs but still open to new understandings.[5]

Once installed as head of the biblical department, Russell hurriedly embarked on his training, which was just as Mills had suggested. First was a four-week intensive course at the Moody Bible Institute in Chicago, a program designed primarily for ministers. Then came six weeks at Lake Chautauqua to study Hebrew. Here Russell encountered his first modernist influence in William Rainey Harper, the president of the University of Chicago, who was one of the guest speakers. The most lasting impression for Russell, who had spent his life almost entirely among Quakers, was exposure to other denominations.[6]

Years later, Russell was appalled by the utter ignorance in which he began his teaching. He sought no help from other teachers or leading Friends because he did not even know what questions to ask. He also came to a realization about why Mills had chosen him—his lack of connection with or training in a seminary freed him from even the suspicion of any taint of "unsoundness." Russell speculated that Mills, who was himself mild and undogmatic, hoped that Russell would become a liberalizing influence among Indiana Friends, but there is no way to confirm his understanding.[7]

Regardless of whether it was Mills's plan, Russell developed in just this direction between 1895 and 1901. He won acclaim at Earlham as a popular and gifted teacher. Among the wider community of Friends, he became known as a preacher and writer. For some he was an inspiring figure. For others he was frightening, a false teacher who was undermining the faith of Friends in the authority of the Scriptures.

By 1900, Russell was identifying himself with the modernist move-ment that was profoundly influencing American Protestantism in the late nineteenth and early twentieth centuries, and with the "higher critics" who were challenging traditional methods of scriptural study. The two, although twin evils in the eyes of fundamentalists, were not the same, nor did commitment to one necessarily mean commitment to the other. "Higher criticism" was a scholarly method, a "scientific" outlook applied to the Bible. Its goal was to use all of the tools of scholarship available—linguistics, archeology, geology, sociology, psychology, and history—to determine the original intent of the writers of each book of the Bible, what they *really* meant, given the circumstances of the time. This was not in itself radical, but higher critics often made it so by pointing out various ahistorical or problematic sections of Scripture—for example, the two somewhat contradictory Creation accounts in Genesis and their incompatibility with geology and paleontology, the writing of the Pentateuch long after the period of Moses, the multiple authorship of the Book of Isaiah, the likelihood that many of the books of the New Testament were not written by the men whose names they bore. Such arguments were usually confined to the pages of mind-numbing schol-arly journals, but conservatives, including scholars with impeccable credentials, saw in them a weakening of the authority of Scripture and thus an undermining of Christianity.[8]

Modernism embraced this "scientific" approach, but it was a wider outlook that did not necessarily reject all traditional Protestant ortho-doxies. Modernists shared three basic views. The first was a belief in progressive revelation, a sense that each succeeding generation has a deeper understanding of religious truth than those that had gone before it. The second was a belief in the immanence of God, that God can be understood not just through the written revelation of Scripture, but through all of creation. Finally, modernists believed in the gradual growth or advent of God's kingdom on earth, that the world was surely and inevitably becoming a better place. These ideas would be vital for Russell in his years at Earlham.[9]

Russell began his journey toward modernism with his reading. Years later, he remembered that when he took over the biblical department virtually all of the theological books in the library were holiness works, mostly by Methodists, although the writings of the Quaker holiness enthusiast Hannah Whitall Smith were prominent. Dougan Clark's pri-mary text had been Field's *Handbook of Systematic Theology,* whose author, an Australian Methodist preacher, "treated all Biblical texts, often regardless of context, as of equal authority and who found an extreme doctrine of holiness everywhere." Russell refused to use it in his classes.[10]

Aware of his ignorance, Russell began to study the Bible systematically. Only gradually did an awareness of "historical and critical problems" dawn on him. According to his own account, he instinctively preferred works that used a scientific approach over the dogmatic ones that Clark favored. Especially important for Russell were those of George Adam Smith, Ernest Burton, and Shailer Mathews, the last two among the leading lights of the University of Chicago Divinity School. A visit to Richmond by Richard Moulton, another Chicago professor, introduced Russell to the idea of the Bible as literature, to be studied for its literary as well as its spiritual elements.[11]

A turning point for Russell was the visit to Earlham early in 1898 of John Wilhelm Rowntree. Rowntree was perhaps the leading young Friend in London Yearly Meeting, an extraordinarily influential voice for a Quakerism that would meld traditional forms of Quaker worship with modernist theology. Russell apparently impressed Rowntree favorably, since Rowntree offered to donate religious books to the library on the condition that he, Rowntree, select them. They arrived a few weeks later, mostly modernist works.[12]

It is difficult to gauge how much these events affected Russell's work in the classroom, since Russell's notes from this period have not survived and his students, largely concerned with defending their teacher against critics, spoke largely of his Christian commitment and reverence for the Bible. Russell was using works by Burton and Mathews as texts, however, and they were frank in their modernism. Certainly the criticism from opponents of liberal theology says much about the thrust of his courses.[13]

By 1897, Russell was ready to take his new insights off campus to Indiana and Western yearly meetings. His efforts were varied. One was to visit quarterly meetings, Sunday school conferences, and pastoral institutes. Another was to speak at the Quaker academies at Vermilion Grove, Illinois, and Spiceland, Plainfield, and Fairmount, Indiana. The most important and visible was the Bible School Institute held at Earlham beginning in 1897.[14]

The Bible School Institute was a week-long summer course designed for "ministers and Bible School teachers, and other Christian workers" in Indiana, Western, and Wilmington yearly meetings. It was the brainchild of Allen Jay, who intended it to deepen the scriptural learning especially of pastors in the yearly meetings, many of whom had limited formal education. Its direction fell to Russell, however, and he moved cautiously to introduce, at least in a limited way, modernist teachings. "I kept as far away as possible from speculative and theological questions," Russell remembered. "My aim was to give a fresh approach to Bible study and interpretation, which would in time open the way for different ideas of its use and meaning." But Russell's "fresh approach" was for many dangerous heterodoxy.[15]

Further exacerbating tensions was Russell's refusal to hold evening evangelistic meetings on campus, a refusal in which the board committee on religious life supported him. Those attending such meetings, Russell argued, were already converted; thus evangelism was unneeded. More importantly, in Russell's view, "the mental attitude of a school room is different from that of a revival meeting." The former assumed an open mind, a willingness to modify or change beliefs when faced with new evidence. On the other hand, the revivalist attitude was "essentially conservative," appealing to believers to "cling to the faith once for all delivered to the saints and to shun doubt as one would resist sin." This was precisely the mindset that would look askance at Russell over the next two decades.[16]

Russell was quite willing to critique the Quaker variety of holiness revivalism publicly. The most notable episode came in 1899, when he and his wife, Lieuetta, attended Western Yearly Meeting. At the Sunday evening session, as distinguished guests, they sat on the platform with the speaker, the well-known evangelist Esther Frame. She preached an emotionally charged sermon, "Homecoming in Heaven," in which she told the audience to wave handkerchiefs to those looking down on them from heaven. She then called on those who wished to go to to heaven to stand. The Russells conspicuously kept their seats, prompting Frame to turn and ask them, "Why, Brother and Sister Russell, don't you want to go to heaven?" It was awkward, but, disapproving of such emotionalism, they refused to answer. Fortunately for the Russells, the meeting later became so unruly under Frame's leadership that David Hadley, the yearly meeting superintendent, abruptly closed it.[17]

In this skepticism about revivalism, Russell joined a group of young modernist Gurneyite Friends who by 1900 were emerging as a powerful force in Quakerism. They included English Friends like Rowntree and William C. Braithwaite, Albert J. Brown, the Quaker pastor who married Russell and his wife, President Thomas Newlin of Pacific College, and, most of all, the philosopher Rufus M. Jones of Haverford, who was a frequent visitor to Earlham and who was making his journal, the *American Friend,* an articulate voice for his vision of liberal Quakerism. In the words of Jones, their acknowledged leader, these young modernists were "quietly, gradually . . . working to broaden the thought of the church." Russell's ties to this group were strengthened in 1900 when he attended the Haverford Summer School. The brainchild of Jones to bring together liberal-minded Friends and give them greater understanding of modernist Bible study, it included on its faculty Rowntree and J. Rendel Harris from England, George A. Barton of Haverford, and Richard H. Thomas of

Baltimore, all influential liberal Friends, and two non-Quaker modernists, William N. Clarke of Colgate and Foote Moore of Harvard. This was a critical experience for the young Russell. As he put it, it "revealed so clearly the deficiencies in my preparation for my work at Earlham that I resolved the following year to devote myself to further study."[18]

Finally, in these years Russell gained more of a sense of himself as a Friend. In 1897, the Gurneyite yearly meetings had held a conference in Indianapolis and there decided to draw up a uniform discipline and form a Five Years Meeting that would more closely align all Gurneyite Friends. This movement, in which Rufus Jones was a central figure, caught Russell's interest, and he began to follow Quaker affairs more closely. In 1900, he contributed his first articles to the *American Friend,* and in 1901 attended the first Friends Peace Conference in Philadelphia. Thus, by 1901, Russell had begun to develop a considerable reputation in Quaker circles as a bright young scholar and gifted teacher. But he was also controversial. Some of the older revival preachers saw him as hostile to and disrespectful of their work. Others were convinced that his advocacy of modern methods of biblical study indicated "unsoundness," an irreverence toward the Scriptures. More specific criticisms from these early years are lacking. Apparently to have a reputation as a modernist was enough to set off some evangelical Friends.[19]

By 1901, Russell was at a turning point in his career. Determined to do doctoral work, he applied to the University of Chicago and received a fellowship. President Mills urged him to take a leave of absence, but Russell, wanting to keep his options open, and uncertain about whether he wished to return to Earlham, submitted his resignation.[20]

Russell's years at Chicago, from 1901 to 1903, confirmed the direction in which he had been heading since 1895. At Chicago, he worked with Shailer Mathews, probably the country's foremost modernist theologian, and Ernest Burton, a renowned New Testament scholar. The two years at Chicago gave Russell new confidence in himself. "I had a sense of being at home in the field of Biblical scholarship and related subjects," he wrote in his autobiography. "I was no longer haunted by the fear that my teaching was vitiated by ignorance of methods of interpretation, theories, and facts which were the common property of scholars." Ironically, Russell left without completing his thesis, and in fact did not receive his doctorate until 1917.[21]

In the spring of 1903, Russell considered his prospects. One Friend suggested him for the presidency of Pacific College. Russell inquired about a post at Haverford, but when no opening appeared began discussing a return to Earlham. He set one condition, that he would have "full academic freedom" in his teaching. A committee of trustees asked to meet with him, and Russell was blunt: "I did not want to teach anywhere

where what I taught was to be censored." Benjamin Johnson, one of the oldest and most influential trustees, asked if that "excluded friendly discussion" about the meaning or implications of his teaching or "conference over its effect on the students or on the church?" That, Russell answered, was very welcome, and the board immediately rehired him.[22]

Since Russell had left for Chicago, however, an important change had taken place on the campus—a new president had arrived. He was Robert L. Kelly, and early in 1903 he had replaced Joseph John Mills. Kelly would be as much of a force for change at Earlham as Russell had been. His vision differed in fundamental ways from Russell's, and it brought the two into bitter conflict a decade later.

President Kelly's Earlham

Kelly was relatively young for a college president, born in 1865. In many respects, his background was in keeping with his predecessors'— born into an old Quaker family (he was a nephew of Eli and Mahalah Jay), educated in the Bloomingdale Academy in Parke County, an 1887 Earlham graduate, a recorded minister. He had spent most of his career teaching in Quaker schools—the Quaker academies at Bloomingdale and Plainfield, Indiana, and Adrian, Michigan, and in 1900–1901 had been the acting president of Penn College in Iowa. He had also been active in Quaker affairs. In 1897 Western Yearly Meeting had appointed him to the Earlham board.[23]

At the same time, Kelly also represented a break with the past, a move in the direction of academic professionalism. He was the first president to earn a bachelor's degree according to what was becoming the normal pattern of graduation at age twenty-two. (Mills and Barnabas Hobbs had no earned degrees, while Joseph Moore received his B.S. from Harvard when he was twenty-nine.) He was also the first Earlham president to have studied in a modern graduate school, for three years at the University of Chicago, where he was a student of the great educational philosopher John Dewey and did experimental work in child psychology. Kelly turned down an appointment in the philosophy department at the University of Illinois in 1901 to come to Earlham. Although he never earned a doctorate himself, Kelly was committed to the emerging academic culture of the university, which valued the Ph.D. as the standard credential for college teaching.[24]

Once president, Kelly began to move the college toward fulfilling his vision—definitely Christian, certainly Quaker, but progressive in all respects. Over the next decade he brought Earlham decisively closer to the non-Quaker academic world.

ROBERT L. KELLY

Kelly heartily approved of one action that Mills had already taken, the abolition of the preparatory department, which came in 1901. Enrollment had dwindled, and there was a growing sentiment that its continuance detracted from collegiate work. So Earlham left secondary education to the high schools and the Quaker academies.[25]

Kelly also tightened entrance requirements for the college. Under Mills, the college had recruited students from the Quaker academies by granting sophomore standing to any of their graduates. While popular with Quakers and a drawing card for the college, the policy was by the turn of the century a problem for students seeking admission to the best graduate schools, which regarded such students as short of credits. (Kelly himself faced such a problem when he applied at Chicago.) So he won permission from the board for the change, which did not significantly affect enrollment.[26]

Kelly moved to develop the faculty, and although he made no radical changes, the impact was apparent. When Kelly arrived, there were but two Ph.D.s on a staff of twenty. When he left, it was nine of thirty-five. In many cases, members of the faculty received repeated leaves of absence for graduate work, some of which resulted in doctorates.[27]

Kelly's hiring favored Quakers. In many cases this continued to mean bringing back bright alumni to teach, like Russell and Murray S. Kenworthy in religion, Harlow Lindley and Walter C. Woodward in history, Martha Doan in chemistry, Millard S. Markle in biology, Laurence Hadley and Florence Long in mathematics, and Arthur M. Charles in German. Most of these had finished work for the Ph.D., and the rest had made at least some progress. The non-Quakers hired in this period probably had to meet a somewhat higher standard of scholarship, and in fact provided the college with some of its best-known professors. Cleveland K. Chase came armed with a degree from Goettingen in 1902 to teach Latin for nine years. Harry N. Holmes arrived fresh from Johns Hopkins to head the chemistry department in 1907, remaining seven years before moving on to Oberlin. Throughout these years, however, most of the faculty were Friends, and most of them were birthright Friends. As was the case in the time of Moore and Mills, most had names that had been familiar to Indiana Friends for a century: Trueblood, Hadley, Mendenhall, Lindley, Hodgin, Marshall, Russell, Kenworthy, Dennis, Doan, Woodward, Charles.[28]

Another indication of the growing professional emphasis on the campus was the construction of a library building. Since the opening of Lindley Hall, it had housed the library. History professor Harlow Lindley, who doubled as librarian, had catalogued the holdings according to the new Dewey system and otherwise had tried to bring it up to professional standards. By 1905, its room was overflowing. Fortunately, the college received an offer from Andrew Carnegie, who was providing funds for college as well as public libraries. Carnegie offered $30,000 for a building if the college would raise an equal amount in endowment. The board accepted the proposition, and engaged a Chicago firm that specialized in library construction to handle the building, which was to be "as nearly perfect as was humanly possible." Planning soon showed that increasing the cost to $40,000 would double the capacity to 70,000 volumes. Carnegie refused to increase his gift, but Kelly and the board decided to depart from usual policy to borrow most of the extra money needed. The new building, opened in 1907, was considered a model library, so much so that the state library commission used it for its summer schools from 1909 to 1913.[29]

The Carnegie gift marked a new direction in fund-raising, one that became increasingly important under Kelly, as the college began to turn to great private philanthropists and the early foundations. Under Kelly, the college substantially increased its endowment while also paying for two new buildings and other improvements.

To be sure, Earlham continued to rely largely on traditional sources of support. The single largest donors between 1895 and 1915 were the brothers Francis T. and Mordecai Morris White, wealthy bankers and Quakers who had been students in the Boarding School. Their combined gifts of $250,000 accounted for about half of Earlham's endowment. The funds to build Bundy Hall, the men's dormitory, came from a Quaker farm family in Hancock County, Indiana. Most of the rest of the college's fund-raising was done by the indomitable Allen Jay, on whose shoulders the task had rested since the 1880s. He was constantly traveling, visiting monthly and quarterly and yearly meetings, calling on individuals, especially in Philadelphia, still bringing in donations.[30]

Nevertheless, under Kelly the college established its first ties with non-Quaker philanthropists and with foundations, Andrew Carnegie being the first when the library was built. The most important foundation support for Earlham came from the Rockefeller-endowed General Education Board, one of America's first great foundations. Closely connected with the Rockefeller Foundation in New York City, it made grants for endowment to colleges that met standards of viability and academic excellence. It was a major force in American education in the early years of the twentieth century.[31]

Kelly early established ties with the General Education Board. In 1907, he rejoiced that Earlham had qualified for the board's eligible list. It showed that Earlham had the "promise of permanency," was one of those schools "which are likely to be educational centers in the future." In 1911, in order to qualify for consideration for a board grant, the trustees authorized an "automobile campaign" to liquidate the college's debt. Morton C. Pearson, the pastor at Indianapolis First Friends, ran the effort, which involved over two hundred volunteer solicitors. By the end of the summer the campaign had succeeded. In October 1911 the General Education Board offered a $75,000 grant for the endowment, if the college could raise $325,000 additional in three years. Coming as it did on the heels of the campaign to erase the debt, the effort failed, securing only about half of the amount needed. The General Education Board agreed to match the funds that Earlham had raised, bringing in about $37,000.[52]

Soliciting Rockefeller money did not sit well with some faculty and alumni. In 1907, when the college was placed on the General Education Board eligible list, there was considerable unrest on campus. In the midst of the Progressive Era, John D. Rockefeller was the incarnation of evil, a "malefactor of great wealth" who had accumulated his riches at the expense of the public good. In the minds of many, to accept his money was to compromise with evil, to benefit from oppression, to admit "moral contamination" to Earlham. Such objections, however, had little impact. The *Earlhamite* stated the official point of view: "Granting that moral contamination would result, would not that be outweighed by the moral growth in new lives and by the increased number of individuals benefited?" Allen Jay was more succinct. Told by one Friend that he did "not like the smell" of money from such sources, Jay, in his inimitable speech, replied: "Thee won't have to thmell it."[53]

A new sensitivity about the evil doings of "robber barons" was not the only manifestation of Progressivism on campus. By 1910 there was apparently a consensus at Earlham that "every form of vice and corruption" had to be fought, and that it was the duty of "college men" to take the lead. Walter R. Miles, a 1908 graduate, struck this note. "Fellow students, the times call for Winkelrieds and Luthers," he said in an oration in 1907, "men who have convictions and who will stand by them, alone if need be; men who scorn bribes and threats and the seductive flattery of public opinion; men who are the sworn foes of injustice, the implacable enemies of dishonesty in public life."[54]

Earlham Progressivism took various forms. The theme most often struck was a commitment to "clean government." As early as 1898 the *Earlhamite* published pieces on the horrors of "bossism." It also gave prominent coverage to alumni like R. Warren Barrett and Thomas R. White, who were prominent in reform politics in Philadelphia, and J. Bennett Gordon, another alumnus who as an editor in Richmond and Indianapolis had "gained quite a reputation by his articles against the political tactics of the Cannon-Aldrich crowd." (The *Earlhamite*'s skewering of autocratic House Speaker Joseph G. Cannon was ironic, since he was a birthright Friend who had been a student in 1850.)[55]

The political activities of students were limited, since women, of course, could not vote, and most of the male students were under twenty-one. They tended to be overwhelmingly Republican. Only in 1912 was there much doubt about the political sentiments of the campus, when there was a three-way race among Democrat Woodrow Wilson, Republican incumbent William H. Taft, and the Progressive party candidate, Theodore Roosevelt. Significantly, in 1916 the *Earlham Press,* which had replaced the *Earlhamite,* concluded that there was not much political awareness on campus, and that that was a good thing. "The college student is, or should be, a busy man. His daily program is too full to allow much time for newspaper reading," it editorialized. "He can get his political point of view just as well if not better after finishing school than at present. He now has before him many other educational advantages that will not then be open. So politics can wait."[36]

At least some faculty were politically active in these years. There was but one Democrat among them, English professor William N. Trueblood, whose Jeffersonian opposition to Prohibition once led a quarterly meeting to petition the board (unsuccessfully) for his dismissal. Kelly is more difficult to peg. In 1905 he was active in the campaign of Richmond Progressives against the Republican mayor, William W. Zimmerman, whom Kelly accused of "aid[ing] and encourag[ing] the practice of adultery, prostitution, abortion, and the countless other sins connected with an impure life." By 1912, however, Kelly was a supporter of President Taft in his feud with Theodore Roosevelt, and was involved in a bitter newspaper exchange with Richmond editor William Dudley Foulke, who was one of Roosevelt's leading supporters in Indiana. In 1917, Kelly, for a time, sought the Republican nomination for Congress from the Richmond district. Russell, on the other hand, was probably the leading Progressive on campus. In 1913 he was elected, as a Progressive, to an at-large seat on the city council, receiving more votes than any other candidate. In 1914, the Progressive party nominated him for Congress. His platform was quite liberal—the initiative, referendum, and recall; primary elections; women's suffrage; child labor laws; minimum wage laws for women; and the eight-hour day. Russell went even further and endorsed federal legislation to guarantee black voting rights in the South, one of the few times that anyone at Earlham showed much interest in racial questions in this period. Russell's candidacy was unsuccessful, but apparently aroused considerable enthusiasm among the students. Other faculty activities were mostly of the "good government" variety. Harlow Lindley, for example, was a councillor of the American Civic Federation, which aimed at healing divisions between labor and management.[37]

The one reform cause that apparently united the campus was Prohi-

bition. Most Progressives favored it, and Earlham was fervently committed. The school papers gave considerable coverage to the activities of S.
Edgar Nicholson, an 1885 graduate, who was a leader in the Anti-Saloon
League. Earlham's sympathies were best shown in March 1914, when
there was a local option election in Richmond on banning all sales of
alcoholic beverages. One hundred male students paraded from campus
to the mass meeting held on the eve of the election. On Election Day,
"class work was practically suspended for the day and all cuts were
excused," so that students could help the cause, "challenging voters,
getting out votes and supporting dry leaders by their presence." Nevertheless the wets prevailed. The enthusiasm was all the more ironic
because the campus was not within the city limits, and even many of the
faculty could not vote.[38]

If Earlham was unanimous in embracing Prohibition, it gave a less
certain note about other aspects of Progressivism. There certainly were
critics of capitalism on campus, advocates of some vague form of Christian socialism. As early as 1897, Bevan Binford, a future teacher at
Friends University, warned that "the revolution will come, the Nazarene
will conquer, and labor and capital shall share in equitable proportion."
Another student, writing about the coal strike of 1902, placed the blame
on "a few coal barons and railway magnates," who were so unchristian
and ungenerous that "human nature rebelled against such oppression
and tyranny." Walter R. Miles diagnosed the disease in a 1908 article:
"Business is made an end, not a means to a broader life; in place of a
servant, men have made it a good to which they sacrifice." An anonymous woman student, writing a year later in the *Earlhamite,* saw "class
struggle" as "inexorable," and concluded that even "the alleviating
panaceas of philanthropy have become a national reproach."[39]

The college's most articulate and persistent critic of the established
economic order was Elbert Russell. By 1907 he had become the campus's
most fervent proponent of the Social Gospel, the Protestant movement
that attempted to transform American society, especially economic relations, on "Christian" lines. "Life has become increasingly social," he told
a Quaker audience in 1907. "It follows from this that religion must more
and more concern itself with social morality, that less and less can the
religious message be merely one of individual salvation, but must be
more and more a statement of social duties and an ideal of cooperation
and brotherhood." By 1912, Russell was taking a position that was
advanced even for an advocate of the Social Gospel. In a series of articles
in the *American Friend,* he scored the ways in which American industrialists treated their workers. He even defended the strikes led by the
Industrial Workers of the World (IWW), a radical group that sent chills

down the spines of much of the middle class. In chapel Russell praised the IWW for seeking to remedy real problems and defended them from charges of anarchism. A year later he argued for the rights of workers to unionize and strike.[40]

In this, of course, Russell was following a course that other young, modernist Friends had embraced, giving Quakerism the social activist tinge that most still associate with it. But it would probably be wrong to conclude that Russell spoke for most of the faculty and students at that time. Even as Russell praised the IWW, Dean of Men William O. Mendenhall was warning students against the dangers of "syndicalism." And while sympathies may have been with the striking coal miners in 1902, it was at least in part because the miners' leader, John Mitchell, was pronounced to be free of any "radical" taint. The hold of Christian socialism on this generation was to be slight.[41]

If Earlham students were uncertain about economics in these years, they were even less interested in another Progressive reform, women's suffrage. "Earlham girls have never been prominent in suffragette movements of any kind," the *Earlham Press* concluded in 1911. Virtually the only stirring of suffrage activities in these years was the appearance in 1911 of Martha Gruening, a Philadelphian who worked for the National College Equal Suffrage League, as a chapel speaker. After her address, about seventy-five women students met with her for discussion, but, according to the *Press*, the dominant question was whether men would still respect women if they voted. No organization at Earlham came out of Gruening's visit. Only one graduate from this period, Sarah Addington, of the class of 1912, was active in the women's suffrage movement, as a publicist for the National Women's Suffrage Association. And when the Nineteenth Amendment granted women the right to vote in 1920, it apparently aroused little interest on campus. In this respect Earlham lagged far behind women's colleges, or even many other coeducational schools.[42]

Recapturing other aspects of women's lives in this period is difficult. Many elements of student life remained separate. There were still men's and women's literary societies, the Ionian and the Phoenix, and although they jointly published the *Earlhamite*, it ceased in 1914, superseded by the weekly campus newspaper, the *Earlham Press*. The Press Club, which published the *Press*, was a male-only group. The YMCA and the YWCA, which dominated campus religious life, operated along similar lines. So did student government, which was not campus-wide, but organized by dormitory councils. Of the elite student groups, only the Anglican, which published a literary magazine, was coed. No one openly questioned such separation. Elbert Russell reflected the mind of the campus in a chapel talk in 1904 when he said that while women had the same rights to education as men, their education should be different, just as men and women were different. An editorial in the *Earlhamite* was more blunt in 1903. "Are not the unwritten rules of propriety beginning to be disregarded when the ladies make their training identical with man's, and glory in their lack of common sense knowledge?" it asked. "Happily, the tide is turning and college girls are becoming more sensible, their eyes are opening to the fact that they are losing their femininity in the rush for degrees and honors." The *Earlhamite* writer echoed the larger society in a closing admonition: "Let the college girl remember that when she goes home at the end of her course, not her knowledge of Greek and calculus, but her woman's disposition, her woman's character, her woman's manner will be tested, and let her reverently train herself for her 'Woman's Sphere.'"[43]

Yet even as the campus embraced the idea of a "woman's sphere," its conception of that sphere apparently was broadening. Women majors were found in all fields, including the natural sciences and mathematics, a deviation from the rule in most schools of the period. Chemistry professor Harry N. Holmes privately confided his distaste for teaching women, but he apparently was alone in that feeling. Women students from the period remembered a sense that no field was closed to them. Caroline Miles Hill, an 1887 graduate who was the first woman to earn a Ph.D. at the University of Michigan, encouraged them. In a 1908 article in the *Earlhamite,* Hill analyzed alumni statistics to blast the popular idea that the marriages of college-educated women were less happy or successful than those of less educated women, pointing out that of the hundreds of women who had attended Earlham since the 1860s, only five had been divorced. "I believe, more and more, that a woman is not fit to be married until she has demonstrated her ability to live alone, that she has no right to impose herself as a helpless burden on a man," she concluded.[44]

It is also unclear how much Progressivism affected the classroom, whether it significantly changed teaching methods or curriculum. The faculty did expand considerably, but this was largely in response to the growth in enrollment, from about three hundred in 1903 to about five hundred in 1915. There were some departments added: economics, education, home economics, and physical education. All of them shared one characteristic, the love of Progressives for turning all human activities, whether business, homemaking, or teaching, into sciences, regulated by laws and principles and the subject of instruction by professionals in the field.[45]

This tendency toward a "scientific" approach can be seen in other areas. Philanthropy had always been a Quaker concern, but now it was presented as "scientific charity." In 1912 the board approved the establishment of a chair in "Philanthropy and Social Ethics," to be endowed from funds raised by the temperance committees of the two yearly meetings. The emphasis would be on temperance and "the relation of intemperance to labor, poverty, crime, insanity, and all other diseases." Also included, however, would be all aspects of philanthropy, with the aim of "reducing the dependency and delinquency of the depressed and defective classes." The yearly meetings, however, never raised the endowment. Even in the natural sciences, there was a new emphasis on experimental work. In 1903, biology professor David W. Dennis proposed setting up a "summer Biological Station . . . for nature study on some lake." In 1907, when J. Herschel Coffin arrived as the college's first psychology professor, he, with Kelly's encouragement, established an experimental psychology laboratory, one of the first college laboratories in the country.[46]

Kelly's final contribution came in bringing Earlham into the world of professional associations that were becoming increasingly vital to higher education, another part of the process of professionalization. In 1915, when the North Central Association of Colleges and Secondary Schools was formed for accrediting purposes, Earlham was on the original list of approved institutions. Kelly himself served as a member of its committee on college standardization. That same year, Kelly was the leading spirit in founding the Association of American Colleges and was elected its first president. Kelly was also active in the National Education Association, and was one of the founders of the Council of Church Boards of Education. He played a leading role in forming an association of presidents of the Quaker schools within the Five Years Meeting as well.[47]

The results of Kelly's efforts are difficult to gauge. Earlham supporters were enthusiastic. William Dudley Foulke expressed their sentiments at the 1917 commencement: "When . . . you became president the College was a rather narrow gauge institution, little known to the world at large . . . conservative, sectarian, and provincial," he told Kelly. But through Kelly's work, "a complete change has come over the face of Earlham, both physically and intellectually. . . . Earlham has become an institution of national reputation." But not everyone agreed. When Harry N. Holmes left for Oberlin in 1914, his ablest student, Ernest A. Wildman, commented that Holmes was taking a step upward. Not a step, Holmes responded, but a "hundred yard dash." In 1915 Earlham was still in debt, its endowment relatively small, and its faculty still poorly paid, even compared to most Indiana colleges. And by 1915 it was torn with controversy over its very identity.[48]

The Flowering of Campus Culture

In order to understand the conflict that had come to divide the campus so bitterly by 1915, one has to understand how student culture was changing in the early years of this century. Earlham moved steadily toward developing what a leading historian of higher education, Helen Lefkowitz Horowitz, has called "campus culture." It was a student world that emphasized social life over the life of the mind, that centered around elite clubs, and that especially venerated athletics. Earlham's religious identity limited this growth in vital ways, most notably in banning fraternities and sororities, but nevertheless campus culture became increasingly powerful. Kelly's support for, or at least his acquiescence in, this growth was part of the issue between him and Russell. Officially, Kelly was insistent about denying the existence of such forces on campus. At his inauguration in 1903, Kelly exalted in the "entire absence of cliques and factions, or of any organizations whose tendency is to establish social strata." Earlham was, he said, "essentially a democracy, and the only aristocracy we know is the aristocracy of character and conscience." Yet Kelly also presided over the events that undermined this vision.[49]

A persistent theme in the student press in these years was summed up in an editorial in the *Earlhamite* in 1907: "The spirit and vim of a college is largely made manifest through the number and character of the interests outside of the regular classroom." The campus, another writer proclaimed three years later, had little use for "the one who studies all the time and refuses to take part in the various activities of student life." An earlier writer in the *Earlhamite* was succinct in 1904: "He is a poor stick who knows nothing but books." Much of the campus apparently internalized these values. Revealing is an open letter on behalf of a Rhodes Scholar candidate that appeared in the *Earlham Press* in 1911. The authors were three seniors, Carl Ackerman, Homer L. Morris, and Paul Furnas, all of whom would have distinguished careers in college teaching or administration. In their letter, the trio enumerated four distinguished characteristics of their candidate: his success as an artist, athlete, campus leader, and "mixer." They said nothing about his grades or scholarship.[50]

This campus life apparently had a number of features. One, which had appeared in the 1880s and 1890s and which the faculty deplored, was the "class scrap," in which various classes competed, at best for each other's banners, at worst in barely restrained brawling. In 1898, one participant actually stabbed another. Thereafter the campus powers, faculty and student, set themselves against it and by 1910 it had disappeared.

Apparently there was also agreement on the more positive aspects of the new campus culture, at least among those who wrote articles for the *Earlhamite* and the *Press.* They urged mindfulness of proper dress and behavior in social settings. "A sweater in the dining room or a flurry in the parlor . . . spreads the report that we are an ill-mannered, boorish lot," one fulminated. The college needed more formal dress affairs. By 1910 at least one student was resentful of Earlham's "snobbishness." There was a need for more college songs: "It is a conceded fact that the singing of spirited college songs is fundamental to real college life. With the introduction of . . . new songs, this should be all the more predominant at Earlham." And there was general condemnation of "knocking" and other negativism, which was all too prevalent.[51]

Much of campus life revolved around clubs and organizations. A number were related to curricular interests, like the History Club or the Polity Club, which do not appear to have been especially prestigious, and which were short-lived. The older literary societies survived, but their reputations apparently fell when the *Earlhamite* gave way to the *Press.* Instead, in this period, the most prestigious organizations on campus were those that involved competition. New organizations like the Press Club and the dormitory councils involved winning elections. Debate, the oratorical contests, and, above all, athletics involved competition with other schools.[52]

If Earlham ever had an elitist organization, it was the Press Club. Leading campus men formed it in January 1911 to publish a weekly newspaper, the *Earlham Press.* They limited membership to men, and put it on a self-perpetuating basis—only members could nominate new ones, and any current member could "blackball" a prospective one. By 1914, the *Press* had replaced the *Earlhamite* as the campus journal, and a Press Club membership had become the most sought-after one on campus. It was also the target of considerable animosity. That same year, the club agreed to give a faculty committee some role in nominating members, and to elect new members by a 4/5 vote. Two years later, the club formed a women's auxiliary, but it was short-lived. The club would remain an elite male group, and a source of considerable irritation, for another decade.[53]

Student government also appeared on campus in this period, but it owed less to an interest in self-government or preparing students for participatory democracy than it did to enforcing discipline. There are indications that the faculty was finding it increasingly difficult to preserve order. Certainly regulations were strict, embracing every aspect of student life. But students, especially men, were becoming more open in rebellion. Most manifestations were mild, such as *Earlhamite* editorials that penalties for missing chapel smacked "of the spirit of the debtors law of colonial days," or playing practical jokes on fellow students, or holding mock prayer meetings. Sometimes, however, rebellion took more serious forms, as in 1914, when two men were suspended for publicly ridiculing the governor of the men's dormitory.[54]

Until 1907, all students living on campus were housed in Earlham Hall, men in the east wing, women in the west. Control lay in the hands of the governor and matron, often a married couple who lived in the building. When Bundy Hall opened as the new men's dormitory, a new arrangement was necessary. Kelly's solution was first to have a faculty member live in Bundy. To aid him, the hall formed a dormitory council. The time was past, one supporter wrote, "when college students believed that it was their privilege, if not their duty, to play as many 'pranks,' to break as many 'rules,' and, in fact, to be as anarchistic to all college authorities as possible." Now, "instead of considering themselves as inmates with a 'governor' to *keep watch* over them," the residents of Bundy "consider[ed] themselves as citizens of a community able to govern themselves." Soon afterwards, a similar system was organized for the women in Earlham Hall. The councils had power to judge and punish infringements of dormitory regulations, such as fighting or curfew violations, although final power was in the hands of the president. It is difficult to say how well it worked, although the system remained in place long after Kelly had left.[55]

A final innovation in student government came in 1915, when Kelly created the positions of dean of men and dean of women. It was consistent with the Progressive emphasis on professionalism. Kelly appointed William O. Mendenhall, the boys' governor and a mathematics professor, to the men's post, while Martha Doan, an 1892 graduate with a doctorate in chemistry, became dean of women.[56]

The final element of campus culture to fall into place was athletics. Oratory and debate still had a strong following, but their appeal did not compare with sports. This, of course, was the period when football especially became a mania on many campuses. It probably never approached that level at Earlham, but football and basketball became central to student life.[57]

In these years, the college press was filled with exhortations to support the teams. "The interest and enthusiasm shown in the athletic sports is a fair standard to judge the general wide-awake condition of the college," the *Earlhamite* editorialized in 1907. Later the same year, it proclaimed that "football is the greatest of all college sports, and there is no true Earlhamite who will not stand by his team." There is some evidence, however, that Earlham's squad was not especially Quakerly on the field. Butler University's players claimed in 1912 that "the Earlham team are the worst sluggers that they ever play." The campus leaders who wrote for the college press were free with advice about what was needed for success. Student support was vital, of course, not only at the games but at practices as well. Cheering had to be organized efficiently. "Yell leaders should be appointed in the near future and several mass meetings held in which to practice all the yells and the Earlham songs," the campus was exhorted in 1902. "Get together, appoint leaders, practice the cutting and slashing yells." Lukewarmness was the worst of sins. And there had to be pep rallies. The 1915 season opened with a "red hot demonstration of what the student body can do to boost the team." Women students joined in, with "snap and ginger galore. They ran through the livest and most popular of the college songs, and they all got into it with a lot of pep."[58]

Thus by 1915 student life at Earlham had become much like that at most other colleges and universities. It exalted the "leader," the "mixer," the athlete or debater who competed successfully with other schools. What was unclear was how compatible this student culture would be with Earlham's Quaker and religious foundations. That question takes us back to Elbert Russell, who would be Earlham's most articulate critic of this new direction.

The Ordeal of Elbert Russell

After he returned to Earlham in the fall of 1903, Russell quickly reestablished himself as one of the college's most popular and influential teachers. He also became increasingly visible and active in Quaker circles. Within a few years, he had become probably the most controversial and embattled Friend in the United States.

By 1903, Russell had begun writing regularly for the *American Friend,* and it is in these early essays that we see the direction his thought took over the next decade. His first article, significantly, was "The Principle of Progressive Revelation in Scripture." He began with a seemingly conservative point of view. For Protestants, he told his readers, the Bible was "the standard of belief and practice." Thus Russell's goal was not to minimize or derogate the importance of the Bible. Instead, he argued that it was vital that it be properly understood. The problem lay with those whose understanding was static, who taught that all revelation had ceased two thousand years earlier. "I am among those who hold that we have not yet exhausted the Bible, and that the Spirit of God will continue to lead his children into fuller knowledge of truth," he wrote.[59]

By 1905, Russell had become more combative. He conducted epistolary wars with several holiness correspondents. He told one that higher critics were those who truly understood the Bible. With a sympathizer he was more blunt. "The Bible has suffered just as much from over-claims for it as from total neglect, if not more," he wrote to Levi T. Pennington, one of his students and a Quaker pastor. "As long as men are forcing a false view of the Bible on our denomination, it is necessary to call attention to the facts that make against the scientific and historical inerrancy of the Bible." But for many Friends, to do that was to question its authority.[60]

As he challenged the way that Friends viewed the Bible, Russell came to restate and challenge a number of doctrines that modernists among and outside Friends also questioned. Critics charged Russell with two "heresies" about Christ: doubting the Virgin Birth, and setting aside the Atonement. Russell always denied the former charge, however, and there is nothing to give it credence. On the other hand, he hardly mentioned the Virgin Birth in his writings or his preaching. Russell was at open odds with evangelical Friends on the Atonement. He insisted that "atonement" was not a scriptural term, and that Christ had only used "blood" once in connection with his death. The value of Christ lay in his life. In Christ, humans could see "the holiness, love, and personal power of the Universal Character we call God." Still, Russell was emphatically Christian. His writings always affirmed both the divinity and uniqueness of Christ. "The world of scholarship has not outgrown the need to sit at Jesus' feet," he wrote in 1909.[61]

Less prominently, but still clearly, Russell challenged older ideas, particularly about Original Sin and Satan. Russell did not question the reality of sin, or the susceptibility of humans to it. "I know too well the strength and terror of sin to offer men a mere human savior or a religion of self-culture," he told one critic. Russell emphasized human capability, not failings. "The modern man does not feel a worm in the dust. He rather feels a strong man, armed, looking for worlds to conquer," Russell told the Five Years Meeting in 1907. "The old preaching belittled and depreciated man that it might glorify God, but the modern preacher will seek to redeem and exalt man that he might serve God." At the same time, Russell effectively discarded the personality of Satan. He argued that what some, including biblical writers, called demonic possession was simply mental illness. As for Satan, people were saved by believing in Christ, not in the devil. For Russell, similarly, hell (as well as heaven) was a state of being, not a place. In short, Russell believed that Christianity had to change, casting off the bonds of Calvinism and Wesleyanism, in order to meet the needs of a new day. "The new conditions of the Twentieth Century demand new methods of stating the gospel, new means of bringing it home to men and of applying it to modern life," Russell told Friends. It was incumbent on Friends to "cast aside every burden of dead ideas and clothe the eternal gospel in the forms of modern thinking."[62]

In Quakerism, Russell found the faith uniquely suited to do just these things. By refusing to bind themselves with creeds, Quakers left openings for the new light that scholarship and modern thought shed on Christian faith. Through their teaching of the Inner Light, "that of God in every soul," they showed the world a source of guidance that was available to all. And with their tradition of social conscience, they were almost uniquely suited to show the world the way to apply Christian teachings to solve its problems.[63]

Still, Russell saw perils ahead. In the nineteenth century, Friends had come close to abandoning their heritage for "a mediocre type of Protestantism." The distinctive Quaker literature had been mostly set aside for books from other traditions. And there were still those who were trying to impose a Puritan creedalism on Friends, those for whom Christianity was not a spiritual way of life, but "a wave of neurotic emotionalism, the more hysterical the more spiritual." It was this Russell opposed, this from which he wanted to "rescue" Friends. His commitment made him a center of controversy.[64]

Russell and the other Quaker modernists faced a powerful holiness group within the Society of Friends, one that was committed not only to the doctrines that modernists challenged, but to their maintenance through a variety of creedal tests, and, if necessary, by "stopping the mouths of false teachers." Within a few years, this group would be part of the larger fundamentalist movement. For holiness Friends, Russell's teaching and ministry were but another sign of the approaching end of the world, the premillennial second coming of Christ, as "evil men and seducers" were "waxing worse and worse, deceiving and being deceived," and "every kind of ism that the devil ever invented" was "captivating the minds of men and laying waste the heritage of God." For these Friends, salvation came only through accepting the inspiration of the Bible, the efficacy of the Blood, second-experience sanctification, and the imminent return of Christ. Souls depended on silencing false prophets like Russell.[65]

Between 1900 and 1910, Russell became the target of increasingly hostile attacks from those committed to this vision. Most came from ministers outside Indiana Yearly Meeting, and they ran along similar lines. Jacob Baker, an elderly holiness minister from Michigan, catalogued Russell's errors, drawn from him "in a personal interview." They included "denial of a personal devil" and of "the substitutionary sacrifice of Jesus Christ" as well as a claim that "the Scriptures contradict themselves and that he has a right to put his own construction on the inspired Word." J. Walter Malone, the most influential of evangelical Friends, wrote to Russell of his hope that "the Lord will show thee the peril in which thee stands," closing darkly that he had heard Russell quoted as saying things he dared not even put into writing. One Quaker student of the period remembered that when she returned home her pastor closely questioned her, "seeking to determine the depth of my fall from grace as a result of Elbert Russell's teaching."[66]

In 1905 the attacks on Russell and other modernist Friends found a focal point. Many of Russell's opponents were associated with the Cleveland Bible Training School, founded by J. Walter Malone in 1892 as an alternative to the Quaker colleges for those preparing for the ministry and other religious work. By 1900 it had become part of the network of Bible colleges that furnished the shock troops for the emerging fundamentalist movement. Malone published a variety of holiness journals, but in 1905 he launched the *Evangelical Friend*. Its editors were two particularly zealous and outspoken holiness ministers, William P. Pinkham, formerly an Earlham professor, and Edward Mott. Their first issue was a call to battle. "There has seldom, if ever, been greater need of faithful watchmen than now," their opening editorial proclaimed. Two months later, the editors took aim at the summer Bible institute that Earlham sponsored. One speaker was characterized as purveying "poison," while Russell was acknowledged to have said "many excellent things," but also to have enunciated some mistaken views of the nature of God and Christ. In a subsequent exchange of letters with Russell, Pinkham was more blunt, telling Russell that he was flirting with "Hicksism" and that Russell was "wholly unwarranted in promulgating opinions" that were "contrary to the faith" of Friends.[67]

There is no evidence that these attacks cowed Russell; he was not afraid to be outspoken. Never did he show signs of doubt, and he was not slow to accuse critics of unchristian conduct. Some he told that they were spreading false information, others that their zeal was not according to knowledge, others that they were behaving like pharisees. He warned Luke Woodard, a persistent critic, that if Woodard did not desist, he would bring charges of "detraction" against Woodard in his monthly meeting.[68]

In 1906 the Cleveland group, with sympathizers from Ohio to California, embarked on a crusade to rescue Friends from "unsoundness." The *Evangelical Friend* became increasingly strident in its attacks on Russell. In July it demanded that Earlham fire him. One of Russell's students was driven out of two Quaker pastorates because he had studied at Earlham. Allen Jay, the much-loved minister who was one of Russell's staunchest supporters, was close to despair by the end of the year. Malone and his sympathizers, "with a zeal born of fanaticism" had resolved "to run the American Friend out of existence, and drive the Board of Trustees to turn Elbert Russell and some others of the Earlham College faculty out of the college." Some of the other Quaker colleges (probably Penn in Iowa and Friends University in Kansas), apparently on the theory that Earlham's loss was their gain, were quietly abetting the campaign, approaching Earlham's financial backers and cutting into the college's income. Already Kelly was seeing the effects. It was a "deep and well laid plan," and Russell's critics, according to Jay, had "gone in to win."[69]

Nineteen hundred and seven, however, was not to be the year of triumph that Russell's opponents anticipated. At the end of the year the *American Friend* was still very much in existence with editorial policies unchanged, and Russell was still very much at Earlham. Just as their plans ripened, the holiness forces found themselves divided and distracted by the issue of pentecostalism. "Tongues" invaded the Cleveland school and church and the resulting excitement apparently gave pause to some Friends who had seen Malone and his faculty as the upholders of "sound" Quakerism.[70]

The holiness group probably would have failed, however, in its war on Russell, since Russell had firm support at Earlham. By 1907, almost a generation of students had passed through his classes, and he was one of the most popular teachers on campus. "When Prof. Russell takes a manuscript from his pocket in chapel, school books and *Saturday Evening Posts* are immediately dropped and closest attention given," the *Press* noted in 1911. Since many alumni were Friends who returned to their hometowns, Russell had a vocal group of grassroots supporters. There is nothing to indicate that, before 1911, any of the trustees attempted to influence what Russell taught, and when disagreement did come it was more political than theological. Kelly was as much a modernist in sympathy as Russell, although he was not as outspoken. It is more difficult to account for the support of the trustees, since they were appointed by Indiana and Western yearly meetings, and several had holiness views. But the board was largely dominated by a little group of elderly Quaker businessmen, especially Timothy Nicholson, along with Allen Jay. Nicholson was a moderate who had battled holiness Friends for decades. The fact that the holiness minister Luke Woodard was one of Russell's chief critics doubtless influenced Nicholson, since Woodard and Nicholson had been at odds since the 1870s. Jay was possibly the single most respected and beloved Friend in America at the time. His personal faith was evangelical, but while he had had considerable success as an evangelist, he had often been at odds with the holiness party. After 1900, he had identified himself with toleration of modernism, and he manifested this most clearly through his steadfast support of Russell. In the case of the other trustees, there seems to be a sort of possessiveness—they looked askance at outsiders implying that their management of Earlham was leading it away from the faith.[71]

Even as he was moving in heterodox directions, Russell remained conventional in other ways, and that doubtless also strengthened him in his battles. A recorded minister, he preached often, and served as the campus pastor. In 1903 he agreed to be the pastor at Knightstown, about forty miles west of Richmond, serving to the satisfaction of Friends there. He regularly supervised religious services on campus, met with students who were troubled about their religious experience, and proudly counted the souls he had won to Christ. Such happy results came not from revivalism; instead, Russell tried to bring about "a quiet, intelligent conversion," which showed "a far larger percentage of converts to Jesus Christ than many of the revivals in our churches or camp meetings." In his home life of family devotions and regular prayer, Russell matched any opponent.[72]

In addition to all of this, everyone, admirers and detractors, recognized Russell's abilities. He was the recipient of a steady stream of requests to interpret difficult passages of Scripture as well as invitations to preach and speak to a variety of groups. "Of course a lecture course in a Friends church in Indiana could not properly be started without having Elbert Russell on board for the first year anyway, could it?" wrote one pastor in 1906, and many other Indiana Friends apparently shared his feelings. Many had either not heard of Russell's heresies or thought them unimportant.[73]

Another factor may have been important—with a few exceptions, the blasts at Russell came from outside Indiana Yearly Meeting. Where Russell was known best, attacks were fewest. This is best illustrated by Russell's relationship with Ira C. Johnson, the superintendent of Indiana Yearly Meeting. Late in 1906, some of Malone's Cleveland coadjutors were trying to win Johnson's support. He wrote frankly to Russell about his fears of liberalism. But Johnson also knew and liked Russell, and it seemed impossible to him that so upright and capable a young man could be "unsound." "Thee don't talk like that to me," he told Russell. And there were undoubtedly many other Friends whose personal affection for Russell proved stronger than their theological doubts.[74]

Thus fortified, Russell went into the 1907 sessions of the Five Years Meeting in Richmond. Before it opened in October, Russell met quietly with Rufus Jones and other modernists to plan strategy. They decided that they would be forthright and aggressive in presenting their views, and left the most daring work to Russell. His paper, "A Ministry for the Present Day," was the fullest statement of his vision of liberal Quakerism. "It is not a new salvation that is needed," he said at the climax, "but a new statement of the eternal gospel of God's saving grace." The minister would not say, "believe or be damned," and the minister would know that salvation did not depend on believing that the first chapters of Genesis were historical, or that Moses wrote the Pentateuch, or in the "outward second advent of Jesus." Christian life was what mattered, not doctrinal belief. When he finished, a woman from California fell to her knees in an agonized prayer for Russell's soul. Opponents tried to exclude the paper from the published proceedings of the conference, but Timothy Nicholson and Rufus Jones immediately rose to Russell's defense, and the holiness Friends were voted down.[75]

Russell and Jones thought that the conference was a great triumph for the "forces of progressive thought," but others had doubts. Sensational accounts appeared in Richmond and Indianapolis newspapers, and holiness Friends launched new attacks. There is some evidence that even Russell's moderate supporters found his outspokenness unsettling or at least ill advised. Timothy Nicholson wrote later that he thought some of Russell's expressions "indiscreet." He and Kelly were worried enough to urge Russell to send his own account to the newspapers. Russell thought that the overall result was healthy for Earlham, but that is not clear. In 1908, Indianapolis pastor Morton C. Pearson warned Russell that support for the summer biblical institute at Earlham was "hanging by a very slender thread," and in 1909 it came to an end. Russell claimed that it was no longer needed because the battle for modern thought had been won in the yearly meetings, but that may be rationalization; certainly the *Evangelical Friend* hailed it as a defeat for Russell.[76]

Meanwhile, the old battles continued. The *Evangelical Friend* kept up its attacks on Earlham and on Russell. "Teachers of error in religion will only weaken the religious and moral influence of Friends, until presently the very best element among the supporters of our colleges are discouraged and disgusted and conscientiously withholding begins and the sooner it becomes general, the better," Mott and Pinkham wrote. Russell, supported by Kelly and Jay, vigorously denied the charges, and Russell wrote acidly about the growth of heresy hunting among Friends. Nevertheless the holiness group did not relent. Russell lost a vital ally when Allen Jay died suddenly in 1910. In 1913, Western Yearly Meeting actually appointed a committee to investigate the teachings in the biblical department, but it apparently had no impact on Russell. Kelly was forthright in defending him: "I guess Pres. Kelly gave it to them pretty heavy," one student wrote home about a meeting between Kelly and some unhappy Friends. The same year a conference of Friends from the two yearly meetings urged that "all instruction given" in the biblical department "be in harmony with the established doctrine of the Friends Church as adjusted by the recent Five Years Meeting." This would not have cowed Russell, since he always insisted that *he* was the one contending for traditional Quakerism. More serious was a battle on the floor of Indiana Yearly Meeting in 1914, when Russell tangled openly with Timothy Nicholson. Nicholson favored the appointment of Truman C. Kenworthy, a Russell critic, as yearly meeting superintendent. Russell made a long speech against Kenworthy. Nicholson responded by accusing Russell of bringing the methods of a political campaign into the yearly meeting. Russell saw nothing personal in it; rather Nicholson, who for decades had been the "unofficial boss of Indiana Yearly Meeting," was annoyed by an "insurgency" in his domain. The yearly meeting confirmed Kenworthy's appointment. At Earlham, however, Russell was apparently safe from attack, and he still had many supporters among Friends.[77]

Security in his position was not enough, however, to keep Russell at Earlham. By 1914, stresses were developing between Russell and President Kelly. Within a year, they broke out into open conflict, probably the most bitter internal strife that Earlham would ever see. It was full of paradoxes. Russell, the liberal, was the defender of maintaining a strong denominational identity for the college, including mandatory church attendance for students and strict campus discipline, like prohibitions on smoking, dancing, and unchaperoned dating. The holiness Friends who sided with Kelly to force out Russell were casting their lot with a leader who wanted to downplay Earlham's sectarian roots and instead encourage the development of "campus culture." Russell, the modernist, was thus defending the moral and personal values of his critics. And his critics were casting their lot with a president who was no less liberal than Russell and who had begun the process of secularizing Earlham. This makes Earlham very different from other schools, where a commitment to liberalism usually coincided with a hostility to denominationalism.[78]

There is every indication that, in spite of his heterodoxies, Russell had had Kelly's firm support, and the support of the trustees. But when the differences between Russell and Kelly became bitter and open, the trustees, conservative businessmen for the most part, instinctively sided with Kelly and established authority. Just as they had refused to accede to the holiness Friends' demands to fire Russell, because to do so would have suggested that they had been tolerating "unsoundness," so they sided with Kelly against Russell, because to accept his charges would have been to admit that they had turned the college over to a president who had led it in the wrong direction.

Nevertheless, between 1911 and 1914 Russell had weakened his position with the trustees in several ways. Some were uncomfortable with a course on the social teachings of Christ that he began to offer in 1911, fearing that it was "socialistic." Others may have been put off by Russell's campaign for Congress in 1914, which was devoted in large part to attacks on "Old Guard" Republicanism, the persuasion of most of the trustees. And Russell had irritated Timothy Nicholson with his opposition to Nicholson's choice for the yearly meeting superintendency. The composition of the board was also changing; between 1913 and 1915 three new trustees, David Hadley, Edward Woodard, and Leander Woodard, the last two more of the innumerable relatives of Luke Woodard, had been appointed. All had anti-Russell leanings.[79]

A final source of irritation was a long-running controversy over erecting a Friends meetinghouse on campus. In 1912 the Five Years Meeting had agreed to locate its central offices in Richmond. There were hopes that Indiana Yearly Meeting would move its annual sessions from the East Main Street Meetinghouse in Richmond to a new building on the campus that would serve both it and the Five Years Meeting. A new meetinghouse and the Five Years Meeting offices on campus would make Earlham the center of most of American Quakerism. A theological school for American Friends that had long been under discussion might also become part of the complex. This would have cemented Earlham's Quaker ties for all time, and Russell naturally favored it.[80]

The East Main Street Friends, led by Nicholson, however, refused to cooperate. With this refusal, the growing group of Friends in West Richmond, who had been meeting on campus, decided to build their own meetinghouse on West Main Street. Kelly encouraged them; he was unalterably opposed to having a meeting on campus whose pastor would not be under his control, a condition that the West Richmond Friends would not accept. Russell argued that even though West Richmond Meeting would not be on campus, it should be the campus meeting. The college's Quaker identity, he was convinced, depended on the required attendance of the students at a regular Friends meeting on Sunday mornings. Kelly disagreed, and wanted to continue to hold Sunday services on campus. Russell felt strongly enough about the matter to submit his resignation as college pastor in March 1915, giving up his post rather than countenance Kelly's decision. Since the college's limited budget made it impossible to hire a campus minister separate from the biblical department, Russell was effectively using his popularity with students and alumni as well as his unquestioned ability as a teacher to bring new pressures to bear on Kelly and the trustees, who would be loath to lose him.[81]

This was more than a controversy over where the college's students would attend church. Russell was convinced that Earlham's identity as a Quaker institution was at stake. Earlham occupied a unique position as Russell saw it. Of the ten Quaker colleges in the United States, five— Penn, Whittier, Pacific, Friends, and Cleveland—were under fundamentalist influence or control. Guilford was geographically isolated, and, along with Wilmington, in a precarious financial position. Haverford and Swarthmore, while prosperous and of high quality, were largely isolated from the rest of American Quakerism. With its stability, able faculty, relative freedom from fundamentalist intolerance, and location in the Quaker heartland, Earlham was ideally situated to lead in molding a new generation of Quaker leaders along thoughtful, intelligent, modern lines.

As Russell read the signs of the times, however, Earlham was moving in the opposite direction. Kelly was open in his desire to make the college less sectarian and more attractive to non-Quakers. As we have seen, Kelly encouraged the growth of a campus culture not much different from that of other colleges. This had a variety of consequences. It did increase enrollment significantly. In 1903, when Kelly became president, it was 276. By 1906, enrollment had nearly doubled to almost 500, where it would remain for the next four decades. As had been the case since the founding, the overwhelming majority of students came from Indiana. Much of the increase, however, came from "Day Dodgers," students from Richmond living at home.[82]

Quakers remained the largest religious group on campus. Statistics were collected sporadically; they indicate that while the percentage of Friends was slowly declining, throughout this period they accounted for a majority of students. Certainly Kelly publicly affirmed the school's ties with Friends. "One of the ideals which we attempt to maintain is to keep Earlham a Quaker institution," he wrote in 1907. "My experience has been that those who are not Quakers who were educated at Earlham are the most enthusiastic ones in favor of maintaining it as a Quaker institution." Years later, however, Kelly admitted that he had wanted to "overcome the provincialism of the college" and "broaden the horizons of Friends." That, he said, "actually helped to emphasize the best in Friends institutions."[83]

Certainly Quakers and Quaker concerns were in evidence under Kelly. Numerous members of the faculty were active as delegates to the Five Years Meeting or as members of its commissions. Prominent Friends like Rufus Jones, Norman Penney, and William C. Braithwaite visited and spoke frequently. Kelly supported scholarships for the children of Quaker missionaries and ministers, and for those preparing for the Quaker ministry. He also proposed one-year scholarships for outstanding graduates of Penn, Wilmington, and Friends University, comparable to the scholarships that Bryn Mawr and Haverford gave each year to outstanding Earlham graduates. A revealing incident took place in 1905, when the heirs of Joseph Elkinton of Philadelphia offered to sell the college his large collection of Quaker books. In 1880, the college had rejected a similar collection as unneeded by the college. This time, however, Kelly jumped at the chance to acquire it, and sent out Harlow Lindley and Allen Jay to raise the funds for the purchase.[84]

Still, it is also clear that the dominant religious influences on campus in these years were not Quaker. Instead, most campus religious activities were in the hands of the YMCA and YWCA. As early as 1899, the board had agreed to abolish the mandatory Sunday school sessions and turn them over the associations. Within a few years, they controlled most of the campus's religious life. Men especially formed "Gospel Teams" that held services at the jail, at city missions, and in country churches. Each held prayer meetings. They were also responsible for an annual series of week-long meetings that were not exactly revivals but which were designed to see that all students "should be crowned with Christ as their King." Typical were those held in the fall of 1915 by "Dad" Elliott, a former Northwestern University football star who exhorted students to follow "our Great Coach." Almost half of the students signed "covenant cards . . . dedicating or reconsecrating their lives to Christ."[85]

Russell was not a foe of the associations. He had been active in the YMCA himself as a student, and gave their activities his hearty support. He was convinced, however, that Kelly slighted Quaker groups. The Young Friends movement, recently inaugurated and headed by Earlham alumnus and Russell student Tom Jones, received little support from Kelly. In fact, Russell charged, the administration actively discouraged any attempt to form Quaker groups as threatening to non-Quaker students.[86]

Russell also thought that he saw moral deterioration taking place on campus. He told Amos K. Hollowell, the president of the board of trustees, that it was becoming an expectation that the girls should learn to dance; at least one student had come to him sorely distressed over the dancing in physical training classes. The boys on campus, however, caused him the most concern. Conditions in Bundy Hall were completely out of control—the residents had "dismissed one governor within a year and run out another." Dean of Men William O. Mendenhall believed that students should not be compelled to obey rules that they disapproved of. Thus the church attendance requirement was becoming a dead letter.[87]

Other tensions had arisen between Kelly and Russell. For several years, Murray S. Kenworthy, a former Russell student, had been his assistant in the biblical department. Without consulting Russell, Kelly dismissed Kenworthy and made Mendenhall part of the biblical department. Mendenhall was a presidential favorite who had no background in religion save YMCA work. Finally, there was open conflict between the wives of Russell and Kelly that, according to rumor, on at least one occasion erupted into a screaming, hair-pulling fight on College Avenue.[88]

On April 8, 1915, Russell offered his resignation to the board, releasing a public statement to the local press that summed up his position. In his autobiography, Russell claimed that when he resigned, he intended to leave quietly, but, as he put it, "I reckoned without my friends and especially the alumni." The alumni had become especially important, since in 1915, for the first time, the two yearly meetings had agreed to allow them to elect three board members. Russell, by his recollection, gave a statement of Kelly's failings to the board "at their insistence." Russell may initially have planned to leave quietly, but by the end of April he was deeply involved in a plan to force the board to fire Kelly.[89]

When Russell announced his resignation, history professor Walter C. Woodward, aided by Harlow Lindley and geologist Allen D. Hole, drew up a petition that a majority of the faculty signed, asking the board not to accept Russell's resignation. Soon the whole faculty was polarized; it was almost impossible to avoid taking sides. Student petitions poured in, as did letters from alumni and members of the yearly meetings. Confronted with this, the board announced that in May it would conduct an inquiry into the Kelly administration.[90]

Thus encouraged, Russell laid out a plan for Kelly's destruction. In an undated memorandum, he listed the steps to be taken. College engineer Marmaduke Gluys was "to be questioned on matters of business in which college affairs and the president's private affairs have been confused." Other professors would talk about conditions on campus; Richmond residents would describe Kelly's poor relations with the community. The board was urged to look at discipline among the students and at Kelly's ability "to command the confidence and respect of Professors and officers inside the college," along with his "personal peculiarities." Supporters gathered evidence. One wrote of how Kelly had hired a professor who smoked cigarettes and another who had publicly advocated toleration of moderate drinking. Others wrote of Kelly's poor relations with a variety of constituents. The local newspapers, edited by friends of Russell, regularly ran helpful stories.[91]

When the hearing came, however, it vindicated Kelly. For three days, the trustees heard sixty people testify and considered a number of letters. Eighty years later, it is difficult to know what to make of the situation. On one hand, the trustees doubtless began with a predisposition to support duly constituted authority, i.e., Kelly. As one trustee told Russell, the college could find another Bible professor without difficulty, but not another president. On the other hand, while Kelly certainly had enemies among the faculty and alumni who resented what they considered to be his autocratic ways, no clear evidence of the kind of wrongdoing for which Russell's supporters searched has survived. The question was one of the direction Earlham would take, and the board sided with Kelly.[92]

The board's action effectively closed the controversy, but scars lingered for years. None of the principals' careers suffered greatly. Kelly left Earlham in 1917 to head first the Council of Church Boards of Education, and then the Association of American Colleges. Russell went first to Johns Hopkins and eventually to Duke, retiring in 1941 as dean of its divinity school. Mendenhall left in 1918 to become president first of

Friends University and then of Whittier. Ironically, he became not only a good friend of Russell in later years, but a leader in a variety of Quaker causes. Two of Russell's closest friends on the faculty, Laurence Hadley and Edwin Morrison, also left out of frustration and anger, as did Walter C. Woodward. Even more ironically, both Hadley and Woodward resumed connections with Earlham as long-serving trustees.[93]

The Russell controversy also confirmed the direction in which Earlham was to move. The motif was, above all, professional. Scholarly credentials would increasingly become the standard by which faculty qualified for employment and renewal. Classes, and not just those in the natural sciences, would place increasing emphasis on laboratory work and experimentation. Earlham would be accredited. It would solicit funds from non-Quaker philanthropists and foundations. It, and its faculty, would be active participants in appropriate professional and scholarly organizations. And it would increasingly take its cues, not from the denomination to which it was tied, but from the larger academic world.

What the conflict of Russell and Kelly did not involve, at least in their minds, was the question of academic freedom. Indeed, even as Russell and Kelly waged their final battle, the new-born American Association of University Professors had issued its first statement on academic freedom. The Association of American Colleges, Robert L. Kelly, president, greeted it with fierce opposition. Russell had returned to Earlham in 1903 with a promise of considerable freedom, but neither he nor any of his colleagues made an issue of formally dedicating the college to full liberty of discussion and inquiry.[94]

Nevertheless, although Earlham might not officially be dedicated to academic freedom, by 1915 long strides had been made. Two presidents and a succession of board members had affirmed that they would not set the bounds of inquiry on campus to suit the narrowest minds in Indiana and Western yearly meetings. Cleveland K. Chase, the former Latin professor, summed up the situation by expressing his "admiration and wonder" at, despite denominational ties, the "breadth of vision, a toleration, a desire to be fair that have allowed the college to develop as few people unacquainted with the facts would believe."[95]

While freedom of inquiry was relatively secure, the religious direction of Earlham was less certain. Earlham's connection with the yearly meetings, through the board and through its students, was still strong. It was also clear that evangelical/holiness Quakerism would not take root on campus. The forms of religion, such as mandatory chapel, were still very much a part of campus life. But that religion was increasingly generically Protestant, vaguely evangelical, certainly not distinctively Quaker. Just how Quakerish the campus would be in future years was still an open question.

Earlham had arrived at this situation through conflicts, however, that were at odds with the processes seen in other church schools of the period. Many other denominational colleges were beginning a process of loosening denominational ties, asserting the right to pursue an intellectual life that was sometimes at odds with church doctrine, and deemphasizing denominational identities. In many of these schools, the first step was often to focus on a "Christian" identity, as opposed to a denominational one. This, in turn, would ultimately lead to a general deemphasis on the role of religion in campus life, especially campus intellectual life. And religious liberals, increasingly devoted to an ideal of academic freedom, were usually leaders in such causes.[96]

Earlham departed from this pattern in critical ways. The vision of President Kelly certainly was in keeping with it; if nothing else, the hard realities of economics, the need for more students, seemed to dictate this course. But this was not the course of Elbert Russell. For him and his supporters, a commitment to freedom of inquiry went hand in hand with a commitment to Quaker distinctiveness. Russell helped set a pattern at Earlham in which those most committed to a sectarian, distinctive identity for the school would be professional-minded, modernist faculty often at odds with administrators for whom sectarianism was poor policy.

The era of Russell and Kelly had also set another pattern. The long process of alienation from the two yearly meetings had begun, as many Friends came to regard Earlham, with its modernist biblical department, with fear and suspicion. These Friends would not give up entirely, however, without making one more effort to wrest control back into their hands.

The Trials of
Liberal Quakerism,
1915–1946

*A*lexander C. Purdy was a popular professor at Earlham, and it was no surprise for him in 1919 and 1920 to find his classes on the Bible and on the life of Christ filled to capacity. But not all of those earnestly taking notes in the Lindley Hall lecture room were there out of enthusiasm or affection. At least one was a member of Indiana Yearly Meeting on a very different mission—gathering evidence that would be used by its fundamentalist members in an attack on Purdy and on Earlham, an attack that finally came in the autumn of 1920. It was an ordeal that ultimately exonerated both the professor and the college, but left deep scars on both. It was a critical step in the long process of alienation of the college from its original constituencies.[1]

At the heart of this alienation were increasingly divergent visions of Quakerism, and of what it meant for Earlham to be a Quaker college. These divergent visions were rooted in differences in the larger Society of Friends, differences that became greater between 1920 and 1940. They were seen first in the theological conflict that climaxed in 1920–1921, but which continued to simmer for decades. By the 1930s, however, a new series of conflicts over the secular college culture, both on and off the campus, especially over smoking and dancing, dwarfed those disputes. Students and faculty heightened these tensions in the 1930s, as some saw Quaker principles impelling them to challenge the status quo on economic and racial matters. This led them into conflict not only with many in the Richmond community, but also with Earlham's president, the staunchly conservative William C. Dennis. These tensions with the community reached a new height during World War II, when the college admitted Japanese American students from the internment camps of the West Coast.

Earlham's history in this period was paradoxical. Two presidents— David M. Edwards from 1917 to 1929, and William C. Dennis from 1929 to 1946—led the college. Edwards verged on socialism in his politics, while Dennis was a stalwartly conservative Republican. Both were theological liberals who incurred the wrath of fundamentalists, but it was Dennis, who shared the social outlook of his opponents, who, by relaxing restrictions on smoking and dancing, was responsible for the greatest changes in the college. And while theological conflict was hardly unique to Earlham in these years, at Earlham it took paradoxical turns. In Earlham's case, most of the theological liberals, in the tradition of Elbert Russell, advocated and emphasized a distinctively sectarian vision of higher education, rooted in Earlham's Quaker heritage. They contended both with students, impatient with all tradition and restraints on the campus culture, and with fundamentalist-leaning Friends, who wanted to banish not only theological liberalism but also smoking, dancing, and other amusements dear to many students, modeling Earlham not as much on its past as on the Bible colleges many Quaker pastors had attended.

At the same time, Earlham remained close to its roots. A majority of students continued to come from Indiana, and those from Richmond continued to be the single largest group. Of religious groups, Friends were still the largest. But even here change was taking place. While a majority of Quaker students still came from Indiana and Western yearly meetings, there was an increasing presence from the East, especially from Philadelphia, New York, Baltimore, and New England yearly meetings. And as the Quaker academies in Indiana faded away, Earlham looked increasingly to Quaker boarding and day schools in the East for students.

The Flowering of Liberal Quakerism

Robert L. Kelly announced his resignation early in 1917. Although the board had stood behind Kelly during the attack by Elbert Russell and his supporters, the controversy left the campus divided and Kelly less able to lead it effectively. Apparently he was determined to remain just long enough to forestall any impression that he was forced out. He considered seeking a seat in Congress, but gave that up when he was offered the position of executive secretary of the Council of Church Boards of Education. The new post brought him a higher salary, and that increased further when he was also appointed the executive secretary of the Association of American Colleges, a position he held until retiring in 1937. Until his death in 1954, he retained close ties with the campus, more so, probably, than any president since Joseph Moore.[2]

When Kelly announced his resignation, Amos K. Hollowell, the chairman of the board, had no doubts about who his successor should be. He immediately wrote to Rufus Jones at Haverford, dropping broad hints that the position was Jones's for the asking. If not Jones, then Hollowell hoped for Haverford professor Richard Gummere. Neither showed any interest in coming west.[3]

Instead, the board chose a Friend who embodied both tradition and change. At the time he accepted Earlham's presidency, David M. Edwards was the president of Penn College in Iowa. Born, appropriately, in Earlham, Iowa, in 1871, Edwards was the first president who had never been an Earlham student. His education had been unconventional—he was married with children when he entered Penn in 1896, but he graduated with honors in four years. He went on to do graduate work in sociology at the University of Chicago and Boston University. His Ph.D. from the latter made him Earlham's first president with an earned doctorate.[4]

There was much in Edwards's background to comfort the strong fundamentalist group in Indiana and Western yearly meetings. He came on both sides from old Quaker families, and was a recorded minister. Iowa Yearly Meeting was a holiness bastion, and Penn had always been considered free from any taint of modernism. Stories circulated of how, when Edwards was in graduate school, he had "spent whole nights on the floor in prayer that God would keep [him] true to the Bible and . . . from following the modernists." Edwards strengthened this impression by preaching at Indiana Yearly Meeting in 1917 a sermon on the Atonement that evangelicals found inspiring.[5]

The fundamentalists, however, misjudged Edwards. He was in fact thoroughly modernist in his sympathies, counting among his favorite students leading young liberal Friends (and future Earlham faculty) like Alexander Purdy and Clarence Pickett. His successor at Penn burned some of the pernicious books that Edwards had allowed into its library. Edwards himself had not always been happy at Penn, and had contemplated leaving as early as 1914. He was, however, a success there, bringing Penn through two successful fund raising campaigns, the second after a disastrous fire destroyed the college's main building.[6]

Arriving at the same time as Edwards was the new professor in the biblical department, Alexander Converse Purdy. Born in 1890 in western

DAVID M. EDWARDS

New York, he was a son of Ellison R. Purdy, who had moved west to become one of Iowa Yearly Meeting's leading pastors (and a relative moderate among its zealous fundamentalists). At Penn, Alexander had been one of Edwards's prize students as well as a star athlete and orator. He went on to Hartford Seminary, where he received his Ph.D. in 1914. Between 1910 and 1914 Hartford had become the favorite destination of bright young Friends from the Midwest who contemplated careers as pastors or teachers of religion. Purdy's contemporaries at Hartford included Earlham alumni Tom Jones and Levinus K. Painter and fellow Penn graduate Clarence Pickett. A few years behind them was a Friend from Wilmington, Ohio, Thomas R. Kelly. All achieved distinction as Quaker leaders, and all but Painter would be Earlham faculty or administrators.[7]

Purdy's arrival showed that Elbert Russell's departure had not changed Earlham's commitment to modernism and critical scholarship in biblical teaching. When Russell resigned, the college replaced him with two of his students, Tom Jones and Francis Anscombe, and with Henry J. Cadbury, a Philadelphia Friend who had just finished a Ph.D. at Harvard. Kelly actually hired Purdy in 1916, but a commitment to the YMCA delayed his arrival for another year.[8]

At Earlham, Purdy joined a group of idealistic young Friends who came into their own in these years, as leaders in the Five Years Meeting and as authors, lecturers, and ministers. Eldest among them was Allen D. Hole, affectionately known as "Daddy" Hole, after the death of David W. Dennis in 1916 the senior natural scientist of the faculty. A recorded minister, he was for many years the executive secretary of the Peace Association of Friends in America. One appreciative student remembered how the kindly, patient Hole helped to free him of "crude, false, and superstitious concepts of the universe." Two other young scientists, both alumni, joined him. Millard Markle in the biology department was a 1910 graduate whom Kelly had hired immediately and who remained forty-four years, with time off to earn his Ph.D. at the University of Chicago. An active Friend, he was also an outspoken evolutionist. "I do not mean to destroy anyone's faith or belief in the least or think that it needs to be just because they do not believe all the Bible to be literal," he told his students. In 1919 Ernest Wildman, a chemist who had left a lucrative position in private industry because his employer was uncomfortable with his pacifist convictions, returned to Earlham. Wildman, a member of a prominent Quaker family in Clark County, Ohio, would ultimately prove more liberal in his religious and political views than almost anyone else on campus.[9]

The religion and philosophy department was the heart of religious teaching on campus, and it was a modernist stronghold. Purdy's colleague was the psychologist J. Herschel Coffin. Ironically, at the turn of the century, his family had moved from Indiana to Iowa so that the Coffin children could attend Penn and thus avoid the pernicious tendencies at Earlham. Coffin, however, had become a committed modernist by 1907, when he came to Earlham after graduate work at Cornell. Those hunting heresy found no lack of it in his classes.[10]

These Friends found support off-campus from Richmond Friends, particularly Walter C. Woodward, Charles M. Woodman, and S. Edgar Nicholson. The most influential of these was Woodward, an 1899 graduate who taught history at Earlham from 1910 to 1915. He had returned to Richmond in 1917 as executive secretary of the Five Years Meeting and editor of the *American Friend*. He staffed his office with liberal Friends, and while admitting all points of view to the columns of the *American Friend*, took a consistently modernist line in his editorials. He immediately became a member of Earlham's board and remained on it until his death in 1942, nearly all of the time as chairman. Woodward's predecessor at the *American Friend* was S. Edgar Nicholson, an older Earlham alumnus who alternated between working for the Five Years Meeting and various Prohibition groups, especially the Anti-Saloon League. The pastor of both, and yet another influential liberal, was Charles M. Woodman of West Richmond Friends Meeting. A New Englander, Woodman came to West Richmond in 1916, and became an Earlham trustee in 1919.[11]

The tie with West Richmond Meeting was important, since its members included Five Years Meeting officials like Woodward as well as most of the Earlham faculty. West Richmond Friends saw their meeting becoming one of the premier Quaker congregations in North America. "I do not know of another Friends meeting anywhere in the country which has proportionally so many representative members filling important places in the church," Nicholson told Woodman. To strengthen ties with the campus, West Richmond made all Earlham students associate members of the meeting.[12]

These Friends shared a number of views. A starting point was a distaste for the holiness orthodoxy that gripped much of midwestern pastoral Quakerism. "There is in this locality,—west of Richmond— about as much Quakerism as there is in a . . . camp meeting in full swing," Thomas R. Kelly, a future member of the faculty, wrote in 1916. "Some meeting houses seem to be infested with 'amens' and 'glory, hallelujahs' and you can scarcely open your mouth without jarring a few loose from the rafters." Woodward took Indiana Yearly Meeting to task in 1918 for having "an excess of dead timber." Although Earlham was in its midst, the college had not produced the leadership that Indiana Yearly Meeting needed. "The ministry, largely untrained, has proceeded in old and impoverished ways, confusing dogmatic evangelistic methods with pastoral care and construction," he wrote, "while in many areas superficial emotionalism and . . . super-heated vagaries . . . have masqueraded under a Friends label." Although "special meetings" continued to be held on campus, and Purdy himself participated in similar services, these Friends had little confidence in revivalism as most of Indiana and Western yearly meetings practiced it. They affirmed the need for a definite Christian commitment, but they saw that as a life-long process rather than an instantaneous experience. Nicholson wrote in the *American Friend* that Friends needed a "wider catholicity in spirit."[13]

In other respects, these Friends were disciples of Elbert Russell. They disputed the holiness understanding of a blood atonement. Purdy also dismissed biblical literalism and inerrancy. Prophecy, for example, especially the prophecies of Christ, had to be understood as directed at the people of the time, not to the distant future. They, especially the scientists, were committed to evolution as the basis of the natural sciences. Purdy told his critics that it was impossible to reconcile the creation narratives in the first three chapters of Genesis with the indisputable findings of modern science. This point of view found its most articulate proponent in Ernest Wildman. "Religion should be based upon experience, upon reality, upon real facts rather than upon imaginary or 'manufactured facts,' he told his students. "Theological dogmas and doctrines are 'manufactured facts,' which were invented by men to systematize, rationalize and explain *their* apprehension of *their* spiritual experiences." Mildred Henley, a 1920 graduate, was blunt in echoing Wildman: "He whose religion was not elastic enough and strong enough to stand the strain of adjustment to certain established and proven facts of science has not a religion." Earlham faculty, however, emphasized that they viewed evolution theistically, as Joseph Moore had. As Edwards put it in 1920, it was "a description of the mode by which God has worked in doing the thing which has been done, in creating and sustaining and bringing the forces of this world in which we live."[14]

In the minds of these liberals, doctrine was a secondary concern. "It is not wise to be unduly disturbed about intellectual conceptions of the principles of religion," Edwards wrote to one Indiana Friend. "The main thing is to be concerned with the way one is living and the way one can serve his day and generation." This certainly was the experience of one of Purdy's students, who wrote that in Purdy's classes one came "not to interpret doctrines and religious beliefs," but to know "religion as a personal thing." Religion had to be modern. As another student wrote, "The 'old-fashioned' religion does not meet our needs today of a vital, *living* religion."[15]

These Friends were united in seeing a great future for Quakerism, especially in the era of World War I. "We shall have to re-examine the postulates of our civilization; and every man must be ready to submit his financial, social, and moral interests to such a readjustment as a critical study of social problems may demand," wrote J. Herschel Coffin in 1917. Friends, as advocates of "christian democracy," were uniquely suited to take the lead in that "readjustment." Walter C. Woodward agreed: "The opportunity which faces us as a church is unparalleled. Never, so far as we know, has a religious denomination been entrusted with such a unique and so tremendous a responsibility," he told readers of the *American Friend*. "It is ours in a very peculiar way to lead the world into paths of that good will which all agree is the only hope of civilization."[16]

To accomplish this, Quakers had to be prepared for leadership, and the liberal Friends tied to Earlham agreed that college-educated Friends would provide that leadership. "The future of the Society of Friends, perhaps more distinctly than that of any other religious group, is dependent upon its institutions of higher education," Edwards wrote to a supporter. Alumnus and former trustee Absalom Rosenberger spoke for these Friends in seeing Earlham as "the strategic point of Quakerism." They pointed out that, alone of the Quaker colleges west of Philadelphia, Earlham was on a relatively sound financial footing and was fully accredited. They believed that Earlham would be, in Edwards's words, "the principal educational institution of the Society of Friends in America, . . . producing a good portion of the leadership for the entire church." It would "prepare them . . . under Christian influences for services for humanity." Woodward rejected the idea that Quaker colleges should be limited by their yearly meetings. "In our colleges must be found that liberalism, that constructive vision, without which there is no progress," he wrote in 1918. Instead, he wanted yearly meetings to reflect the broad vision of the colleges: "For the college merely to reflect the yearly meeting would destroy the very fundamental purpose of our denominational colleges."[17]

The Earlham group did not agree, however, about the state of contemporary Quakerism. Tom Jones, the 1912 graduate who was field secretary for the Young Friends, was confident: "We are in a better position to move forward as a united body than we have been for two hundred years," he wrote in 1917. S. Edgar Nicholson agreed, at least as far as Indiana Yearly Meeting was concerned. "The elements that are represented in West Richmond Meeting will increase influentially," he wrote to Woodman, "and in the near future will certainly be the dominant elements." Others were not so sure. Woodward thought that the Society of Friends needed to "reconstruct itself on a world frontage." Elden H. Mills, a 1917 graduate, lashed out in 1920: "If the members of the Friends' Church had spent the same amount of energy in seeking the leading of the 'Inner Light' themselves and following it out, as they have in picking out the things in others with which they did not agree, and haggling over them, the story of the Society of Friends would have been different, and we would be vastly more influential."[18]

Whatever their assessment of contemporary Quakerism, these Friends were convinced that they saw the Quaker future. It was definitely Christian—all affirmed their commitment to Christ, to the need of all humanity for a savior. But their primary concern was service. "Jesus' whole life, from its beginning to its close, was one continuous expression of social service," Woodman told the Five Years Meeting in 1917. The problem of Christianity, in Nicholson's eyes, was that it "defined religion in terms of words and phrases rather than in terms of life and service." Homer J. Coppock, a 1904 graduate active in the Five Years Meeting, labeled social service "the acid test of Quakerism." By 1920 Woodward was fending off complaints that too much of the *American Friend* was devoted to service concerns and not enough to spirituality.[19]

What is not clear is how much impact these Friends had on Earlham students. A majority of the student body from 1915 to 1920 were Friends, most from Indiana and Western yearly meetings. For every major Quaker event of the period, there was a considerable Earlham contingent present—the annual conferences of the Young Friends, the meetings of the Forward Movement, the 1920 All-Friends Conference in London, the activities of the Five Years Meeting. There was a steady procession of liberal Friends as speakers in chapel and at commencement; Rufus M. Jones, the pillar of Quaker modernism, was a frequent visitor. Students had little use for revivalism, with its "long discourses on sanctification and other vague terms." Until the late 1920s, the campus YMCA sent out "gospel teams" to hold special meetings in Quaker communities, but they eschewed "the old-fashioned type of revival." Typical was a visit to Kingman, Indiana, in December 1916. "The team found . . . that the town had been preached and revivaled to death," the *Press* editorialized, so "the policy of the Earlham men immediately was not to give the town another revival, but rather to present Christianity in the light of life problems and their solution, trying to fit the talks to the most apparent needs of the people." In the same year, when a group of students from Western Yearly Meeting organized to serve their home meetings, they emphasized young people's clubs and courses in Quaker history, not the more traditional types of evangelism.[20]

On the other hand, there is abundant evidence that many, perhaps a majority, of students either rejected this vision of Quaker activism and distinctiveness or paid it little attention, just as Elbert Russell had claimed in 1915. Indeed, there were consistent complaints about student attitudes toward religion, particularly lack of attention in chapel and the widespread nonattendance of the Sunday morning services on campus. In 1924, the college dropped the mandatory Sunday service, and reduced chapel to three times a week. Students from the period are divided in their memories of whether attendance at off-campus churches was common, but they are agreed that the chapel attendance requirement was unpopular. By 1933, the college was frank in admitting that most of the chapels were not devotional, with addresses on topics like "Student Life in Japan" or "Our Promised Land, the Corn Belt." When chapels were devotional, they were "distinctive and free from sentimentality."[21]

Perhaps even more significant was Earlham's response to World War I. When the United States did enter the war in 1917, some on the campus tried to keep up the traditional Quaker position. The editors of the *Press* blasted the sentiment that "all efforts [should] be turned toward militarism." They worried that Friends were being stampeded into embracing the call to arms. They urged Quakers to "stand by their principle, not by inactivity, no, nor by long-faced pacifism, but by the enlistment of lives into the service of mobilizing the spiritual forces of this old world, and show our colors for the Kingdom of God." In other words, they would do their duty by embracing the liberal Quaker ethic of service. Many at Earlham did. Faculty like Allen D. Hole continued to be open and forthright in advocacy of pacifism. As many as thirty-four students registered as conscientious objectors and joined the Friends Reconstruction Unit in France that the newly formed American Friends Service Committee had organized.[22]

Taking such a stand certainly involved risks. In 1917–1918 a wave of suspicion of anyone not fervently behind the war effort swept the nation. Richmond newspapers attacked Quaker pacifism, and pacifist addresses at the 1917 sessions of the Five Years Meeting in Richmond attracted considerable negative comment. Several Bureau of Investigation agents were in the gallery, waiting to hear treasonable sentiments. There is no evidence, however, that anyone on campus suffered harassment, although one student, Paul Whitely, was imprisoned when he could not satisfy his draft board of his sincerity as a conscientious objector.[23]

For most, however, pacifism was not an issue. Earlham had five times the number of men in the military—178—as were conscientious objectors. Throughout the spring of 1917 men dropped out to join the army. The first, Tom Barr, was the son of Daisy Douglas Barr, a well-known Quaker pastor and evangelist. President Kelly, in one of his last acts, left the decision to the conscience of each student faced with military service with a statement that the board endorsed: "Each man is answerable before God as to his duty in the situation which now confronts him. Every man ought to be able to find in his own heart his duty in the present crisis." (Kelly himself was not above a little German-baiting, pointing out that while Germany had inspired the university, the denominational college was purely American.) Edwards, while seeing Reconstruction as the natural outlet for the energies of Friends, thought that Earlham could provide everything but "technical military training." Until the end of the war, the *Press* gave equal attention to reports of the experiences of students in the armed services and to those in the Reconstruction unit in France. When the war ended, a number of veterans returned to campus, often wearing their uniforms. For a time, there was tension between them and the campus pacifists.[24]

The war was not the only source of tension on campus in these years. In fact, the confidence of the Earlham liberals in their own power and influence was unjustified. In 1920, Earlham came under the most pointed and concerted attack that it would ever face. At issue were Earlham's liberal Quakerism and its very methods of teaching both the Bible and science.

The Heresy Trial of 1920–1921

Between the end of World War I and 1925, American Protestantism saw conflict between conservative evangelicals, generically labeled fundamentalists by most historians, and liberal modernists. The conflict was most intense in the great national denominations, especially the Presbyterians, Methodists, and Baptists. Ultimately, the liberals achieved at least toleration for their views, and many of their conservative opponents departed to found new denominations or movements.[25]

Essentially, the conflict was the result of the efforts of theological conservatives to purge their denominations of ministers and teachers who did not hold to what they considered scriptural faith. Typically, fundamentalists based their position on some creedal document, an historic statement or confession, which they set up as the definition of orthodoxy for the denomination. The movement was given impetus by the publication from 1910 to 1915 of a series of pamphlets, *The Fundamentals;* hence the label *fundamentalist.*[26]

There is disagreement among historians about the bases of the fundamentalist movement. All historians agree, however, that antipathy to modernism united fundamentalists. They saw evolution as completely contrary to Scripture. They insisted on the inerrancy of the Bible, the centrality of the doctrine of the Virgin Birth of Christ, and the imminence of his premillennial return. They were skeptical about the potential of the Social Gospel, although by no means entirely opposed to reform work. And they were certain that no one who did not hold these beliefs could be considered a Christian. Thus they sought to impose their vision as the minimum that God required.[27]

Quaker fundamentalism followed much these same lines. Between

1900 and 1920, it had risen as the old holiness revival party in the Gurneyite yearly meetings responded to the growing visibility and influence of modernist Friends like Elbert Russell and Rufus Jones. The rallying point for these Friends was the Richmond Declaration of Faith, drafted in 1887 as a unifying document for the Gurneyite yearly meetings. Modernists never liked it, and when the Five Years Meeting was formed in 1902 they made its inclusion in the Uniform Discipline optional with the constituent yearly meetings. Most, Indiana and Western among them, had included it in their versions. This, in fundamentalist eyes, made it the statement by which all Quaker ministry and teaching should be judged.[28]

The heart of fundamentalist Quakerism in these years was the Cleveland Bible Institute of Walter and Emma Malone. It was probably the single greatest source of pastors for the Five Years Meeting, and was above suspicion in the doctrinal "soundness" of its graduates. By 1920, Cleveland alumni and former associates of the Malones had formed a network of evangelical Friends from North Carolina to Oregon and California. Central to that network were Bible colleges founded on the Cleveland model by Friends. Most important to Indiana Friends was the Union Bible Seminary in Westfield, Indiana.[29]

Union was led by William M. Smith, an uncompromising fundamentalist who had been a student of the Malones and had taught for a time in their school. In 1911 he founded the seminary, which was also uncompromising in its holiness and fundamentalist orthodoxy, "the old tried truth of Christian doctrine as held by Orthodox Friends." Within two years of its establishment, Smith students were pastors in thirteen Friends churches in Indiana and Western yearly meetings. Their number grew steadily. By 1920, for example, nearly all of the pastors in Portland Quarter of Indiana Yearly Meeting had been students at Westfield.[30]

Smith gave no quarter in his attacks on "unsoundness" among Friends. Smith even condemned Robert Barclay's *Apology,* long considered the standard work of Quaker theology, as inadequately evangelical. Smith's influence also grew through his publications. In 1913 he began publishing the *Friends Minister,* which was, if possible, even more conservative than Walter Malone's *Evangelical Friend.* (In 1921 he changed its name to the *Gospel Minister.*) Almost every issue contained some blast at heresy. Colleges were infected with "evolution and higher criticism, the handmaids of infidelity, so much so that the Holy Ghost has abandoned them."[31]

Smith did not speak for all of the antimodernist, evangelical Friends in Indiana and Western yearly meetings. There was another group that shared his antipathy to modernism, but which was less strident in its rhetoric and less given to public attacks on fellow Friends. Its adherents, unlike Smith, were active in their yearly meetings and in the Five Years Meeting. They included men like Truman C. Kenworthy, the former superintendent of Indiana Yearly Meeting, E. Howard Brown, the pastor at East Main Street Meeting in Richmond, George N. Hartley, a well-known minister and missionary, and R. Aaron Napier, then the Indiana Yearly Meeting superintendent. Often they had ties to Earlham; Hartley, Brown, and Napier were former students, while Kenworthy's children were alumni. But, like Smith, they wanted to root "unsoundness" out of Quaker institutions.[32]

By 1919, these tensions were becoming apparent to the leaders of the Five Years Meeting, including Woodward. "Right now there is manifest in some sections a great diversity of opinion and belief among Friends," Woodward editorialized in September. Because of the war, he thought, there was a combative spirit prominent, seen in "a studied propaganda of carping criticism, hesitating not at gross misrepresentation." Indeed, some Friends seemed to have as their goal "another separation." Woodward compared them with "medieval zealots," proceeding "on the assumption that defense of the faith (their faith) makes holy an unholy spirit and unholy tactics in the defender."[33]

This sentiment reached its head in the Portland Quarter of Indiana Yearly Meeting. Portland was a fundamentalist stronghold which had never had many ties with Earlham. In April 1920 it noted "unrest among our members, caused by the many conflicting reports in our midst about certain teachings and methods among us." It called for an examination of "such questions as may arise about the teachings, policy, etc. of Earlham College and the *American Friend*" by the yearly meeting. S. Edgar Nicholson was then clerk of the yearly meeting, and he sought to head off the matter by suggesting the appointment by the Yearly Meeting of Ministry and Oversight of a Committee on the State of the Church, to consider the condition of the whole yearly meeting and thus deflect attention from Earlham. By the time of the yearly meeting, however, it had become a committee, formed under the relevant provisions of the college charter, to investigate Earlham. At the request of Indiana Yearly Meeting, Western Yearly Meeting appointed its own committee, and the joint group met at the East Main Street Meetinghouse in Richmond December 7 and 8, 1920.[34]

The joint committee had five members from each yearly meeting: S. Edgar Nicholson, Ida T. Parker, William J. Sayers, Ira C. Johnson, and S. Adelbert Wood from Indiana; and Albert J. Brown, J. Brandt Wolfe, Mary M. Harold, George H. Moore, and Charles T. Moore from Western. Of these, only Wood and Charles T. Moore had strong fundamentalist leanings. Parker was a pastor of moderate views who was both an Earlham graduate and a former member of the staff at the Cleveland

Bible Institute. William J. Sayers was the pastor at Muncie, a moderate like Parker. Johnson was a much-loved minister of evangelical views, past seventy, who instinctively disliked controversy. Albert J. Brown, the clerk of Western Yearly Meeting, was the most liberal of its delegation, a former president of Wilmington College and a sympathizer with Elbert Russell and Rufus Jones. Wolfe's views are hard to peg; at times he sympathized with fundamentalism, but he also appears inclined to follow Brown's lead. Harold, the pastor at Danville, Indiana, was a moderate like Sayers and Parker, skeptical about some modernist teachings but also thinking that there was room for them in her yearly meeting. George H. Moore was an Earlham graduate and the president of the Five Years Meeting Mission Board; he had taught for a time at Westfield, and was then serving as a pastor. Not all appeared in Richmond; business detained Brown and Parker, while bad weather kept Wolfe away.[35]

A group that called itself the "Committee of Ten" conducted the "prosecution." A meeting of antimodernist Friends in Richmond on October 22 had named them to represent its concerns. At its heart were were Truman C. Kenworthy, E. Howard Brown, and Albert J. Fuerstenberger, who appeared at the hearing to press the case against Earlham. Fuerstenberger emerged as the group's chief witness. A product of Ohio Yearly Meeting who had been a pastor in several places, in 1920 he was at the Carthage, Indiana, meeting. Three years before, at age forty, he had left Wabash, Indiana, where by all accounts he had been a successful minister, to come to the small North Tenth Street Meeting in Richmond and to take courses at Earlham. His experiences as a student accounted for much of the case against Alexander Purdy.[36]

When the hearing began on December 7, order broke down almost immediately. The accusers were to present their case first. The yearly meetings' committee had decided to hear but one witness at a time, but the "Committee of Ten" insisted on attending as a group. Fuerstenberger did most of the talking, with help from Brown and Kenworthy. Thomas R. Woodard, a dentist and recorded minister from Knightstown, Indiana, and a nephew of Luke Woodard, also appeared to plead against "unsoundness," as did Percy Thomas, the pastor at Dublin, Indiana; Lois Pitts, an evangelist; Frank Long, the pastor at Farmland, Indiana; Mildred Allen, the pastor at Mooreland, Indiana; Lydia Inman, a Friend from Portland, Indiana; and George N. Hartley. Fuerstenberger, Brown, and Kenworthy provided most of the attack. They opened with a long statement of Earlham's shortcomings: "For a number of years, and up to the present time, in common with much of the unguarded educational system of today, the integrity and authority of the Holy Scriptures have been discredited at Earlham," it began, "both by certain text books used, and by verbal teaching, especially in the biblical department, by an appeal to the unscientific and unproven 'Evolutionary Hypothesis.'" These had created unrest in the two yearly meetings. Through the use of books by "destructive higher critics" Earlham was "tearing the Bible to pieces to fit the theory of Evolution" and had "caused many young people to lose their childhood faith in God and the Bible." It was the responsibility of the two yearly meetings to put things right: "Friends generally do not want these things taught at Earlham . . . and Friends ought to be allowed to have what they want and what they pay for."[37]

The Committee of Ten's indictment was significant in other ways. They praised the recently held World Christian Fundamentals Conference in which Friends had participated. They found it easy to explain the errors of the modernists; they were "very largely teachers and those who have failed in the ministry, doubtless because they have lost their passion for souls." They also raised the old charge that the modernists were tainted with "Hicksism." The solution, then, was for the yearly meetings to change the trustees, and then for the trustees to change the college.[38]

Fuerstenberger was the first witness. He had refused to take any course in which evolution was taught, but he had had the Old Testament and the Life of Christ under Purdy, as well as a course with J. Herschel Coffin. Fuerstenberger's indictment was wide-ranging and vehement. The modernist texts that Purdy used, by C. F. Kane, Ernest Burton, and Shailer Mathews, were an "outrage." Purdy was guilty of a long list of errors in teaching. "The Bible was set at naught as an authority on scientific facts concerning the creation of the world and of man." Adam and Eve, Cain and Abel, the Flood, and Jonah were dismissed as mythical. Purdy had even suggested that the Pentateuch was not the work of Moses, and that the Jews had taken certain ideas from pagans. In the Life of Christ, Purdy had not mentioned the Virgin Birth, and had denied the Second Coming. The class, Fuerstenberger claimed, "many a time compelled me to hang my head in shame as I saw my Lord lowered to the level of a man." He had complained to President Edwards and to Amos K. Hollowell, the board chairman, but had received no satisfaction; Edwards had "insisted that we had to interpret the Bible in the light of scientific facts." Earlham, Fuerstenberger concluded, was guilty of deception.[39]

Others of the Ten followed and elaborated on these themes; various faculty like J. Herschel Coffin and Millard Markle were indefinite about conversion, or doubted the biblical account of creation, or questioned miracles, or embraced evolution. Truman Kenworthy wanted the work of all higher critics banished from campus; based on correspondence with Wheaton College and Taylor University, both sound evangelical schools, he knew that "plenty of books can be found to fill the courses." Of course, that would mean new faculty and new courses.[40]

Two other themes emerged in the testimony of the critics. One source of resentment was a report that Edwards had privately said that most of the ministers in Indiana Yearly Meeting were "ignorant." Edwards denied it, but this outlook certainly underlay the oft-stated liberal desire to raise the educational standards for pastors. S. Adelbert Wood admitted that pastors often could not understand Earlham faculty. Fuerstenberger was the most blunt. Earlham students, he said, made fun of "pastors who preach the Bible as historical and without error in the original writings." It was offensive, he told the committee, "to have students come from the college and make light of you." Aaron Napier, the yearly meeting superintendent, charged that at Earlham "there was not a thing said . . . against the ministry, yet it was treated in such a way that made you just a little bit ashamed of the fact that you were a preacher." Thus it was not surprising that Napier claimed, on the basis of a canvass of Indiana Yearly Meeting pastors that 82 percent "were lukewarm towards or radically opposed" to Earlham, and that it was "almost an impossibility to place an Earlham student, while he is a student in Earlham College, around this yearly meeting." There were only five Indiana Yearly Meeting pastors who were Earlham graduates.[41]

The other constant of the critics' testimony was the need to impose doctrinal tests and standards and expect adherence to them. Thomas R. Woodard was the most direct in this—Friends did have a creed in the Richmond Declaration. It was clear and uncompromising. S. Edgar Nicholson continually pressed the critics on this point. Was it possible that Earlham could reconcile its teachings with Indiana Yearly Meeting's Discipline? Was there room for differences in interpreting and understanding Quaker beliefs? The Ten categorically rejected that. Friends could not "parley" or "interpret the Discipline from different angles." That would make it appear that "we don't know how to interpret plain words in the Discipline." Their interpretation was the only one possible.[42]

On the second day Earlham presented its case, led by Edwards and aided by a sympathetic Nicholson. Edwards aggressively affirmed the college's Christian and Quaker foundations. Earlham was proud of what it did, and he would hold nothing back.[43]

The first thing that Edwards did not hold back was an attack on some of the Committee of Ten. While they had advertised most of the group as being former Earlham students, Edwards pointed out that four had had a "very meager amount of Biblical work" and thus would "not be prepared . . . to express an opinion that would be of any particular value." They had been admitted in spite of inadequate preparation, and none remained more than three semesters; Mildred Allen, for example, stayed only ten days. Edwards directed a particular swipe at Aaron Napier, the yearly meeting superintendent, who lived a block from campus, but never attended campus events or talked with students. (At this point

Napier protested that the Committee of Ten had used his name without his consent.)[44]

Edwards then embarked on a threefold argument. One was that teaching at Earlham followed lines that were standard in American colleges. Edwards introduced letters from the presidents of eleven church schools including Oberlin, Grinnell, and Carleton that he considered similar to Earlham, showing that evolution and critical study of the Bible were the accepted methods. He also called on Robert L. Kelly, who sent a strong statement. "I am rather surprised to learn that there is any considerable number of Friends who wish to go back to the methods which prevailed decades, if not centuries ago," Kelly wrote. "I hope that the friends of Earlham will not allow the prestige it has won both in the world of religion and the world of education to be shattered in this suicidal way."[45]

Edwards's second line of defense was to assert that Earlham had to be judged by the Christian character and commitment of its students. He was blunt in stating the college's goal. It did not tell its students: "This is the way you must think," or, "There are the things you must believe." Instead, it taught them "how to think logically, and . . . operating along normal lines or processes of thought, arrive at . . . truth for themselves." He then introduced letters from a number of students who affirmed the education that they had received and who scored Earlham's critics. Typical was Kent Morse, then teaching at Friends University: "I am all out of patience with those who, instead of praying with Christian faith for the success of an institution, seek with wagging tongues to bring about its destruction."[46]

Edwards concluded by arguing that the teaching at Earlham was consistent with Quakerism, including the "Discipline as interpreted by the Five Years Meeting of 1912." This was vital—the Five Years Meeting had reaffirmed that the Richmond Declaration was a statement of Quaker faith, but was not to "be taken as constituting a creed." Edwards expanded on this before the committee. "If we are going to say, notwithstanding the fact that the reputable world is doing a certain way, we are going, because of traditional adherence, to stick to some stereotyped set phrases of some past generation," he argued, "then we have cut loose from the spirit of Quakerism, which has always been the spirit of progress and the spirit of the search for truth."[47]

Purdy followed Edwards. Purdy was somewhat more conciliatory, emphasizing the points of agreement between himself and his critics. For example, when E. Howard Brown accused Purdy of denying the need for the New Birth because he questioned the historicity of Adam and Eve, Purdy responded with a ringing affirmation of "the reality, the power and awfulness of sin. I am conscious of personal guilt . . . and I am abundantly conscious of the need of a Saviour." At Earlham, he said, all "look the truth squarely in the face, because there is no real conflict between science and the Bible." All science at Earlham, he asserted, was theistic in its basis. He even announced that he was dropping the Kane textbook that critics found so objectionable, although only because he had independently decided that it had weaknesses.[48]

On the other hand, Purdy handed critics plenty of ammunition with his candor. The Bible, he said, must be seen "for what it is—a book of religion and not a book of science or history." The writers of the books of the Bible spoke as they understood; in light of modern science, they had clearly erred, as in the first three chapters of Genesis, or the account of the parting of the Red Sea in Exodus. Purdy also said that it was clear that Jesus had expected to return to earth soon after the Crucifixion. New methods of scriptural study involved terrible adjustments for some, yet in the end a faith consistent with scientific fact would be stronger. Thus he urged his students not to try to change their parents' minds. Instead, he told them, "the thing for you to do is to enter actively into the work of the church and prove that your faith has not been weakened." He would not change his teaching methods, and he knew that he had the board behind him "because they were going to teach the truth."[49]

Other faculty—J. Herschel Coffin, Allen D. Hole, Millard Markle— followed, speaking of their Christian commitment and church activities and of the spiritual atmosphere of the college, while denying that their teaching could undermine anyone's faith. At least one of the investigating committee, Wood, was not impressed. Their teaching could still be wrong and the students deluded, he argued, making the situation worse.[50]

The last witness for the college was Charles M. Woodman, the West Richmond pastor and the chairman of the board's Committee on Religious Life. Woodman was unsparing in his attacks on the college's critics. He scored the Committee of Ten for ignoring the hearing's rules, refusing to answer questions, telling untruths, and including Aaron Napier's name without his consent. There were rumors, he said, that they had a five-thousand-dollar fund to use against Earlham. Kenworthy, Brown, and Fuerstenberger had done everything possible to undermine and harm Purdy and Earlham. And that was tragic, because Earlham was a place where students found Christ. "The real seat of unrest may be found in the spirit of Indiana Yearly Meeting itself, reflected in its evangelistic board, which makes little or no effort to understand the Earlham atmosphere," Woodman argued. Instead, there had been "a deliberate effort to place in churches all over Indiana Yearly Meeting men and women as ministers who have come from William Smith's meeting, and Walt Malone's school, and others of a similar type." A handful of pastors at larger meetings were Earlham supporters.[51]

At this point, some of the yearly meeting committee began to discuss what they had heard. Wood and Sayers clashed openly when Sayers said that the "pastors of a good deal over half of the membership of Indiana Yearly Meeting are friends of Earlham, and encourage their young people to go there." Wood responded that he knew of three quarterly meetings where Earlham had no supporters and argued that if the committee found in favor of the college, it would discredit the complaining pastors. Woodman replied that the committee must seek truth, regardless of the consequences. On that discordant note, the hearing ended.[52]

Over the next four months, the committee members from the yearly meetings pondered their decision. The surviving evidence, mostly letters to Nicholson, suggests that the committee was divided from the beginning, and that both Earlham and its critics tried to influence their deliberations. S. A. Wood and Charles T. Moore sided with the Ten; Wood thought that they had proved their case. Charles T. Moore was even more definite. "I won't send my boys there and I am bound to tell every person who asks me if Earlham College is a safe place to send their children," he wrote to Nicholson. J. Brandt Wolfe, who had not attended the hearing, also seemed to edge that way. William J. Sayers, George H. Moore, and Ira Johnson focused on trying to conciliate the two sides. "I fear separation," Johnson told Nicholson. "If we all would come together in the spirit of meekness and humility something might be accomplished without the aid of Bailiffs to keep order."[53]

That spirit was not much in evidence in the new year. Mary M. Harold reported that Enos Harvey, the superintendent of Western Yearly Meeting, was sympathetic to the Ten, and that their supporters in Western were "determined to drag in all the trouble they can." Edwards worried that "there is so much rumour and supposition floating about and such things grow by leaps and bounds." In February Fuerstenberger called Thomas R. Woodard to Carthage to grill Mildred Henley, a 1920 graduate and biology teacher in Carthage High School, about her letter in support of Purdy and her teaching of evolution. It served little purpose save to anger her large and influential family and other Earlham supporters when word spread. The Ten tried to convince the Indiana Yearly Meeting Evangelistic Board that Woodman's testimony showed that he was "unsound" and should be investigated. They also sent a fierce letter to the joint committee arguing that the hearing showed "a gross betrayal of trust we had" in Earlham. "The real question involved is this—are we . . . going to mutilate our Bible, virtually discard it for a false theory of so-called science, and throw away our Declaration of Faith," they asked, "or have we the wisdom to discipline and correct Earlham College, which is our child, before it is forever too late?"[54]

In March the joint committee began drafting its report. Nicholson asked each member to come with a statement embodying his or her conclusions, but the members used Nicholson's, which supported Earlham on every disputed point. The committee discussed it and voted on it paragraph by paragraph. Finally, all but Wood and Charles Moore gave it their approval. Wood was vociferous, saying that pastors would oppose the finding and that it would make matters worse. According to Wood, Nicholson was the only member of the joint committee who wholeheartedly supported Earlham's religious and evolutionary teaching, a charge Nicholson denied.[55]

Nicholson released the report late in March. "Earlham College Strongly Endorsed by Committee of Investigation" was Walter C. Woodward's headline in the *American Friend,* and that was a fair estimate. The report did gently urge "in view of the existing situation" that "Earlham instructors should endeavor to express themselves in the classroom in the more customary Quaker phraseologies." On every major issue, however, it found for the college. It defended the biblical and biology departments with comparisons with other schools, just as Edwards had done. It judged the criticism of Purdy to be due to "questions which involve only technical theological definitions" and "misunderstandings." It called the charge that evolutionary teachings were *per se* irreligious "a perversion of facts." Most importantly, it scored the insistence of Fuerstenberger, Brown, and Kenworthy "that the Discipline and the Richmond Declaration of Faith mean a particular thing and only that thing, and that a particular interpretation of them is the standard by which all Friends must be judged, and exclude all others from church fellowship."[56]

Reactions to the report were predictable. Woodward announced that the report settled the matter, and that henceforth the *American Friend* would not carry material on the topic. Old Timothy Nicholson, now past ninety, broke with his former ally Kenworthy after reading the transcript of the testimony, commenting that the assault was "an astounding assertion unworthy of belief by anyone." Earlham triumphantly published the report.[57]

The critics struck back with their own pamphlet, consisting largely of statements by Charles Moore and S. A. Wood. It reiterated the charges that Fuerstenberger and Kenworthy had made in the hearing, highlighting statements from Purdy and Coffin, which, according to their critics, showed them admitting "that there are parts of the Bible that they do not believe." They also blasted S. Edgar Nicholson, claiming that he had "whitewashed" the college's offenses and had thus shown contempt for "accredited ministers of the Friends Church." The central issue was, in their eyes: "Shall the Church control and correct the College, or shall the College be allowed to control the Church and blast away the foundation stones of its Declaration?"[58]

Throughout the spring, the agitation continued. In April, Portland Quarterly Meeting hosted a conference with at least thirty ministers present to endorse the "minority report" by Wood and Moore. The printed version "circulated quite generously" at the Western Yearly Meeting pastoral conference in April. Charles Moore was busy handing out copies. William M. Smith gave it his endorsement. Kenworthy also gave an interview to the Richmond newspapers in which he made "caustic charges." Soon Nicholson and the Ten were accusing each other of bad faith. Nicholson saw their actions as "part of a concerted plan that is developing in several yearly meetings to force a particular doctrinal issue upon the next Five Years Meeting." Nicholson warned Kenworthy that he was ready "to go to the last limit" in responding. Mary M. Harold, however, counseled leaving the critics to God. "If there are those who even leave the church, it may work for good," she told Nicholson.[59]

The controversy left scars at Earlham. Purdy left in 1923 to teach at Hartford. He had seen the hearing as little less than an inquisition directed at him, and it haunted him. J. Herschel Coffin also left the same year to become the academic dean at Whittier, where he would soon be embroiled in controversy with the strong fundamentalist group in California Yearly Meeting. The natural scientists, Hole and Markle, continued at Earlham, teaching as they always had, and continuing to be active in both the yearly meeting and the Five Years Meeting.[60]

On the other hand, there is nothing to indicate that the controversy changed teaching on campus. At the 1921 session of Indiana Yearly Meeting, Edwards endorsed, on behalf of the college, the Richmond Declaration of Faith and pledged the faculty "in so far as God will give us the wisdom to do so to make our teaching and preaching conform to what we believe to be the fundamental principles of Friends." Just as Russell had not, so neither Edwards nor any of the faculty under attack explicitly raised claims of academic freedom. That, apparently, was an idea still foreign to the campus. But Edwards was edging that way, as became clear in 1925. Early that year, Edwards outraged Albert L. Copeland, the clerk of Western Yearly Meeting and the board's most theologically conservative member, by inviting Harry Emerson Fosdick, an outstanding modernist preacher and author who was a lightning rod for fundamentalists, to speak at commencement. When Copeland demanded that the invitation be withdrawn, Edwards refused, saying that if the board imposed doctrinal tests for speakers or faculty, he would resign. In fact, the board tabled just such a proposal later in the year. Then that summer, a sermon by Edwards, saying that parts of the Bible were probably mythological and unhistorical, received wide publicity. Several pastors sent withering protests. One called it "the biggest piece of infidelity he ever heard of." Another said that it put Edwards in the same class as gamblers and cigarette smokers. Charles T. Moore raged that "you certainly will lose your own soul in this present course you are going." Another pastor called Edwards an "apostate" and told him that his leadership had "literally damned individuals in their spiritual life." Edwards remained defiant, and unrepentant, even urging alumni to "bring some pressure to bear" on his critics.[61]

It is difficult to determine how much damage these controversies did to the relationship between Earlham and the two yearly meetings. They probably only strengthened pre-existing feelings, heightening antagonism where it had existed since the days of Elbert Russell but alienating few supporters. Certainly enrollment from the two yearly meetings did not drop, and there is no evidence of any attempt to displace liberal board members like Woodward and Woodman. Earlham supporters continued to hold positions of influence in Indiana Yearly Meeting—Nicholson continued as clerk until 1925, with German professor Arthur M. Charles succeeding him. Faculty were frequent speakers and preachers, often serving as interim pastors. And certainly the controversy had no discernible impact on the college's finances. In 1920 Edwards had launched a half-million-dollar endowment campaign in Wayne County that realized only $62,000. The Committee of Ten had pointed to this as evidence of widespread disaffection. By 1924, however, with the impetus of a challenge grant from the General Education Board, Edwards had added $600,000 to the college's endowment, bringing it to $1,250,000, and making Earlham the best-endowed college in the Five Years Meeting. When a fire destroyed Lindley Hall in October 1924, Edwards was once again successful in raising the money to replace it with a new building, Carpenter Hall, still the campus's largest classroom building.[62]

Still, the impact of the controversy of 1920–1921 should not be underestimated. The greatest effect may have been psychological, and on both sides. After this attempt, the fundamentalist faction of the two yearly meetings never again tried to regulate the academic side of the campus. They simply gave up on Earlham, and supported schools more in line with their views, especially Anderson and Marion colleges and Taylor University, all soundly evangelical and all within Indiana Yearly Meeting's bounds, but none of them Quaker institutions. It was hard for Earlham to have much influence, English professor Ruby Davis lamented in 1929, when "Earlham's beliefs and standards are under such suspicion that in many communities its representatives are not welcome as speakers."[63]

On the other hand, the events also heightened a kind of siege mentality at Earlham, a sense that Indiana Yearly Meeting in particular was increasingly unfriendly territory. "I feel that the relationship between the college and the church is not ideal," Edwards wrote understatedly in 1928. The faculty agreed. Arthur M. Charles, while he was the Indiana Yearly Meeting clerk, described the yearly meeting as "somewhat narrow-visioned, opinionated, [and] fundamentalist." Warren Barrett, a former faculty member and alumni trustee, was even more blunt. The membership of the yearly meetings, he told a fellow alumnus, "did not listen to reason. They have some kind of inspiration that takes the place of reason." In his last years at Earlham, Edwards stopped even reading an Earlham report at Indiana Yearly Meeting because "the meeting did not seem to be interested." The long process of alienation had advanced significantly.[64]

The Roots of Quaker Radicalism

Even as the Committee of Ten was arousing strong emotions with its crusade against higher criticism and evolution, a more subtle change was beginning at Earlham. Under Edwards, a new group of young Quaker faculty, along with a small but growing number of Quaker students from the East, began to move Earlham's understanding of Quakerism in new directions, away from pastoral, Orthodox Quakerism and closer to the unprogrammed, Hicksite tradition. Earlham became even more closely tied to Friends in Baltimore, New York, Philadelphia, and New England yearly meetings. It became increasingly focused on social activism as an expression of Quaker faith, especially in the areas of peace, race, and economics. In these years, a search began for a distinctively Quaker philosophy of education. Thus between 1920 and 1930 a group of Quaker faculty carried forward the outlook that Elbert Russell and his students had introduced to campus. They were liberals in the twentieth-century understanding of the term—modernist in theology, progressive if not vaguely socialist in politics, admirers of Russell and Rufus Jones, committed to social and economic change. But unlike their counterparts at other church schools, they did not advance their cause by deemphasizing denominational identity. They saw Earlham's Quaker heritage as something to guard and strengthen.

Between 1922 and 1925 five new Quaker faculty arrived who would have a tremendous impact on the campus. In 1922 came one of the most remarkable couples since George Fox married Margaret Fell, Howard and Anna Cox Brinton, to teach physics and classics, respectively. Howard Brinton had been acting president at Guilford; he had met Anna Cox while both were working for the AFSC in Europe. While Howard was an extraordinarily talented individual, Anna was by most accounts even more gifted. It was an innovation to have a married couple on the faculty; it was even more of one to have a pregnant woman. A concerned President Edwards suggested to Anna that she might want to use a back path from her house to her office to avoid becoming a spectacle, a suggestion that she ignored, but she did become a legend on campus by having her three children born in Richmond on weekends, never missing a class.[65]

In 1923, Clarence Pickett replaced Purdy in the biblical department. Pickett was another student of Edwards at Penn who had gone on to Hartford Seminary and had been principal at Pickering College, a Quaker boarding school outside Toronto, before becoming the Friends pastor in Oskaloosa, Iowa, during World War I. There his articulate pacifism got him mobbed. In 1919 Pickett came to Richmond to join the Five Years Meeting staff. An old friend of Purdy who had traveled with him in Europe, Pickett was Purdy's choice as his successor.[66]

CLARENCE PICKETT (LEFT) AND ALEXANDER PURDY (RIGHT)
while students at Hartford Seminary.

In 1924 Edwards hired Harry N. Wright as his academic dean. Wright, a 1904 graduate who had gone on for a Ph.D. in mathematics, had from 1918 to 1923 been the president at Whittier. Wright took over day-to-day administration at Earlham, as Edwards became increasingly occupied with fund-raising after the Lindley Hall fire in the fall of 1924. Wright was not an especially active Friend, but he was supportive of the activism of the younger Quaker faculty.[67]

Perhaps the ultimately most influential of the Quaker faculty to arrive under Edwards was Thomas R. Kelly, who came to teach philosophy in 1925. Yet another midwestern Friend who had studied at Hartford (but no relation to Robert L. Kelly), Kelly had also been in France in Reconstruction work during World War I. A protege of Rufus Jones, he had returned to Hartford to finish his doctorate. Edwards hired him in January 1924 to teach philosophy, but then gave him leave to work with the AFSC in Germany and begin at Earlham in the fall of 1925.[68]

At Earlham these new faculty made common cause with others who had come before them, like Ernest Wildman, Millard Markle, E. Merrill Root in English, and Homer L. Morris in economics, or who arrived in the same years, Quakers like Anna Eves and Charles Cosand in English, Murvel Garner in biology, Clyde Milner in psychology (and later the dean of men), and Perry Kissick in history. Root was especially important. A New Englander and Amherst graduate, the son of a Congregational minister, he had been a conscientious objector during World War I and had converted to Quakerism. Well thought of as a poet, he was also the campus's most outspoken socialist in the 1920s.[69]

Most of these had been reared as pastoral Quakers; virtually all became members of West Richmond Meeting. Several, like Merrill Root, Murvel Garner, and Millard Markle, served as part-time pastors; by the 1920s a few small meetings near Richmond had become dependent on Earlham students and faculty. But the 1920s also saw the Brintons, whose roots were in the unprogrammed tradition, begin an unprogrammed meeting on campus that met in the faculty parlor and attracted a few other faculty and students. Some of the students were from the East, others from the Ohio and Western Conservative yearly meetings, and thus were accustomed to silent worship. Other attenders were curious pastoral Friends.[70]

These Friends also brought a hint of political and economic radicalism to Earlham. Root was the firebrand. His outspoken defense of the (many thought unjustly) condemned anarchists Sacco and Vanzetti, one of the great leftist causes of the 1920s, brought demands for his dismissal, demands that Edwards ignored. "The wage system, with its emphasis on money as the sole aim of work, and its ruthless tyranny because of the threat of withholding money, is atrocious, and must eventually go," he had written while in France. "War, race hatred, poverty, and industrial tyranny" were the fruits of capitalism. For a while, enlightened souls had looked with hope to the Russian Revolution, "a great free wind from the steppes," but reaction had restored itself with bayonets from Italy to the West Virginia coalfields. Root was not the only person at Earlham willing to see some good in communism. Homer L. Morris, for example, told students that "the Soviet and Bolshevistic system of government is not necessarily dangerous, but needs an open-minded attitude . . . in its trial." Even Edwards took a swipe at "the present industrial order" in a baccalaureate sermon, drawing fire from the editors of the *Palladium*, Richmond's leading newspaper.[71]

While these Friends looked to advance change in society, they wanted to do so peacefully. They were committed pacifists. Frederick J. Libby, the head of the National Council for the Prevention of War, called Earlham "a candle giving light on the peace movement to the whole region which it serves." Root branded military action "cannibalism," and the military "pathetic" and "stupid." Attacking proposals for a "National Day of Mobilization" in 1924, Root proclaimed: "For me it is a day of revolt. I will not mobilize; I will not bow the knee to Baal; I will have no physical or spiritual part in its Mumbo-Jumbo mummeries."[72]

Many of the faculty found a natural outlet for their commitments in the American Friends Service Committee (AFSC), which had been founded in 1917 to coordinate Reconstruction work in France. While the driving forces behind the AFSC were Philadelphia Friends like Rufus Jones and Henry J. Cadbury, Earlham faculty and graduates played a critical role in the AFSC's early years. Vincent Nicholson, a 1910 graduate, was the first executive secretary, while Wilbur K. Thomas, a native of Amboy, Indiana, with numerous Earlham ties, was his successor. Tom Jones and Paul Furnas, 1912 and 1911 graduates respectively, were the first field secretaries, and Charles M. Woodman, Walter C. Woodward, and Allen D. Hole were board members. Faculty like the Brintons, Purdy, Morris, Pickett, and Charles, among others, played important roles in AFSC work between 1918 and 1930. A 1933 survey showed that Earlham had supplied more AFSC workers than any other college, about 29 percent of all to that date.[73]

The last statistic is important, because it suggests that at least some of their professors' views affected the students. Certainly there was agreement that leading faculty liberals like Purdy, Pickett, Root, Kelly, Wildman, and the Brintons were gifted and popular instructors. A 1929 graduate, Paul G. Kauper, for example, remembered Root as a "scintillating teacher who almost literally bubbled over in class." The Brinton and Pickett homes became favorite resorts of students for discussion of religious and social problems. Carl J. Welty, a 1924 graduate, recorded in his diary for

February 18, 1924: "At Prof. Brinton's tonight I heard John Fletcher relate some of his experiences as an English CO in prison for two years. Made me proud of attending a Quaker school." Sunday evening discussions at the Pickett home left a lasting impression on a generation of students.[74]

From the standpoint of a liberal Friend, the 1920s have almost the appearance of a golden age at Earlham. Yet, however gifted its faculty and vibrant its spiritual life, the college still faced real problems.

One problem was financial. While Edwards had been a successful fund-raiser, he and the board agreed that the college's $1.25 million endowment was half of what it needed to be. Salaries were low, compared even with other Indiana colleges. On one occasion Edwards had to call an emergency board meeting to authorize a $500 raise to keep Homer Morris from going to Miami University. It was probably inevitable that talented faculty would look elsewhere.[75]

There is also evidence that some of these faculty found Earlham intellectually stultifying, its students provincial and unmotivated. That was especially true of Thomas R. Kelly, who spent most of his ten years on the faculty trying to find ways to leave what he called "the sticks." One of Kelly's more gifted students remembered Kelly's "dissatisfaction with teaching students who were less than warmly interested and his longing to teach only those who were deeply dedicated to the search for truth." At least a few students admitted the justice of such criticisms, noting how current periodicals and books lay dusty in the library in favor of "collegiate activities, athletics, buzzing, and at times studying." A different discontent drove away Clarence Pickett, who found Indiana Yearly Meeting fundamentalists harassing him, although not with the same vehemence they had directed at Russell and Purdy.[76]

Little of this discontent was initially directed at Edwards. By all accounts, he was popular with the faculty. But this may be because Edwards, preoccupied with financial matters, left campus governance in the very capable hands of Harry N. Wright, who in turn leaned heavily on Ernest Wildman and Clarence Pickett for advice. By 1927, perhaps encouraged by this and by the model of other colleges, the faculty tried to formalize their role in the governance of the college. To meet this challenge, the board appointed a survey committee of trustees to study ways to increase the effectiveness of the school. In February 1928 the committee brought in eight recommendations, largely the work of Homer L. Morris. Some were financial—that the endowment be increased so that Earlham could reject unqualified students and raise faculty salaries. Most, however, related to governance—that a faculty council be formed, that a tenure system be established, that there be an appeals system for terminated faculty, and that a faculty committee be involved in hiring. Today these practices are a given in higher education, and were in fact becoming common at the time. In June 1928, the board, at its request, received a delineation of the powers of the proposed faculty council—it would work with the administration on "faculty appointments, faculty dismissals, salaries, [and] budget." This was so audacious in the eyes of the board that it appointed another committee to investigate what could lie behind such requests. In October that committee reported back that there was "a lack of confidence" in the board's Committee on Teachers and Officers, which controlled hiring, and "a desire to circumvent the power and authority of the President of the College." The board absolutely refused to relinquish any power over finances. It sent the other recommendations back to the Survey Committee.[77]

The ultimate victim of this unhappiness was the president. Between 1924 and 1928 enrollment fell from five hundred to four hundred. Finances became untenable as the college faced deficits. The unrest spread to the students as morale generally declined. Increasingly, faculty resentments focused on the president. Early in 1928 Edwards wrote candidly to his old friend Walter Dexter, the president of Whittier, that he was tired and was thinking of resigning when Carpenter Hall, which replaced the burned Lindley, was completed. By the end of the year Edward D. Evans, the Indianapolis businessman who was a formidable presence on the board, was telling Edwards bluntly that "some change will have to be made in the present management of the college." Edwards also apparently lost the critical support of Walter C. Woodward. Thus when a small group of trustees met with Edwards in January 1929 and urged him to resign, it surprised no one when he complied. Only a few days later he was badly injured in an automobile accident, and the board made Harry N. Wright the acting president.[78]

Edwards's departure forced the board to move quickly to name a successor, and in four months they did. Their choice was in certain respects a break with tradition, and certainly a break with Edwards, both in personality and in outlook.

The new president was William Cullen Dennis, the son of the much-loved botanist David W. Dennis. Will Dennis had graduated from Earlham in 1896 at eighteen, had gone on to Harvard for a second A.B., and then graduated with honors from Harvard Law School. He had taught law at Illinois and George Washington, had been a counselor for the State Department, and at the time of his selection was in a prosperous private practice in Washington, D.C. A recognized authority on international law who had spent considerable time abroad as a mediator, his professional reputation certainly equaled and probably surpassed any of his predecessors. In contrast with previous presidents, he had never taught in a Quaker school.[79]

No one who knew William C. Dennis lacked strong feelings about him. All acknowledged his integrity, his intellectual acumen, his gift for logical analysis, and his decisiveness. Few who met him in debate ever forgot the experience. "There may be a degree of satisfaction which comes in one's ability to completely pulverize an argument or criticism, but this does not necessarily mean good college administration," Homer Morris warned him after Morris joined the board. Students generally respected him, although some found him aloof, and few would have thought of him as a "buddy." Above all, Dennis was a staunch political and social conservative who regarded many events in the 1930s and 1940s with a hard, keen skepticism.[80]

Dennis's arrival coincided with major changes in the faculty. The Brintons and Morris left in 1928, the Brintons for Mills College and then to head the Quaker study center, Pendle Hill, Morris for a private job and then to teach at Fisk University before joining the AFSC staff and the Earlham board. A year later, in 1929, Clarence Pickett departed to become executive secretary of the AFSC. In 1930 Dean Harry N. Wright also left, apparently unable to get along with Dennis. He went to the City College of New York, eventually becoming its president. (Dennis had a succession of academic deans. His first choice, Arthur M. Charles, had to resign for health reasons, while E. D. Grant died suddenly and M. O. Ross and H. Randolph Pyle left for other schools before 1940.)[81]

Dennis worked hard to replace these men and women with equally capable faculty. He was particularly concerned with the biblical department. Pickett's successor, A. D. Beittel, was not a Friend but was an outspoken political liberal and religious modernist who left in 1931, unhappy with Dennis. His successor, Merle Rife, while quite competent, was a Methodist whom students found distant and rather solemn. Dennis was dissatisfied; he was determined "to bring an outstanding Quaker spiritual leader to the college," a project in which the board encouraged him. Significantly, Dennis, with the trustees' support, made strenuous efforts to entice Alexander Purdy back to Earlham, and even obtained pledges to offer Purdy a $5,000 salary, almost twice the Earlham norm. After consideration, however, Purdy remained at Hartford. Dennis then tried to bring the Brintons back, and then focused on Elden Mills, an alumnus and birthright Friend who was a successful Congregationalist minister in Connecticut. Earlham could not begin to match his salary, so Dennis had to make do with a program of visiting preachers. Finally, in 1936, he hired William E. Berry, a well-known Friend who had been the dean at Penn and the teacher of both Purdy and Pickett. Modernist in sympathies, his life at Penn had accordingly been difficult. Berry's field was classical languages, however, and he was past sixty and plagued by

WILLIAM C. DENNIS

health problems. While the gentle Berry was liked and respected on campus, he never attained the influence or popularity of Purdy or Pickett.[82]

Dennis's failure to attract the sort of leading Quaker he wanted may reflect growing tensions on campus between the president and certain faculty, mainly the liberal Friends who had been so influential in Edwards's last years. The sources of tension were varied—politics, educational philosophy, racial attitudes, and questions of governance.

To a faculty that had been increasingly restive and assertive of its rights, Dennis's style often seemed authoritarian. He quietly discontinued the survey committee, and showed absolutely no inclination to yield any control over hiring and firing. The onset of the Great Depression made at least some of the questions raised in 1927–1928 moot. There was little likelihood of becoming more selective when financial hardship was forcing out good students. For much of the 1930s, the faculty "donated" up to a quarter of its salary back to the college to avoid a deficit. The board had to approve any exceptions. It was not an atmosphere in which there were abundant alternatives to consider or in which one jeopardized one's position. The proposal for a tenure system was another casualty of Dennis's arrival. There was in fact something like it; long-time faculty remained in their positions. In only one case did Dennis dismiss a senior professor, and that did not come until the end of his presidency.[83]

Dennis was no friend, however, to faculty rights as many were coming to understand them. This was best seen in 1939, when Dennis was a member of the Association of American Colleges Commission on Academic Freedom and Tenure, which was working with a like committee of the American Association of University Professors. The AAC committee, headed by Henry M. Wriston of Brown University, recommended a three-year probationary period for the tenure decision, while Dennis argued that the period should be four years. The committee also resolved that professors "should be free from institutional censorship or discipline" for expressing opinions as private citizens. Faculty "should exercise appropriate restraint" but "the judgment of what constitutes fulfillment of these obligations should rest with the individual." When an institution wished to discipline a faculty member for some public expression, there should be a right of appeal to a joint faculty-board committee. This Dennis also condemned, arguing that "it permits the teacher with impunity to inflict untold and immeasurable damage upon the institution which furnishes him his livelihood and which he is supposed to serve." Dennis also blasted the provisions for the appeal committee as "an elaborate and expensive set-up for a trial" unless colleges were given the same rights when accused of "unjust practices."

Ultimately, Dennis prevailed. The final AAC policy omitted the sentence he found objectionable, and six years, an even longer period than Dennis proposed, became the norm for tenure evaluation.[84]

Dennis also was straightforward in his views on pedagogy. He was willing to strike out in certain new directions; in 1930 he inaugurated the annual Institute of Polity, later the Institute of Foreign Affairs, which for over three decades brought leading diplomats and academics to campus. He taught a course in international law every year himself. His methods were traditional, and he was suspicious of innovation. Millard Markle characterized him as stuck in "inertia and conservatism, . . . obsessed with the idea that we shall get into trouble by 'tinkering with the curriculum.'" Markle may have been harsh in his assessment, but not overly so. Dennis was frank in conceding that he did not encourage experimentation in the classroom. "I have relatively little confidence in the latest 'new methods,'" he wrote in 1931. "I do not think the educational methods of Christ and Socrates can be improved on."[85]

Dennis's convictions soon brought him into conflict with some of the Quaker faculty who were convinced that part of the mission of Earlham should be to base its teaching on a distinctively Quaker vision of education. This impulse received considerable stimulus in 1935, when J. Herschel Coffin, now the dean at Whittier, published a lengthy report, advocating that the Quaker colleges find a distinctive basis in emphasizing social science, peace, and education. As might be expected, it saw education as a means of social change. Faculty proponents succeeded in having a committee appointed to consider drafting a new statement of the college's aims with the Coffin report in mind. "The Quaker point of view should be more in evidence in our teaching," they argued. By early in the next year, however, Ernest Wildman told Homer Morris, an enthusiastic supporter of Coffin's ideas, the report was "in bad repute" at Earlham, "even . . . the subject of jokes." According to Wildman, it was "anathema" to Dennis, and since Dennis had "packed" the Curriculum Committee with his supporters, there was little chance of change.[86]

Dennis was convinced that this tendency to seek a distinctively Quaker philosophy of education was pernicious. "There is not, cannot, and should not be any specific pattern of Quaker education," he said in his report to the two yearly meetings in 1936. Dennis argued that while there were many characteristics of good teaching, above all were "freedom of thought and freedom of expression, the right to examine and proclaim the truth." The great enemy of this freedom was regimentation, which was, in Dennis's view, "equally disastrous, whether it proceeds from the Right or the Left." Joseph Moore and David W. Dennis had spent much of their lives "preaching to our membership that there is no Quaker botany. I am equally convinced that there is no Quaker economics." In

1934, at Dennis's urging, the board resolved that no one could "commit the College . . . to any statement, whether referring to Quaker belief, philosophy, or Quaker educational technique." The debate at Earlham thus ran counter to trends in the larger academic world, where liberal Protestants were increasingly suspicious of attempts to incorporate "sectarian" views into teaching, viewing such tendencies as antithetic to the life of the mind. At Earlham, in contrast, faculty like Wildman and Kissick saw Quaker traditionalism promoting social change and academic freedom.[87]

There were also political differences between Dennis and some of the Quaker faculty. Dennis was a conservative Republican, an unrelenting critic of the New Deal and active in state Republican politics. Anything that smacked of socialism horrified him. In contrast, the liberal Friends were quite sympathetic to the New Deal, and in some cases were open in socialist views. Wildman, for example, for several years operated a cooperative store out of the basement of his house on College Avenue.[88]

These differences, however, do not explain why there was so much antipathy toward Dennis on the part of some faculty. Dennis felt it almost immediately. In 1931 he actually drafted a letter of resignation (never sent) on the grounds that he was unable to gain the cooperation that he needed. At times the problems flared up in faculty meeting. In 1933, for example, Dennis had to spend part of one meeting defending himself from a charge that he was making Earlham "too conservative." At times faculty like Wildman and Kissick openly expressed their disappointment.[89]

Few ever charged Dennis with heavy-handed suppression of dissenters. As has been pointed out, lack of formal tenure did not move him to purge critics. There is nothing to indicate that he consciously tried to intimidate those who disagreed with him. At times he was forthright in defending them, as in 1939, when he upheld Wildman's right to operate his cooperative enterprise after Richmond businessmen complained about campus "collectivism."[90]

The problem was probably best glimpsed in 1931 by W. C. Allee, a member of the board and University of Chicago professor, when he cautioned Dennis that Dennis "personified" problems, that he saw differences of opinion over policy as personal or as attempts to undermine his authority and leadership. Dennis may well have come into office with a fatalistic attitude. Friends warned him that Earlham had been "noted for its jealousies." Former professor Edwin Morrison wrote that "to my knowledge only one president has ever left Earlham under happy conditions." Dennis apparently thought that this would be his fate. He told Allee that "nearly all presidents, like wild animals, died violent deaths in their official capacity."[91]

Dennis escaped that fate, but his critics did feel that he singled them out in unkind ways. Perry Kissick charged that Dennis treated him poorly, ridiculing his teaching methods and siding with discontented students in his classes. Ernest Wildman thought that the faculty who had "a concern for the Quaker way of life" had dwindled under Dennis. The president had "publicly belittled" him and Kissick in faculty meeting, and referred to Wildman in committee meetings as "our socialist member." Between 1936 and 1946, Dennis had never asked him to speak in chapel (although students occasionally did when they were responsible for choosing speakers). The result of this tension was a steady stream of departures between 1930 and 1935—Wright, Milner, Beittel, Thomas R. Kelly—although Dennis did his best to retain Kelly.[92]

By the end of the first year of the Dennis administration the president's opponents had informally organized, meeting weekly for lunch in a group that became known as the "Cave of Adullam," a scriptural reference to the gathering place of the discontented. Kelly, Root, Kissick, Wildman, Garner, Markle, and Charles Cosand were stalwarts, as were Clyde Milner and A. D. Beittel before their departure. Board chairman Walter C. Woodward was also a regular attender. Woodward's relations with Dennis were friendly, but his sympathies were with the Quaker faculty. The Adullamites found a sympathetic ear in two other trustees, Homer Morris and Allee, especially Morris. Now with the AFSC, and regularly reelected to the board by the alumni, Morris peppered Dennis with acerbic comments and gave what support he could to the faculty dissidents.[93]

The "Cave" was mainly a place to "cuss it out," as Root put it. However much the Adullamites annoyed him (and they did), throughout his presidency, Dennis had strong support from the board. And as the decade wore on, the Quaker group in the "Cave" began to splinter. Markle and Garner, never as strident as the others, focused on teaching and church work. Kelly left for the University of Hawaii in 1935. Root began an intellectual journey (described in the next chapter) that ended with him to the right of Dennis. Only Kissick and Wildman were willing to challenge the president openly, and their taste for battle was fading. By the second half of the 1930s, questioning the status quo on campus would come mainly from students. And they focused not on pedagogy or governance but on what a small but active and articulate group of students saw as fundamental Quaker concerns: economics, peace, and race.[94]

Earlham's record on racial matters before 1930 was not particularly noteworthy. There were few black students, and few faculty or students had shown much interest in or concern for racial justice. In this they probably reflected the attitudes of most Friends, in Indiana or elsewhere.

The Quaker heritage on race was an ambivalent one. Friends had been critical in the great shift of the eighteenth century in North America in which many came to view slavery as wrong, and in the nineteenth century produced abolitionists far out of proportion to their numbers. Before the Civil War, Indiana Yearly Meeting had shown more solicitude for the rights of free blacks than any other white group in the state. It hired lawyers to rescue kidnapped freed people, helped set up schools and libraries in black settlements, and petitioned the Indiana and Ohio legislatures to repeal discriminatory laws. There were a few black members, and blacks were admitted to Quaker schools. There was no segregation in schools, meetinghouses, or burying grounds. Indiana Friends were kindly, but also paternalistic and rather distant. They were less so than Friends east of the Appalachians, where Quakers were usually cool to black members. Eastern Friends supported numerous charities and schools for blacks, but did not admit them to Quaker ones well into the twentieth century.[95]

We know almost nothing about black students at Earlham before 1920. The first, Osborn Taylor, entered in 1880, attracting no comment from classmates. Only a handful of African Americans followed him before 1920, but we know nothing about their experiences, only their occasional appearances in campus photographs leaving any record of them.[96]

The record of racial attitudes on campus before 1920 is as ambiguous as that of the larger Society of Friends. Certainly Earlham reflected the larger society. Essays in the *Earlhamite* fully accepted prevalent ideology about the "racial superiority" of the Anglo-Saxon and the Anglo-Saxon's duty to teach and elevate less fortunate races. Occasionally there would be black-dialect short stories in the *Earlhamite,* and between 1915 and 1920 the YMCA put on minstrel shows.[97]

On the other hand, there were just as many expressions of more enlightened views. There were black speakers in chapel as early as 1887; in 1899 Booker T. Washington spoke to an enthusiastic audience of seven hundred. Over the years, the editors of the *Earlhamite* condemned school segregation and lynching and praised Frederick Douglass and Toussaint L'Ouverture. They acknowledged that blacks lagged behind whites in wealth and education, but that was the result of white oppression. Time and education would resolve such inequalities. And many Earlham graduates went to Southland, Indiana Yearly Meeting's college for blacks in Arkansas, as teachers.[98]

This uneven record continued into the 1920s. The Ku Klux Klan was strong in Indiana, perhaps more so than in any other northern state, and Quakers were not immune to its appeal. Its commitment to Prohibition may have been the critical factor, but Klan membership undoubtedly indicated at best an indifference to racism. Research has shown that about a quarter of the adult male Friends in Wayne County were Klan members at one time, about the same proportion as among other denominations. Tom Barr, a 1921 graduate and the son of Daisy Douglas Barr, the Quaker pastor who was a national Klan leader, did some recruiting on campus, although only two students, both Quakers, appear on local Klan membership rolls. At least seventy-nine alumni or former students in Wayne County, however, were Klan members at one time.[99]

On the other hand, the Klan also provoked considerable opposition among Friends. In 1922 Indiana Yearly Meeting condemned it as unpatriotic and un-Christian. Some fundamentalist Quakers blasted it because of their antipathy to secret societies. Liberal Friends, slowly coming to embrace the cause of racial equality, also opposed the Klan.[100]

The first glimmerings of interest in racial justice at Earlham had come under President Robert Kelly. In 1912, Elbert Russell had devoted a chapel address to the "race question." According to the *Earlham Press,* "after showing how impossible it is to give the two races equal rights, he showed that in the true spirit of Christianity it should be done." In 1915 a black resident of Richmond wrote to thank Kelly for speaking at the local memorial service for Booker T. Washington. A true Quaker, he wrote, was "the negro's most true and devoted friend." The *American Friend* noted in 1920 that the *Richmond Blade,* Richmond's black newspaper, spoke highly of Friends.[101]

There were a few black students during Edwards's time. The first African American to graduate from Earlham was Clarence Cunningham in 1924. Cunningham, a member of the Friends meeting at New London, Indiana, had been warned by another black student that he would "face such racial prejudice as to make it virtually intolerable." President Edwards encouraged him to enroll, and professors treated him well, but Cunningham had to face a constant stream of indignities. The only black in the men's dormitory, he was always assigned to room by himself. Even as a senior, he did not "head" a table in the dining hall, as was the custom. The Glee Club and Mask and Mantle, the dramatic group, rejected him. Traveling with the track team, he stayed in ramshackle boarding houses and ate in the kitchen and no one protested. Still, Cunningham found Earlham, all in all, to be "a pleasant place," and he was impressed enough with Friends to remain one the rest of his life. Most of the other black students of the time did not live on campus; the few who did usually seemed lonely and unhappy. Edwards admitted that black students faced special problems in Richmond, especially finding the part-time jobs that most needed to survive.[102]

Under Edwards, and with the work of Clarence Pickett, perhaps encouraged by the model of the AFSC, change slowly began. Edwards signed a public condemnation of the Klan in 1924, which he hoped was destined for "a most humiliating fall and final destruction." Between 1926 and 1929 several black speakers appeared on campus; in 1927, for example, the Anglican Society, which published the campus literary magazine, sponsored a visit by the black poet Countee Cullen. That same year the board noted that "there is an evident conviction on the part of the students that Christian faith must find through them more expression in conduct and social responsibility"; race relations were becoming one expression of that. Pickett began holding an annual interracial Sunday chapel service, which local blacks attended and afterwards met with students. Pickett also hosted a Sunday evening discussion group for students. During his last year at Earlham, they were particularly interested in race relations and wanted to meet with a group of black students their own age. Thus in the spring of 1929 they visited Wilberforce University near Xenia, Ohio. They expected a group from Wilberforce to come to Earlham that fall.[103]

By the fall, Pickett was gone and President Dennis had arrived, and Dennis was not one to encourage anything that smacked of radicalism. His racial policy for Earlham would be, in his own mind, "a middle of the road policy, neither radical nor reactionary but liberal," as he called it in a 1943 statement. "It is not the sort of policy that makes anybody stand up and cheer. It will, I believe, command the long run support of solid and respectable people. . . . It distinguishes between liberal aims and radical means." Dennis thought that some of Earlham's faculty when he arrived were "a little extreme in [their] preaching of racial equality." So he began to lay down policies, most of them informal. Black students would continue to be admitted, but in limited numbers. They could live on campus, although, for reasons that are unclear, Dennis discouraged women from living in the dormitory. There would be no segregation, but anything that even hinted at interracial dating was unacceptable. Black speakers would continue to come to campus, but they would not speak on race relations.[104]

This put Dennis squarely in the path of the Wilberforce students' visit. A. D. Beittel, Pickett's successor, who later became president of Tougaloo College, was working with the Earlham students planning the Wilberforce visit. Dennis's initial attitude on the matter is not clear, but when he discovered that "interracial marriage and similar sex topics" might be part of the students' discussion, he cancelled the visit. Dennis was convinced that "to extend an invitation to a delegation of negro students to come over to Earlham and engage in a miscellaneous free-for-all discussion of race and sex with our students" would be a "disaster." Instead, Dennis thought that students should be content "to show our interracial brotherhood at Earlham by our daily conduct, without continually dissecting and analyzing it." Dennis conceded that interracial marriage was a proper subject for classroom discussion, but he saw no benefits from the student proposal. His suggestion was that two professors from Wilberforce visit Earlham and meet informally with faculty, which did happen.[105]

The Earlham community quickly and definitely split over Dennis's decision. The board upheld it. Edward D. Evans, one of its most influential members, told Dennis that he would "be supported by every one other than some of these extraordinary persons who are intent upon changing the structure of the whole world." Anna Eves, a former teacher at Southland and a member of Richmond's Inter-Racial Council, agreed. "It is our serious obligation to avoid unfortunate circumstances," she wrote. "We [must] protect our susceptible students from their desire to further great causes by outstanding and unwise sacrifice of themselves." She reported that Henry Richardson, perhaps Richmond's leading black citizen, thought that discussions of interracial marriage seldom served any good purpose.[106]

Not everyone agreed. The students who had visited Wilberforce were outraged. Beittel bluntly told Dennis that five of the six members of the faculty Committee on Religious Life opposed his decision. (They would be the nucleus of the Adullamites.) Tom Kelly concluded that Dennis was hopelessly conservative. "He seems afraid to have race relations discussed!" Kelly wrote to his brother-in-law. "You'd writhe. So would Clarence Pickett. I don't see anything ahead." Pickett did protest to Dennis, but to no avail.[107]

After 1930 interest in racial matters on campus declined. This may reflect the graduation of students who had been under Clarence Pickett's influence. Without someone on the faculty to spur them, students continued to reflect the attitudes of their hometowns. "It has been my observation that Friends groups in local communities go about the matter of bettering race relations in a most half-hearted, superficial fashion," Paul K. Edwards, a 1920 graduate and the son of the former president, wrote in 1936. There was an occasional condemnation of segregation in the *Post,* and praise for racial equality. But interest would not revive for another decade.[108]

It is also likely that the Depression distracted the campus. As it hit bottom between 1931 and 1935, an increasing number of students were concerned mainly with survival—remaining in school and paying bills. Departures for financial reasons were common. Dennis constantly searched, not only for economies, but for donors to support needy students on an individual basis.[109]

The Depression, however, also saw the rise of a nationwide student movement that produced unprecedented political activism on campuses. Much of it focused on economics, demanding government action to provide employment and correct what many perceived as a flawed distribution of wealth. On many campuses the center of such activism was the National Student Association, which was in turn the subject of a fierce struggle for control between socialist and communist factions. By 1938, the communist group had gained control of the national organization.[110]

The first stirrings of leftist politics came early in 1931, and they came, ironically, with William C. Dennis's direct participation. A group of students had asked Dennis to have a socialist speaker in chapel, suggesting several they knew. Dennis pronounced none to be up to the intellectual level necessary, and told the students that he would try to arrange a visit by Norman Thomas, the Socialist party leader and future presidential candidate. Thomas came in February 1931, staying at the Dennis home and speaking in chapel on socialism. A furor arose afterwards, when a small group of local socialists arranged for Thomas to speak that evening in the high school auditorium. They drove Thomas through town in a car draped with red flags. Some irate onlookers tore the flags from the car. The Daughters of the American Revolution and the American Legion blasted Thomas and organized a series of "Americanism meetings" to counteract whatever evil influence he might have had. The *Indianapolis News* scored Earlham for the invitation; one Indianapolis attorney told the president of DePauw University that there were dangerous communist sympathizers at Earlham. Dennis did not back down, defending Thomas as a "perfectly law-abiding man" who was fiercely opposed to communism. Dennis told one of the students that he hoped that Thomas would return to campus. The board backed Dennis.[111]

The immediate result of Thomas's visit was the organization of an Earlham chapter of the socialist student group, the Student League for Industrial Democracy, with Merrill Root as the faculty sponsor. Its accomplishments, other than meeting for discussions, were few. A planned investigation of the problems of workers in Richmond apparently never took place. Sixteen alumni did sign a 1932 statement endorsing Thomas's presidential candidacy and praising the Socialists as the only political party that embodied Quaker ideals. Dennis's sole criticism was that "we ought not to electioneer in our capacity as members of the Society of Friends." That was a position that Dennis would stress increasingly for the rest of the decade, most notably in a speech to the 1935 sessions of the Five Years Meeting that received considerable publicity.[112]

SLID languished until the fall of 1935, when a newly arrived firebrand from New York City reinvigorated it. Mathew Amberg was an unlikely Earlham student. A committed socialist, he had been expelled from City College for taking part in a student demonstration against fascism the year before. Dennis agreed to admit him if he promised to abide by college policies, and in fact awarded him a scholarship.[113]

After City College, Amberg found Earlham a "never never land—a source of amazement, delight, puzzlement." Even though he quickly established himself as the campus radical, he encountered little hostility, and in fact participated in everything from debate to track. Occasionally he would spend an evening with Dennis himself arguing politics. Politically, he judged Earlham "dead," and thus took the lead in reorganizing the SLID chapter and affiliating it with the American Student Union. Although the ASU had led demonstrations and "strikes" as early as 1933, none had taken place at Earlham. In April 1936 SLID sponsored a "Student Strike against War" on campus, with about forty-five students and three faculty, including Merrill Root and Murvel Garner, holding a meeting in Goddard Auditorium during a class hour. At the end of the year, however, Amberg, running short of money, went back to City College, with a letter of recommendation from Dennis facilitating his return.[114]

SLID disintegrated after Amberg's departure. It was never large; the *Post* reported twenty members in 1934, and by 1936 it was rapidly losing supporters to the Democratic party and the New Deal. In 1932, for example, a student straw poll for the presidential election went Hoover 265, Thomas 66, Roosevelt 44. In 1936 it was Landon 141, Roosevelt 91, and Thomas 7. The same polls showed 14 faculty for Thomas and only 1 for Roosevelt in 1932; in 1936 the statistics were reversed. Students from the period remember that while some were politically active and aware, most were not. And some students were fiercely critical of the socialists. When SLID urged a boycott of the 1936 Berlin Olympics as a protest against Hitler, another student blasted their "Socialist-Communistic movement that is being spurred on by alien agitators and their American stooges." Nevertheless the socialist presence, small as it was, had an impact. It, along with the cooperative store, raised tensions in Richmond. By 1938 Dennis himself referred to the "prevalent belief . . . that Earlham College is a radical, Socialist institution if not worse."[115]

After 1936, activism at Earlham became increasingly focused on problems of peace. This was full of paradoxes. Insofar as it was directed at keeping the United States out of a European war, it united Dennis and the most radical socialists on campus. It also drew on traditional Quaker pacifism, and, at Earlham, could claim the sanction of custom and hoary theology. Isolationist in tendency, it brought together anti–New Deal Republicans and erstwhile Roosevelt supporters. Yet ultimately its leftist connections made it suspect in Dennis's eyes, and the result was conflict.

Dennis's position was, as usual, both principled and complex. He was not a pacifist, but he felt it incumbent not to challenge Quaker tradition and the pacifism of many alumni. He respected the idealism of the conscientious objector, and used his influence against legislation that penalized those who opposed war. As he told one Friend, the motives of the pacifist were sound, "the motives which must govern the world." But Dennis was intensely suspicious of the ways in which pacifism had become entangled with leftist politics in the 1930s. He thought that the cause of peace was far more likely to flourish if "isolated from radicalism and sovietism." He had little faith in the sincerity and commitment of nonreligious pacifists. He sniffed at the spectacle of "our so-called 'pacifist' Friends getting ready to fight another war to make the world safe for 'popular front democracy.'" Behind many, he suspected, were not respectable if misguided socialists like Norman Thomas but pro-Soviet communists. These fears conditioned Dennis's response to peace activism.[116]

In fact peace activism nationally in the 1930s was hopelessly entangled with politics. Disillusionment in the wake of World War I had produced widespread antiwar sentiment; a poll of 19,000 Protestant clergy in 1931 showed that a majority would oppose American participation in *any* future war, no matter what the reason. Leftist antiwar feeling was heightened by a conviction that U.S. entry into World War I was largely the fruit of manipulation by armaments manufacturers and bankers. When the American Student Union was formed in 1935 by a merger of SLID and another organization, it took a firm pacifist stance, but as fear of fascism grew, so did resistance to a pure pacifism. ASU conventions became stormy as pacifists and advocates of mutual security battled over the best way to resist Hitler.[117]

At Earlham, peace activism took a variety of forms, but nearly all were connected in some way with SLID or the ASU. From the time he entered Earlham in 1934 until his graduation in 1938, Tom Jones, a New York Friend (not to be confused with the future Earlham president), was a leader. A member of SLID, Jones at first was uncertain about a "strike." As an alternative, in the fall of 1935 he tried to organize a student chapel program on peace. SLID also raised money on campus for the National Council for the Prevention of War. In the summer of 1936 several students and faculty joined the AFSC's emergency peace campaign of caravans around the Midwest to present antiwar lectures and plays. By 1938 there was an Earlham Anti-War Club. It is also clear, however, that the impact of pacifism on the campus was limited. In 1938 the *Post* charged that "Earlham peace groups just talk and never start anything materially constructive." The core group of activists, mostly remnants of SLID and ASU, was made up of pacifists with socialist leanings like Jones, Edwin Sanders, Kenneth Ives, and Marian Binford. Almost all had Quaker ties and attended the unprogrammed meeting that still survived. They were also active in a wide variety of campus organizations, from the ASU to the Foreign Relations Club. Ives recalls meetings at which the same small coterie of participants would facetiously ask: "And what group are we today?"[118]

Before 1938, President Dennis gave peace activities on campus little attention, but the Student Strike against War in April 1938 upset him. It was a national movement, directed by the ASU, which by this time was no longer committed to pacifism but to mutual security against fascism. The Earlham group, however, was still strongly pacifist, and wanted in some way to commit Earlham to such a position. On April 15, Jones asked Dennis to set aside the 11:00 hour on April 27 for a meeting in Goddard Auditorium to discuss opposition to war, the meeting to be held in lieu of chapel that day. Three days later, Jones, Sanders, and Esther Winder made the same request in faculty meeting. The president and faculty refused. The faculty was moderate in its response, recognizing "high motives and idealism," but arguing that it would be improper for the college to take sides in a contentious public debate. Individual instructors were left to decide whether they would excuse absent students who wanted to participate in the "strike." Dennis took a harder line. Perhaps because Charles Woodman, W. C. Allee, Laurence Hadley, and Homer Morris of the board were sympathetic to the students, he did not try to stop the meeting on April 27, but in remarks to administrators he lashed out at the strike as a "grave menace." The American Student Union was communist-dominated, and the strike was "nothing less than a dress rehearsal for a conspiracy against the government of the United States." At least one student agreed, writing in the *Post* that participants in the strike were "cowards and weaklings" who had no faith in God: "If they did they would live peacefully day by day and endeavor to spread the gospel of peace by pacific means, rather than stirring up strikes and issuing propaganda, which by the way may be traced to communistic headquarters." The meeting itself, with about 150 in attendance, almost a third of the student body, passed without incident.[119]

These events portended future directions. Increasingly, students at Earlham would be politically active, and that activism would be on the liberal side of the political spectrum. Usually, Earlham activists would take their cues from larger, national organizations—the Student League for Industrial Democracy, the American Student Union, the American Friends Service Committee. Earlham's Quaker heritage and ties, however, gave campus activism some unique twists. The AFSC was moving in much the same direction as liberal advocacy groups in the 1930s, and its links to Earlham were strong. In their pacifist commitments, moreover, the activists could claim a foundation in Quaker tradition.

These movements were student led and initiated. A few of the liberal

Quaker faculty—Markle, Garner, Wildman, Kissick, Root, Kelly—were willing to aid the students, but they did not set the terms of discussion and action. Students in the 1930s began a tradition that would continue down to the present day. It is difficult to place them into simple categories. The peace activists and SLID members of the 1930s did not feel themselves that different from their classmates. The categories that historians like Helen Lefkowitz Horowitz have proposed for students of the period—college man, outsider, rebel—did not apply to Earlham. Tom Jones, for example, was not only a peace activist but the captain of the cross country and track teams (and a member of the 1952 U.S. Olympic team), president of the Varsity Club, editor of the *Earlham Post,* and a member of the Ionian and Anglican societies. Marian Binford Sanders remembers that "we made a broad swath and were not only *social* 'radicals.'" By her account, "we were visible in *all* college activities—sports, plays, debates, literary and writing groups." Certainly their activism had its limits. The small meetings and the speeches in Goddard Auditorium were tame even by the standards of the 1930s, where at other campuses socialists and communists warred for control of organizations and peace activists marched and even picketed the homes of college presidents.[120]

Student activism and demands would be felt in other, less political ways. By the 1940s they would heighten the hostility between the college and many in Indiana and Western yearly meetings.

The Last Triumphs of Campus Culture

This political and social activism took place against a backdrop of student life that also took its cues from the larger world. David M. Edwards was the last Earlham president to attempt to halt its development. It was the stalwartly conservative William C. Dennis who would raise tensions with the yearly meetings by giving students a final victory and relaxing the campus bans on dancing and smoking.

While Edwards may have been liberal in theology, his views on campus discipline were as traditional as any of his predecessors'. Students remember him as kind but strict in his dealings with them. Even those who blasted Edwards on doctrinal grounds commended his moral and disciplinary leadership of the campus.[121]

Edwards was very willing to take strong action when he thought the situation demanded it. By the time he became president, the college had developed a series of "precedents," mild forms of hazing aimed at freshmen: wearing beanies, entering chapel and the dining room after juniors and seniors, not using certain parts of the campus. At times special committees, at times the dormitory councils, administered them. Punishments for men usually involved whacks with the "precedent paddle," similar to those fraternities used. In early October 1924, a group of juniors and seniors staged a mock meeting of the Bundy Hall Dormitory Council to haze some freshmen. It involved what the faculty called "objectionable and even indecent practices"; at least one of the freshmen was seriously injured. Edwards suspended or expelled eight of the perpetrators. He was equally relentless in dealing with students accused of drinking or suspected of any kind of sexual impropriety. In one case, Edwards urged a student to leave school just for joking about having a "social disease." Otherwise, Edwards told him, he would be "pretty largely socially ostracized."[122]

In 1925 Edwards and the faculty tackled a far tougher issue that embodied the elitist side of the campus culture, the Press Club. Founded in 1911 to publish the campus newspaper, the *Earlham Press,* the Press Club admitted only men, and by a virtually unanimous vote. Its members quickly became a campus elite. As one member, its last president, put it, the club "took the ideals of a 'Rhoades [*sic*] Scholar' man for its own." It was not so much interested in "mere journalistic ability" as it was in "qualities of manhood, leadership, and the ability to work hard for an ideal." It was the "'he-man' organization" at Earlham.[123]

The club naturally aroused resentments—from women, from unsuccessful applicants, from officers of other organizations who saw it as a clique that tried to dominate student life. Edwards and the faculty viewed it as an increasing threat to their authority. The club, Edwards argued, "brought together a type of college student that was difficult to manage, and who, buttressed in by the rest of his group made a solid phalanx of opposition to the educational ideals of the institution." Other Quaker faculty, like Homer Morris, opposed it as having all of the features of a fraternity, particularly the influence that Press Club alumni exerted over the organization. In the fall of 1924 Edwards asked Clarence Pickett to investigate privately whether the Press Club "had developed into a secret society."[124]

Pickett's report apparently confirmed Edwards's fears, since the faculty acted in the spring of 1925. It concluded that the Press Club had become "virtually a fraternity" that was "incompatible with Earlham spirit." It gave the club the choice of opening up membership to all students, including women, on the basis of try-outs, or dissolving, an ultimatum that Edwards firmly supported. This brought howls of protest from alumni members. Thirty held a meeting on campus at Commencement time in June 1925 and resolved that they were entitled to a say in the club's future. The faculty in turn saw this as a direct challenge to its authority over student organizations.[125]

All summer Edwards received a stream of indignant letters from Press Club alumni. Paul Furnas, one of the founders, wrote that he was "sick at heart" and that Edwards's action was a "catastrophe." Others warned Edwards that his actions would alienate alumni and make recruiting more difficult. "It has been hard enough for us of the Alumni to 'talk Earlham' during the last ten years without you removing the most attractive feature left on campus," one old member told him. More significant were admissions that the Press Club was much of what its enemies charged, and that that was good. "Many strong men have been drawn to Earlham with the hope that they might make the Club, held there by the high spirit of the Club, and have maintained a greater loyalty to the College because of their loyalty to the Club after graduation," one former member wrote. Another claimed that jealousy was behind the attacks. Charles G. Blackburn, the senior who had been elected the club's president, defiantly told the Rotarian Edwards that the Press Club was elitist in the same way that Rotary was: "If it is undemocratic for a man to strive for membership in such a group then all life is undemocratic."[126]

Ultimately, the faculty prevailed. A student referendum showed that most favored preserving the club, but on the conditions required by the faculty. The admission of women was apparently particularly offensive to Press Club members, and they voted, against the advice of the alumni, to dissolve the club. In 1926 a new group began publishing the *Quaker Quill* as the campus newspaper.[127]

The Press Club battle is significant in several respects. It shows how the faculty, and Edwards, still saw Earlham as different because of its Quaker ties. It also says something that there was some inclination among women students to object to unequal treatment. The ratification of the Nineteenth Amendment may have drawn little attention on campus, but Earlham women would resent the existence of a closed men's organization for which there was no women's counterpart, and could apparently command the support of most of the student body in their resentment. On the other hand, at least some Earlham men wanted Earlham to have the sort of elite organizations that dominated campus culture at other schools, and which were defined in part by their "he-man" masculinity.

Edwards's response to other aspects of student culture of the 1920s was mixed. On one hand, he apparently had no reservations about athletics. He had won the applause of the student body in his first chapel address in 1917 when he made building a new gymnasium one of his two top priorities. It was completed in 1924. Interest in athletics remained strong on campus, although by 1930 basketball was threatening to replace football as the dominant spectator sport. Women's athletics, especially field hockey, were also drawing more participants. Clara

Comstock, the coach of most of the women's teams and later Dennis's dean of women, became a national figure in women's athletics.[128]

Edwards held firm in resisting the changes that students after 1920 apparently wanted most, the end of the bans on dancing and smoking. In his eyes, dancing was not inherently evil, but it was "out of harmony and not compatible with Earlham life." Edwards admitted that by 1925 students were constantly asking him to allow dancing. For a time he hoped that providing a skating rink would distract them. Instead, he had to deal with a procession of students who attended dances in town, often with parental approval, and showed no remorse. The faculty supported the ban, partly because of the traditional Quaker attitude against dancing, partly because they worried that if admitted to campus it would crowd out other activities and encourage an unhealthy emphasis on couples. Dancing as an "educational" activity, however, was different, and by 1929 "folk dancing," supervised by Clara Comstock, took place occasionally. Moreover, the faculty stopped trying to control off-campus dancing. Women could attend with written permission from their parents; there were no restrictions on men.[129]

It was left to Dennis to end the ban. In some ways, he found student behavior difficult to comprehend, never having been a typical student himself. (He was, after all, only eighteen when he graduated from Earlham.) He handled disciplinary matters with lawyerly deliberation and attention to detail, carefully drafting memoranda weighing the evidence and recording the verdict in each case before him. He was just as strict as Edwards in dealing with anything suggesting sexual impropriety, but was inclined to be merciful when he discerned signs of genuine regret in other offenders.[130]

Dennis's standing as a Quaker was important, and it was different from his predecessors'. Unlike previous Earlham presidents, Dennis had spent his life in non-Quaker worlds of law schools and government. While temperamentally conservative, he did not view amusements like dancing with the horror of most Indiana Friends. He had kept his membership with Friends while living in the East, and when he accepted the presidency stated a desire to "bring about a sympathetic understanding between the College and the plain people of the country communities." He wanted the college to "be the center of a vibrant and oncoming, but at the same time solid and cultured, Quakerism in the Middle West." As he was the first president who was not a recorded minister, he did not preach or write on controversial theological topics. Nevertheless, he was in the tradition of Kelly and Edwards, committed to "the widest practicable individual freedom of opinion and expression." Dennis was proud of his Quaker forebears, and made it clear that he would not let opponents on the left or right define him out of the Society of Friends. "I will not be driven from the House of my Fathers," he told them.[131]

With this background, Dennis approached the vexed question of dancing. He polled students to determine their opinions, and appointed a faculty committee to study the implications of the question. Dean Comstock urged a policy change, arguing that dancing was "a means of acquiring social grace." The student poll showed that 65 percent favored allowing dancing, with only 11 percent opposed. The support among Quaker students was slightly smaller, 56 percent to 18 percent. In February 1930 the faculty presented a proposal to the board that was filled with safeguards. There would be no dancing on campus. Women could attend dances organized by campus groups in town only with written permission from their parents and from the dean of women. Each request had to be made three days in advance. Both deans had to approve each proposal for an off-campus dance. "Satisfactory" chaperones were required, and no dance could take place on a school night. The board approved the proposal, and by the spring of 1930 dancing had become a staple of campus social life. Almost immediately pressure began to build to allow dancing on the campus. By the summer of 1933, Dennis had concluded that it would be easier to supervise dances if they took place at the college. The board agreed, and dancing came to campus. Dennis was quite sure that the change was "socially and morally beneficial." Instead of having students "bootleg dancing" in suspect places, they were "amid beneficial associations either on campus or at suitable places off the campus." Students hailed the decisions, and dances became a fixture of student life.[132]

The change did bring criticism. Western Yearly Meeting of Ministry and Oversight sent a minute of opposition in the fall of 1929. One of the Western trustees, E. T. Albertson of Indianapolis, told Walter Woodward that dancing would be acceptable on campus only when Friends allowed it in their local meetings. Another pastor and alumnus condemned dancing as a relic of barbarism that served only to excite dangerous lusts. A few other alumni complained about such "worldly vanities," as did a few pastors. Such criticism was exceptional; overall, Dennis reported that there had been little opposition. And in fact Earlham was not out of line with other Quaker colleges. By 1939, only one still completely banned dancing by students.[133]

The other great change of the Dennis years was far more controversial. By 1942, for the first time in Earlham's history, smoking was allowed on campus, and that brought more contention than any event since the heresy investigation of 1920.

Earlham had banned all forms of tobacco use since 1847. There was always resistance, as records of disciplinary actions show. In 1879 the editors of the *Earlhamite* noted that while tobacco was forbidden, "a glance . . . into some of the boys' rooms at the beginning of vacation would have convinced anyone that the rule had not been strictly observed." Edwards upheld the ban while he was president. He did not believe smoking to be immoral, but he did think it "disgusting." Nevertheless the college had to contend with a shift in social standards and the mass marketing of cigarettes. By 1924, Edwards was fending off reports that many women students were "addicted to and practice on the campus and in Earlham Hall the cigarette habit." By the time Edwards left, the college no longer enforced rules against off-campus smoking by men, although Dean Comstock struggled a little longer with the women, giving up in 1933.[134]

Dennis moved slowly, maintaining the ban on campus tobacco use but acquiescing in smoking off campus. This had the grudging assent of the board. "If they must smoke, my judgment is that they smoke in the graveyard with the other dead ones," E. T. Albertson told Dennis. Students were taking the matter into their own hands. There was a considerable increase in the proportion of student smokers between 1930 and 1939. By 1939, students had taken over for smoking a vacant lot at the east edge of campus that became known as "Camel Corner." The cemetery on the west side of the campus was also a favorite spot. By the end of the decade there was a well-worn path from the west door of Carpenter Hall into it, and at the conclusion of chapel there would be a mass exodus to the cemetery's east edge for a few puffs before class. Dennis also tolerated faculty smoking, although only in private and not in the presence of students.[135]

By 1939, Dennis had decided that some sort of change was necessary. There were constant complaints from lot holders and officials of the adjacent Earlham Cemetery about cigarette butts and other trash left on graves. Dennis also worried about the safety of women students going out at night for a cigarette. Like dancing, Dennis saw smoking not as a moral question but one of evolving tastes. In the spring of 1939 students began agitating for change, spurred by the expulsion of a coed for repeatedly smoking on campus. Her supporters plastered trees and buildings with signs reading: "We Want Smoking Rooms." The students claimed that the administrators were guilty of "absolute disregard of students' wishes and utter lack of democratic spirit." They also presented Dennis with a petition bearing four hundred student signatures asking for a smoking area on campus. On April 24 the faculty meeting recommended to the board that it set up an "unheated shelter, artistic and inexpensive" for smokers on campus. The board, in turn, sent the matter back to the faculty for decision.[136]

Dennis saw the matter as amenable to some compromise that would recognize the desires of most students without unduly arousing the yearly meetings. He pointed out to critics that "regular" smokers were a minority, and that most of them had acquired the habit before they arrived on campus. The two yearly meetings no longer expelled members for smoking; in fact, many student smokers came from prominent Quaker families. Dennis and the faculty took two years to make up their minds, before recommending to the board in 1941 that a "Commons" be established behind Earlham Hall where smoking would be allowed.[137]

Toward the end of his presidency, Dennis wrote that the smoking debate "caused a sharper division in our Board than any other decision." Some students opposed change; "no thinking student of Earlham ever wants smoking allowed on the campus," one wrote in 1941. When the discussion began in 1939, it aroused a few Friends. "The [newspaper] story about smoking was read in our prayer meeting, and the members protest," wrote two Quakers from Fountain City, Indiana. Western Yearly Meeting formally condemned any change in policy the same year. The most vehement opposition, in fact, came from three Western trustees. E. T. Albertson took the lead. In 1939 he blasted Dennis and the faculty for cowardice in dealing with the students and their "insidious propaganda." In 1942 Albertson, along with Albert L. Copeland and Charles A. Reeve, argued that the board had a "sacred obligation" to ban smoking as bad for health and morals and offensive to Friends. Nevertheless the board voted ten to five to approve the faculty proposal, and the Commons opened that year.[138]

The decision to allow smoking brought a storm of protests from the two yearly meetings. Indiana Yearly Meeting of Ministry and Oversight condemned it, throwing in denunciations of dancing and of card playing, which had been allowed on campus for two decades. Most of the protests came from areas in which fundamentalist sympathies were strong. Typical was Anderson Monthly Meeting, which condemned the Commons as a snare "which sanctions and gives approval of ensnaring vices and habit forming corruptions, that tend to physical, mental, moral, and spiritual injury." Van Wert and Portland quarterly meetings made similar statements; both had been at the center of the 1920 complaints about the college. Dennis had especially unpleasant exchanges with some members of Walnut Ridge Quarterly Meeting, which condemned the Commons and objected to Quaker pastors being educated in a place that allowed such immorality. Dennis asked to present Earlham's position to the quarterly meeting. The critics responded that since Earlham was doing things clearly against Scripture, there was no point in hearing him. One turn-of-the-century graduate wrote to Dennis that Earlham students obviously needed a "Christian experience that takes away even the desire for such things." E. Howard Brown, one of the Committee of Ten, resurfaced to point out the smoking decision as only the latest of Earlham's numerous derelictions. Protests continued to arrive on Dennis's desk well into 1943.[139]

The battle had deeper meaning. One should not underestimate the moral issue that the critics of the decision saw involved. But also involved was a growing fear that Earlham was slowly drawing away from the two yearly meetings. This was the subtext for many alumni and other Friends in Indiana and Western.

Certainly Quakerism continued to be prominent in the life of the campus under Dennis. In 1939, a majority of the faculty were still Friends. Of 500 students, about a third were Quakers, down from the proportion at the turn of the century, but still higher than at any other Quaker college except Penn in Iowa. It and Earlham were the only schools where Friends made up over 30 percent of the student body. Still, this meant that Quaker students were now a minority on the campus. Two shifts had taken place. One was that about 40 percent of the students were from Wayne County, and most of them were non-Quaker "Day Dodgers." This percentage had been growing steadily since the turn of the century, and attracted little comment.[140]

The other change was more important for the future of the college—the slow but steady growth in the number of students from the East Coast, particularly from New York, New Jersey, and Pennsylvania. In 1910, they had accounted for 14 of 480 students. By 1930, they were 49 of 449 students, and in 1940, 63 of 519. Still relatively small in numbers, they nevertheless exerted considerable influence on the campus.[141]

It is difficult to say how much this influx reflects a calculated strategy on Earlham's part. As early as 1929, Loren C. Petry, a 1907 graduate who had gone on to teach at Cornell and help found the Friends meeting in Ithaca, had proposed just such a course. "The support of the college by western Friends, both individually and as Yearly Meetings, has fallen away and may be expected to continue to fall away," Petry wrote to friends on the faculty. It was inevitable, and Earlham could not reverse it. Instead it should look for opportunities among eastern Friends. Haverford did not admit women, and Swarthmore was small and highly selective, so there were many Friends who were looking toward Earlham. Petry also argued that such a course would work to Earlham's benefit: "To make connections with the east would result in changes at Earlham, particularly in point of view," he wrote, "but I think it would help set up the educational standards." That, in turn, would increase enrollment.[142]

Most, although not all, of the students coming from the East were from the Quaker boarding and day schools, especially Oakwood in Pough-keepsie, New York, Westtown outside Philadelphia, and Moorestown, New Jersey. In the case of Oakwood and Moorestown, Earlham graduates William and Chester Reagan were the principals, while there were several Earlham alumni on the Westtown staff. Robert E. Fatherley, an Oakwood alumnus and 1928 Earlham graduate, remembered that William E. Simkin, who had graduated from Oakwood a year ahead of him, led a series of Oakwood football players to Earlham. Earlham graduates who were pastors in New York Yearly Meeting also played an important role in sending students west. Earlham was probably a last resort for some—for many years the question at Westtown was: "Are you going to college, or are you going to Earlham?" Some at Westtown saw Earlham as hopelessly "rah-rah," rustic, and unsophisticated. But others saw it as a healthy, moral place far from the influences of the city. And in many cases, the "eastern" students coming to Earlham were the children of parents born in Indiana or Ohio who had attended Earlham and had moved east after graduation.[143]

The easterners had a clear impact on the campus. They brought new ways to the college—soccer and field hockey, for example. They were, as a rule, better dressed and more prosperous—one Indiana student remembered that the girls from Philadelphia were the ones who could afford to visit a hairdresser. They often were among the best students on campus—in 1934, for example, six of ten honors scholarships for the freshman class went to graduates of eastern Quaker schools. This generated some resentment, since many of the Indiana students saw the easterners as a clique, although groups based on home ties tended to break down over time. The easterners were not afraid to press for changes; in 1933, for example, Dennis told the trustees that agitation to allow smoking on campus came largely from a "valuable contingent of eastern Friends." This tendency to challenge rules apparently did not faze Dennis—the next spring he made a round of speaking engagements at the Quaker schools in New York and the Delaware Valley.[144]

Not a few Friends viewed this influx with misgivings. E. T. Albertson told Dennis that the eastern Friends wanted to "push around everyone"; they should instead obey the rules and benefit from the superior morals of Indiana. "These individuals and students that insist upon personal liberty at the inconvenience and dissatisfaction of all other Friends have a tendency to get on my nerves," he fulminated. Other Indiana Quakers echoed Albertson's views. Homer G. Biddlecum, the pastor at Charlottesville, told Dennis that he was "alienating from Earlham College large numbers of Indiana Quakers, as you seek to liberalize the College to appeal to Eastern Quakers." Bruce Siler, a 1929 graduate, echoed Biddlecum, but was more personal: Dennis was himself an easterner who had lost the confidence of the "rank and file of Quakers west of Indianapolis."[145]

It was not just critics who worried about Earlham's direction in the late 1930s and early 1940s. Friends and alumni whose commitment was beyond question were unsettled. "In my mind . . . to some degree for a number of years we have been getting away further and further from some of the old Quaker principles," Isaac E. Woodard, Indianapolis businessman and future trustee, told Dennis. W. C. Allee agreed. "The distinctive genius of Quakerism [is] to live at once practically and prophetically. I have not found this prophetic spirit in the forefront at Earlham, at least in recent years," he wrote in 1942. The complaints were various: Earlham was too expensive. The faculty who visited local meetings talked "far above the heads of the young people." The children of influential Friends had had run-ins with college authorities and thus their parents were unhappy; "Indianapolis will be a poor place for you to come for help if G. does not graduate," a trustee warned Dennis about one problem student. There were complaints that Quaker students had become a minority, and that the college did not work hard enough to draw students from the two constituent yearly meetings. One alumnus reported that in the yearly meetings, Earlham graduates appeared to be "an exclusive group."[146]

These worries made an impression. In 1939, to try to improve relations with the two yearly meetings, and especially with their pastors, William E. Berry organized a two-day conference for ministers on campus. Over sixty attended the first in February 1939, and Milo Hinckle, the Indiana Yearly Meeting superintendent, praised it as a great success. Dennis in his reports to the two yearly meetings began to emphasize the college's Quaker commitment and the activities of the faculty in Indiana Yearly Meeting and the Five Years Meeting. He also encouraged more faculty to attend both yearly meetings. Early in 1940, the faculty appointed a committee to study Earlham's standing as a Quaker institution. Including some of the weightiest Friends on the faculty, with Allen D. Hole as its head, it apparently lapsed when Hole died suddenly that summer. Two years later, however, the faculty agreed that it needed "greater participation in the activities of the church."[147]

Thus it was that Earlham's Quaker identity appeared problematic by 1941. There were tensions and uncertainties on all sides. Relations with the two yearly meetings were cool, as not only campus theology but also morality seemed in question. The growing numbers of eastern Friends were doubtless strengthening the basically modernist, liberal Quaker flavor of the college, but there was no one Quaker leader to serve as a leader or as a lightning rod, as Elbert Russell, Alexander Purdy, and Clarence Pickett had. It would be the coming of World War II that would bring the campus to a new awareness of its Quaker foundations.

Earlham and World War II

The Second World War affected Earlham more than any previous conflict. Two years or more of campus debate, in which President Dennis took a leading role, preceded American entry into the conflict. It was brought home to students by the arrival of refugees from Europe, by the opposition of most of the students to American involvement in the war, by debates over conscientious objection versus participation in the armed forces, and by the coming to Earlham, after the United States entered the war, of a group of Japanese American students. The last raised a variety of issues, including all of the questions of race that Dennis had tried to deflect.

From 1933, Earlham students had had reminders of the troubles of Europe in a succession of refugee students who came to the campus under the auspices of the AFSC. Two Earlham graduates, Alice Shaffer and Leonard Kenworthy, worked in Berlin in the 1930s, trying to aid persecuted Jews, and Arthur M. and Carrie Charles for a time directed a refugee camp in New York. The first German refugee at Earlham, Etta Albrecht, arrived in 1933. In 1938 the faculty voted to provide a scholarship for a German Jewish student, "without expressing any opinion upon any controversial international question, but as an expression of sympathy for suffering." A year later, the school hired a refugee zoologist as a visiting professor. Two other refugees made a deep impression on the campus, both through their personalities and their stories of persecution—Rudolph Blitz, a Jewish student from Vienna who arrived in the fall of 1939, and Norbert Silbiger, another Viennese who became a much admired teacher and director and one of Richmond's most beloved citizens after a year on the faculty.[148]

Neither the presence of the refugees nor the antipathy of the campus community toward Nazism, however, moved most faculty and students to favor intervention in the affairs of Europe. In fact opposition to intervention probably fractured the New Deal group on campus, as Roosevelt's interventionist sympathies alienated former supporters like political science professor Arthur Funston. A few faculty, most notably Merrill Root, now moving away from pacifism, advocated U.S. entry into the war after 1939, but they were a distinct minority. President Dennis was one of Indiana's leading isolationists. "Every day I am more convinced that this is not our war," Dennis wrote to his congressman in July 1940. He vociferously opposed the Lend-Lease program of aid to Great Britain, saying that it "makes directly for war and for the breaking down of our ordered system of constitutional government." Dennis was involved with isolationist groups like the America First Committee, giving antiwar speeches from coast to coast in 1941.[149]

Students were equally active in opposing American intervention. The editors of the *Post* warned against being drawn into war by propaganda, as had happened in 1917. By 1938 a group calling itself the Student Peace Volunteers, later the Peace Fellowship, had formed on campus. It raised money for the war relief efforts of the AFSC and sent out delegations to Quaker meetings to present antiwar plays. By 1941 the group had seventy-five members, most of them Friends.[150]

When U.S. entry into the war did come in December 1941, it presented the campus with problems. Some were financial—with most men of college age in the armed forces, enrollment inevitably declined. There was the challenge of determining how closely Earlham could cooperate with the war effort and still maintain the peace testimony. And there was the hostility the college faced because of the presence of a small group of Japanese American students from 1942 to 1945.

After Pearl Harbor, there was a massive shift of sentiment. "There is a minority which still holds that conflict was avoidable and to be regretted, but what was for the most part a previously more or less isolationist campus swung quickly over to the band-wagon with the national collapse of isolationist leadership," the *Post* noted. Finances became critical; had all eligible men rushed to enlist after Pearl Harbor, the drop in enrollment would have been devastating. The faculty and administration urged students to remain until drafted. Meanwhile the faculty decided to switch from semesters to quarters, to make it easier for drafted men to complete units of work when called. The faculty estimated that with allowances for circumstances and summer sessions (which faculty would teach at nominal salaries), men could graduate in two and one-half years. Even with such allowances, by 1945 the number of men on campus had dropped 80 percent compared with 1941 and total enrollment was only about 225.[151]

The college made no attempt to influence student decisions about whether to enter the armed forces, following much the same policy as in World War I. Three absolute pacifists who graduated before the war began chose prison rather than to compromise their principles by registering for the draft. Sixty students registered as conscientious objectors, compared with about six hundred who entered the armed forces. Of the latter, 38 percent were Friends. This was probably typical of pastoral Friends generally. In 1943, for example, Western Yearly Meeting reported four hundred members in the armed forces. There continued to be pacifist sentiment on the campus, but it was muted.[152]

The college's options for dealing with the loss of so many students were limited. Dennis presented the general philosophy in his report to the yearly meetings in 1942: "A Quaker college should not, as a college, participate directly in the war effort, but it should do everything short of direct participation to cooperate with and facilitate the work of the government." This meant that the choice of many schools, including some of the Quaker colleges, to establish officer training units was not an option, but early in 1943 Dennis suggested the establishment of a Provost Marshal training unit. Although in uniform and under army command, its members would not drill or train for combat. Instead they would be trained to administer occupied territories; their training would be similar to that of AFSC Reconstruction workers who would enroll in the same classes. The advantage was that it would bring badly needed revenues to the campus without, in Dennis's view, compromising any fundamental principle.[153]

This suggestion badly divided the campus. The faculty was evenly split between supporters of the plan and those who saw it as inconsistent with the peace testimony. The board, recognizing how sensitive the subject was, met with faculty and spouses and "certain prominent Friends from the community" before making a decision. A majority of the board favored the project, but because there was so much opposition decided not to proceed with it. Edward D. Evans was outraged; although a Friend, he had no use for "individuals who are too good to have U.S. army men on the campus." However, many alumni and local Friends were so pleased that they increased their giving to the college to such a degree that cutbacks were minimal.[154]

Earlham's other option was to try to secure a Civilian Public Service camp. CPS had been established by the Selective Service Act of 1940 to provide conscientious objectors with an opportunity for alternative service. Since religion was the only acceptable basis for claiming CO status under the act, administration of the CPS units was turned over to churches. The units performed various tasks of "public importance," from fire spotting in national parks to working in mental hospitals. Friends placed their units under the AFSC; Thomas E. Jones, a 1912 graduate and then the president of Fisk University, ran the program, with Paul Furnas, a 1911 graduate, as his assistant. Ernest Wildman and Murvel Garner were given leave from teaching duties to head CPS camps.[155]

Early in 1943 Selective Service director Lewis B. Hershey announced that he had approved Earlham as the site of a CPS unit. The faculty had facilitated it by setting up a new program in "Relief and Reconstruction." Up to 260 men from other CPS camps would be trained for overseas work similar to that done in France during World War I. About 20 arrived early that summer, only to have Congress deal the Earlham program a fatal blow. Two riders to an appropriations bill were aimed at CPS, one limiting COs to work in the United States, the other banning CPS units from being located on college campuses. Thus the CPS men were dispersed to other sites and the Earlham unit came to an end.[156]

There was one other source of new students for the college: Japanese Americans from the West Coast, forcibly removed from their homes to internment camps early in 1942 because some in government feared that they would engage in espionage and subversion. Their enrollment at Earlham was doubly significant. It reaffirmed the college's long-standing interest in Japan. It also was the beginning of Elton Trueblood's long and fruitful relationship with Earlham.[157]

Earlham's ties with Japan went back to the 1880s when Joseph Cosand, a Friend from New London, Indiana, and a former Earlham student, became the first Quaker missionary in Japan. He, in turn, was responsible for the arrival of Earlham's first Japanese student, Chuzo Kaifu, in 1890. From the 1890s into the 1930s there was usually at least one Japanese student on the campus, almost always a graduate of the Tokyo Friends School that Cosand had helped found. In turn, other Earlham alumni went to Japan as teachers and missionaries. By 1923 there were eight in Tokyo alone. A student from this period, Bonner Fellers, later an aide to Gen. Douglas MacArthur, would play a critical role in the preservation of the Japanese monarchy after World War II.[158]

As anti-Japanese sentiment grew in the United States in the 1920s and 1930s, Earlham remained an exception. Perhaps the best evidence is student reaction to the Japanese Exclusion Act of 1926, which ended Japanese immigration to the United States. Thomas R. Kelly and a group of students proposed sending an Earlham student to the Imperial University in Tokyo as a gesture of friendship and fellowship. Wilfred V. Jones, the son of Quaker missionaries to Cuba, was selected. Students raised money to pay his travel expenses, and Jones sailed in October 1927. Jones was the first American student to enroll in the Imperial University, and his presence received considerable favorable publicity in Japan.[159]

When the decision came to move West Coast Japanese Americans to internment camps in January 1942, President Dennis was in California. William O. Mendenhall, the president of Whittier, contacted Dennis about accepting the Japanese American students who had been enrolled there. Meanwhile, the AFSC had sent Homer and Edna Morris to oversee relief work in the internment camps. By the spring, authorities in Washington had agreed that Nisei might enroll in midwestern colleges that were not near military installations or plants where sensitive defense work was done. Earlham immediately announced that it would accept twelve Nisei. Morris and D. Elton Trueblood, a Friend then on the faculty at Stanford, handled many of the arrangements. Earlham was one of fifty-three colleges to enroll Japanese Americans during the war.[160]

Dennis and the board knew that they faced a ticklish situation, and he was determined to take every possible precaution to avoid trouble. If Dennis had any doubts about his course, he did not record them. "I never felt more convinced that I was right about any action which I have taken at Earlham College than I do about this matter of the Japanese students," Dennis wrote to one Quaker. "If we do not do our best to help these students, I do not see why we should be called a Quaker college." Dennis himself thought the relocation unnecessary; "an unfortunate minor tragedy," he called it. But he was rigorous in his requirements for enrollment. Nisei students had to provide "proof of absolute loyalty and financial capacity." They would receive no scholarships, nor would they have jobs on campus, so that there would be no question of "other American students" being deprived of anything. Dennis pointed out that all but one of the first group were church members, that he had personally interviewed the two transferring from Whittier, and that the two coming from Oregon had letters of recommendation from the governor and from the publisher of Portland's leading newspaper. Dennis also took the precaution of consulting with the mayor and other Richmond community leaders, and even met with the local American Legion post and offered to allow its officers to inspect the students' files.[161]

The presence of the students engendered hostility. One petition from Richmond told Dennis that "no Japanese can be trusted except a dead one." A delivery man bringing supplies told a secretary that the packages contained poison for the "Japs." Especially in the fall of 1942, the president's office received a number of "anonymous and scurrilous communications." In October, when Richmond's mayor faced a tough reelection campaign and sensed resentment in the city, he began to claim that he had opposed the coming of the students, but that the federal government had given him no choice. In the spring of 1943, out of the blue, the local daily, the *Palladium-Item*, ran an especially vicious attack on the Nisei.[162]

The most heated exchange came in the fall of 1943, and initially it did not even involve Earlham. It began instead in Spring Grove, a suburb of Richmond that was still an independent corporation. There Indianapolis Quaker businessman and Earlham graduate Isaac F. Woodard had turned the old family home into Quaker Hill, which he hoped would become a Quaker study center. It was for a time used to house refugees, and there was talk of a CPS unit being based there. In the fall of 1943 a young Nisei couple with a baby were living there with Milton and Freda Hadley, the Quaker Hill directors.[163]

The presence of the Nisei greatly exercised some Spring Grove residents, especially Lena Hiatt, the town board president. Late in September she dispatched a ferocious letter to Indiana Yearly Meeting. "Many of our boys have been called to fight the Japanese, who are the most brutal inhuman people on the face of the Earth. Our tax payers object to harboring them here, regardless of where they were born, while their own sons are having to give their life blood . . . in war against Japan," she charged. Dennis was a disgrace, Hiatt continued, "and if he is more for Japan than for Americans he had better go over and help them first-handed." Hiatt warned of mob action if the Nisei remained in Richmond.[164]

One did not intimidate William C. Dennis, and Hiatt's threats roused him to action. He pondered filing a libel suit or having Hiatt prosecuted for sending a threatening letter. Hiatt later claimed that Dennis told her that "he had always believed in war, and had declared war on me, and war it will be." Dennis did go to the next town board meeting, where he forced it to disclaim any ill intention toward the students at Earlham. When a local lodge announced that it would discuss the subject, Dennis appeared to defend Earlham's position and in fact won the group to his side. The November elections swept Hiatt and all but one of the Spring Grove board members out of office. Hiatt blamed Earlham and "outside money"; Dennis made no secret of his satisfaction.[165]

While there was opposition, however, there was also vocal support for Earlham's position. No one was ever more forthright than Dennis. When the *Palladium-Item* launched its attack in the spring of 1943, he replied immediately. "It would be cowardly for me to sit by without a protest while you endeavor to hold all Japanese, including those young Americans of Japanese descent, responsible for the horrible misdeeds and thereby injure these young people in spirit and endanger their personal safety," Dennis wrote to publisher Rudolph G. Leeds. "I do not wish to argue this matter with you. I do not think I could add anything to the Declaration of Independence, the Constitution of the United States, and the Sermon on the Mount. . . . When you tell me that because the Japanese war lords have committed a terrible crime, and all Japanese are 'congenitally deceptive and treacherous,' I reply that I do not believe it; that I prefer to agree with Edmund Burke, who 'did not know how to draw an indictment against an entire people.'" Students responded favorably to the Nisei presence. When the decision to admit them was announced, the *Post* hailed it as a way of showing "those guiding the war efforts that here students are determined to look forward after the settlement of this war by promoting good will and a spirit of friendliness NOW !" *Post* editors dismissed critics as ex–Ku Klux Klan members. Quarterly meetings, pastors, the Western Yearly Meeting Peace Committee, Indiana University President Herman B Wells, and alumni all commended the college. "Give 'em hell. . . . You keep those students! *Stand your ground!* You are right!" wrote one 1938 graduate, himself an army officer. In one case, one of the Nisei actually confronted the publisher of the *Palladium-Item* in person.[166]

The Nisei found their life on campus happy. There was an occasional display of hostility, but it was exceptional. One told a classmate that Earlham was "the closest thing I know to Utopia." They were active in campus activities and organizations. Henry Tanaka, for example, was elected to the Bundy Hall council, the Precedents Committee, and the Ionian Society as well as being active in the Earlham Peace Fellowship, the choir, and the YMCA. Others had similar records at Earlham.[167]

The one "problem" to vex Dennis with the Nisei grew at least in part from the idealism of the students, in part from the peculiar conditions of wartime. It was interracial dating. For Dennis, the trustees, and at least some of the faculty, it represented a full-blown crisis, particularly when it came to involve not only whites and Nisei but whites and blacks.

The war years saw a resurgence of interest in racial equality and justice on campus. The editors of the *Post* linked segregation and racial discrimination with fascism, and groups like the YWCA and the Peace Fellowship increasingly focused on such questions. Students were probably responding as well to increased activism by blacks during the war. The goal of the students was "to find ways to develop understanding and to apply the Earlham ideals of no race or creed discrimination." They wanted to see Earlham "take a definite Christian stand on racial equality comparable in courage and vigor to that already taken . . . on a military unit and the admission of Nisei students."[168]

This was one issue, however, where Dennis was certain that Earlham had gone as far as it could go. Since 1931, Dennis had relaxed a bit; black speakers now came to campus to speak on race-related matters. Dennis, in his own mind, was trying to pursue a "middle of the road" policy that was "liberal in aims but not radical in . . . methods." For Dennis, that involved "a distinction between educational equality and racial equality" and so he had "not endeavored to force racial social equality upon those of our students who were not ready for it." That meant, for example, that whites who objected did not have to live on the same dormitory hallways or sit at the same dining room tables as blacks. Black students could play football, but in basketball Earlham "bowed to the informal state rule that Negroes are banned from indoor sports in Indiana." Dennis opposed the rule, "but we have not felt called upon to strike any attitude about this matter and to withdraw from basketball with DePauw, Wabash et al., because they will not play basketball with Negroes on the team." He was convinced that Earlham had "just about the best racial situation that I know of anywhere." He was also convinced that that would continue "only . . . so long as we do not admit too many Negroes." Five or ten were acceptable; twenty-five would be too many.[169]

By 1943, a black student from New Castle, Indiana, James Turner, had come to trouble Dennis. Turner had enrolled at Earlham with the encouragement and financial help of New Castle Quakers, and was majoring in political science with the hope of going on to law school. His academic advisor remembers him as perfectly self-controlled and polite, but inwardly seething at racial injustice. As early as April 1943, Dennis received reports that Turner was dating white coeds. Early in December, Turner occasioned a minor crisis when he asked one to the Ionian dance. A number of students had encouraged him, partly out of idealism, partly to have more men at the dance. Dean Comstock "counseled" the woman involved and Turner met with Dennis himself. Turner apparently backed down, fearful of losing his scholarship.[170]

When word spread of the incident, a number of students and some of the more liberal faculty, like Murvel Garner and Francis D. Hole, the son of "Daddy" Hole, were appalled. There were rumors that Dennis and Comstock had banned even interracial dancing, which Dennis denied. For the students in the Peace Fellowship, it was a clear case of "unmerited suppression." Early in December, a student delegation accompanied by three faculty met with Dennis to protest. The president warned them that "by stirring things up and drawing lines and calling for declarations of policy they could only divide us into two camps and make the situation worse." Coming on the heels of the Spring Grove battle, Dennis was sure that the whole question was "full of dynamite," and could better be dealt with after the war, when emotions were not running as high.[171]

No sooner did the Turner controversy fade than Dennis became aware of a growing relationship between Edward Uyesugi, one of the Nisei, and Ruthanna Farlow, a Quaker student from Paoli, Indiana. When Dennis learned of it, he called her in for a talk. According to Dennis, she said that the relationship was "intellectual only." Dennis was concerned enough to report to the board that he would "take quiet but efficient methods, through her people if necessary, to end it." By January 1944, however, he was receiving new reports and calling on the Farlow family for help. For Dennis, the case was "not . . . a matter of racial superiority but simply a matter of hard common sense." In fact Dennis failed here; Uyesugi and Farlow married after graduating.[172]

Faced with such cases, Dennis proposed to the board the policy that would bedevil the college for a decade. Earlham would "quietly" discourage interracial dating "apt to lead to love and marriage." The board gave overwhelming approval. One trustee from Western Yearly Meeting thought the problem was "not enough white boys to help the others 'know their place.'" Indeed, she thought that Earlham had treated black students too leniently. An Indiana trustee told Dennis that students "need to be jolted out of their smugness and conceit in thinking they are so absolutely right." Only the new alumni trustee, Birk Mendenhall, a Friend and education professor at Ohio State University, protested that the college should not tolerate "social and economic injustice" to appease "the reactionary element in the immediate college environment."[173]

As backward as the college's policy appears now, Earlham undoubtedly compared favorably with other schools. In 1945 an official with the Rosenwald Fund, a New York foundation with a special interest in black education, told Dennis that Earlham's record with minorities was "about as good as any that we know of." In fact, even compared with other Quaker schools, Earlham looked good. Of all of the Quaker secondary and boarding schools, only one, Oakwood in New York, admitted black students in 1944. Westtown was preparing to do so, although in the face of substantial opposition from some alumni. George School near Philadelphia had refused even to allow a black commencement speaker. In a study done for the Friends World Committee in 1944, Thomas E. and Esther B. Jones concluded that "Friends have become separated from the thinking and planning of Negro youth today." Thus, given the pervasive segregation even of the North in the 1940s, it is not surprising that many students found Earlham relatively enlightened. One black student, Edmund Casey, wrote in a theme: "I have known that social equality could exist. . . . This year my associations with my class-mates have shown to me that it can exist here in the United States and apparently without any ill feelings among the people." A white student wrote back from the army that "the spirit at Earlham really approached democracy. The friendliness among Jewish, white, colored, and yellow has a desired quality almost considered an oddity in our age." It made him want to become a Quaker. In fact the questioning and idealism of the war years would become one of Earlham's distinguishing features over the next half century.[174]

As the war came to an end, so did William C. Dennis's presidency. Sixty-seven years old in 1945, he announced that he would retire no later than the end of the 1946–1947 school year, preferably earlier. He was tired, but he, and Earlham, had survived. In fact his prophecy that his presidency would end in "violence" was not fulfilled—he was the first president in the history of Earlham to retire flat out.[175]

The college, however, was also tired. A trustee recalled a decade later that in 1945 "Earlham had a wartime enrollment of 225 students. The faculty was the smallest in modern times. Their pay, compared with wartime salaries, was barely liveable. No new buildings had been built for about twenty years. It took real conviction to teach and work at Earlham." Physically, the campus was run down and, as one administrator recalled it, "shaggy." As for the faculty, many of its best teachers had left for CPS, the armed forces, or other "war work"; Dennis was grateful that health problems had kept Arthur Funston, whom he regarded as his best professor, out of the army. One 1943 graduate remembered how *old* her teachers all seemed; she was studying under many of the same professors who had taught her parents a quarter of a century before. Earlham was at a turning point, and everyone realized that the end of the war, and the arrival of a new president, must bring change.[176]

The Creation of
Modern Earlham,
1946–1958

"As I see it Earlham College has been at the fork of the roads," wrote alumnus, former professor, and trustee Homer L. Morris in the autumn of 1946. "The College could very easily, in view of the increasing competition of state supported institutions, slip into a position of mediocrity and lose its position of leadership. On the other hand there is . . . unparalleled opportunity for Earlham to become one of the outstanding church-retained colleges in the Mid-West, and make a distinct contribution not only to the Quaker way of life but to the cause of liberal arts education."[1]

Morris was right to see Earlham facing critical choices at the end of World War II. Physically, the campus would have to build and expand. Enrollment, at its lowest level in fifty years, would have to be rebuilt. An aging, depleted faculty would have to be replaced. The new president, Tom Jones, would have to take hold. Most of all, the college would have to wrestle with what it meant for Earlham to be a Quaker institution.

Twelve years later, when Tom Jones retired, his presidency was a success by almost any standard. Enrollment was edging close to one thousand. Jones had raised ten million dollars for new facilities. The faculty had been transformed. And what was once a respectable midwestern church school was moving toward becoming a national institution.

What was still unresolved was the question of Earlham's Quaker identity. In some ways, it was stronger in 1958 than in 1946. For the first time in decades, Earlham had in Elton Trueblood an international Quaker figure whose evangelical piety was beyond question and who was respected and welcomed by the masses of members of Indiana and Western yearly meetings. Earlham had again become a place where Quaker pastors were educated and trained. The number of students from the two yearly meetings had remained large.

On the other hand, the liberal Quaker impulse at Earlham had also become stronger. Most of the Quaker faculty hired in these years were firmly in the liberal, unprogrammed camp, theologically and politically. They had few ties with Indiana or with pastoral Quakerism. They and a growing number of Quaker students would express their faith through social activism that focused on peace and racial equality. A growing number of these Quaker students would likewise come from the unprogrammed yearly meetings of Friends, especially in the East. Their sympathies were not with the conservative politics and culture of Richmond, Indiana. The result was growing friction, even as Earlham grew and prospered.

In a vital way, Earlham, in these years, took an almost unique path. While many colleges eschewed denominational identity, Earlham's became stronger. It was strengthened because a variety of Friends on campus found in that identity a vision for education. At times some elements of that vision would come into conflict.[2]

"The Earlham Idea"

In the summer of 1945 the trustees began their search for William C. Dennis's successor as president. They restricted their search to Friends, ranging from Elbert Russell's old adversary William O. Mendenhall, forced out at Whittier for his opposition to military training on campus, to young veterans of Civilian Public Service. Three candidates emerged as front-runners, two without Earlham ties. David E. Henley had been the dean at Whittier and had been active in the Five Years Meeting, while D. Elton Trueblood had taught at Guilford and Haverford before going to Stanford University. Dennis was already negotiating with him to come to Earlham as a member of the faculty and as the successor to Elbert Russell, Alexander Purdy, and Clarence Pickett as the campus's spiritual leader. The trustees' search committee found Henley solid but unexciting, while they perceived Trueblood as more interested in writing, teaching, and lecturing than in administration.[3]

The board's choice was Tom Jones, a 1912 graduate and at that time the president of Fisk University. He came from a background that reassured almost all of Earlham's constituencies. Jones was born in the solidly Quaker community of Fairmount, Indiana, in 1888, the descendant of a long line of North Carolina Quakers. His education was what was expected of a bright young Quaker at the turn of the century—the Fairmount Academy, then working his way through Earlham. He was recorded a Quaker minister while still in college, and after Earlham went on to Hartford Seminary. There he decided that his future was not as a Quaker pastor. Instead he served as executive secretary of the Young Friends movement. He also made a fortunate marriage to Esther Balderston, a member of a prominent Philadelphia Quaker family.[4]

Jones's academic credentials were equally impressive. From Hartford he had gone to Columbia University for graduate work in sociology and economics. After their marriage, he and Esther went to Japan, where she had committed herself to a term of missionary work. There he did research for his Ph.D. thesis, one of the first to challenge the "scientific" bases of widely held ideas of Anglo-Saxon racial superiority. This work, and his Quaker background, led to a call in 1926 to the presidency of Fisk University. Jones found the black college torn by strife. When he left twenty years later, it had doubled its enrollment, was well endowed, and had become the first accredited black college in the South.[5]

Jones initially had doubts about leaving Fisk—Earlham was offering a considerably lower salary, and the challenges seemed daunting. Loyalty to his alma mater and to Quakerism won out, and in the fall of 1945 Jones accepted the Earlham board's offer, to take office in July 1946.[6]

Jones was very different from the president he succeeded. While Dennis was cool and calculating, Jones was, as one of his faculty wrote, "a man of swift and violent emotions, of intuitive and sudden judgments." His temper was notable; one professor gauged how Jones was responding to provocation by watching the color rise upward from his shirt collar to his forehead. His greatest talent was probably fundraising; he was a "financial ball of fire." This activity took him away from campus frequently, so he depended heavily on subordinate administrators. Critical was Paul Furnas, a 1911 graduate who was one of Jones's closest friends. Jones persuaded him to come back to Earlham from Philadelphia as business manager. Perhaps just as importantly, Furnas was a calming influence who, as another administrator put it, kept "the volatile Jones from apoplectic fits." But Jones's dominant mood was not angry. He was affable, garrulous, and generous, with a gift for meeting people. Informal by nature, his insistence on dispensing with titles and using first names quickly became the campus practice. No one ever questioned his decisiveness or that even his swift judgments were usually sound.[7]

Even while still at Fisk, Jones became actively involved in planning at Earlham. It was a sign of things to come that his closest confidant on the board was Homer Morris. They had been good friends while students, and Jones had hired Morris to head the economics department at Fisk. Morris had been a persistent critic of Dennis, but now Morris had Jones's ear, and Jones was open to his advice on hiring, curriculum, and other matters. Morris, in turn, served as a conduit for the concerns of faculty like Millard Markle and Ernest Wildman, who had felt powerless under Dennis.[8]

Jones, however, was not afraid to make decisions that ruffled feathers among some of the faculty even before he arrived. He told Arthur M. Charles, past seventy and on the faculty since 1904, that the time had come to retire. And Jones upheld Dennis's decision to terminate history professor Perry Kissick, who had been at Earlham since 1928. Kissick was a committed Quaker and pacifist whom some students found inspiring but others rigid and dull. He and Wildman had been Dennis's most persistent faculty critics. Even Morris thought him a poor teacher, and acquiesced in Dennis's decision. The dismissal of such a veteran stirred considerable consternation among many faculty, who saw it as Dennis's final revenge on his opponents.[9]

When Jones arrived at Earlham, he had a clear vision of what he wanted to accomplish and what Earlham's future would be. He called it "The Earlham Idea." One administrator who arrived near the end of his presidency remembered how Jones "with face flushed and his fist clenched, talked about the Earlham Idea, the Earlham Idea. . . . If you don't agree with the Earlham Idea, you don't belong here." For Jones, it was "an idea which lies at the very heart of American faith," born in England, brought across the Atlantic, then up to Indiana from North Carolina. There, in the "Friendly Valley" of the Whitewater, in "the revealing presence of the living God," Friends had "found that which makes a nation great." That was a peculiar blend of intuition, science, and faith, "the germinal force which both maintains and spreads civilization." In order to maintain that vision, they had founded Earlham, which merged "a Quaker meeting and a scientific laboratory." There they had nurtured values of freedom, integrity, discipline, and faith. And in a world in which those values seemed to be under relentless attack, Jones and Earlham were committed to their defense and development.[10]

While idealistic, Jones was also hard-headed and practical. There was much to be done. He knew that Earlham, after Haverford and Swarthmore the best-endowed of the Quaker colleges, was still in a financially precarious state. In the fall of 1946, enrollment exploded to 600 students, 250 of them veterans enrolling under the G.I. Bill. Dormitories and classrooms were filled to capacity, and since many of the veterans were married, for the first time the college provided housing for students with families. Dennis had already planned a new women's dormitory and natural sciences building, the latter to be named for David W. Dennis. Jones began fund-raising with a million-dollar campaign to mark the college's centennial. By the time of his retirement in 1958, he had raised ten million dollars and had physically transformed the campus. There were new men's and women's dormitories, a new science building, and a residence for the president, in addition to lesser structures. Most importantly, Earlham Hall, which had stood since 1847, had been replaced by a near-duplicate structure. The plan had originally been to remodel the old building, but it was in such poor condition that it was demolished.[11]

Not all of the funds raised went into building. Jones did much to expand the faculty and to raise salaries. The size of the faculty doubled between 1946 and 1958. The student-teacher ratio, which in 1945 was 17 to 1, by 1954 stood at 11 to 1. Salaries, long a concern, grew substantially. The average for a full professor, which had been $3,000 in 1945, increased to $4,500 in 1949, and to $7,000 in 1958, which, even allowing for inflation, reflected a significant increase. The college budget, which was $250,000 in 1946, nearly tripled in just two years, and had reached almost $1,500,000 in 1958.[12]

Jones proved innovative in raising money. Dennis had embarked on a new course in 1942 by engaging a fund-raising firm, Marts and Lundy, in Philadelphia, but the war had kept much from being accomplished. Jones tried several methods. He continued to use Marts and Lundy. He realized that the Richmond area was the single most important one for Earlham fund-raising, and so he assiduously cultivated well-to-do residents like Rudolph G. Leeds, the publisher of the *Palladium-Item*, C. Edgar Hamilton of the Richmond Gear Works, and Ralph Teetor, an inventor and part-owner of the Perfect Circle Corporation in nearby Hagerstown. The last two became members of the Earlham board. Jones also brought onto the Earlham board Paul Davis, a nationally known consultant on college finance and fund-raising. In these years Earlham, largely through Elton Trueblood, formed its relationship with the man who would become Earlham's single largest financial benefactor, Eli Lilly of Indianapolis. By 1954 the Lilly Endowment was giving $100,000 a year to Earlham. Jones was also one of the cofounders of the Associated Colleges of Indiana (ACI), which coordinated fund-raising for all of the private colleges in the state.[13]

One route that Jones steadfastly refused to consider was direct government subsidies (although he did take advantage of certain federal loan programs). His experiences as a conscientious objector during World War I and with CPS during World War II had made him skeptical about the influence of the federal government. Jones was suspicious even of scholarships funded by the federal government. In his eyes, the "free and untrammeled search for truth, essential to the preservation of democracy and the private enterprise system," was best "safeguarded in the present arrangement of balance between the church-related and independent colleges and the tax-supported and public institutions." Jones, in contacts with businessmen, unabashedly celebrated the ACI's "Hoosier demonstration of faith in the American system of self-help, individual initiative, and creative enterprise" which would "prevent federal subsidy and ultimate control of the free higher educational system of this country."[14]

These and other accomplishments, as impressive as they were, were hardly unique. Other colleges also flourished between 1945 and 1960, as total college enrollment in the United States increased fivefold. What distinguished Earlham in these years was its adherence to, even its strengthening, of its sectarian identity, even as other church-related schools were weakening denominational ties. By any standard, Earlham's understanding of itself as a Quaker institution in the minds of faculty and students was stronger in 1958 than it had been when Jones arrived.[15]

The Quaker Oasis

When Jones accepted the presidency of Earlham, he returned with a sense that Earlham was losing its Quaker identity. "We had swung away from a deep spiritual interpretation," he told the trustees when they interviewed him, "and were he ever to have anything to say about it he would do his best to swing Earlham back into line with the highest type of Quakerism." Once on campus, Jones set out to strengthen Quakerism on the campus. He elaborated his vision in his first address to Indiana Yearly Meeting. Earlham would be "an oasis of the purer form of Quakerism." Friends had "been so influenced by others that we have come to let them do our thinking for us," he told his hearers. "In our confusion, we have forgotten our Quaker principles."[16]

Jones came back to Indiana with a sense that Quakerism was in trouble there. The Quakers of the Midwest, he wrote to John D. Rockefeller, Jr., in 1947, "had suffered much erosion of spirit and loyalty during the depression and war years." He continued to feel that throughout his presidency; as late as 1956 he wrote of the need for the college to contribute to "the revitalization of Quakerism in the Middle West." This may have been the result of his consciousness of the yearly meetings' steady numerical decline with the movement of Friends out of the old Quaker farming communities and the slow growth of meetings in urban areas. But his desire for a renewal of midwestern Quakerism led by Earlham came from his sense that he was not just a bridge between the yearly meetings and the college, but that he was really part of both.[17]

Jones's own religious vision was very much an attempt to find a

middle way between modernism and fundamentalism. Although semi-
nary-trained, he made no pretense of theological sophistication. Yet in
his speeches, his writings, and his communication with various elements of the college's constituency, Jones did present a clear spiritual
vision. Writing to Rufus Jones (no relation) in 1946, the Earlham president said that "the time is right to plant Midwestern Quakerism in the
line of mystical religion, social concern, and evangelical commitment."
Ultimately, the first two came to dominate the third at Earlham. But for
Tom Jones, all three were vital.[18]

TOM JONES

Jones's own pronouncements on the nature of Quakerism blended evangelical and liberal elements. On one hand, he was quite capable of holding forth in a way that gladdened the hearts of the faithful. As one of Jones's faculty put it, he could preach on conversion and salvation to Indiana Quakers not just because he understood Indiana Quakerism, but because he himself had known conversion, had been born again. "Earlham is both interested in the saving grace of Jesus Christ and in the way of holiness," he told one small-town Friend. When he preached in local meetings, he struck similar notes. Enticing a potential contributor, he claimed that he, Paul Furnas, and Elton Trueblood were three men who saw "eye to eye in the matter of bringing to the world, both by preaching and by practice, the gospel as propounded by Fox, in the firm conviction that this is the balm in Gilead for the sick and confused world." They would maintain Earlham on a firmly Christian basis.[19]

Still, in most situations when Jones tried to define Quakerism and what Quakerism meant at Earlham he spoke in a language more liberal than evangelical. He made no secret of the fact that he was not a fundamentalist; his communications with confidants show that he thought of Earlham's relationship with more stridently evangelical Friends as an "us-them" situation. At the heart of his own Quaker vision was the Inner Light, a central principle of liberal Quakerism and the *bete noire* of fundamentalist Friends. The foremost Quaker values, he told the faculty and student body at their opening assembly in 1948, were self-discipline, wholeness, integrity, simplicity, and belief in "that of God in every man." It is worth noting that Jones never put "conversion" among Earlham's goals—not that he would have denigrated it, but he did not see it as part of the college's mission.[20]

Perhaps the best evidence of this is Jones's articulation of the place of religion in the curriculum. "Earlham is unapologetically religious in its approach to modern educational problems," he wrote in 1949, but that religious approach was put more in terms of ethics and philosophy than experiential faith. The religion courses presented Christianity as "a philosophy and a way of life the value of which has been attested by the great minds of the world." Similarly, when Jones defined Earlham as a "Christian community" in a 1954 speech, he said that Earlham believed "that there is an intelligence behind the world, that the life and teaching of Jesus is important, and that God works both through scientific discovery and creative revelation."[21]

Many of the ways, moreover, that the Jones administration sought to translate this theory into practice were liberal. Jones himself as a young man, of course, had manifested his own faith through the Young Friends Movement, the AFSC, and education rather than as a pastor. When a student asked Jones to comment on the future of Quakerism in 1955, the

Earlham president gave three reasons for his optimism: the success of the Quaker colleges in "relating high scholarship to individual and community needs"; the work of the AFSC; and the activities of the agencies and boards of the Five Years Meeting. All of these were at best suspect, at worst anathema, to many Indiana Friends, especially those with fundamentalist sympathies.[22]

Jones saw himself striking a balance, a balance of all of the best elements found in the diversity of Quakerism, and avoiding its worst extremes. "Holding to the belief that there is 'that of God in every man,' a balance between experiential and revealed truth and that which is experimental and technical, dealing with facts, is being maintained," he wrote of the college's program in the spring of 1947. "Evangelical by nature, this spirit avoids fanatical preaching, uncultivated teaching, and vain argumentation."[23]

Probably no one better exemplified this blend of evangelical faith, intellect, and cultivation than Elton Trueblood. His importance to Earlham was incalculable. He was probably the best-known faculty member that Earlham has ever had. Author, preacher, and teacher, Trueblood made contacts that brought millions of dollars to the college, and won for it and for himself an audience that went far beyond the bounds of Quakerism. At the same time, he helped to repair some of the damage caused by previous battles between the college and the two yearly meetings.

Trueblood's life paralleled Jones's in many ways. Like the president, Trueblood came of an old North Carolina Quaker family, which had moved first to Indiana and then to Iowa, where he was born in 1900. Trueblood attended Penn College, where he graduated in 1922 with every possible honor. Alternating graduate study in divinity and philosophy at Brown, Harvard, and Johns Hopkins with ministerial work, by the late 1920s he had been marked as one of American Quakerism's rising stars. This was confirmed in 1933, when he was invited to Haverford as one of the successors to the retiring Rufus Jones, and to become editor of American Quakerism's most venerable periodical, the Philadelphia *Friend.* After two years, however, he left for Stanford University to become the university chaplain and to teach courses in the philosophy of religion.[24]

Trueblood eventually became discontented at Stanford, and by 1945 had decided to leave. In his autobiography, Trueblood explained his decision by referring to his desire to teach in a small college, "an institution of manageable dimensions in which an individual can make a real difference," and to be where there was an "unapologetic Christian commitment." Trueblood's discontent coincided with William C. Dennis's renewed desire to find a Friend for the religion department of the stature of Elbert Russell and Alexander Purdy. Dennis's idea was for a "roving professorship" under which Trueblood would teach half-time and be free to write, travel, and speak. Earlham would be for Trueblood "a teaching base for spiritual leadership in the Society of Friends." At first Trueblood resisted, indicating an interest instead in the presidency, but by the fall of 1945 Dennis had persuaded him. The coming of Jones and Furnas to the college, along with other plans, excited Trueblood. "With enough gathered sticks we should have quite a fire," he wrote to Homer Morris. Trueblood received the highest salary that Earlham had ever given any faculty member, partly raised by special contributions.[25]

At Earlham, Trueblood found his niche. He was immensely popular as a teacher, his lectures finely crafted and impressively delivered and always crowded with students. He was in constant demand for occasions ranging from Rotary lunches to meetinghouse dedications to college commencements to scholarly endowed lectures. He also produced a steady stream of books. On and off the campus, he was legendary for his ego; it drove some colleagues almost to distraction. Probably the fairest evaluation came from Jones's secretary, Opal Thornburg: "The only criticism we can make of Elton, or that we have heard others make, is that he has the same opinion of himself as his most ardent admirers have. However, he is just as generous in his good opinion of other people, and, as President Jones says, he really is as good as he thinks he is." But Trueblood's friends and admirers far outnumbered the detractors, and he brought Earlham an abundance of good will and favorable publicity at a time when both were critical. His 1956 *Reader's Digest* article, "Why I Chose a Small College," probably did more than anything else to bring Earlham national exposure in these years.[26]

The sources of Trueblood's influence and popularity were complex. Once a modernist liberal in faith, in the 1940s Trueblood had begun to move toward a more evangelical vision of religion. Many of his views, particularly on politics and pacifism, made him controversial among liberal Friends. Trueblood's writings, however, obviously struck a nerve in Cold War America, and they did so because they were articulate, uncompromising reassertions of the values that most Americans found familiar and comforting but perceived to be in danger. Two consistent themes run through Trueblood's works. One is that the survival of the American way of life and democratic institutions was dependent on moral values, and that moral values depended on religion. The other, closely related, was that the West found itself in danger because it had slipped away from its religious foundations and thus was morally adrift. Only religious revival could bring the United States and other democracies back to the strength that would enable them to withstand the communist onslaught.[27]

Events in the world around him—World War II and the early days of the Cold War—clearly underlay Trueblood's writing. In the first of "A

Trilogy for Our Times," *The Predicament of Modern Man,* published in 1944, Trueblood reflected on the world that would emerge from global conflagration. He was not optimistic about the results. "Something has gone wrong," he wrote; the United States was a "sick" society, a "cut-flower civilization," as he called it in a memorable phrase.[28]

Diagnosing the source of this malaise was no problem for Trueblood. "Our worst troubles," he claimed, "arise primarily from psychological rather than purely physiological sources." And at the heart of those ailments was the decline of religious faith and commitment. At the beginning of the century, in the English-speaking countries, he wrote, "nearly everyone read the Bible and engaged in public and private prayer, as well as family prayer, and great numbers heard, once each week, sermons that expounded the gospel." Those happy days were gone. Contemporary faith, in contrast, was "Christianity and water," with both the urgency and vigor gone. Clearly influenced by Neo-Orthodox theologian Reinhold Niebuhr, Trueblood saw the roots of this "mush and milk" faith in the modern fixation on tolerance, lack of discipline, and the loss of a sense of the reality of sin. The churches in 1950 did not realize that the West faced "the accumulated sins of Western man over the whole period of modern history." Instead, the mainline denominations had gone whoring after the strange gods of popularity, the "silly cult" of freedom, and, most of all, the false deity of tolerance, which for Trueblood was in most cases simply an indifference to truth.[29]

The stakes were enormous. Virtually all of Western civilization, especially those things that were most important to the democratic tradition—progress, reform, human rights—lay rooted in the Judeo-Christian tradition. And opposed to that was the faith of communism, which was not so much an economic or political system as it was a moral system, a moral system that had no place for God. That explained its brutalities. Thus the recovery of Christian faith became an imperative since, as Trueblood told an audience at Brown University in 1954, "the only way to meet a perverted faith is by the clarification and exemplification of a better faith."[30]

Trueblood had no lack of ideas on how to achieve that faith. The key, he wrote in 1947, was "a vigorous evangelical Christianity," one that eschewed materialism and the nonmiraculous. Trueblood's own mission was devoted to what he called "the recovery of discipline." In practical terms, his most obvious success at Earlham came in the regular assemblies and chapel services. Trueblood had no sympathy for colleges that had "secularized" such services or had made them voluntary for students. Because young people lacked "a rational basis of choice" and appreciation of spiritual things, they routinely ignored such opportunities unless required to take advantage of them, thus losing opportunities for spiritual growth. Trueblood was a vocal advocate of mandatory attendance at the Earlham assemblies, arguing that required attendance helped to develop spiritual discipline.[31]

Most of Trueblood's energies in this direction, however, went to the Yokefellow project. A direct outgrowth of his interest in a disciplined life, Trueblood modeled this "order," as he called it, both on medieval monastic brotherhoods and on Protestant intentional communities. The Yokefellows were to be a "horizontal fellowship," cutting across denominational lines and working for spiritual renewal in all. They would be marked by the "intensity of their fellowship and by their spiritual self-discipline." The movement was formally launched in 1949, and within a decade had attracted thousands of adherents.[32]

Trueblood's influence outside Earlham was enormous. His prestige among midwestern Quakers was unrivaled. It would be an oversimplification to say that he was Earlham's emissary to the fundamentalist-leaning Quakers of Indiana, since Trueblood, while a gifted preacher, was not a revivalist, and while evangelical, was definitely not a fundamentalist. Rather, Trueblood had his widest following among the middle classes of midwestern Quakerism, too respectable for emotional religion but socially and politically conservative. Trueblood also had thousands of non-Quaker admirers, among them a number of important businessmen and industrialists, of whom the wealthiest was Eli Lilly of Indianapolis. In 1954 President Dwight D. Eisenhower appointed Trueblood, a staunch Republican, religious advisor to the United States Information Agency, a key player in the Cold War. Trueblood's Republican politics may explain some of his popularity, especially in the McCarthy era. McCarthyism, after all, had at its roots a deep suspicion by millions of the loyalties of intellectuals, academics, and "striped-pants boys." At a time when colleges were widely perceived as "red nests," when Earlham was the focus of unfavorable publicity because of the activities of draft resisters and integrationists, it was doubtless comforting for many to see at Earlham a man like Trueblood, whose faith and patriotism were not only beyond question, but who could match the academic credentials and intellectual accomplishments of the liberals.[33]

Raising the yearly meetings' level of comfort with Earlham was important for Jones and the trustees. As Isaac E. Woodard wrote of Trueblood's hiring: "We are starting something [that is]. . . very important . . . and feel . . . is linking up our Yearly Meetings with Earlham to a much closer degree. Instead of being skeptical, we want these members everywhere to speak of it as 'our college.'" Jones and his administrators were constantly aware of the sensitivities of their socially and theologically conservative yearly meeting constituencies. Earlham did not reverse the policies on smoking and dancing that had caused Dennis so much trouble. Instead, the college resolved on a three-part strategy of outreach to individual meetings, training for pastors with continuing education for those already in the ministry, and quiet handling of complaints.[34]

One way that Jones tried to do good for both Earlham and Indiana Quakerism was by cultivating contacts with Friends meetings. Publicly he claimed that the "disinterest and distrust which exists is mostly based on lack of information." Some of this was pure recruiting and fund-raising; Jones and other administrators traveled constantly, looking for likely students and potential contributors. Still, many in the yearly meetings had the feeling that few Earlham faculty were "interested in our church work." A few professors continued to serve as pastors, and a few others were active on yearly meeting boards and committees. Most, however, especially of the new faculty, seemed rather distant from their constituency. Those most involved were veterans like Millard Markle, George Scherer, and Murvel Garner who were now near retirement.[35]

Jones tried to change this situation. Conceiving of Earlham as a cross between a meetinghouse and a laboratory meant that there were always new ideas to be tested, and he was convinced that ideas coming out of the college could make a difference in the lives of Indiana Friends. Thus he encouraged faculty involved in college programs like Community Dynamics and soil science to offer their services to Quaker communities, although the results were at best mixed. Better received were the deputations of Earlham students who visited local meetings. These involved anywhere from fifty to one hundred students and faculty a year. In 1946 a student group attempted to revive the nearly dormant Friends meeting at Webster, a village near Richmond that had a wonderful antebellum meetinghouse but only one resident family left in the meeting. The students took over the meeting with enthusiasm and kept it up for several years, unfortunately in the process driving out the last resident family. Thereafter the deputations confined their efforts to work with existing meetings. By 1955 over fifty meetings were being visited annually, with students preaching, singing, teaching Sunday school, and leading youth groups. The committee in charge reported generally good reactions, although there was always some anxiety that students might give embarrassing answers to certain questions, and some complaints that the students were "nice, but not very spiritual."[36]

The college under Jones also attempted to improve the condition and quality of the Quaker ministry. This had been a problem for Indiana Friends since the inception of the pastoral system. Horace P. Cook, an alumnus and the clerk of Anderson Monthly Meeting, summed up the situation in 1946: "The majority of [Quaker pastors] are products either of the green woods or from such schools as the Cleveland Bible School," the stronghold of fundamentalist Quakerism. Cook expressed a hope that Indiana Yearly Meeting would have a "loyal Earlham graduate" in every pulpit. Here was an opportunity for Earlham, but also an implicit problem: the expectation by many in the yearly meeting that the college should serve as a "preacher factory." Adding to the pressures were the fears of more liberal Friends that unless Earlham turned out more ministers, Friends would be left with no choice but to look to such fundamentalist bastions as Marion, Asbury, and Cleveland, and what remained of Quaker distinctiveness would be lost.[37]

After Jones's day, these concerns led to the founding of the Earlham School of Religion. In this period, however, Jones had more modest ambitions. One was to sponsor a series of pastoral conferences, partly to allow ministers to spend time with experts who could advise them on everything from the latest marriage counseling techniques to the impact of the discovery of the Dead Sea Scrolls on understanding the Old Testament. Jones approached them with trepidation at times, especially when some liberal faculty and guest speakers verged on dangerous territory. "I must say," he told Charles Woodman, one of the organizers of the 1949 conference, "I rather shuddered when I knew that these questions were going to come before some of the fundamentalist preachers that were present." There is no evidence, however, that any of the conferences produced negative repercussions for the college.[38]

Attempts to steer Earlham students toward careers as pastors brought more mixed results. Jones himself had some doubts about the characteristics that seemed to make for success in the Indiana Quaker ministry. Writing to a sympathetic alumnus in 1956, Jones expressed his preference for a "genuine Quaker pastor who has a concern to keep our Meetings Quaker" over the "vigorous doorbell pusher" who seemed to be the type most admired in the yearly meetings. But Jones also believed that a new generation of liberally educated Quaker pastors might be able to bring new life to American Quakerism, especially in the Midwest, a conviction that Trueblood shared. So together they raised money for scholarships, cajoled a cantankerous but well-heeled Spiceland Friend into donating the endowment for a preaching prize, and lectured Indiana Quakers at every turn on the need for a sound liberal arts education for everyone entering the ministry. The results of their efforts were uncertain. On one hand, some of the most influential and successful Quaker pastors of the post–World War II era, such as Lorton Heusel, Wayne Carter, Jack Kirk, and Thomas Mullen, were alumni of this period. On the other hand, there was a consensus in the 1950s that the Quaker colleges were not meeting the demand for ministry.[39]

Finally, Jones tried to be sensitive to the yearly meetings by bowing, whenever possible, to their moral standards and sentiments. Thus he continued the limits on campus smoking and the ban on campus drinking and the expectation, made clear to faculty, that they were not to serve alcohol to students at social events in their homes. Public meetings and athletic events did not take place on Sunday. Card playing was banned in the Commons, and gambling all over campus. Even plays with suspect titles like T. S. Eliot's *The Cocktail Party* had to be screened and cleared by the administration before they could be performed. Jones brought fervent evangelical ministers like Paul S. Rees, an associate of Billy Graham, to campus, and joined a committee to invite Graham himself to Indiana in 1956.[40]

Still, problems appeared. Some Friends complained that faculty were allowed to smoke at all, anywhere, at any time. Others condemned sanctioning anything but religious events on campus on Sunday. A Friend from Ridge Farm, Illinois, criticized the college for no longer holding revivals with altar calls. One minister was outraged by the performance of James Thurber's *The Male Animal* at Homecoming in 1948 because it included scenes of drinking without concluding with a clear total-abstinence statement. Individual faculty came under attack for un-Quakerly appearance or habits. And there were always fundamentalist preachers presenting highly colored versions of events on campus. Typical was one who told a very conservative Friends meeting in Howard County, Indiana, that he had been bodily ejected from the campus for preaching second-experience holiness, a subject dear to many Indiana Quakers. Jones dismissed the story as pure fabrication, but such problems persisted throughout his presidency.[41]

It is not clear how much Jones affected relations with the yearly meetings. The number of students from the two yearly meetings in 1958 was about one hundred, lower than in 1940, and those from the East now outnumbered those from Indiana. Five years into his presidency, financial support from the yearly meetings was still meager and limited to scholarships for their own students. In 1956, Dean of Students Eric Curtis was still noting the "fairly frequent reports we get of ruffled relations with our Quaker area." In some ways, Jones's success in other areas probably undermined his effectiveness in this one—as the base of financial support and students expanded steadily throughout his presidency, dependence on the yearly meetings declined.[42]

Perhaps the most delicate work that Jones undertook with the yearly meetings was the expansion of the board of trustees. Its composition had not changed since 1915—Indiana and Western yearly meetings each appointed six members, while the alumni association elected three.

Jones saw the board as one of the college's weaknesses. Homer Morris reinforced his opinion, arguing that the board often needed certain types of experience or expertise that the two yearly meetings could not provide. Jones also worried about the quality of the yearly meeting trustees. In his view, far too often they were Friends pushed by factions because of their pronounced evangelical views and willingness to support an agenda, usually relating to smoking or dancing.[43]

There were various ways of dealing with the situation. The alumni advocated increasing the number of alumni trustees to six. That, however, was acceptable to Western Yearly Meeting only if the yearly meetings confirmed them. The alumni association, on the other hand, was wary of giving the yearly meetings any power over its appointments; they feared that fundamentalist factions would force narrow appointments. The fears of both sides were probably unjustified, as Homer Morris pointed out at the time. Between 1915 and 1947 all of the fifteen elected alumni trustees were Friends, all but two members of Indiana or Western yearly meetings. The yearly meetings, in turn, nearly always appointed alumni to the board. The result was that the number of alumni trustees increased only by one while Jones was president.[44]

Instead, Jones moved on two other fronts. One was to add at-large trustees. The board would nominate them and the two yearly meetings would confirm them. Morris's argument about the need for special expertise apparently was convincing. Charles A. Reeve, an Indianapolis Friend who had been on the board for two decades, commented that now there was an opportunity to have more businessmen and fewer Ph.D.s. The first at-large trustee was Hagerstown industrialist Ralph Teetor, appointed in 1949. He was followed in 1950 by Harry J. Carman, dean emeritus of the college at Columbia University, chosen for his ties with foundations. By 1956 there were four at-large trustees.[45]

As for the yearly meeting trustees, Jones moved cautiously but definitely. One change that the board made was to limit appointments to three three-year terms, making for greater flexibility and ending the tendency of the yearly meetings to appoint the same people indefinitely. A "grandfather clause," by which limits did not apply to current trustees, shielded the feelings of current board members. Jones also took steps to influence the yearly meeting appointments. He convinced the yearly meetings to place board nominations in the hands of special nominating committees. Publicly Jones said that this put the decision in the hands of "the most thoughtful and experienced members of the yearly meetings" who "asked the Earlham Administration and Board to make suggestions for the Committee to consider." In practice it meant that Jones and his confidants in the two yearly meetings acquired considerable influence over appointments. For example, in 1946 Jones arranged to have an old classmate, Lester C. Haworth, then a vice president at Haverford, appointed to the board as a Western Yearly Meeting trustee. Haworth was a birthright member of the yearly meeting, but had transferred his membership to Philadelphia years earlier. Jones persuaded him to move it back to Danville, Indiana, then arranged for supporters in Western to propose Haworth. Western approved it, but some Friends felt that he had been forced on them. Jones had a number of such opportunities between 1946 and 1950, as several veteran trustees retired or died.[46]

The new members of the board often presented a striking contrast with their predecessors. When Albert L. Copeland retired as a Western trustee, his successor was Howard S. Mills, Sr., a 1920 graduate from West Newton, Indiana, who was building a milk route into a multimillion-dollar business. The Millses were neighbors and supporters of Elbert Russell, and Howard had been a devoted student of Alexander Purdy and Allen D. Hole. Thus he had little sympathy for the fundamentalist varieties of Quakerism, but was a wise and gentle presence on the board for half a century. Similarly, the ever-acerbic Edward D. Evans was replaced by his cousin, Isaac E. Woodard, another Indianapolis Friend. Although a grandson of Luke Woodard, Isaac was more open-minded. He enthusiastically endorsed Jones's ambitious plans. Others who came on the board in these years were as important. In 1951 Dwight Young, a Portland, Indiana, garment manufacturer was elected an alumni trustee. Ironically, he was a step-grandson of George N. Hartley, one of the Committee of Ten who had bedeviled Alexander Purdy. Young, however, was a steadfast supporter of intellectual freedom on the campus. Jones was also pleased by the election of another alumni trustee, Dorothy Quimby Peaslee, a Philadelphia Friend whose husband was a leader of the Philadelphia bar and an Eisenhower administration official. The Peaslees' social, business, and political connections, as well as their wealth, gave them considerable influence with Jones. When, in 1955, the yearly meetings agreed to add two more at-large trustees Jones saw to it that Dorothy Peaslee, who had served the maximum three terms as an alumni member, received one of the appointments.[47]

Thus Tom Jones sought to reaffirm Earlham's Quaker identity. By any standard, it was stronger when he retired in 1958 than it had been in 1946. The relationship with the yearly meetings had improved, partly from Jones's assiduous attention, partly from the power and energy of Elton Trueblood. For the first time in two generations the very visible leader of Earlham's religion program did not raise theological hackles with most midwestern Friends. But, in reforming the board, Jones was reducing the influence of the yearly meetings on the college. And Jones also presided over a transformation of Earlham's faculty, and the beginning of a transformation of its student body, that would decisively change the campus and its understanding of itself as a Quaker place.

The CPS Generation

In the spring of 1953 a young Haverford English professor, Wayne Booth, received an offer from Tom Jones to head the Earlham English department. Booth, not long out of the University of Chicago, had never heard of either Jones or Earlham, but many of his Haverford colleagues had, and they assured him that it was academically mediocre and that its president was an autocratic conservative. Acceptance would be committing professional suicide. Booth had no intention of doing that, but Jones was offering a substantial raise, and so Booth agreed to visit campus for one day. He still did not want to leave Haverford, but one day at Earlham became two, and then three, and finally four. And at the end of the fourth day, Booth accepted the Earlham position.[48]

What changed Booth's mind was the sense of intellectual excitement and commitment that he found among many of the Earlham faculty. For the most part unconcerned about publishing or academic career-building, they were instead totally dedicated to teaching. They had a strong sense of community; cooperation was the keynote of campus relationships. And allowing for the usual faculty skepticism about administrators, there was loyalty to and affection for Tom Jones.[49]

In Booth's mind, at the heart of this remarkable group were the faculty who had come to Earlham since 1946, particularly the conscientious objectors who had served in Civilian Public Service (CPS) during World War II. Historians of twentieth-century pacifism and social activism have seen the concentration of pacifists in alternative service as critical for a wide variety of postwar reform movements. CPS men who had worked in mental hospitals exposed abominable conditions and helped bring change. They were also uncompromising opponents of racial segregation. And they showed themselves quite willing to challenge authority through strikes and work slowdowns. As Charles Chatfield has noted, "The C.P.S. experience had a radicalizing effect on a significant minority of C.O.s. From witnessing to their social beliefs, these men began to act for social justice."[50]

Earlham had strong ties with CPS. Jones had been in charge of the American Friends Service Committee's administration of the CPS camps, with Paul Furnas as his chief aide. Other Earlham faculty, like Ernest Wildman and Murvel Garner, had been camp administrators. As CPS men were for the most part well educated, and a significant number were Quakers, it was natural for Jones to look to CPS veterans as potential faculty.[51]

The CPS men whom Jones hired did set the tone for the campus for a generation. Allen D. Hole (son of "Daddy" Hole) in French, Howard Alexander in mathematics, Warren Staebler in English, James McDowell in psychology, William Fuson in sociology, Thomas Bassett in history, Arthur Little in speech and drama, James Cope in biology, John Sweitzer in buildings and grounds, and Harold Cope as head of the food service were also CPS men. They also proved to be, by and large, among the campus's most effective and popular teachers. They brought to campus superb academic credentials, a willingness to experiment and innovate, and a high sense of idealism. Little, for example, told Jones that he wanted to use his drama teaching to advance the "brother-hood of man." That idealism would often bring them into conflict with Jones and the Richmond community.[52]

Not all of Jones's hiring was of CPS men. Indeed, he made it clear "that we can make a mistake by overloading the faculty with C.P.S. trainees." Several new faculty were veterans of the armed services, such as Leonard Holvik and Lawrence Apgar in music and Grimsley Hobbs in philosophy. Jones was always on the lookout for Quakers; some of his most distinguished faculty were Friends like David E. Henley, the sociologist who became academic dean in 1951, James Thorp in geology, Laurence Strong in chemistry, David Telfair in physics, and Hugh Barbour in religion. But he expanded his hiring horizons considerably beyond those of his predecessors. When he hired Wayne Booth in 1953, he was somewhat anxious because Booth was nominally a Mormon. Jones arranged for Booth to meet with some of the board. The trustees accepted Booth only after repeated promises that he would not proselytize in the classroom. When Jones hired William Stephenson, a biologist whose religious views were decidedly unorthodox, Jones persistently referred to him as "our Christian humanist," not because such a label was accurate, but because that was how Jones was comfortable categorizing Stephenson. In 1955, Jones hired Edward Bastian, an erudite University of Chicago instructor. Bastian was an agnostic, and was candid in his interview. After questioning Bastian and hearing nothing reassuring, Jones finally asked: "But you believe in integrity, don't you?" Bastian's affirmation was enough for Jones.[53]

Jones was also willing to do some unconventional things. In 1946, Elton Trueblood, on his way to Germany for the AFSC, encountered a journalist who identified himself as a fellow Quaker. The shipboard conversation convinced Trueblood that Landrum Bolling was someone who should be teaching at Earlham. Bolling had no doctorate and limited college teaching experience, but Jones subsequently hired him to teach political science; ten years later he succeeded Jones as president. A prime example was Arthur Little, who arrived to teach drama and speech in 1947 and to be one of the "weighty" campus Friends until his death. Several CPS compatriots had recommended Little, a Georgian who had become a Quaker during World War II. The iconoclastic Little lacked even a bachelor's degree, having been thrown out of the University of North Carolina during his junior year. Jones liked him, however, and gave him a post (at an exceedingly low salary). Little quickly established himself as a nonconformist, even returning in the fall of 1950 with a beard.[54]

Jones, however, also made appointments of non-Quakers that were more attentive to traditional academic qualifications and prestige. He was overjoyed to bring in Leonard Holvik with his Harvard degrees. Jones was also willing to scrape up a competitive salary for Joseph D. Coppock, a Harvard-trained economist who had been a State Department staffer. When Jones interviewed John Hunt, a Ph.D. candidate at the University of Chicago, he thought that he was hiring someone for an art position, when in fact Hunt's work was in literature. But he hired him and let him teach art history for a year before moving him to the English department.[55]

Relatively few of Jones's new faculty were women. The proportion of women faculty declined steadily in the 1940s and 1950s, as long-time Quaker women faculty like Ruby Davis and Anna Eves in English, Auretta Thomas and Martha Pick in languages, and Florence Long in mathematics retired. For the most part, mirroring national trends, which saw the proportion of women faculty steadily declining, men replaced them. Jones did hire some women. When he discovered that Kathleen Postle, the wife of Indiana University Center director Arthur Postle, had a doctorate in English, he offered a temporary position that became a twenty-five year appointment. Jones even broke his rule not to hire married women with children at home when he appointed Helen Hole, the wife of Allen D. Hole, Jr., to the English department. Helen Hole would prove to be one of the campus's leaders, retiring as Earlham's first provost. The faculty was not entirely free of sexism. One woman faculty member was quite sure that neither Jones nor most male faculty would have tolerated the same kind of assertiveness in a woman that they expected of a man. But another hired about the same time thought that Earlham compared quite favorably in this respect with other schools.[56]

Jones took great pride in the faculty he assembled. In 1956, reviewing his first ten years, Jones summed up: three out of four members of the Earlham staff had been hired since 1946. One out of four was an alumnus. One out of three had studied or taught abroad. People like

Arthur Funston, hired by Dennis without doctorates, were finishing them. Jones saw them as special in their dedication: "There is scarcely a faculty member who has joined the staff since the first of last July who has not assumed a financial loss and in some instances a lower status," he wrote in 1947. Two outside consultants concluded in 1956 that "there are so many manifestations of faculty alertness at Earlham that it is difficult to review all of them." Yet this celebration of the new wore on some of the senior faculty; "they feel that all the later administrations—the brash young men—may not adequately appreciate them," William Fuson noted.[57]

Not surprisingly, these new faculty were often determined to shake up teaching methods and introduce new pedagogies and programs to the campus. In this they had Jones's support. Although traditional in outlook himself, Jones also liked innovations, in marked contrast to his predecessor, and he publicized and praised them. There were many innovations under his presidency. One of the first was the Community Dynamics Program, which began in 1947, directed by William Biddle, a Columbia Ph.D. formerly of the U.S. Department of Agriculture. It attempted to apply theories and knowledge, especially from the social sciences, to community problems as close as Richmond and as distant as Puerto Rico, attracting national attention. Similar was a program in soil science that involved a number of faculty from the natural sciences, led by Ernest Wildman, who in 1941 had moved to a small farm, both as an experiment in simple living and as a demonstration of the possibilities of soil restoration. In 1952, James Thorp, a 1921 graduate whose wife was a granddaughter of Eli and Mahalah Jay, and one of the leading figures in the field, took over its direction. There were also new programs in elementary education, agriculture, and nursing, the last in cooperation with Reid Hospital in Richmond.[58]

Perhaps more important were improvements in the traditional disciplines, making them more rigorous and exacting. After Wayne Booth took over as chairman of the English department, he established a freshman humanities program modeled on one that he had directed at Haverford. Its basic features were a diverse reading list, small group discussions, and tutorials in which students critiqued each others' papers. Similarly, the Social Science Division set up a wide-ranging introductory survey, but it proved short-lived. Across the curriculum, new faculty experimented with discussion techniques, in-class debates, and new textbooks. In some cases, change meant cuts. When Joseph Coppock assumed direction of the economics department in 1953, he eliminated bookkeeping and stenography classes and replaced them with more coursework in economic theory and statistics. Sometimes attempts to be innovative were the stuff of campus folklore, such as when Thomas D.S.

Bassett introduced a lecture on westward movement in an American history class by wearing a coonskin cap and playing a guitar while singing "The Ballad of Davy Crockett."[59]

The Jones years saw a fundamental shift in Quaker spirituality on the campus. While the presence of Elton Trueblood strengthened, at least for a time, an evangelical understanding of Quakerism, the ultimate effect of Jones's new Quaker faculty was to head Earlham's Quaker spirituality away from that of Trueblood and pastoral Friends.

From his arrival, Trueblood was charged with revitalizing chapel and worship on campus. Under Jones, the chapel program, now officially "assembly," was cut back to twice a week from three, with Tuesday's "convocation" being secular and Thursday's chapel religious in nature, and attendance required at both. By all accounts, Trueblood succeeded, at least in the first few years. He used his far-flung connections to bring in a wide variety of speakers. Trueblood saw the "unapologetically devout" chapel program as vitally important. "In my own college we probably put more concentrated effort into this program than into any other single aspect of college life, and we feel justified in the results," he wrote in 1949. Some students appreciated the programs. One argued that there was a clear divide between "Chapel BT (Before Trueblood) and AT (After Trueblood), and greatly for the better." By 1957, however, a writer in the *Post* demanded more variety. Chapel, she said, was boring, a mixture of the missionary, the educator, and what another student called "The Learned Fog." The first possessed "the shrinking timidity of a rhinoceros, and a voice like a two-handed saw," while the last, "an intoxicated kangaroo," said "absolutely nothing coherent—though in a most convincing fashion." Most of the speakers, however, were "the Methodist, Baptist, and Presbyterian ministers of identical small town communities."[60]

Trueblood also played a critical role in building a meetinghouse, something that had been discussed for literally a century. A gift from the Stout family of Paoli, Indiana, made possible its construction, which was completed, in large part by volunteer labor, in 1951. For many, the experience of students, faculty, and administrators working with Friends from local meetings was a vital element in community building. In 1952 Trueblood began regular Sunday services after the pattern of a pastoral Friends meeting. He was the most frequent speaker, but there were numerous guest preachers as well. Attendance was high when Trueblood preached, with numerous townspeople turning out.[61]

Despite the heightened profile of pastoral Quakerism on campus, it was the unprogrammed meeting that grew most rapidly during Jones's tenure.

The number of students from eastern yearly meetings increased steadily, strengthening this tendency. So did the new Quaker faculty, whose sympathies were overwhelmingly with the unprogrammed tradition.[62]

The most potent symbol of liberal Quakerism's place at Earlham was the creation of Clear Creek Monthly Meeting. The small, unprogrammed worship group that met in Carpenter Hall took on new life after World War II with the influx of new Quaker faculty. Most, although not all, of the CPS men and their families joined, as did the Truebloods, Joneses, and Furnases. As Elizabeth Furnas, Paul's wife, put it: "Our main interest . . . is to have in these parts a Friends meeting based on silent worship which can represent that historic testimony of Friends." Some pastoral Friends resented what they perceived as an air of superiority on the part of some Clear Creek people. Millard Markle, no longer a "heretic" but the clerk of Indiana Yearly Meeting of Ministry and Oversight and a senior West Richmond Friend, argued that Earlham needed to accept and improve the pastoral pattern, not disparage it, even implicitly.[63]

These questions remained relatively minor so long as they involved only an informal worship group. The rub came when the group decided to regularize its existence and become a monthly meeting. The prospect made Jones and some other Friends on campus nervous. He feared that to have the meeting take on official status would discourage non-Quaker students from attending. More vexing was the problem of affiliation. Indiana Yearly Meeting was entirely pastoral, and many questioned how well an unprogrammed meeting would fit into its structure. Markle told Jones that to set up a meeting "alien in its loyalties to Indiana and Western Yearly Meetings" would "seriously jeopardize the best interests of the college." Others were open to the new monthly meeting, but opposed suggestions that it follow the model of many new Quaker meetings established after 1910 and be independent and unaffiliated. That, they worried, would convey "aloofness, separateness, and independence" from Indiana Yearly Meeting, "as [though] neither we or they were worthy of Christian fellowship," as one concerned Friend put it. The result would be more strain. The solution was ultimately to form Clear Creek as subordinate to West Richmond, then have West Richmond "set off" Clear Creek as a monthly meeting. After the Stout Meetinghouse was completed, it became Clear Creek's home. The place of the Clear Creek Friends in Indiana Yearly Meeting was always awkward. The meeting quickly established itself as the most liberal in the yearly meeting. Nevertheless a number of Clear Creek Friends became active in both the yearly meeting and the Five Years Meeting.[64]

The Quaker faculty manifested their faith in various ways on campus. Some Quaker commitments clearly nettled Jones, even though the issues were minor. In the fall of 1946 Jones asked the faculty to wear academic regalia for the opening assembly. Ernest Wildman asked to be excused, saying that "such finery was not in agreement with Quaker ideals of simplicity and democracy." Jones granted his request, but grumbled to Wildman that such scruples were relics of the days of broad-brimmed hats. William Fuson, the CPS veteran and sociologist, thought it unacceptable to have a formal presidential residence on campus. It "would tend to make a President the symbol of Earlham in the way in which a bishop is the symbol of a hierarchical church." The stated aim of "simple elegance" was to him "uncongenial with Earlham standards." Others objected to financial contributions from sources they thought inappropriate, such as the American Legion.[65]

When faculty discussed matters of faith, they usually, with the notable exception of Elton Trueblood, were found on the liberal-modernist side of the theological spectrum. They normally did not speak openly of personal faith in classes; students even of Trueblood are hard-pressed to recall him dealing with it in the classroom. In more private settings, however, it was common. Faculty were also often called on to discuss the nature of Quakerism and Christianity. A good illustration is found in the Quaker Lectures delivered at Western Yearly Meeting by David Henley, Thomas Brown, and William W. Clark, in 1948, 1951, and 1952, respectively. In his address, Henley embraced classic modernist positions: the love of God manifested in Christ, that of God "in every person, regardless of place, race, or class," God's use of "the peace-making, spiritual, democratic method for men's salvation," and "the creation of a world of Democratic Brotherhood." Brown told his audience that people were at their best when they loved each other, and that the best examples in recent times were Albert Schweitzer and Mohandas Gandhi. Clark, speaking on "The Practice of Jesus," blasted the increasingly influential neo-orthodoxy of Reinhold Niebuhr and argued that to follow Christ was to be a pacifist and visionary on the side of the underdog, rather than to do the "practical thing."[66]

Such expressions were, for the most part, not especially controversial. The problems came when some faculty and students sought to translate these beliefs into actions. To be sure, Jones and the trustees encouraged this in many cases; Jones pointed proudly to "the emphasis we place on Christian social attitudes in the training of students." He urged David Henley to explore the possibility of a college program in industrial peacemaking. He made the development of an interest in race relations in the two yearly meetings a priority, and he encouraged students to volunteer at the Townsend Center, which served poor blacks in Richmond. Students and faculty went to Cuba and Jamaica under the auspices of the AFSC to help build meetinghouses and community centers. Jones regarded the Campus Peace Fellowship and the Earlham chapter of the Fellowship of Reconciliation as firmly within the Quaker tradition, even when he disagreed with them on specific issues. As will be seen, he had his limits, limits that the trustees shared. As one of them put it, the challenge was for Earlham to emphasize "the basic philosophy of Quakerism . . . without being *stinkingly nice.*"[67]

There were many students especially who were determined to be, in these years, "stinkingly nice." For them, activism for racial justice and peace was the essence of Quakerism. They would provide Jones with some of his worst headaches and Earlham with some of its most pointed controversies.

Race and Peace

The first of these controversies involved a revival of interest on campus in combating racial segregation. It was ironic in casting Jones in a relatively conservative role, applying brakes and declaring limits to student activism, since he had come to Earlham amidst fears that he would be a radical on racial matters.

One of the hard questions that the trustees posed to Jones while interviewing him in 1945 concerned his attitudes toward Dennis's racial policies. Pauline McQuinn, one of the Indiana Yearly Meeting trustees, worried that Jones would invite problems. "The very fact that he has been president of a Negro college will cause many patrons of Earlham to fear that he would use Earlham as an experimental ground for interracial relations," McQuinn warned Charles Woodman, "or what is more probable that he would be a drawing card for many negro students and frankly I don't think we are ready to go that far." Woodman assured McQuinn and Lilith Farlow, another doubter, that "Jones told us that he would have no inclination to make Earlham an experiment station on inter-racial issues." Jones was "thoroughly aware of the position which a great majority of Earlham's alumni and constituents holds on this question," and thus would uphold Dennis's policy.[68]

Such fears proved unfounded. The number of black students remained small, proportionately about the same in 1958 as it had been in 1946. Most were "Day Dodgers" from Richmond, many of them veterans. The nursing program with Reid Hospital also brought a few black women onto the campus for classes, but they also did not live in the dormitories. The greatest change was the arrival of blacks from Africa and the Caribbean who did live on campus. Still, they were few. Edd Lee, a black 1950 graduate who lived in Bundy Hall, remembered his happiness when there finally was a black woman living in Earlham Hall whom he could date. The conflicts that arose were largely the fruit of the idealism of some of Earlham's white students.[69]

Jones's racial attitudes are critical for understanding these events, but even contemporaries who knew him well disagreed in their assessment of them. Many expected that he would break with Dennis's policies; after all, he had been president of a black college for twenty years, and had long been interested in racial problems. In 1938 Jones had traveled in South Africa, reporting on conditions there for Friends in England. Yet at least some of the faculty found Jones a distinct disappointment. One described his racial attitudes as those "of a person who grew up in Fairmount, Indiana, in the time in which he did . . . *very* patronizing, very patronizing." They were "attitudes you would not have expected in a Quaker, much less the president of a Quaker college, much less the president of a Quaker college who had been president of Fisk University for twenty years." But this was not the prevalent view on campus. Most of the faculty thought that Jones was quite free of racial prejudice. It is significant that in the first catalog he produced after becoming president he emphasized that one of the fundamental facts about Earlham was being a place in which students of different races lived, ate, and learned together. And most black students of the period, when they objected to his policies, thought that the policies reflected the pressures on him from others, not his own convictions.[70]

Black students coming onto campus found relatively little overt prejudice. The college admitted black applicants on the same basis as others, and housed them in dormitories without regard to the race of their roommates, with one exception—new black students roomed alone until they found roommates. Jones justified this as avoiding unpleasant situations for the blacks involved. One black who lived in Bundy described the campus as an accepting place in which he felt no different from anyone else. Another found it a "friendly atmosphere." The faculty were unanimously opposed to racial discrimination; Trueblood spoke for them in writing that "the end of segregation is practically as certain as was the end of slavery a hundred years ago."[71]

Earlham was, in fact, in advance of many Indiana colleges of the period. Some did not even admit black students. Hanover College, for example, considered admitting an African American student in 1948, but reversed itself under pressure from students and alumni. Wabash College still refused to enroll blacks as late as 1952. Other schools, like Indiana and Purdue universities, allowed blacks to attend, but did not allow them to live in dormitories.[72]

Richmond in the 1940s was still a largely segregated city in a largely segregated state. Indiana's black residents, many of whom had come from the South to escape desperate poverty, "suffered the burdens of discrimination, segregation, and second-class citizenship in every aspect of their relationship with white Hoosiers," as one historian of the state has put it. Richmond was not in advance of the rest of the state.

Custom restricted blacks to the north side of town, with its "old and deteriorated houses" and "unpaved, undrained, unlighted" streets. Realtors routinely steered black customers away from certain neighborhoods, no matter how affluent they might be. Most blacks worked, as one remembered, in the "fire department, mail carriers, then you could get in the foundry and then a janitor." Another resident agreed. "Richmond was like other places when it comes to employment. There were very few minorities hired and generally when they were hired they were not given the best jobs." Schools were not legally segregated, although housing patterns concentrated blacks. The high school opened activities to all students, but it set a racial quota for the basketball team. Almost all public accommodations were segregated. The YMCA did not admit blacks, although the YWCA did. No hotel in town took black customers, nor did most of the restaurants. It was a particular affront to some that the city's leading restaurant, owned by an Earlham graduate and Friend, did not serve African American customers. The roller skating rink, bowling alleys, theaters, and swimming pools were for whites only.[73]

After World War II, there was an unprecedented commitment at Earlham to challenging these norms. That determination brought tension and conflict between the administration and the rebellious students. There was controversy over the desire of some students, mostly Quakers, to use "direct action" to combat segregation. Even worse, in terms of what Jones considered bad publicity, was the persistent interest of some students in interracial dating.

The first open tensions erupted in the spring of 1947. A number of students, working with members of the Richmond NAACP, embarked on a campaign to challenge racial discrimination in local restaurants, theaters, and businesses. Integrated groups entered restaurants and asked for service, or went to theaters and demanded to be seated together. They drew on the earlier efforts of pacifist groups like CORE (Congress of Racial Equality) during World War II. Several of those involved were CPS veterans. The activism of the students upset Jones, who believed it both unwise and contrary to Quaker principles. To him, such "direct action" tactics were unduly confrontational and coercive. When groups picketed two restaurants in May 1947, Jones responded harshly. He forbade students to take part in such demonstrations, at least as Earlham students. He would encourage them to discuss and study racial problems, but would not condone attempts to change local conditions through any means other than discussion.[74]

Thereafter, student confrontations with Richmond's segregation were more low key and spontaneous, but they did continue. Robert Goens, a black student in the late 1940s, remembered one occasion when an integrated group of football players, most weighing over 220 pounds, went to the Tivoli Theater and sat down together in the white section of the balcony. An usher promptly appeared to tell them that the section was "reserved." "Where do you recommend we sit, it's full over there?" Goens asked. "I really don't care," the usher replied. Goens nodded to his football buddies and then told the usher, "You can take your ass downstairs or we're going to throw you over the banister." The usher disappeared.[75]

The most divisive, if not inflammatory, racial issue in these years was interracial dating. For many alumni of this era it is still an exceedingly sore point; they find it incomprehensible that Earlham bowed to the standards of a racist society and officially "discouraged" it. The policy was at the center of considerable debate on campus, and often put the administration on the defensive with liberal Friends.

The college's policy received the endorsement of the faculty in April 1948, with the hearty approval of Jones and the board, including relatively liberal members like Homer Morris. While affirming that Earlham did not discriminate in admissions, housing, or participation in all aspects of campus life, it would act to discourage "repeated interracial dating likely to lead to love and marriage." There was considerable argument over what lay behind the college's policy. Jones, both publicly and privately, defended it as an exercise of the college's parental role: "It is too serious a matter to enter into lightly." Jones himself said that he did not think that two mature people were incapable of entering into such a relationship, but that college students were not that mature. "Without maturity, interracial and intercultural contacts become dangerous or impossible," he wrote. "Complicated social processes involved in immature interracial and intercultural situations often lead to heartbreak." Lester Haworth agreed; interracial marriage was so stressful a commitment that undergraduates could have no conception of what they faced. Others close to Jones advanced other justifications; William J. Reagan, an alumnus and close friend of the president, worried that too many interracial relationships would bring a reaction in the two yearly meetings that would limit black enrollment. Fear of negative reactions off campus probably was important; even those who bitterly opposed the policy assumed that donors drove it. As one student put it, Earlham had "sold its soul for a million dollars."[76]

The administration saw itself as gentle and long-suffering in enforcing the policy, but students perceived it differently. One woman remembered that just for walking across campus holding hands with a black man after a dance she was called in by the dean of women and sternly warned never to do such a thing again. "It made me feel dirty and it made me feel angry," she recalled. One black student wrote indignantly to the Administrative Council that "social relations at the College have reached a new low. If I can no longer go to a dance, or any other college function with a person of my own choosing . . . then I think Earlham College does discriminate against Negro students." Some black men admitted that they took pleasure in tormenting administrators. Robert Goens remembered being called into the Dean of Men's Office with some friends after they were seen walking with white girls. "You can't be seen walking across campus with a white girl," the dean told them. "So she's white. What's that got to do with it?" Goens replied. "We always had an answer. Hey, we were all loaded for bear when we'd go in there, . . . and by the time we'd leave this guy'd be pulling his hair out."[77]

Three cases became serious, in the administration's eyes. The first, in 1948, involved Veronica Giessler, a white Quaker, and Madison Shockley, a black veteran. When the couple ignored warnings from the deans, Elton Trueblood was called in to "counsel" them. When that failed, he called Giessler's mother, only to be thrown into consternation when she sided with her daughter. A conversation with Jones went equally badly. Finally, faced with a threat of expulsion, Giessler backed down. Another interracial romance in 1950, again involving a white woman, Elsa Carter, and a black man, Wilfred Doty, ended when Jones refused to allow Carter to return to campus until after Doty graduated.[78]

The greatest controversy, however, came in the spring of 1952, when Grace Cunningham, the daughter of Clarence Cunningham, the college's first black graduate, and Robert McAllester, a white conscientious objector from Ithaca, New York, announced their engagement. Both were seniors, and did not plan to marry until after graduation, but Jones viewed their action as an act of defiance, a situation "created deliberately by the couple with a lack of care for the problem of the college." In fact the administration was torn and uneasy. Dean of Men Eric Curtis was willing to enforce the policy for consistency's sake, but privately told Jones that he thought it unchristian. Allen D. Hole asked Jones if the college would act against an unwise engagement by members of the same race. Still, the Administrative Council backed Jones, and on the evening of Sunday, April 19, summoned Cunningham and McAllester to tell their story. The administrators present emphasized three themes. The first was that the two had no conception of the problems they would face. David Henley told them that "you will have tragedy and suffering, and you may blame us for not interfering earlier." Curtis worried that hundreds of students would be withdrawn by anxious parents, and that the reaction of alumni would be overwhelmingly adverse. Paul Furnas agreed. "It came as a shock to me to learn alumni and parents would feel so strongly about interracial matters," he told those present, "but I have either to work with that fact or turn over the administration to someone else." Jones was blunt: "I will not override constituencies." Finally Jones saw a clear violation of college rules that demanded some action. Faced

Addendum

Following the publication of this book, Veronica
Giessler Nicholson offered the following version of
the events related on page 206:

"Veronica Giessler Nicholson adamantly denies that she
backed down under pressure from Jones, Trueblood,
and other administrators. After numerous conferences
with authorities, she and Madison Shockley agreed to
modify their on-campus contacts to situations in which
other people were present, but not to limits on contacts
off campus. She was clear that she was not compromising her convictions, which were in opposition to
Earlham's interracial dating policy. Indeed, by her
account, she responded to Jones by threatening to
expose Earlham's practices in the black press."

with an implicit threat of expulsion halfway through the last semester of college, McAllester left campus with the understanding that both would be allowed to graduate in June, which they did. Soon afterwards they were married in the Ithaca Friends Meeting, and, Jones's fears to the contrary, remain so.[79]

The Cunningham-McAllester case attracted nationwide publicity. Newspapers around the country picked up the story, as did *Time* magazine. Warren Staebler, in Rome on sabbatical, read about it in an Italian newspaper. The faculty, board, and alumni association all endorsed the administration's handling of the situation. But there were numerous and vociferous critics, on and off the campus. While faculty doubters muted their opposition, students, alumni, and liberal Friends generally did not.[80]

There had been protests against the policy as early as 1948. A survey by one of William Fuson's sociology classes showed that a majority of students favored permitting interracial dating. (Day Dodgers were the most likely to object.) A religion professor claimed in 1950 that a majority of the faculty opposed the policy. Criticism ebbed and crested; in 1951 one writer in the *Post* hopefully opined that the question had "settled down into a satisfactory compromise." But the Cunningham-McAllester case "set off a wave of protest and feeling." One student blasted the administration for perpetrating a "legal injustice" and began fasting in protest. When rumors spread that the couple would not be allowed to attend commencement there were calls for a boycott. Quakers across the United States protested, as did AFSC officials, African American newspapers, and the NAACP. A testy Jones dismissed his chief critic, the *Indianapolis Recorder*, as a "radical negro newspaper," when in fact it was relatively conservative by the standards of the black press. But it was blistering in its criticism of Earlham on this matter.[81]

Interracial dating continued to unsettle the campus for the rest of Jones's presidency. A year later Jones removed the editor of the *Post* for running a story that Jones thought unduly critical of college policy. Criticism from Quakers around the country continued. One Friend in Columbus, Ohio, told Jones that "the finest tenets of Quakerism are being violated so as to increase the appeal of Earlham to your building program. This seems very like selling one's birthright for a mess of pottage." Another called the policy "downright reprehensible"; yet another compared Jones to Sen. Joseph R. McCarthy. There was persistent student protest. In 1953 and 1956 Henley and Curtis met with student groups to hear their criticisms. When the two deans cited "outside social pressures," the critics responded that "if Earlham is to be a leader among colleges, then she is being hypocritical if she yields to pressures of society. . . . She must go all the way or close to maintain her standards and ideals." A 1958 survey showed that 82 percent of the student body were now opposed to the policy. In fact it did not long survive Jones's retirement that year.[82]

It is important to view these events in context. Jones was apparently convinced that he was moving as fast as he could without alienating alumni and midwestern Friends who were, he always pointed out, also a part of the Earlham community. He always had before him the example of Cecil Hinshaw and his "Holy Experiment" at William Penn College in Iowa. Hinshaw, in his commitment to pacifism, integration, and modernist theology, had alienated Iowa Friends and had been fired in 1949. Much of the faculty and student body had left with him, Robert McAllester among them. Jones was also convinced that Earlham "radicalism" was *hindering* integration in Indiana; he had been told that Earlham's interracial dating "notoriety" had convinced the trustees at Hanover and Wabash to continue bans on black students. One faculty member at another Indiana college, herself active in the Indianapolis NAACP, remembered her reaction to the Cunningham-McAllester case: wonder, not that Earlham discouraged interracial dating, but that there was *any* college in Indiana in 1952 where students wanted to engage in it. And there was always the overwhelmingly negative response of Richmond residents to the mere *sight* of an interracial couple. "Richmond is more akin to the South in its traditions, mores, and beliefs, than to the North," one student wrote in 1958. "The very strong reactionary elements in and around Richmond would *not* have to call in Klan reinforcements from points further south to disrupt the academic life of the college. There is the strength and determination to do so right here in this area. *A number of Quakers would be right beside them.*"[83]

So the college continued to be divided. On some racial issues there was broad agreement. A variety of black speakers came to campus: the chemist Percy Julian, Fisk University President Charles Johnson, the activist Quaker Bayard Rustin. Student groups visited Flanner House in Indianapolis, worked at Richmond's Townsend Center, and formed interracial "caravans" to visit local nearby Quaker meetings, "acquainting Friends meetings with Earlham's race policy and presenting a concern for the brotherhood of all peoples." Jones was convinced that "if you visited our campus, you would find as little racial prejudice here as on any campus in America." He thought that if he could only get students "out of the pressure group psychology," then "through love and reconciliation," progress would be made.[84]

There were other, less patient voices on campus. John Sweitzer, a CPS veteran and the head of buildings and grounds, urged Jones to recruit more black students and to hire a black faculty member. By 1958, the school was searching for one. Henry L. Anderson, a black student from Philadelphia, spoke for many on campus when he expressed his hope that "Earlham should be a generator that produces electric charges. . . . Every student should leave Earlham College with fifty percent of his future work devoted to bettering race relationships." In fact the two sides were now in place that would remain for the next four decades on a variety of issues. On one were the administration and some of the faculty, sensitive to what they perceived as hard realities, ever counseling patience and restraint. Other faculty and students would not wait, and were determined to press for what they perceived as justice regardless of the consequences. At least one sympathizer with the latter, Arthur Little, nonetheless counseled patience, since the triumph of justice was inevitable. As he put it, "the time and the temper of the faculty and student body, the very atmosphere of the place, move us on . . . toward a goal of real equality."[85]

If the Quaker commitment to racial equality presented Earlham with a challenge, that challenge was minor compared to the problems that the Quaker peace testimony presented. The determination of some students to take an uncompromising position of resistance to the draft divided the student body, created fierce resentments in Richmond, and left Jones scrambling to find some acceptable compromise. To aggravate tensions, Jones's refusal to give unqualified support to the resisters brought attacks from more fervently pacifist Friends. The onset of the Korean War brought new tensions and divisions. Even after the war's end in 1953, peace and pacifism continued to be contentious, emotionally debated issues on the campus.

One of the ironies of Tom Jones's presidency was that World War II was at least indirectly responsible for the college's great enrollment spurt. By 1946, the number of students had reached a record high, and a majority of the men were veterans attending under the G. I. Bill. Some had been students whose careers were interrupted by World War II, and who had now returned to finish. Others were new students.[86]

The veterans had a definite, albeit temporary, impact on the campus. For the first time, the college arranged to accommodate married students. Campus Village, better known as "Vetville," constructed from Army surplus materials, became a fixture back of the fieldhouse. The veterans had a definite impact on campus student culture. Those with families, often with jobs, had little interest in extracurricular activities. They certainly had little patience with Precedents or the mild hazing that was standard for freshmen. And some understandably looked askance at campus prohibitions on drinking, particularly in their own homes. They were overwhelmingly a steady, serious group who won the respect of the faculty and fellow students.[87]

Also coming to campus with the veterans of the armed forces were CPS veterans. The CPS men were ineligible for government aid, so Earlham itself offered them reduced tuition. The CPS veterans were far fewer in number than those from the armed services—there were seven times as many of the latter on campus-but the CPS men were bright, articulate, idealistic, and very open in their pacifist views. From 1946 to 1948 there was some tension between the two groups of veterans, never breaking out into any kind of incident, but very much present. In the eyes of most of the veterans, pacifism was entitled to respect as part of Quakerism. For that reason they voted overwhelmingly not to organize a veterans club or an American Legion post on campus. But many perceived a condescension on the part of the pacifists, and they resented it. After two years together, however, tensions eased, noticeably so in the opinion of Fred Valtin, Vetville's "mayor."[88]

But in the summer and fall of 1948, trouble broke out anew. The source was the Selective Service Act of 1948, passed that summer in response to heightened tensions over the Soviet Union. It reinstated the peacetime draft, with provisions for college students to be deferred until the end of the school year. Exemption for conscientious objectors was limited to religious objectors. Various pacifist groups, especially the AFSC and the recently formed Friends Committee on National Legislation (FCNL), had strenuously opposed it. They feared that worse might follow. Proposals for Universal Military Training, which would have required several months of military training at age 18 and reserve service until age 27, were also considered by Congress.[89]

In July, just after the new draft law was passed, a long-planned peace conference, sponsored by the Five Years Meeting and Friends General Conference, took place on campus. In the course of the conference, wide divisions became apparent, mirroring splits in the national peace movement. More conservative pacifists were determined to tie pacifism as closely as possible to religion, and to take advantage of the provisions for conscientious objectors in the new draft law. More radical Friends, many veterans of CPS, wanted to bear witness against the evil of the draft by refusing to register. The conference participants, struggling to find consensus, before adjourning delegated power to a subcommittee to summarize the conference's conclusions. The result was radical. Especially controversial was the sentence: "We warmly approve civil disobedience under Divine Compulsion as an honorable testimony fully in keeping with the history and practices of Friends." The advices saw refusal to register for the draft or to pay taxes used for military purposes as natural outgrowths of Quaker beliefs. Many Indiana Friends found such recommendations unsettling. Their standing as "law-abiding citizens" was important to them, and willful disobedience to law smacked of radicalism if not communism. Thus a number of midwestern Friends, like Errol T. Elliott, the editor of the *American Friend,* and Tom Jones, distanced themselves from the conference, claiming that it had no authority to speak for all Friends.[90]

Worse from the college's point of view was the presence at the conference of members of Peacemakers, a new interdenominational group committed to absolute pacifism. Someone placed a box of their pamphlets, an open letter to draft-age men calling on them to refuse to register, on one of the literature tables. When a college employee complained about its contents, Jones ordered it removed. Conference officials acquiesced, since the Peacemakers did not have permission to use the literature tables. By this time, however, at least a dozen had been picked up, and one fell into the hands of the local American Legion post. It called for an investigation of the college and the Peacemakers, labeling the pamphlet's circulation as a possibly "criminally seditious act," and hinting that the Peacemakers were a subversive group. The Legion did not contact the college before acting, and Jones pointed out that its statements were in error: Earlham certainly had not distributed the pamphlet to anyone. By this time, however, the Legion's protest was in the press, and Jones's denials never caught up.[91]

Had this been the end of the case, the tensions between the college and the American Legion might have faded away. But when classes resumed in the fall, the college faced a small group of students who, on grounds of conscience, refused to register for the draft. They were at the center of the most divisive controversy, as well as the most publicized incident of Jones's presidency.

Earlham's fall semester began on September 22, four days after the deadline for registration under the new draft law. Within a week, the college authorities learned that eight students had refused to register for the draft. Each of the men had informed his draft board that he was, for reasons of conscience, refusing to register. Jones had some hint that summer of what was to come when Ralph Cook, a student from Maine, was convicted of refusing to register and sentenced to two years in prison. Cook's father was a Quaker pastor, and both of his parents came from large and well-known Indiana Quaker families, so the case received considerable attention in Quaker circles. Jones privately expressed sympathy, and Cook's letters from prison won him considerable respect on campus. He saw himself following in the footsteps of the early Friends, and opposition even at Earlham did not deter him. "I can just hear them laughing at this letter and calling me hopelessly naive," he wrote. "I should rather be a little fool of God than a disillusioned worldly-wise."[92]

The eight other men still on campus shared Cook's idealism, although they were quite diverse otherwise. Five were Friends, one a Presbyterian, one a member of the Church of the Brethren, and one of the Evangelical United Brethren. In age they ranged from nineteen to twenty-five. Two were seniors, three juniors, two sophomores, and one a freshman. Four had been in CPS during World War II. At least two were married men with families. Several of the single men were living together at Quaker Hill. Ironically, probably all would easily have won exemption, if not as conscientious objectors, then as heads of families or ministerial students.[93]

Most of the nonregistrants left statements about their beliefs. Identical strains run through them—strong religious faith and a determination that as followers of Christ they could do nothing else. "I am convinced that the life and teachings of Jesus of Nazareth are the most practical and effective methods for destroying evil and redeeming people to the way of love," Lorton Heusel told his draft board. "I cannot visualize Christ walking into Selective Service headquarters and putting his signature on the draft law, one that denies the dignity of human personality and strikes at the root of individual freedom." The resisters felt that they were under no obligation to obey such a law. As Francis Henderson put it at his trial: "I believe there is a Higher Law, a Law of God . . . which all laws made by governments should conform to and in most cases, in my thinking, do, but in a few cases when that law does violate the law of God, as I see it, I must obey the law of God." The law of God commanded them to live as Christ had lived, forbade them to kill. "Since I believe that God is in every man, to kill a man would mean destroying part of God. Therefore, I believe that a man should never be killed by another under any circumstance," Steve Simon wrote to his draft board. Even to take advantage of the law's provisions for conscientious objectors would be an unacceptable compromise. As Armin Saeger wrote, "I feel that willfully to register under such a law would be to participate in and justify the government's act of preparation for war and by so doing deny the spirit of Christ as the guide of all human relationships." They denied any contempt for law. They were not, as Richard Graves told Tom Jones, "advocating a society in which anyone who disagrees with a certain law can simply disobey it." Instead, they wanted "a society in which everyone seeks to do that which is morally right, regardless of the consequences."[94]

The presence of the nonregistrants on campus left Jones and the board with decisions to make, and the position they took was the kind of compromise that Jones so loved to find in hard situations. The official stance was a formula that Jones used again and again in correspondence and press releases:

> As a college and a Quaker institution Earlham upholds the law, believing that representative government can only be maintained by democratic processes arrived at by intelligent and noncoercive methods. In accord

with its traditional position of respecting individual conscience, it holds in love and sympathetic understanding not only those who register under the present Selective Service law but even those who for conscientious reasons feel they cannot register.

While this position apparently satisfied most students, faculty, alumni, and Quakers, there were numerous critics. Jones himself found the nonregistrants' position difficult to understand. He spent considerable time trying to persuade at least some of the resisters that registration would involve no compromise of principle. He was not above pleading with them, arguing that they might well harm Earlham through their actions. But he never threatened any kind of disciplinary action against them, and he steadfastly resisted calls by some for their expulsion.[95]

While the presence of the nonregistrants on campus was common knowledge, nothing appeared in the press until November. The FBI was investigating, but the first arrests did not come until January 27, 1949, when three men were taken into custody. Three more were arrested on February 4, with the last two arrests taking place on March 4 and April 8. Once the arrests were made, the campus hotly debated the actions of the nonregistrants, while the eight men became the target of fierce attacks from the American Legion and from Rudolph G. Leeds, the owner and publisher of the *Palladium-Item*, Richmond's daily newspaper.[96]

Leeds was one of the wealthiest and most powerful men in Richmond. An exceedingly conservative Republican, he used the editorial page (and often the news columns) of his newspaper to score his enemies. "For . . . hatred at its best, particularly of Mr. and Mrs. Roosevelt, Joe Stalin, and the British, ask Rudy Leeds," a competing newspaper editorialized. One Earlham faculty member, himself conservative in his politics, thought Leeds simply malicious; Bernhard Knollenberg, the Yale librarian who had grown up with him, dismissed Leeds as "a spoiled boy who has grown old without maturing." Leeds had been a student at Earlham in 1901–1902, but before Jones became president he had shown little interest in the college. Jones, however, had assiduously cultivated him and had won Leeds's support for his early fund-raising.[97]

Leeds numbered "draft dodgers" among his numerous hates. When the arrests of the nonregistrants began, Leeds saw that the *Palladium-Item* covered them in highly unfavorable terms. "FBI NABS DRAFT DODGERS" was a typical headline. More than one story hinted that draft resisters had communist connections. When Jones gently protested, Leeds responded that the nonregistrants were "law breakers, criminals for what amounts to an attack on their country during hours of peril." He hoped that they would "serve time in the penitentiaries with other criminals."[98]

Leeds probably spoke for most Richmond residents. The nonregistrant position was beyond the understanding even of many local Quakers. Robert N. Huff, the college's development director, wrote that most alumni saw the nonregistrants as a "new breed of ingrates," and considered Earlham to blame for them. The American Legion once again launched a barrage of criticism, passing resolutions denouncing those who "openly flaunted their disregard" for the draft law, and demanding that the college expel them. A group of Richmond business leaders urged Jones not only to expel the nonregistrants but also to fire their faculty supporters. Even the campus and Indiana Quakers were badly divided. On campus, feelings ran high, especially in "Vetville." A *Post* poll showed that about 75 percent of respondents disapproved of the nonregistrants' stand. "If you are so against fighting for your country & your freedom, why then do you demand the right to vote? Some way of protecting your freedom," one critic commented. A writer in the *Post* called for their expulsion, arguing that because of the nonregistrants Earlham was "losing much of the respect and integrity it has built up."[99]

On the other hand, the nonregistrants also found supporters. Earl Robbins, a local attorney, volunteered his services. Several Indiana Friends contributed to legal expenses. A group of faculty made up a bail fund. Lorton Heusel remembered how, riding to Indianapolis on U.S. 40 with two federal marshals, he saw chemistry professors Ernest Wildman and George Scherer pass his car. He knew that they would be waiting at the federal courthouse with his bail money. One student sympathizer compared the nonregistrants to Christ. Clyde Harned, a 1926 graduate and leading member of Richsquare Meeting, even took on Rudolph Leeds, telling him bluntly: "Your editorials stink."[100]

It was in this atmosphere that the first trial in Indianapolis, that of Steve Simon and Rollin Pepper, took place on February 25. A group of sympathetic faculty and students had planned to attend the trial at the federal courthouse, a prospect that angered and worried Tom Jones. In the faculty meeting on Thursday, February 24, he blasted participating faculty for canceling their classes without permission. After considerable discussion, Jones backed down, and there was agreement that after seeing Simon and Pepper before the trial, the group would adjourn elsewhere to hold a Quaker meeting for worship, "to pray the defendants into probation," as one put it. That evening, however, Tom Jones called the faculty to tell them that no one would be able to see the two men before the trial, and so he had arranged for the group to hold a meeting at Indianapolis First Friends. About fifty assembled there the next morning. Those who had gone to the courthouse found an angry Tom Jones there, ordering them to leave. When he arrived at First Friends, Jones explained that the prosecutor had told him that the presence of a large group of supporters in the courtroom would anger the judge and bring a harsher sentence. Most of those present were skeptical, convinced that Jones was interested only in avoiding bad publicity. The trial did not go well. The judge knew little about Quakerism and had no sympathy for the two men. Both, pleading guilty, were released on bail by the mystified judge while he had a sentencing investigation conducted.[101]

The college, in fact, did escape bad publicity over the trial, but four days later, March 1, the Tuesday morning assembly raised tensions to new heights. The speaker, long scheduled for that day, was Milton Mayer, a Quaker, a former member of the faculty at the University of Chicago, and a staffer at Robert M. Hutchins's Great Books Foundation. W. C. Allee, the former trustee, wrote that Mayer had "a high reputation for being provocatively truthful"; Fuson called him "the most outspoken Peacemaker in the country." Mayer was an articulate, uncompromising pacifist with little tolerance for differing views. Jones, away from campus for the day, was worried about Mayer's appearance; he left instructions that William W. Clark, the religion professor in charge of the assembly, was to tell Mayer about the recent trial of the nonregistrants and plead with him "under the circumstances [not] to introduce anything of a controversial nature."[102]

Mayer, however, arrived with a speech in hand on "The Individual and the State," which, he claimed, Elton Trueblood had agreed would be his topic. Although he did not specifically mention nonregistration, Mayer's address was a brief for "absolute pacifism, absolute socialism, absolute democracy, and absolute Christianity." In his view, the United States was "a menace to the world." Answering questions afterwards, Mayer called one student who disagreed with him a Nazi, and another a bigot. As one faculty member put it, Mayer "blew the roof off Goddard. . . . The campus seethed for two days." All over it were groups of arguing students, with furious exchanges on the Opinion Board. The *Palladium-Item* once again went on the attack, and the American Legion had new reasons to call for investigations.[103]

Partly to undo the public relations damage, partly in the interest of "balance," the administration hurriedly arranged for a very different point of view to be presented by Col. Melvin J. Maas, the national president of the Marine Corps Reserve Officer Association. His subject was defense policy. Notice of the speech appeared widely, and Jones invited officers of the American Legion to have lunch with him and Maas after the assembly.[104]

There were about 850 people present for Maas's appearance on March 22. He was blunt in his remarks, arguing that "the worst warmongers are those who say they will not fight in defense of their home and country." Anyone who would not bear arms for his country had forfeited any right to share in the privileges of citizenship, Maas argued. As Maas proceeded, suddenly there fell from the top of the Goddard Auditorium stage a dead cat. Attached to a rope, it hung suspended a few feet above the colonel's head. Maas smiled broadly, saying only, "Well, at least someone fell for this speech." He continued without further comment, and received a huge ovation, probably more for his good humor than for the speech itself.[105]

Everyone assumed that the dead cat was some kind of pacifist protest. An infuriated Tom Jones, as red-faced and angry as anyone had ever seen him, was on his feet immediately at the conclusion of the assembly, calling the action "despicable and insulting" and promising stern punishment for the culprits, a sentiment the president of the Student Senate echoed. The immediate publicity, in Jones's words, was "disastrous." "DEAD CAT HALTS COLONEL IN ADDRESS AT EARLHAM" was the headline in that evening's *Indianapolis News.* Everyone's assumptions turned out to be wrong, however, both about the perpetrators and the long-term impact of the incident.[106]

The dead cat was not a political statement or protest, but a simple prank by four men: Howard Mills, Jr., James Fowler, Steve Edgerton, and Bill Ross. All were considered campus leaders; none was a nonregistrant or political activist. Maas had been scheduled at the last minute, replacing an Anglican Society program that was the cat's target. When they learned of the change, the four men tried to retrieve the cat (a stuffed specimen from the biology department), but found it stuck in the rafters. They were horrified when it somehow dislodged itself during Maas's speech. After the assembly, they went to Douglas Hoyt, the president of the Student Senate, and asked to be suspended. After talking with them, Jones agreed; they were removed from campus until the end of spring vacation on April 18, but did not lose any credits. The combination of circumstances—the basic humor of the prank, Maas's good-natured response, and the voluntary confession by the students—had what Jones called "a miraculous effect on public opinion both on the campus and in the Richmond community." By early April, Jones was writing that the incident had been "a blessing in disguise," turning "some of our unfortunate publicity into a rollicking laugh."[107]

In fact, nonregistration became less of an issue after March 1949. There were other trials of nonregistrants; some escaped prison sentences, while others did not. A few other students before 1955 found themselves with difficulties with the Selective Service. At least one from Richmond, Edwin White, whose application for conscientious objector status was rejected by his draft board, also went to jail. Jones took precautions against more bad publicity; he pressured Arthur Little not to produce Paul Green's *Johnny Johnson,* an antiwar drama, and he cancelled a 1949 visit by Bayard Rustin, the black Quaker and radical pacifist, on the grounds that his point of view had already been adequately presented on campus. Most of the college's constituents were satisfied. One alumnus, now a professor at Beloit College, wrote Jones that he would have enjoyed telling the American Legion to "go sit on a tack," but that Earlham's course was wise in "these days of low income, high prices, and now, accelerated witch-hunting." Peace activities continued on campus, with leading pacifists like Cecil Hinshaw, A. J. Muste, and (later) Rustin visiting.[108]

The most vehement criticism came from the most radical elements of the national pacifist community. The Fellowship of Reconciliation criticized Jones for not giving the nonregistrants "clear wholehearted support"; Marian Binford Sanders, the old American Student Union leader, called Jones's course "appeasement rather than action on principle." Mayer, who felt that the college had misrepresented him, berated Earlham in an article in the *Progressive*, accusing it of flagrant immorality in its policies on interracial dating and nonregistration. "They begin by betraying the Gospel of Jesus Christ; they wind up worshiping a pickled cat," Mayer concluded acerbically.[109]

Earlham and the Cold War

After 1949, issues of war and peace on campus became increasingly entangled with questions of Cold War politics and the response of Quakers to them. The outbreak of the Korean War in the summer of 1950 tied problems of peace to the quandaries of how to deal with communism and the Soviet Union.

At first glance, Earlham would appear to be the sort of place that the very atmosphere of the United States in the McCarthy Era should have devastated. The presence of the draft resisters, problems with patriotic groups like the American Legion (usually in the forefront of red hunting), the generally liberal outlook of the faculty, all boded ill. Yet in fact the college, with a few exceptions, came through relatively unscathed.[110]

The reasons for this were several. Jones was adamant in avowing that he would never hire a communist, since communist minds were closed to truth. This was by no means an uncommon position at the time; its victims were most often not those who were still party members, but rather those who had been involved in communist activities in the 1930s and early 1940s. The Quaker nature of the school also made a difference. The Quaker faculty, including the CPS men, because their pacifist and liberal views grew out of religious belief, had no such skeletons in their closets. Ironically, the only member of the Earlham faculty ever publicly accused of complicity in communist subversion was Elton Trueblood.[111]

Debates on and off campus, instead, were more limited. They involved questions that the college had confronted before—how far a
Quaker school could cooperate with the national fight against communism and still respect the Peace Testimony. They would test the limits of
dissent and free speech and loyalty. Probably most visibly, they would
focus on the faculty member who would, in the 1950s, become one of the
nation's leading academic defenders of McCarthyism.

Interestingly, communism had not been central to the controversy
over the nonregistrants. Subversion first became a major issue on
campus in the spring of 1950 through the *Indianapolis Star*, which,
under publisher Eugene S. Pulliam, was well known for its aggressive
red-baiting. In May, two of its reporters came to campus to interview two
German exchange students. Neither student spoke English very well,
and the reporters, in the words of trustee Ralph Teetor, "deliberately
irritated the individuals involved in the interview and misused their
statements." A sociology professor sitting in was so worried that he
called Tom Jones, who ordered the reporters off the campus, threatening to call the police if necessary. The next day an indignant Pulliam
telephoned Jones: "What in the hell do you mean by ordering my
reporters off your campus? Don't you know this is a free country and that
newspapermen can go wherever they wish to get a story?" Jones responded gamely: "I didn't know that your reporters were in hell, although they behaved a great deal as if they were. And I'll give you to
understand that no one can slander my faculty and students." Pulliam
was taken aback, telling Jones: "Well, you don't talk like a Quaker."
Pulliam in fact sent another reporter to campus who produced a much
more favorable story. The first account, however, again aroused the
interest of the American Legion, which asked Jones to explain the
article. Jones sent Robert N. Huff to present Earlham's side in what
amounted to a trial. This time the Legion was convinced and pronounced
the college free of any taint of subversion.[112]

The outbreak of the Korean War that summer brought a new element
of uncertainty to the campus. There were obvious challenges to face—
with the nation once again at war, there surely would be new draft
callups. With no debate, the board resolved that Earlham would "serve
the nation and the world," but "must be careful to provide that particular
contribution which its own heritage makes appropriate."[113]

In Jones's mind, the war in Korea was different from past conflicts,
since it was a "police action" under the auspices of the United Nations,
and Jones was passionately committed to the U.N. as the world's best
hope for lasting peace. To him, it offered the possibility of "world

community and peace through education and persuasion . . . backed up by police power." In his eyes, since this was a "police action" rather than a war, participation might not be a violation of the Peace Testimony.[114]

This enthusiasm led Jones later that summer to accept the chairmanship of the Wayne County division of the Crusade for Freedom, a nationwide effort to rally popular support for the war in Korea and to oppose communism. Although Homer Morris warned him that the Crusade was "a technique of the cold war, which is being used by the military," Jones refused to reconsider. Revealingly, he told Morris that "I have gone all out to do something positive to demonstrate that I am just as patriotic as those who feel that they must resort to military service." On September 27, Jones gave the main speech in a Crusade program broadcast on the Richmond radio station. With the strains of "The Battle Hymn of the Republic" in the background, Jones praised the Crusade and the efforts of the "United Nations police force in Korea."[115]

Three weeks later, Jones's devotion to the United Nations caused a major controversy on campus. On October 19, Jones spoke at an elaborate convocation at which the faculty presented a United Nations flag to the college. Jones praised U.N. actions in Korea with much the same rhetoric as his radio address, and at the conclusion invited all present to join him in a procession to the center of campus to raise the U.N. flag over Earlham. Some students were outraged; one claimed on the Opinion Board: "We have overthrown the accumulated wisdom of the ages for the accumulated wisdom of the Palladium-Item, and the teachings of Jesus of Nazareth for those of Senator [Homer] Capehart [a conservative Indiana Republican]." More upsetting to Jones was criticism from the faculty. Some of the CPS men dismissed Jones's parade as "the old rigmarole." Drama professor Arthur Little actually sent Jones his resignation that evening. To Little, the "plain sophistry" of Jones's actions that day would "lead the sensitive and intelligent student directly to cynicism, and it is not right for me to seem to give it backing by my silent preference." Jones talked Little into remaining. English professor Norma Bentley released an open letter to the faculty in which she denounced the presentation as unsuitable for a Quaker college. Finally Jones met with objecting faculty, but that left him still angry over what he perceived as unreasonable and personal attacks. The faculty, in turn, thought that Jones was "taking an American Legion, super-patriotic line." By winter, however, the internal feuding faded away in the face of a very public controversy.[116]

That controversy centered on Hsin-Yuan Tien, a Chinese student who had enrolled in the fall of 1949, transferring from William Penn after the failure of Cecil Hinshaw's "Holy Experiment." His father was an official in Chiang Kai-Shek's nationalist government who had fled to Formosa after the communist takeover in 1949. By his second year, Tien had attracted some notice on campus for his criticism of the Chiang government and willingness to defend some of Mao Zedong's policies; although Tien adamantly denied being a communist, in the atmosphere of the time that was enough for some to brand him one. The blow-up came in December 1950, when Tien was part of the evening Current Events course that William C. Dennis taught. The discussion focused on the Chinese intervention in the Korean War that autumn. Tien interposed a stark question: "What's wrong with communism?" This apparently struck a raw nerve with some of the Day Dodgers in the class, who afterwards called a *Palladium-Item* reporter to share the news of this "communist sympathizer" in their midst. The reporter, in turn prepared a story on the "Red Chinese" at Earlham; Leeds agreed to hold it up only when Jones argued that since the case involved questions of security and subversion, premature publicity might be harmful.[117]

The college thought that it had little choice but to bring in the State Department, which was supplying Tien with funds, and the Immigration and Naturalization Service. As Jones told the *Palladium-Item,* "the present international situation is so critical . . . [that] the college feels the necessity of keeping the government informed of this student's attitude." The INS, in fact, did begin a long interrogation of Tien, who was quite frank in acknowledging that he saw some good things in the communist revolution in China; by the end of January at least one INS official had branded Tien a "subversive" and was recommending that he be deported. To aggravate the public relations problem, Tien also was open in his agnosticism. This apparently was the last straw for Jones, who decided that Tien would have to leave Earlham because his "attitudes" were "hopelessly at variance with the ideals and purposes for which Earlham stands." Meanwhile, Tien's mere presence on campus made some nervous. Friends arranged for him to go to Thorntown, Indiana, to stay with a Quaker family, where a mob came close to forming when it learned of his presence.[118]

Neither Jones nor the college appears in a very good light in this incident. Jones moved relentlessly ahead with plans to expel Tien, despite pleas from professors who described him as a "serious, conscientious, courteous student" with "an openness and tentativeness of mind." Writing privately to Lester Haworth, Jones admitted that "ordinarily Earlham would stand on its reputation and again run the gauntlet of local criticism," but the case appeared so hopeless that the best solution was for Tien to transfer to another college. Tien's relationship with Corine Gray, a fellow student, which had been an annoyance to Jones long before, doubtless did not encourage him to do more on Tien's behalf. It was not difficult for critics to sense that fear of bad publicity drove Jones. "It is distressing to heart-sickness to observe the head-long pace at which our national democratic life is deteriorating today," one Friend wrote, "but one is double heart-sick when one observes . . . a Quaker college becoming a party to this unhappy process." The careful brief that Dean Edward Allen gave the faculty not to "be drawn into controversy or to provide chances to be misquoted" supports such an appraisal. Fortunately, the case came to a happy resolution. Tien was able to transfer to Haverford, where he graduated in 1953, and he did marry Corine Gray. Jones and other Earlham officials did offer aid in Tien's battle against deportation. After graduate study in Australia, Tien was able to return to the United States for a distinguished career as an academic sociologist.[119]

The only other incident involving direct accusations of subversion was almost comical, involving as it did Elton Trueblood, whose religious commitment and patriotism were absolutely beyond question. Early in 1954, Trueblood had taken a leave of absence from Earlham to become the head of religious affairs for the U.S. Information Agency. That summer, he found himself under attack as a communist sympathizer by a right-wing newspaper in Texas and by the American Council of Christian Churches, a small group of extreme conservatives headed by Carl McIntyre, a fundamentalist who was a fixture of the McCarthyite right. They cited comments that Trueblood had made about communal sharing of goods among the early Christians, calling his appointment "a slur upon us and our God-fearing people." Trueblood dismissed them with contempt; the group did "not have enough standing in American church circles to warrant further comment." In fact the incident was soon forgotten.[120]

The most notorious faculty member at Earlham in the 1950s was one who was at odds with most of his colleagues and who horrified not a few students and alumni. Once an uncompromising socialist and pacifist, E. Merrill Root became one of the nation's leading academic defenders of McCarthyism, winning the praise of such stalwarts of the postwar right as William F. Buckley, Jr., Max Eastman, Brent Bozell, and J. B. Matthews. In many ways, Tom Jones found Root useful in appealing to certain types of donors and in defending the college against charges that it was overly liberal. But he would also prove to be the focus for more outrage and demands for dismissal than any faculty member since Elbert Russell.[121]

Late in the 1930s, Root began an intellectual pilgrimage that transformed him from the campus's most outspoken leftist to its most prominent conservative. Root himself claimed that he had not changed; the world had. Colleagues remembered him speaking of the Spanish Civil

War from 1936 to 1939 as opening his eyes to the dangers of communism. Root himself left only a cryptic account, in which the "mediocrity of 'liberal' colleagues, their easy acclaim of the fashionable in life and literature, their conformity to the novel, the outre, the avant-garde" impelled him to the right. Like many other socialists, he was outraged by the Soviet-German Non-Aggression Pact of 1939. He also credited George Orwell's *1984* and Arthur Kostler's *Darkness at Noon,* both powerful anticommunist novels, as major influences.[122]

Root first attracted attention with a letter that appeared in the *New York Times* on February 28, 1949. By this time the nation was absorbed with questions about the extent of communist influence in American life, an absorption that eventually became McCarthyism, with its irresponsible tarring of the innocent in the pursuit of evil. Such fears had already led some states to impose loyalty oaths on teachers, and some private colleges and universities to move against faculty who were judged to be bad influences because of perceived communist ties. These actions drew protests from many anticommunist liberals, who saw them as an infringement on academic freedom.[123]

Root's letter was an articulate and biting statement of the extreme anticommunist position. "Membership in the Communist Party automatically disqualifies a man from intellectual integrity, and makes him an alien to truth. One might as well expect one of Hitler's storm troopers to instruct youth intellectually about theories of race," Root wrote. A communist was a member of a "militant power group" with a "fixed dogmatic scheme of rigid doctrine." Thus communists had no intellectual commitment to pursue truth wherever it might lead. For Root, the conclusion was inescapable: "All communists should immediately, without excuse, qualification, or argument, be dismissed from every scholastic and academic position in America." They were not, Root argued, "a vitamin but a disease of the mind and spirit . . . a mortal malady." As for those "dupes" who defended their right to teach, they were worse than communists, and deserved the "scorn of living intelligence and the contempt of all free minds."[124]

Root's letter attracted considerable attention and comment. The Committee for Constitutional Government, a vocal conservative group, circulated it as a pamphlet. Tom Jones told Root that he agreed with his views and planned to send copies of the letter to friends. But at least one old friend of Root, Homer Morris, was appalled. "I have difficulty reconciling this statement with the opinion of Merrill Root as I knew him twenty years ago," Morris wrote to him. In Morris's mind, the great threat to the United States was not internal communist subversion but the "fear hysteria" that was "spreading like creeping paralysis over the college campuses." In a reversal of the usual situation, board member Morris lectured Professor Root on responsibility: "Your letter will be a source of comfort and encouragement to the F.B.I. and every American Legion Post and reactionary heresy hunter in the country. Make no mistake about it; the heresy hunt is on. Your letter will give encouragement and stimulation in this movement." Root was unrepentant. "Would you allow a Nazi Bundist, or a Kleagle of the Ku Klux Klan to teach in school or college?" he asked Morris. Root countered Morris with his own warning: "I have found the forces of the Left far more hostile, far more intolerant, and far more underhanded than the forces of the right have ever been." Root concluded on a note that he would often strike over the next few years, that of the lonely individualist: "As a free mind, I have to speak the truth as I see it; if friends are unable to agree with me . . . that is the price I have to pay for being true to myself and to the truth that is more than myself."[125]

For the next three years, Root was quiet, but in 1952 he again burst into the public eye, and never left it while he remained at Earlham. In July, he published an article in the far-right weekly *Human Events*, "Darkness at Noon in American Colleges." It went beyond the abstract point of his *New York Times* letter—communists were unfit faculty—to argue that "collectivism is rampant in almost all colleges and universities in the United States." Anyone who believed in "economic freedom . . . and . . . hostility to the State" was an "academic outcast." The climate of American colleges, he claimed, favored "all that socializes, collectivizes, encroaches; all that reduces the uncommon individual to the hideous caricature called 'the Common Man.'"[126]

This article, along with others in a similar vein, made Root the most controversial person at Earlham. Over the next two years Root emerged as one of the Right's favorite professors. Root gave effusive praise to Sen. Joseph McCarthy, became a close personal friend of the House Committee on Un-American Activities investigator J. B. Matthews, and considered an offer to become the assistant editor of *Human Events*. His work drew accolades from prominent conservatives. "I wish we had an Earlham College in every state and a Professor Root on every college campus in this Republic!" wrote Sen. Karl Mundt of South Dakota, one of the Senate's leading McCarthyites.[127]

In 1953, Root received a grant from the Volker Foundation to develop his ideas into the book that was published in 1955 as *Collectivism on the Campus: The Battle for the Mind in American Colleges.* The foundation required that Root not reveal his source of funding, leading some on campus to speculate that Root's money came from "fascists." Jones cautioned Root that he had some concerns about "whether your study will be objective and fair or merely the collection of data to prove a point that you have already led yourself to defend." (In fact, when he saw

Root's finished work, Jones privately concluded that *Collectivism on the Campus* was deeply flawed.) Root claimed to find evidence of communist sympathies everywhere in colleges and universities, not just among outright communists but also among "fellow travelers" and "state liberals." In 1957 he followed this with another book, *Brainwashing in the High Schools,* which concluded that U.S. history textbooks were filled with subversive, anti-American sentiments. As two reporters for the *Chicago Sun-Times* summarized it, the book claimed that "most historians and college professors, most textbook authors and publishers, and a high percentage of public school teachers and administrators, some wittingly and others unwittingly, are distorting history, defaming the American heritage, turning the country into a collectivist and perhaps communist state."[128]

It is difficult to determine just how much influence Root's work had. Numerous speaking invitations came to him, mostly from conservative groups, although he also received invitations to debate leading liberals at places like Yale. *Collectivism on the Campus* generated relatively little interest; by 1955, when it appeared, repeated attacks and investigations had virtually obliterated open communists from college faculties. On the other hand, *Brainwashing in the High Schools* had considerable impact. One observer thought that Root had "more influence than any other in textbook censorship efforts." In Mississippi, the American Legion, along with the DAR and the White Citizens Council, actually hired Root to examine the textbooks on the state's approved list.[129]

While Root became a favorite of conservatives, he was a horror for liberals. Complaints poured in on Jones from around the country. "It is something of a body blow when one of our own group seems to say, 'amen' to the attacks being made against the colleges and universities," the executive secretary of the Association for Higher Education wrote to Jones. The president of Occidental College labeled Root "so intemperate as to be of questionable fitness for teaching in a liberal arts institution." Although Root remained a member of West Richmond Meeting, Quaker journals stopped publishing his poetry. On campus, fellow faculty were aghast over Root's views. One colleague even took to the Opinion Board to jab at the English professor. Root did find some student supporters, but most who were aware of his politics simply dismissed him as bizarre. When he ventured occasionally into the *Post,* other faculty responded with "blasts." Wayne Booth, the head of the English department, told him bluntly: "I wish you would stop writing your political articles." Even the relatively conservative Elton Trueblood avoided association with Root.[130]

Through all of this, Tom Jones was firm in supporting Root's academic freedom. Jones came up with a formula that he used in letters to Root's critics; he was "one of the most beloved and effective teachers on the

Earlham staff. . . . We agree with his right to speak, as we agree that persons who hold another point of view have a similar right to speak." At first, Jones enjoyed the flurry that Root caused among "collectivistic pressure group thinkers." He constantly assuaged Root's ruffled feelings, even while admonishing him to "stay close to the facts." But even Jones's heir apparent, Landrum Bolling, thought it "a terrible thing that Professor Root has associated himself with such lunatic fringe people as he has." Bolling charitably opined that Root, "something of a babe-in-the-woods in this political arena," was being used by others. Yet Jones was apparently never tempted to silence Root. "In dealing with a controversial subject like this, we will get it from both sides," he told Dean David Henley. "In the long run freedom of expression and concern pay off."[131]

Root's declining effectiveness as a teacher complicated the situation. Although he told a supporter that he hoped "to fill many young souls with a sense of eternity, to help them be free spirits who abhor collectivism," he did not bring his politics into his courses. But he was increasingly erratic, telling a reporter that a sure sign of communist sympathies was "a preference for British poetry over American." Root no longer corrected papers, emphasizing instead the unfettered "stimulus of creative powers." Since he almost never gave a grade below "C," advisors routinely directed their weak students into his classes. In 1958, 90 percent of the students on academic probation at the college were taking a course with him. Root himself may have sensed his declining power. By 1955, he was actively seeking ways to support himself by writing and teaching so that he could give up "the academic grind."[132]

There is no sign that Root ever had any doubts about his course. "I'd much rather write poetry than polemics," he wrote to a friend in 1955. "I hate awfully to be the one called to do the dirty work but I felt I had to do it." Yet Root himself seems to have had a strong sense that he was ever fated to be an outsider. "I have always been in the minority that is against every status quo," he told an admirer, "and a 'conservative' status quo would still find me afoot and light-hearted upon the new open roads of the world." He remained at Earlham until he retired in 1960.[133]

There were other manifestations of pacifism and peace activism during Jones's presidency, other times when red-hunters scented subversion on campus, but they were relatively inconspicuous. In retrospect, it seems difficult to perceive, given the fears and passions of the times, how the college might have proceeded differently. Most of the nonregistrants returned quietly to campus to graduate after serving their prison sentences, receiving little attention, even from the *Palladium-Item*. Faculty of the period, while well aware of the dangers of appearing procommunist or "subversive," never felt particularly threatened. In this Earlham apparently *was* different from many other campuses of the period, but this was probably because its "radicalism" on issues of peace obviously stemmed from religious commitment rather than subversive tendencies, and involved students rather than faculty. It was ironic that the faculty member most under attack in these years was the stalwart McCarthyite Merrill Root, but Root was never in danger of losing his job. Writing of the principles by which he was trying to lead the college, Tom Jones had told two alumni in 1949 that "insofar as these principles cause us to carry water on both shoulders, we gladly carry it. Insofar as they cause us to spill the water off of those shoulders, we also spill that water." In retrospect, it appears that relatively little was spilled.[134]

Toward Quaker Governance

Tom Jones liked to speak of Earlham as a combination of Quaker meetinghouse and scientific laboratory. From his arrival at Earlham, he pictured the Earlham idea as making the campus a "Quaker meeting writ large." That meant changes in the ways that trustees, administrators, faculty, and students did business on campus. The result, the conduct of the college's business by seeking "the sense of the meeting" in Quaker fashion, would become one of Earlham's most distinctive and jealously guarded practices.[135]

Jones's years at Earlham saw the culmination of the long struggle for institutional acceptance of the norms of faculty rights that had become standard in American colleges. By 1950, there was finally a sabbatical policy. The college joined the nationwide pension system for higher education, what is now TIAA-CREF. Group insurance was provided, as were scholarships for faculty children. Special funds were set up for travel abroad and to aid faculty in purchasing homes.[136]

The most significant development in this respect was the adoption, in 1955, of a policy on tenure and academic freedom. The first faculty Jones hired after the war were not anxious about these subjects. Jones assured them that the college effectively had a tenure system, even if it was not in writing. Anecdotal evidence is somewhat in conflict on this point. One professor remembered that his tenure decision in 1951 came after Jones had consulted discreetly with a number of people on campus. On the other hand, it became part of campus folklore how in six successive years Jones told Arthur Little: "Arthur, this year we can't afford to give you a raise, but I am going to give you tenure."[137]

There were few overt worries about academic freedom in these years. In 1948, several faculty, led by William W. Clark, formed a chapter of the

American Association of University Professors. This action was not in response to anything at Earlham, but instead grew out of a case at Evansville College, which had fired a professor for supporting the presidential candidacy of Henry A. Wallace amidst widespread charges that Wallace's campaign was tinged with communist support. Faculty at several Indiana schools joined the AAUP as a way of protesting the Evansville action. Jones's initial response was almost apoplectic, but he came to accept it.[138]

Faculty hired after 1950, however, were uneasy with Earlham's informality in regard to tenure and academic freedom, and urged the adoption of more formal policies. In 1953 a joint committee of faculty and trustees began a study of tenure and academic freedom. In February 1955 the board adopted a formal policy. The tenure system was the standard one for American higher education. The statement on academic freedom was the one that William C. Dennis had resisted so strenuously in 1940. These changes had the effect of moving the college closer to the rest of American higher education. The other changes in governance in these years, however, strengthened the college's Quaker distinctiveness.[139]

When Jones became president in 1946, he urged both the board and the faculty meeting to discard parliamentary procedure and instead use the methods of the Quaker meeting for business. Instead of motions and votes, it would be left to the presiding officer of the meeting to discern when the group had reached consensus. There were certain problems inherent in such a procedure. The Quaker business meeting was based on attempting to reach unity through the leadings of the Holy Spirit, with the clerk of the meeting discerning the "sense of the meeting," and, through it, the will of God in the particular matter at hand. It was one thing to do this in a group with a shared spirituality, quite another to attempt it in a secular setting. Versions of consensus decision-making had been employed in CPS campus, however, so Jones had the enthusiastic support of many of the new faculty. In both the board and the faculty meeting, the change was made almost without remark, and without any change in written regulations or bylaws.[140]

Even while Jones was making these changes in the name of democracy on campus, he kept other types of power firmly in his own hands. He was especially jealous of his control over hiring and retaining faculty. While his decisions were usually sound, there were some disasters, like Edward J. Allen, the academic dean whom Jones brought to Earlham in 1949 and who fled the campus after only two years. At first Jones also presided over the faculty meeting, although by 1950 he had largely delegated that duty to the academic dean. His secretary, Opal Thornburg, still served as recording clerk; some faculty grumbled that no matter

what happened in the meeting, her minutes reflected the president's
wishes. And as one English professor remembered, "When Tom Jones
wanted to take over and be autocratic, he did." Meanwhile, Jones's own
style created headaches for subordinates. While attractive in theory, his
open-door policy often meant in practice that the impulsive Jones over-
ruled decisions that other administrators had made, particularly the
long-suffering Paul Furnas and the academic deans.[141]

Early in 1955 the college, considering the possibility of applying for
several grants and having just completed a major self-study of the
faculty, decided to undertake a "management" self-study. Five "weighty"
faculty, all Quakers, were named to the committee: Paul Furnas; Harold
Cope, now the head of Accounting; John Sweitzer, the head of buildings
and grounds; Laurence Strong, a recent arrival in the chemistry department; and William Fuson of sociology. The study was exhaustive and
quite critical of certain aspects of the college's workings. It took the
faculty to task, for example, for endlessly second-guessing and debating
the findings of its own committees "so that Faculty Meetings have
achieved a regrettable reputation for verbiage and procrastination." It
made a number of suggestions about a new committee structure. Most
importantly, it called for the faculty to elect its own presiding officer,
pointing out that it was awkward, if not impossible, for the dean, often
appearing as an advocate of some policy, to discern the sense of the
meeting on it.[142]

It was Tom Jones, however, who was the subject of the most telling
criticism. While giving Jones ample credit for his accomplishments, the
report also detailed failings. As Jones himself summarized them, they
focused on his tendency to make quick decisions that conflicted with
those of other administrators. Moreover, the report concluded, "In his
effort to practice 'Quaker democracy' and to draw instructional staff into
various areas of policy making and administration, the President is
sometimes interpreted by the Faculty as having delegated more extensive authority to the Faculty and the committees than is always adminis-
tratively possible."[143]

Just before classes began in the fall of 1955, the committee invited
Jones and other administrators to hear a preliminary summary of the
report. An increasingly angry Jones listened to the criticisms; when Paul
Furnas finished, the president burst out: "Well, after this I'll have to
resign!" Some of the committee thought that Jones's threat was purely
rhetorical, but they agreed to soften some of the language. Meanwhile
Jones, on reflection, was forced to admit the justice of the criticisms. He
agreed to the changes proposed, including the formation of a Faculty
Affairs Committee to offer recommendations on hiring and tenure. Thus,

a generation later, and four years after his own death, the faculty governance plan that Homer Morris had first proposed in 1928 came to the campus. Characteristically, the once-affronted Jones promoted it as a model for other colleges.[144]

*

While attempts to bring Quaker procedure to faculty governance were, in the opinion of all concerned, quite successful, the impact of the "Earlham Idea" on student governance was much less certain. Jones and Trueblood valiantly struggled to convert the student body to their vision of a community of learning, and they won support from many students who found the ideals of a community run on Quaker principles appealing. The result was a new type of student government and an experiment with an honor system. But there were other students who were sure that "Quaker democracy" had no room for a strong-willed president like Tom Jones. And there were still others for whom high idealism held little appeal, who simply wanted to be typical college students, or to finish their degrees and get on with their lives, as was the case with most American college students between 1945 and 1960. The result was tension between different student groups, between what one called "the meetinghouse crowd and the Commons crowd." By the late 1950s, there was an increasing mood of student restlessness.[145]

By the 1950s, some of the older campus culture was breaking down. The Precedents Committee continued to exist, but its regulations were milder and were no longer enforced with corporal punishment. Class antagonisms had disappeared. Athletics, especially football, were less and less the focus of student interest and enthusiasm. There were new "traditions," the most worrisome of which for faculty was "Hell Day," the Friday before Homecoming when the sophomore class elected a "Hell Hag" to reign in competition with the Homecoming queen and embarked on a wave of pranks and practical jokes. The administration always disliked it—in 1951 the deans of men and women described Hell Day as a "mob-mentality" that included property destruction, smearing the campus entrance and the president's house with paint, tampering with fire-fighting equipment, moving bulldozers being used on construction projects, and even burning a cross! That fall the sophomores outdid themselves, actually setting fire to the newly tarred entrance drive and detouring traffic from U.S. 40 around the Heart. That was the end of "Hell Day," which became a much more restrained "Hecky Dern Day."[146]

The college's instruments for reining in mischief like "Hell Day" and making the "Earlham Idea" an integral part of student life were two, a change in student government and the institution of an Honor Code.

Elton Trueblood was intensely interested in both, especially the formulation of the campus Honor Code, and the latter embodied his vision of what a college should be.

A student senate had been formed under Dennis in 1944, but its constitution underwent extensive revision in 1946 and 1947. As the faculty approved it in the spring of 1947, the senate was a joint faculty-student group, with five faculty and twenty-one students representing various constituencies—the dormitories, the Day Dodgers, and Vetville. Perhaps most importantly, one of its committees had jurisdiction over disciplinary cases, making recommendations to the deans and the president, recommendations that they usually followed.[147]

The Honor Code was the subject of considerable discussion in the fall of 1948 before approval by the faculty meeting finally came. In its final form, it was similar to those at a number of other schools; Haverford's seems to have had the greatest influence on the Earlham drafters. The preamble emphasized the "Earlham Idea." The code itself enjoined students to act "honorably in all relations and areas of life." Those who witnessed a violation of campus regulations were required to confront the offender "and request that he report to the Honor Court." If that failed, then the Honor Court was to be informed. The court, made up of two faculty and five students, was to have jurisdiction over all aspects of "non-academic life." Trueblood hailed it as a "delicate balance of order and freedom." It would emphasize counseling, but could recommend expulsion or suspension to the administration, which had ultimate power.[148]

It is difficult to say how "Quakerly" these developments were. The senate constitution as adopted in 1947 and revised in 1950 assumed voting rather than Quaker business procedures. While the Honor Code made reference to Earlham's "sense of the meeting of the minds of faculty and students," it was clearly more indebted to the honor codes common at other elite colleges than to Quaker tradition. Indeed, while Quakers had always emphasized a high standard of integrity, "honor" was a word that was not commonly a part of the Quaker vocabulary. Significantly, the code did not attempt to define what "honor" meant.[149]

It is also difficult to judge how successful these attempts to make students embrace the "Earlham Idea" were. Jones publicly proclaimed that the honor system had succeeded admirably, but his private files show that he was often concerned that the senate Honor Court was lax in enforcing campus rules. After a few years, the "honor system" of not checking attendance at chapels and convocations was abandoned. Two consultants in 1951 found that many students rejected or ignored it. From the beginning there were student critics. In 1949 one blasted the code as a "sham"; honor, he said, could come only from moral conviction, not regulation. Another student two years later saw the Honor Code only as further proof that Earlham was "obsessed with the idea of sin." By 1957, it was the center of considerable controversy. The *Post* claimed that half of the students ignored its injunction to confront wrongdoers, while on the Opinion Board critics flayed it as "an informer system reminiscent of the Spanish Inquisition." That same year the faculty concluded that enforcement was far too lax. As for the senate, while elections were sometimes hard fought and the officers usually dedicated and responsible, there were periodic complaints about late starting, irregular procedure, poor attendance, and other signs of apathy.[150]

The result was a rising tide of student discontent. The *Post* pronounced campus life "dead." "Only a few show up for football games, and activities like Mask and Mantle, the band, and even the *Post*, recruit members with difficulty," it editorialized in 1957. Wayne Booth sensed a sour mood growing. "It's been four years since I heard of a practical joke at Earlham that couldn't have been invented by Faulkner's Benjy— except that there was no cruelty in his nature," Booth wrote on the Opinion Board.[151]

Such opinions, while pronounced, were not the only ones on campus. One student critic, while blasting administrators for paternalism, admitted that Earlham had a strong sense of community, offset by an excess of conformity. *Community* was something on the minds of many faculty and students in these years. Almost never mentioned in campus discourse before 1946, it was now at its center. It was a chief concern of Elton Trueblood. "A college is a society," he told the Association of American Colleges in 1949. "Ideally, the members of college, both teachers and taught, *work* together, *think* together, *play* together, and *pray* together." In 1951 he urged that faculty be allowed to build homes on campus, in order to further "friendly relations between faculty and students." Such relations were critical, he thought. "If we do all else and fail in this, our failure is complete," he told Jones. The CPS men agreed. The faculty had to "keep clear our vocation as a religious community for living, teaching, and learning, accepting its costs in time, consultation, and mutual forbearance," Fuson told the faculty meeting in 1947. There was a danger, which Warren Staebler described in 1955 as the "morbidity of constant self-examination." He urged the faculty that it should "simply agree we are good, but not so good as we think, and try to be better." As he concluded, "the important thing . . . is to develop the right kind of community."[152]

There was another vision of community at Earlham, however, one that appealed to a growing number of students and faculty. "My acquaintance with Quakers at Earlham makes it difficult for me to imagine a group of Friends . . . not welcoming with respect and consideration both the opinions and association of individuals of diverse creeds and experi-ence," one departing faculty member wrote in 1950. Two freshmen echoed that sentiment in 1957. "The Quaker undertaking and toleration of different beliefs *should* be, and is, the basic moral foundation of Earlham College," they wrote on the Opinion Board. The debate on campus was beginning, a debate that would pit two visions of the nature of a Quaker community against each other. On one side were Tom Jones and Elton Trueblood, with a vision of learning and service as the outgrowth of discipline and Christian faith, a vision of Earlham as a place where "the religious atmosphere should so pervade the entire place that most of the students are not really aware of religion as being anything strange." For a decade, by the force of their personalities and the power of their intellects, they had led in the transformation of Earlham from a respectable midwestern church school into a national institution. But in so doing they brought to Earlham the advocates of another vision of Quakerism, one that spoke mainly of tolerance and activism. This, and the conflicts that grew out of it, would be the central battle of Earlham's next decade.[155]

6

"The Sixties"
1958–1973

*I*t is an oft-deplored practice to organize college histories by presidencies. All too often, such an organization is frightfully artificial. Landrum Bolling's fifteen years as Earlham's president, from 1958 to 1973, however, were a discrete and critical period in the college's history. That period was, moreover, probably the most turbulent and eventful in the history of American higher education, roughly corresponding to what we generically label "the Sixties." At Earlham, "the Sixties" would be eventful, but, in striking contrast with many of its peer institutions, change would come with relatively little turbulence, and with considerable growth in the stature of the school.

Most college and university campuses were very different places in 1973 from what they had been in 1958. The changes would have been apparent even to the most obtuse observer. Students *looked* different. The men's hair was longer, and many were now bearded. Women were as likely to be in shorts or slacks as skirts, and blue jeans were the most favored article of dress. No longer was housing strictly separated by gender. More and more dormitories were coeducational, and those that were not usually allowed "visitation." Students were far more politically aware; especially between 1965 and 1970, dozens of campuses had seen unprecedented waves of political activism and protest, activism that helped bring down at least one president of the United States, not to mention more than a few college and university administrators. At its best, "the movement" that emerged from the campuses in these years was idealistic; at its worst it was violent and nihilistic.[1]

The impact was definite, although not as dramatic, in the classroom. There was a growing demand for "relevance," with rebellion against required courses and impersonal methods of teaching. Growing numbers of students and faculty began to see the classroom and the curriculum as means of social and political change. And students were increasingly demanding more control over their own lives and the government of their schools.[2]

These changes were exceedingly controversial. More than one politician advanced his career by blasting campus protesters and activists as communistic and un-American. On the campuses, administrators found themselves fending off complaints from unhappy alumni who were horrified by the changes they saw taking place. The general population was often incredulous over what it saw as the antics of a spoiled, self-centered generation.[3]

These national currents did not leave Earlham or Quakerism untouched. Its students resembled those on other campuses. What had always been a lively political atmosphere had become fiercely and lopsidedly liberal and Democratic. Earlham now also had coed dorms, and all of the perceived problems of sexuality that they involved.

Yet in other, important ways, Earlham was different. Although it had an active antiwar movement, that movement never turned violent in the ugly ways that it did in other places. Earlham was one of a handful of campuses in the country with an active antiwar movement where in 1968 the head of Selective Service could have appeared without an explosion. While there was curricular innovation aplenty, much of it extraordinarily creative, it came without much relaxation of requirements. An experiment in abolishing grades proved short-lived. And some prohibitions on student "lifestyle" remained in place, particularly that on alcohol, much to the anger of many students. Yet while many campuses would by 1970 describe themselves as "traumatized," few at Earlham would have used such language.

The roots of that difference lie in large part in the fact that Earlham was still a self-consciously Quaker school. Maintaining a Quaker identity involved a struggle. There was less agreement about what it meant to be a Quaker school than in 1958. The number of Quaker students was declining, and the number from Indiana and Western yearly meetings was lower than it had ever been before. Yet Earlham was now home to the nation's only accredited Quaker seminary, the Earlham School of Religion, which was an increasingly important source of leadership for Quakers around the world. Campus groups were, if anything, more likely to base their actions on their understanding of Quaker processes and ethics. And the Quakerly commitment to decision-making by consensus became, if anything, more central to life on the campus. It was also a brake on some of the more radical proposals for change.

This change, and continuity, sprang from complex sources—a growing and able faculty, an increasingly gifted and diverse student body, patient and wise leadership on the board of trustees. Yet, as in any college, the president was vital. And it is the consensus of all connected with Earlham in these years that it was fortunate to have as president Landrum R. Bolling.

Earlham Transformed

Landrum Rymer Bolling represented a break with tradition in important ways. He was Earlham's first president who was not a native of the Midwest, and its first who was not a birthright Quaker. He was also unusual among college presidents in not having an earned doctorate. None of these "handicaps," however, would prove significant.

Bolling was a native of Parksville, Tennessee, born in 1913. An able and precocious student, he graduated from the University of Tennessee in 1933, then went on for an M.A. at the University of Chicago. He taught political science at Beloit College and Brown University for six years before spending World War II as a foreign correspondent for the Overseas News Agency. A chance shipboard meeting with Elton Trueblood brought him to Earlham to teach in 1948, and he alternated teaching with journalism until 1955, when Tom Jones made him the college's general secretary, responsible especially for fund-raising. Bolling had become a Friend as a young man, influenced by his wife Frances, who was the daughter of Arthur Morgan, the Quaker Tennessee Valley Authority administrator and the influential president of Antioch College.[4]

Many saw Bolling as Jones's heir apparent, with his appointment as general secretary as a chance to hone his skills. Bolling was not at all sure that that was what he wanted, at one point asking not to be considered. In the spring of 1957, Jones announced his intention to retire the following year—he would be seventy, and he considered his work done. Quickly the choice for president narrowed down to Bolling and Samuel Marble, the president of Wilmington College, the Quaker school in southwestern Ohio. For a while, the board was evenly split, with Bolling's opponents arguing that it would be awkward to appoint a current member of the faculty. In the end, however, worries about Marble surfaced, while Bolling's supporters held firm. In the minds of the faculty, Bolling's qualifications were clear: "His popularity, his teaching and oratorical skill, his experience in the development program, his

LANDRUM BOLLING

knowledge of 'the world,' his fertility of ideas, were all outstanding within our community," one faculty member wrote in 1958.[5]

Bolling proved to have all of these attributes. One of his faculty described him as "a gifted improvisor and inspired crisis manager" who was "overflowing with new ideas." His energy was boundless; it was not uncommon for him to return at 5:00 P.M. from a full day off campus to spend the evening in his office handling correspondence. He preferred to be in motion, however; if he had been cooped up in his office and found that he needed to consult with a colleague, he was much happier leaving the office to find the person himself rather than using the telephone. He had a gift for public relations. A local admirer commented that Bolling possessed "the disarming ability, almost a genius, of giving extemporaneous remarks the quality of finished prose." In his first few years, he had appeared on the "Today" show, had made the college one of the centerpieces of an N.B.C. special program on Quakerism, and had been the subject of stories in *Time* and *Reader's Digest.* Politically astute, and well connected in both of the major parties, he provided advice on educational policy to the Kennedy campaign in 1960 and to the Nixon forces in 1968. Admirers touted him as a Democratic candidate for Congress and the United States Senate.[6]

Above all, Bolling was a diplomat. He did not fear taking decisive action; sometimes other administrators grumbled over how he would overrule what they thought was a hard-won consensus. English professor (and later trustee) Wayne Booth put his finger on one of Bolling's abilities as "a great skill thinking about how the other person feels." Bolling put this skill to good use in his first years in office, easing out a few tenured faculty who had become ineffective teachers.[7]

Jones's retirement marked a general turnover in the college administration. Paul Furnas also retired, going back to his farm outside Philadelphia, but Jones remained in Richmond, consulting for the Association of American Colleges and continuing to cultivate donors for Earlham. While Jones and Furnas departed with fanfare, Dean David Henley was quietly eased out, much to his disgruntlement. For a time, on the advice of Swarthmore College president Courtney Smith, Bolling served as his own academic dean in order to have a better sense of educational policy and planning, delegating certain duties to two assistants. For other positions, Bolling blended older, traditional Earlham ways with new ones, sometimes bringing in people from other schools, sometimes choosing people already on the staff. Harold Cope became the business manager, for example, and William Fuson the assistant for academic affairs. Eric Curtis, Jones's dean of men, was moved up to vice president. Bolling often hired alumni—Charles Johnson and Hugh Ronald in the

Development Office, Thomas Mullen as dean of students, Margaret Grant Beidler as dean of women, and John Owen, Ben Carlson, and Darrell Beane in the Admissions Office. Although most of these were Quakers, not all were.[8]

Probably Bolling's most important appointment was to bring Joe Elmore into the administration. Elmore, a Methodist from Texas educated at Southern Methodist University, Union Theological Seminary, and Yale, had come to Earlham in 1957 for what he thought would be a short stay. (By his own admission, he did not want to live in the Midwest.) His original duties were teaching religion and counseling students. In 1961 Bolling appointed him his assistant for faculty affairs, with Fuson continuing to handle curricular matters. In 1964 the two positions were consolidated with Elmore becoming academic dean, with the position being upgraded to vice president in 1967. Elmore would continue until 1981, winning extraordinary respect and affection from faculty and students alike.[9]

Bolling also brought change to the college's governance structure. Under the old system, the senior member of each department had served as chair. Now, the chair went in turn to all members of the department. In addition, Bolling reconfigured committee memberships, opening them to all faculty as individuals, rather than as representatives of departments, and with regular rotation. Predictably, some senior faculty were dubious, but younger ones were enthusiastic, and the changes were accepted.[10]

The faculty by 1973 was larger and much more diverse than it had been when Bolling became president. It was less Quakerly. Most of the CPS men remained, although now near retirement, and they were the core of the faculty, although there were murmurs of discontent among the young. There were, to be sure, new Quaker teachers. Paul Lacey, hired for the English department in 1960, had already made a reputation for himself in Quaker circles, as had Wilmer Stratton, an alumnus who returned to teach chemistry in 1959, and Jackson Bailey, another alumnus who came to the history department the same year. There was delicious irony in the return of Alexander Purdy in 1960, retired from Hartford Seminary and now part of the new Earlham School of Religion faculty. And, as had been the case for a generation, there were new faculty who became convinced Friends.[11]

Most new professors were not Friends, and there were quickly departures from old patterns. Earlham had acquired its first Jewish faculty member, Harold Hyman, under Jones; Bolling hired others without attracting notice or comment. Joe Elmore worked through the Danforth Foundation and the Society for Religion in Higher Education to try to find faculty with Christian commitments, but that was no longer a *sine qua non*. Faculty hired in the 1960s do not remember religious views being an issue. And it was in these years that the first African American faculty came to the college. The first hired was William Cousins, a sociologist, in 1966.[12]

If in some ways the faculty was becoming diverse, it was also becoming more male. Following national trends, in the 1950s the percentage of women on the faculty had begun to decline, and that continued in the 1960s. As veteran women like Florence Long in mathematics, Undine Dunn in English, and Mary Lane Charles in French retired, men replaced them. The college abolished a rule against hiring faculty spouses in 1959, but that had little effect. Most of the women who came to campus in these years were at the lower levels of the administration. There were notable exceptions, of course. When the office of provost was created in 1970, the first to hold it was Helen Hole, an English professor and one of the faculty's "weighty" Friends. It was not until the early 1970s, however, that concern was openly expressed that at a Quaker school there should be more of a balance of the sexes.[13]

As the faculty grew, and became more diverse, so did the student body. It was in the 1960s that Earlham became a national institution.

That change came gradually, and was not entirely the result of any one conscious decision. For nearly half a century, the percentage of students from Indiana had been declining. In 1920, it was 80 percent; by 1943 it was 65 percent. In the Jones years, Hoosiers ceased to be a majority, and by the first years of Bolling's presidency they accounted for about one third of the student body. The slide slowed thereafter but did continue. In 1965, Indiana students were about a quarter of all students at Earlham. They have hovered between 20 and 25 percent since then. By 1971, almost half of each entering class was at least 500 miles from home.[14]

This statistic reflected several changes. One was the near disappearance of the "Day Dodgers," town students who continued to live at home. By 1970, there were few left. Earlham's steadily rising costs (it was now cheaper to pay room and board plus tuition at one of the state universities than to live at home and attend Earlham) were one reason. Edward G. Wilson, the chairman of the trustees, concluded in 1967 that students of Earlham's caliber from Richmond who could afford the school would probably prefer to get away from home. Those who could not afford Earlham could also join the growing enrollment at the local Indiana University extension campus, which in 1970 moved out of the basement of Carpenter Hall and became Indiana University East. The extension of the college's recruiting also played a role. What had been a one-person operation in 1946 became a full-scale admissions office under Bolling. The growing number of students from the Northeast, between Washington, D.C., and Boston, compensated for the decline in Indiana enrollment. The college had attracted students from Quaker prep schools in this area for decades, but in 1954, faced with a budget deficit, Tom Jones had decided to recruit intensively in Philadelphia, New Jersey, New York, New England, and Baltimore. As a result, enrollment from the East grew substantially. "We are embarrassed by so many applications from the East that we see grave dangers in significantly distorting our student body," Bolling wrote in 1961. By that time, total enrollment was near one thousand.[15]

By 1960, in fact, competition for admission had become, in Bolling's word, "terrific." Because of dormitory arrangements, the college tried to admit roughly equal numbers of men and women, but because the number of women applicants was greater, the college rejected more women than it accepted. In 1961, for example, it accepted only one in five. In these years the college settled on the policy still in place down to the present: to strive for a geographical mix of students while giving preference to Quakers and the children of alumni. In the early 1960s, that meant that Earlham accepted three quarters of all Quaker applicants but only 45 percent of others. While the decline in the number of baby boomers made competition less intense by the early 1970s, never again would the college have open admissions.[16]

The result of this growth and increased competition was a student body that was, in general, more able than any in Earlham's history. Faculty agree that it improved significantly between 1950 and 1960. Writing in 1961, Fuson noted that there were no longer students on campus clearly unsuited to college. The "superlative" students probably still went to the elite eastern schools, but Earlham could now fill its classes with what Fuson called "the upper middle brow." Statistics support Fuson's view; composite scores on the Scholastic Aptitude Test, which averaged 1,045 in 1959, were 1,207 in 1965, far above the national average. Others thought Earlham even better; in 1959 one consultant opined that Earlham and Occidental College in California had the two best student bodies of any small college in the country. One trustee was admonishing Bolling that he did not want Earlham to become "too big or too brainy," and Bolling was forced to issue denials that "Earlham is determined to become known as an elite intellectual institution."[17]

The third leg of Earlham's success in these years, along with faculty and students, was money. While Earlham's tuition rose steadily, and the college remained, after Notre Dame, the most expensive in Indiana, its endowment grew even more quickly, at least in the latter half of Bolling's presidency. Here Bolling's success as a fund-raiser, and especially his relationship with Eli Lilly, were critical.

There had been complaints at least since the 1920s that Earlham was too expensive. During Bolling's tenure, total charges rose about 6 percent annually, from about $1,600 to almost $3,700. This steady rise made many unhappy, especially in the two yearly meetings, and led to claims that most Quaker and alumni children were being systematically priced out of Earlham. Steady growth in financial aid offset the rise in large part, and that went disproportionately to Quaker students.[18]

As costs increased, however, the school was becoming increasingly successful in attracting the foundation grants that Bolling saw as critical to higher education in the 1960s, fearing that the widespread faculty perception of Earlham's genteel poverty would hamstring proposals for innovation. It had been one of Tom Jones's great regrets that he had never been able to win funding from any of the major eastern foundations. Bolling was more successful. One of the first grants was $25,000 from the Kresge Foundation for the construction of the new library. In 1962 came two major grants from the Ford Foundation, $275,000 jointly to Earlham and Antioch for a program in "Non-Western Studies," and a $1.6 million grant for endowment and programs to be matched on a 2 to 1 basis, a match that the college successfully completed in 1964. It was, to date, the largest gift that the college had received. Other Ford grants followed, including $150,000 for undergraduate program innovations in 1973. The college was also successful in winning support from other sources, most notably large grants from the Danforth Foundation for innovations in philosophy teaching and $375,000 from the National Endowment for the Humanities for the Program in Integral Education. Bolling also encouraged individual faculty to develop contacts and write grant proposals, bringing him in at appropriate times. By 1973, more faculty were involved in such activities than ever before.[19]

The largest donor in the college's history, however, would be Eli Lilly, the Indianapolis pharmaceutical magnate. His generosity was critical in the expansion of the college in these years. Lilly had, with his brother Josiah, built his family's patent medicine business into one of the country's largest drug companies. An intensely private and modest man who abhorred publicity and had little interest in society, Eli Lilly was an avid amateur historian and archaeologist, with several highly respected publications to his credit. He was as happy in the company of professors and academics as businessmen.[20]

Lilly was a devout Episcopalian, and his first contacts with Earlham came through Elton Trueblood, whose books he admired. He also became a supporter of Trueblood's Yokefellow project, and through the family foundation, the Lilly Endowment, directed considerable financial support to it. Lilly's interest was heightened by one of his associates, Tillman Bubenzer, who was an active Yokefellow. Lilly also admired Quaker beliefs and idealism; his first dealings with Trueblood involved a gift of vitamins for the American Friends Service Committee to distribute in Europe after World War II. Another Quaker tie came through Harold Duling, an Endowment official who was a member of Indianapolis First Friends Meeting. Originally, Endowment support of Earlham came through unrestricted grants to several private Indiana colleges; between 1958 and 1962 the Endowment dispersed $8.5 million in grants. The hope of more led to naming the new library for the Lilly family when it opened in 1963.[21]

It was Landrum Bolling, however, who drew Eli Lilly himself close to Earlham, as opposed to the institutional interest and support of the Lilly Endowment. Lilly liked Bolling, finding him energetic, intelligent, and dedicated. The two men became good friends, with Bolling one of the group Lilly invited to his summer home in northern Indiana. This relationship was critical, since Lilly himself told an interviewer in 1972 that he chose his philanthropies "simply . . . on the basis of personal interest and often on the basis of friendship." The friendship of Bolling and Lilly would be one of Lilly's most intimate.[22]

Lilly's first great gift, his Conner Prairie Farm near Noblesville, Indiana, was a controversial one on campus. Lilly had purchased the farm in 1934 and had set out not only to make it a profitable working farm but also to restore the 1823 William Conner home, which had been one of the first brick houses in central Indiana and an important trading post. Lilly had a deep interest in historic preservation and happily combed the country for antiques and artifacts.[23]

Late in 1963, Lilly decided to turn Conner Prairie, including almost 1,400 acres of land, over to Earlham. Bolling, realizing how important Conner Prairie was to Lilly, and that Earlham's future relationship would be tied up inextricably with it, never thought of rejecting it. But there were profound doubts on campus about it, stemming from fears that administering such a complex operation was beyond Earlham's capabilities, or, worse, that it would be a constant financial drain on the college. Lilly tried to provide a cushion with a promise of a $50,000 annual subsidy for four years.[24]

Over the next decade, Lilly watched Earlham's handling of his gift with approval, and with growing regard for Earlham. James Cope, the head of Earlham's Joseph Moore Museum, became the liaison among the college, Conner Prairie, and Lilly, winning Eli Lilly's respect. By 1970, Earlham had made the major decisions about Conner Prairie. It would become a living history museum, similar to Colonial Williamsburg or Sturbridge Village, interpreting life in an Indiana settlement in 1836. Lilly provided nearly $4.5 million to develop the site, and watched with pleasure as the number of visitors grew from 1,500 in 1963 to over 125,000 in 1976. Today it is one of the nation's most respected institutions of its kind.[25]

Lilly was also generous to the college, with the largest gifts coming near the end of his life. One of Bolling's last official acts as president was to announce what became known on campus as "the magnificent gift" of $17 million, the largest Earlham has ever received. And when Lilly died in January 1977, Earlham was in his will for a tenth of his estate, about $13.5 million.[26]

Lilly was not the college's only major benefactor in these years, of course. Despite the tumult of the late 1960s, and fears about its impact on donors, the college's budget and endowment grew steadily. The budget, about $1.2 million in 1958, was almost $6 million by 1973. And the endowment, less than $2 million in 1958, was over $20 million when Bolling left in 1973.[27]

Thus it was that Earlham laid the foundations of its future in the 1960s. It had been one of William Cullen Dennis's favorite aphorisms that "Earlham is a better college than it is on paper." But, even on paper, Earlham was coming to look more and more impressive. One administrator may have been overenthusiastic when he told Bolling in 1964: "We are no longer kidding when we say that Earlham College is the best small, coeducational, church related college in the Midwest." But its reputation grew steadily in these years, not least because of innovations and improvements in the academic program.[28]

Academic Life

Ultimately, of course, the success of the campus was dependent on its intellectual life, what took place in the classroom. From all accounts, the college was far stronger academically and intellectually when Bolling left than when he became president.

Some of this strength was certainly due to the quality of the faculty. As has already been seen, the able teachers of the CPS generation were still on campus, only beginning to retire in the mid-1970s. Now at the height of their powers were the second generation that Jones had hired in the 1950s, people like Wayne Booth in English or William Stephenson in biology or Laurence Strong and Theodor Benfey in chemistry or Edward Bastian in history. Joining them was a generation of newly minted Ph.D.s, some of them Quakers, some of them alumni, but most of them with no previous connection with Earlham or with Friends. As Bastian remembered them, they arrived with their "rambunctiousness, and the smell of their graduate school . . . still strong upon them." Benfey thought them a "world-class" group who, if anything, gave older faculty a feeling of inferiority. A group of Danforth faculty interns was impressed in 1972 with their commitment to teaching—"Earlham faculty vocalize their concerns about their teaching mission all the time." By 1967, over half of the faculty had been at the college five years or less.[29]

The ability of the faculty doubtless accounts for the growing interest in innovation on campus. Bolling was at the heart of several of these proposals, and in fact began his presidency with a plan for radical change in the college's calendar.

Bolling's idea was to move from semesters to trimesters, or what became known known on campus as the "3–3" system. Under it, the school year would be divided into three terms, and students would take three courses each term, compared with four or five under semesters. Bolling's argument was that by taking fewer classes, students could concentrate more intensively on the material and retain more. Some faculty were convinced that at least part of the president's motivation was a desire to shake up the whole curriculum. As Bolling himself told a colleague, "I think the trick in this job is to come in, shake everybody out of their old academic ruts, introduce radical new methods and programs, and then move on." The change would force departments to examine and in many cases redesign their courses. Debate in the faculty meeting was fierce. Some of the older faculty in the Natural Sciences Division were especially opposed, convinced that it was impossible to teach their courses adequately in ten weeks. Younger faculty, on the other hand, the "young bucks," as Wayne Booth called them, were fervently in favor. Ultimately, a third group, not really committed to either side, tipped the balance by deciding that Bolling deserved a chance to try his ideas. In the January 22, 1959, faculty meeting, the faculty approved the change, to begin in the fall of 1960. The results were generally satisfactory to most on campus, and the new calendar did coincide with, if not force, considerable curricular change.[30]

Some of the changes early in Bolling's tenure involved the demise of some programs and departments. Home economics, which was regarded as insufficiently academic, was abolished, with a new program in Family Relations replacing it. The nursing program with Reid Hospital also came to an end. Elementary education survived, but with little support. Public speaking also disappeared, as drama became part of the fine arts department and speech courses were offered only irregularly. Intercollegiate debating, a fixture of the campus since the 1890s, survived only a little longer. The agricultural science program also was laid down, although an interest in agriculture on campus survived in other ways. The community dynamics program disappeared with the departure of its director, William Biddle. Once one of the centerpieces of curricular innovation on campus, it fell victim to declining student and faculty interest.[31]

On the other hand, these years witnessed the inauguration of several of the most distinctive of the college's programs. Three would become outstanding: off-campus study, Japanese studies, and the library's program in bibliographic instruction.

Earlham, of course, had long-standing ties with Japan. Since 1890, there had usually been at least one Japanese student on the campus, and a number of Earlham graduates had lived and worked in Japan, most typically as teachers or missionaries. Earlham's acceptance of Japanese American students during World War II had reinforced those ties, as had the fact that Tom Jones had lived in Japan before becoming the president of Fisk. The first work in fact had been done under Jones, when Earlham had begun discussions with Antioch about the possibility of a program in international relations, focusing especially on the "non-Western" world. A request for funding to the Ford Foundation, however, brought rejection with the comment that the two schools were too far apart geographically to have an effective relationship.[32]

This rejection did not faze Earlham. Early in 1959 the man who would be the center of Earlham's efforts arrived on campus, Jackson Bailey. A 1950 graduate and member of an old and influential Maine Quaker family, Bailey had worked in Japan for the AFSC before going to Harvard to take his doctorate in Japanese history under Edwin O. Reischauer, the leading American figure in the field. Although Bailey had his choice of positions, Bolling persuaded him to return to Earlham. Bolling acted over the vociferous objections of the Educational Policy Committee, which was convinced that the college had greater need in several fields other than Japanese history. The resistance, however, was not long lived.[33]

Once Bailey was on campus, he and Bolling decided to continue collaborating with Antioch, in the hope that if they could demonstrate a successful relationship, that would change minds at the Ford Foundation. For four years, Bailey taught a course in East Asian history at Antioch, while the two institutions agreed on a division of activities— Earlham would develop Japanese resources, while Antioch would focus on China. The strategy was successful. In the summer of 1960, the two institutions received a $35,000 Ford grant for a three-year program of faculty seminars on both campuses. Visiting specialists would meet with the seminars, teach classes, and give a major public address. The program brought most of the leading East Asian scholars in the country to the two campuses. In the three years of the grant, nearly a third of Earlham's faculty participated.[34]

The success of this program brought encouragement from the Ford Foundation to apply for a much larger, $275,000 grant for a two-year program. It not only continued the faculty seminar and expansion of library holdings, but envisioned more intensive work by individual faculty, in Bailey's words, through "a summer study program in Japan with each . . . working with a mature scholar and colleague, helping him pursue a project related to his own field of specialty."[35]

Seven members of the teaching faculty—Milton Kraft in education, Leonard Holvik in music, Arthur Funston in political science, William Darr in art, Arthur Little in drama, Grimsley Hobbs in philosophy, and Bailey—along with librarian Philip Shore, spent the summer of 1962 in Japan, with some remaining longer. The group studied together in Kyoto and Tokyo before pursuing individual projects in different parts of the country. Their return had considerable impact on campus. Holvik and Little became respected experts on Japanese Noh drama. Courses in Japanese art, music, philosophy, and politics became part of the curriculum.[36]

The other two important elements of the program were a foreign study program and teaching Japanese language. There was general agreement that language instruction was essential, so Bailey made arrangements with the International Christian University in Tokyo to supply a teacher. Misako Hagino came to Earlham in the fall of 1962 as the college's first instructor in Japanese language. The methods of teaching were also different from those in most American universities. As Bailey put it, Earlham "pioneered in our approach to Japanese language instruction at a time when other institutions were sticking rather rigidly to ethnocentric Indo-European linguistic principles and refusing to teach beginning Japanese through the medium of the Japanese script." In fact, Earlham always taught using the Japanese characters, and, initially, even created its own textbooks because no others were available.[37]

By 1973, Japan had become an important element in the college's life. Two years earlier, the Lilly Endowment had given the Great Lakes College Association a half million dollars for an East Asian Center, the Japanese component of which was based at Earlham. The library had a *tokonoma* area on the first floor, with a *kotatsu* at which students studied surrounded by Japanese scroll paintings. The library's holdings on Japan were recognized as one of the best undergraduate collections in the country, as was its instruction in their use. There was a succession of visiting Japanese faculty, particularly in the fine arts. And Bailey successfully brought new faculty into his orbit, like Edward Yates in art and future president Richard J. Wood in philosophy. The result was a national reputation in Japanese Studies both for Earlham and for Bailey.[38]

One important element in the Japanese program, of course, was sending students to Japan. Concurrent with, in fact tightly linked with, the developments in Japanese and "non-Western" fields was the flowering of Earlham's off-campus study program. Bound up with that was the creation of the Great Lakes College Association (GLCA).

Bolling, working with Samuel J. Gould, the president of Antioch, was the moving force in the creation of the consortium that became known as the GLCA. Bolling was impressed with the work of the Associated Colleges of the Midwest (ACM), which was made up of liberal arts colleges in Illinois, Wisconsin, Minnesota, and Iowa, like Knox, Carleton, Grinnell, and Beloit. Its premise was that by pooling resources, the schools supported programs that they lacked resources to mount individually.[39]

Bolling and Gould saw great advantages in such a cooperative effort. They focused on ten institutions in addition to their own: DePauw and Wabash in Indiana; Kalamazoo, Albion, and Hope in Michigan; and Oberlin, Kenyon, Ohio Wesleyan, Denison, and Wooster in Ohio. All of these schools shared certain qualities—they were highly respected liberal arts colleges, relatively well endowed, and had either church ties or strong religious traditions. Oberlin was the critical institution; since its resources were much larger than those of the other schools, it was by no means certain that it would see advantages in joining. But Oberlin did join, and in April 1961, supported by a grant from the Ford Foundation, representatives from the twelve schools met in Cleveland and approved a provisional constitution. Bolling became the first chairman of the board of directors, and Eldon L. Johnson, who had been president of the University of New Hampshire, became the first president of the association.[40]

Over the next decade, the GLCA embarked on a variety of initiatives. Its impact was probably not was great as some had hoped it would be. Many Earlham faculty of the period recall that it had little effect on what or how they taught. Plans for regular meetings of students, like student government officers, were short-lived, much to the disappointment of some students. In many ways the move into the GLCA was symbolic—Earlham now publicly identified its peer group not so much as other independent colleges in Indiana or other Quaker schools, but schools like Oberlin and Kenyon. But in other areas, especially in off-campus study, the impact was considerable.[41]

Earlham students had been studying abroad for some time before Bolling, but usually as individuals in foreign universities. The first formal Earlham program had begun in 1956, when French professor Mary Lane Charles, supported by funding from trustee Dorothy Peaslee, who had a special interest in international relations, took fifteen students to France, leaving in July and returning in January 1957. They began with language study in Geneva and Tours before settling down in Paris. All lived with French families. In the next four years, Charles took two more groups to France, and Warren Staebler one to Italy. Faculty also led trips to Mexico and Scandinavia, with planning done for other groups to visit Russia and Japan.[42]

Other schools were developing foreign study programs at this time, but Earlham's was distinctive in several ways. The typical pattern nationally was "junior year abroad," most often in France, Germany, or England. Students would take much the same courses that they would have taken at home; Stanford University, for example, established "mini-campuses" in Europe where Stanford professors offered Stanford courses to Stanford students. Many faculty at other schools saw such programs as of dubious value, a glorified vacation that detracted from real learning.[43]

This was not the view at Earlham. Bolling set the tone. He was the most widely traveled president Earlham had ever had, with years of living abroad, including time in Japan, Africa, and the Middle East as well as most of Europe. He was convinced that greater understanding of diverse cultures and international affairs should be critical elements of a liberal education. This was one of his arguments for the "3–3" reform — by allowing students to spend a spring and summer, or a summer and fall off-campus, they could have a six-month experience and still spend only one term away from Earlham. Bolling saw foreign study, moreover, as in keeping with Quaker tradition. Quaker faculty played a critical role in the development of the program, including early program leaders like Charles, Staebler, William Fuson, and, of course, Jackson Bailey. The first director of the International Programs Office, Lewis Hoskins, came to Earlham after several years as executive secretary of the AFSC. These faculty shared an understanding of the Inner Light that taught that, since the Light was in all people, no matter the race, nationality, or ethnicity, anyone could learn from anyone else. Indeed, openness to the Light found in others was a critical part of their vision of Quaker education. Thus open doubters were scarce among the Earlham faculty. When one natural scientist told a student that foreign study was a waste of time, there was genuine consternation among his colleagues.[44]

On this basis, the Earlham program began to bloom. In 1961, the college committed itself to Lewis Hoskins's recommendation that "the foreign study program be regarded as an integral part of the Earlham College academic program and budgeted within the overall Earlham budget in the same way departments or other special programs are handled." Other principles were quickly established—that students would bear only travel costs; that in Earlham programs a faculty member would usually accompany the students; that whenever possible, students would live with families in the host country rather than in student hostels or university dormitories. Many of the programs that Earlham set up had language at their center—those in France, Mexico, Russia, Japan, Spain, and Germany and Austria. In 1961, however, the first program in London was set up, partly to serve English and history majors as well as those whose foreign language skills were uncertain. Students could also choose from a variety of GLCA programs, each administered by a different GLCA school. Antioch, for example, took responsibility for the Yugoslavian program.[45]

Not all of the off-campus programs were foreign. During the 1960s, Earlham established ties with the Merrill Palmer Institute in Detroit to take advantage of its resources for students in sociology, psychology, and family relations. With Kalamazoo and Coe College, Earlham set up a study center in Washington, D.C., with an emphasis on politics and public affairs. An "arts term" was created in New York City, and in 1968 the GLCA set up a program in Philadelphia to study urban problems that attracted many Earlham students.[46]

Virtually everyone involved saw the off-campus study program as having considerable impact. One student found her experience in Japan, through its contact with people of other faiths, strengthening her own Quaker commitment. For many, it was their first experience outside the United States, and the college's policy was to "choose mature students and then turn them loose—within limits." This, in Wayne Booth's words, would produce "the kind of growth in independence which is one of the chief rewards of getting away." Bolling agreed; experiences abroad would "help develop the qualities of initiative and self-reliance." Perhaps most important, growing numbers of faculty and students found themselves with an appreciation of a different way of life or point of view, what Allen Hole, Jr., called a "cultural experience." And it was a measure of Earlham that that was now fully within its understanding of its mission.[47]

Still another direction for off-campus study, of a somewhat different nature, was the Wilderness program, which began in 1071. It was designed not so much to expose students to a different culture as to teach them about themselves and to heighten their sense of community.

The program took a group of students, usually about fifty, into a wilderness setting for about one month. The first group went to the mountains of Utah in the summer of 1971. Field study was an integral part of the experience, as students gained knowledge of geography, geology, meteorology, physiology, and ecology. But more important, in the minds of those who developed it, was that it offered an alternative to "traditional, active teacher/passive student learning situations." It was "aimed at education and development of the whole person." A typical day might involve hiking, climbing, and canoeing, while students collected and observed botanical and geological phenomena. The program proved successful. By 1976 it had given rise to a "water wilderness" in northern Minnesota and a winter term program that became Southwest Field Studies, with over fifteen faculty and three hundred students participating in the first five years.[48]

Surveys of alumni from 1960 onward have consistently shown that some of their best memories are of the library. Today, peers generally agree that Earlham's is the best college library in the country. Most of the credit must go to the head librarian who arrived in 1962, Evan Farber.

The library was a clear priority when Bolling became president. The old Carnegie facility of 1907 had long since passed its capacity, and it was outmoded and badly dated in almost every way. Even in the last years of Tom Jones's presidency there had been discussions of how to replace it, with debate focusing on whether to remodel the old building or replace it entirely. (One overenthusiastic, innovative architect wanted to construct a new building over the main drive.) Finally the decision was made for a new building on the west side of the campus.[49]

By 1961, Bolling had also decided that the college needed a new head librarian, and so did not renew the contract of the incumbent, who had been at the college since 1950. The library had been competently but unimaginatively run, and Bolling wanted someone more aggressive. Philip Shore, the associate librarian, took over for a year while the college conducted its search.[50]

Ironically, Evan Farber, who would have the longest tenure of any Earlham librarian, was not the college's first choice. Farber had recently been divorced. The college had never hired a divorced person; the position of the two yearly meetings was still not to record divorced people as ministers, and Tom Jones had always held up as proof of Earlham's basic morality that there had never been a divorce among its faculty. Custody of his four daughters further complicated Farber's situation; several administrators for whom divorce was not a bar were worried about whether he would be able to give full attention to the library. Fortunately for Earlham, the search group's first choice rejected its offer, and so Farber was hired.[51]

Farber was a break with Earlham's past in several ways; not only was he divorced, but he was also Jewish. A native of New York City, he had graduated from Chapel Hill and had done graduate work in political science at Princeton before deciding that library work was his real interest. When Earlham hired him, he was on the staff at Emory University in Atlanta.[52]

The new Lilly Library was still under construction when Farber arrived, and he almost immediately put some of his ideas to work. He wanted the library to be inviting, very much a center of the campus's intellectual life, but above all well used by students. A 1971 visitor caught Farber's vision: "a library must be a place for students not only to do research, but to browse, dream, and nap, and certainly not a jail with check-out counters and guards inspecting briefcases." He purposely put down deep carpets so that patrons could sit or lie on the floor. To collect art to decorate the new building, he began a senior art prize, with winning work purchased for display in the library. He worked on the reference desk evenings and weekends like the other staff. He also cajoled the administration into providing staffing for the sorely neglected science library, and eventually new quarters.[53]

Farber's best-known contribution to library science was bibliographic instruction, a fruit of work at the reference desk. One night he was dealing with a procession of students from an English class, all writing papers on William Faulkner's "The Bear." Repeating the same advice, and directing students to the same reference works over and over again, it occurred to Farber that it would be much simpler to meet with the whole class and introduce them to the most useful guides and reference books together. Faculty proved open to the idea, and over the next few years it became a feature of most classes. New staff, especially reference librarian James Kennedy and science librarian Thomas G. Kirk, were important in building the program. In 1973, Farber marshaled some statistics on how his methods had changed library use. In 1972-1973, students checked out over 45,000 books, compared to 24,000 in 1964-1965. Interlibrary loan requests had increased tenfold. Even more rewarding were less tangible results. "The references used in term papers today are much more varied and erudite than those used . . . ten years ago," he concluded. Most heartening was how students viewed the librarians, as "full-fledged partners in the teaching and learning process."[54]

As Farber published accounts of the Earlham program, it attracted considerable attention, and numerous other colleges began to emulate Earlham's methods. Librarians from all over the United States came to see how the library operated, and Farber found himself greatly in demand as a speaker and consultant. By 1970, Earlham's library was one of the best known in the United States, and Farber had become a national leader in the field. More importantly, the library had become a central part of the lives of Earlham students.[55]

Not every new program on campus proved successful. The late 1960s and early 1970s were a heady time for education in the United States. Curricular innovation was the order of the day. Especially in favor were ideas that broke down traditional boundaries among disciplines, which blurred distinctions between teachers and taught, and which emphasized "experiential" learning. "Relevance" was the order of the day. At its best, this urge opened the way for exciting syntheses in interdisciplinary work. At its worst, it led to the wholesale dismantling of course requirements, leaving students to choose from a smorgasbord of courses with little intellectual coherence.[56]

The college embarked on a variety of short-lived curricular innovations. One of the first was the Reading Program, inaugurated in 1960.

Under it both faculty and students were to read one book in common every year, with several other common readings according to the class year. The chosen reading usually related to education or world affairs, such as Jacques Barzun's *The House of Intellect* or Barbara Ward's *Five Ideas That Change the World*. Often one of the authors would be a convocation speaker. Students were required to pass an examination on the readings. The program was unpopular from its inception. Many students resented the extra work, for which they did not receive credit. Others did the reading only in a cursory way, absorbing just enough to pass the exam. After a few years the program faded away.[57]

In 1967, the college began a more ambitious experiment in alternatives to the traditional curriculum, Program II. Aimed at freshmen, it emphasized self-paced learning and tutorials as a way of meeting requirements in five areas—literature, fine arts, behavioral sciences, natural sciences, and philosophy and religion. In addition to attending some regular classes, students met with tutorial groups of six to twelve students for discussion, heard special presentations from faculty, and met individually with instructors and student tutors. All grading was Pass/Fail, with only passing grades recorded.[58]

Program II lasted only two years—critics charged that it did not provide enough structure for many students, who consequently failed to complete courses in a timely way. It did, however, have consequences for the grading system, the college's brief experiment with abolishing traditional letter grades. As early as 1936, Ernest Wildman had advocated this; in the late 1960s it seemed to many to be an idea whose time had come. One faculty member argued that grades involved a "false precision." Without letter grades on transcripts, employers and graduate schools would have to look carefully at a student's "whole record." Andy Weiser, the Senate president in 1970, was outspoken; the traditional grading system was "plainly barbaric and immoral." As early as the fall of 1967, the faculty discussed changing most grades to Pass/Fail. By the 1968–69 school year, a number of introductory courses, including the required Humanities and History sequences, were Pass/Fail. A headline in the *Post* summed up the student case for change: "Pass/Fail Relaxes Classroom, Eliminates Competition." In the spring of 1970, the faculty approved abolishing the old system of A, B, C, D, and F grades and replacing it with a system of Honors, High Pass, Pass, and Not Pass, with the last not recorded on transcripts. No grade point averages would be calculated.[59]

This grading experiment lasted only two years. For purist critics of the traditional grading system, it still made too many judgments and distinctions. More telling were complaints from students seeking admission to graduate and professional schools. Although the transcript stated specifically that "Honors" did not correspond to an "A," "Pass" to a "C," etc., graduate schools made precisely those calculations, and that hurt Earlham students. A comparison of grade distribution in the fall of 1968 and 1970 shows why:

Fall 1968	*Fall 1970*
A 23%	Honors 11%
B—42%	High Pass—32%
C—26%	Pass—43%
D—5%	
F—3%	Not Pass—5%

If "Honors" was considered an "A," then only half as many were being given under the new system. With so many of the campus's best students vociferously unhappy, and faculty doubters energized, the faculty gave up the experiment and returned to a letter grade system in the fall of 1972. There were no "D" grades, however, on the ground that credit should not be given for unsatisfactory work. And "Not Pass" replaced "F," it not being recorded on transcripts.[60]

What some saw as the fiasco of the grading changes did not deter interest in new programs. Although Program II had not lived up to everyone's hopes, the college embarked in 1972 on the Program in Integral Education, better known as PIE. The work largely of two young philosophy professors, Richard Wood and Len Clark, who oversaw a successful grant application to the National Endowment for the Humanities for its support, PIE was the fruit of growing interest in interdisciplinary and multidisciplinary work on campus, rejecting what one professor called "artificially structured knowledge." The idea was to bring together a relatively small group of students, twenty or thirty, in their freshman year, to examine a single topic from a broad range of perspectives. Plans included integrating psychology, biology, history, sociology, literature, political science, philosophy, and religion. Thus, the program began in the fall of 1972 with William Fuson of sociology, Andrea Jacoby of English, and Jerry Woolpy of biology leading "Women and Men: Sexual Identity and Roles in Society." In winter and spring terms, the students, with different faculty, took up "Contemporary Japan" and environmental studies. PIE was sometimes two thirds of, sometimes the entire course load for those involved. In the sophomore and junior years, students did traditional course work, but retained a PIE advisor. In their senior year, they would integrate their experiences in three interdisciplinary seminars. The faculty and students who took part judged the program rewarding and successful, but the cost of such intensive team teaching was prohibitive, and when the NEH grant ran out in 1976 the program came to an end.[61]

Other initiatives had more lasting impact. One was a successful application to the Danforth Foundation for a program to integrate philosophy teaching into the rest of the curriculum. It brought a number of young faculty to the campus part time, teaching what became known as "Philosophy of" courses: Philosophy of Art, Philosophy of Science, Philosophy of Literature, Philosophy of Social Science. Even after the funding came to an end, several of these courses remained as an integral part of the curriculum. Another undertaking had considerable influence beyond the campus. This was the Chemical Bond Approach project, begun late in the 1950s, the work of Laurence Strong, which tried to bring "coherence and structure" into the teaching of secondary school chemistry through conferences for science teachers and writing model textbooks. Drawing considerable funding in the Sputnik-era quest to improve scientific education, its influence was considerable, helping focus the teaching of secondary school chemistry more on experimentation and less on rote memorization.[62]

There is no question that in the 1960s Earlham was an intellectually vibrant place, one where a dedicated faculty took delight in teaching and students were, mostly, serious about learning. One 1963 graduate from Terre Haute, Indiana, remembered how different Earlham seemed from the colleges her high school friends were attending—Earlham was so much more serious, especially about classes. A 1960 graduate found herself undergoing a kind of culture shock after leaving the campus: "Gosh, I thought everyone was concerned about the population explosion, nationalism in Africa, nuclear test bans."[63]

Certainly the college's reputation was steadily improving. A few headlines from the *Earlhamite* and the *Post* tell the story: "Chicago Tribune Lists Earlham College as One of Twenty Best Liberal Arts Colleges in Midwest"; "New York Times Cites Earlham"; "Earlham among Top 3% in Who's Who Listing." The *Times* judged Earlham on a par with Ivy League institutions; *Harpers* named Earlham one of the best small colleges in the country.[64]

There was a price for this success. Many students complained about overwork. Typical was an Opinion Board writer in 1961 who declaimed against classes that took too much time; Earlham, he said, was "a school whose prestige, standards, and tuition are rising at an unparalleled rate." In 1967 the *Post* editorialized that the "large quantity of work assigned" was taking away from extracurricular activities and "such simple activities as just talking to people or taking a walk just for the fun of it." By 1972, at least one member of the faculty agreed, attacking the "'work the student to death' ethic" that "piled on more papers, more pages to read, and more quizzes to take."[65]

Some faculty shared such worries about what Earlham was becoming. Wayne Booth caught it when he compared the campus he joined in 1953 with that he left in 1963. "In '53 nobody, except a very few, could worry about national image because we knew we didn't have any. It's really a great thing . . . to be in a place where people are not thinking about quality on the inside," he remembered. "We talked about it in the late fifties. 'Are we going to come to the point where we're just like those other places—thinking more about reputation than quality?' We worried about that." This was the college's challenge, and would continue to be.[66]

Race

As Earlham was becoming academically stronger, it was also becoming more racially diverse. The vibrant student commitment to fighting segregation and discrimination of the 1940s and 1950s continued, and, if anything, grew stronger in the 1960s. The proportion of black students increased considerably, and Earlham hired its first black faculty and administrators. African and African American history, literature, and culture became part of the curriculum. For the first time, there was an active, articulate black student group on campus.

On the other hand, these changes did not come without conflicts— conflicts that mirrored those taking place on campuses across the country. Some who were at Earlham in these years remember real racial tension. Others perceived a college that, while occasionally failing to live up to its high ideals, still experienced less racial conflict than most schools. But there was no doubt that a change had taken place. Earlham now had a black student population that was quick to challenge what it perceived as injustice, both in the larger American society and at Earlham.

The most controversial race-related issue of Tom Jones's presidency, the interracial dating policy, soon disappeared under Bolling. He thought that counseling would be appropriate in certain situations, concluding that it was "the widely held judgment of experts in family relations that most such romances are doomed to end in extremely serious problems for the individuals involved." By 1962, the college's public position was that Earlham would offer counseling when it saw students in situations likely to lead to problems. Interracial dating might be one, but not always. The Senate gave its approval. A writer in the *Post* in 1965 still saw problems: "any white girl or boy who dates a Negro is immediately 'labeled,' sometimes as a 'show-off,'" the author claimed. But after 1965, interracial dating was not an issue on campus.[67]

Students and some faculty also continued their battle against segregation in Richmond. Pressure from students played an important role in forcing a local skating rink to integrate. Students fought a running battle for several years with Connie's, a local restaurant that first refused to serve blacks, then interracial couples, and finally "draft dodgers."[68]

These actions aroused little antagonism, but a renewed student interest in "direct action" by 1960 was more controversial. The Civil Rights Movement was entering a new phase of fighting discrimination. The "sit-in" movement, which began with the actions of college students in the spring of 1960, caught the imagination of students at Earlham. A few decided to act locally by picketing the Kresge and Woolworth stores in downtown Richmond. Neither engaged in segregation, but they were part of national chains whose southern stores did, and some activists felt that picketing northern stores would bring more pressure to bear on national headquarters. Early in April, a few Earlham students, along with students from Antioch and Central State University in Ohio, and Richmond NAACP members, began their protests.[69]

The actions against Kresge and Woolworth split the campus. Bolling, on the verge of gaining a grant from the Kresge Foundation for the new library, was appalled. While sympathetic to the goals of the demonstrators, he thought that this "tiny fringe" was more likely to arouse antagonism than support for the cause. The "picketing business," as he called, was, he claimed, a "fad" that would soon pass away. Some students agreed. "An anti-segregation protest demonstration by a few students at an integrated store merely because that store has the same name as a segregated store does not help mutual understanding between the town and college," one wrote. Another opined that it would be better to focus on "*educating* people through movies, newspaper and radio, speakers, and the public library." Many other students, however, rejected such arguments as "a cloak for timidity and comfortable opinion." Even one faculty member, to Bolling's consternation, joined the picketing one afternoon.[70]

After 1960, skeptics were less and less prominent on campus. Students and faculty continued to work against discrimination in the Richmond community. Some local white residents were certain that "a bunch of nigger-lovers" at Earlham was responsible for any racial tension in Richmond. And some Richmond blacks were equally sure that Earlham students were "a bunch of rich Easterners who want to change our way of life." But the battle against segregation and racism was increasingly focused on acting both on campus and in the larger American society.[71]

On the campus, students, faculty, and administrators took up a variety of activities to advance the cause of equality. Martin Luther King, Jr., visited Earlham in the spring of 1959, the first in a series of speakers who included such leading figures from the southern Freedom Movement as Aaron Henry, Marian Wright, James Bevel, James Lawson, Septima Clark, and Jack Greenberg. (At the other extreme, George Wallace spoke on campus while campaigning in the Indiana Democratic presidential primary in 1964. Students greeted his states rights rhetoric with stony silence.) For a few years, the college set up an exchange program with Tougaloo College in Mississippi. In 1961, four students went to the Highlander School in Tennessee, a center of training for racial activism all over the South. The *Post* and the Opinion Board monitored events in the South closely, and students held fund-raisers, like a "hootenanny" in the fall of 1963, for the Congress of Racial Equality (CORE) and the Student Non-Violent Coordinating Committee (SNCC), which were in the forefront of the movement.[72]

By 1963, Earlham students were joining other idealistic, largely affluent white students, usually from elite schools, going south to work with SNCC, CORE, and other groups on voter registration and desegregation projects. In the summer of 1963, for example, Pete Titleman was in Albany, Georgia, a particular target of activists. John Stevenson went to Mississippi for the "Freedom Summer" of 1964, working near Philadelphia, which became the center of national attention when three northern students were murdered near there. Another student, Ralph Engleman, was a civil rights veteran by 1964, with service in sit-ins in Nashville in 1961, in Martin Luther King, Jr.'s campaign in Birmingham in 1963, and in the Freedom Summer. He was a close friend of one of the murdered students, Andrew Goodman. By 1966, students were working with the Southern Christian Leadership Conference and other civil rights organizations on projects in such northern cities as Chicago and New York.[73]

None of these actions proved controversial on campus, nor did they attract negative comment from any of the campus constituencies. But when a race-conscious frame of analysis was applied to the campus, it did raise tensions, tensions that were subdued compared with those that many schools experienced, but very real and painful.

When Joe Elmore became academic dean in 1963, he made increasing the number of black students at Earlham a priority. At that time, black enrollment was low, thirteen Americans and two from overseas. A year later it was up to twenty-three and five, respectively, 2.2 percent of the student body. In 1965, the college decided to make a concerted effort to increase black enrollment as part of a Quakerly commitment to the "disadvantaged." Certain students, like Sybil Jordan, who had been one of the African Americans who integrated Little Rock Central High School,

Frances Moore, who would achieve an international reputation in the 1970s, and Marilyn McNabb, one of the organizers of the Earlham chapter of Students for a Democratic Society (SDS), took the lead in encouraging the college to act.[74]

Aside from more intensive recruiting, some remedial work would probably be needed for students coming out of segregated southern school systems or struggling urban ones. Here Earlham was able to draw on a new Great Society program, Upward Bound, which, with funds from the Office of Economic Opportunity, attempted "to enhance the self-image of the high school participant and his ability to relate to others so that he may picture himself as part of a college experience." In fact Upward Bound was not designed solely for blacks. The first sessions were held on campus in the summer of 1966, with students from Richmond, Cincinnati, Dayton, Troy, and Lewisburg, Ohio. Lincoln Blake and Paul Lacey, two English professors with a special interest in African American students, were the directors.[75]

That fall, nineteen black students, the largest group in the college's history, entered Earlham. In the next few years, black enrollment grew substantially. By 1969, it was up to fifty-nine, or 4.2 percent of the college's enrollment, the highest percentage of any private school in Indiana. By 1972, it had grown to 75, or 6 percent of the student body.[76]

While there was now a significant black presence on campus, the experience of these students was mixed. For some, it was a happy place. Sybil Jordan, the black woman from Little Rock who graduated in 1966, found Earlham "fun, challenging, and exciting." Gwen Weaver, who arrived from Washington, D.C., in 1967, thought that Earlham was everything that she had wanted in a college, and affirmed her experience by becoming a Quaker. Even such Earlham supporters, however, acknowledged that many black students had different experiences, and many were open in voicing their disappointments about certain facets of Earlham.[77]

Unhappiness centered on three aspects of the college. The first was the lack of black faculty. The first black professor, William Cousins in sociology, joined the faculty in 1966, remaining two years. Bolling and Elmore tried to attract others, but without success. Elmore blamed the unwillingness of black professors to come to a relatively small city like Richmond, as well as the intense competition for minority faculty. At least one decision proved extremely controversial, when Bolling in 1969 rejected a candidate with Black Panther ties who arrived on campus with two bodyguards but who had enthusiastic support all over campus.[78]

Bound up with the problem of recruiting black faculty was the question of a Black Studies Program. Earlham was a little ahead of most schools in teaching African history—that began in 1965—and by 1968

Paul Lacey was teaching a seminar on African American literature. Overall, however, Earlham was simply joining the pack of schools hurrying in the late 1960s to establish such programs.[79]

For many on campus, this effort was far from adequate. They demanded a full-fledged Black Studies Program, headed by a black person. In the fall of 1968, a special Black Studies Committee, headed by Helen Hole, studied how to set up a program. The committee reported its recommendation to establish the program to the faculty meeting on May 1, 1969. Outside Stout Meetinghouse, where faculty meetings were held, over one hundred students participated in a vigil, gazing in at the faculty meeting. As the faculty discussed the proposal, the students broke up into black and white caucuses. After a few minutes, the black students announced: "We're going in," and moved into the meetinghouse, congregating in the hallway outside the entrances to the meeting room while the faculty debated whether they should break with tradition and allow students to observe. Few faculty approved; it was clear to Paul Lacey, the clerk, that most were unwilling to proceed under circumstances they perceived as coercive. Instead, the faculty adjourned for ten minutes as the students withdrew outside. Some were angry, calling for a class boycott if the faculty meeting rejected the Black Studies proposal. After the meeting reconvened, however, the students were content to send in one student with a petition to observe, agreeing that they would withdraw if there was even one objection. There was, and the students gave up their attempt to enter. By now, even faculty sympathetic to the protesters felt that it would be unwise under these circumstances to attempt to reach consensus, and so postponed a final decision until May 6. At that meeting they approved the proposal, with a few professors who had doubts about the design of the program standing aside.[80]

Over the next year, planning proceeded for the program, but its start was rocky. Funds had to be raised, and enrollment in some of the courses was disappointing. One history course in the spring of 1971, team taught by three professors, had only five students. A director who was hired to begin in the fall of 1970 withdrew at the last minute. It was not until 1972 that T. J. Davis arrived as the permanent director of the program.[81]

There were other attempts to incorporate the experiences of black people into the curriculum. About 1970, some students began to demand a required course in Black Studies. There was also an attempt to set up an Urban Studies Program. George Sawyer, a black 1955 graduate and local attorney, was hired to coordinate it. It proved short-lived, however, due to lack of funds, lack of support from other departments on campus, and the doubts of some faculty that Richmond was sufficiently "urban" to make such a program work.[82]

The last area of conflict grew out of the experiences of many of the black students on campus. By 1965, African American students were beginning to voice complaints—while Earlham was better than the larger American society, blacks found "some prejudice and (though very rarely) even rude insults." At that time, they blamed them on ignorance, especially among new students.[83]

Within five years, the complaints were becoming more pointed and explicit. English professor Lincoln Blake perceived "an undercurrent of unexpressed racial tension on this campus." A black Quaker found a "wall of racism." Simba Lewis, one of the most outspoken African American students, pronounced "the whole atmosphere here . . . very covert but very hostile." Another black student agreed. "Earlham is a microcosm of the overall sick and inhuman American society," he wrote. "Overt and covert racism is just as prevalent here as it is in the rural and urban societies of this country." Critics pointed to what they said was an unacceptably small number of black students, an unacceptably higher attrition rate among them, and the lack of black faculty as proof.[84]

One of the sources of this alienation was the ideological direction of many black students in the late 1960s. Across the country, many embraced not integration, but separatism, based on the ideology of Black Power. Many proponents of such views were contemptuous of white liberals. "I suppose the idea of white liberals is all right, but I can't see getting into a deep personal relationship with one," a student commented. "In order to escape from the supremacy of white culture, blacks intellectually and emotionally need to feel our own roots, . . . to rediscover our own community," another wrote.[85]

This new militancy manifested itself in various ways. In 1967, the Black Leadership Action Coalition (BLAC) was formed to expose "elements of racism which are hidden by the false atmosphere of brotherhood." It advocated the establishment of a Black House, which began in 1969 in one of the campus houses, and giving a seat on the Community Council to any group "that could prove past discrimination."[86]

The reaction from the rest of the campus was mixed. Many white students and faculty found the BLAC's tactics and demands understandable and reasonable. Bolling, for example, defended the formation of Black House as giving African American students a chance to find an identity. Others thought that any kind of separatism was incompatible with the Quaker mission of the college. Helen Hole watched with "a sense of defeat that we have to have a black house." William Fuson protested official recognition of BLAC on the grounds that it was based on race, "a specious category, intellectually indefensible." When BLAC held an observance of Martin Luther King, Jr.'s birthday in 1971 restricted to blacks, and posted guards in Nation of Africa uniforms outside

Goddard Auditorium to control admission, Warren Staebler decried it. "The terrible tensions straining our large society we should refrain from reproducing in our little society," he wrote. "Whatever militant separatism may be justifiably contained in the complex meaning of Black Power outside our gates has no place inside them." In the era of Black Power, George Sawyer noted, many at Earlham were longing for the days of King. But for many campus blacks, those days were past.[87]

Still, one should not overstate the degree of racial alienation or hostility at Earlham in these years. While rhetoric from the most militant activists was occasionally ferocious, rhetoric was usually not translated into action. The vigil at the May 1, 1969, faculty meeting was the closest any group ever came to disruptive action, in contrast to the racially charged protests that scarred other colleges, and the utter failure of that effort apparently made an impression. When a few BLAC members considered disrupting a board meeting to press grievances, cooler heads persuaded them to send in a request for one representative to address the board, which happened. Even the more outspoken black leaders thought that most African Americans on campus were "soft spoken and patient." Solidarity was not absolute. When administrators charged one outspoken BLAC leader with burglarizing the Earlham Bookstore, the initial reaction of other members was loudly to cry frame-up and persecution and make life miserable for some administrators. Yet when persuaded by the evidence, they not only acquiesced but themselves told the perpetrator to leave. Meanwhile, the faculty and administrators tried to deal patiently with tensions, real and perceived, by encouraging dialogue and considering a testimony on race.[88]

Ironically, the most explosive racial confrontation involving Earlham students took place off campus, at Richmond High School. Racial tensions had run high in the community in the 1960s. The high school was a center of resentment because of the small number of black teachers, the absence of blacks from groups like the pom-pom corps, and a series of racial incidents. The spark came with a confrontation between a white teacher and a black student in March 1971. With the support of their parents and black community leaders, black students walked out of classes and began a sit-in to protest conditions and policies at the high school.[89]

The walk-out was the climax of years of frustration, but Earlham students and faculty were actively involved. Some joined the protesting students; Ken Martin, a black English professor, carried a sign reading: "Free your mind and your ass will follow." The emphasis was on keeping the protest nonviolent. Here Bolling was convinced that George Sawyer and students from the college played a critical role. There was some scuffling when police tried to carry protesters out of the building. The confrontation ended when the school board agreed to examine black grievances.[90]

As racial tensions had increased in Richmond, many white residents blamed Earlham. In the spring of 1966, for example, local realtors spread rumors that Earlham was "pushing housing integration." (When Earlham had developed part of its holdings on the southeast edge of the campus early in the 1960s, it had intentionally sold building lots to blacks, breaking local housing patterns.) When trouble broke out at the high school, many were sure that Earlham people were the cause. "Earlham is behind the whole thing," one woman claimed. "Sawyer started it, the Earlham College kids started it, and then the kids [at the high school] backed them up." This became the prevailing opinion among white residents; town-gown relations were probably never worse. Bolling and other administrators pointed in vain to the thousands of hours of volunteer work in the community by Earlham students and their attempts at mediation during the sit-in.[91]

Overall, Earlham did not escape tensions from a more racially diverse student body in the 1960s. The complaints were those that broke out on campuses across the United States, and Earlham's solutions—to try to increase black enrollment, find black faculty, create a Black Studies Program, and heighten racial sensitivity—were much the same as those at other schools. Yet, for whatever reason—the Quaker influence, the commitment of all parties to keep the peace—Earlham made the transition better than most.[92]

Earlham and the War

The Vietnam War, and the antiwar movement, were defining events for American higher education between 1965 and 1972. Earlham shared fully in "the movement"; by 1968 opposition to the war was probably as full and as widespread as on any campus in the country. Yet the antiwar movement at Earlham was always peaceful; rhetoric might be strident, but actions were never violent.

The antiwar movement on campus did not spring up overnight, of course. It found fertile ground in the pacifist commitments of many of the faculty, both the CPS men who were now its senior members, and the newer arrivals. Successive groups of students, some Quaker, some not, also lent support. Often other students, who were showing a growing interest in leftist politics, joined them. In 1961 such interests found expression in the Earlham Political Issues Committee (EPIC). A 1963 survey of incoming freshmen showed that political awareness and rebelliousness had increased greatly since 1960.[93]

These faculty and students were often at odds with Landrum Bolling, who shared at least one characteristic of William C. Dennis: he was not a pacifist. He described himself instead as a "maverick Quaker who does not feel that pacifism has very much immediate practical relevance to the foreign policy of the United States." Privately, Bolling was impatient with those he labeled "naive political pacifists," seen most publicly at the AFSC. And Bolling was not alone on campus. Debates on pacifism and disarmament, on the Opinion Board and elsewhere, were lively.[94]

There were numerous occasions for debate in the early 1960s. Earlham students took part in an AFSC-led vigil at the army chemical weapons facility in Newport, Indiana, in the spring of 1961. In the fall of 1962, when the Cuban Missile Crisis was at its height, a group of seventeen students joined a protest in Indianapolis against U.S. policy, much to Bolling's chagrin. On campus, controversy erupted over accepting scholarship money provided by the National Defense Education Act. Some objected to anything involving "defense," others to the requirement of a loyalty oath from recipients. A few years later, there was debate over allowing the campus to be part of local civil defense planning. "A Friends' College must ask itself what psychological effect its action . . . will have," wrote chemistry professor Theodor Benfey. "If we become too soon a cog in the machine of readiness for the war to come, we will be seriously hampered in doing those things which Quakers have a vocation to do: to build the conditions for peace." In both cases, however, Bolling made the decision to participate in the programs.[95]

Clearly related to this peace activism was a new interest in the politics of the Left. In the early 1960s, Earlham still had a vibrant two-party system. In the 1960 election, for example, Nixon narrowly edged Kennedy on campus. There was an active Earlham Conservative Club which, while often the target of pacifist ire, was uncowed. It was the self-described radicals of the Left, however, who increasingly set the terms of discourse on campus. One unhappy alumnus grumbled that Earlham showed every sign of becoming "a second-hand Antioch."[96]

This political activism was murky in its ideology. It was part of a nationwide movement, sometimes vaguely Marxist, committed to non-violence, civil rights, disarmament, and economic change. In 1962, it found expression in the Port Huron Statement of the newly formed Students for a Democratic Society (SDS), which early attracted interest at Earlham. What was needed was some cause around which to rally. In early 1963, Earlham sympathizers found it in free speech.[97]

The issue was whether or not to allow an avowed communist to speak on campus. In 1963, with Cold War tensions still running high, this was an exceedingly controversial issue. In Indiana, for example, state law prohibited communists from appearing at state universities. At Earlham, a small group of students, mostly associated with a new student literary magazine, *Prism,* wanted to invite a Polish diplomat to speak. Bolling thought them "naive" and mostly interested in stirring up controversy, but nevertheless set faculty and board committees in motion to study the whole issue of controversial speakers. That spring, the Polish diplomat did come to campus to speak on Marxism, with historian Edward Bastian offering a critique afterwards.[98]

That fall, the issue became far more complex when Christopher Clausen, the editor of *Prism,* invited Herbert Aptheker to campus. Aptheker, a Columbia-trained historian whose book *American Negro Slave Revolts* was a landmark work, was also an open member of the Communist party, in fact one of its chief American theoreticians. Aware of potential trouble, the faculty spent several meetings discussing Aptheker's appearance. They were divided. Some, like Laurence Strong, feared the "predicament of being able to discuss nothing to which we do not already subscribe." For many this was a fundamental issue of free debate and discussion. Others, like Elton Trueblood, saw little intellectual value in the visit of a defender of Stalinism. Bolling was nettled, convinced that he was "dealing with great numbers of immature adolescents who are in rebellion against almost any kind of parental authority." Clausen and the editors of the *Post* saw a blatant double standard. "The Conservative Club, over the past few years, has brought a whole menagerie of racists, unreconstructed Luftwaffe pilots, and other anti-democratic speakers," the *Post* editorialized. Clausen deplored what he saw as a lack of intellectual integrity by which only leftist speakers were judged "controversial." After long discussion by a faculty committee, the decision was made to postpone Aptheker's appearance until the spring. (Ironically, he would have been postponed regardless, since he was originally scheduled for November 25, the day of John F. Kennedy's funeral.)[99]

By the end of the year, the college had settled on a policy that affirmed "free discussion." Aptheker was rescheduled to speak April 6, 1964, as part of a series of three speakers, "sandwiched" between a Roman Catholic philosopher and the anticommunist intellectual Sidney Hook. Aptheker himself pronounced Earlham to be "like the beginning of a Chekhov play." When he completed his acerbic dissection of American capitalism, Bolling, to the dismay of some faculty and students and the happiness of many trustees and alumni, followed him with a rebuttal. Cuban exiles arrived to picket, and the *Palladium-Item* was nearly apoplectic in its outrage over Aptheker's presence.[100]

After Aptheker, there were no limits on campus speakers, and few attracted much attention off-campus. An impression had been sealed, however, in the minds of many local residents that Earlham was a "pro-communist" place. The next few years would not change such minds.[101]

The Vietnam War first reared its head on campus in a *Post* article in 1963. The first signs of opposition to the war surfaced in 1965. At Earlham, the antiwar movement took its cues from the larger, national movement. Campus activists drew basic tactics of protests and vigils, teach-ins and draft resistance, from off-campus. But at Earlham the antiwar movement was different from that at many other campuses: it never turned nihilist or violent. The SDS had disappeared from campus by 1968, even as the national organization was entering its most vio-lence-prone and in some cases terroristic phase. Nothing remotely similar ever emerged at Earlham.[102]

Here the college's Quaker identity was critical. While the antiwar movement was tied to other forms of activism on campus, and by 1970 many Earlham students advocated radical change in American society, they always did so peacefully. At Earlham more than most schools, the peace movement was bound up as much with older commitments to pacifism as it was with the New Left.

There were, to be sure, a few students and faculty who saw them-selves as part of the New Left. Such committed radicals dismissed the rest of the student body as "a very tame group." One alumnus went on that popular leftist pilgrimage, a journey to Cuba to help with the sugar harvest. A temporary instructor, after leaving Earlham, really did go on to try to manufacture bombs with the Weatherman faction of the SDS, fortunately unsuccessfully. There was an SDS chapter on campus for a time, with Paul Lacey as its faculty sponsor, but, as mentioned above, it soon faded away. The few faculty who attempted to bring confrontational tactics to campus found little support. Even committed opponents of the war were appalled when an English professor led a small group of students in heckling conservative author Russell Kirk during a campus appearance. More typical of Earlham was the stance in 1969 of an antiwar group calling itself Concerned Students for Communication: "We have absolutely ruled out disruptive confrontation tactics."[103]

Nevertheless, opposition to the war on campus was real and intense. The first stirrings came in the spring of 1965, as organized antiwar protests were getting underway elsewhere. For the next five years, events on campus generally followed national trends. Earlham saw teach-ins and vigils and protests on and off-campus. Beginning as a distinct minority, by 1968 opponents of the war were the overwhelming majority at Earlham. The first demonstration on campus took place in May 1965, a month after mass antiwar protests in Washington, D.C., led by the SDS with several Earlham students participating. The Earlham SDS chapter organized the local action. Significantly, two of its leaders, John Stevenson and Ralph Engelman, were civil rights activists who had been in Mississippi. They handed out a letter at the May Day celebration, and on May 12 organized a silent vigil on the Heart, with about 150 people, including 10 faculty, participating. After the vigil concluded, an open discussion took place in the meetinghouse. As the new school year began in the fall of 1965, activities intensified, in a pattern that they would follow for the next four years. Vigils on the Heart now were held every Thursday at noon. The first teach-in, part of a national event, took place on October 9. Arthur Kanegis and Robert Meeropol (the latter the son of Julius and Ethel Rosenberg) took the lead in forming the Earlham Committee to End the War in Vietnam. Twenty students attended the demonstrations in Washington over Thanksgiving weekend that the National Coordinating Committee to End the War in Vietnam had organized. Protesters called for "a halt to bombing, torturing, and other war atrocities." Those attending the Thursday vigils made a cease-fire, with U.S. withdrawal and international arbitration to follow, their goals. Some protesters were more pointed: "I am disgusted with this country; it is rotting, externally and internally," Meeropol wrote in the *Post*.[104]

In the fall of 1966, students decided to take the antiwar movement into Richmond. They cautiously began with a vigil along U.S. 40 at the north edge of campus before actually venturing to the courthouse square on November 23. The mayor, Corky Cordell, had been leery of such an event; that spring he had met privately with Paul Lacey and two students, imploring them not to cause trouble. Lacey's response was that as long as the war continued, protest was inevitable, and that Cordell would have to decide who was in the charge of the town, the mayor or the high school hoodlums. The vigil took place, with a few onlookers, mostly Richmond High School students, hurling obscenities, but police prevented any direct confrontation. This was the first of many such demonstrations in town.[105]

The draft was at the heart of student concerns. Some students did go to Vietnam; at least one, Bruce Shaffer, was killed in action soon after he graduated in 1968. There were long discussions among the men about the best ways to fail draft-board medical screenings, such as "chopping off a toe, or by drinking something that would make your urine purple," one remembered. Burning draft cards was, of course, a favorite form of protest, but few on campus went that far. Faculty offered draft counseling, and in fact conscientious objectors from Earlham encountered few problems. Here Jackson Bailey's work in Japanese studies proved invaluable, winning a statement from appropriate authorities that it was "in the national interest" to improve the teaching of English in Japan. This provided an opportunity for alternative service for a number of Earlham students. By 1969, some on campus wanted to offer draft counseling to Richmond High School students, while others handed out literature to inductees at the local draft board office. Still, there were a few students who chose the course of draft resistance. The first was Tim Zimmer, an absolute pacifist who had mailed his draft card to President Johnson and had refused even to apply for CO status. Sentenced to three years in prison in the spring of 1967, he served part of his sentence and returned to campus in 1969. Compared with the draft resisters twenty years earlier, Zimmer's support on campus was overwhelming.[106]

Initially, there was significant opposition on campus to the antiwar movement. One 1968 graduate estimated that in 1965 opponents of the war were less than 20 percent of the student body. A writer in the *Post* that year concluded that there was a consensus on campus that "public political involvement" by students was a bad thing. Handing out literature at the May Day celebration brought sharp criticism. When one campus peace group scheduled an outdoor rally in May 1966, sixty counterprotesters threatened to pelt the "peaceniks" with water balloons. When rain forced the rally into Goddard Auditorium, the opponents came in with signs reading: "Back Our Boys in Vietnam." After listening a short time to the antiwar speeches, they left. Some faculty remained skeptical about the peace activists, like Edward Bastian, who thought them hopelessly naive about Ho Chi Minh and communism. Elton Trueblood was always critical of the antiwar movement, especially after his personal friend Richard Nixon became president. As late as 1967, one student thought that most students viewed "the weekly vigils as being silly and of no importance and scoff at anyone who is a part of them."[107]

Yet views were changing. The student who thought that 20 percent of the campus opposed the war in 1965 felt that the proportions were reversed by 1968. By that year faculty counseling students found that those deciding to serve, not conscientious objectors, were the targets of most campus criticism. Many students from conservative middle class families who arrived contemptuous of demonstrators had been transformed by the time that they graduated. A case in point was Eric Berg of the class of 1968. In the spring of 1966, he was one of the organizers of the counterdemonstration in Goddard. Two years later, he was a conscientious objector working for Robert F. Kennedy's presidential campaign in Indiana. In this, he was much like Landrum Bolling, who in 1965 was critical of the protesters. By February 1967 he was writing to Sen. J.

William Fulbright, a leading "Dove," about his "strong feeling about the war in Vietnam, and particularly about the tragic and foolish continuation of the bombing." In 1969, Bolling was signing public statements against the war.[108]

By 1968, the antiwar movement at Earlham was at its height. Vigils and demonstrations continued on campus and in town. Many students and faculty threw themselves into the antiwar challenges of Eugene McCarthy and Robert F. Kennedy for the Democratic presidential nomination. The nominally Quaker Republican nominee, Richard Nixon, drew almost no public support on campus, and his victory plunged many into gloom.[109]

In November 1968, Earlham had the chance to show how real its commitments to free speech and nonviolence were. On November 11, the Richmond Classroom Teachers Association was to use the dining hall for a meeting. There were many conservatives in the school system who disapproved of Earlham, and many on campus were sure that they were responsible for the invitation to Selective Service Director Lewis B. Hershey to address the meeting. Probably no one was more unpopular on college campuses in 1968, and the teachers saw this as a way of embarrassing the college, by provoking either a cancellation or an incident. Bolling first learned that Hershey was coming to campus from the local newspaper two weeks before the meeting. The teachers association innocently protested that it had no idea that Hershey's presence might cause a problem.[110]

In fact, the college handled the situation better than anyone could have hoped. "Earlham students met the flaunting of Lewis B. Hershey . . . with such power and equanimity that we should all be proud," one local observer wrote. Bolling invited Hershey to a question-and-answer session with students, an invitation that Hershey accepted. The day before his appearance, several hundred faculty and students paid for a full-page advertisement in the *Palladium-Item*, a condemnation of the war that Paul Lacey had written. When Hershey spoke to the teachers, a group of faculty and students held a silent vigil outside the dining hall. In the meeting with students, the questions were pointed but polite, with no disruptions. Even Hershey praised student behavior.[111]

The final test came in the spring of 1970, with the Cambodian incursion and the killing of four students by National Guardsmen at Kent State University. Across the country, colleges and universities exploded in protest; many simply closed down. Anger and consternation ran just as deep at Earlham, but the college's reaction was significantly different. On May 6, the day after the Kent State shootings, classes were cancelled and faculty and students met to decide on a response. That response was peaceful, imaginative, and successful.[112]

The faculty had always resisted making any kind of corporate statement on the war, holding that such actions should be left to individuals. On this occasion, however, they acted as a body, stating their "profound opposition to the use of live ammunition by police or military units in efforts to control student demonstrations." They continued on, "in keeping with this college's longstanding Quaker opposition to the use of violence in any form," to appeal "to the dissident critics of our society, on and off the campus to refrain from those acts of violence which might provoke violent retaliation."[113]

The same day, most faculty and students gathered at Chase Stage. Bolling was away from campus, and Joe Elmore left direction of the gathering to the faculty. "Ted Benfey, Jerry Woolpy, Bill Stephenson, lots of faculty would go up and engage in the free-for-all," Elmore remembered. "It was a very passionate but very good debate." Several possible courses of action emerged from the discussion.[114]

One course was to go to Washington to try to impress members of Congress with the depth of student concern after Kent State. It made a deep impression on many that, along with the students and faculty on the buses, rode Landrum Bolling. The faculty set up options for students who wished to withdraw for the rest of the term or who wished to focus on current events in their courses. Finally, students decided to try to reach out to the local community. About twenty five met at the Holiday Inn with an equal number of community leaders. They made arrangements for students to engage in more community service. Perhaps the most unusual result was a program in which students rode on patrol with Richmond police to gain a better understanding of the problems that police faced. Unfortunately, the program came to an end a year later after the confrontations at Richmond High School.[115]

As was the case across the country, the spring of 1970 marked the crest of the antiwar movement at Earlham. The wind-down was gradual, to be sure. Demonstrations, vigils, and participation in national protests continued, as did draft resistance. But as the number of American troops in Vietnam steadily decreased, so did the passions on campus. By early 1971, Bolling judged that the "fire" was "out." The pacifist and social justice commitments behind that "fire" never died out completely, however, and in the 1980s would burst forth again.[116]

The Transformation of Campus Culture

By 1973, the institutionally guided student culture that had dominated Earlham for a century had come to an end. The college had relinquished much of its regulation of the lives of students. No longer were men and women barred from each other's living quarters. No longer was convocation attendance mandatory. Dress codes were gone, as were the served meals that had been a feature of the dining hall for generations. To a degree that many found distressing, sex and drugs became part of the lives of many students. Meanwhile, venerable campus customs disappeared. The old literary societies, the Phoenix, Ionian, and Anglican, all died. Homecoming became an event almost completely for alumni. Interest in spectator sports waned, despite some of the most successful teams in the college's history. The result was friction, especially with alumni, townspeople, and some members of Indiana Yearly Meeting.[117]

Early in Bolling's presidency, a few students assumed the style and manners of the "beats," the cultural rebels who drew increasing attention in the late 1950s and early 1960s. The very novelty of their appearance, especially the long hair and beards of the men, attracted considerable attention, much of it disapproving. Typical was a local resident who complained to Bolling about the "creeps and queeries and the unwashed bearded that are cluttering up your campus." As early as 1959, a visiting group of academics, generally complimentary of Earlham, commented that it seemed to "have an excessive number of 'odd-balls'" among its male students. In 1961, Director of Admissions Darrell Beane worried that "the impressions of Earlham (in terms, mainly, of physical appearances of students and some faculty)" were hurting recruiting in Indiana. Such nonconformists annoyed Bolling, but he never took any harsh action against them, other than refusing to allow them to be pictured in campus publicity materials. By 1966, he was conceding that they were often the college's best and most thoughtful students.[118]

These nonconformists were the wave of the future. In some cases there were real problems—faculty charged that some students were not just unkempt, but absolutely dirty. A 1965 visitor complained that she thought she was in Greenwich Village. There was friction among the students, especially between groups that by 1966 were becoming known as "jocks" and "grubs." There was a minor blow-up in May 1966, when eleven men took an especially long-haired "grub" from his dormitory room and forcibly cut his hair. By 1967, the Senate was criticizing the college's publicity materials for the "clean-cut" image that they tried to present. By 1970, virtually every rule or tradition about dress, such as not going barefoot to class, was gone. Administrators worried about the impact on prospective students and donors—Tom Jones, still raising money, would bring visitors to campus only during vacations when students were not visible—but college authorities applied no coercion to force changes. Both trustees and administrators concluded that regulations would be counterproductive and would "close the channels of communication."[119]

If student dress disturbed many, changes in living arrangements, especially "visitation" and coed dorms, were the source of even more criticism. Here again Earlham followed nationwide patterns in the 1960s, as the traditional strict separation of the living quarters of the sexes broke down on campuses. That, in turn, was inextricably linked in the minds of many with the "Sexual Revolution" of the late 1960s and early 1970s.[120]

In some respects, Earlham was ahead of most American schools. In 1961, the school adopted an "open section" policy, whereby men and women could visit each other on Sunday afternoons in their dormitory rooms. Doors were to be left open, and at least three of any couple's four feet were to be on the floor at all times. Students justified the visiting with arguments that it made for a "homelike" atmosphere and showed trust of students. In the summer of 1963, however, the administration ended the experiment. Campus rumor blamed a spate of student pregnancies; the official explanation was that "dating situations behind closed doors in dormitory bedrooms" had been abused "by some irresponsible persons." Privately, Bolling wrote that "this 'open dorm' nonsense has gotten completely out of hand clear across the country." There were strenuous student protests, but Bolling was sure "that most of the girls are very much relieved to have this kind of thing eliminated."[121]

Agitation for change continued, however, growing in intensity after 1965. Student groups put forward a variety of proposals. The men's dormitories, setting their policies through the Association of Men Residents (AMR), went back to open sections, with individual hallway units setting their own policies. Some limited the hours that women could visit, while some were open seven days a week, twenty-four hours a day. The women were more conservative, not moving to allow such options in dormitories through the Association of Women Students (AWS) until 1969. Thereafter they quickly loosened their regulations.[122]

The other great change was the creation of coed dormitories. In the spring of 1969, the Senate presented the board with a "plan for [an] Ideal Earlham Living Situation." It included cooperative houses organized around themes (like a Spanish House), with such houses and dormitories being coed. In the fall of 1969, the first Earlham coed unit opened in one of the houses that the college owned. It proved so popular and successful that in the fall of 1970 there were three such houses, all coed, and Hoerner, the newest dormitory on campus, also became coed. By 1972, coed housing was the rule in three of the five dormitories. Some students, mostly women, expressed reservations, but they were a distinct minority. A 1972 survey showed that only 12 percent of students wished to live in single-sex housing. Coed housing was now the Earlham norm.[123]

Bound up closely with coed housing were worries about student sexuality. Official college policy was clear: "premarital and/or extra-marital sexual relations on the part of members of this community are intolerable. Persons insisting on practicing them are in effect dissociat-ing themselves from the Community." The administration frowned on even public discussion. When two married students jokingly inquired on the Opinion Board if the prohibition on sex applied to them, Bolling removed their note as "an offense to the community." There was some sex education in the 1960s. For most of the decade, a frank lecture on sexuality by the director of the Family Relations Program was part of New Student Week. One visiting counselor in 1962 found Earlham students very self-conscious about sex.[124]

There was evidence, however, of changing attitudes. One faculty member as early as 1963 sensed sentiment for "free love" on campus. That fall, a writer in the *Post* claimed that premarital sex was normal and healthy. By 1966, other writers were blasting the campus's "unrealistic restrictions" that impeded "healthy, uninhibited attitudes toward sex." By the end of the decade, the *Post* was running stories with headlines like: "Survey Reveals Students Ignore Sex Regulations." The survey in question, admittedly unscientific, showed that 63 percent of the students responding thought that premarital sex could be a good thing.[125]

The faculty and administration and even some students faced this revolution with a mixture of resignation and concern. Board members especially worried about the breakdown of traditional standards. Some students of the period had the impression that the college was concerned only with avoiding harmful, exploitative sexual relationships. Faculty had the impression that sex was causing problems. Officially, college policy remained the same: "Earlham College cannot endorse or approve premarital sexual relations," was the statement in the college catalog in 1969. Administrators felt that even implicitly to take any other position would break faith with other constituencies, especially the yearly meet-ings. At times it took public action to enforce that stand, as in 1972, when officials sanctioned six men and a woman who had been involved in what the administration described as a flagrant and unhealthy sexual relationship. By that year, some students were openly contemptuous of the school's attitude. "It is disgusting that Earlham continues to feel the need to protect its students from sex," one wrote. "At what magic age is a person able to handle sex? Upon graduation from Earlham?" Sex would continue to be a source of tension on campus down to the present.[126]

One of the most tragic aspects of the changes that "the Sixties" brought to college campuses was drug use. By 1970 Earlham, in some quarters, had the reputation of being a center of both the use and sale of illegal drugs, a reputation that was probably not deserved. Earlham, however, did not escape the challenges that most colleges had to confront.[127]

In 1960, there was no doubt that for those who cared to indulge, alcohol was the drug of choice on campus. No one claimed that the campus was entirely dry—one of the most memorable incidents of Tom Jones's presidency had been his dismayed discovery that some senior men had brought beer to the senior picnic. Bolling continued the traditional ban on alcohol, and assured concerned Friends in the two yearly meetings that offenders were expelled: "What criticism there can be on this point is beyond my imagination," he wrote to one.[128]

Over the next few years, student impressions were that many students, perhaps a majority, were drinking at least occasionally. One 1963 graduate remembered that while many students used alcohol, they always did so off campus, in one of the town bars or in the cemetery. In 1965, Bolling fervently denied that the campus had a drinking problem, but Dean of Students Eric Curtis thought otherwise. The *Post* reported that "a great many . . . do drink in their rooms on weekends."[129]

After 1965, drinking probably did increase. One woman who arrived in 1967 remembered students often drinking behind closed doors: "Well, we know we're not supposed to do it, but let's do it anyway." That same year, the Faculty Affairs Committee recorded that some faculty were challenging the college's total ban as unrealistic, but this did not move Bolling or the board. By 1968, one faculty member was deploring what he saw as a "more casual acceptance" of alcohol, a movement from "a policy of disapproval to one of indifference." By 1971, the *Post* was editorializing about the problem of loud, "dumb drunks" on campus.[130]

Other drugs arrived more slowly. As late as 1968, a student from Marion, Indiana, could graduate without ever having encountered them. In 1966, the college began attempts at drug education, but the impact was uncertain. Students of the late 1960s and early 1970s remember the use of marijuana—"not a big deal at all," as one put it—and some LSD. But other hard drugs were uncommon. A 1973 graduate, "a Puritan by resolution," remembered some "experimenting" friends who went to great lengths to acquire some peyote, but then had no idea of how to use it. A 1971 *Post* survey, undoubtedly not representative, found that over half of students responding had tried marijuana. It quoted one that "an awful lot of jocks are giving up vomiting on Saturday or Sunday . . . in favor of turning on." It found no heroin use, however, and considerable caution about hallucinogenic drugs.[131]

The college's response was often uneven. Officially, drug use was grounds for suspension or expulsion, and there were times when the college imposed such penalties. The emphasis, however, was on counseling and prevention. Students who sought help voluntarily did not face sanctions. Enforcement, however, was difficult, and only the most flagrant cases were taken up. On one occasion a number of students tried to force the issue by organizing a "confess-in," on the theory that if the hundreds who had used drugs at least once confessed, the administration would either have to give up the policy or expel most of the student body. Instead, the Office of the Dean of Students turned the names of confessed users over to the FBI, which took no action.[132]

Rumor and impressions in Richmond and elsewhere undoubtedly made the problem seem worse than it was. One administrator remembers constant charges that Earlham was the source of Richmond High School's drug problems, when in fact investigation consistently showed that students at the high school were usually the suppliers for Earlham. This impression, however, was never dispelled, and undoubtedly was a cause of the alienation of some of the college's local constituency.[133]

Even as new problems were appearing on campus, many traditions were passing away. Student life underwent a sea change between 1958 and 1973. In 1958, a graduate of a generation before would have found much that was familiar on campus. Freshmen still wore beanies and jumped through the Precedents Committee's hoops. Homecoming was still a major event, with floats for the parade, the "Tiv Rush" procession from campus to downtown and the Tivoli Theater, and the election of the Homecoming Queen. Students were still expected to dress for served dinners in the dining hall. The autumn All-College Outing was still a major event, as was the Senior Picnic just before Commencement. Attendance was still required at the twice-weekly convocations. The venerable Ionian, Phoenix, and Anglican still held places of honor on campus.[134]

By 1973, virtually all of these were gone. Beanies disappeared in 1968, and the Precedents Committee evolved into a New Student Week Committee whose function was to be warm and welcoming, rather than even slightly threatening. Homecoming was now for alumni; the election of the queen continued, but even that was under increasing attack. Served dinners and the dress code for dining had come to an end — critics blasted the distinction between served and servers as undemocratic. No longer did the All-College Outing take place, killed by student and faculty disinterest due to academic pressures, and the same fate soon met the Senior Picnic. The Ionian, Phoenix, and Anglican had all collapsed.

Mandatory convocation attendance, after considerable debate among the faculty, came to an end in 1969. Even caps and gowns had disappeared from commencement—the 1969 graduating class set a precedent by deciding not to wear them and use the money saved for black scholarships. Students saw these changes as an adjustment to the times—life was too serious for such frivolity. Frances Bolling, the wife of the president, saw it differently: "Students seemed to have no time or conscious desire for fun. All life was very earnest, almost grim."[135]

In fact, students did create new customs of fun and commitment (other than those under official ban). The first of a series of student-run coffee houses, the Guarded Well By, opened in Paul Lacey's garage in 1964, only to fall afoul of zoning and health regulations. Concerts by visiting folk and rock artists became increasingly popular. Students played an important role in the 1971 founding of a cooperative store that emphasized natural foods.[136]

A survivor of the older student culture, somewhat battered, was competitive athletics, especially the men's football and basketball teams. In these years, the college had some of its most successful teams. The 1961 football squad lost only one game, while in 1962 it went undefeated. From 1965 to 1974, under Coach Del Harris, later a fixture in the National Basketball Association, the basketball team was a consistent winner, advancing to the national NAIA finals in 1971. But student interest and support were declining. The football and basketball players, now the "jocks," tended to be politically and socially more conservative than the rest of the student body, and thus in disfavor in many quarters. In 1970 the Student Activities Board, which allocated funds to student groups, actually cut off money for the cheerleading squad, and football games went uncovered that fall because the *Post* could not find a sports editor. On the other hand, interest in other team sports, especially volleyball and soccer, grew steadily.[137]

Perhaps the greatest change in student life was for women. Their lives had been more restricted than men's, both in terms of the rules that the college imposed and the limits that society set. By 1973, the former had disappeared forever, while the latter had diminished considerably.

Alumni have somewhat different memories of Earlham's possibilities and expectations for women early in Bolling's administration. One 1958 graduate, an English major with an almost-perfect grade point average, remembered that her advisor apparently never thought of recommending graduate school to her. More common were women who found that Earlham treated them as well as it did men, both inside the classroom and in planning for careers. Several recall advisors who steered them away from "women's careers" to less traditional graduate and professional fields. Faculty were honest about problems that women would face. William Stephenson in biology, for example, coached women applying to medical school about the sexist attitudes they would immediately encounter. Particularly before 1965, the atmosphere at Earlham was far better than in most colleges and universities.[138]

In other ways, Earlham mirrored the larger society, but in less restrictive ways. Many, perhaps most, women came to the college expecting to find a husband there, and many did. One 1962 graduate remembered that "if there were no possibles [for marriage] by senior year, women started to feel desperate." Yet they also had the feeling that education came first, and that there was not the same pressure for an "MRS." degree as at many other schools.[139]

If Earlham gave women more intellectual freedom than most schools, it carefully controlled them in other ways, far more than it did men. In this respect, Earlham was much like other colleges, and patterns of change in such regulations mirrored the processes elsewhere.[140]

In 1958, as had been the case for a generation, women on campus had "hours"—they had to be in their dormitories by 10:30 on weeknights, and by midnight on weekends. There was also a "sign out" policy—applicable whenever women left dormitories, no matter what the reason, and even preceding spring break. Neither policy applied to men. The college justified these as security measures for the women's own safety, and only a few students, at least before 1965, publicly questioned them. They were accustomed to such restrictions at home, and friends at other colleges almost always reported similar rules. Theoretically, the AWS, with the oversight of the administration, set the regulations, and AWS was responsible for punishing violators.[141]

Early in the 1960s, a few women, often with backing from the men, did begin to challenge the rules that bound them. One woman took to the Opinion Board in 1961 to urge change:

Part of the process of maturation is learning to make one's own decisions as to whether one should stay out late or not. . . . If the College cannot trust a student's better judgment as to the hour of their return to the dorm here on campus, what do they expect will happen when a girl student leaves campus for a summer job in New York or some other large city? . . . I feel very strongly that it is time for a revamping of women students' dormitory rules! Certainly by the time a student has reached her senior year and is twenty-one years of age, she should not be penalized if she is one minute late!

In the spring of 1965, when the college suspended a woman for an hour's violation, there was considerable protest.[142]

In fact, the regulations did change. By 1967, junior and senior women could, with parental approval, set their own hours, although they still had to sign out. Of ninety-eight eligible women, only three had parents refuse permission. And most women seldom stayed out after the traditional closing hours. In the 1969–1970 school year, women got keys to let themselves into the dormitories, rather than depending on a staff member to allow them in after doors had been locked. Hours continued only for first-term women, with the limit that all women had to be in their dormitories by 6:00 A.M. In March 1971 that rule was abolished.[143]

Much of the change was due to the first glimmerings of the women's liberation movement on the campus. By 1964, one of the arguments put forth for change in women's rules charged that they stemmed from a "double standard . . . based on the archaic concepts of feminine inequality and fragility." By 1969, one student was writing in the *Post* that "we're not battling just specific rules, but the whole attitude of society toward women." Another woman student agreed. "Earlham girls are facing an identity crisis," Anne Minor wrote in the same year. "As of now, according to many female Earlhamites, she is floundering in the middle, caught between the safer-sounding traditional role and the exciting, but widely unaccepted ideas of women's liberation groups." By 1970, there was an Earlham Women's Liberation Group "to change the traditional roles and images of women and to affect the social, political, and economic conditions under which women live and work." The next year, the Women's Center was formed, and in January 1973 it began publishing a newsletter. By this time, the AWS and the AMR had merged, ending distinctions based on gender.[144]

One of the causes of change was one of Earlham's brightest features the off-campus study programs. By their nature, they involved considerably more freedom than was customary on campus. Faculty noticed that some women went through a period of shock, after being on their own in Paris or Rome or London, then returning to face a 10:30 curfew. Margaret Beidler, the dean of women for much of the sixties, was certain that foreign study had made change inevitable.[145]

Earlham as a Quaker Place

Those who were on campus in the 1960s differ in their impressions of how the school's Quaker identity changed in those years. On some points there was broad agreement. The founding of the Earlham School of Religion, the world's first Quaker seminary, was a notable event. Still at the core of the college's faculty was an active and articulate group of Friends. The college continued to attract a large number of Quaker students. There was also agreement that ties with the yearly meetings were much weaker by the end of the decade, weaker than they ever had been. On other points, especially a critical one, there was debate. It was unclear in the minds of many how much impact the college's Quaker identity had on its intellectual life. Some saw it as a foundation, others as a significant hindrance. There was also disagreement over the very nature of religious life on campus. Many perceived a significant decline, even a growing hostility to the more conventional forms of spiritual life.

Bolling himself was the second president of Earlham who was not a recorded Quaker minister, and the first who was not a birthright Friend. He and his family became members of West Richmond Meeting. He did not write extensively about Quakerism, and he did not preach, as Jones had, although he was a frequent speaker to Quaker groups on topics related to education. Privately he did reflect on Quakerism, and particularly about what it meant for Earlham to be a Quaker school.[146]

Bolling thought that the Quaker identity of the college had to be founded on religion. "We believe as a College that religion is central in human experience," he told the faculty in 1958. Bolling continued, however, in a solidly liberal way. Earlham would eschew "dogma" and "indoctrination"; the college would be "guided by spiritual insights" and a "common life" that would "bear some meaningful relationship to moral, ethical religious concerns and values." Bolling held to this vision throughout his presidency. Earlham was a *Christian* school, he wrote in 1971, which he defined as one that emphasized caring for one another and "balanced human development." The problem that many church-related schools faced was smugness: "The pretense that a Christian College is where everyone looks neat and clean and never makes a mistake, or violates a rule—and if he does is automatically thrown out." That pretense, Bolling argued, was "the curse hanging over the church-related college . . . the source of much of its failure to be truly Christian—in the spirit of the First Christian who consorted with publicans and sinners and so lived that ordinary, weak, fallible men and women might have life and have it more abundantly."[147]

Bolling had an acute awareness of the diversity of Quakerism. "There are so many brands of Friends in the world and they differ so widely in views on just about every subject that it is almost never possible to say what Friends think about anything," he wrote to one Quaker. For that reason, he was "inclined to be very generous about allowing anybody to claim the Quaker label . . . but very resistant to the claims of any individual or group which presumes to speak for *the* Quaker viewpoint."[148]

Within a year of becoming president, Bolling had to face a full-blown crisis of relations with Indiana Yearly Meeting, one of uncertain origins. After the 1958 yearly meeting sessions, Bolling had thought that "though we had a few rough spots, I had the feeling that the general attitude toward Earlham was as fine as I have ever known it to be." Later that same year, however, a new agitation broke out over smoking and dancing, issues that had seemingly been dormant for fifteen years, and a new accusation of widespread drinking on campus. At the Indiana Yearly Meeting sessions in August 1959, there was a rancorous discussion. Three years earlier, both Indiana and Western yearly meetings had agreed to include Earlham in their budgets, the money to be used for scholarships for students from the yearly meetings. At yearly meeting in 1959, however, New Garden and Van Wert quarterly meetings, both strongly fundamentalist, objected to providing any funds to Earlham. New Garden, in addition to condemning smoking, drinking, and dancing on the campus, criticized Earlham for liberal theology, questioning the divinity of Christ, not emphasizing the Blood Atonement, and teaching evolution. Bolling responded that he had offered to meet with the two quarterly meetings to discuss their concerns, but he had received no response. He was blunt in his comments: "If Earlham had depended on the financial support of the yearly meeting it would have gone out of existence long ago."[149]

The ensuing discussion followed lines that would have been familiar to Elbert Russell and Alexander Purdy, as did a subsequent meeting held in October in Fairmount, Indiana. Critics claimed that Earlham did not hold to "the original teachings of Friends—George Fox, William Penn, and others." There was particular unhappiness over reports that "the Garden of Eden" was "taught as a *myth* at Earlham." The critics, however, differed from the previous generation in a vital way. As one New Garden Friend put it, there was no desire "to control Earlham's policy or to dictate class instruction." They did object, however, to being assessed by the yearly meeting to support teachings and practices that they opposed. One Friend from Van Wert made the issue one of liberty of conscience. The college, instead of relying on assessments that local meetings and churches had to pay, should "draw its own support."[150]

Earlham did not lack defenders. One student, James G. Johnson, the son of a pastor, and himself then the pastor of the Dublin Friends Meeting, pointed out that it was Earlham and not his yearly meeting that had drawn him to the ministry. Alumni challenged critics about how much they knew firsthand and how much they were relying on rumor. Elton Trueblood, then the clerk of the yearly meeting, was blunt—he headed Earlham's religion department, and any blame for its failings was his. He considered the attacks "a moral issue . . . a dishonest device, disgusting, a disgrace to our Yearly Meeting."[151]

Bolling was also blunt in responding to such criticism. He pointed out that the financial support from the yearly meetings for Earlham was minimal, compared with the $125,000 that the United Brethren gave Indiana Central College, or the $200,000 annually that Anderson College received from the Church of God. The relationship of Earlham with the yearly meetings was not "warm." He was convinced that the attacks came from "people who know little about the standards, values, practices, and beliefs of faculty and students at Earlham." Privately, he was even more outspoken. "There are certain 'Earlham haters' in the Yearly Meeting, who miss no occasion to condemn the College for real and fancied wrongs," he wrote to one Friend, "and . . . one of their favorite charges is to accuse the College of being 'too liberal' and too much influenced by the 'liberal wing' of Quaker ministers." Bolling thought it better to handle such conflicts openly. In the end, however, he agreed to a compromise that left support of the Earlham scholarships to the decision of each meeting, thereby releasing objectors from support.[152]

No other such conflicts erupted during the rest of Bolling's tenure, but there were certainly signs of strain. The number of students from the two yearly meetings gradually declined. About one hundred in 1958, it was less than twenty by 1973. The reasons were complicated. One was that the college stopped automatically admitting every applicant from Indiana and Western yearly meetings. One pastor who was well disposed toward Earlham wrote of the despair of one rejected student: "I have never witnessed such a tragic scene as the day Earlham's dean sent the letter informing him *he was not* [admitted], that his records did not indicate he was college material." In fact the college still gave "clear-cut priority to Quaker students from our Yearly Meetings," and it was easier for Indiana Quakers to gain admission than anyone else. The problem was that fewer and fewer were applying. Cost was one consideration— more and more, Friends from the yearly meetings felt that, despite scholarships, Earlham was just too expensive for them.[153]

But there was also a growing feeling that Earlham was an alien place, dominated by those whose values were different. The student deputation visits to local meetings ended by 1970, amidst complaints about the appearance and spirituality of participants. "The message was not a gospel message; prayers were read, mechanically, not spontaneous," one Friend wrote. Another told Bolling that "we have yet to really see a spiritually enlivened person to come from the school and wonder what is the matter with the religion that is supposed to be at Earlham." One alumnus was prescient in writing to Bolling in 1962: "As the eastern students become more plentiful, I believe an antagonism will develop toward Indiana's way of life, Indiana's weather, Indiana's politics, in short, to Indiana," she wrote. "Quakerism and Indiana's plain ways will become downgraded, misunderstood, and unwanted." Part of the problem, however, was that it was often *Quakers* from the East who were most problematic for Indiana Friends. And the changes of the late 1960s, especially coed dormitories, heightened such concerns. As the board noted, for many in the yearly meetings, "the idea of academic excellence is still of less concern than is the idea of a guarded education." By 1971 William Fuson, himself active in Indiana Yearly Meeting, was noting that if Earlham was established to serve "the children of the meeting," now it needed "to discern the larger meeting whose children we may wisely serve."[154]

To be sure, Earlham continued to have numerous supporters, financial and spiritual, in the two yearly meetings. And Earlham faculty continued to play a role, although not as central as in the past, in Indiana Yearly Meeting—Hal Cope, for example, succeeded Elton Trueblood as clerk in 1966. The composition of the board continued to reflect the yearly meetings' considerable influence. By 1967 they had approved the addition of three additional at-large trustees, raising the number to seven. The yearly meeting trustees continued to be the majority of the board. There were suggestions that the time had come to cut ties: "We have got to quit kidding ourselves that Yearly Meeting influence really helps the on going thrust of the college," one of the other trustees said in 1965. Another thought that the yearly meetings had forfeited their rights by their lack of support. Others pointed out, however, that there were seldom questions that polarized the board along yearly meeting/non-yearly meeting lines. One at-large trustee thought the yearly meeting trustees had never taken any action detrimental to the college. Edward G. Wilson, the president of the board after 1969, considered it desirable to reduce the number of yearly meeting trustees, but concluded that it would not be worth the hurt feelings.[155]

In fact, in the college, there was growing uncertainty about how it should serve the yearly meetings. In 1958, at his first faculty retreat, Bolling had expressed his hope that Earlham would "make a significant and needed contribution to Quakerism, particularly to the two yearly meetings with which Earlham is affiliated." But the two yearly meetings did not perceive that happening. William Fuson was candid in 1971: "A good case could be made that many things have been going on at Earlham these last few years which, if they were fully known by . . . the Quaker Yearly Meetings, might well have led them to close the college!" Fortunately, Fuson continued, "our communication screens are fairly effective and the indifference of the Yearly Meetings fairly pervasive."[156]

Fuson probably exaggerated. If the college had become increasingly less relevant to the yearly meetings, another Earlham enterprise was becoming more important. That was the Earlham School of Religion.

Ever since Friends moved to the pastoral system late in the nineteenth century, there had been discussion of the need for the establishment of a Quaker seminary to train pastoral ministers. Elbert Russell had hoped to see it at Earlham, and in 1920 a group of leading Friends, including David M. Edwards, had called for the establishment of such a school. None of these plans ever came to fruition. Instead, Friends interested in seminary work attended a variety of institutions. Many of fundamentalist sympathies were educated at undergraduate schools like Marion, Anderson, or Taylor in Indiana, or Bible colleges like the Cleveland Bible Institute, God's Bible College in Cincinnati, and especially Asbury, a school with a long holiness tradition in Wilmore, Kentucky. More liberal Friends, especially Earlham graduates, looked to eastern schools, studying at Harvard, Yale, or Colgate. The favorite seminary, however, was Hartford, which had attracted Friends like Charles Woodman, Tom Jones, Alexander Purdy, and Elton Trueblood since the turn of the century. The presence, after 1923, of Purdy and Moses Bailey on its faculty especially drew fledgling Quaker pastors.[157]

One of the changes Trueblood and Jones had initiated was a masters program in religion, intended especially for pastors. It never attracted many students; by 1958 it had granted only seven degrees. At the same time, interest in a seminary in the Five Years Meeting was growing. Errol T. Elliott, the executive secretary, and others, however, proposed setting up a Quaker chair in an established seminary, preferably at the Butler School of Religion, a Disciples of Christ institution in Indianapolis. While president of Earlham, Tom Jones had also been doubtful about the prospects for a Quaker seminary.[158]

When Bolling became president, he began actively to explore the idea of a seminary. "Friends have a special mission still to perform within the Protestant Church and . . . a Quaker School of Religion could give something of real value to those who are going ahead in leadership among Friends," he wrote to one supportive Quaker pastor. Bolling persuaded the Lilly Endowment to provide money for a feasibility study. To conduct the study, Bolling hired Wilmer Cooper, a staffer from the Friends Committee on National Legislation with a doctorate from Vanderbilt.[159]

Cooper found considerable support for the seminary idea in a year of traveling among Friends in most of the yearly meetings. There were skeptics, to be sure. One Indiana monthly meeting announced its opposition because of the "unsoundness" of Earlham's theological teaching. Alexander Purdy at Hartford was "quite positive that the Society of Friends would not and could not afford it." But Cooper and Bolling found the response encouraging enough to make a formal proposal to the Earlham board in February 1960 to establish a school of religion.[160]

The proposal proved extremely controversial on campus. Several college faculty were adamantly opposed, as were some of the students. The main worries were financial. Opponents were certain that the seminary would prove to be a terrible drain on the already precarious college budget. One student argued that the seminary would draw more Quakers to the campus, making Earlham a "prep-school for Quaker ministers," thus "subtracting from the present stimulating atmosphere." The discussion in the board meeting was intense. Two alumni trustees, Lawrence Leland and Edward G. Wilson, were outspoken critics. Wilson, a birthright Friend from Richmond who spent his career in New York City, considered "saving" pastoral Quakerism a lost cause, and was "aghast that Earlham, an outstanding liberal arts college with very limited financial resources, would consider also adding a theological seminary." Finally, after two days of discussion at its February 1960 meeting, the board reached consensus to proceed, with Wilson's unlikely benediction that Earlham should "have the best damned school of religion there is."[161]

The school offered its first classes in the fall of 1960. There were eleven students, although only four were actually M.A. candidates, the rest being enrolled as "special" students, some through extension courses offered in Indianapolis and Fairmount, Indiana. The school was fortunate in its faculty. The presence and active support of Elton Trueblood was critical. Cooper, the administrative secretary, also scored a major coup when he persuaded Alexander Purdy, who had retired from Hartford, not only to give up his reservations but to join the faculty. For Purdy it was a triumph to return, given the circumstances of his departure in 1923; he remained five years. The fourth founding member of the faculty was Hugh Barbour, whose soon-to-be-published Yale dissertation, *The Quakers in Puritan England*, would became the standard work on seventeenth-century Quakerism. The non-Quaker contributing was the Methodist Joe Elmore. The first class of three graduated in 1964.[162]

Over its first decade, ESR grew slowly in enrollment and financial support. The number of students was usually between twenty and thirty, hitting a high of thirty-eight in the fall of 1970. Finances were usually precarious, and more than once Cooper, who after 1962 had the title of dean, looked gloomily at the school's future. Money did not come easily. Tom Jones, now a supporter, took charge of raising funds, and a matching grant from Lilly Endowment helped in the first few years. Still, Jones found this money the most difficult he had ever tried to secure. In 1966, the school embarked on a campaign to raise $1.3 million. That proved far more difficult than anticipated; by the summer of 1967 the professional fund-raisers had given up. Nevertheless, by the end of 1967 ESR reached its goal.[163]

By the end of the decade, ESR had begun to find its identity. Although ultimate authority lay in the hands of the Earlham trustees, it had its own board of advisors, mostly drawn from the Five Years Meeting (which in

1965 became Friends United Meeting), but with a few Friends of other persuasions as well. Most of the students came from the pastoral yearly meetings, with most interested in careers as Quaker pastors. That, of course, was the motivation for founding the school. An increasing proportion, however, came from the unprogrammed yearly meetings of Friends General Conference. This was in keeping with the outlook of the faculty. Purdy was probably the most liberal, with Trueblood the most evangelical. None was a fundamentalist Christian, however, and the school did not appeal to fundamentalist-leaning Friends. On the other hand, many liberal Friends, especially alumni in the unprogrammed yearly meetings, were extremely skeptical about the school and its mission. Typical was one 1934 graduate who wrote that the school was dispensing "warmed over Methodism." As late as 1967 there was criticism in *Friends Journal,* the organ of Friends General Conference.[164]

Still, by 1973, the school had demonstrated its staying power. Provisional accreditation came that year. Finances, while always uncertain, were stable, as was enrollment. Most of all, the school could point to a growing group of students and alumni who were filling important pastorates and administrative positions in the Quaker world. That was giving Earlham vital new Quaker ties even as many pastoral Friends became increasingly skeptical about many aspects of the college.[165]

The religious atmosphere of the campus changed in the 1960s. In some ways, Earlham mirrored national trends. By 1970, most college students were showing less interest in conventional, organized religion. On the other hand, as many denominational colleges lost much of their denominational identity, Earlham's understanding of itself as a Quaker place remained strong. The rub came in finding agreement about what it meant to be a Quaker college.[166]

Bolling and Elmore continued Tom Jones's policy of seeking Quakers and other active Christian faculty, but without any kind of church membership requirement. As Bolling told the Senate in 1961, he looked for "some degree of Christian commitment." Edward G. Wilson, an increasingly influential board member, wrote in 1964 that he could see the value of having a Hindu or Muslim on the faculty, and that there was "no harm in having an atheist or agnostic." That same year, responding to a questionnaire, Bolling wrote that the college did hire Jews and nonbelievers, but that the college had "some concern . . . to keep the percentage of [such] faculty members . . . a relatively small proportion of our faculty." Jewish faculty hired in these years, however, remember no questions about their religion.[167]

More disturbing for some faculty and administrators was a growing anti-Christian sentiment among some students that they first detected in the early 1960s. Typical was a student who blasted religious services in convocation as "an intrusion not in keeping with Quaker liberalism." Some of it was a dislike of "codifying systems of doctrines." But there was something more at work. "Some students feel to be identified as a Christian on our campus is unpopular," Wilmer Cooper worried in 1961. Joe Elmore agreed: "From my own classes and discussions, I am disturbed about the lack of openness, the dogmatism against a fancied 'dogmatism,' and a host of emotional blocks against a consideration of the Christian faith." The college responded in various ways. Campus meeting for worship continued, as did various student religious groups. Probably more important was the influence of individual faculty members as spiritual guides, mentors, and role models. By the early 1970s, there was a "Jesus Movement" on campus that had "Watered-Down Christianity" as its target. Still, the dominant atmosphere of the campus, given to questioning and skeptical of organized religion, was definitely not evangelical.[168]

Many at Earlham, both faculty and students, wrote and spoke of their understanding of what it meant for Earlham to be a Quaker school. Some saw details as critical. Bolling, for example, argued that the physical appearance of the campus should be Quakerly, with "an air of simplicity, cleanness, neatness." Some saw it in holding to Quakerly peculiarities, such as avoiding honesty oaths on exams. Still others thought that it had to involve a certain way of teaching, with "simplicity, humility, and devotion to truth." The 1963 catalog was explicit in its Quaker language: "If all human beings are made in God's image, each with a measure of the Light which shone fully in Christ, men must be treated accordingly."[169]

There was consensus that Earlham as a Quaker school should turn out men and women with certain moral and intellectual characteristics. Bolling, in 1958, described Earlham's central aim as developing "young people who have acquired within themselves a genuine thirst for knowledge and understanding, and such disciplines of mind and spirit that they can carry mature, independent responsibility in their homes, their vocations, and in the broader community, with intellectual competence, spiritual awareness, and a sense of social concern." Many saw this as best being done by an openness to new ideas; as Wilmer Cooper wrote in 1964, "part of the genius of Quakerism is to be ready to break out of old molds." The faculty and board affirmed this in 1970, stating officially that one of Earlham's goals was to be the search for truth "through honest questioning and open listening, through rigorous reasoning and calm reflection."[170]

What was increasingly absent was a sense of Quakerism as a religion. Some still spoke of the religious side of campus, but even they usually spoke of religion as a search, a quest. One student wrote that she appreciated the college's Quaker spirit because it had "the amazing ability to make the Catholic a better Catholic, the Jew a better Jew, etc. down the line." It is significant that when Elton Trueblood retired in 1966, his replacements were academic philosophers rather than campus religious leaders. Increasingly, some on campus saw secularization as an impending danger. Even students perceived that the "shared faith" that had once seemingly united Friends on campus was gone.[171]

Two themes are prominent in campus discourse about Quakerism in these years: community and consensus. Decision-making by consensus was, of course, one of Tom Jones's innovations, but by the 1960s it was seen as almost sacred, the heart of the Quaker process, as Helen Hole put it. Both veteran and younger faculty affirmed it; newcomers assumed that the college had always governed itself thus. It may well have given the faculty more power than at most institutions, although that is unclear. Even student groups, which in Jones's time had often stuck with parliamentary procedure, were by 1970 equally committed to the consensus process.[172]

Consensus was not an end in itself, however; its value lay in the strengthening of the campus's sense of community. Virtually everyone saw this community as one of Earlham's great strengths, but there was considerable disagreement about the sources and nature of the community, and there was constantly expressed fear that community was diminishing on campus.

Some, like William Fuson, saw the essence of community in a shared commitment to Quakerism, as he put it in 1972: "an educational community derived (somewhat) but still drawing significantly from and contributing . . . to the inspiration of a lively experiential community of faith." Warren Staebler agreed; the college had to "resist the blandishments of 'togetherness.'" Genuine community, he argued, lay "in a sense of corporateness, not in the fact of congregating." Others, however, viewed common experiences, like served dinners in the dining hall, as critical. The board saw the faculty as central, the body that "created and sustained that sense of community that is the basis for the character of the college."[173]

Almost everyone on campus worried, however, that Earlham's sense of community was endangered. As early as 1959, as enrollment neared one thousand, some faculty worried that the college had become too big. Some saw the decline of student government as a contributing problem—in 1950 the Senate had enforced regulations, but by 1965 that was left to the dean of students and staff. Some students agreed that widespread violations of certain rules contributed to a breakdown. By 1970, many saw political activism as polarizing—it had encouraged athletes, for example, to form their own subculture. Some mourned "an insufficient amount of free interaction and communication between various segments of the community." Helen Hole noted in 1972 how it had once been common for faculty to invite student groups to their homes, but now faculty were less willing, and "students don't respond to this sort of thing." Some blamed the end of shared experiences, like mandatory convocations. Even improvements on campus bore some of the blame— the construction of Runyan Center as the college's first real student union meant that students and faculty no longer congregated together around the post office and Opinion Board in Carpenter Hall. Still others blamed problems endemic in the larger society, like racism. Chemistry professor Theodor Benfey probably identified a more critical problem— a growing divergence between the "tightly knit idealistic group" of CPS veterans on the faculty, and the younger teachers "who had less interest in Quakers and less interest in the community."[174]

There was sometimes disagreement even among the faculty about what it meant to be a Quaker place. A notable case was the debate over Earlham's application for a Phi Beta Kappa chapter in 1961. It was not the college's first attempt; the national honorary society had turned down the school in 1928 and 1935. A discussion in the faculty meeting in 1950 had revealed some difference of opinion on the desirability of applying. By 1961, Bolling and many faculty saw a Phi Beta Kappa chapter as one of the finishing touches on Earlham's achievement of a national reputation. But there were opponents, almost all Quakers. Helen Hole thought that membership, which was based on grade point averages, was far too mechanical. Fuson was outspoken in his criticism. He blasted Phi Beta Kappa as a "status symbol" that was not needed to attract good students or faculty. Its membership, moreover, would be chosen by a small group of faculty whose standing depended on "election made elsewhere from five to fifty years ago." Phi Beta Kappa would be contrary to "Quaker testimonies of truth and simplicity." Supporters on the faculty, however, were not persuaded. Economist Joseph Coppock saw Phi Beta Kappa as a "symbol of intellectual excellence," and charged that opposition was "a form of anti-intellectualism." English professor Leigh Gibby saw the question as one of tolerance. Objectors had every right not to join, but they had no right to forbid others, "just because it is his conscience, and not his reason which speaks." The supporters prevailed, and Earlham received its chapter in 1964.[175]

Not everyone on campus saw the college's sense of itself as problem-free. Occasionally a radical student would mount a head-on assault. "The prizing of apparent consensus over conflict assumes the object of education is accommodation into the social system," one wrote in 1964. A *Post* editorial agreed in 1971, accusing Earlham of "clinging to the ideals and traditions of an erstwhile era" while "merely ignoring the sickness of this country." Faculty doubters were more measured, but their concerns about the direction of the campus were real. Some thought that at times the "weighty" Friends on the faculty were engaged in a "deliberate effort towards mystification," and muttered about the "Quaker mafia." Many worried that the emphasis on Quaker values got in the way of good, hard thinking. History professor Edward Bastian, for example, was open in his opinion that too often on campus sentiment was valued over critical analysis. Gordon Thompson, a popular English professor who saw Quakers making an extraordinary contribution to the world, nevertheless worried that "if we can keep going the way we're headed we can become a truly loving community in which 'Academics Isn't Anything.'" In a talk at Faculty Retreat in 1971, Thompson summed up the fears of many faculty. Some Quakers really did appear "hostile to the life of the mind." Some asked, in perfect seriousness, "if we weren't being un-Quakerly in trying to attract good students to Earlham." Then there were admissions procedures that would reject outstanding academic prospects "because they may not fit into the community," while allowing in "a number of creatures who enter our classrooms swinging on vines." With unerring wit, Thompson focused on the often bizarre results of the union of liberal Quakerism and the 1960s counterculture: "mindless students whose idea of bliss was to get married in the meetinghouse in one of those ceremonies where the participants dress like peasants, eat dandelion bread, and read passages from *The Prophet* to each other." Even committed Friends like Fuson worried about the widespread "functioning myth" at Earlham that Friends were so "open" that "they can perceive no boundaries, affirm no findings, and state no themes upon which they may approach agreement."[176]

Still, these fears and disagreements seldom broke into open conflict. Often older faculty pointed out that it had been left to each generation of faculty to redefine the nature of the campus community, and that the process was often messy. Many visitors to the campus found it an extraordinary place. "I've never encountered a pervading spirit—including the Friendly sense—such as your college," one Philadelphia Friend wrote to Bolling in 1964. The headmaster of a Quaker secondary school agreed in 1965: "The Quaker world is indebted to Earlham for many, many things. How shall we list them?" he asked. A visitor from MIT in 1971 found "a decent, human environment, one that asks not for boundless love, for eternal convergence, nor even an insipid brotherhood, but for respect and care." He discovered no consensus, however, about many aspects of Earlham's future. "Some would make it even more insulated, others would borrow a Fellini helicopter and drop the college on the outskirts of Boston or San Francisco," he concluded. "Some would pump Quaker ideals and rituals out of the college, others would die for these very same ideals, and still others are uncertain of the viability of any religious college." These were Earlham's questions as the 1960s ended.[177]

These questions, however, would be asked on a campus that was a stronger place, academically and financially, than it had ever been. The generosity of donors, especially Eli Lilly, meant that for the first time in its history Earlham was no longer on the edge of poverty. Its student body was larger, more geographically and racially diverse, and better in every measure of academic ability than before. Its reputation had never stood higher.

Earlham did not escape the stresses of the time. "All colleges sit on powder kegs these days," Bolling had written to another educator in 1969, and by that time many of the country's leading institutions of higher education had exploded into disorder and violence. Some of the elements that had yielded such a harvest were present at Earlham—a growing and increasingly assertive group of African American students, a strong antiwar movement, a significant number of students at least experimenting with drugs. Some faculty saw real scars by 1973. Yet Earlham kept the peace. Part of the credit must go to the people on campus, administrators, faculty, staff, and students. But part must also go to a century of Quaker tradition that made a politics of violence and confrontation simply out of place.[178]

Earlham and the
Culture Wars

1973–1996

lthough few on the faculty realized it at the time, commencement at
Earlham in June 1991 would be a turning point for the institution.
President Richard J. Wood, on sabbatical in Japan that term, was not
present. The graduating class was mostly in cap and gown. The parents
were visibly divided between those in the suits and dresses that they
thought appropriate for such an occasion and those in shorts and jeans
who scorned such trappings of bourgeois respectability. The senior class
speaker, as usual, offered a critique of certain college policies, especially
regarding homosexuality, that he thought deficient and intolerant. The
popping of champagne corks, so common at other commencements, was
absent here. For many of those present, save for the president's absence,
this was unremarkable, and the informality and diversity were the
essence of a Quaker college.[1]

This year, however, there were others present who saw the ceremony
with very different eyes. With Sadie Vernon, a much-respected Quaker
missionary and graduate of the Earlham School of Religion, receiving an
honorary degree, for the first time in years a number of members of
Indiana Yearly Meeting were attending. What they experienced that
Sunday afternoon left them shocked and appalled. None of the prayers
was explicitly Christian. Two male graduates appeared in what seemed
to be dresses, complete with jewelry and high heels. Some of the most
radical graduates saluted gay and lesbian students with shouts of "queer"
and "dyke." The senior speaker declared himself to be a gay man.[2]

The 1991 commencement would have consequences that no one on campus foresaw—a bitter controversy in Indiana Yearly Meeting that involved the first attempt in three quarters of a century to change the board of trustees in order to change college policy. The arguments would have been familiar to any observer of American society— on one side, socially conservative evangelical Christians battling what they perceived as flagrant immorality, on the other, liberals fighting what they saw as narrow-minded fundamentalist intolerance, with a number of Friends caught unhappily in between. What sociologist James Davison Hunter called the "Culture Wars" had come to Earlham.[5]

This incident embodied many of the themes of the past two decades of Earlham's history. Every group affiliated with the college, whether students, faculty, board, or alumni, affirmed its Quaker identity. They appealed to it in arguing for and against the alcohol policy, for and against divestment from companies doing business in South Africa, for and against the existence of a homosexual group on campus, for and against even presidential candidates. Few, if any, would openly question the centrality of Quaker *values* in Earlham's life. The campus's values were those that the liberal wing of the Society of Friends increasingly embraced.

Those Quaker values, however, were increasingly different from the values and the faith of many, probably a majority, of the members of Indiana and Western yearly meetings. Tension between the yearly meetings and the college was chronic, and on at least four occasions between 1976 and 1994 broke into open conflict. The immediate issues usually involved sexuality, but those in turn were rooted in disparate understandings of Quakerism and of what a Quaker institution should be. Earlham's campus culture was at odds not only with "the world," but with many Quaker neighbors.

At the same time that it debated its Quaker identity, Earlham was also, by most standards, strengthening itself as an academic institution. The endowment grew steadily, giving Earlham financial resources almost inconceivable a generation earlier. The faculty and staff were larger than ever before. The library won national acclaim as one of the best, if not the best, undergraduate libraries in the country. As ratings of colleges and universities proliferated in the 1980s, Earlham fared well, capped by a 1995 *U.S. News and World Report* survey that named it one of the nation's six best colleges in teaching quality and effectiveness. Virtually every evaluator applauded the college for its academic excellence, sense of community, and faculty commitment to teaching.

Some of this, to be sure, grew out of new programs. In the 1970s and 1980s the college added a variety of initiatives to the curriculum, some reflecting what the college perceived as its Quaker identity—Peace and Conflict Studies, Human Development and Social Relations, Women's

Studies—others the outgrowth of long-standing Earlham work, such as Japanese Studies. Some were variants on long-standing courses, like the reconfigured Humanities Program that became part of the curriculum in the fall of 1977.

Finally, Earlham faced many of the problems that other schools were experiencing in the past two decades. Black students perceived racism on campus. Women perceived sexism. Some faculty perceived a wave of political correctness threatening to overwhelm Earlham. As the baby boom generation graduated, financial pressures grew. In the 1980s, leadership became a crisis. The class of 1986 graduated having seen four presidents in four years.

Administration

As was the case in many colleges and universities, the nature of administration at Earlham changed, both in size and in its nature, in the 1970s and 1980s. Once quite small in relation to the teaching faculty, the number of administrative faculty increased to a point almost equal to the number of professors.[4]

Much of this change was due to increasing demands for certain types of services. As the college's budget grew steadily, so did the need for effective fund-raising: thus the growth in the Development and Alumni offices. The situation was similar in admissions. As competition for a shrinking pool of potential students became far more intense, the need for recruiting grew. As the college tried to draw and retain black students, and improve the quality of their life on campus, so Earlham gained an associate dean for minority affairs. Similarly, as the college's interest in grant writing grew, there was an associate academic dean for program development. Numerous other examples could be cited.[5]

The nature of administrators also changed. Most positions became increasingly specialized and professionalized. As late as the 1970s, for example, most of the senior administrators in Student Development had Ph.D.s and taught part-time. Tony Bing, the dean, was half-time in the English department, while his successor, Robert Ubbelohde, held a joint appointment in Education. By the 1990s, however, such arrangements were less common. Administrators were more likely to hold specialized degrees and to have careers that did not include classroom teaching, although a number were still found at least occasionally in the classroom.[6]

Perhaps the most striking changes were in what had once been the Dean of Students' office, whose name, significantly, was changed to Student Development. Beginning in the late 1960s, and especially with

Bing's appointment, the emphasis was less on enforcing rules and regulations than on supporting students in their personal and intellectual growth. One popular innovation was the introduction of "Living/ Learning" courses, in which residents of a dormitory hallway all enrolled in a certain class, which was often taught in the dormitory.[7]

The Living/Learning concept was the foundation for one of Earlham's most unusual initiatives of the past quarter century, the yurt project. In the fall of 1973, Bing brought to campus Bill Coperthwaite, a New England environmentalist, "to talk about simple living, respect for nature, social design, different ways of learning, folk wisdom, and, of course, yurts." Coperthwaite advocated the Mongolian structures as environmentally sound. That summer, a group of students went to Maine to study yurt construction with Coperthwaite, and in the spring of 1974, about one hundred built one on back campus behind Runyan Center. Bing hailed it as an opportunity for students to "explore the relationship between physical and mental work, to work with faculty in new ways, to gain new respect for space, materials, and tools, and to significantly test some theory against experience." Some students actually advocated building a yurt village as dormitory space. For many faculty, however, the whole idea was "just too weird," and the skeptical board of trustees refused to fund it. So the yurt village died.[8]

There was also reconfiguration at the highest levels of the administration. In 1970, the college created the position of provost to oversee the academic and student sides of the campus, in part because of the increasing complexity of running the campus, more than the president could oversee on a day-to-day basis. The first provost was Helen Hole, the English professor and nationally known Quaker figure who was one of the most beloved and respected people on campus. When she retired in 1972, an English department colleague, Paul Lacey, succeeded her. Relatively young, not yet forty, Lacey found himself facing, as will be seen, the most controversial tenure case in Earlham's history as well as a major confrontation with some constituents over the formation of a Gay People's Union. He returned to full-time teaching in 1975—three years in administration was enough.[9]

When Lacey resigned, a reorganization took place which has endured to the present. Joe Elmore, the academic dean, also assumed the provost position. He handled it with the same wisdom and effectiveness he had brought to the deanship. When he announced his intention to resign at the end of the school year in a fall 1980 faculty meeting, one member of the faculty observed that the collective dismay was reminiscent of a funeral. After a national search, Len Clark, a philosophy professor since 1967 and an Indiana native, replaced Elmore, and remains in the position.[10]

The president, of course, remained the single most important campus leader. In October 1972 Landrum Bolling announced his resignation. He became the executive vice president of the Lilly Endowment at the request of Eli Lilly himself, taking up half-time duties in January 1973 before completely leaving Earlham in June.[11]

With Bolling's departure, Paul Lacey acted as president for over a year while the board searched for a new chief executive. At one point, the search committee almost despaired of finding a qualified and available Friend. When it did make its choice, the presidency went to someone who marked another departure from the past.[12]

A native of Michigan, Franklin Wallin was the first president of Earlham in half a century who did not have any previous connection with the college. A specialist in French history, he had graduated from the University of Wisconsin and then took his Ph.D. at Berkeley. His career included teaching experience as well as stints as an administrator at Wayne State University and Swarthmore. Before coming to Earlham he had served as dean, provost, and acting president at Colgate. No president of Earlham had ever brought such a strong and diverse background to the college. Like Bolling, Wallin was a convinced Friend, but Wallin's sympathies were with the unprogrammed tradition. He and his wife Florence became attenders of Clear Creek Meeting.[13]

Evaluations of Wallin's years at the college were and are still varied. Financially, they were often trying times. He arrived just in time for the deep recession of 1974–1975, and was still at Earlham for the even worse economic downturn of 1981–1982. There were also the chronic headaches of inflation and energy crisis. Enrollment fluctuated, ranging from about nine hundred to almost eleven hundred. Thus much of Wallin's time had to be devoted to grappling with financial problems, considering cuts or planning for cuts that were never needed. Some faculty thought that this colored Wallin's whole vision of Earlham's future, "an entrapping vision," as one professor called it. As such faculty perceived it, Wallin saw Earlham as "a very parochial Midwestern school. . . . He thought Earlham could not expand and had to get used to being smaller than it was."[14]

However much some faculty may have disagreed with Wallin's perception of the future, they respected his abilities. Joe Elmore said that he "had never met or worked with anyone in a close working relationship who was more straightforward, open, and honest and who would never intentionally hurt or undercut another person." Other administrators especially respected him. He was willing to delegate authority, and to trust the judgments of his subordinates about the proper conduct of their areas. And there were many on campus who saw Wallin as just what Earlham needed after the often frenetic pace of the Bolling years. In their minds, the college now had to focus on consolidating and preserving its gains. The gains were real. The endowment by the time Wallin left had tripled, to nearly $65 million, and in significant ways the academic program was more diverse and stronger.[15]

Wallin retired in the spring of 1983. The two final competitors to succeed him were Paul Lacey and Dewitt C. "Bud" Baldwin, an associate dean at the University of Nevada Medical School. In the minds of many, Lacey was the natural choice—a "weighty" Friend and popular professor respected by a generation of alumni and students who through his writing and speaking had won an international reputation among Quakers. As former provost and acting president, he had administrative experience. But in those capacities he had also found himself in conflict with many of the college's constituents, board members as well as faculty, which worked to his disadvantage. So Baldwin was Wallin's successor.[16]

Baldwin was yet another departure from Earlham's past patterns of choosing a president. The son of Methodist missionaries and a Swarthmore graduate, he had been a conscientious objector during World War II and had become a Quaker after the war. He was not a conventional academic but a medical doctor who had spent a successful career in medical schools. When he became president, he was sixty-three, with an understanding with the board that he would not remain past seventy.[17]

Baldwin's presidency was brief—in less than a year, at the 1984 commencement, he announced his resignation. Baldwin was popular with many students and younger faculty and even with some members of the two yearly meetings; "You're the first president of Earlham I could talk to," one Western Friend told him. Everyone found Baldwin kindly, friendly, and approachable, even charming.[18]

From the time he arrived on campus, Baldwin also faced problems. He raised hackles when he asked for remodeling in the president's residence. More serious was a conflict of expectations between Baldwin and members of the board, especially the chairman, Gerald Mills, a member of the family that had been so important to the college for half a century. Baldwin wanted time to get to know the college, perhaps six months, before he undertook any fund-raising, but Mills, with the early, critical stages of the first capital campaign in a decade being planned, insisted Baldwin could not wait. Baldwin also found himself at odds with Len Clark, the provost, and G. Richard Wynn, the vice president for financial affairs. He wanted his own people, but that was not Earlham's way. They in turn perceived him as not having realistic expectations about the duties of an Earlham president.[19]

Finally, there was tension between Baldwin and many of the senior faculty. He perceived them as often insensitive to the needs of younger faculty and students; they saw Baldwin as allowing the college to drift. As one professor summed up his perception, Baldwin seemed to see himself as a turn-of-the-century college president, a wise, amiable figure who sat under elm trees and chatted with students. Early in the 1984 spring term, there was a meeting of about a dozen senior professors who had served on the Faculty Affairs Committee over the previous five years. The group deputed three of those present—Gordon Thompson from English, William Fishback from mathematics, and William Stephenson from biology—to meet with Baldwin. The meeting was amiable, but, as one of the faculty recalled, "it was clear to us that he had no conception of the job."[20]

Baldwin did in fact have an agenda, an aggressive one that included changes in the athletic program and in recruiting students, the renovation of the library and the construction of an art gallery, as well as the long-planned capital campaign. Before embarking on these tasks, however, he wanted his own people in place in the provost's office and in financial affairs. When he again raised the subject with certain board members in April 1984, they refused to allow it. So Baldwin, faced with pressures from all directions, including an unhappy board, decided to resign. Popular with many students, Baldwin took some comfort from the dozens of rosebuds that graduates handed him as they passed over the stage.[21]

With Baldwin's departure, there were real fears that the college faced a crisis of confidence. Words like "fiasco" and "debacle" were current. While a search committee began the work of finding a new president, the board named Lawrence "Pete" Leland, a former trustee and 1938 graduate who had been one of the most respected students of his generation, acting president. A retired insurance executive from Vermont, Leland had been a trustee from 1958 to 1967. Len Clark took charge of academic operations, while Leland focused on raising money and trying to rebuild morale. His good nature and enthusiasm did much to help heal the campus.[22]

Meanwhile, a search committee of four trustees, two faculty, and two students was doing its work. The faculty had been uneasy when the search began, sending a letter to the trustees asking for assurance that the trustees would keep in mind faculty needs and urging that if non-Quaker candidates were considered, that it be ascertained that they were committed to maintaining the college's Quaker identity. The search committee worked methodically, contacting virtually every influential Quaker in the United States to compile a list of possible candidates. In April 1985, three visited campus: Robert Johansen of the World Policy

Institute, Arthur Chickering, a Memphis State University educational theorist, and Richard J. Wood, the academic vice president at Whittier College and a former Earlham professor.[23]

After the on-campus interviews, the search committee met to review what they had heard. After discussion, although that was not their charge, they decided to seek consensus on recommendation to the board. Johansen was their choice. The board did not accept it. After a long discussion in executive session, it decided to offer the presidency to Wood, who accepted almost immediately.[24]

When the board's decision was announced, "widespread concern and dissatisfaction were expressed," in the understated words of the faculty meeting minutes. Faculty concerns focused on a worry that the consensus process had been "lost, and trust and confidence . . . violated." At a special faculty meeting called on April 17, the faculty could not even reach consensus to send a welcoming letter to the new president. There was outspoken student protest, led by members of the Lesbian and Gay People's Union (LGPU), who charged that Wood was insufficiently sympathetic to gay rights. His refusal to support divestment from companies doing business in South Africa also drew criticism. A student letter urging him to reconsider coming drew 110 signatures, and a protest vigil on the Heart attracted 250 participants.[25]

The protests moved neither Wood nor the board. The trustees responded to the charges of violated consensus with a reminder that the decision was ultimately theirs to make, and that they had made it by consensus—of the board. Several things drew them to Wood—his knowledge of Earlham, his administrative experience, his Quaker commitment, and what the board saw as his capacity for constructive work with faculty and students.[26]

In some ways, Wood was a return to an older tradition. Unlike his immediate predecessors, he had Earlham ties, and he was a seminary graduate—a few years later he would be the first president of Earlham ever recorded a Quaker minister while in office. His academic credentials were impressive—undergraduate work at Duke, a B.D. at Union Theological Seminary, and a Ph.D. in philosophy from Yale. He had first joined the Earlham faculty in 1966, developing a deep interest in Japanese philosophy and aesthetics. In 1980, he had left for Whittier. Wood had been drawn to Quakerism while at Earlham, although he did not join a Friends meeting until he went to Whittier.[27]

Wood did his best to try to dispel at least some of the anxiety that his appointment created. In May 1985, he came to campus to meet with a variety of groups, especially the LGPU and black students, who had been his most outspoken critics. But he was also not afraid to embark on new courses. The board acknowledged the duties that inevitably fell to a presidential spouse by appointing his wife, Judy, assistant to the president. Wood was willing to risk accusations of high-handedness by cutting back functions of the Administrative Council, which had in his opinion become balky and ineffective. He was blunt in telling the campus that it needed to give more attention to off-campus constituencies like the yearly meetings. And he tackled controversial subjects almost immediately, like calendar reform.[28]

In his years as president, Wood was no stranger to controversy. Early in his administration, he and new Vice President for Financial Affairs Richard K. Smith convinced the board that Earlham was underpriced, and thus presided over significant increases in tuition. By 1995, total costs for one year exceeded $20,000, twice the 1980 figure. Several actions brought charges of exceeding authority, as in 1990, when he told the faculty that if it could not reach consensus for or against calendar change, he would act. As will be seen, there were vociferous attacks on his qualms about South African divestment. At the same time that some campus gay activists charged him with homophobia, some Indiana Friends were blasting him as a radical advocate of homosexuality. In the fall of 1993, arguing that the days of being able to raise funds for faculty salary increases and program initiatives through higher-than-inflation tuition increases were gone, he launched an intensive examination of almost every facet of Earlham's operation. In his last year at Earlham, Wood faced intense criticism when he initially denied tenure to a popular economics professor. The case involved the invocation by Wood and the board of a residency policy whose existence many if not most faculty denied. Many feared that the heated debate and anger the case aroused would cripple Wood's ability to lead the campus. The impasse was resolved when a group of senior faculty mediated a solution that satisfied the concerns of Wood and the board of trustees and gave the professor, Jonathan Diskin, tenure.[29]

But while there was controversy, there was also undeniable accomplishment. Even Quaker critics acknowledge that Wood was committed to preserving and strengthening Earlham's Quaker identity, and that he improved ties with important Quaker constituencies. In 1987, he launched the college's first capital campaign in over a decade. A consulting firm had estimated that it might be able to raise $4 or $5 million. Instead, the campaign brought in nearly $38 million, exceeding the goal. There was a wave of favorable publicity for Earlham under Wood, most recently the *U.S. News and World Report* ranking of Earlham as one of the nation's best teaching colleges. Honors came to him, like the offer of the chair of the Association of American Colleges and Universities and the chairmanship, through presidential appointment, of the United States–Japan Friendship Commission. And in January 1996, the college was almost halfway to its $30–million goal in a new capital campaign.[30]

At the end of March 1996, Wood announced his resignation at the end of the school year to accept the post of Dean of the Divinity School at Yale University, where he had done his graduate work. As the college launched the search process for a new executive, it secured as interim president for 1996–1997 Eugene S. Mills, a 1948 graduate who was the former president of both the University of New Hampshire and Whittier College. Mills returned to Earlham with a rich heritage of connections. His father, Sumner Mills, was a former trustee, and his brother, Gerald, had served for a decade as chair of the board. His wife, Dorothy, also an alumnus, is the daughter of longtime chemistry professor and weighty campus Friend Ernest A. Wildman.

The National Liberal Arts College

In the past two decades, Earlham has consolidated the repositioning that took place in the 1960s. From an institution that once saw its peer schools as the colleges of Indiana and the Five Years Meeting, Earlham now views itself, and is viewed, as a national institution. Its "overlap group," the other colleges with which it competes most intensely for students, is now made up of Oberlin, Grinnell, Carleton, Macalester, and Haverford. Not everyone on campus has been comfortable with such company—there are continuing fears of becoming too much of an elite institution, "too much like Swarthmore," as the reservation is sometimes expressed. As in previous years, Earlham's achievement of such excellence was the fruit of a combination of students, faculty, and financial resources.[31]

Earlham's student body has shown considerable consistency over the past two decades. As was the case with the last years of the Bolling administration, about 20 percent of Earlham's students have continued to come from Indiana, with another 30 percent from other midwestern states. Usually between 35 and 40 percent come from the Northeast, with the rest evenly divided among the South, West, and overseas. With the end of the entry of the baby boomers in the 1970s, competition for admission became somewhat less intense, although the college continued to be selective. Some faculty worried that the quality of students overall declined in the 1970s, but the median SAT levels never went below 1,050, consistently about 200 points above the national median. In the last decade, the median at Earlham has risen to over 1,100, leading to a new debate about whether the college has become too selective.[32]

Enrollment for the past two decades has swung between 950 and 1,150. Currently, it is close to 1,000, although the college has set a goal of 1,200. The number of applicants has grown steadily. By 1990, it had doubled in five years, and has continued to rise, although at a slower rate.[33]

The heart of any college is its faculty. Virtually all observers have praised Earlham's for the past two decades as measuring up to the highest standards set by its predecessors. "Brilliant and demanding" were the words of one of the popular college guides; another wrote of "their excellence in teaching and their ability to cross curricular lines." Yet another praised Earlham for "a scholarly faculty whose main joy is teaching." All observers give Earlham faculty high marks for dedication to teaching, accessibility, and commitment to their students.[34]

For the past two decades, the college has put considerable effort into faculty development. In the early 1970s, there was widespread national concern over the state of college faculties, a worry that many tenured faculty had become "deadwood," settling into stagnation or at least failing to grow. At Earlham, both administrative and teaching faculty put considerable energy into preventing this concern from becoming reality.[35]

One of Paul Lacey's most important acts as provost and acting president was to set aside half of the $150,000 grant the college received in 1973 from the Ford Foundation for innovation as a kind of "internal foundation," both for curricular projects and for individual faculty work focused on personal intellectual growth. The latter might involve travel for research, the acquisition of a new language, or even retooling to teach a new subject area. Under Wallin, the Professional Development Fund became a regular part of the budget, with grants administered by a standing committee of the faculty.[36]

The establishment of the Professional Development Fund involved little controversy; the case was very different with a proposal that Wallin, Elmore, Lacey, and the members of Faculty Affairs Committee (FAC) advocated, first discussed in the spring of 1974 and taken up in the faculty meeting early in 1975. That proposal mandated regular reviews of tenured teaching faculty at five-year intervals. It generated heated debate. While the authors presented it as "a cooperative program between the College and individual faculty members designed to encourage career-long growth and to maintain teaching effectiveness," some senior professors saw it as an assault on the tenure system. One branded it an "inescapable inquisition" that would create a "climate of over-busyness" and produce "an unwholesome competitiveness" among the faculty. Others saw in it a dangerous presumption that age inevitably engendered lack of dedication or intellectual dexterity, and feared that, to the extent it relied on standard student evaluation forms, it would be overly mechanical. Supporters argued that the program would simply enhance accountability and would be a "stimulus to periodically renew a faculty member's own sense of self-evaluation." There was also an appeal to Earlham's basic sense of fair play—if junior faculty had to be reviewed every two years before tenure, then why not give senior faculty

at least some scrutiny? Lacey, Elmore, and the members of FAC volunteered to be the first to go through the process so that their cases would
illuminate any problems with it. After three months of debate, in May
1975, after most skeptics were convinced that the proposal really was not
an attack on the tenure system, but still with obvious reluctance on the
part of others, the proposal was accepted.[37]

Yet another development along these lines was approved by the
faculty at the same time as the plan for five-year reviews, the creation of
the Teaching Consultant position. The brainchild largely of chemistry
professor Gerald Bakker, the proposal grew out of a conviction, in his
words, that "good teachers are *made*, not *born*, and that many people can
become better teachers if they have the support of colleagues to help
them reflect on and experiment with their teaching." Because there was
a desire to have someone familiar with Earlham, and trusted by colleagues, it was decided that the consultant should be a member of the
faculty released half-time to offer advice to fellow faculty members. That
might involve observing classes, reading course evaluations, examining
syllabi, or even offering career advice. To heighten confidence in the
consultant, all consultations were voluntary and strictly confidential,
with the teaching consultant ineligible to serve on any body making
decisions about teaching faculty for three years after serving. In the first
four years, consultants reported that in a given year, they met with
between two-thirds and three-fourths of the teaching faculty. After the
first was appointed, a grant from the Fund for the Improvement of Post-
Secondary Education came for support. Bakker served as the first consultant, succeeded by Paul Lacey. Consultants serve for two years,
coming from a wide variety of disciplines.[38]

These initiatives set the standard for the next two decades. More
efforts to enhance teaching effectiveness have come through Earlham's
participation in the Great Lakes College Association (GLCA), with
Earlham faculty as regular participants in its teaching workshops. In
1984, largely through the work of German professor Richard Jurasek, the
college received a major grant from the National Endowment for the
Humanities for Foreign Languages in the Curriculum (FLIC). It provided funds for twenty-four faculty to renew their knowledge of a foreign
language, or learn a new one, for use in the classroom. As one faculty
member noted, this typified Earlham's approach—not narrowly focused
on a particular discipline or on pure research, but rather crossing
disciplinary lines and fostering intellectual growth in ways that would be
useful in teaching and learning.[39]

The third leg of the Earlham triad was, of course, financial. In the
Bolling years, Earlham finally escaped the near penury under which had
operated for a century. In the past two decades, the college has placed

itself among the top echelon of American liberal arts colleges in endowment and expense.

As noted earlier, Earlham faced financial trials in the 1970s. At that
time, its salaries were usually toward the bottom of the GLCA schools; a
1978 *Post* story claimed that faculty pay had, on average, lost 20 percent
of its purchasing power to inflation since 1968. Some recovery began in
the early 1980s, and in the late 1980s there were several years of above-
inflation increases. Since 1992, as enrollment has fallen, increases have
been 3 percent annually or less, with one year in which there was none
at all.[40]

Over the past twenty years, the college's budget has grown steadily,
fueled by rising tuition and successful fund-raising. In 1974, when
Wallin became president, total charges were a little over $4,000 a year.
By 1983, when he retired, they stood at $8,700. As noted earlier, when
Wood became president, he and other high administrators argued that
Earlham was underpriced, and convinced the board that that justified a
series of above-inflation tuition hikes. Thus since 1985, total costs have
doubled to about $20,000 annually. Meanwhile, the college's budget,
about $6 million in 1975, was over $20 million in 1995.[41]

While Earlham has remained more tuition-driven than most of the
institutions it considers its peers, it has also seen dramatic growth in
endowment. In the 1970s, largely through the influence of Chairman
Edward G. Wilson, the board followed the model of the Common Fund
and adopted a rule allowing a 5 percent return from the endowment for
use in the regular college budget, thus securing greater growth. Recently, the board decided to use a 4 percent rate, which, while pinching
in the short term, will mean significant long-term endowment growth.
Through the work of the Alumni Development office, successful management, and a growing stock market, the value of the endowment has
increased steadily. About $20 million when Wallin became president, it
was $65.8 million when he left. Today, with the addition of funds from
another capital campaign in the late 1980s, it stands at about $212
million. Some moves, however, proved controversial. When the college
received large blocks of Eli Lilly corporate stock after Eli Lilly's death in
1977, it incurred the displeasure of both company and the Lilly Endowment by putting much of it on the market in order to keep Earlham
holdings diversified.[42]

One of the fruits of successful fund-raising has been physical improvement of the campus. While no subsequent president has tried to
equal the pace of the Jones years, each, save Baldwin, has left some new
facility behind him. The last years of the Bolling administration saw a
new natural sciences building, Stanley Hall. Under Wallin, the college's
athletic facilities were substantially upgraded, with major additions to

Trueblood Fieldhouse. The past ten years under Wood have seen an addition to the library, renovation of Bundy Hall and Goddard Auditorium, and the construction of two new dormitories, Warren and Wilson Halls. The last were named in honor, respectively, of Clifton Warren, a 1927 graduate and one of the college's most generous donors, and Edward G. Wilson, a 1929 graduate who was for many years one of the most influential members of the board. For most current faculty, however, a social science building remains the most pressing priority, and it was part of the capital campaign opened in 1995.[43]

A final factor in the school's general financial growth has been success in attracting grants. Although, unlike research universities, no one's future at Earlham has depended on grant writing, a number of faculty have proved successful. Three applications to the National Endowment to the Humanities since 1980 have brought significant sums for the FLIC program, an endowed chair in multidisciplinary studies, and for a series of summer seminars for participants in the Humanities program. As will be described later, grants in 1985 and 1989 from the Ford and Knight Foundations have funded joint faculty-student research projects. There has also come a large grant from the Hughes Medical Foundation to purchase equipment and fund positions in the biology department. The Lilly Endowment has continued to be generous to Earlham, with grants for a variety of purposes ranging from strengthening the African and African American Studies program to studying the impact of information technology on teaching. Funds from several sources, including the Hewlett Foundation and the Fulbright Scholar-in-Residence program, have brought twenty-five international scholars to campus since 1989. In 1990, a $300,000 grant from the Joyce Foundation was used to provide support for sabbaticals for third and fourth-year teaching faculty.[44]

Today, with budgets in higher education universally tight, and public concerns over costs growing, Earlham still faces considerable uncertainty. The drying up, in the Reagan years, of federal funds has played a role—while the college received $2.4 million in federal grants between 1975 and 1979, that declined to about $67,000 between 1986 and 1990. Today the campus is the scene of vigorous debates over how to maintain financial viability.[45]

The result of Earlham's commitment to teaching and its success in fund-raising has been a generally enviable reputation. The 1974 North Central Association accrediting report called Earlham "one of America's well-established, deeply rooted, almost classical liberal arts colleges." Beginning in the mid-1980s, with the increasing popularity and influence of college rating and ranking guides, there was a steady stream of favorable publicity for the college. In 1985, *U.S. News and World Report* ranked Earlham fourteenth in the nation in overall reputation among liberal arts colleges; two years later it was sixteenth. In 1987, Earlham made *Money* magazine's top ten list of best bargains in college education; four years later the *Kiplinger Report* named Earlham among its top twenty buys. In 1992, the *Fiske Guide to Colleges* gave Earlham five stars for overall quality of campus life. The 1994 edition of *Barron's 300 Best Buys in College Education* called Earlham "one of the nation's more distinctive, selective liberal arts colleges" at "the top of the academic roster."[46]

Academic Life

In many ways, Earlham has seen remarkable continuity in its academic programs. While many colleges relaxed or entirely abolished requirements in the 1970s, Earlham did not. It still requires a year of foreign language, four courses in the natural sciences, a year-long Humanities sequence, and courses in social sciences, fine arts, religion, and philosophy, and physical education. Departments that have long been Earlham's strongest, like biology and English, remain so. But there has also been change in the past two decades, with the creation of new programs, especially interdisciplinary programs, the recasting of others, like Humanities, and the decision to return, in the fall of 1996, to a semester calendar.

Calendar would be one of the most fractious issues that Earlham confronted. By the 1970s, there was some discussion about the desirability of returning to semesters. When Wood became president, he asked the faculty to look at the question. Proponents of change argued that the college's schedule, with fall term extending from Labor Day to Thanksgiving, a long break until New Years, then winter and spring terms hard on each other, was draining and debilitating for faculty and students alike, and that it was costly as well. Supporters of the "3–3" system responded that it offered the advantages of more opportunities for foreign study and was less intense, since students took only three courses at a time. In most departments, it allowed faculty to do only two classes per term. Biologists and geologists were especially concerned about the implications of change, since semesters assumed ending the school year in mid-May, and that would effectively end opportunities for local fieldwork. The discussions in 1986 ended without consensus; those in 1990, after a long debate that sometimes verged on rancor, reaffirmed, with great reluctance on the part of some, the 3–3 system. In the fall of 1994 a task force brought a new proposal for semesters to the faculty meeting. After extended debate, the faculty approved the change. Earlham would go back to semesters in the fall of 1996.[47]

Perhaps the most important curricular change since 1973, or at least the one that affected the largest number of students, was the reconfiguration of the Humanities program in which all students take part in their first year at Earlham. Thousands have now passed through it, the one unifying experience that all members of an entering class share.

During the 1976–1977 school year, two historians, Douglas Steeples and Robert Southard, and three English faculty, Dan Meerson, Leigh Gibby, and Gordon Thompson, began discussion of some kind of joint effort by the two departments. Both faced cutbacks, and both had required courses—a world history survey and the Humanities classes that dated back to the 1950s—with which both were increasingly dissatisfied. After months of discussion, they brought forward a proposal to conflate the history and English requirements into a four-term Humanities sequence, which the faculty approved in April 1977.[48]

The program's basic functions were set at the inception. It was, with a few exceptions, half of the teaching load of faculty in English, history, and classics. Professors from other departments, especially religion and philosophy, also took part regularly. The focus was on intensive reading, writing, and discussion with the first three terms in the first year. In Humanities I, students wrote seven or eight papers on the assigned readings before discussing them in class. The pace in Humanities II and III was somewhat less demanding, with only four papers. The Humanities I reading list changed every year, while there was some carryover in the other terms. The reading lists were consciously designed not as "Great Books," although some "canonical" works were always included. Students completed the sequence by taking a history, English, or classics course designated as a Humanities IV.[49]

Generally, responses to the Humanities program have been positive. Many, probably most students, found it impossibly demanding and time-consuming, but acknowledged its value; it was a "stretching experience," as one called it. Such praise came especially from alumni, who credited it with honing analytical and writing skills. "I'm the one in the office who always does the writing," was a typical comment. Similar praise came from faculty. Within a decade, the program was attracting national attention, and participating faculty found themselves in demand as consultants for programs at other colleges. Administrators pegged it as one of the anchors and stellar features of the college.[50]

Such feelings were far from unanimous. Some faculty saw the program as far too demanding, one that drove away students. Some criticized it as unfair to those whose abilities were not in writing or discussion. There were charges that the reading list, with its focus on history, literature, and philosophy, was far too narrow. As will be seen later, the reading list was also the target of attacks from both faculty and student critics who blasted it for being far too male and Eurocentric. In fact, the program has changed over the years, and will change more with the switch to semesters. But the changes contemplated will probably not be enough to mollify critics.[51]

Humanities was like other curricular innovations in the past two decades in crossing departmental and disciplinary lines. Three other such programs became part of the curriculum—Peace and Conflict Studies (PACS), later Peace and Global Studies (PAGS), Human Development and Social Relations (HDSR), and Women's Studies.

PACS went back to Landrum Bolling's presidency, growing out of a conviction, not unique to Earlham, that peace as well as war was an appropriate subject for academic study. After a time of discussion and experimentation, in the fall of 1971 Dale Noyd, a psychology professor who, while serving in the Air Force, had been court martialed for his opposition to the Vietnam War, convened a workshop to plan such a program. A proposal came to the faculty in February 1972. It excited considerable discussion and at least some opposition; one skeptic argued that setting up a program to study peace at Earlham was much like expecting the critical study of dialectical materialism at Moscow State University. Most faculty, however, agreed with the Peace Studies Committee that it was "peculiarly appropriate that Earlham College, with its active Quaker tradition, should be in the forefront in establishing a truly significant Peace and Conflict Studies program." The faculty approved the proposal, with the understanding that the PACS program would be as broad as possible in scope, not limited to conflict resolution.[52]

Between 1972 and 1975, eleven PACS courses were offered as plans were made for the full implementation of the program. In 1974, Howard Richards, educated in philosophy and law at Yale, Stanford, and Berkeley and with a long career as an activist, was hired as its director. In 1975, the faculty approved the creation of three core courses in economics, philosophy, and sociology/anthropology. There were additional upper division courses, a senior seminar, and a field component. At this time, the program was not a major, since it was the hope of the participating faculty that "most students will have some contact with the application of several disciplines to problems of peace and war, and that they will then choose to make their own personal contribution to the building of peace through a major in one of the existing disciplines."[53]

The program has retained these basic features, but with some important changes. The name was changed to Peace and Global Studies (PAGS) in 1981, with the argument that this recognized the theme of global interdependence that was central to the program. It also began offering a major. In recognition of the vitality of Earlham's program and commitment, in 1994 the college became the headquarters for the Peace Studies Association.[54]

The second new interdisciplinary program, Human Development and Social Relations (HDSR), dated back to 1966, when the college set up a program in Human Relations. In 1975, the college received a grant from the Lilly Endowment to establish a Center for Human Development and Social Relations. The proposal depicted it as an innovative program that would "combine theory and practice, and intellectual and occupational competencies," to help prepare students for "careers in social service." It would do so by drawing mainly on the psychology and sociology departments, but on biology and philosophy as well. With perspectives from these disciplines, HDSR would "integrate field knowledge and the acquisition of occupationally useful skills" and help students "clarify and deepen their awareness of values and ethical judgments." It began its first year of full operation in the fall of 1976. The faculty approved its formally becoming a part of the curriculum in May 1977.[55]

Since its inception, HDSR has consistently been one of the three or four most popular majors at Earlham. It continues to rely heavily on contributions from the psychology and sociology/anthropology faculty. Field experience through an internship is still a requirement. The expectation of those who created the program that it would provide an occupational alternative for those who did not plan on graduate work has not proved well founded; most HDSR majors go on for graduate or professional work.[56]

A formal Women's Studies program came relatively late to Earlham. Classes in women's history and women's literature were offered in the mid-1970s, but for several years there was little movement toward anything more formal. By the mid-1980s, a number of courses focusing on the experiences of women were being offered in a variety of depart-ments, ranging from religion to English to history. Many on campus considered it unconscionable that a Quaker school would so lag behind other institutions. Others argued that while it was desirable to incorpo-rate women's and feminist points of view into the curriculum, this could be done without a formal major or program that would create pressures for additional staffing and new burdens for already overworked faculty.[57]

Early in 1987, a group of faculty who had functioned as the Women's Program Committee proposed the creation of a formal program and a major. The point of view was avowedly feminist, focusing on "the inadequacy of norms and expectations derived from *man* as the measure of all things," and showing "the established body of knowledge" to be "not neutral and unbiased but rather . . . the product of exclusion . . . of certain groups and perspectives." Instead, the program would, through "new perspectives and values," encourage changes "in ways of thinking, acting, and creating." The program relied mostly on classes already being taught in a number of departments, but also created introductory courses, including one in feminist theory, and a senior seminar as well as an internship. The faculty approved the creation of the program in the spring of 1987, and its first group of majors graduated in 1991.[58]

The library continued to be one of the college's outstanding features. After 1966, there was relatively little change in the staff for almost a quarter of a century.

Part of the library's reputation rested on the continuing success of the bibliographic instruction program. By the late 1970s, it had become a fixture in the life of the campus. Librarians from around the nation visited Earlham to study it, and Library Director Evan Farber traveled with faculty for presentations at numerous college libraries. There were other distinguishing features as well—the abundance of recreational reading and periodicals, the relaxed, informal atmosphere, the easy relations of the library staff with most students and faculty.[59]

There were changes, naturally. The most notable involved technology. For years, Farber resisted installing the electronic security system that had become standard in most college libraries, out of a feeling that it communicated a suspicion inappropriate to a Quaker institution. But in the fall of 1979, because of the problems missing books caused, he gave in. There were a few protests; one student wrote in the *Post* that the system was a "disgrace to humanity" and a "ghoulish harbinger" that "mocks the school's vital concept of consensus." Most students, however, tired of books that they needed disappearing, supported the change.[60]

The more noticeable changes came in the late 1980s. Early in 1989, the college replaced its traditional card catalog with an electronic one. In 1992, Earlham helped found a consortium, originally funded by the Lilly Endowment, called the Private Academic Library Network of Indiana (PALNI). PALNI created a computerized network that linked the catalogs of almost every private college library in the state. It also provided funding to automate circulation, which took place in the fall of 1995.[61]

Attracting national attention was an experiment that began in the fall of 1990. Farber had long argued that the increasing access of students to masses of information through electronic searching, especially on-line searching, would make for fundamental changes in teaching, as students would have to focus more and more on choosing what they needed from the overwhelming quantity of information available. He organized a conference in Richmond on this subject in 1989, and it was the subject of the Faculty Retreat in 1990. That same year, Farber arranged for

Dialog, a national on-line service with over four hundred data bases, to provide a year's free service (later expanded to two) to the college as an experiment to study the impact of access to information on teaching. The experiment drew complimentary coverage in the media, including the *New York Times* and the *Chronicle of Higher Education.*[62]

Farber's final project was a new library wing. Planned since the late 1970s, it provided badly needed space for additional stacks, new computing facilities, and a greatly expanded area for the Friends Collection and Archives. Farber himself retired in 1994, replaced by an Earlham alumnus and protege, Thomas G. Kirk, the college's first full-time science librarian, who returned to Earlham from Berea College.[63]

Other technological changes took place rapidly on campus. There had been demands for a computer center as early as 1966, about the time that the campus acquired its first computer. By 1979, there was discussion of using computers in the classroom, which became common, especially in natural sciences courses, in the 1980s. The computing center, which had a staff of 4 in 1974, had grown to 9 positions with 28 student workers by 1993. Statistics show how central microcomputers have become at Earlham. In 1983, there were 26 college-owned microcomputers on campus; by 1993 that had grown to 430, and conventionally typed papers were almost unknown. In some classes, by 1995, computer use and exploitation of the Internet were givens. The college used budget surpluses beginning in 1991 to provide almost every member of the faculty with a desktop computer. By 1993, e-mail had become a fact of life, and a lively medium for faculty debate.[64]

There have been numerous other curricular changes since 1973. Changes in accrediting regulations caused the demise of the elementary education program in 1976. Similar accrediting changes led to the creation of an innovative new program in 1992 for those pursuing secondary teaching licenses. Some new programs, like the special program in Senior Year Studies, lasted only a few years. Others, like the Management program, Environmental Studies, and Jewish Studies, are still trying to establish themselves. Still other innovations lasted longer, like the FLIC initiative first funded by the NEH in 1984.[65]

These decades also saw the growth of programs whose roots lay in the Bolling years. Off-campus study continued to be one of Earlham's attractions. By 1990, about 60 percent of all Earlham students took part in such a program. New ones were added, mostly reflecting a curricular or multicultural interest: Kenya in 1979, Jerusalem in 1984, Northern Ireland in 1991, and Martinique in 1995. International education, to be "at home in the world," was an increasingly critical element in the college's self-perception. The college also built on its strengths in Japanese studies. East Asian Studies became a major in 1974. Early in 1987, the college combined several Japan-related programs under the rubric of the Institute for Education on Japan, with Jackson Bailey as director. It included the college's foreign study programs in Japan, English teaching programs there, and the Studies in Crosscultural Education program, as well as coordinating programs for the study of Japan in Indiana schools. Meanwhile Bailey won numerous honors for his work, including, before his retirement from teaching in 1994, awards from the Japanese government and the American Historical Association. Public officials praised Bailey and Earlham's services generally as some of the state's vital resources in attracting Japanese businesses to Indiana. Bailey's untimely death in August 1996 was mourned in both Japan and the United States.[66]

One of the most popular and attractive innovations on campus in the last decade was the result of a successful application to the Ford Foundation in 1985. That year Ford had invited a select group of colleges to submit proposals for innovative programs in teaching and learning. Earlham received a major grant for joint faculty-student research projects, in which faculty and students work together on a topic proposed by the faculty member. This built on a long heritage of such activities in the college, especially in the natural sciences. A similar grant from the Knight Foundation in 1989 brought another half million dollars. The latter is focused on projects related to the mission of the college, especially its Quaker identity; the results of projects are reported directly to the board for that reason. In the past decade, over two hundred projects in every discipline have explored subjects ranging from street gangs in Los Angeles to peace-making in Northern Ireland to Quaker music to African weaving to the history of AFSC peace initiatives in the Middle East to abortion policy in Great Britain to the Human Genome Project.[67]

If there is consensus on anything at Earlham today, it is on this paradox—the curriculum is strong, but needs constant attention, examination, and questioning to remain so. Some of the most fervent challenges to it would come in the name of multiculturalism.

Multiculturalism and Its Discontents

Most observers have identified Earlham with political activism since the 1960s. More than one visitor has described the campus as being in a kind of "Sixties time warp." Much campus activism was focused, as will be seen, on questions of peace and foreign policy. But increasingly over the past two decades it has come to center on issues of race, gender, and sexual orientation. Student activists have created controversy with their often fiery denunciations of what they brand racism, sexism, and homophobia at Earlham and in the larger society. They have pushed for affirmative action policies, for responses to what they labeled acts of discrimination, and for incorporating their concerns into the curriculum. They were able to bring about some changes, but never enough to satisfy the most militant. They also found some allies on the faculty, but other faculty, and some students as well, saw this activism as a stultifying political correctness that threatened free discussion and academic freedom.

Since the 1960s, the college has attempted to attract and retain both black students and faculty. In 1973, the college adopted an affirmative action policy focused on racial minorities. A decade later, there was a grant from the Joyce Foundation to enhance the effectiveness of minority recruiting. In 1984, the college set up the position of assistant dean for minority affairs, in part to aid minority student recruiting. In 1978, a college house was formally dedicated as the Cunningham Cultural Center, in honor of Clarence Cunningham, Earlham's first black graduate, and for the use of the Black Leadership Action Coalition. In 1989, to attract more African American students from Indiana, the college announced that it would replace loans with outright grants. When the U.S. Department of Education challenged such race-based scholarships in 1991, the college refused to back down.[68]

In 1984, a faculty report concluded that "minority students tend to leave Earlham with a bittersweet view of their college years." Some had happy experiences, while others found at Earlham the same problems that they had encountered in the larger American society. It was the latter, and their white supporters, who were the most vocal, and who dominated campus discussion of race.[69]

Occasionally there were open outbreaks of racial tension. In a few cases they have involved racial epithets—in intramural basketball, in a student election, in an "underground" campus newspaper—directed at individuals. A particularly horrendous case came in April 1989, when racist graffiti was found in a Runyan Center bathroom. Usually the perpetrators were never identified. The incidents always brought some official administrative action, and sometimes wider response from the campus. Hundreds turned out for a meeting to denounce the graffiti in the spring of 1989, for example. For the most militant critics, however, the response was never enough: "Every time a racial incident occurs, we get a race seminar," one complained in 1991. "No action is being taken. We just keep getting these seminars."[70]

Such outbreaks were relatively rare, and never involved the rancor that a number of other schools experienced in the 1980s and early 1990s. More common complaints involved more subtle problems. There were charges of "intellectual hypocrisy," that the college wanted to be an "all white upper-middle class nursery." Among the complaints from time to time were the lack of blacks in the *Sargasso,* inadequate black enrollment, high black student attrition, racist attitudes among faculty, inadequate funding for the BLAC and the Black Cultural Center, and "naive, racist statements coming from the college's leading spokepersons."[71]

The administration did acknowledge problems, problems that it tried to combat—advisors who assumed that all black students came from impoverished inner cities; lack of career-planning advice; the need for more courses that incorporated African American materials and perspectives. More disturbing was the finding, by a visiting group of black alumni in the spring of 1977, of "an almost total lack of meaningful communication between Black students and the rest of the college."[72]

One of the most often voiced complaints was over the small number of black faculty. The college hired several in the early 1970s, but the first two to come up for tenure did not receive it, which critics were quick to cite as evidence of racism. The rejection of Thomas J. Davis, the director of the Black Studies program, was especially unpopular. It would be 1984 before a black professor at Earlham received tenure; two others have since, including, for the first time, the director of the African and African American Studies Program. When the contract of a black woman Quaker in the English department was not renewed in 1994, that again brought protests and charges of institutional bias.[73]

After 1980, the race-related issue that energized the largest group on campus was divestment from corporations that did business in South Africa. Intended as a tactic to weaken the apartheid regime there, it became a national movement in the early and mid-1980s.[74]

The issue first surfaced in a concerted way at Earlham in the fall of 1978, when a group of students held a vigil for divestment at a board meeting. They argued that the college should sell its stock in any company that did business in South Africa. The board took such concerns seriously. Instead of divesting, it chose to follow the Sullivan Principles, which allowed investment in companies doing business in South Africa that met certain standards for black employees there. The board position was that divesting would mean giving up any leverage over conditions in South Africa, a stance that it never changed. The board and administrators gave considerable time and effort to monitoring the policies of companies in which Earlham held stock.[75]

Such arguments did not convince the campus activists, who bitterly criticized what they saw as Earlham's complicity in the apartheid system. "Please Earlham divest now and wipe the blood from your hands," one alumnus wrote. From 1986 to 1989, campus protests grew increasingly urgent. In the spring of 1988, the senior class decided to put its traditional gift to the college in escrow until the college divested. Leaders and New York City alumni formed the National Alumni Movement for Earlham Divestment (NAMED). It demanded complete divestment, especially of the college's large holdings of Eli Lilly stock. When the board responded that the Lilly stock had been a gift that brought with it special responsibilities, critics replied that it was the moral equivalent of a gift of slaves. The controversy died down somewhat after 1989, finally becoming moot with the end of apartheid in South Africa.[76]

Thus Earlham faced the same problems of race that most American colleges confronted over the past two decades. While certainly it knew tension from time to time, it never experienced the kinds of flare-ups that plagued many other campuses. One BLAC president commented that the battle at Earlham had basically been won, leaving campus blacks to focus on the larger society. A 1985 faculty survey showed the feelings of black students to be generally positive about Earlham, especially about the academic program. Complaints focused on social life and the lack of black faculty. Earlham could not escape completely the problems of the larger society of which it was a part, but it had much in its struggle in which it could take pride.[77]

A second source of agitation for change on campus over the past two decades was the rise of a vibrant, articulate, and vocal feminist movement at Earlham. Its roots went back to the 1960s; by 1973, when Landrum Bolling left, there was already a Women's Center and newsletter. By the 1990s, with the renamed Womyn's Center, a Women's Studies program, and a variety of competing feminisms, the movement was one of the chief intellectual and political forces on campus. It manifested itself in a variety of ways.

One of the first women's concerns to find expression in the 1970s was the relatively small number of women faculty. As has been seen, when many older female professors retired in the 1960s, men replaced them. By 1974, this had become a real concern, especially for Joe Elmore, and adding women to the faculty became priority. It was justified in various ways. Many thought it unthinkable for a Quaker college, committed to the equality of the sexes, not to have a significant number of women faculty. Others pointed to the need for female role models for students. And so between 1974 and 1995 the percentage of women on the faculty increased steadily; for the past decade, most of the faculty hired for tenure-track positions have been women.[78]

These women reported mixed experiences. Paul Lacey found in reviewing student evaluations in 1980 that women faculty were often subjected to "painful and brutal" comments. One woman claimed that "sexist attitudes" were "so pronounced" that many students refused to treat women professors with the same respect that they gave to men.

Another woman professor claimed that women faculty at Earlham were "cautious and anxious not to tread on any toes." Other women faculty, while occasionally encountering such treatment, thought it the exception rather than the rule. Such tensions have continued down to the present. An April 1989 faculty meeting, for example, became a wide-ranging discussion of how women faculty felt that they were categorized by gender, leading to efforts by some male faculty to try to become more sensitive to such concerns.[79]

Women's concerns also made their way into the curriculum. As was noted earlier, various courses in women's history and literature became part of the curriculum in the 1970s, and in 1987 the major in Women's Studies was approved. The library began to focus on acquiring women's and feminist materials. Some feminist faculty attempted to transform teaching methods, discarding what they perceived as authoritarian male models for more nurturing, discussion-based feminist ones.[80]

The most urgent women's voices on the campus were usually those of students. Beginning in the late 1970s, often with support from sympathetic men, they offered a critique of various aspects of campus life that drew on feminist theory to measure Earlham and find it wanting.

The institutional locus of student feminism was usually the Women's Center, which by 1981 had been rechristened the "Womyn's Center," since, as one activist put it, "womyn are not an extension of men." It was a place for workshops, lectures, and "consciousness-raising discussions." Proponents found it "empowering and supportive." For many, men and women, however, as one student put it in 1988, the "Womyn's Center is becoming one of the largest jokes on campus," a stronghold of "aggressive, angry and intimidating womyn who are hostile toward anyone, male or female, who does not share their views on women's rights." Supporters disputed this depiction, but admitted that usually less than 10 percent of women students on campus were actively involved with the Womyn's Center. And even some women faculty mourned bad experiences with students who insisted that all teaching be done according to their particular feminist ideology.[81]

Whether or not they were overly strident, students certainly were vocal on a variety of women's issues. A prochoice position on abortion became campus orthodoxy; the brave souls who posted antiabortion views on the Opinion Board could rely on a torrent of response, some measured, some not. Any abortion rights demonstration, local or national, could depend on a sizeable Earlham contingent. By 1990, there was an organization, Students for Choice. Other national issues, like comparable worth, while discussed on campus, did not arouse the same passions.[82]

On campus, feminists offered a variety of criticisms. There were demands that courses, especially Humanities, include more books by women. There were demands for the use of inclusive language; in fact the college did stop using generic male pronouns in official publications. There were demands for a gynecological clinic, staffed by a woman physician. There were demands that the bookstore not stock works that feminists considered demeaning to women. There were demands for more women faculty, and especially for more women as high administrators.[83]

At times, the language and attitudes were harsh. In 1989 and 1992, there were furious denunciations of some administrators, growing out of rumors that they were hiding or ignoring cases of rape. While many students were convinced of the truth of the claims, concerted efforts by the administration during the 1989 controversy produced nothing to substantiate them; President Wood pointed out that the chief sufferers from the rumors had been the Student Development staff, who had the highest proportion of women of any unit on campus. One positive result was the organization of Earlham Action against Rape, a student group that tried to promote discussion of sexual assault issues and organized a campus escort service. The 1992 incident involved a finding of not guilty in a sexual harassment case between two students; the verdict produced fierce attacks in the *Word*, the campus newspaper, and a wave of vandalism. Some campus feminists embraced an extreme separatism. Even answering men's questions about feminism, one argued, "puts the onus back on the woman. She questions her actions, her feelings, and once again begins to doubt herself." A few dismissed men entirely. "I do not care how liberated a man claims to be," one wrote in the *Word*. "What I do appreciate is a view that sees womyn as able to carry on without men." Some women complained that to question such views brought accusations of disloyalty and betrayal.[84]

The institution's response to this range of feeling was restrained. As has been seen, it was a priority to address some of these concerns—for example, setting up an affirmative action program for women faculty. Joe Elmore was willing to be innovative to attract them. He experimented with spouses sharing an appointment; at one time Earlham had ten faculty involved in five such appointments, making it a national trend-setter. That in the history department held by Randall and Alice Shrock is now the longest-running in the United States. In 1985, the campus established a sexual harassment policy. On other issues, it acted more slowly—for example, it took almost fifteen years to outline an official policy on parental leave. And, as was the case on other campuses, the college's actions were usually not enough for the most outspoken critics.[85]

Dealing with women's issues was relatively uncomplicated, compared to dealing with homosexuality. That was the most explosive and controversial matter to face Earlham in the past two decades.

It seems certain that there were gay people at Earlham before 1960, but they have left no written records behind them. In the 1960s, some faculty remember a few students approaching them with a fear whose expression was always the same: "I'm afraid that I may be a homosexual." At the time, there was little to do besides recommending counseling and silence.[86]

In 1971, following national trends, the first campus gay group, the Gay People's Union (GPU), formed. It kept a low profile for its first year of existence; the *Post* did not notice its founding. Then in the fall of 1972, it began to meet publicly. One administrator thought it morally repugnant and feared a backlash from alumni and the yearly meetings; he argued that the group should be banned from campus. Other administrators agreed with Hugh Ronald, the financial vice president, that "you can't be a college and forbid people to talk about any topic." Bolling, still president, decided to allow the GPU to continue to meet. When the board took up the issue in the spring of 1973, Paul Lacey, the provost and soon to be acting president, went into the meeting with a letter of resignation in his pocket, prepared to submit it if the board banned the group. But the board gave its assent with relatively little debate. By the spring of 1974 the GPU had secured recognition as an official student organization.[87]

Over the next few years, the group remained relatively small, what a *Post* writer called "a forgotten minority." Meetings were held regularly, with an occasional speaker from off campus. In 1978, the GPU sponsored a convocation address by Elaine Noble, the first lesbian member of the Massachusetts legislature. The *Post* was generally sympathetic, and there was no attempt by the college to abridge the group's rights. Members, however, thought that most gay people on campus were too afraid to identify themselves publicly.[88]

On the other hand, there was clear ambivalence about the GPU and gays and lesbians at Earlham. The *Earlhamite*'s editors decided not to publish a "coming out" notice from an alumnus in 1976, and it was not until 1984 that the GPU was listed as a student organization in college publications. Some objected to student activity fees subsidizing the GPU, and college administrators were clear that while they considered sexual orientation a private matter, it would be "problematic" for the college to employ an openly gay person.[89]

More disturbing were expressions of rank prejudice. Many gay students in the 1970s and 1980s could tell such stories. As the backlash to the gay liberation movement grew nationally in the 1970s, Earlham was not immune. "Faggots" and "queers" were epithets hurled. GPU signs were sometimes torn down or even set on fire. "Last year, when the guy who was my boyfriend came up and we walked into SAGA [the campus food service], some guy said, 'I think all fags should be shot,'" one student wrote. It is not clear, however, how common such verbal assaults were.[90]

In the last decade, gay and lesbian activism on campus has ebbed and flowed. Certainly there were still expressions of prejudice, if not hatred. "You . . . will rot in Hell. I know you will get there before I do because of you that don't have AIDS I will kill you" was one message that appeared on e-mail in 1993. There was a sense of wariness among many students. "Walking on this campus is constantly a challenge because I don't know when some homophobic attack might be directed towards me," one student wrote in 1989. On the other hand, such incidents may have attracted attention because they were exceptional at Earlham. In 1994, an LBGPU statement (the name had evolved to Lesbian, Bisexual, and Gay People's Union by the early 1990s) included an outsider's evaluation of Earlham as a "Queer-friendly" place.[91]

The response from some in the campus homosexual community to any perceived attack was often vehement. By 1991, new, more radical alternatives to the LBGPU were forming, with names like the Queer Collective. A short-lived Earlham chapter of the militant gay organization ACT-UP also appeared. The AIDS crisis added urgency to the activism of many. Demands for condom dispensers in dormitories involved charges that "the absence of condoms is silence . . . Silence = Death," a favorite ACT-UP slogan. There was insistence that Earlham was a "status quo of Hatred and Intolerance," of "blatant homophobic harassment." In the minds of some gay activists, to express even the slightest reservation was to side with the enemy. "If you have the point of view that queers need counseling or that queer people have an immoral lifestyle, it is a short step to ignoring the murder or abuse of someone who is beat up," one student wrote. When biology professor Jerry Woolpy published an *Earlhamite* article about new research on the biology of homosexuality, one campus activist denounced it as the moral equivalent of scientific racism.[92]

The college, meanwhile, gradually became more open in its tolerance. Gays and lesbians were not added to the affirmative action statement, as many demanded, but neither were they discriminated against in hiring. In 1992 sexual orientation was included in the campus harassment policy. In February 1994, as will be seen, the college endured angry criticism to host the Midwest Bisexual Lesbian and Gay College Conference. Attempts at dialogue on homosexuality on campus, however, often fell victim to the conviction of many gay activists that even discussion was a compromise of principle. When a trustee, a Quaker minister, gave a tempered talk in April 1991, arguing that the Bible condemned homosexual acts, campus rumor turned it into a demand for expelling gay students. Two years later, when a Denver Quaker involved in a "ministry" to gay people visited campus as part of a series of speakers from all points of view, there were again angry denunciations of tolerating any doubt. Free expression, wrote one ESR student, "loses its meaning and its moral justification when it is used to perpetuate oppression." The maintenance of an atmosphere of tolerance and free discussion on campus would face challenges from all sides.[93]

By the late 1980s, these concerns about racism, sexism, and homophobia, and some others, were finding expression under the rubric of multiculturalism. Supporters at Earlham were part of the larger, national movement that agitated for substantial change in higher education. As befits an intellectual movement that prizes diversity, generalizations about multiculturalism are difficult to make. Proponents advocated changes in both the substance and methods of teaching and in the climate of higher education to make it more open and hospitable to "marginalized" groups. This meant criticism of "the canon," especially in literature, as overly focused on the works of white European men. Similarly, multiculturalists criticized other disciplines, like history, for excluding the contributions of women, people of color, and non-elites generally. Efforts to improve campus climates often focused on "hate speech" codes, proscribing conduct deemed offensive or oppressive to certain groups, especially women, gays, and minorities. At its best, multiculturalism made real contributions to knowledge in a variety of fields. At its worst, the movement degenerated into the left-wing dogmatism that critics labeled "political correctness." Both kinds of multiculturalism could be found at Earlham.[94]

Earlham, of course, had a long-standing interest in other cultures. As early as 1949, one student had argued that Tom Jones's "Earlham Idea" would "only become meaningful when we bring to our campus in ever larger numbers, Negroes and Indians from South Africa, Jews and other homeless from D. P. camps, communists from China, Jugoslavs and Russians, and all those who at present cannot live in harmony with one another." In the 1960s, Earlham was a national trendsetter in "Non-Western Studies" and off-campus programs. In the 1960s and 1970s, the college attempted to diversify both students and faculty. In 1975, the faculty approved, from "concern about cultural diversity and international dependence," a requirement for a cross-cultural component in its education program. In 1981, a new major in International Studies was created.[95]

For some faculty and students, this was not enough. As early as 1976, there were calls for some sort of required course in Black Studies. Three years later, a Nigerian student criticized the reading list in the East African history course for not including enough works by African authors. There were also demands to do away with the election of the Homecoming Queen as sexist, which in fact did happen in 1977. In the spring of 1980, with language that would be passé for the next generation of activists, some students blasted Earlham as an "oppressive, sexist, racist, capitalist, and heterosexist institution." It needed to "respect new and different ways to construct and present knowledge."[96]

In the last decade, the multicultural push at Earlham has taken several directions. The Humanities program has been central; its reading list has received considerable criticism from those, including some faculty, who argue that it needs more works by women and people of color. When the Humanities faculty attempted a discussion of the issues raised by Allen Bloom's *The Closing of the American Mind,* a best-selling attack on multiculturalism, in a summer seminar in 1989, the disagreements were so sharp and unpleasant that future seminars avoided directly dealing with such topics. Some faculty criticized the Humanities program's focus on finding an "authorial voice" as old-fashioned and wrong-headed. No matter the subject of the assigned text, there would be demands from some students that the discussion focus on racism, sexism, and homophobia.[97]

Other areas have also been the subject of multicultural critique. In 1989, for example, one student demanded that the college end all of its foreign study programs in "Western" countries, and instead require all students to live and study in the Third World. A succession of groups - the Student Union, the Progressive Student Union, the Activist Alliance, the Multicultural Alliance—formed and faded as student leaders graduated. Their demands usually included a more racially and ethnically diverse faculty and student body, a more multicultural curriculum, more support especially for the AAAS program, inclusion of gays and lesbians in the college affirmative action program, and, as a 1992 manifesto put it, action against "racially oppressive remarks and behavior." In 1992 and 1994, groups briefly occupied the president's office to draw attention to their causes. In the latter case, the Multicultural Alliance demanded that normal governance procedures be bypassed to institute their reforms by given deadlines, a demand the administration and faculty flatly refused to accept.[98]

Probably no issue better embodied these concerns than Big May Day and the battles it inspired from 1969 onward. By the 1960s, May Day was one of Earlham's most venerable traditions, with roots going back to 1875, when a group of women students had staged a spring festival. Until the turn of the century, only women participated. By 1902, it had begun to assume the character it would have for the next ninety years, "Old English May Day," with most students and faculty taking part.[99]

By the 1930s, Big May Day had become the great campus spectacle. Staged every four years, so that theoretically every student would have a chance to take part before graduating, it involved casting the campus as the sixteenth-century English village of Earlham, receiving a visit from Queen Elizabeth I, traditionally portrayed by the president's wife. Faculty and staff and their families as well as students played hundreds of roles, from lords and ladies to milkmaids and shepherds. After World War II especially, the celebration drew thousands of spectators and considerable press coverage, all of it favorable. In 1961, for example, the *Louisville Courier-Journal* wrote: "It is likely that nowhere else on this continent is an amateur production more competently handled in both planning and execution."[100]

All of this came at a cost. Costuming, rehearsals, assigning parts, and hundreds of other details of preparation took thousands of hours, many supplied by the unpaid labor of faculty wives. The 1955 observance was postponed until 1957 to allow time to study the whole question. Still, a survey that year showed that faculty attitudes were overwhelmingly favorable, while almost 85 percent of students favored continuation. And so May Day went on.[101]

By 1969, however, campus activists were actively questioning Big May Day. There was picketing that year; one freshman argued that Earlham should give its time and energy to "world affairs, political events, and social concerns." That led another student to retort: "Why does a person have to be socially concerned every second of his existence?" By 1973, there was noticeable alienation; one opponent sprinkled thumbtacks around the May Pole for the benefit of the barefoot dancers. By 1981, criticism had changed from focusing on the event as a waste of time to emphasizing what critics saw as its exclusive aspects. May Day, they charged, was an embrace of "racism and ethnocentrism," since it supposedly ignored and marginalized other, non-English cultures. It also glorified Elizabethan England, which was held guilty of a host of sins. Critics demanded instead an "international spring celebration, drawing from many cultures."[102]

By the 1989 observance, the whole multicultural arsenal of analysis was being turned on May Day. It was a "disgusting display of status" that created "a stratification between classes." Its pageantry was "a mockery of the values we try to achieve," while the roles contributed "to the stereotyping and degradation of persons." It was inappropriate because it celebrated only one culture, and that a culture that embodied racism, sexism, homophobia, imperialism, slavery, anti-Semitism, and the persecution of "witches." (One historian noted that the number of witches executed in the critics' pronouncements kept climbing to the point that there would have been no one left living in Elizabethan England, male or female.) Although most faculty and students chose to participate in the 1989 observance, the protests were worrisome enough that it was decided to try to address such concerns head-on. Thus as plans were made for the 1993 celebration, the co-convenors of the supervisory committee, Registrar Lavona Godsey and junior SaraAnne Acres, held a series of meetings to invite comments and ideas.[103]

The committee's solution was a compromise. The celebration would be called simply "May Day." While most participants would play the traditional English roles, they would not have precedence in the procession, and others would be encouraged to take part representing their own cultures. While traditional events like the May Pole and Morris Dances would take place on the Heart, scattered around it would be "villages" representing other cultures.[104]

As is often the case with compromises, this one left many unsatisfied. A number of long-time participants saw it as a "politically correct hodge podge"; some decided not to take part. But it was far too traditional for critics, who saw in it a "'dominant' Anglo culture and token villages." About forty-five protestors delayed the start of the festivities to read a list of objections. They kept up their barrage afterwards. "May Day was not a show," one wrote in the *Word.* "It was a political act of racial domination, an exercise of power. It was just as political as modernity's capitalist system where the hegemonic First World societies rule over the poorer peoples who live away from the 'Heart' of civilization." Reaction from spectators, mostly alumni, ranged from chuckles over the protest, which some saw as venerable tradition in itself, to anger at being a captive audience. And in fact a majority of students still participated. "Why it is fair for all cultures to be celebrated except white Europeans?" one asked. The 1993 celebration, however, may well have been the last at Earlham. Under the new semester calendar, there may not be enough May for May Day.[105]

The institutional response to multicultural pressures varied. Some faculty were supportive of the multicultural impulse. A number had been influenced themselves in their teaching by debates about the nature of the canon and had responded by trying to make their own courses more inclusive. In the English department, for example, courses in emerging, postcolonial, and women's literatures joined more traditional offerings like Shakespeare, and reading lists in the latter showed a much wider range. When the faculty discussed strategic goals for the campus in 1989, one included using "gender, race, and class" as categories of analysis. On the other hand, many faculty remained skeptical. An attempt in the Curricular Policy Committee to require new course proposals to address these sorts of criteria failed in 1992 amidst concerns over academic freedom.[106]

More controversial was the long effort to draft a code on racial harassment. Beginning in 1990, a committee of faculty and students had struggled to balance two goods. One was the conviction that no one in a Quaker school should be subjected to harassment; the other was avoiding the chilling effects on free discussion that "hate speech" codes had allegedly created on other campuses. When the committee brought a proposal to the faculty meeting in the fall of 1991, debate bogged down amidst competing fears. Some questioned the desirability of distinguishing between intentional and unintentional acts, or of even presuming innocence. Such concepts, one argued, had traditionally been supportive of white male power; like-minded faculty, echoing arguments at other institutions, asserted that free speech was too often an instrument of oppression. Opposed were faculty who saw in such views clear and present dangers to academic freedom. With such a gulf of opinion, consensus proved impossible to reach. At that point, Sara Penhale, the clerk of the faculty meeting, asked two faculty of opposing views to convene a group that would attempt to draft a new, compromise document. Working with several colleagues of all views, they wrote a focused statement informed by American Association of University Professors guidelines that targeted all types of harassment but which also distinguished between intentional and unintentional acts and between the merely offensive and the harmful. Although some on both sides of the debate have expressed reservations about its construction and operation, the faculty accepted it in April 1992.[107]

Today, there is no consensus at Earlham about the impact of multiculturalism. Some see it as the source of a stifling political correctness, while others insist that Earlham remains a deeply traditional, elitist institution in which minorities and "the other" are still effectively disempowered and marginalized. Still others think that Earlham has, by seeking to make policy through consensus, found a middle way that has worked to the benefit of all. This method of resolving the issues that multiculturalism raises is deeply ingrained in Earlham's understanding of its Quaker identity.

Earlham as a Quaker Place

Earlham's president, Dick Wood, was fond of saying that Earlham is almost unique among nationally ranked liberal arts colleges in retaining a strong religious identity. Virtually every college constituency—alumni, faculty, staff, students, trustees—affirms it. Yet there was, and is, considerable disagreement among them about what it means for Earlham to be a Quaker college. And there have been periodic attacks from area Friends who have found aspects of Earlham's understanding of itself directly contrary to their convictions about Quaker faith and practice.

Over the past two decades, Earlham has faced a variety of tests of its Quakerism—some from students, some from faculty, some from the yearly meetings. Some have involved the nature of the Earlham community. Some have grown out of Earlham's commitment to peace and nonviolence. Some have involved questions of sexual morality. Some have involved the number of Friends on the campus, and the nature of its religious life. Most vexing have been yearly meeting relations, especially with Indiana Yearly Meeting.

One of the most persistent themes in Earlham's conversations about itself has been *community*. Earlham governs itself, for example, by a *Community* Code. Numerous visitors to campus have noticed the value that Earlham places on its sense of community. Faculty speak of how they came to Earlham in part because they wished to participate in a college that was an intentional community. Scarcely a year passes that a faculty meeting does not devote considerable time to the subject. Most recently, a long statement from Dick Wood on Earlham as a Quaker, residential college, focusing in large part on strengthening community, has been at the center of considerable debate. Students fully share in the conviction that Earlham's sense of community is precious. As one student leader put it in the spring of 1994: "The building of community at Earlham is of supreme importance to this institution. Not only is it an important part of the way we understand ourselves and our lives, but it is also deeply related to the mission of the college."[108]

If there is consensus on the centrality of community, there is also a constant fear that it is being eroded. One student in 1983 saw the cause as insufficient dialogue among groups on campus. In 1989, another student saw the chief threats to community at Earlham in the college's failure to divest and the possession of guns by campus security. Older faculty bemoaned the sparse attendance at convocations and occasions like lectures and teas. Still others pointed to what they saw as pervasive apathy over student government and campus activities. Many athletic events were poorly attended. It was difficult to find staff for the newspaper and the *Sargasso*, the yearbook. The *Earlham Post* collapsed in 1984, and it was the fall of 1986 before the *Earlham Word* took its place. Many faculty focused on "busy-ness"; they felt that they simply no longer had the time to be as involved in the campus community as they should be.[109]

There has been no lack of prescriptions for strengthening the campus community. Franklin Wallin's 1974 inaugural address was centered largely on his vision of making Earlham a religious, ethical, and intellectual community. Some have focused on strengthening student involvement in decision-making. Most campus committees, in fact, do have student members, and a few have had student convenors, although there is considerable debate about their effectiveness; skeptical faculty point to often poor student attendance at meetings, while student critics respond that students have little power. For a time in the 1970s, there was experimentation with town meetings for the entire campus; some found them, however, a "forum for undisciplined rhetoric by a few vocal persons" rather than "an opportunity for serious community-wide discussion. Still others saw the Community Code as central, and it underwent regular revision, most recently in 1991. Many administrators saw student-faculty interaction outside of the classroom as the key, and there was no lack of ideas about how to encourage that.[110]

Today, evaluations of the campus's sense of community run the gamut. One faculty member in 1995 pronounced community "dead" at Earlham. Others share fears that it is headed in that direction, but find the situation still reversible. Still other faculty argue that fears often come from a misperception of the nature of a college community. They mostly seek intellectual community based on an interchange of ideas, rather than the social community that many faculty miss. Perhaps the safest statement to make is that the continued interest in discussing the subject shows how important it continues to be to many on campus.[111]

Less chronic than the discussion of community, ebbing and flowing with events in the larger world, was the peace movement on campus. After the end of the Vietnam War, it lost much of its impetus, but it did not disappear. The creation of the PACS Program institutionalized it. When a new Community Code was drafted in 1976–1977, it included a section on nonviolence as one of Earlham's distinctive values. The faculty softened the statement to remove the impression that pacifism was a sine qua non of the Earlham community. There was considerable debate in 1974–1975 and 1978–1979 about security carrying guns on campus. Critics thought it indefensible for a Quaker school; others responded that it was a necessary concession for the protection of the security personnel, on whom pacifist values were not necessarily binding.[112]

Events in the winter of 1979–1980 re-energized campus peace activism. The combination of the Iranian Hostage Crisis and the Russian invasion of Afghanistan moved the Carter Administration to revive draft registration, a move that the Reagan Administration continued. The Reagan emphasis on increasing defense spending and using military force generally re-energized peace activists, and those at Earlham were no exception. Their activities took several forms.[113]

One was draft resistance, which again became a hotly debated topic on campus. Both the institution officially and students generally were far more sympathetic to nonregistrants than they had been thirty years before. The college took the position that registration or nonregistration was a matter of individual conscience, and that it would support students in whatever decision they made. Meanwhile, Earlham would offer counseling, would not release student records to the Selective Service without student permission, and would continue not to allow military recruiting on campus. When the Solomon Amendment withheld student aid from nonregistrants, Earlham joined the court challenge, and pledged to make up from other sources anything that a nonregistrant might lose.[114]

Only a handful of students actually refused to register, but they received so much support on campus that Earlham's reputation for radicalism and nonconformity received a significant boost. Various groups formed to campaign against the draft, with names like Earlham against Registration (EAR) and Richmond against the Draft (RAD). "Earlham is so pro-draft (registration) resistance in its publications that it makes those who did register, which is probably the majority on campus, feel we are the bad guys," one student complained. The reasons that nonregistrants like Michael Frisch and Steve Gillis gave for their actions echoed the nonregistrants of 1948–1949—they could not take any action that seemed to justify war.[115]

Earlham peace activism found other expressions in the early 1980s. Some renewed the Vietnam-era resistance to paying taxes that might be used for military purposes. There were rallies, protests, even sit-ins in congressional offices. For some, civil disobedience was now a tactic to be employed routinely. There was considerable support for the nuclear freeze movement on campus. The Earlham School of Religion did declare itself a nuclear-free zone, but the college faculty could not reach consensus to do so. Indeed, some of the faculty argued that it was inappropriate for the faculty meeting to act "on a political issue upon which reasonable people may and often do disagree." By 1983, there was an annual Peace and Justice Festival, which eventually evolved into Peace with Justice Week.[116]

Yet while some antiwar activism grew out of a pacifist commitment that proponents saw as natural to a Quaker college, there were other, angrier voices. One student caught that drift in 1983: "You will find a strange combination of despair and grim hope," she wrote. "The despair rises out of a sense of powerlessness; the grim hope out of the necessity to act, to be humane in an inhumane world." Students would "not be inclined to starry-eyed idealism," but would "adopt a realistic attitude, marked by cynicism and unbelief." Nowhere was this more clearly seen than in the angry blasts at Reagan policy in Central America. Some became so committed to their conceptions of justice that they dismissed "nonviolent purists." Others warned against the dangers from the "growing intolerance between extremist factions of the student body."[117]

Such antipathies died down somewhat in the late 1980s, as the campus focused on other concerns. The outbreak of the Gulf War in 1990–1991, however, re-energized antiwar activism. PAGS head Tony Bing received national attention when he traveled to Iraq in October 1990 as part of a delegation sponsored by the Fellowship of Reconciliation. When the U.S. offensive began on January 16, 1991, the campus found itself divided. Even opponents of the war were split between those who acted out of pacifist conviction and those who saw the conflict as yet another example of American imperialism, driven by the insatiable demands of oil companies and the American "war culture." Others were supportive. On the night that the U.S. offensive began, three hundred opponents held a candlelight protest vigil on the Heart, while a smaller group of supporters sang the National Anthem nearby.[118]

The campus debate over the Gulf War was heightened by the long-standing interest on campus in the Middle East and Palestinian issues. There has been a Quaker school at Ramallah on the West Bank since the 1870s; numerous Earlham alumni have taught there, and a number of Ramallah graduates have come to Earlham, many on a scholarship designated specifically for them.[119]

As early as 1957, there had been debate on campus about the rights of Israelis and Palestinians. Such interest was heightened in 1970, when Landrum Bolling was part of an AFSC group that produced a proposal for peace in the Middle East that most viewed as sympathetic to the Palestinians. Throughout the 1970s and 1980s, there was always a significant group on campus pushing Palestinian concerns. Some Jewish students claimed that their actions and rhetoric often crossed the line into anti-Semitism. Such activists gave the opposition to the Gulf War much of its edge.[120]

Thus Earlham kept up its heritage of antiwar activism. Some participants doubtless were inspired by a Quakerly pacifism; others by nonreligious political conviction; many doubtless could not always distinguish between the two. Even some Quakers looked askance at the combination on campus. That concern was nothing, however, compared to the struggles about sex on campus.

The 1970s confirmed the sexual revolution that began in the late 1960s. For millions of Americans, the widespread availability of birth control devices, especially "the pill," led to an unprecedented degree of sexual experimentation, especially among college students. For some, this activity was simply healthy and natural. For others, especially Indiana Friends, it was flouting basic principles of morality that could not be compromised. For so private a matter as sexual activity, for the most part we have only impressionistic evidence. But this period of Earlham's history opened with what many saw as one of the defining moments in the campus's history, the tenure case of Jerry Woolpy.[121]

Questions about sex and sexual morality were at the heart of the Woolpy case, and, as messy and complicated as it was, it marked a turning point in the history of the college. Woolpy had come to Earlham in the fall of 1967 to teach biology, especially genetics, direct from the

University of Chicago. He quickly established himself as one of the most popular and effective professors on campus. He also quickly found himself entrusted with a number of difficult and delicate committee tasks that he carried off with similar success. He was not averse to making waves; at one point Bolling was on the verge of firing him in a dispute over a departmental search procedure. In the minds of most on campus, however, he was a strong candidate for tenure when he came up for consideration in the fall of 1973.[122]

The situation, however, was not normal. Recently divorced, Woolpy had begun living with Sara Penhale, a 1971 graduate, two years after her graduation. They planned to marry, but since her plans for graduate work were uncertain, they had decided to wait. For Bolling when he learned of it, the situation was completely unacceptable. Not only did it defy what he considered basic moral convention, but it also showed extremely poor judgment. It was a bad example for students. Woolpy did accept the importance of being a role model, but obviously did not see his life as fundamentally immoral or meriting dismissal.[123]

Bolling left in the spring of 1973, handing on the case to Paul Lacey, Joe Elmore, and the Faculty Affairs Committee (FAC). Meanwhile, the entire campus was aware of what was going on, and it found itself polarized. Many faculty thought that, whatever Woolpy's gifts as a teacher, "living in sin" was something that the college could not countenance, and that to tenure him would do just that. Lacey, facing the issue head-on in convocation, although without naming Woolpy directly, made it clear that he thought to give him tenure involved troubling questions. Most students, and many other faculty, found it equally inconceivable that the college would refuse to keep such an effective and gifted professor. The five elected members of FAC reached a strong consensus in favor of tenure. They argued that to tenure the biologist was similar to tenuring divorced people, which the college had already done—just as that action did not necessarily endorse divorce, so the college would not be endorsing Woolpy's lifestyle. Lacey and Elmore could not join in the recommendation, although they made it clear that they did not feel that they should have the last word, phrasing their doubts as being unconvinced that Woolpy should have tenure, rather than convinced that he should not. So the case went to the board of trustees to examine the questions of policy and precedent involved.[124]

The board's handling of the case was, by its own admission, extraordinary. In December 1973 it invited Woolpy and Penhale to a special meeting. Both found the experience unnerving, especially when out of the opening silence one elderly member, not a Quaker, prayed for sinners to be damned to hell. For about forty-five minutes, the board members quizzed the two, pressing the question of why they did not marry. Both responded that they would probably have been married by this time had their lives not been so disrupted by the controversy. That afternoon, Lacey, Elmore, and Edward G. Wilson, the board's chairman, came to see them. They shared an unprecedented resolution—Woolpy would have the 1974–1975 year as a sabbatical year, to be followed by another year on the faculty, during which the tenure decision would come.[125]

The board saw itself bending as far as it could bend, avoiding either outright acceptance or rejection of Woolpy. Its minute noted that the board could not reach consensus on tenure, but did not "wish to take a position that severs abruptly and permanently Jerome Woolpy's relationship with the Earlham community." Woolpy and Penhale saw the message as clear—go away and come back married. Some students saw the decision as a cunning ploy to postpone the decision until many of Woolpy's strongest supporters had graduated. In fact, Woolpy and Penhale did marry during the sabbatical year, and he did return to receive tenure. A few years later Penhale also joined the faculty, where both remained until he retired in 1996.[126]

Everyone involved stated explicitly that circumstances made this a unique case. Even Woolpy's faculty supporters argued that they did not see any kind of precedent being set, and the board certainly agreed. Yet there was a clear sense that something had changed. As Lacey, Elmore, and the FAC members noted, this was "the first personnel matter in which sexual conduct is openly mentioned; previous to this, any faculty member engaging in unconventional sexual behavior was quietly sent away without a single voice being raised in protest." Now Earlham, uncertainly but surely, had bent.[127]

No other individual case on campus ever became so public. For student behavior we have only impressionistic evidence. Certainly some administrators and faculty had the impression that many, perhaps most, students were experimenting sexually, often with unhappy results emotionally. A highly unscientific survey of students in the fall of 1982 showed that 90 percent of men and 52 percent of women reported some sort of sexual experience (although there was no indication whether it took place on campus or not). Occasionally some student would comment publicly, such as a writer on the Opinion Board in 1987 who claimed that on campus "people often decide on the spur of the moment to have sex." In a 1976 speech to the board, Elton Trueblood bemoaned what he saw as "great evidence of unchastity."[128]

The college administration struggled early in the 1970s to uphold a traditional view of the merits of abstinence. In 1971, a section on sexuality was added to the college catalog. It affirmed "healthy, positive attitudes ... toward sexuality and honest and open communication about all sexual matters." It also affirmed "the conviction that complete sexual relations of men and women should be confined to the marriage partnership." Many students objected to this position as an invasion of their rights and privacy, often with support from parents, while some faculty thought that the college was being utterly unrealistic. In 1976, a task force of trustees, faculty, and students undertook drafting a new community code. Sexuality quickly became a point of contention. Some favored retaining the old statement condemning sex outside of marriage; some thought it pointless for the college to try to regulate it; still others wanted some recognition of the legitimacy of sexual relationships outside marriage. The debate would go on for six years, with the board of trustees especially opposed to anything that implied condoning of premarital sex. Finally, in the fall of 1982, the board approved a code that said nothing on the subject.[129]

Officially, the college remained committed to the position that it could not and did not condone sex outside of marriage. Dick Wood made this clear in a number of public statements, and Len Clark, the provost after 1981, gave prospective faculty what was known as "the lecture," telling them that to live with a person of the opposite sex openly would be a major impediment to renewal or tenure. Many members of the faculty remained personally committed to those standards.[130]

The pressure to erode such standards, however, was constant. Beginning in the late 1980s, a number of students, and some faculty and staff, began to press for condoms or "latex barriers" to be made freely available on campus. The need for birth control, which had been available through Health Services since the late 1970s, was not so much the reason as the necessity of preventing the spread of AIDS. The latter gave the campaign a deadly urgency in the minds of "latex" supporters. "I want condom machines in bathrooms and health services, without any sort of notation on medical records. . . . The college needs to face facts that students are going to have sex," one student argued in 1992. "I was enraged by the policy—that the administration put their sense of morality in front of issues of health." Various groups distributed condoms to mailboxes to publicize their cause. To suggest abstinence brought ferocious responses, usually accusations that those supporting a more traditional morality were really advocating death for those they disliked. As one student put it, on this issue Earlham was "not a safe place for people who felt differently."[131]

There was in fact some give. The new Community Code, approved in 1991, included a long section on "Expressions of Sexuality." It acknowledged the "lack of consensus in the community concerning sexuality," conceding the "diverse viewpoints of Friends." While noting that Quakers traditionally had "held that sexual intimacy should be fully expressed only within the spiritual, emotional, and physical commitment that the community publicly affirms in marriage," it also noted that some contemporary Friends were affirming other standards. It also stated an awareness that "sometimes, by mutual choice and understanding, interpersonal relationships do take the form of sexual intimacy." In 1992, after months of debate, compromise was reached on a "latex policy": there would be no more campus-wide distribution, but each dormitory would set its own policy on installing machines to make such devices available. Campus opinion was divided. Some activists saw the compromise as grudging and inadequate, especially in the era of AIDS. Others, especially in the yearly meetings, were pained by what they saw as Earlham's implicit endorsement of immorality.[132]

For the past two decades, the college has attempted to keep up a spiritual witness. As Dick Wood put it in a 1990 convocation address, Earlham aspired to be a place that "welcomes people of all faiths and people of no faith to be in a college that takes religious faith seriously." Few publicly challenged the desirability of that, but there was considerable debate on campus about what that should involve. Some openly questioned whether it was necessary for the campus to be religious in order to be Quakerly.[133]

Certainly there was considerable effort to keep up a strong, diverse Christian religious life. Campus meeting for worship was held every Sunday morning during the school year. There was a Young Friends group, usually small but vibrant. A variety of faculty groups interested in spiritual matters have existed, mostly recently a Faculty Faith group. Worship twice weekly is an integral part of the Earlham School of Religion. For the past two decades, there has been a campus minister. There have also been student groups, like the Earlham Christian Fellowship, the Fellowship of Christian Athletes, and the Intervarsity Christian Fellowship.[134]

At the same time, there was official recognition of the religious diversity of the campus. For a time, there was an attempt to make Campus Meeting for Worship more welcoming to non-Christians by making it an interfaith service, avoiding "exclusive" language and hymns. After a few years of feeling that the result was vague and "wishy washy," in 1985–1986 it was decided to pattern it more after a pastoral Friends meeting and hold separate Jewish services. In 1986 Beit Kehillah, the Jewish Cultural Center for the campus, opened on College Avenue. There was also interest in less conventional types of spirituality. In the 1993–1994 school year, there was a "Spiritual Lifestyles House" on campus that included study of Buddhism, Hare Krishna, Shamanism, Bahai, Dream Workshops, and a "Weekly Drumming Circle."[135]

On the other hand, religion could be a source of friction. By the 1980s, about a third of each entering class reported no religious affiliation. Humanities instructors found that whenever the reading list included explicitly Christian texts, like St. Augustine's *Confessions* or Blaise Pascal's *Pensées,* some students could always be counted on to be openly contemptuous. Jewish students also complained of ignorance and hostility that bordered on anti-Semitism. At times such disagreements extended to the faculty. In the spring of 1995, the idea of congregational hymn singing in the baccalaureate service was the occasion for considerable faculty debate. Some objected to it as un-Quakerly, while others found the public visibility of choosing to sing or remain silent, faintly coercive. One saw it as the first step on the slippery slope toward a religious test, to which Wood replied that the most dangerous slope the campus faced was secularization.[156]

On the specific subject of Earlham's Quaker identity, there has been no lack of vision. Presidents Wallin, Baldwin, and Wood all made Earlham's Quaker roots and aspirations the focus of their inaugural addresses. Wallin saw Earlham as a "continuing educational experiment." The college's mission was a "corporate search for spiritual truth" by "an open community of teachers and students who mutually shared high expectations," and who "valued each person's potential for growth." Baldwin emphasized following the Inner Light and providing service to the world, based on preparation at Earlham. Wood aspired to Earlham's becoming "a model for a Christian, church-related college that is not a narrowly sectarian Bible college." Noting that many Quaker colleges had lost their Quaker identities, he thought that Earlham should live out the testimonies of Friends, but needed to remember that it was "a college, an educational institution, not a lobbying group or a therapeutic institution."[157]

The college tried to live out its Quakerism in several ways. One was through consensus decision making, which virtually everyone on campus saw as vital. "I don't think I can over-emphasize the value of consensus in speaking of the reason for Earlham," one professor told new students in 1984. By the 1970s, virtually every group on campus operated on that basis. Many faculty conceded its difficulties and frustrations. One clerk of the faculty noted how hard it was to transfer to a secular setting "the Quaker ideal of religious experience." Much time had to be spent correcting misconceptions—that consensus required unanimity, that a single person could exercise a veto, that a new consensus had to be reached on every subject with each new class of students. As one frustrated new faculty member put it, trying to influence decisions sometimes felt like "beating your fist against a pillow." Paul Lacey was equally direct: trying to get the Earlham faculty to reach consensus was like "trying to take a herd of kangaroos for a walk." Yet virtually all faculty affirmed the process.[138]

The other notable way in which the college tried to affirm and guard Earlham's Quaker identity was through the Community Code. Beginning with revisions in 1976–1977, the code was expressed in terms of testimonies, the historically Quaker understanding of the nature of Truth. The version that year opened with a section on "Quaker Roots" that reviewed Quaker understandings of God and the Inner Light as the foundations of Friends. It then discussed simplicity, equality, nonviolence, and social justice as the Quaker values that Earlham especially tried to exemplify in its life. The 1991 revision of the Community Code was even more detailed. Under five headings—Respect for Persons, Building Community, Academic Integrity, Peace and Justice, and Simplicity—it presented sections of Testimonies, Expectations, and Queries.[139]

There were other affirmations of Earlham's Quaker identity, especially in the classroom and in scholarship. Arthur Little, the theater professor who retired in 1976, thought that the Quaker professor should aim "at education for the service of man and the glory of God." Paul Lacey hoped that through teaching literature he would not only enter into a "double dialogue, with text and with student," but would hope for a "third dialogue . . . one which gathers the other two into itself, the dialogue with the Eternal Thou, the Inward Teacher, who can bring all things into clarity and truth." Franklin Wallin argued that the point of Quaker teaching should be questioning verities like growth, technology, competition, nation states. Still others point to a curriculum that includes International Studies, PAGS, and an emphasis on cooperative learning and service learning. Now Earlham supports a nascent Institute for Quaker Studies. Again and again debates in the faculty meeting, ranging from grading to the Honor Code to community, turned on how individuals understood Quaker values.[140]

Students showed considerable enthusiasm for certain Quaker values, especially those that melded with their own concerns. Advocates of multiculturalism argued that a Quaker school could take no other course than the particular pattern that they recommended. When the Earlham Environmental Action Coalition formed in 1989, it portrayed its activities as an extension of the Quaker testimony of simplicity. One student in 1988 argued that no Quaker college should fly the American flag, since Friends "place almost no trust in symbols." That same year, a faculty member condemned the demolition of Jones House, the old presidential residence, as "extravagant behavior incompatible with Quaker principles." Other critics argued that Quaker principles demanded everything from abolishing the Homecoming Queen election to banning meat from the cafeteria to ending work study to doing away with letter grades.[141]

Still, many on campus perceived threats to Earlham's Quaker identity. In the early 1970s, a discussion about the number of Quakers on campus began that continued for a decade. It grew out of a conviction, expressed succinctly by chemistry professor Theodor Benfey in 1972, that a Quaker College needed "a significant number of live, fallible, cantankerous, real-life Quakers." While seeking Quakers had always been a priority in hiring, it acquired more urgency with the realization that in the next few years nearly all of the CPS men whom Tom Jones had hired would be retiring. In fact, many of the "weightiest" Friends on the faculty were gone by 1980—Arthur Little, Warren Staebler, William Fuson, Howard Alexander, Helen Hole. Hugh Barbour and James Cope were the last, and they had retired by 1990. In response, in the late 1970s, a concerted effort began to recruit more Quaker faculty. Administrators saw this as a fundamental matter of identity. Because Friends did not define themselves by creedal statements, Earlham needed Quakers to "give testimony to their theology by the way they live," Len Clark argued in 1984. "If you don't have Quakers you're always wondering what the response of Friends should be."[142]

Impelled by such concerns, the college and ESR made progress in recruiting Quakers. Under both Wallin and Wood, Friends have become one of the college's three affirmative action categories. Wallin especially looked to the American Friends Service Committee and the new Friends Association for Higher Education as sources. The college and ESR were able to secure for a joint appointment John Punshon, an English Friend and perhaps the most distinguished living thinker and writer in the Gurneyite Quaker tradition. In 1988, Wood decided to commit more resources to the college's Friends Collection through the creation of a full-time position of archivist and curator with a joint appointment in the history department. A new core of younger Quaker faculty also emerged, although they were far more diverse than the men of the CPS generation. By 1990, with the percentage of Quaker faculty at about 20 percent, there was general agreement that the college's identity was safe in this respect.[143]

The number of Quaker students proved more problematic. By 1980, Earlham was receiving relatively few from the pastoral yearly meetings—most came from meetings affiliated with the liberal, unprogrammed Friends General Conference. The percentage of Quaker students hovered between 10 and 15 percent. This was higher than most Quaker colleges, but still caused concern.[144]

Not everyone on campus fervently embraced Quaker values, or Earlham's interpretations of them. From time to time, one student noted in 1976, it was "chic" to be "Anti-Quaker" and thus "anti-Earlham." The continued policy forbidding alcohol on campus came in for frequent and bitter attack. One student critic saw consensus as merely a "means of thwarting progress and maintaining authority." Another in 1994 questioned whether one had to accept a spiritual basis for the campus; for him, "Friends' process is not necessarily about God or Quakerism in as much as it is about integrity, mutual investment, respect, and a certain degree of selflessness." From time to time, students, upset by some decision, would angrily declare: "Earlham as an institution no longer makes much attempt to live up to the high goals set by Quakerism."[145]

Yet, in spite of all of these doubts, most on campus shared a basic conviction that Earlham should remain a Quaker place. As one faculty member put it, there was "something about being a Quaker college, something about the Quaker ethic, that really informs the way in which we do business and think about each other." That made, and makes, Earlham special for many of its people.[146]

While the college debated its Quaker identity, the Earlham School of Religion was also seeing changes. The founding dean, Wilmer Cooper, has referred to the period from 1975 to 1985 as the "years of maturing." In 1975, after fifteen years of effort, ESR achieved full accreditation by the Association of Theological Schools of the United States and Canada. It remains the only fully accredited Quaker theological seminary in the United States. Three years later, a "blue ribbon" committee of faculty and administrators from both the college and ESR, as well as board members, undertook an intensive study of ESR's situation and prospects. It concluded that ESR had proved itself "a valid, permanent member of the Earlham complex" that was making "a substantial contribution to the educational and spiritual ethos of the campus," as well as to the Society of Friends.[147]

Part of ESR's maturity was financial. In the mid-1970s, Franklin Wallin and Richard Wynn insisted that the school had to set its financial house in order. In 1975, the Earlham board set up a three-year plan to increase giving through the ESR Annual Fund to create balanced budgets. This was vital, since in 1974, tuition revenue accounted for less than 20 percent of the budget. By 1978, the budget was balanced, and by 1980 the accumulated debt of $281,000 had been wiped out. Higher enrollment helped; between 1975 and 1985 it was healthy, usually between 65 and 75 students.[148]

There was considerable continuity in the faculty. Four of its five founding members—Hugh Barbour, Joe Elmore, Wilmer Cooper, and Elton Trueblood—continued to teach at least part-time into the 1980s. Perhaps the most influential member of the faculty in the 1970s was Miriam Burke, whose emphasis on spirituality had an extraordinary impact on both faculty and students. Cooper retired as dean in 1978, replaced by Alan Kolp, a Friend originally from Winchester, Indiana, with a Harvard Ph.D. Kolp returned to full-time teaching in 1984, replaced by Tom Mullen, an alumnus of the college who had been one of Indiana Yearly Meeting's most respected pastors before returning to Earlham in 1966. Mullen served until 1991, when Andrew Grannell, a 1965 graduate of the college and a 1969 ESR B.D., left an administrative position with New England Yearly Meeting to become dean.[149]

In the school's first years, it emphasized training Quaker pastors. By the 1980s, while pastoral students continued to be an important element in the school, a majority looked to other careers as chaplains, counselors, social workers, and administrators. This shift in student interests was reflected in what Mullen in 1976 called the school's "amazing diversity." At ESR, he wrote, "Friends with widely differing theological views regularly debate their beliefs and their methodologies with one another, and the dialogue is enriched by the input of other Christians to help sustain an ecumenical perspective." While students from Friends United Meeting remained the backbone of the pastoral student group, an increasing number of other students came from the yearly meetings of Friends General Conference. More fundamentalist Quakers, especially in Evangelical Friends International, have by and large eschewed ESR, but there have been important exceptions, like Paul Anderson, the editor of the *Evangelical Friend.*[150]

By its fourth decade, ESR had become a central Quaker institution. Its faculty were in constant demand as speakers and workshop leaders for yearly meetings. When Friends on the ESR faculty are combined with those in the college, they form what is unquestionably the largest and most distinguished group of Quaker scholars in one institution anywhere in the world. ESR alumni, in turn, have become what one astute Quaker observer, Chuck Fager, in 1981 called "a new Quaker establishment." ESR graduates were, he wrote, "already well represented in key pastorates in Friends United Meeting and the Evangelical Friends Alliance, and their number here is increasing." They also, he noted, were on the staffs of Friends United Meeting, several larger unprogrammed yearly meetings, the Friends Committee on National Legislation, and the Quaker study center Pendle Hill. Fager concluded that "the present and potential contribution of the ESR generation to American Quakerism seems at this point almost wholly positive, almost too good to be true."[151]

The last decade has seen two major changes for ESR. The first was long-planned, the construction of a new classroom building. The school's facilities, three old houses at the northeast edge of campus, had long been recognized as inadequate. After some debate about whether to build near Stout Meetinghouse, the decision was made to construct a new building at the site of the largest of the old residences, Jenkins

House, which was demolished to make way for it. The new building, in gray fieldstone resembling a Friends meetinghouse from the Delaware Valley, was opened and dedicated in the fall of 1989.[152]

The other change came in the fall of 1994, when ESR began a new partnership with Bethany Theological Seminary. Bethany, a Church of the Brethren school in Oak Brook, Illinois, a suburb of Chicago, had been seeking a new site closer to centers of Brethren population. Ties between the Brethren, one of the historic peace churches, and Friends dated back to the early years of this century, and intensive study showed considerable potential in a cooperative arrangement between the two institutions. The outcome of discussions was Bethany's decision to sell its Chicago-area campus and build next to ESR. While cooperating on courses and sharing faculty, both schools have maintained their separate institutional existence.[153]

Other Friends have been concerned about Earlham since 1973. Their concerns have usually been quite different from those on campus. For many members of Indiana Yearly Meeting, Earlham was a real problem that sometimes flared into open conflict. In 1976, 1984–1985, 1992, and 1994, some feared that the relationship was near the breaking point.

The conflicts between Earlham and Indiana Yearly Meeting were part of a larger conflict within American Quakerism. Between 1975 and 1995, some perceived American Friends as becoming increasingly polarized. Part of the polarization involved theology, part politics, part social change.

Doctrinal issues were related largely to the increasing appeal of a universalist viewpoint among more liberal Friends, especially those in Friends General Conference (FGC). Quaker universalists argued that no religion held a monopoly on truth, that insight could be found in all faiths. Thus they often were openly critical of the Orthodox Quaker argument that Quakerism was Christian, or that the Inner Light was the Light of Christ. In some unprogrammed meetings, the use of explicitly Christian language became a point of contention. Significant numbers of liberal Friends by the 1990s objected to being characterized as Christian; often they would describe themselves as Quaker Jews or Quaker Buddhists or Quaker Bahais, for example.[154]

Such doctrinal disputes found their flash point in Friends United Meeting (FUM), the largest of the international Quaker bodies and the successor to the old Five Years Meeting. It represented the middle ground of American Quakerism—the Evangelical Friends Alliance (later Evangelical Friends International) was fortified behind explicit doctrinal statements with a strong holiness tinge, while FGC repudiated any attempt at doctrinal regulation. FUM cut across the spectrum of American Quakerism. It included most of the pastoral yearly meetings that had been part of the Five Years Meeting, like Indiana and Western. It also included a significant nonpastoral element, sometimes meetings like Clear Creek that belonged to predominantly pastoral yearly meetings, sometimes in yearly meetings like New York or New England or Baltimore where nonpastoral Friends were the majority. To heighten the diversity, in the 1950s and 1960s some yearly meetings that had split at the time of the Hicksite separation, such as New York and Baltimore, reunited, bringing more unprogrammed Friends into FUM. Meanwhile, several pastoral yearly meetings had strongly evangelical, if not fundamentalist, wings that were growing in strength and influence. Thus FUM was in an almost unique situation to be torn by conflicting currents.[155]

One of the results of the increased diversity in FUM was to bring Friends in Indiana and Western yearly meetings into more contact with liberal Friends than they had had before. The presence of several meetings in the Chicago area that were part of both Western and the Illinois Yearly Meeting (FGC) heightened such awareness. The contacts were often unsettling. Many in the two yearly meetings were startled when liberal Friends raised questions about foreign missions, for example. Liberal Friends, in turn, were horrified when evangelical Friends insisted that to be a Quaker one had to be a born-again Christian.[156]

Political issues also increased the tensions. Most unprogrammed Friends tended to be very liberal politically, identifying with the left wing of the Democratic party. Many pastoral Friends, on the other hand, were politically conservative, often sympathetic to groups like the Moral Majority or the Christian Coalition. In some yearly meetings there were churches with tendencies toward ultrafundamentalist, millenarian causes like Christian Reconstruction. Abortion and homosexuality were usually flash points, especially homosexuality. Some pastoral yearly meetings, among them Indiana, broke ties with the AFSC when it included homosexuals in its affirmative action statement and endorsed a prochoice position on abortion. FUM had to wrestle with a variety of issues involving homosexuality—one program, Quaker Volunteer Witness, was destroyed when FUM decided that it could not countenance the involvement of "practicing" homosexuals. On the other hand, many liberal meetings were by the 1980s sanctioning same-sex unions.[157]

Finally, there were social splits. Unprogrammed American Friends tended to be well-educated and urban. More evangelical Friends were often rural, although the stereotype of them beloved by many liberal Friends—that they were poorly educated—does not bear close inspection. In Indiana Yearly Meeting, for example, some of the most outspoken critics of Earlham and of liberal positions on doctrinal and social issues have been teachers and other professional people of deep evangelical faith.[158]

These conflicts inevitably raised questions for Earlham. It was affiliated with two yearly meetings in the pastoral tradition. Both were
diverse, but since the 1970s Indiana Yearly Meeting has grown more
doctrinally evangelical and conservative, often to the dismay of its more
moderate minority. In 1991, there was fierce struggle in the yearly
meeting over "Realignment"—a proposal to merge FUM and EFI, pre-
sumably shedding the liberal, unprogrammed yearly meetings in the
process. In Western, Realignment found little support, but diversity has
brought knotty problems there to resolve, especially involving homosexuality. In 1988, 1993, and 1995, Western found itself grappling with
the question of same-sex unions in its own meetings. With most of
Earlham's Quaker students coming from unprogrammed yearly meetings after 1970, Earlham often found itself in an awkward position. That
year the board noted the problem of the "growing disparity between the
Mid-Western Quaker philosophy and life styles and those of the Eastern
unprogrammed meetings."[159]

For the past two decades, there has been a considerable degree of
alienation from Indiana and Western Friends. As one Earlham person
wrote hopefully in 1976 of yearly meeting relations: "members . . . look
upon the college with a combination of awe and admiration and with a
bit of suspicion"; most Earlham students and faculty in turn were
"completely unfamiliar" with area Quakers. Probably for most members
of Indiana and Western yearly meetings, Earlham had lost its relevance.
This was in part because so few students from either yearly meeting
were attending Earlham, in part because by the 1980s only a handful of
Earlham faculty were active in Indiana Yearly Meeting. By 1979, for
example, there were only about twenty-five students from the yearly
meeting attending. That year's entering class had ten, but six came
either from West Richmond or Clear Creek, and four were the children
of faculty. By 1990, the number on campus was less than a dozen. The
sources of those realities were complex. As observers noted, Earlham
had "image" problems generally in Indiana, in part because of its high
price, in part because of its academic rigor, in part because of its
reputation of being "a radical, hippie school." By the 1990s, even many
usually supportive alumni were expressing fears that Earlham was no
longer interested in Indiana students generally and Indiana Friends in
particular. The college responded that it especially wanted such students, but faced often hostile meetings, pastors, and high school counselors. In the late 1970s, for example, when the admissions staff simply
requested a list of high school–age students from Indiana Yearly Meeting's office, the lack of cooperation was disheartening. The dearth of
students was reflected in declining financial support from local meetings; by 1980 only a handful included Earlham in their budgets.[160]

Members of the yearly meetings had no trouble identifying issues about which they were dissatisfied. Richard P. Newby, the Indiana Yearly Meeting clerk who was considered relatively liberal, summed them up in 1981: "The College has become too tolerant. The board members have been too liberal and lenient and efforts must be made to develop a strong Quaker image." There was a variety of problems: accommodations for Indiana Yearly Meeting when it held sessions on campus; the lack of evangelical Christians on the faculty; the teaching in ESR; books in the bookstore; drinking, smoking, and issues of sexuality, especially homosexuality. When the college attempted to recruit within Indiana Yearly Meeting, these problems came to a head. One "College Night" for Quaker students in Indiana, for example, according to a student, "escalated into a violent denouncement of the degeneration and permissiveness of the world in general and Earlham in particular."[161]

On the other hand, Earlham continued to have a significant body of supporters in both yearly meetings. The yearly meeting trustees tended to be alumni and generally supportive of the college's direction. Real hostility has come largely from Indiana Yearly Meeting. The only serious case involving Western Yearly Meeting took place in 1982 when two meetings objected to the presence of the *Dungeons and Dragons* fantasy game in the bookstore, calling it something that "Satan has connived up to bring about war on God's Kingdom." Although some on campus considered these objections a case of blatant censorship, the administration took the position that "encouraging fantasizing about the use of violence is a serious question for a Quaker college." A student member of the Bookstore Committee, noting that the meetings also wanted *National Lampoon* removed, called giving in on *Dungeons and Dragons* a "political compromise."[162]

Thus conflict has largely been between Earlham and members of Indiana Yearly Meeting. Proximity may be the cause. Some see the explanation in the presence of three evangelical Christian schools— Taylor University, Anderson University, and Indiana Wesleyan University (formerly Marion College)—within the yearly meeting's bounds. For many members of the yearly meeting, these are models of what church-related schools should be, and thus Earlham's deficiencies are all the more glaring.[163]

The first open flare-up of the last quarter-century began in 1975. In the yearly meeting sessions that year, one member asked about "the reason for some literature in the college bookstore." Franklin Wallin responded with a general defense of academic freedom. In spring 1976, some members of Mooreland Friends Church, a strongly evangelical group not far from Richmond, visited the bookstore and came back with copies of *Playboy*, *Playgirl*, *Penthouse*, and *Oui*, which they exhibited to a horrified monthly meeting. By the summer, there were rumors that the college would be "hauled into court" over the presence of "soft" pornography in the bookstore. In fact, the magazines disturbed some on campus. In the yearly meeting sessions, there was, as the official minutes put it, "a rather intense discussion." It concluded with a charge to the yearly meeting clerk and superintendent to meet with Wallin and the Bookstore Committee to discuss the situation. When the meeting took place, the Bookstore Committee members agreed that there was no reason for the bookstore to carry the magazines, since they served no academic purpose and were offensive to many. In turn, the Friends from the yearly meeting did not demand a blanket policy on "objectionable" works.[164]

Almost a decade passed before another open problem appeared. It came in the 1984 yearly meeting sessions, with a concern from Van Wert Quarterly Meeting, probably the most fervently evangelical quarter in the yearly meeting. By this time, Indiana Yearly Meeting had been holdings its sessions on campus for thirty years, and that was part of the problem. The Van Wert concern included, in the yearly meeting's words, "alcohol on campus, lack of hospitality, profane language, non-Christian religious groups allowed on campus, emphasis on Friends beliefs but a dearth of books about Jesus Christ, and coed dorms." Others in the yearly meeting, often with considerable vehemence, condemned allowing smoking and again objected to "pornographic" books and posters in the bookstore. There were more practical criticisms made as well: college staff were difficult to locate or not especially helpful when problems arose during yearly meeting sessions. As a result, the yearly meeting approved the formation of a committee to study the issues between the yearly meeting and the college and to work toward new understanding and reconciliation.[165]

The committee was clerked by E. Stanley Banker, a long-time pastor with considerable college administrative experience who also joined the Earlham board in 1985. It made its report in the August 1985 sessions, specifying three recommendations: the appointment of a liaison for communication between the college and the yearly meeting during its sessions, direct involvement of the two yearly meetings in the search for an assistant to the college president focusing on Quaker relations, and continued dialogue over specific problems. The committee divided those problems into three areas. The first was moral issues, such as the GPU, coed dormitories and bathrooms, the use of tobacco and alcohol, and "literature and art materials in the bookstore which could well be viewed as pornographic in nature." The second was philosophic. The college, the committee worried, was "strangely out of touch with evangelical Friends," reluctant "to articulate Quaker roots and experience from their historical and contemporary Christian basis." Finally, there were problems with facilities during the yearly meeting sessions, especially discourteous behavior by some college staff. Banker hopefully noted that even on the committee there had been "widely varying views" and yet "real communication." Responding for the college, the new president, Dick Wood, emphasized that he did not wish to see Earlham "lose its Christian and Quaker character." He argued that Earlham was "less secular than many had thought" and that it was working on some of the stated concerns—alchohol was still banned, for example.[166]

Some changes did come from the discussions of 1984-1985. After 1985, special attention to accommodating yearly meeting visitors yielded results. For the next few years complaints were minimal. The college finished a project begun in the late 1970s to install separate men's and women's bathrooms on every floor of every coed dormitory. The college also set up a task force on Quaker relations that made a number of suggestions for strengthening the college's Quaker identity, such as hiring a full-time archivist and curator for the Friends Collection and giving more attention to recruiting Quaker students.[167]

After 1985, tensions continued to simmer, but did not break out again until after the 1991 commencement, with its open affirmation of gay pride by some students. The 1991 yearly meeting sessions were characterized by an unusual degree of strife. Most centered on the "Realignment" proposal that would have made radical changes in Friends United Meeting, an idea that the yearly meeting declined to endorse. In his report opening the yearly meeting sessions, however, Horace Smith, the yearly meeting clerk who had been at commencement, bluntly stated his disappointment over what he had experienced. His words caught the college administration off guard; it hastened to prepare a statement addressing the concerns, and in fact Smith later said that his report had been perceived as more critical than he had intended. Smith's concern was moderate compared with what was to come.[168]

One challenge came almost immediately, when the yearly meeting executive committee approved a proposal to establish a loosely defined "alternative" program to ESR at the Anderson School of Theology, a Church of God institution. The yearly meeting staff argued that this was simply to provide more choices for people in the yearly meeting interested in training for pastoral ministry. It would involve paying the salary of a Quaker professor to teach courses in Quaker history and polity. Critics were clear about dissatisfaction with ESR, claiming that its biblical courses were insufficiently evangelical, that its faculty had limited pastoral experience, that many Indiana Yearly Meeting pastors had had unsatisfactory experiences there, and that at least one faculty member was tainted with "New Age" errors, all charges that ESR disputed. The final straw for some was ESR's hiring as its Old Testament professor a non-Quaker woman rather than a well-qualified Quaker man with pastoral experience, which critics saw as an example of misapplied affirmative action and generally misguided priorities. The yearly meeting clerk described Anderson as "more Christian." Little came of the proposal. There was never enough money to begin to pay a full-time salary, and the one Quakerism class at Anderson, although ably taught, attracted only three students. The Anderson debate, however, provided the backdrop to a far more rancorous dispute.[169]

That fall, a group of eight Indiana Friends, mostly from the Muncie or the Marion area, began discussions about trying to bring about change at Earlham. Some were alumni, others had strong Earlham ties through children who had attended. None was a fundamentalist, and they did not start with a clear agenda other than a conviction that Earlham needed to curb aggressive gay and lesbian activism. Some of its members came to campus for a meeting on September 14, 1991, with Wood and Stephanie Crumley-Effinger, the campus minister charged with particular responsibility for Quaker relations. What happened then is still in dispute. Wood, Crumley-Effinger, and Kirsten Bohl, a student government leader present, understood the critics to urge "releasing" homosexual students and faculty, something the critics deny they ever suggested. The members of what was now known as the "Unofficial Committee" came away dissatisfied, and attempts to set up another meeting failed.[170]

Instead, the group decided on another course: unhappy with Earlham policies, they sought change in the Earlham board. Wood and the college first learned of this tack when some of the committee approached Imogene Holloway, a 1948 graduate and active member of Fairmount Meeting. She declined to join them, and notified Wood about what had happened. There was considerable uncertainty on campus about just what critics wanted; many Earlham supporters believed that the goal was ultimately to fire Wood and replace him with someone more theologically conservative.[171]

Conflict on these issues was almost certainly inevitable. In 1982, Indiana Yearly Meeting had adopted a minute condemning homosexual acts as sinful. The clerk had accepted it over the objections of a number of Friends, and many liberal Friends, especially at Earlham, always considered its validity questionable. For the rest of the decade, homosexuality was a driving force in criticism of the AFSC and Friends United Meeting. Wood gave critics ammunition in an interview with the *Word* in February 1991 in which he stated that "it would help a great deal if the Society of Friends did what it ought to do and recognize single sex marriages," a position that dismayed some trustees. Wood was careful to point out that he spoke personally, not for the college on that issue, and that he had only expressed his opinion when asked. For many in Indiana Yearly Meeting, however, Wood's position was the ultimate affirmation of what they considered terrible sin.[172]

In the spring of 1992, the Indiana Yearly Meeting Nominating Committee became the focal point of the battle. As was yearly meeting procedure, the other yearly meeting trustees had recommended that the two incumbent trustees, Harry Treber of Amboy Meeting and Jean Reller of Clear Creek, who were eligible for reappointment, return to the board. The "Unofficial Committee" urged the Nominating Committee not to be bound by Earlham's recommendations. Some members of the Nominating Committee argued for replacing Treber and Reller with two other well-respected Friends from the Marion area. The Nominating Committee found itself deadlocked. At one point, Wood threatened that the board could change its bylaws to end Indiana Yearly Meeting appointments entirely, a legally tenuous position from which he had to retreat. Supporters of change argued that the yearly meeting had the right to appoint its own choices and that Earlham had dominated the appointment process too long. Even Earlham critics did not agree on what changing trustees should mean. The members of the "Unofficial Committee" argued that they would be content with the two new trustees encouraging more civility and circumspection among students. Other Earlham critics apparently saw this as the first step in remolding Earlham along the lines of fundamentalist institutions like Bob Jones University. One was quoted as saying that when "Christians" had control, they would turn Earlham into a Bible college or close it. Wood and the board pointed out that that was impossible, but they did object to singling out two individuals to pay for Earlham's perceived faults, and also worried about the precedents being set.[173]

Throughout the spring and summer, tensions rose. Wood and at least one member of the "Unofficial Committee" found themselves in a war of words over what had taken place in the September 1991 meeting. Commencement in June, which had been the subject of considerable worry and work by a faculty-student committee, was subdued compared to the previous year, but a number of students and faculty wore small "I'd be fired" buttons, in reference to the supposed "Unofficial Committee" demand. Meanwhile, the Nominating Committee remained deadlocked, and Charles Heavilin, its clerk, was determined not to report any nominations until there was unity. Heavilin, a long-time pastor, had himself been critical of Earlham, but privately thought the move against Reller and Treber unjustified. There was some effort at a compromise under which only Reller would be reappointed, but both Treber and the board rejected that.[174]

When the yearly meeting opened on Saturday, August 1, one of the first items on the agenda was a discussion of the trustee issue that continued into the afternoon. Despite the admonition of Horace Smith, the clerk, that the discussion should focus on the trustee appointments and not Earlham policies, critics often focused on just that, especially the 1991 commencement and the presence of the LBGPU on campus. They also attacked the wording of the Community Code's section on sexuality, which they said implicitly condoned premarital sex. Some of the most fervent critics of Earlham also tried to hold up the reappointment of Thomas Gottschalk, one of the at-large trustees, apparently on the ground that no one who had been on the board when the code was accepted was a fit trustee. A strong endorsement of Gottschalk by David Brock, the yearly meeting superintendent, ended the discussion and Gottschalk was reappointed. A special session set aside that afternoon to discuss general Earlham concerns brought more attacks on Earlham's policies, and spirited defense from supporters of the college. Friends on both sides left pessimistic that any middle way could be found.[175]

On Monday afternoon, August 3, the yearly meeting took up the issue again. Supporters of the college argued that making views on homosexuality a litmus test would set a terrible precedent; opponents urged the qualifications of the proposed replacements and again scored Earlham policies. Gradually, the tide in the room shifted in favor of the college. One turning point was an address by SaraAnne Acres, a junior student who spoke movingly of her experience of the campus's Quaker atmosphere. Another was the appearance of Jean Reller, one of the trustees under attack, who pointed out that none of the critics who wanted to replace her had ever contacted her with their concerns. Finally, a particularly vehement attack on Dick Wood and the college from one critic brought protests from Friends of all views, including many of unquestionable evangelical faith who were critical of college policies. Some of them also questioned the wisdom of making Treber and Reller bear the brunt of the yearly meeting's difficulties with Earlham. After a period of silence, the clerk gave a powerful narrative about his own struggles on the subject, and of his feeling that it would be wrong to remove the two trustees when the yearly meeting had never formally voiced its concerns to the board. He was now convinced that the college indeed was hearing the yearly meeting, and drew a minute reappointing the two. Moved by his words, and by an experience that some described as a clear leading of the Spirit, the meeting united in support.[176]

The discussion did have consequences. One was the 1993 appointment, with the board's full support, of J. R. Reece, one of the Friends put forward as an alternative to Treber and Reller, as a trustee. The 1992 yearly meeting had ended with a clear expectation that there would be discussions between Earlham and the yearly meeting to resolve the difficulties. Don Garner, the new clerk of the yearly meeting, formed a subcommittee from the yearly meeting Executive Committee that met with college officials and board members over the winter of 1992–1993. From their discussions, a proposal emerged for a new Earlham relationship with the yearly meetings. They would give up the appointment of trustees entirely, and the board would become entirely self-perpetuating, save for the alumni trustees. Three would continue to come from both Indiana and Western, however, and a majority of the board would always have to be Friends. To many Indiana Friends, this offered the advantage of allowing Friends who wished to disclaim any relationship with Earlham to do so, while preserving some local influence on the board. To date, while it won the backing of the Earlham board, neither yearly meeting has acted on the proposal. It proved unpopular with many in Western Yearly Meeting, while reaction in Indiana has been uneven.[177]

The future of the proposal was clouded by yet another controversy in February 1994. In 1993, a group of gay activist students from Earlham had attended the Midwest Bisexual Lesbian and Gay College Conference at Iowa State University. They offered Earlham as the site for the 1994 conference. The college administration agreed, as long as it was made clear that this was an entirely student-run affair. The conference certainly was enough to raise the hackles of moral traditionalists. A number of nationally known gay activists were to be present for workshops on topics like "Getting Lesbian/Gay/Bisexual Studies at Your School," "Fighting Internalized Homophobia/Biphobia," and "Fighting the Growing Christian Right." The conference would conclude with a performance by the Flirtations, "the world's most famous openly gay, politically active, multi-cultural a cappella singing group." (A previous appearance at Earlham had drawn objections from Indiana Yearly Meeting.) The conference brochure described Earlham as "a great Queer positive and accepting environment."[178]

Late in January, one of the conference organizers sent out information to all of the colleges in Indiana. That directed to Indiana Wesleyan University fell into the hands of a Friend who faxed it to the yearly meeting office. David Brock, the yearly meeting superintendent, immediately sent a strong protest to the trustees appointed by Indiana Yearly Meeting, characterizing the conference as a "slander" on the Quaker name and asking that it be cancelled. That drew an equally strong response from Dick Wood and from Quaker members of the faculty, who protested what they saw as a clear attempt to limit freedom of discussion on campus. After careful deliberation, and with misgivings on the part of some trustees, the board refused to cancel the conference, which took place without incident.[179]

The conference outraged many members of Indiana Yearly Meeting. One pastor, in a column in the *Palladium-Item,* called the conference a betrayal of Quakerism, an "implicit sanction of sin." A series of meetings that the college had arranged to discuss the proposal to change trustee appointments came to focus largely on the issue, with expressions of anger common. Interestingly, one of the criticisms most often voiced was of the conference's attacks on the Christian Right, of which many Indiana Friends said that they were a part. There was a demand by some meetings that future yearly meeting sessions not be held at Earlham, and that even the yearly meeting records be removed from the Friends Collection. The yearly meeting executive committee rejected those proposals, but did issue a statement saying that it did not "condone what goes on" at Earlham.[180]

This rupture, and other tensions, led both yearly meetings to act. In 1995, the two approved a proposal drafted by their clerks and superintendents for a joint committee to be established under the 1881 charter that would consider relations between the college and the yearly meetings and seek ways to work toward reconciliation. Readily accepted by the college administration, which had proposed a variant, it is forming as this book goes to press.[181]

And here, with the two yearly meetings pondering the future of their relationship with the college they founded a century and a half before, this history comes to its appropriate end. Earlham was established in a time of flux and change for Quakers, trying to adjust to a changing world. This period of its history finds them, and the Friends and non-Friends at Earlham, still grappling with what it means to be a Quaker school, to live in an often hostile world and yet not be part of it.

Postscript

In December 1996, the board of trustees named Douglas C. Bennett the sixteenth president of Earlham. A Friend and Haverford graduate, a political scientist by training and since 1994 a vice president of the American Council of Learned Societies, Bennett took office in July 1997.

Notes

Preface

1. In the past few years, this subject has been of interest to scholars of both religion and higher education. Of considerable influence have been George M. Marsden and Bradley J. Longfield, eds., *The Secularization of the Academy* (New York: Oxford University Press, 1992); and George M. Marsden, *The Soul of the American University: From Protestant Establishment to Established Nonbelief* (ibid., 1994).

2. See Wilmer A. Cooper, *The Earlham School of Religion Story: A Quaker Dream Come True* (Richmond, Ind.: Earlham School of Religion, 1985).

3. See Willard C. Heiss, ed., *Abstracts of the Records of the Society of Friends in Indiana*, 7 vols. (Indianapolis: Indiana Historical Society, 1962–1977), I, xiii–xv.

1. Friends Boarding School, 1832–1859

1. Bernhard Knollenberg, *Pioneer Sketches of the Upper Whitewater Valley: Quaker Stronghold of the West* (Indianapolis: Indiana Historical Society, 1945), 18; Stephen B. Weeks, *Southern Quakers and Slavery: A Study in Institutional History* (Baltimore: Johns Hopkins University Press, 1896), 286–87; Thomas D. Hamm, *The Transformation of American Quakerism: Orthodox Friends, 1800–1907* (Bloomington: Indiana University Press, 1988), 12–15.

2. James Harris Norton, "Quakers West of the Alleghenies and in Ohio to 1861" (Ph.D. diss., Case Western Reserve University, 1965), 22–24; Malcolm J. Rohrbough, *The Trans-Appalachian Frontier: People, Societies, and Institutions, 1775–1850* (New York: Oxford University Press, 1978), 89–114.

3. Rufus M. Jones, *The Later Periods of Quakerism* (2 vols., London: Macmillan, 1921), I, 385–403.

4. Howard Beeth, "Outside Agitators in Southern History: The Society of Friends, 1656–1800" (Ph.D. diss., University of Houston, 1984), 461–64; Jean R. Soderlund, *Quakers & Slavery: A Divided Spirit* (Princeton: Princeton University Press, 1985), 103–25, 187; Thomas E. Drake, *Quakers and Slavery in America* (New Haven: Yale University Press, 1950), 68–84.

5. Borden Stanton, "A Brief Account," in *Friends' Miscellany*, ed. John Comly and Isaac Comly (12 vols., Philadelphia: J. Richards, 1831–1839), XII, 217; George Carter letter, *Christian Worker*, 12th Mo. 1, 1874, pp. 362–63; Harlow Lindley, "The Quaker Contribution to the Old Northwest," in *Children of Light: In Honor of Rufus M. Jones*, ed. by Howard H. Brinton (New York: Macmillan, 1938), 321; John Belton O'Neall and John A. Chapman, *The Annals of Newberry* (Newberry, S.C.: Aull & Houseal, 1892), 35; David Brion Davis, *The Problem of Slavery in Western Culture* (Ithaca: Cornell University Press, 1966), 492–93.

6. The best account of Quaker migration to Ohio is Norton, "Quakers West of the Alleghenies," 18–126. For Quaker settlement in the Richmond area, see Knollenberg, *Pioneer Sketches*, 18–22; and Henry Hoover, *Sketches and Incidents, Embracing a Period of Fifty Years* (Indianapolis: John Woolman Press, 1962), 7.

7. *Proceedings of the Celebration of the Establishment of Whitewater Monthly Meeting of the Religious Society of Friends* (Richmond, Ind., n.p., 1909), 31–42; Willard C. Heiss, *Abstracts of the Records of the Society of Friends in Indiana* (7 vols., Indianapolis: Indiana Historical Society, 1962–1977), I, xxv.

8. Hamm, *Transformation*, 5–7, 9–11.

9. Ibid., 3–9; Paul K. Conkin, *The Uneasy Center: Reformed Christianity in Antebellum America* (Chapel Hill: University of North Carolina Press, 1995), 120–21.

10. Hamm, *Transformation*, 7–9.

11. For the Discipline in use at this time, see *The Discipline of the Society of Friends, of Indiana Yearly Meeting* (Cincinnati: A. Pugh, 1839). For a wonderful memoir of a life lived under it, see James Baldwin, *In the Days of My Youth: An Intimate Personal Record of Life and Manners in the Middle Ages of the Middle West* (Indianapolis: Bobbs-Merrill, 1923). For other other Protestants, see Conkin, *Uneasy Center*, 85–86.

12. Hamm, *Transformation*, 10, 14; Thomas D. Hamm et al., "Moral Choices: Two Indiana Quaker Communities and the Abolition Movement," *Indiana Magazine of History*, 87 (June 1991), 141.

13. Hamm, *Transformation*, 53; Lemuel Baldwin to Naomi P. Curl, 11th Mo. 19, 1854, Naomi P. Curl Papers (Friends Collection, Earlham College, Richmond, Ind.); Thomas Arnett, "A Solemn Address to Youth," [1823], in Thomas Arnett, *Address to the Christian Traveler, in Every Denomination* (Cincinnati: Achilles Pugh, 1872), 11–39.

14. See, generally, H. Larry Ingle, *Quakers in Conflict: The Hicksite Reformation* (Knoxville: University of Tennessee Press, 1986).

15. *Journal of That Faithful Servant of Christ, Charles Osborn, Containing an Account of Many of His Travels and Labors in the Ministry, and His Trials and Exercises in the Service of the Lord, and in Defense of the Truth, as It Is in Jesus* (Cincinnati: Achilles Pugh, 1854); Indiana Yearly Meeting, *Testimony and Epistle of Advice* (N.p., 1827), 1.

16. Hamm, *Transformation*, 18–19; Norton, "Quakers West of the Alleghenies," 150–53; Duck Creek Monthly Meeting Men's Minutes, 4th Mo. 28, 1828, Indiana Yearly Meeting Archives (Friends Collection, Earlham College, Richmond, Ind.); Indiana Yearly Meeting for Sufferings Minutes, 10th Mo. 3, 1834, 10th Mo. 2, 1835 (ibid.); Mary Coffin Johnson and Percival Brooks Coffin, *Charles F. Coffin: A Quaker Pioneer* (Richmond, Ind.: Nicholson, 1923), 72–73; Ingle, *Quakers in Conflict*, 183–246.

17. Hamm, *Transformation*, 23, 25–26.

18. *The Works of George Fox* (8 vols., Philadelphia: Marcus T. C. Gould, 1831), I, 74. There is a vast literature on Quaker education, but a good synthesis is desperately needed. The best available is Helen G. Hole, *Things Civil and Useful: A Personal View of Quaker Education* (Richmond, Ind.: Friends United Press, 1978), 7.

19. W. A. Campbell Stewart, *Quakers and Education: As Seen in Their Schools in England* (London: Epworth, 1953), 46–49; Hole, *Things Civil and Useful*, 5; Howard H. Brinton, *Quaker Education in Theory and Practice* (Wallingford, Pa.: Pendle Hill, 1949), 23.

20. Hole, *Things Civil and Useful*, 6–8; Leonard S. Kenworthy, *Quaker Education: A Source Book* (Kennett Square, Pa.: Quaker Publications, [1987]), 6–7.

21. Stewart, *Quakers and Education,* 25, 27, 31.

22. Hole, *Things Civil and Useful,* 6.

23. Thomas Woody, *Early Quaker Education in Pennsylvania* (New York: Teachers College, Columbia University, 1920), 41–83; Stephen Allott, *Lindley Murray, 1745–1826: Quaker Grammarian of New York and Old York* (York, Eng.: Sessions, 1991); J. William Frost, *The Quaker Family in Colonial America: A Portrait of the Society of Friends* (New York: St. Martin's, 1973), 93–132.

24. For the "Reformation" generally, see Jack D. Marietta, *The Reformation of American Quakerism, 1747–1783* (Philadelphia: University of Pennsylvania Press, 1984). For philanthropy, especially education, see Sydney V. James, *A People among Peoples: Quaker Benevolence in Eighteenth-Century America* (Cambridge: Harvard University Press, 1963), 253–54, 272–78.

25. James, *People among Peoples,* 272–76.

26. For the school in Portsmouth, which, after being relocated in Providence, became the Moses Brown School, see Rayner Wickersham Kelsey, *Centennial History of Moses Brown School, 1819–1919* (Providence, R.I.: Moses Brown School, 1919). For the Nine Partners School, see Hugh Barbour et al., eds., *Quaker Crosscurrents: Three Hundred Years of Friends in the New York Yearly Meetings* (Syracuse: Syracuse University Press, 1995), 150–51. For Westtown, see Helen G. Hole, *Westtown through the Years* (Westtown, Pa.: Westtown School, 1942). For Guilford College, see Dorothy Lloyd Gilbert, *Guilford: A Quaker College* (Greensboro, N.C.: Guilford College, 1937).

27. *Journal of Charles Osborn,* 175–76; "Report of Makefield Monthly Meeting," 1828, box 2, Evans Family Papers (Ohio Historical Society, Columbus). For the founding of denominational colleges in this period, see Frederick Rudolph, *The American College and University: A History* (Athens: University of Georgia Press, 1990), 44–67.

28. Ethel Hittle McDaniel, *The Contribution of the Society of Friends to Education in Indiana* (Indianapolis: Indiana Historical Society, 1939), 17–19; Richard G. Boone, *A History of Education in Indiana* (New York: D. Appleton, 1892), 129–42.

29. McDaniel, *Contribution,* 19; *Indiana Yearly Meeting Minutes, 1830,* pp. 18–20.

30. Opal Thornburg, *Earlham: The Story of the College, 1847–1962* (Richmond. Ind.: Earlham College Press, 1963), 28–32; Thomas Stewardson to Aaron White, 2nd Mo. 2, 1837, box 1, Furnas Family Papers (Friends Historical Library, Swarthmore College, Swarthmore, Pa.); Elijah Coffin to Aaron White, 2nd Mo. 22, 1836, ibid.

31. Thornburg, *Earlham,* 32–33.

32. Ibid., 33–34.

33. Ibid., 34–35.

34. Hamm, *Transformation,* 20–22. For Joseph John Gurney generally, see David E. Swift, *Joseph John Gurney: Banker, Reformer, and Quaker* (Middletown, Conn.: Wesleyan University Press, 1962). For his visit, see James A. Rawley, "Joseph John Gurney's Mission to America, 1837–1840," *Mississippi Valley Historical Review,* 49 (March 1963), 653–74.

35. Hamm, *Transformation,* 20–22.

36. Ibid., 22–28.

37. Thornburg, *Earlham,* 37.

38. Ibid., 35–37.

39. Barbara Miller Solomon, *In the Company of Educated Women: A History of Women and Higher Education in America* (New Haven: Yale University Press, 1985), 27–41; William Phillips Bickley, "Education as Reformation: An Examination of Orthodox Quakers' Formation of the Haverford School Association and Founding of Haverford School, 1815–1840" (Ed.D. diss., Harvard University, 1983).

40. *Indiana Yearly Meeting Minutes, 1837*, p. 19.

41. Thornburg, *Earlham,* 38–39; Boarding School Committee Minutes, 1838 (Friends Collection).

42. Thornburg, *Earlham,* 40–42.

43. Ibid., 44–46.

44. Boarding School Committee Minutes, 2nd Mo. 22, 4th Mo. 3, 1847; Elijah Coffin to Eleazar Beales [*sic*], 4th Mo. 6, 1847, Letterbook 1, box 1, Coffin Family Papers (Friends Historical Library); Thornburg, *Earlham,* 49.

45. Elizabeth H. Emerson, "Barnabas C. Hobbs: Midwestern Quaker Minister and Educator," *Bulletin of Friends Historical Association,* 49 (Spring 1960), 21–35; Minnie B. Clark, "Barnabas Coffin Hobbs," *Indiana Magazine of History,* 19 (Sept. 1923), 282–90; Baldwin, *In the Days of My Youth,* 139–40.

46. Thornburg, *Earlham,* 55–56.

47. Coffin to Thomas Evans, 4th Mo. 10, 1847, Letterbook 1, Coffin Papers; "Teachers and Officers of Friends' Boarding School," *Earlhamite,* 3 (Jan. 9, 1897), 99; Stewart H. Holbrook, *The Yankee Exodus: An Account of Migration from New England* (Seattle: University of Washington Press, 1950), 297–312.

48. Coffin to Huldah C. Hoag, 3rd Mo. 31, 1847, Letterbook 1, Coffin Papers; Coffin to Nathan C. Hoag, 2nd Mo. 26, 1847, ibid.; Barbour et al., eds., *Quaker Crosscurrents,* 113–14.

49. Thornburg, *Earlham,* 50.

50. Ibid., 56–60.

51. Information on students was taken from the student registers, 1847–1858, in the Friends Collection.

52. Ibid. For the distribution of Quaker schools in Indiana, see McDaniel, *Contribution,* 64–97. For Quaker settlement patterns, see the map on the inside front cover of Heiss, ed., *Abstracts,* VII.

53. Student Registers, 1847–1852; Heiss, *Abstracts,* I, 278, IV, 57, 336, 341–43, V, 316; William Wade Hinshaw, ed., *Encyclopedia of American Quaker Genealogy* (6 vols., Ann Arbor: Edwards Brothers, 1950), V, 610.

54. Coffin to Nathan C. Hoag, 2nd Mo. 26, 1847, Letterbook 1, Coffin Papers.

55. Thornburg, *Earlham,* 47–48; Oliver Smith to Tamar Thorn, 12th Mo. 21, 1851, Student Letters Collection (Friends Collection).

56. Frederick Rudolph, *Curriculum: A History of the American Undergraduate Course of Study since 1636* (San Francisco: Jossey-Bass, 1977), 54–98; Laura M. Bachelder, *Indiana Alma Maters: Student Life at Indiana Colleges, 1820–1860* (Fishers, Ind.: Conner Prairie, 1995), 26–29.

57. Boarding School Committee Minutes, 9th Mo. 21, 1847; Coffin to Evans, 11th Mo. 9, 1847, Letterbook 1, Coffin Papers; Thornburg, *Earlham,* 61; "The Science Department and the Men at Its Head," *Earlhamite,* 21 (Nov. 1893), 17–21.

58. Coffin to Evans, 8th Mo. 16, 1847, 11th Mo. 9, 1847, 2nd Mo. 1, 1848, Letterbook 1, Coffin Papers; Boarding School Committee Minutes, 9th Mo. 27, 1848; "Catalogue of Books Belonging to the Library of Friends' Boarding School near Richmond, Indiana," 1847 (Friends Collection); *Indiana Yearly Meeting Minutes, 1839,* p. 22.

59. Mary Coffin Johnson, ed., *Life of Elijah Coffin* (Cincinnati: E. Morgan, 1863), 30; Clarkson Fulghum Diary, 10th Mo. 29, 1858 (Friends Collection); Governing Committee Minutes, 8th Mo. 6, 1860 (ibid.); Benjamin F. True-blood Reminiscences, Feb. 29, 1916, p. 2, Reminiscences Collection (ibid.); Boarding School Committee Minutes, 9th Mo. 22, 1851; David Hunt to Curl, 1st Mo. 30, 1854, Curl Papers; Thornburg, *Earlham*, 69; George P. Emswiler, *Poems and Sketches* (Richmond, Ind.: Nicholson, 1897), 245–46.

60. Boarding School Committee Minutes, 10th Mo. 2, 1848, 5th Mo. 25, 1852; Margaret White to Josiah Forster, 4th Mo. 2, 1849, box 4, Furnas Papers; Thornburg, *Earlham*, 63–64.

61. Boarding School Committee Minutes, 1st Mo. 1, 1856, 2nd Mo. 26, 1856; Harlow Lindley, "History of Earlham College," typescript, ca. 1947, ch. 1, p. 21 (Friends Collection); Mary D. Hunt to Curl, 6th Mo. 12, 1855, Curl Papers; *Life of Elijah Coffin*, 67; Thornburg, *Earlham*, 48; Coffin to Thomas Kimber et al., 2nd Mo. 7, 1857, Letterbook 2, box 1, Coffin Papers; Coffin to George W. Taylor, 9th Mo. 7, 1847, Letterbook 1, box 1, ibid.

62. Boarding School Committee Minutes, 1st Mo. 27, 1857, 11th Mo. 9, 10, 1858, 12th Mo. 28, 1858, 8th Mo. 9, 1859.

63. William Tallack, *Friendly Sketches in America* (London: A. W. Bennett, 1861), 60–61; "Education," *Hoosier State*, [ca 1858], Miscellaneous Periodical Collection (Friends Collection).

64. Mary D. Hunt to Curl, 6th Mo. 12, 1855. For other schools of the period, see Bachelder, *Indiana's Alma Maters*, 20–21; and Burton J. Bledstein, *The Culture of Professionalism: The Middle Class and the Development of Higher Education in America* (New York: Norton, 1976), 235–36.

65. Mary D. Hunt to Curl, 6th Mo. 12, 1855; Smith to Mother, Feb. 2, 1851, Student Letters Collection; Dorothy Gilbert to "Home Friends," 11th Mo. 4, 1855, ibid.; Opal Thornburg, "Day Before Yesterday at Earlham," *Earlhamite*, 55 (July 1934), 8; Thornburg, *Earlham*, 70, 75; Boarding School Committee Minutes, 1st Mo. 1, 1856.

66. Thornburg, "Day Before Yesterday"; Gilbert to "Home Friends"; Boarding School Committee Minutes, 6th Mo. 24, 1847.

67. Boarding School Committee Minutes, 7th Mo. 27, 1852, 10th Mo. 3, 1851; Joseph Doan, "Earlham in 1851," *Earlhamite*, 18 (Nov. 1890), 30; Almira Hadley Wilson to Rebecca H. Hadley, 12th Mo. 14, 1851, Student Letters Collection; Oliver Smith to Thorn.

68. Thornburg, *Earlham*, 47, 68–69; Arnaldo Letter, *Oriental*, 2nd Mo. 1859, Miscellaneous Periodical Collection.

69. Oliver Smith to Thorn; William Wilson Diary, 2nd Mo. 2, 1857 (Friends Collection); Letitia Smith to Mother, Feb. 2, 1851, Student Letters Collection; Fulghum Diary, 12th Mo. 1, 1858; Doan, "Earlham in 1851," 30. For student riots in the period, see Bledstein, *Culture of Professionalism*, 228–35; and Helen Lefkowitz Horowitz, *Campus Life: Undergraduate Cultures from the End of the Eighteenth Century to the Present* (Chicago: University of Chicago Press, 1987), 24–25.

70. Boarding School Committee Minutes, 1st Mo. 23, 1849, 1st Mo. 22, 1850, 3rd Mo. 2, 1859; Arnaldo Letter; Laura E. Fetters to Opal Thornburg, June 24, 1959, Reminiscences Collection.

71. Mordecai M. White, "Reminiscences," *Earlhamite*, 18 (Jan. 1891), 76; Miriam Jane Hill to John P. Parker, July 30, [1850], Student Letters Collection.

72. Amos Mills to ?, 12th Mo. 6, 1851, Student Letters Collection; Fulghum Diary, 1st Mo. 30, 1859; Enos Kendall Autobiography, typescript, n.d., Reminiscences Collection.

73. I computed ages by comparing names found in the Student Registers, 1847–1852, and 1858 with Heiss, ed., *Abstracts;* and Hinshaw, ed., *Encyclopedia.*

74. Lydia Thomas to Emma Thomas, 11th Mo. 18, 1856, Student Letters Collection; Mary Russell to George Allen, 5th Mo. 10, 1854, ibid.; Elizabeth Ann Watkins to Curl, 12th Mo. 3, 1854, Curl Papers.

75. I made this comparison by using the statistics in Hamm, *Transformation*, 52–58, with the sources in note 73.

76. Thornburg, *Earlham*, 51–52.

77. Henry B. Hill to William P. and Allen Hill, 2nd Mo. 13, 1850, Student Letters Collection; Hiram Hadley Reminiscence, n.d., Reminiscences Collection; *Indiana Yearly Meeting Minutes, 1850*, pp. 35–36; ibid., *1851*, pp. 19–21.

78. Thornburg, *Earlham*, 64–65; *Indiana Yearly Meeting Minutes, 1855*, pp. 31–33; Boarding School Committee Minutes, 1st Mo. 27, 1857.

79. *Indiana Yearly Meeting Minutes, 1851*, p. 30; ibid., *1852*, pp. 23, 44–45; ibid., *1853*, pp. 36–40, 50–51.

80. Caleb Johnson, "Bible Schools among Friends," *American Friend*, 5th Mo. 30, 1898, p. 525; "Early Days of Friends Boarding School," *Earlhamite*, 3 (Oct. 31, 1896), 35; "A Student of 1847 Writes Home," ibid., 59 (April 1938), 10–11; Tallack, *Friendly Sketches*, 32–33. See also Levi Jessup, "Earlham College," *Earlhamite*, 4 (July 1880), 231–32.

81. Hugh Moffitt to Mary Barker, 7th Mo. 12, 1855, 10th Mo 14, 1855, box 5, Coffin-Baxter Papers (Friends Historical Library); Thornburg, *Earlham*, 66.

82. Thornburg, *Earlham*, 66–67.

83. Tallack, *Friendly Sketches*, 32; Hamm, *Transformation*, 37–42.

84. Hamm, *Transformation*, 38; Knollenberg, *Pioneer Sketches*, 138. For the market revolution generally, see Charles G. Sellers, Jr., *The Market Revolution: Jacksonian America, 1815–1846* (New York: Oxford University Press, 1991); and Sean Wilentz, "Society, Politics, and the Market Revolution, 1815–1848," in *The New American History*, ed. Eric Foner (Philadelphia: Temple University Press, 1990), 51–68.

85. Addison Coffin, *Life and Travels of Addison Coffin* (Cleveland: William G. Hubbard, 1897), 115; Hamm, *Transformation*, 37–42.

86. Hamm, *Transformation*, 42–63.

87. Sarah Ann Hampton, "Novel Reading," 3rd Mo. 1855, Sarah Ann Hampton Commonplace Book (Friends Collection); Ionian Society Librarian's Book, 1858 (ibid.); Boarding School Committee Minutes, 12th Mo. 30, 1856.

88. Thornburg, *Earlham*, 72–73. For the relationship between education and social change, see Bledstein, *Culture of Professionalism*, 248–86. For literary societies and their roles in other schools, see Bachelder, *Indiana's Alma Maters*, 32–35; and Thomas S. Harding, *College Literary Societies: Their Contribution to Higher Education in the United States, 1815–1876* (New York: Pageant Press International, 1971).

89. Hesperian Junto Minutes, 1856 (Friends Collection); Ionian Society Record Book I (ibid.); Mary Pickett, "History of Phoenix Band," *Phoenixian*, 2 (Dec. 1892), 100–02.

90. Hesperian Junto Minutes, 6th Mo. 27, 1857; Gilbert to "Home Friends"; Thornburg, *Earlham*, 72–73; Rudolph, *American College and University*, 144–49.

91. For Haverford's transformation into a college, see Rufus M. Jones, *Haverford College: A History and an Interpretation* (New York: Macmillan, 1933), 25–34.

92. "Education, No. 1," *Friend*, 3rd Mo. 13, 1830, pp. 169–70.

93. Sarah Ann Hampton, "Address," 3rd Mo. 14, 1857, Hampton Commonplace Book; Elbert Russell, ed., "Diary of Rebecca Russell for the Year 1861," typescript, vol. I, p. 200 (Friends Collection); Eli Jay, Autobiography, Oct. 24, 1899, box 1, Eli and Mahalah Jay Papers (ibid.); "Matthew Charles," *Earlhamite,* 33 (Nov. 10, 1906), 37; William B. Morgan to Samuel Bettle, Jr., 9th Mo. 7, 1854, box 1, Bettle Family Papers (Friends Historical Library); Allen Furnas to "Friend," 2nd Mo. 9, 1845, box 7, Treasurer's Papers (Oberlin College Archives, Oberlin, Ohio); *Autobiography of Allen Jay, Born 1831, Died 1910* (Philadelphia: John C. Winston, 1910), 57–58.

94. Jay Autobiography; Jonathan Messerli, *Horace Mann: A Biography* (New York: Knopf, 1972), 549–89.

95. Thornburg, 57–59; "Matthew Charles," 37; Hamm, *Transformation,* 40.

96. Wilson Diary, 1st Mo. 9, 1857; Boarding School Committee Minutes, 12th Mo. 30, 1856, 1st Mo. 27, 2nd Mo. 4, 1857.

97. *Indiana Yearly Meeting Minutes, 1856,* pp. 24–25; ibid., *1857,* p. 40; William B. Morgan, "E Pur Si Muove," *Earlhamite,* 8 (Dec. 1880), 56–57.

98. *Indiana Yearly Meeting Minutes, 1859,* p. 98; Morgan, "E Pur Si Muove," 56.

99. Thornburg, *Earlham,* 79.

2. Earlham's Surrender to the Larger Culture, 1859–1895

1. For Dougan Clark, see Thomas Hamm, "The Quaker Tradition of Young Walter Malone," in *Hope and a Future,* ed. David L. Johns (Richmond, Ind.: Friends United Press, 1993), 8–9. The only copy of Clark's speech that I have located, *Address by Dr. Dougan Clark* (N.p., 1858), is in the Nathan Hunt Clark Papers at the Indiana Historical Society, Indianapolis.

2. [Clark], *Address.*

3. Dougan Clark, "A Plea for Orthodoxy," *American Friend,* 1st Mo. 13, 1898, pp. 39–42. Clark delivered this lecture between 1888 and 1892.

4. Thomas D. Hamm, *The Transformation of American Quakerism: Orthodox Friends, 1800–1907* (Bloomington: Indiana University Press, 1988), 37–42.

5. *New Castle* (Ind.) *Courier,* Oct. 10, 1867, p. 2; *Indiana Yearly Meeting Minutes, 1864,* p. 8.

6. Hamm, *Transformation,* 36–73.

7. Ibid., 42–45.

8. Ibid., 75–76, 85–87.

9. Ibid., 77–85.

10. See generally, ibid, esp. 107.

11. Ibid., 109; C. W. Pearson, "Has Earlham a Mission?" *Earlhamite,* 9 (July 1882), 232–33.

12. Ibid., 111–20; Allen Jay to Martha A. Jay, 1st Mo. 28, 1875, G-L box, Allen Jay Papers (Friends Collection, Lilly Library, Earlham College, Richmond, Ind.).

13. Timothy Nicholson to Joel Bean and Hannah E. Bean, 5th Mo. 2, 1881, box 4, Joel Bean Papers (Friends Historical Library, Swarthmore College, Swarthmore, Pa.); Barnabas C. Hobbs, *Earlham Lectures* (Richmond, Ind.: Nicholson, 1885), 20–23.

14. Dougan Clark, "The Society of Friends and Holiness," *Christian Worker,* 1st Mo. 14, 1886, pp. 13–14.

15. G.N. Hartley Reminiscence, n.d., Reminiscences Collection (Friends Collection); Ida Parker, "The Religious Element of the College," *Earlhamite,* 33 (June 12, 1907), 254.

16. "Mt. Pleasant Boarding School," *Earlhamite,* 2 (9th Mo. 1874), 3; Esther

B. Tuttle, "Friends Western Colleges," ibid., 12 (Feb. 1885), 102. Students who were children of leading holiness Friends were identified from "List of Students in Friends' Boarding School and Earlham College, 1847–1886" (Friends Collection).

17. Editorial, *Earlhamite*, 7 (July 1881), 238–39; ibid., 3 (10th Mo. 1875), 15; "Obituary," ibid., 11 (June 1884), 239.

18. J. H. Douglas, "Protest," ibid., 11 (June 1884), 214; "College Influence," ibid., 2 (11th Mo. 1874), 35–36; Editorial, ibid., 20 (May 1893), 123; *Catalogue of Earlham College* (Richmond, Ind.: Telegram, 1884), 24–25. For a marvelous example of a student's religious questioning, see the Diary of Ruth J. Hinshaw for 1874 in the Friends Collection.

19. *Catalogue of Earlham College* (Richmond, Ind.: Telegram, 1878), 13; ibid. (1869), p. 18.

20. Earlham College Faculty Minutes, 10th Mo. 26, 1881 (Friends Collection); Opal Thornburg, *Earlham: The Story of the College, 1847–1962* (Richmond, Ind.: Earlham College Press, 1963), 222–23.

21. Hamm, *Transformation*, 90–91; "Joseph Moore," *Phoenixian* 4 (May 1894), 4; "Report," *Earlhamite*, 9 (July 1882), 219; Robert L. Kelly, "The Educational Work of Allen Jay," ibid., 36 (May 21, 1910), 242–43; Clark, "Plea for Orthodoxy," 41; Lucile Carter Inke to Alumni office, June 1967, Reminiscences Collection; Elbert Russell Reminiscences, Typescript, n.d., ibid.; Irene U. Baker to Opal Thornburg [ca. 1965], Joseph Moore Presidential File (Friends Collection).

22. "Locals," *Earlhamite*, 6 (March 1879), 140; ibid., 7 (May 1880), 188; ibid. (June 1880), 213; *Officers and Students of Earlham College. Catalogue* (Richmond, Ind.: M. Cullaton, 1888), 64–65; *Catalogue of Earlham College* (Richmond, Ind.: Daily Palladium, 1880), 53–54.

23. "Commencement Week," *Earlhamite*, 14 (July 1887), 237; W. S. D., "Quakerism," ibid., 13 (Jan. 1886), 85–87; G. E. H. "Quakerism, Past and Present," ibid., 9 (Jan. 1882), 79–81.

24. "Letter from M. P. Wright," ibid., 11 (Feb. 1884), 108–09; "Earlham College—A Quaker Institution," ibid., 14 (March 1887), 141; "Exchanges," ibid., 13 (Oct. 1885), 22.

25. Editorial, ibid., 13 (Feb. 1886), 113; ibid., 12 (Jan. 1885), 90; *Catalogue of the Officers and Students of Earlham College* (Richmond, Ind.: T. D. De Yarmon, 1885), 49; *Elbert Russell, Quaker: An Autobiography* (Jackson, Tenn.: Friendly Press, 1956), 56–57, 71.

26. *Catalogue of the Officers and Students of Earlham College* (Richmond, Ind.: T. D. De Yarmon, 1887), 21–22; Joseph John Mills, "The Friends College," *Earlhamite*, 9 (June 13, 1903), 264; Editorial, ibid., 14 (April 1887), 160.

27. "Locals," *Earlhamite*, 11 (March 1884), 140; Editorial, ibid., 20 (May 1893), 122; Chalmers Hadley, "Earlham," ibid., 65 (Jan. 1944), 12; *Elbert Russell*, 36; "Report of Statements and Arguments Made before a Joint Committee Appointed by Indiana Yearly Meeting and Western Yearly Meeting of the Society of Friends, at Hearings Held in the East Main Street Friends Church, in the City of Richmond, Indiana, on December 7, and December 8, 1920," typescript, pp. 321–22, Religious Controversies File, Controversial Issues Collection (Friends Collection).

28. George M. Marsden, *The Soul of the American University: From Protestant Establishment to Established Nonbelief* (New York: Oxford University Press, 1994).

29. *Catalogue of the Officers & Students of Earlham College* (Cincinnati: Gibson & Co., 1862), 8; *Catalogue of Earlham College* (Richmond, Ind.: Daily Palladium, 1881), 7, 27; *Catalogue of Earlham College* (Richmond, Ind.: M. Cullaton, 1893), 19; "Report of the President of Earlham College," *Earlhamite,* 2 (Oct. 1, 1895), 5–6; Editorial, ibid., 5 (May 1888), 186; M. P. Wright, "Friends Academies," ibid., 8 (Feb. 1881), 102–03.

30. See the catalogs in note 29.

31. "United States Census of Friends, 1890," *Christian Worker,* 4th Mo. 7, 1892, pp. 211–13; Elbert Russell, "Friends Secondary Schools," *Quaker,* 11th Mo. 12, 1921, pp. 171–72.

32. See the citations in note 29 and "Remarks of President Dennis," *Earlhamite,* 52 (Dec. 1930), supplement.

33. "United States Census of Friends."

34. Pearson, "Has Earlham a Mission?"; Editorial, *Earlhamite,* 13 (Dec. 1885), 65; Ethel Hittle McDaniel, *The Contribution of the Society of Friends to Education in Indiana* (Indianapolis: Indiana Historical Society, 1939), 82.

35. Thomas C. Kennedy, "Southland College: The Society of Friends and Black Education in Arkansas," *Arkansas Historical Quarterly,* 42 (Autumn 1983), 207–38; Lindley D. Clark, "Up from Slavery—A Link between Two Eras," *American Friend,* Aug. 8, 1935, p. 325.

36. Thornburg, *Earlham,* 132. For somewhat different views of Quaker work among Native Americans, see Rayner Wickersham Kelsey, *Friends and the Indians, 1655–1917* (Philadelphia: Associated Executive Committee on Indian Affairs, 1917); and Clyde A. Milner II, *With Good Intentions: Quaker Work among the Pawnees, Otos, and Omahas in the 1870s* (Lincoln: University of Nebraska Press, 1982).

37. David L. Johnson and Raymond Wilson, "Gertrude Simmons Bonnin, 1876–1938: 'Americanize the First American,'" *American Indian Quarterly,* 12 (Winter 1988), 27–28.

38. Chalmers Hadley, "Earlham," *Earlhamite,* 64 (July 1945), 14. For Gertrude Simmons's life at Earlham, see, for example, "Personals and Locals," ibid., 2 (Nov. 1, 1895), 47; ibid. (March 15, 1895), 255; ibid. (April 1, 1896), 207; "Hallowe'en Party," ibid. (Nov. 15, 1895), 61; and "Music Recital," ibid. (Jan. 1, 1896), 108.

39. Zitkala-Sa, "The School Days of an Indian Girl," *Atlantic Monthly,* 85 (Feb. 1900), 193.

40. Ibid; Gertrude Simmons, "Side by Side," *Earlhamite,* 2 (March 16, 1896), 177–79; William C. Dennis to Cora Marsland, Feb. 9, 1938, Gertrude Simmons file, Alumni Collection (Friends Collection).

41. "At the College," *Earlhamite,* 2 (March 16, 1896), 186–87.

42. Johnson and Wilson, "Gertrude Simmons Bonnin," 28–40.

43. Thornburg, *Earlham,* 85–87.

44. Ibid., 119–20.

45. *Catalogue of the Officers and Students of Earlham College* (Cincinnati: Gibson & Co., 1865), 3; *Earlham College, Richmond, Indiana, Catalogue* (Richmond, Ind.: M. Cullaton, 1890), 6–7. The ancestry of all four men can be traced in William Wade Hinshaw, ed., *Encyclopedia of American Quaker Genealogy* (6 vols., Ann Arbor: Edwards Brothers, 1936–1950), I; and Willard Heiss, ed., *Abstracts of the Records of the Society of Friends in Indiana* (7 vols., Indianapolis: Indiana Historical Society, 1962–1977).

46. *Earlham College* (1890), 6–7.

47. Ibid.; Thornburg, *Earlham*, 90. Laurence R. Veysey, *The Emergence of the American University* (Chicago: University of Chicago Press, 1965), 175–76.

48. Mahalah Jay, "Earlham College," *Earlhamite*, 7 (July 1881), 237–38; "Report," ibid., 8 (July 1882), 218; Editorial, ibid., 240; Thornburg, *Earlham*, 445; *Catalogue of Earlham College* (Richmond, Ind.: Telegram, 1884), 4; *Catalogue of the Officers and Students of Earlham College* (Richmond, Ind.: T. D. De Yarmon, 1885), 6; Barbara Miller Solomon, *In the Company of Educated Women: A History of Women and Higher Education in the United States* (New Haven: Yale University Press, 1985), 78–93.

49. Chester Allen, "Woman's Suffrage," *Earlhamite*, 12 (Nov. 1884), 55–58; [Absalom Knight], "Woman and Government," ibid., 10 (Jan. 1883), 82–84; Faculty Minutes, 3rd Mo. 4, 1873.

50. *Catalogue of the Officers and Students of Earlham College* (Cincinnati: Gibson & Co., 1864), 14; W. B. M[organ], "Is Earlham College Failing?" *American Friend*, 2 (12th Mo. 1868), 284–85; Editorial, *Earlhamite*, 1 (3rd Mo. 1874), 56.

51. Mattie Dennis, "The World's Congress of Representative Women," *Phoenixian* 3 (June 1893), 9–11; Anna M. Moore, "Lucy Stone," ibid., 3 (Feb. 1894), 132–35; Anna Birdsall, "What Girls Can Do," ibid., 3 (May 1893), 186–88; Caroline Miles, "An Open Letter," *Earlhamite*, 19 (Jan. 1892), 51–52; Barnabas C. Hobbs, "Address to the Graduating Class," ibid., 1 (9th Mo. 1874), 5–6. For the women's rights movement in this period, see William R. Leach, *True Love and Perfect Union: The Feminist Reform of Sex and Society* (New York: Basic, 1980).

52. "Commencement Day," *Phoenixian*, 1 (July 1891), 43; Josephine M. Hadley, "Woman's Education," ibid., 1 (June 1891), 20–22; Elvira Hester, "The Education of Women," *Earlhamite*, 11 (July 1884), 219–23; Mary Coggeshall Sackett, "The College Girl in the Home," *Earlhamite*, 5 (April 1, 1899), 127–28; J. J. Mills, "Earlham's Testimony," ibid., 13 (Oct. 1880), 14–15; William N. Trueblood, "To the American Women," ibid., 1 (1st Mo. 1874), 6–8. For these issues in the larger society, see Barbara Leslie Epstein, *The Politics of Domesticity: Women, Evangelism, and Temperance in Nineteenth Century America* (Middletown: Wesleyan University Press, 1981).

53. [Morgan], "Is Earlham College Failing?" 267.

54. *Catalogue of Earlham College* (Richmond, Ind.: Telegram, 1876), 31–32; *Catalogue of the Officers and Students of Earlham College* (Richmond, Ind.: T. D. De Yarmon, 1887), 69–82.

55. "Letter from M. P. Wright," 108; R. W. Barrett, "Relation of the Student to Money Making," *Earlhamite*, 5 (May 27, 1899), 174.

56. Burton J. Bledstein, *The Culture of Professionalism: The Middle Class and the Development of Higher Education in America* (New York: Norton, 1976); W. Bruce Leslie, *Gentlemen and Scholars: College and Community in the "Age of the University," 1865–1917* (University Park: Pennsylvania State University Press, 1992).

57. John Edwin Jay, "But for the Grace of Earlham?" typescript, n.d., Reminiscences Collection.

58. I based this on a comparison of alumni lists with the lists of Quaker college presidents in Errol T. Elliott, *Quakers on the American Frontier: A History of the Westward Migrations, Settlements, and Developments of Friends on the American Continent* (Richmond, Ind.: Friends United Press, 1969), 387–88. William W. Birdsall, a Hicksite Friend and 1873 graduate, was president of Swarthmore College from 1898 to 1902. Ibid., 388. Guilford was

founded as New Garden Boarding School in 1837, but did not become a college until 1888.

59. Other small, church-affiliated colleges offer an interesting comparison with Earlham in this period. See, for example, Leslie, *Gentlemen and Scholars*; David B. Potts, *Wesleyan University, 1831–1910: Collegiate Enterprise in New England* (New Haven: Yale University Press, 1992); John Barnard, *From Evangelicalism to Progressivism at Oberlin College, 1866–1917* (Columbus: Ohio State University Press, 1969); and Thomas Leduc, *Piety and Intellect at Amherst College, 1865–1912* (New York: Columbia University Press, 1946).

60. Hamm, *Transformation*, 66–69; [Julianna Harvey], *Memorial of Cyrus W. Harvey* (Philadelphia: Friends' Book Store, 1920); Back Creek Monthly Meeting Men's Minutes, 9th Mo. 13, 1866, Indiana Yearly Meeting Archives; Caroline Carpenter Diary, July 30, 1863, box 1, Carpenter-Wright Family Papers (Friends Collection); Steve Valentine, "Amidst the Bloody Strife: Earlham College during the Civil War Era," *Indiana Military History Journal*, 2 (Jan. 1977), 9–11.

61. Amy Ann Sanders to Louzena Sanders, Feb. 19, 1867, Student Letters Collection, Earlham College Board of Trustees Minutes, 12th Mo. 19, 1865 (Friends Collection).

62. Board Minutes, 3rd Mo. 23, 1866, 1st Mo. 21, 1869; Amy Ann Sanders to Louzena Sanders, Feb. 7, 1868, Student Letters Collection; "Locals," *Earlhamite*, 20 (Nov. 1878), 44; Advertisement, ibid., 20 (May 1893), 3; *Catalogue of the Officers and Students of Earlham College* (Richmond, Ind.: Telegram, 1871), 22.

63. Board Minutes, 12th Mo. 19, 1865; Faculty Minutes, 1st Mo. 30, 1873; "Locals," *Earlhamite*, 3 (11th Mo. 1875), 37.

64. Thornburg, *Earlham*, 73–75, 159–60; "Ionian Society," *Earlham Annual for 1902* (N.p., n.d.), 26–28; "Phoenix Band," ibid., 28–30; W. T. D., "The Early Ionian," *Earlhamite* 5 (June 1878), 201–03; Mary Pickett, "History of the Phoenix Band," *Phoenixian*, 2 (Dec. 1892), 100–02.

65. Thornburg, *Earlham*, 130–31, 209, 201–03.

66. See, generally, the *Earlhamite* for 12th Mo. 1873; *Catalogue of Earlham College* (Richmond, Ind.: Telegram, 1877), 18; William B. Morgan, "Earlham College," *Earlhamite*, 3 (6th Mo. 1876), 194.

67. Faculty Minutes, 9th Mo. 29, 1880; D. W. Dennis, "The Ionian Hall Fund," *Earlhamite*, 2 (Nov. 1, 1895), 36.

68. *Autobiography of Allen Jay, Born 1831, Died 1910* (Philadelphia: John C. Winston, 1910), 67; Thornburg, *Earlham*, 163–65.

69. Faculty Minutes, Nov. 16, 1887; Board Minutes, 6th Mo. 16, 1891, 10th Mo. 7, 1891, 6th Mo. 13, 1893.

70. Thornburg, *Earlham*, 219; Board Minutes, 6th Mo. 17, 1890; "Athletics," *Phoenixian*, 3 (Nov. 1893), 77; "Prof. Trueblood, Veteran Earlham Gridder, Reiterates Football History of the Gay 90s," *Earlham Post*, Oct. 30, 1943, p. 5; "Who and What They Are," *Earlhamite*, 20 (Dec. 1892), 33–35; "Athletics," ibid. (Nov. 1892), 26–28; Henrietta Stanley, "Three Cheers for the Yellow and Cream," *Phoenixian*, 2 (May 1892), 13. For football and its impact on other schools, see Leslie, *Gentlemen and Scholars*, 190–94; and Frederick Rudolph, *The American College and University: A History* (Athens: University of Georgia Press, 1990), 373–93.

71. *Catalogue of the Officers and Students of Earlham College* (Richmond, Ind.: M. Cullaton, 1886), 39; Thornburg, *Earlham*, 215–16.

72. Editorial, *Earlhamite*, 11 (July 1884), 233; ibid., 20 (May 1893), 122; "Should the Library Be Opened on Sunday Afternoon? A Reply," ibid., 19 (Feb. 1892), 71–72; Helen Lefkowitz Horowitz, *Campus Life: Undergraduate Cultures from the End of the Eighteenth Century to the Present* (Chicago: University of Chicago Press, 1987), 98–150.

73. "The Day-Dodger," ibid., 20 (May 1893), 121; Editorial, ibid., 21 (Jan. 1894), 61.

74. "Report of the President of Earlham College," ibid., 2 (Oct. 1, 1895), 6; Homer Carey Hockett, "A Quaker Boy and Earlham College," 1960, Reminiscences Collection. Compare the situation at Earlham with that found in Leslie, *Gentlemen and Scholars*, 189–213; and Horowitz, *Campus Culture*, 98–150.

75. *Catalogue of the Officers and Students of Earlham College* (Cincinnati: Gibson & Co., 1865), 18; ibid. (Richmond, Ind.: Crawley & Maag, 1868), 20.

76. *Catalogue of the Officers and Students of Earlham College* (Cincinnati: Gibson & Co., 1863), 11; ibid. (1864), 15; ibid. (Richmond, Ind.: Telegram, 1870), 20; *Catalogue of Earlham College* (ibid., 1875), 25; ibid. (1887), 64; *Officers and Students of Earlham College. Catalogue* (Richmond, Ind.: M. Cullaton, 1888), 74.

77. E. H., "The College Government," *Earlhamite*, 11 (April 1884), 159; James Bradley to B. C. Hobbs, June 12, 1867, Student Letters Collection; Horowitz, *Campus Life*, 32–34.

78. Serepta A. Pearson to Mahalah Jay, May 6, 1866, Student Letters Collection; Walter T. Carpenter to Thomas and Catherine Newby, 7th Mo. 10, 1866, ibid.; Faculty Minutes, April 20, 1893.

79. Faculty Minutes, 11th Mo. 6, 1870, 10th Mo. 29, 1874, March 26, 1883; Charles Mather to William B. Mather, Feb. 7, 1890, Mather Family Collection (Friends Collection). For concerns about alcohol in Richmond generally in this period, see James Clyde Sellman, "Visions of Community in Conflict: Richmond, Indiana, 1806–1890" (Ph.D diss., Harvard University, 1993).

80. Thornburg, *Earlham*, 154; *Catalogue* (1864), 10–14; *Catalogue of the Officers and Students of Friends' Boarding School* (Richmond, Ind.: Johnson & Morgan, 1858), 9–10; *Catalogue* (1865), 16; ibid. (1868), 15; ibid. (1876), 15–16. On curricular change generally in this period, see Frederick Rudolph, *Curriculum: A History of the American Undergraduate Curriculum since 1636* (San Francisco: Jossey-Bass, 1977), 99–202. On the centrality of moral philosophy, see Donald H. Meyer, *The Instructed Conscience: The Shaping of the American National Ethic* (Philadelphia: University of Pennsylvania Press, 1972).

81. "President Moore Invites William N. Trueblood to Establish Department of English," *Earlhamite*, 44 (Oct. 1923), p. 6; Opal Thornburg, "Shakespeare in American Colleges and at Earlham," 62 (July 1941), 14–15; *Catalogue* (1888), 23; ibid. (1885), 30–31; Board Minutes, 3rd Mo. 17, 1897; J. B. U., "College Curriculum," ibid., 3 (1st Mo. 1876), 65.

82. Mickie Franer and Rhonda Curtis, eds., *Marcus Mote and Eli Harvey: Two Quaker Artists from Southwest Ohio* (Oxford, Ohio: Miami University, 1992), 29; J. A. Thornburg to Carrie Brown, March 7, 1863, Student Letters Collection; "Locals," *Earlhamite* 2 (2nd Mo. 1874), 106; Thornburg, *Earlham*, 89.

83. Editorial, *Earlhamite*, 10 (Dec. 1882), 64; ibid., 16 (Dec. 1888), 65; ibid., 2 (Oct. 1, 1895), 24; *Catalogue* (1888), 60–61.

84. See, for example, *The Discipline of the Society of Friends, of Indiana*

Yearly Meeting (Cincinnati: A. Pugh, 1839), 35; "Memoranda," *Phoenixian,* 2 (April 1893), 168; *Catalogue* (1878), 30.

85. "From the Phoenix and Ionian Record Books," *Earlhamite,* 12 (March 3, 1906), 137; "Alumni," ibid., 34 (Feb. 8, 1908), 136; Opal Thornburg, "Day before Yesterday at Earlham," ibid., 55 (July 1934), 6; "A Commencement Greeting," ibid., 4 (June 15, 1898), 198; "Locals," ibid., 6 (Nov. 1878), 43; Board Minutes, 12th Mo. 27, 1866, 10th Mo. 5, 1878; "Marmaduke Gluys," *Earlham Press,* March 12, 1921, p. 2.

86. Editorial, *Earlhamite,* 9 (Feb. 1882), 135; ibid., 10 (Dec. 1882), 64–65; Emily W. Mills, "The Practical *versus* the Ornamental in Quaker Education," ibid., 9 (July 1882), 234; "Report," ibid., 227.

87. *Catalogue* (1886), 41; "Locals," *Earlhamite,* 10 (May 1883), 189; Editorial, ibid., 18 (Jan. 1891), 87; ibid., 17 (April 1890), 163; ibid., 19 (May 1892), 137; "Commencement," ibid., 17 (July 1890), 241; Board Minutes, 10th Mo. 13, 1883; J. J. Mills to William Edgerton, Dec. 20, 1892, Letterbook, Joseph J. Mills Collection (Friends Collection).

88. Hamm, "Quaker Tradition," 11–12; "Field Notes," *Friends' Expositor,* 2 (Oct. 1888), 208; ibid., 6 (Oct. 1892), 718; Dougan Clark to Rhoda M. Coffin, 4th Mo. 18, 1872, box 1, Coffin Family Papers (Friends Historical Library, Swarthmore College, Swarthmore, Pa.).

89. Hamm, "Quaker Tradition," 11–12.

90. Board Minutes, 10th Mo. 7, 1885; *Catalogue* (1885), 39; ibid. (1886), 90; Editorial, *Earlhamite,* 16 (Nov. 1888), 40; "Commencement Week," ibid., 20 (July 1893), 57–58; "Harrison Home," ibid., 21 (Nov. 1893), 28; "Locals," *Earlhamite,* 20 (Nov. 1892), 30; Editorial, ibid., 21 (Dec. 1893), 43.

91. Hamm, "Quaker Tradition," 13–16.

92. See, for example, *Stenographic Report of the Funeral Services of Dr. Dougan Clark, Held in the Friends Yearly Meeting House, Richmond, Indiana, October 13th, 1896, at 2 p.m.* (Richmond, Ind.: J.M. Coe, 1896).

93. Anna Moore Cadbury, "Joseph Moore," in *Quaker Biographies. Series II* (5 vols., Philadelphia: Friends' Book Store, n.d.), IV, 3–5.

94. William Cooper, "Joseph Moore: Quaker Evolutionist," *Indiana Magazine of History,* 72 (June 1976), 126–31; Paul F. Boller, Jr., *American Thought in Transition: The Impact of Evolutionary Naturalism, 1865–1900* (Washington, D.C.: University Press of America, 1981), 28–35.

95. Cooper, "Joseph Moore," 132–37.

96. "Report of Statements and Arguments," 321; David W. Dennis, "Annual Address before the Christian Associations of Earlham," *Earlhamite,* 6 (June 16, 1900).

97. S. J. Wright, "The 'Review of Huxley's Lectures,'" *Earlhamite,* 5 (Oct. 1877), 11–13; "Commencement," ibid., 15 (July 1888), 244; D. W. Dennis, "Address to the Earlham Class of '76," ibid., 2 (1st Mo. 1875), 75–79.

98. [William L. Pearson], "Is the Theory of Evolution Anti-Christian?" *Earlhamite,* 7 (July 1880), 223–25; Editorial, *Christian Worker,* 9th Mo. 23, 1886, p. 450; Dougan Clark, *The Holy Ghost Dispensation* (Chicago: Publishing Association of Friends, 1891), 145–46; Dougan Clark and Joseph H. Smith, *David B. Updegraff and His Work* (Cincinnati: M. W. Knapp, 1895), 78–79.

99. "Joseph Moore," *Earlhamite,* 49 (March 1928), 3.

100. Thornburg, *Earlham,* 143.

101. The college catalogs list trustees from this period. For Timothy Nicholson, see "Timothy Nicholson," *Earlhamite* 6 (Oct. 1924), 5; and,

generally, Walter C. Woodward, *Timothy Nicholson: Master Quaker* (Richmond, Ind.: Nicholson, 1927).

102. For lists of trustees, see Thornburg, *Earlham*, 437–39. For Mordecai Morris White, see J. J. Mills, "An Earlhamite Financier," *Earlhamite*, 6 (June 2, 1900), 213–15. For Mary Hough Goddard, see "Mary Hough Goddard," *American Friend*, 6th Mo. 2, 1908, p. 427; and Donald E. Bivens, "Joseph A. Goddard: Muncie Businessman and Quaker Leader" (Ph.D. diss., Ball State University, 1989).

103. See, generally, the minutes of the board for 1860–1880; and, specifically, Visiting Committee Minutes, 1st Mo. 12, 1864, 5th Mo. 19, 1870 (Friends Collection). For the student view, see Walter Roberts to E. H. Walker, 12th Mo. 29, 1866, Student Letters Collection.

104. B. C. H[obbs], "Earlham College," *American Friend*, 2 (11th Mo. 1868), 263; M[organ], "Is Earlham College Failing?" 267.

105. D. C., "Indiana Yearly Meeting," *American Friend*, 1 (11th Mo. 1867), 266.

106. M[organ], "Is Earlham College Failing?" 268.

107. H[obbs], "Earlham College," 263; Board Minutes, 10th Mo. 18, 1870, 10th Mo. 16, 1877, June 9, 1909.

108. Editorial, *Earlhamite*, 1 (12th Mo. 1873); ibid., 2 (10th Mo. 1874), 27; Earlham College Alumni Association Minutes, 1877 (Friends Collection).

109. Editorial, *Earlhamite*, 2 (10th Mo. 1874), 27; ibid., 6 (Oct. 1878), 18.

110. Board Minutes, 4th Mo. 11, 1878, 9th Mo. 26, 1878.

111. Thornburg, *Earlham*, 135–36.

112. *Incorporation, Constitution and By-Laws of Earlham College* (Richmond, Ind.: Daily Palladium, 1884).

113. *Autobiography of Allen Jay*, 321–23.

114. On Moses C. Stevens, see Thornburg, *Earlham*, 60. For William L. Pyle, see *Minutes of Western Yearly Meeting of Friends, 1907*, pp. 101–02. For Absalom Rosenberger, see S. Arthur Watson, *Penn College: A Product and a Producer* (Oskaloosa, Iowa: William Penn College, 1971), 284. For Charles F. Coffin, see Mary Coffin Johnson and Percival Brooks Coffin, *Charles F. Coffin: A Quaker Pioneer* (Richmond, Ind.: Nicholson, 1923). For Joseph R. Evans, see Opal Thornburg, "The Evans-Woodard Family and Earlham," *Earlhamite*, 79 (April 1958), 8.

115. Board Minutes, 6th Mo. 3, 1883; E. H., "The Moore Reception," *Earlhamite*, 12 (Dec. 1884), 170.

116. J. J. Mills biographical sketch, n.d., Mills Papers; Board Minutes, 10th Mo. 3, 1883.

117. Board Minutes, 1st Mo. 18, 1884; Editorial, *Earlhamite*, 11 (Feb. 1884), 112–13; "Professors McTaggart and Pearson," ibid., 110–11; *New Castle* (Ind.) *Courier*, Oct. 10, 1884, p. 8.

118. "Reminiscences of Charles F. Coffin," n.d., typescript, p. 230, box 1, Charles F. and Rhoda M. Coffin Collection (Friends Collection); Thornburg, *Earlham*, 173–74; Editorial, *Earlhamite*, 12 (Oct. 1884), 17. When the alumni association was organized in 1871, Alpheus M. McTaggart was its first president, and Calvin W. Pearson was a member of its executive committee. See Alumni Association Minutes, 7th Mo. 27, 1871. Ironically, late in 1884 Charles F. Coffin had to resign as yearly meeting clerk and flee Richmond when his bank failed. Whitewater Monthly Meeting disowned him in 1886 for improper business practices. Hamm, *Transformation*, 220.

119. Editorial, *Earlhamite*, 11 (July 1884), 233; "Recent Board Meeting," ibid., 11 (May 1884), 181–82.

120. Board Minutes, 10th Mo. 3, 1888, June 15, 1915.

121. Thornburg, *Earlham*, 180–82.

122. Barnabas C. Hobbs, "Earlham College. Its Future under the New Management," *Earlhamite*, 7 (July 1881), 248; Editorial, ibid., 11 (April 1884), 160–61; Editorial, ibid., 14 (Nov. 1886), 38; Thornburg, *Earlham*, 180–82.

123. For the lack of faculty security in this period, see Walter P. Metzger, *Academic Freedom in the Age of the University* (New York: Columbia University Press, 1964), 186–93.

124. Board Minutes, 9th Mo. 16, 1868. Faculty minutes begin in 1859.

125. Faculty Minutes, 7th Mo. 5, 1860, 11th Mo. 22, 1876, 1st Mo. 24, 1877 (Friends Collection).

126. Board Minutes, 3rd Mo. 23, 1866, 10th Mo. 24, 1882; Faculty Minutes, 11th Mo. 3, 1875, 2nd Mo. 19, 1879, 10th Mo. 24, 1882.

127. See the list of faculty in Thornburg, *Earlham*, 440–51.

128. "Zaccheus Test," *Earlhamite*, 12 (Nov. 18, 1905), 37–38.

129. Eli Jay Diary, April 5, 1866, box 1, Eli and Mahalah Jay Papers (Friends Collection); Jacob Baker, *Incidents of My Life and Work of 84 Years* (Richmond, Ind.: Nicholson, 1911), 33–34.

130. Jay Diary, April 5, 1866; "Zaccheus Test"; Thornburg, *Earlham*, 94–96. Edward Taylor, an 1865 graduate, wrote later that Zaccheus Test's "literary taste was too exacting. He could not bear it to use a word in the slightest degree inappropriately." See Edward Taylor to Henry C. Wright, Nov. 19, 1905, Edward Taylor File, Alumni Collection.

131. Hamm, "Quaker Tradition," 11, 16–17; Hamm, *Transformation*, 107–08, 132.

132. Hamm, *Transformation*, 130–37; *Richmond Item* clipping, Sept. 13, 1894, Dougan Clark File, Earlham Faculty Collection (Friends Collection).

133. Hamm, "Quaker Tradition," 17, Elliott, *Quakers on the American Frontier*, 376–78; "The Baptism of Dr. Dougan Clark," *American Friend*, 9th Mo. 17, 1894, pp. 146–48.

134. *Elbert Russell*, 80.

135. E. C. Siler to Timothy Nicholson, 9th Mo. 15, 1894, Timothy Nicholson Papers (Friends Collection); Robert W. Douglas to Nicholson, 9th Mo. 12, 1894, ibid.; "Propositions Submitted to Dr. Dougan Clark," [1894], Clark file; clipping, n.d., ibid.; W. B. Hadley letter, n.d., clipping, Clark file; Allen Jay to Rufus M. Jones, 9th Mo. 5, 1895, box 1, Rufus M. Jones Papers (Quaker Collection, Haverford College, Haverford, Pa.); Nicholson to Jones, 1st Mo. 12, 14, 4th Mo. 6, 6th Mo. 24, 7th Mo. 3, 19, 27, 8th Mo. 1, 1895, ibid.

3. Quakerism, Modernism, Professionalism, 1895–1915

1. *Elbert Russell, Quaker: An Autobiography* (Jackson, Tenn.: Friendly Press, 1956), 79–80.

2. Ibid.

3. Ibid., 10–13.

4. Ibid., 17–75.

5. Ibid., 56–57.

6. Ibid., 82–86. For the importance of the Moody Bible Institute, see Virginia Lieson Brereton, *Training God's Army: The American Bible School,*

1880–1940 (Bloomington: Indiana University Press, 1990), vii–ix. For William Rainey Harper, see George M. Marsden, *The Soul of the American University: From Protestant Establishment to Established Nonbelief* (New York: Oxford University Press, 1994), 236–62.

7. *Elbert Russell*, 82, 89.

8. For an excellent summary of the basics of the Higher Criticism, see William R. Hutchison, *The Modernist Impulse in American Protestantism* (Cambridge: Harvard University Press, 1976), 76–110. For the conservative response, see George M. Marsden, *Fundamentalism and American Culture: The Shaping of American Evangelicalism, 1870–1925* (New York: Oxford University Press, 1980), 17–18.

9. Hutchison, *Modernist Impulse*, 6.

10. *Elbert Russell*, 89.

11. Ibid., 92–93; Creighton Peden, *The Chicago School: Voices in Liberal Religious Thought* (Bristol, Ind.: Wyndham Hall Press, 1987),12–23.

12. *Elbert Russell*, 92–93. For John Wilhelm Rowntree, see Stephen Allott, *John Wilhelm Rowntree, 1868–1905, and the Beginnings of Modern Quakerism* (York, Eng.: Sessions, 1994).

13. Significant in this respect is the testimony of Albert L. Copeland, a long-time Quaker pastor who was clerk of Western Yearly Meeting for many years. Copeland had strong evangelical views, yet wrote that Russell's "reverent spirit was notable." See Albert L. Copeland, "An Account of Experiences and Impressions as a Student at Earlham College," April 1960, Reminiscences Collection (Friends Collection, Earlham College, Richmond, Ind.)

14. *Elbert Russell*, 92–93, 97.

15. Ibid., 91–92.

16. Ibid.

17. Ibid., 102.

18. Ibid., 98–100; Thomas D. Hamm, *The Transformation of American Quakerism: Orthodox Friends, 1800–1907* (Bloomington: Indiana University Press, 1988), 146–60; Rufus M. Jones to Elbert Russell, 8th Mo. 15, 1898, box 3, Elbert Russell Papers (Friends Collection).

19. *Elbert Russell*, 101–06, 120.

20. Ibid., 105.

21. Ibid., 106–13.

22. Ibid., 107; Isaac Sharpless to Russell, 1st Mo. 27, 1903, box 5, Russell Papers; R. W. Kelsey to ibid., 1st Mo. 5, 1903, box 3, ibid.

23. "Our New Professors," *Earlhamite*, 8 (Oct. 5, 1902), 2; "President Robert L. Kelly," ibid., 9 (March 14, 1903), 153–55; Robert L. Kelly Autobiography, typescript, ca. 1940, Robert L. Kelly Papers (Friends Collection).

24. Kelly Autobiography; "Our New Professors"; Laurence R. Veysey, *The Emergence of the American University* (Chicago: University of Chicago Press, 1965), 175–76. On John Dewey's influence, see Alan Ryan, *John Dewey and the High Tide of American Liberalism* (New York: Norton, 1995).

25. *Catalog of Earlham College in Richmond, Indiana, for 1900–1901* (Richmond: Nicholson, 1901), 24.

26. Kelly Autobiography.

27. Opal Thornburg, *Earlham: The Story of the College, 1847–1962* (Richmond, Ind.: Earlham College Press, 1963), 227–29.

28. Ibid., 233–39.

29. "The Library," *Earlhamite*, 5 (Nov. 26, 1898), 55; "Library Notes," ibid.,

7 (March 23, 1901), 175; "Students Benefit from Evening Library Period," *Earlham Press*, Jan. 9, 1915, p. 4; Kelly to Harlow Lindley, [1941], Kelly Papers; Thornburg, *Earlham*, 245–46.

30. Thornburg, 246, 249; *Autobiography of Allen Jay, Born 1831, Died 1910* (Philadelphia: John C. Winston, 1910), 396–406.

31. On the influence of the General Education Board, see Frederick Rudolph, *The American College and University: A History* (Athens: University of Georgia Press, 1990), 431–34.

32. Robert L. Kelly, "Attitude of Philanthropists toward Earlham," *Earlhamite*, 33 (Feb. 13, 1907), 235–36; Earlham College Board of Trustees Minutes, June 20, Oct. 4, 1911 (Friends Collection).

33. Editorial, *Earlhamite*, 33 (Feb. 9, 1907), 123; Levi T. Pennington, *Rambling Recollections of Ninety Happy Years* (Portland, Ore.: Metropolitan Press, 1967), 129.

34. Carl Ackerman, "Progress in Journalism," *Earlhamite*, 36 (Dec. 25, 1909), 84–85; Walter R. Miles, "Fraternalism and American Culture," ibid., 33 (Feb. 9, 1907), 120.

35. Le Roy Dennis, "Bossism," ibid., 4 (June 1, 1898), 170–71; R. L. Sackett, "Honesty Is the Best Policy," ibid., 12 (Dec. 2, 1905), 47–48; "First Chapel Exercises," ibid., 33 (Oct. 13, 1906), 5; "Alumni," ibid., 36 (Feb. 26, 1910), 149. For a student essay, see T. E. Jones, "Democracy and Co-Operation," ibid., 38 (Feb. 24, 1912), 147–49.

36. "Earlham College Political Turmoil," *Earlham Press*, Feb. 3, 1912, p. 1; "Hughes Wins Day by Narrow Margin," ibid., Oct. 28, 1916, p. 1; "College Men and Politics," ibid., Sept. 23, 1916, p. 2.

37. R. L. Kelly to J. Frank Hanley, Oct. 25, 1905, Kelly Papers; "Earlham College Political Turmoil"; "Pres. Kelly Retires from Political Race," *Earlham Press*, May 26, 1917, p. 1; "Alumni," *Earlhamite*, 34 (March 7, 1908), 161; clipping, [1914], box 5, Russell Papers; Elbert Russell, 136–41; Thornburg, *Earlham*, 238–39. For the Progressive Movement in Indiana, see Clifton J. Phillips, *Indiana in Transition: The Emergence of an Industrial Common-wealth, 1880–1920* (Indianapolis: Indiana Historical Bureau and Indiana Historical Society, 1968), 85–131. On the American Civic Federation, see James Weinstein, *The Corporate Ideal in the Liberal State, 1900–1918* (Boston: Beacon, 1968).

38. "Old Earlham Votes Dry," *Earlham Press*, March 21, 1914, p. 4; "False Impression Spreads," ibid., April 1, 1914, p. 4; "Earlham Men Aid Drys," ibid., March 28, 1914, p. 2; "Local Prohibition Club Organized," ibid., Nov. 19, 1914, p. 2. In this section, I am indebted to a paper by Kathy Carey, "Changing Attitudes towards Temperance at Earlham College: 1847–1919," typescript, June 7, 1991, Earlham History Collection (Friends Collection). On S. Edgar Nicholson, see K. Austin Kerr, *Organized for Prohibition: A New History of the Anti-Saloon League* (New Haven: Yale University Press, 1985), 121–23.

39. Bevan Binford, "The Galilean Reformer," *Earlhamite*, 3 (Jan. 23, 1897), 113–15; A. E. Martin, "The American Toiler," ibid., 9 (Nov. 22, 1902), 62–65; Walter R. Miles, "Co-Operation and Modern Life," ibid., 34 (June 10, 1908), 184–86; "The Social Revolution," ibid., 35 (March 6, 1909), 146–49.

40. Elbert Russell, "The Quakerism of the Future," in *Centennial Anniversary of West Branch Monthly Meeting of Friends, Established 1st Month 1, 1807* (n.p., n.d.), 111; Elbert Russell, "The New Struggle for Liberty," *American Friend*, 7th Mo. 25, 1912, pp. 470–72; ibid., "The Massacre of the Innocents," ibid., 8th Mo. 22, 1912, pp. 538–39; ibid., "The Shadow of

Anarchism," ibid., 8th Mo. 1, 1912, pp. 486–87; ibid., 8th Mo. 8, 1912, pp. 502–04; "Russell Defends Labor," *Earlham Press*, May 11, 1912, p. 4; "Delivers Strong Address," ibid., June 25, 1913, p. 2. For the Social Gospel, see Ronald C. White, Jr., and C. Howard Hopkins, *The Social Gospel: Religion and Reform in Changing America* (Philadelphia: Temple University Press, 1976). For the Industrial Workers of the World, see Melvin Dubofsky, *We Shall Be All: A History of the Industrial Workers of the World* (Chicago: Quadrangle, 1969).

41. Luther M. Feeger, "John Mitchell," *Earlhamite*, 9 (March 28, 1903), 163–68; "'Syndicalism' Is Expounded," *Earlham Press*, April 13, 1912, p. 3.

42. "A Suffragette to Come," *Earlham Press*, April 22, 1911, p. 4; "Votes for Women," ibid., April 29, 1911, p. 1; "Earlham and Suffrage," ibid., p. 2; "Alumni and Personals," ibid., March 11, 1916, p. 2. In my writing on women students in this era at Earlham, I am indebted to a paper by Killian Barefoot, "A Struggle for Equality: A History of Women's Education at Earlham College, 1901–1965," May 1991, Earlham History Collection. For women and higher education generally in this period, see Lynn D. Gordon, *Gender and Higher Education in the Progressive Era* (New Haven: Yale University Press, 1990).

43. Elbert Russell, "The Parson on Woman's Education," *Earlhamite*, 11 (Oct. 8, 1904), 1–4; "Woman's Sphere," ibid., 9 (Feb. 14, 1903), 133–34; Thornburg, *Earlham*, 256–57. The *Earlhamite* resumed publication in 1919 as the college alumni magazine.

44. "The Forum," *Earlham Press*, April 1, 1916, p. 3; Ernest A. Wildman Autobiography, 1962, p. 126, box 5, Ernest Atkins Wildman Collection (Friends Collection); Caroline M. Hill, "A Quaker Woman on Marriage and Divorce," *Earlhamite*, 35 (Dec. 19, 1908), 77–78. Compare the Earlham situation with Gordon, *Gender and Higher Education*.

45. *Catalogue of Earlham College* (Richmond, Ind.: Nicholson, 1903); *Earlham College Bulletin* (Earlham, Ind.: Earlham College, 1915); Robert Wiebe, *The Search for Order, 1877–1920*, (New York: Hill and Wang, 1967), 133–63.

46. Anna L. Doan, "The Associated Charities," *Earlhamite*, 11 (Dec. 3, 1904), 57–60; Board Minutes, June 10, 1903, Dec. 10, 1912; Thornburg, *Earlham*, 242.

47. Kelly Autobiography; "In Appreciation of Robert L. Kelly," *American Friend*, 4th Mo. 12, 1917, p. 296; Mark Curtis, "Crisis and Opportunity: The Founding of the American Association of Colleges," in *Enhancing Liberal Education: American Association of Colleges at 75* (Washington, D.C.: AAC, 1988), 7–8; Hugh Hawkins, *Banding Together: The Rise of National Associations in American Higher Education, 1887–1950* (Baltimore: Johns Hopkins University Press, 1992), 16–20.

48. Wildman Autobiography; Thornburg, *Earlham*, 273–74.

49. Helen Lefkowitz Horowitz, *Campus Life: Undergraduate Cultures from the End of the Eighteenth Century to the Present* (Chicago: University of Chicago Press, 1987), 23–55; Robert L. Kelly, "Inaugural Address," *Earlhamite*, 9 (June 13, 1903), 242.

50. Editorial, *Earlhamite*, 11 (Nov. 5, 1904), 37; Editorial, 36 (April 23, 1910), 215; Editorial, ibid., 34 (Nov. 9, 1907), 33; "Big Scholarship Event," *Earlham Press*, Jan. 28, 1911, p. 3.

51. Editorial, *Earlhamite*, 9 (May 9, 1903), 216; ibid., 33 (March 16, 1907), 173; ibid., 35 (Feb. 20, 1909), 137–38; "Our Open Column," ibid., 12 (Feb. 17,

1906), 125; "Fundamental to College Life," *Earlham Press*, Nov. 29, 1913, p. 2; E. P. Trueblood, "Sketches in the Life and Memory of E. P. Trueblood," Sept. 29, 1940, Reminiscences Collection; Elizabeth H. Emerson, "They Make a Difference," n.d., ibid. On the 1898 "scrap," see Russell to William C. Dennis, July 26, 1935, box 5; William Cullen Dennis Presidential Papers (Friends Collection); and E. P. Trueblood to Dennis, [1935], ibid.

52. Compare with Horowitz, *Campus Life*, 118–50.

53. "The Publishers," *Earlham Press*, Jan. 21, 1911, p. 2; "Club Regulations Made," ibid., June 6, 1914, pp. 1, 4; "No Earlham Magazine Published This Year," ibid., Oct. 24, 1914, pp. 1, 3; "Girls to Become Members of Press Club Temporarily," ibid., Jan. 15, 1916, p. 1.

54. "Another Precedent," *Earlham Press*, Oct. 28, 1916, p. 2; "Two Students Suspended," ibid., Oct. 31, 1914, p. 1; Editorial, *Earlhamite*, 12 (Nov. 18, 1905), 38; "Vandalism," ibid., 36 (March 12, 1910), 158; Pauline Pritchard to Parents, 1914, Student Letters Collection (Friends Collection); O. H. Folger, "Earlham Reminiscences," n.d., Reminiscences Collection.

55. "Student Government in Bundy Hall," *Earlhamite*, 36 (June 4, 1910), 260; Florence Long Reminiscence, May 27, 1951, Reminiscences Collection. For student government in other schools in this era, see Rudolph, *American College and University*, 369–70.

56. Thornburg, *Earlham*, 237, 288.

57. "The I.U.-Earlham Debate," *Earlhamite*, 5 (April 29, 1899), 141; "State Oratorical Contest," ibid., 8 (Feb. 22, 1902), 131; "College News," ibid., 40 (Feb. 1914), 81; Rudolph, *American College and University*, 373–93.

58. Editorial, *Earlhamite*, 33 (May 4, 1907), 214; ibid., 34 (Oct. 12, 1907), 6; "Football," ibid., 9 (Oct. 11, 1902), 25; "Butler Question," *Earlham Press*, Nov. 2, 1912, p. 2; "Pep," ibid., Oct. 2, 1915, p. 1.

59. Elbert Russell, "The Principle of Progressive Revelation in Scripture," *American Friend*, 1st Mo. 25, 1900, pp. 77–79; Elbert Russell, "The Unfolding of the Scripture Doctrine of Peace," ibid., 2nd Mo. 22, 1900, pp. 176–78; Russell to Esther T. Pritchard, Jan. 1, 1901, box 4, Russell Papers.

60. *Elbert Russell*, 106; Russell to Irvin H. Cammack, July 25, Oct. 20, 1905, box 1, Russell Papers; Russell to Levi T. Pennington, Feb. 25, 1907, box 4, ibid.

61. George A. Barton to Russell, March 13, 1907, box 1, Russell Papers; Luke Woodard to Russell, 3rd Mo. 28, 1914, box 5, ibid.; Russell to Charles D. Roberts, April 4, 1904, box 4, ibid.; Russell to Cammack, July 25, 1905; Elbert Russell, *Jesus of Nazareth in the Light of Today* (Philadelphia: John C. Winston, 1909), 47, 109–11, 156–57.

62. Russell to William P. Pinkham, Dec. 24, 1905, box 4, Russell Papers; *Minutes and Proceedings of the Five Years Meeting of the American Yearly Meetings of Friends Held in Richmond, Ind., Tenth Mo. 15, to 10th Mo. 21, 1907* (Philadelphia: John C. Winston, 1908), 417–26; Russell to Cammack, July 25, 1905.

63. Russell to Cammack, July 25, 1905; Elbert Russell, "The Interpretation and Use of the Bible," *American Friend*, 7th Mo. 2, 1908, pp. 423–24; ibid., 7th Mo. 9, 1908, pp. 436–39.

64. *Proceedings . . . 1907*, 424; Elbert Russell, "The Problem of a Consistent Quaker Pastorate," *American Friend*, 9th Mo. 26, 1907, pp. 621–23; E. J. R., "Converted—To What?" ibid., 5th Mo. 9, 1907, p. 296; Elbert Russell, "Our Quaker Literature," ibid., 1st Mo. 5, 1905, pp. 4–7.

65. Hamm, *Transformation*, 160–64.

66. *Elbert Russell,* 102–03, 147; E. Howard Brown to Jones, Jan. 8, 1905, box 5, Jones Papers; Edward Mott to Russell, Feb. 12, 1907, box 4, Russell Papers; J. Walter Malone to Russell, Jan. 5, 1905, box 4, ibid.; Cammack to Russell, 8th Mo. 18, 1905, box 1, ibid.; Jacob Baker, *Incidents of My Life and Work of 84 Years* (Richmond, Ind.: Nicholson, 1911), 153; Amy Winslow, "Earlham— 1905–1910," 1960, Reminiscences Collection.

67. Hamm, *Transformation,* 160–61; Editorial, *Evangelical Friend,* June 1, 1905, pp. 1–2; "Notes of Earlham Institute," ibid., Aug. 24, 1905, pp. 193–94; Pinkham to Russell, Oct. 4, 1905, Jan. 25, 1906, box 4, Russell Papers.

68. Russell to Esther T. Pritchard, Jan. 1, 1901, box 4, Russell Papers; Russell to Pinkham, Sept. 2, 1905, Feb. 18, 1906, ibid.; Russell to Luke Woodard, Jan. 12, 1901, box 6, ibid.; Elbert Russell, "A Citizen of Richmond," pp. 10–11, box 8, Russell Papers. This is a draft of Russell's autobiography that contains material not in the published version.

69. "Hard to Explain," *Evangelical Friend,* July 26, 1906, p. 466; Allen Jay to James Wood, 1st Mo. 4, 1907, box 5, Jones Papers; Jay to Jones, 1st Mo. 16, 1907, ibid.; L. Oscar Moon to Russell, March 14, July 15, Aug. 8, 1907, box 3, Russell Papers.

70. Hamm, *Transformation,* 168–72.

71. *Elbert Russell,* 107–08, 147; Thornburg, *Earlham,* 263; Elizabeth H. Emerson to Opal Thornburg, Nov. 18, 1961, Kelly-Russell Controversy: Opal Thornburg Correspondence file, Kelly Papers; Hamm, *Transformation,* 131– 32, 154; "Diogenes Perplexed," *Earlham Press,* Feb. 24, 1912, p. 4; "Life of Christ Class Is Unusually Popular," ibid., Feb. 6, 1915, p. 1.

72. *Elbert Russell,,* 116–18; Richard Haworth to Russell, 4th Mo. 4, 1907, box 3, Russell Papers; Jesse Overman to Russell, Oct. 5, 1905, box 4, ibid.; "Religious Life in Our Educational Institutions," *American Friend,* 2nd Mo. 27, 1913, p. 139; Allen Jay letter, ibid., 3rd Mo. 9, 1905, p. 168; R[ussell], "Converted."

73. Thornburg, *Earlham,* 263; Leonard S. Kenworthy, *Living in a Larger World: The Life of Murray S. Kenworthy* (Richmond, Ind.: Friends United Press, 1986), 35; Levi T. Pennington to Russell, June 19, 1906, box 4, Russell Papers; Lucy Hill Binford to Russell, Jan. 5, 1905, ibid.; Myrtle E. Winslow to Russell, 11th Mo. 5, 1906, box 6, ibid.; Cressie Elizabeth Ellis to Russell, March 27, 1906, box 2, ibid.; Isaac H. Hollingsworth to Russell, 5th Mo. 7, 1907, box 3, ibid.; "Rustle for Russell," *Earlham Press,* Oct. 17, 1914, p. 1.

74. Ira C. Johnson to Russell, 12th Mo. 5, 1906, box 3, Russell Papers.

75. *Elbert Russell,* 119–20; Albert J. Brown to Russell, Oct. 8, 1907, box 1, Russell Papers; Hamm, *Transformation,* 171–72; *Proceedings . . . 1907,* 423– 24, 427, 446–50.

76. *Elbert Russell,* 120; Hamm, *Transformation,* 172; Thomas R. Woodard to Russell, Oct. 31, 1907, box 6, Russell Papers; Morton C. Pearson to Russell, May 1908, box 4, ibid.; Edgar H. Stranahan to Russell, 12th Mo. 3, 1907, box 5, ibid.; Edward Mott, *The Friends Church in the Light of Its Recent History* (Portland, Ore.: Loomis, 193–), 141–42; Timothy Nicholson to Charles E. Tebbetts, [1915], Kelly-Russell Controversy Correspondence file, Kelly Papers; "Friends Bible Institute," *Evangelical Friend,* Aug. 26, 1909, pp. 12–13; "A Peculiar Conclusion," ibid., 2; "Timely Topics," ibid., Sept. 19, 1909, p. 2.

77. "Will Our Colleges Clear Themselves?" *Evangelical Friend,* Oct. 15, 1908, p. 657; "Some Necessary Corrections," ibid., Dec. 3, 1908, pp. 769–70; "Where Rests the Burden of Obligation?" ibid., Nov. 5, 1908, pp. 713–14; "Correspondence," *American Friend,* 10th Mo. 29, 1908, p. 703; Elbert

Russell, "An Open Letter to Friends in America: The Theory and Practice of Detecting 'Unsoundness,'" ibid., 12th Mo. 3, 1908, pp. 780–82; Nicholson to Tebbetts; Russell to Charles F. Coffin, March 24, 1915, box 1, Charles F. and Rhoda M. Coffin Collection (Friends Collection); "Hearings," 325; Board Minutes, Feb. 11, 1913; Russell, "Citizen of Richmond," 101; Pauline Pritchard to Parents, Jan. 19, 1912, Student Letters Collection.

78. Marsden, *Soul of the American University*, 219–91.

79. *Elbert Russell*, 143; Nicholson to Tebbetts; *Richmond Item* clipping, April 9, 1915, Kelly-Russell Controversy file; *Richmond Palladium* clipping, April 6, 1915, ibid.

80. *Richmond Item* clipping, June 16, 1915, Kelly-Russell Controversy Correspondence file; Nicholson to Tebbetts; Kelsey to Russell, Nov. 19, 1905, box 3, Russell Papers; Elliott, *Quakers on the American Frontier*, 279–80; *Elbert Russell*, 145–46.

81. *Elbert Russell*, 146–51; Mildred Henley Calvert interview by Thomas D. Hamm, April 23, 1994, Oral History Collection (Friends Collection).

82. *Richmond Palladium* clipping, April 8, 1915, Kelly-Russell Controversy Correspondence File; *Elbert Russell*, 150–51; "More Represented Than Last Year," *Earlham Press*, Oct. 23, 1915, p. 3.

83. Kelly, "Attitudes of Philanthropists," 136; Kelly to Lindley.

84. "Dr. Jones Lectures," *Earlhamite*, 33 (Feb. 13, 1907), 137; "College News," ibid., 38 (Nov. 18, 1911), 63; "Friends Give Talks," *Earlham Press*, Oct. 26, 1912, p. 1; *Autobiography of Allen Jay*, 400; Board Minutes, June 3, 1905; "Alumni and Personals," *Earlham Press*, Nov. 3, 1917, p. 3.

85. Wildman Autobiography, 134–35; Editorial, *Earlhamite*, 6 (Nov. 11, 1899), 50; "Annual Report of the Y.M.C.A. President," ibid., 33 (April 6, 1907), 194; "College News," ibid., 38 (Dec. 16, 1911), 95; "Christian Associations," ibid., 38 (April 6, 1912), 200; "Y.M.C.A. Prepares for Special Meetings," *Earlham Press*, Nov 6, 1915, p. 1; "Elliott Meetings Highly Successful," ibid., Nov. 20, 1915, p. 1.

86. *Elbert Russell*, 71, 148–49; For the Young Friends, see Thomas E. Jones, *Light on the Horizon: The Quaker Pilgrimage of Tom Jones* (Richmond, Ind.: Friends United Press, 1973), 31–40.

87. *Elbert Russell*, 147–48.

88. Ibid., 147; "New Course in Religious Work," *Earlham Press*, May 23, 1914, p. 1. Alexander C. Purdy related the story of the altercation between Cecilia Kelly and Lieuetta Russell to Wilmer Cooper, who shared it with me in an interview, Oct. 18, 1994.

89. *Palladium* clipping, April 8, 1915.

90. *Elbert Russell*, 150; Catherine H. Woodward to Opal Thornburg, Nov. 20, 1961, Kelly-Russell Controversy: Opal Thornburg Correspondence file; Student Petitions, n.d., Kelly-Russell Controversy file; Indianapolis Alumni to Board, April 20, 1915, ibid.; Baltimore Alumni to Board, March 7, 1915, ibid.; Philadelphia Alumni to Board, April 26, 1915, ibid.; Charles A. Morrison to Russell, May 23, 1915, ibid.

91. Strategy memorandum, n.d., Kelly-Russell Controversy file; Leroy Jones to Russell, 4th Mo. 30, 1915, ibid.; Jerome O. Cross to Russell, April 15, 1915, ibid.; Florence Hanson Morgan to Board, 4th Mo. 30, 1915, ibid.; Thornburg, *Earlham*, 269; Opal Thornburg, "Notes on a Conversation with Esther Griffin White," June 26, 1951, Reminiscences Collection.

92. Percy O. Clark to Mrs. R. L. Sackett, June 2, 1915, Kelly-Russell Controversy file; *Elbert Russell*, 150.

93. Thornburg, *Earlham*, 271–72, 438–39; Elliott, *Quakers on the American Frontier*, 387–88; Russell, "Citizen of Richmond."

94. Walter P. Metzger, *Academic Freedom in the Age of the University* (New York: Columbia University Press, 1964), 206–11; Hawkins, *Banding Together*, 58–60.

95. Cleveland K. Chase to Amos K. Hollowell, April 29, 1915, copy in Opal Thornburg Earlham Notes (Friends Collection).

96. Marsden, *Soul of the American University*, 292–316.

4. The Trials of Liberal Quakerism, 1915–1946

1. "Survey Shows Biblical Department Best in State," *Earlham Press*, Jan. 22, 1923, p. 1; Mildred Henley Calvert Interview by Thomas D. Hamm, April 23, 1994, Oral History Collection (Friends Collection, Earlham College, Richmond, Ind.); Wilmer Cooper Interview by Thomas D. Hamm, Oct. 18, 1994, ibid.

2. Richard Warren Barrett to Robert L. Kelly, March 24, 1917, Robert L. Kelly Papers (Friends Collection); William C. Dennis to Kelly, Jan. 29, 1932, box 5, William C. Dennis Presidential Papers (ibid.); "In Appreciation of Robert L. Kelly," *American Friend*, 4th Mo. 12, 1917, p. 296; Opal Thornburg, *Earlham: The Story of the College, 1847–1962* (Richmond, Ind.: Earlham College Press, 1963), 273. There is considerable correspondence between Robert L. Kelly and William C. Dennis in Dennis's papers.

3. Amos K. Hollowell to Rufus M. Jones, April 21, 1917, box 16, Rufus M. Jones Papers (Quaker Collection, Haverford College, Haverford, Pa.).

4. "Quakerdom at Large," *American Friend*, 6th Mo. 21, 1917, p. 491; S. Arthur Watson, *Penn College: A Product and a Producer* (Oskaloosa, Iowa: William Penn College, 1971), 286.

5. E. Howard Brown to David M. Edwards, July 29, 1925, David M. Edwards Presidential Papers (Friends Collection); Catherine H. Woodward to Opal Thornburg, Jan. 10, 1962, David M. Edwards File, Presidential Collection (ibid.); Thomas D. Hamm, *The Transformation of American Quakerism: Orthodox Friends, 1800–1907* (Bloomington: Indiana University Press, 1988), 167.

6. Edwards to Perry Kissick, Sept. 2, 1924, Perry Kissick Personnel File, Earlham Faculty Collection (Friends Collection); Edwards to Jones, June 24, 1914, box 13, Jones Papers; Watson, *Penn College*, 159–65, 146–48; "Report of Statements and Arguments Made before a Joint Committee Appointed by Indiana Yearly Meeting and Western Yearly Meeting of the Society of Friends, at Hearings Held in the East Main Street Friends Church, in the City of Richmond, Indiana, on December 7, and December 8, 1920," typescript, pp. 88–89, Religious Controversies File, Controversial Issues Collection (Friends Collection).

7. "Alexander C. Purdy," *Earlham Press*, Jan. 15, 1921, p. 2; Hugh Barbour and J. William Frost, *The Quakers* (Westport, Conn.: Greenwood Press, 1988), 340–41, 344–45, 360–61.

8. "Several Changes Made in Faculty," *Earlham Press*, Sept. 18, 1915, p. 1.

9. Francis C. Anscombe Reminiscence, n.d., Reminiscences Collection (Friends Collection); Mary B. Ellis to George H. Moore, Nov. 2, 1920, Religious Controversies File; Ernest A. Wildman Autobiography, 1962, p. 167, box 5, Ernest A. Wildman Papers (ibid.).

10. Theron Coffin to Thornburg, Aug. 22, 1973, Coffin Family File, Friends Pamphlet Group VI (Friends Collection, Earlham); "Joseph Herschel Coffin, Ph.D.," *Earlham Press*, Jan. 22, 1921, p. 2.

11. Elizabeth H. Emerson, *Walter C. Woodward: Friend on the Frontier* (n.p., 1952); "Quakerdom at Large," *American Friend*, 1st Mo. 10, 1918, p. 38; "In Memoriam: Charles M. Woodman," ibid., Jan. 18, 1951, p. 25; Caroline Nicholson Jacob, *Nicholson Family History* (West Chester, Pa., 1970), 71–74.

12. S. Edgar Nicholson to Charles M. Woodman, Jan. 20, Feb. 21, 1916, West Richmond Monthly Meeting Collection (Friends Collection); Woodman to Nicholson, Feb. 12, 1916, ibid.; "Associate Membership Given Earlham Students," *Earlham Press*, Oct. 31, 1914, p. 3.

13. Thomas R. Kelly to Rufus M. Jones, July 18, 1916, box 1, Thomas R. Kelly Papers (Quaker Collection); "Church at Work," *American Friend*, 2nd Mo. 15, 1917, p. 136; "'New Occasions' in Indiana Yearly Meeting," ibid., 10th Mo. 3, 1918, p. 819; S. E. Nicholson, "Friends and World Reconstruction," ibid., 1st Mo. 23, 1919, p. 66; "Report," 346–48.

14. J. Herschel Coffin to Nicholson, Jan. 27, 1921, Religious Controversies File; "Report," 357–68, 371–74, 304, 267–69; E. A. Wildman, "Implications of the Scientific Method," April 27, 1925, box 3, Wildman Papers.

15. Edwards to C. V. Osborn, May 1, 1928, Edwards Papers; "Notes from the President's Desk," *Earlhamite*, 47 (Sept. 1925), 9; "Report," 269; David M. Edwards, "The Problem of Leadership," *American Friend*, 12th Mo. 20, 1917, pp. 1012–13.

16. Amy Winslow, "Suggested Applications of Quakerism to Modern Life," *American Friend*, 7th Mo. 1, 1920, pp. 596–98; Joseph Herschel Coffin, "The Challenge of the Present Crisis to Friendly Education," ibid., 8th Mo. 23, 1917, pp. 664–68; W. C. W., "All Honor to the Friends," ibid., 12th Mo. 16, 1920, p. 1107.

17. W. C. W., "The Exemplar of 'Western Quakerism,'" ibid., 9th Mo. 19, 1918, pp. 775–76; David M. Edwards, "The Problem of Leadership," ibid., 12th Mo. 20, 1917, pp. 1012–13; Earlham College Advertisement, ibid., 8th Mo. 23, 1917, p. 666; Edwards to A. S. Rogers, Dec. 31, 1925, Edwards Papers; Edwards to E. A. Stuart, March 7, 1924, ibid.; Absalom Rosenberger to Robert L. Kelly, April 9, 1917, Robert L. Kelly Papers.

18. Thomas E. Jones, "In the New Year—What?" *American Friend*, 2nd Mo. 8, 1917, p. 109; Nicholson to Woodman, Feb. 5, 1916, West Richmond Collection; "Report," 261–62.

19. "Caught on the Wing," *American Friend*, 11th Mo. 1, 1917, p. 876; Paul J. Furnas, "A Message from Our New Chairman," ibid., 11th Mo. 15, 1917, p. 919; W. C. W., "How Large a Christ Do We Worship?" ibid., 2nd Mo. 21, 1918, p. 147; S. E. N., "The Young Friends Conference as a Turning Point in the Church," ibid., 8th Mo. 21, 1919, p. 719; "The Acid Test of Quakerism," ibid., 12th Mo. 16, 1918, pp. 1075–76.

20. "Notes from the President's Desk," *Earlhamite*, 42 (Oct. 1920), 4; "Alumni and Personals," *Earlham Press*, Jan. 10, 1920, p. 3; "Members of College to Attend Conference," ibid., May 29, 1920, p. 1; "College Campus to Witness Numerous Scenes This Summer," ibid., June 9, 1920, p. 1; "Misconception," ibid., Feb. 24, 1917, p. 2; "Gospel Team Reports Very Successful Trip," ibid., Jan. 6, 1917, p. 1; "Gospel Team Reports a Successful Trip," ibid., April 14, 1917, p. 1; "Members of Western Yearly Meeting Organize," ibid., Oct. 27, 1917, p. 1.

21. "Sunday Chapel Attendance," *Earlham Press,* Nov. 5, 1923, p. 2; "Compulsory Chapel Attendance Dropped," ibid., Jan. 7, 1924, p. 1; "Order in Chapel," ibid., April 28, 1917, p. 2; Edwards to Albert Panhorst, Jan. 14, 1925, Edwards Papers; Robert L. Kelly, "Chapel in Friends Colleges," *Earlhamite,* 54 (July 1933), 6–7; Arnold Vaught Interview by Thomas D. Hamm, April 25, 1994, Oral History Collection (Friends Collection); Howard S. Mills, Sr., Interview by Thomas D. Hamm, April 1990, ibid.; Louis and Mary Ruth (Brown) Jones Interview by Thomas D. Hamm, May 30, 1995, ibid.

22. "Shall the College Decline?" *Earlham Press,* June 2, 1917, p. 2; "The Quaker Drummer," ibid., May 12, 1917, p. 2; "Earlham to Be Identified with Unit in France," ibid., June 13, 1917, p. 2; "Wilmington Page," *American Friend,* 5th Mo. 3, 1917, p. 356; "Friendly Gossip," ibid., 5th Mo. 17, 1917, p. 381; Allen D. Hole, "Conscientious Objectors and Alternative Service," ibid., 4th Mo. 26, 1917, pp. 324–26; Edwards to John S. Surbaugh, Oct. 25, 1928, Edwards Papers. For the Friends Reconstruction Unit, see Rufus M. Jones, *A Service of Love in War Time: American Friends Relief Work in Europe, 1917–1919* (New York: Macmillan, 1920).

23. "Five Years Meeting Echoes," *American Friend,* 11th Mo. 8, 1917, p. 892; "Present Condition of Conscientious Objectors in the Military Camps," ibid., 11th Mo. 7, 1918, p. 938; William Dudley Foulke to William P. Bancroft, Oct. 26, 1917, Miscellaneous Quaker Letters Collection (Friends Collection); Esther Griffin White to Timothy Nicholson, [1917], box 2, Esther Griffin White Papers (ibid.); H. C. Peterson and Gilbert C. Fite, *Opponents of War, 1917–1918* (Seattle: University of Washington Press, 1968), 194–207.

24. "Twenty-Three Men Will Leave School," *Earlham Press,* May 12, 1917, pp. 1, 3; "Physical Preparedness Work Is Discontinued," ibid., June 2, 1917, p. 1; "President Kelly States Policy of Earlham," ibid., April 14, 1917, pp. 1, 3; "Alumni and Personals," ibid., Sept. 28, 1918, p. 3; "Earlham's Honor Roll," ibid., Feb. 2, 1918, p. 1; Warren Beck, "An Earlham Retrospective," 1960, Reminiscences Collection; Edwards to Surbaugh; David M. Edwards, "Friends Colleges and National Service," *American Friend,* 8th Mo. 29, 1918, pp. 722–23; Allen D. Hole, "Earlham College and National Service," ibid., 6th Mo. 6, 1918, pp. 466–67; Edith Morton Bohner, "An Earlham 'Misfit' Remembers 1917," *Earlhamite,* 99 (Summer 1978), 6.

25. For a good general overview, see Ferenc Morton Szasz, *The Divided Mind of Protestant America, 1880–1930* (University: University of Alabama Press, 1982).

26. George M. Marsden, *Fundamentalism and American Culture: The Shaping of Twentieth-Century Evangelicalism, 1870–1925* (New York: Oxford University Press, 1980), 43–62, 118–23; Timothy P. Weber, *Living in the Shadow of the Second Coming: American Premillennialism, 1875–1982* (Chicago: University of Chicago Press, 1987), 3–12.

27. Marsden, *Fundamentalism,* 141–84.

28. Hamm, *Transformation,* 137–39, 160–72; Mark Minear, *Richmond 1887: A Quaker Drama Unfolds* (Richmond, Ind.: Friends United Press, 1987); Elbert Russell, *The History of Quakerism* (New York: Macmillan, 1942), 494.

29. Edward Mott, *Sixty Years of Gospel Ministry* (N.p., 1947), 56; Arthur O. Roberts, *The Association of Evangelical Friends: A Story of Quaker Renewal in the Twentieth Century* (Newberg, Oreg.: Barclay, 1975), 5; Barbour and Frost, *Quakers,* 232–33.

30. Hamm, *Transformation,* 169–70; Simeon O. Smith, comp., *Biography of William Martin Smith and History of Union Bible Seminary, Inc.* (Westfield,

Ind.: Union Bible Seminary, 1982), 25–74; "Bible Seminary Needs," *Friends Minister,* 1 (Oct. 1913), 5; "Report," 109–10.

31. "The Way to Revival," *Gospel Minister,* Jan. 6, 1921, pp. 2–3; "Barclay's Apology," ibid., May 19, 1921, pp. 4–5; "The Bible Training Schools," ibid., Aug. 18, 1921, p. 1; "Decadence of Friends," *Friends Minister,* 1 (Jan. 1914), 1–2.

32. "Report," 109–10, 115.

33. W. C. W., "Taking the 'Schism' Out of 'Criticism,'" *American Friend,* 9th Mo. 18, 1919, p. 807.

34. "A Proposition from Portland Quarterly Meeting to Indiana Yearly Meeting," [1920], Religious Controversies File; Indiana Yearly Meeting to Western Yearly Meeting, Aug. 17, 1920, ibid.; *Minority Report on Earlham College Investigation* (Knightstown, Ind., 1921), 5.

35. S. Adelbert Wood, "Quakerism," *American Friend,* 3rd Mo. 10, 1921, p. 186; "George H. Moore," ibid., May 19, 1932, p. 367; Ida T. Parker, "The Minister and the Sermon," ibid., 7th Mo. 4, 1918, p. 550; "J. Brandt Wolfe," ibid., Jan. 15, 1931, p. 55; "In Memoriam: William J. Sayers," ibid., Jan. 8, 1948, pp. 10–11; "Seminary Notes," *Friends Minister,* 1 (Oct. 1913), 8; Hamm, *Transformation,* 154; Mills Interview.

36. S. Edgar Nicholson to Joint Committee, Oct. 23, 1920, Religious Controversies File; "Quakerdom at Large," *American Friend,* 9th Mo. 27, 1917, p. 781.

37. "Report," 2, 5–7.

38. Ibid., 8–10.

39. Ibid., 20–22, 34, 27, 41–52.

40. Ibid., 48–49, 54, 71, 75–80, 98–103, 110–11, 145–46, 153–55, 163–69, 175–79.

41. Ibid., 9, 11–13, 15–16, 153–55, 165, 464–65.

42. Ibid., 81–88, 106–07, 157–60, 220–21.

43. Ibid., 236–37.

44. Ibid., 237–39, 242.

45. Ibid., 244–45, 254–55.

46. Ibid., 255–57, 260–95, esp. 270.

47. Ibid., 480, 482–83.

48. Ibid., 346–48, 376, 353, 467–68.

49. Ibid., 91–92, 341–43, 335–36, 350, 366–68, 371–74.

50. Ibid., 304–06.

51. Ibid., 426–27, 429, 431–32, 438, 441–3, 447, 460–61.

52. Ibid., 462–64, 471–72.

53. S. Adelbert Wood to Nicholson, Dec. 13, 1920, Religious Controversies File; Charles T. Moore to ibid., Jan. 7, 1921, ibid.; J. Brandt Wolfe to ibid., Dec. 6, 1920, ibid.; Ira C. Johnson to ibid., Dec. 16, [1920], Jan. 5, 1921, ibid.; William J. Sayers to ibid., Dec. 21, 1920, ibid.

54. Nicholson to Committee, March 10, 1921, ibid.; Mary M. Harold to Nicholson, Dec. 14, 1920, ibid.; Edwards to ibid., Dec. 23, 1920, ibid.; Charles M. Woodman to ibid., Feb. 10, 1921, ibid.; Committee of Ten to Joint Committee, Feb. 2, 1921, ibid.; Calvert Interview.

55. S. Edgar Nicholson Notes on Committee Hearings, 1920–1921, Religious Controversies File; Nicholson to Charles T. Moore and Wood, April 4, 1921, ibid.; Wood to Nicholson, April 6, 1921, ibid.

56. *American Friend,* 3rd Mo. 31, 1921, pp. 253–55; "Report of the Investigating Committee," *Earlham College Bulletin,* 4 (April 1921), 8–14.

57. Aaron M. Bray letter, *American Friend,* 4th Mo. 28, 1921, p. 339;

Timothy Nicholson Notes, Dec. 1920, Religious Controversies File; Walter C. Woodward, *Timothy Nicholson: Master Quaker* (Richmond, Ind.: Nicholson, 1927), 171.

58. *Minority Report*, 2–4, 8.

59. Ibid., 8; "Earlham College Investigation," *Gospel Minister*, May 5, 1921, pp. 4–5; Nicholson to Truman C. Kenworthy, T. R. Woodard, and Albert J. Fuerstenberger, April 23, 1921, Religious Controversies File; Nicholson to Indiana and Western yearly meetings, [1921], ibid.; Harold to Nicholson, April 29, May 18, 1921, ibid.; Nicholson to Wood, April 12, 1921, ibid.; Walter C. Woodward to Nicholson, April 21, 1921, ibid.

60. Cooper Interview; Earlham College Board of Trustees Minutes, Oct. 3, 1925 (Friends Collection); Charles W. Cooper, *Whittier: Independent College in California* (Los Angeles: Ward Ritchie Press, 1967), 196–99.

61. *Indiana Yearly Meeting Minutes, 1921*, p. 57; Edwards to Albert L. Copeland, Jan. 27, 1925, Edwards Papers; Charles Moore to Edwards, Dec. 1925, ibid.; J. I. Phillips to ibid., July 29, 1925, ibid.; Brown to ibid., July 29, 1925, ibid.; Edwards to Brown, Aug. 1, 1925, ibid.; Edwards to Marie Sumption, May 1, 1925, ibid.; Clipping, [July 1925], ibid. Fosdick declined the invitation. For Harry Emerson Fosdick, see his autobiography, *For the Living of These Days* (New York: Harper and Row, 1956), 144–76.

62. Thornburg, *Earlham*, 279–81, 301–02, 305–06; Thomas R. Kelly to "Folks," Jan. 29, 1928, box 4, Thomas R. Kelly Papers; Errol T. Elliott, *Quakers on the American Frontier: A History of the Westward Migrations, Settlements, and Developments of Friends on the American Continent* (Richmond, Ind.: Friends United Press, 1969), 392.

63. Loren C. Petry to Arthur M. Charles, [1929], box 1, Dennis Papers; Ruby Davis to Dennis, May 20, 1929, box 3, ibid.; Raymond Elliott to Landrum R. Bolling, Dec. 30, 1963, box 21, Landrum R. Bolling Presidential Papers (Friends Collection).

64. Edwards to Richard R. Newby, Oct. 4, 1928, Edwards Papers; Charles to Dennis, April 7, 1929, box 3, Dennis Papers; Barrett to Dennis, May 14, 1929, ibid.; Dennis to Milton H. Hadley, Aug. 11, 1939, box 6, ibid.

65. Edwards to William E. Berry, Dec. 7, 1928, William E. Berry Personnel File (Friends Collection, Earlham); "Two Department Heads Secured for Next Year," *Earlham Press*, Feb. 20, 1922, p. 1; Dan Wilson, "Howard and Anna Brinton: Translucent Teachers and Minders of the Light," in *Living in the Light: Some Quaker Pioneers of the 20th Century* (2 vols., Kennett Square, Pa., 1984), I, 41–59; Eleanore Price Mather, *Anna Brinton: A Study in Quaker Character* (Wallingford, Pa.: Pendle Hill, 1971), 10–17; Mary Lane (Charles) Hiatt Interview by Thomas D. Hamm, April 20, 1994, Oral History Collection.

66. Lewis M. Hoskins, "Clarence E. Pickett: Servant of Humanity," in *Living in the Light*, ed. Kenworthy, I, 177–89.

67. Harry N. Wright Obituary, clipping, 1969, Harry N. Wright Personnel File, Earlham Faculty Collection (Friends Collection); Margaret Grant Beidler to Hamm, Aug. 18, 1994 (in Hamm's possession).

68. Richard M. Kelly, *Thomas Kelly: A Biography* (New York: Harper and Row, 1966).

69. "New Faculty Members," *Earlhamite*, 47 (Sept. 1925), 6; E. Merrill Root to Talmadge Root, May 1918, box 1, E. Merrill Root Papers (Special Collections, University of Oregon Library, Eugene); "Facts Concerning E. Merrill Root," [1948], E. Merrill Root Personnel File, Earlham Faculty Collection.

70. E. Merrill Root Personal Data Sheet, May 1950, Root Personnel File; Carl and Lois (Harned) Jordan Interview by Thomas D. Hamm, May 5, 1994, Oral History Collection (Friends Collection); Edith Pickett Stratton Interview by Thomas D. Hamm, June 27, 1994, ibid.; Pauline Binkley Cheek, "A Flame Still Burning: The Story of Salem Friends Meeting," typescript, 1992, p. 129 (ibid.); Jones Interview.

71. Edward G. Wilson to Bolling, Aug. 13, 1965, box 26, Bolling Papers; Bolling to F. Adrian Robson, June 4, 1959, box 8, ibid.; E. Merrill Root to Family, April 1918, box 1, Root Papers; E. Merrill Root, "From Genesis to Exodus," *World Tomorrow*, Jan. 1927, pp. 7–9; "College Clubs," *Earlham Press*, Dec. 11, 1922, p. 4; Thomas R. Kelly to Edgar Thompson, July 1, 1929, box 4, Thomas R. Kelly Papers. Edwards, however, worked actively for Herbert Hoover in 1928. See Edwards to William B. Harvey, May 3, 1928, Edwards Papers.

72. Frederick J. Libby to Edwards, May 1, 1924, Edwards Papers; E. Merrill Root, *Dies Irae—Day of Wrath* (Richmond, Ind.: Peace Association of Friends, 1924).

73. "Personals," *Earlhamite*, 1 (May 1920), 7; "Homer L. Morris to Sail for Germany," *Earlham Press*, March 12, 1923, p. 1; "Quaker Social Is Held," ibid., Feb. 9, 1918, p. 1; "Alumni and Personals," ibid., Jan. 15, 1923, p. 3; "Dr. Hole, Prof. Morris, and Reverend Woodman Attend Meeting in Philadelphia," ibid., Nov. 20, 1920, p. 1; "Quakerdom at Large," *American Friend*, June 29, 1933, p. 322. For the founding of the American Friends Service Committee, see J. William Frost, "'Our Deeds Carry Our Message': The Early History of the American Friends Service Committee," *Quaker History*, 81 (Spring 1992), 1–51.

74. "Memorandum of Conversation with Helen Harper," n.d. [before 1935], box 3, Dennis Papers; Paul G. Kauper, "Some Earlham Reminiscences," 1960, Reminiscences Collection; Carl J. Welty Diary, Feb. 18, 1924, typescript, ibid.; Carolyn Carter Kellum Interview by Thomas D. Hamm, June 7, 1994, Oral History Collection; Stratton Interview.

75. Thornburg, *Earlham*, 286–87; Board Minutes, April 30, 1927; *Indiana Yearly Meeting Minutes, 1921*, p. 124.

76. Thomas R. Kelly to Thompson, Jan. 4, 1929, box 4, Thomas R. Kelly Papers; O. Herschel Folger to Richard M. Kelly, Jan. 9, 1963, box 12, ibid.; "The Forum," *Earlham Press*, May 3, 1919, p. 3; Walter C. Woodward to "Dear Friend," 1929, Clarence E. Pickett Papers (American Friends Service Committee Archives, Philadelphia). I am indebted to Larry Miller for a copy of the last item.

77. Edwards to Walter F. Dexter, July 13, 1925, Edwards Papers; Edwards to Elwood C. Perisho, July 14, 1924, ibid.; Board Minutes, June 9, Oct. 6, 1928.

78. Dennis to Alexander C. Purdy, Jan. 9, 1932, Alexander C. Purdy Personnel File, Earlham Faculty Collection; Edward D. Evans to Edwards, Dec. 1, 1928, ibid.; Harry N. Wright to Root, Feb. 22, 1929, Root Personnel File; Emma Dennis to William C. Dennis, May 11, 1929, box 3, Dennis Papers; "President Dennis," *Earlham Post*, Sept. 22, 1931, p. 2.

79. Thornburg, *Earlham*, 315; Beidler to Hamm.

80. Homer L. Morris to Dennis, Aug. 16, 1939, box 31, Homer L. and Edna Morris Papers (Friends Collection); Anna Langston Interview by Thomas D. Hamm, Dec. 5, 1994, Oral History Collection; Martha Calvert Slotten Interview by ibid., April 23, 1994, ibid.; Imogene Cuffel Holloway Interview by ibid., June 21, 1994, ibid.

81. Wilson, "Howard and Anna Brinton," 44–47; Thornburg, *Earlham*, 291, 337–38.

82. Langston Interview; C. Wayne Carter Interview by Thomas D. Hamm, Feb. 24, 1995, Oral History Collection; Donald McKinney Interview by Thomas D. Hamm, Nov. 3, 1994, Oral History Collection (Archives, Earlham); Dennis to Purdy, May 24, July 16, 1930, Purdy Personnel File; Purdy to Dennis, Jan. 21, 1932, ibid.; Dennis to Robert L. Kelly, Oct. 13, 1945, Robert L. Kelly Papers; Dennis to Warder C. Allee, July 25, 1930, June 25, 1932, box 1, Dennis Papers; Dennis to Laurence Hadley, May 21, 1932, box 5, ibid.; Clarence E. Pickett to Dennis, Feb. 5, 1934, William E. Berry Personnel File, Earlham Faculty Collection; Berry to Dennis, July 31, 1936, ibid.; Purdy to Dennis, Aug. 13, 1936, ibid.; Morris to Dennis, Aug. 18, 1936, ibid.; Board Minutes, Feb. 7, 1931; *Indiana Yearly Meeting Minutes, 1929*, p. 72; ibid., *1936*, pp. 72–73.

83. Langston Interview; Marian Binford Sanders to Hamm, Jan. 5, 1995 (in Hamm's possession); Earlham College Faculty Meeting Minutes, Feb. 12, 1934, May 7, 1936 (Friends Collection); *Indiana Yearly Meeting Minutes, 1932*, pp. 60–62.

84. "President Dennis Wins Point with National Group," *Earlhamite*, 61 (Jan. 1940), 12; "Split on Plan to Safeguard Academic Freedom," ibid., 60 (April 1939), 11; *New York Times* clipping, Jan. 13, 1939, box 31, Morris Papers; Dennis to Robert L. Kelly, Dec. 8, 1938, Robert L. Kelly Papers; Faculty Minutes, Oct. 16, 1939.

85. Thornburg, *Earlham*, 318; Millard Markle to Morris, March 2, 1936, box 32, Morris Papers; Dennis to Association of American Colleges, 1931, box 1, Dennis Papers; J. Arthur Funston Interview by Thomas D. Hamm, May 15, 1994, Oral History Collection.

86. Ernest A. Wildman to Morris, March 25, 1936, box 32, Morris Papers; "Summary of Program Committee of Faculty," Nov. 4, 1935, box 3, Wildman Papers.

87. Yearly Meeting Report, 1936, box 32, Morris Papers; Board Minutes, June 9, 1934; George M. Marsden, *The Soul of the American University: From Protestant Establishment to Established Nonbelief* (New York: Oxford University Press, 1994), 332–50.

88. Dennis to Chalmers Hadley, Sept. 3, 1936, box 4, Dennis Papers; Dennis to Edward E. Browne, Nov. 13, 1937, box 2, ibid.; George E. Scherer, *Ernest Atkins Wildman: A Biographical Sketch* (Dublin, Ind.: Prinit Press, 1984), 58–62.

89. Dennis to Board, [1931], box 1, Dennis Papers; Faculty Minutes, May 15, 1933; Opal Thornburg Diary, October 27, 1937, box 12, Opal Thornburg Papers (Friends Collection).

90. Elmer D. Grant to Edwards, March 2, 1930, Edwards Papers; Faculty Meeting Minutes, 1939.

91. Allee to Dennis, Feb. 3, 1931, Dennis to Allee, May 19, 1939, ibid.; box 1, Dennis Papers; Edwin Morrison to Dennis, Aug. 28, 1930, box 3, ibid.

92. W. P. Kissick to Morris, April 1, 1936, box 32, Morris Papers; Grant to Edwards; Thomas R. Kelly to Edwards, Nov. 26, 1929, Edwards Papers; Wildman to Morris, April 21, May 11, 1946, Kissick File. Dennis gave Thomas R. Kelly a series of leaves to study at Harvard and to teach at Wellesley. See correspondence in the Thomas R. Kelly Personnel File, Earlham Faculty Collection.

93. Morris to William E. Armstrong, Jan. 17, 1939, box 31, Morris Papers;

Morris to Dennis, Feb. 20, 1939, ibid.; Alsa Root to Richard M. Kelly, Feb. 19, 1963, box 12, Thomas R. Kelly Papers; Funston Interview; David Telfair Interview by Thomas D. Hamm, May 9, 1995, Oral History Collection; Kissick to David Telfair, May 6, 1984, Cave of Adullam File, Controversial Issues Collection; Thornburg, *Earlham,* 336.

94. Root to Thomas R. Kelly, 1936, box 12, Thomas R. Kelly Papers; Kelly, *Thomas R. Kelly,* 76; Markle to Jones, April 9, 1946, Kissick Personnel File; Kissick to Jones, March 17, 1946, ibid.; Markle to Morris, April 23, 1946.

95. The relations of Quakers and blacks have received considerable attention. For Indiana Yearly Meeting, see Thomas D. Hamm et al., "Moral Choices: Two Indiana Quaker Communities and the Antislavery Movement," *Indiana Magazine of History,* 87 (June 1991), 119–22; John William Buys, "Quakers in Indiana in the Nineteenth Century" (Ph.D. diss., University of Florida, 1973), 180–227; and H[iram] H[adley], "The Education of Our Colored Population,"*American Friend,* 1 (6th Mo. 1867), 147. More generally, see James Harris Norton, "Quakers West of the Alleghenies and in Ohio to 1861" (Ph.D. diss., Case Western Reserve University, 1965), 199–242; Henry J. Cadbury, "Negro Membership in the Society of Friends," *Journal of Negro History,* 21 (April 1936), 151–213; Jean R. Soderlund, *Quakers & Slavery: A Divided Spirit* (Princeton: Princeton University Press, 1985), 183–86; and Philip S. Benjamin, *The Philadelphia Quakers in the Industrial Age, 1865–1920* (Philadelphia: Temple University Press, 1976), 145–71.

96. Lindley D. Clark, "Up from Slavery—A Link Between Two Eras," *American Friend,* Aug. 8, 1935, p. 325. Class portraits before 1900 show a handful of black students.

97. W. Rufus Kersey, "The Supremacy of the Anglo-Saxon," *Earlhamite,* 15 (June 1888), 208–10; "In the Haunts of the Negro," ibid., 18 (Nov. 1890), 26–29; Isadore Wilson, "The Mystery of the Pride Mansion," ibid., 21 (May 1894), 119–20; "Y.M.C.A. Minstrels to Perform," *Earlham Press,* March 20, 1915, p. 1.

98. "Locals," *Earlhamite,* 14 (June 1887), 215; "Lecture," ibid., 6 (Oct. 14, 1899), 21–22; Editorial, ibid., 10 (Oct. 1882), 9; "Alumni," ibid., 38 (March 30, 1912), 192; Joseph W. Kenney, "The First Emancipator," ibid., 8 (May 10, 1902), 216–18; "Educational," ibid., 10 (Nov. 1882), 39; George H. Moore, "A Self-Made Man," ibid., 16 (March 1889), 130–32; R. W. Barrett, "The Saxon of the South," ibid., 3 (Feb. 1, 1897), 129–32.

99. Leonard J. Moore, *Citizen Klansmen: The Ku Klux Klan in Indiana, 1921–1928* (Chapel Hill: University of North Carolina Press, 1991), 72–73; Dwight W. Hoover, "Daisy Douglas Barr: From Quaker to Klan 'Kluckeress,'" *Indiana Magazine of History,* 87 (June 1991), 195; Membership Records, 1921–1925, Wayne County Ku Klux Klan Collection (Indiana Historical Society, Indianapolis); Calvert Interview.

100. *Indiana Yearly Meeting Minutes, 1922,* p. 126.

101. "Chapel Exercises," *Earlham Press,* June 1, 1912, p. 3; Walter Polk De Soto to Robert L. Kelly, [1915], Kelly Papers; Leon R. Harris, "The Voice of the Freedman," *American Friend,* 5th Mo. 13, 1920, p. 451; "Quakerdom at Large," ibid., 8th Mo. 12, 1920, p. 736.

102. Clarence M. Cunningham, "Being Black at Earlham in the Early Twenties," *Earlhamite,* 100 (Spring 1979), 1–2; Edwards to J. Barnard Walton, Nov. 20, 1924, Edwards Papers; Anna Saylor Morris Interview by Thomas D. Hamm, April 19, 1994, Oral History Collection; Melvin Gilchrist, "First Black Earlham Graduate Experience," *Earlham Post,* Feb. 5, 1981, p. 8.

103. "Inter-Racial Services at Sunday Chapel," *Quaker Quill,* Feb. 14, 1928, p. 4; "Countee Cullen at Dennis Thursday," ibid., May 9, 1927, p. 1; "Adventure Open Now to Negro," ibid., March 20, 1928, p. 1; "Joint Association," ibid., March 21, 1927, p. 2; "Interracial Conference Held at Indianapolis," ibid., Feb. 15, 1926, p. 1; "Miss Brown Speaks on Negro Heroines," ibid., Feb. 21, 1927, p. 1; Pickett to Dennis, Jan. 15, 1930, box 6, Dennis Papers; Edwards to Carleton B. McCulloch, Sept. 20, 1924, Edwards Papers; Board Minutes, Feb. 5, 1927.

104. Dennis to Board, Dec. 27, 1943, box 5, Dennis Papers; Dennis to Association of American Colleges, [1931], box 1, ibid.

105. Dennis to Pickett, Jan. 25, Feb. 4, 1930, box 6, Dennis Papers; Harry N. Wright Memorandum, May 26, 1930, ibid.; Kellum Interview.

106. Edward D. Evans to Dennis, Feb. 6, 1930, box 6, Dennis Papers; Dennis to Pickett, Feb. 12, 1930, ibid.; Anna Eves to Dennis, Jan. 26, 1930, ibid.

107. A. D. Beittel to Dennis, Jan. 25, 1930, ibid.; Pickett to Dennis, Jan. 30, 1930, ibid.; Thomas R. Kelly to Edgar Thompson, Jr., Jan. 4, 1929 [should be 1930], box 4, Thomas R. Kelly Papers.

108. Paul K. Edwards to Thomas E. Jones, Dec. 5, 1936, Thomas E. Jones Papers (Quaker Collection, Haverford); "Race," *Earlham Post,* Nov. 12, 1935, p. 2; "Conference Delegates," ibid., Sept. 21, 1937, p. 2.

109. Sanders to Hamm; Langston Interview.

110. See, generally, Robert Cohen, *When the Old Left Was Young: Student Radicals and America's First Mass Student Movement, 1929–1941* (New York: Oxford University Press, 1993).

111. *Richmond Palladium-Item* clippings, Feb. 24, March 2, 1931, box 6, Dennis Papers; Dennis to Mrs. Arthur O. Harold, March 21, 1931, ibid.; Albert L. Copeland to Dennis, March 26, 1931, ibid.; Dennis to Alfred H. Cope, n.d., ibid.; *Indianapolis News* clipping, March 2, 1931, ibid.; G. Bromley Oxnam to Dennis, April 21, 1931, box 5, ibid.; "Problems in Our Town," *American Friend,* March 12, 1931, p. 195.

112. "Liberals Plan Action," *Earlham Post,* March 15, 1932, p. 3; Dennis to Chalmers Hadley, Dec. 9, 1935, box 5, Dennis Papers; W. Bruce Hadley to "Dear Friend," Oct. 3, 1932, ibid.; Dennis to W. Bruce Hadley, Oct. 27, 1932, ibid.; *New York Times* clipping [1935], ibid.

113. Matthew K. Amberg Interview by Thomas D. Hamm, April 25, 1994 (notes in Hamm's possession); Dennis to Joseph Broadman, Feb. 10, 1936, box 2, Dennis Papers.

114. Amberg Interview; "S.L.I.D. Chapter," *Earlham Post,* Nov. 12, 1935, p. 1; "Students Hold Peace Meeting," ibid., April 28, 1936, p. 1; "Statement Authorized by Executive Committee," April 21, 1936, box 4, Dennis Papers; Amberg to John Ackley, Dec. 28, 1935, box 2, ibid.; Dennis to Broadman.

115. "Hoover Wins in Straw Vote," *Earlham Post,* Nov. 1, 1932, p. 1; "Newly Formed A. S. U. Meets," ibid., Jan. 21, 1936, p. 2; Herbert Hadley, "Student Opinion," ibid., Dec. 10, 1935, p. 2; Dennis to Barrett, Nov. 3, 1936, box 2; "Remarks to Executive Committee," April 16, 1938, box 31, Morris Papers.

116. For Dennis on pacifism and peace movements, see Dennis to Albert Johnson, March 8, 1930, box 6, Dennis Papers; Dennis to Stanley P. Smith, May 31, 1937, ibid.; Dennis to Allee, March 26, 1932, June 5, 1934, box 1, ibid.; Dennis to James P. Mullin, Aug. 5, 1944, ibid.; Dennis to Elizabeth Henderson, Feb. 27, 1941, box 5, ibid.; Dennis to Paul E. Fisher, Oct. 11, 1941, ibid.; "Memorandum of a Conversation between President Dennis and Mrs. Gertrude Simms Hodgson," Dec. 13, 1935, ibid.

117. Lawrence W. Wittner, *Rebels against War: The American Peace Movement, 1945–1960* (New York: Columbia University Press, 1968), 1–33; Charles Chatfield, *For Peace and Justice: Pacifism in America, 1914–1941* (Knoxville: University of Tennessee Press, 1971), 259–61, 295–96.

118. "Student Strike," *Earlham Post,* April 26, 1935, p. 2; "S.L.I.D. Backs Peace Bond Sale," ibid., Dec. 17, 1935, p. 2; "We Want Peace," ibid., Oct. 22, 1934, p. 2; "Winder Reports Peace Congress," ibid., June 1, 1938, p. 1; "Help for Needy Chinese," ibid., Dec. 6, 1938, p. 2; "Several Earlhamites Are in Emergency Peace Campaign," *Earlhamite,* 58 (April 1936), 2; Sanders to Hamm; Ives to Hamm.

119. Letter, *Earlham Post,* May 3, 1938, p. 2; "Approximately 150 Students Attend Strike," ibid., p. 4; Faculty Minutes, April 18, 1938; Dennis to Executive Committee, April 14, 1938, box 4, Dennis Papers; "Remarks to Executive Committee"; Dennis to Morris, April 27, 1938, box 31, Morris Papers.

120. Helen Lefkowitz Horowitz, *Campus Life: Undergraduate Cultures from the End of the Eighteenth Century to the Present* (Chicago: University of Chicago Press, 1987), 151–73; Sanders to Hamm; *The 1938 Sargasso,* p. 40; Cohen, *When the Old Left Was Young*; "Among the Earlhamites," *Earlhamite,* 79 (Jan. 1958), 25.

121. Wendell M. Stanley Reminiscence, May 14, 1960, Reminiscences Collection; Florence L. Moyer Interview by Thomas D. Hamm, April 27, 1994 (Notes in Hamm's possession); Robert E. Fatherley Interview by Thomas D. Hamm, Feb. 3, 1995 (ibid.); Charles McCoy to Edwards, July 24, 1924, Edwards Papers; Daniel Whybrew to Edwards, Jan. 29, 1924, ibid.

122. Faculty Minutes, Oct. 7, 1924, Feb. 7, 1929; Edwards to A. Boyd, Oct. 7, 1924, Edwards Papers; Franklin O. Marshall to Edwards, Oct. 8, 1924, ibid.; Edwards to E. A. Kendall, Oct. 7, 1924, ibid.; Edwards to Elisha McFarland, Feb. 10, 1925, ibid.; Fatherley Interview.

123. Charles G. Blackburn to Edwards, Sept. 6, 1925, Edwards Papers.

124. Ibid.; Josiah C. Russell to Edwards, Aug. 14, 1925, Edwards Papers; Edwards to Chester L. Reagan, Sept. 10, 1925, ibid.; Edwards to Mr. Beckitt, Nov. 13, 1924, ibid.; S. Francis Nicholson Interview by Thomas D. Hamm, June 7, 1996, Oral History Collection.

125. Faculty Statement, Aug. 10, 1925, Edwards Papers; Herbert Carey to Edwards, Aug. 9, 1925, ibid.

126. F. G. Wood to Edwards, Aug. 25, 1924, ibid.; Paul J. Furnas to Edwards, Aug. 22, 1925, ibid.; Ralph Nicholson to Edwards, Sept. 24, 1925, ibid.; Vernon Hinshaw to Edwards, Aug. 25, 1925, ibid.; Leslie Pennington to Edwards, Sept. 3, 1925, ibid.; T. S. Raiford to Edwards, Aug. 30, 1925, ibid.; Blackburn to Edwards.

127. Edwards to Carroll Kenworthy, Sept. 14, 1925, ibid.; Thornburg, *Earlham,* 303–04.

128. Thornburg, *Earlham,* 295–96; "Edwards Demands New Gymnasium at Once," *Earlham Press,* Sept. 29, 1917, p. 1; "Fatherley Elected," *Quaker Quill,* Dec. 13, 1920, p. 4; "Earlham's Athletic Policy," *Earlhamite,* 6 (Oct. 1924), 7; Edwards to Copeland, Nov. 18, 1925, Edwards Papers; Edwards to J. O. Hoerner, Dec. 11, 1924, ibid.; Fatherley Interview. For Clara Comstock, see *Palladium-Item* clipping, Oct. 31, 1966, Clara Comstock Personnel File (Friends Collection).

129. Thornburg, *Earlham,* 293; "Freshman Week Successful," *Earlhamite,* 47 (Sept. 1925), 2–3; Edwards to Cassie W. Kelsay, Nov. 10, 1925, Edwards Papers; Edwards to Franklin Raymond, July 8, 1925, ibid.; Virginia Unthank

to Edwards, June 10, 1924, ibid.; Survey Committee Report, April 30, 1927, box 3, Wildman Papers; Dennis to W. O. Trueblood, Nov. 25, 1930, box 5, Dennis Papers.

130. This paragraph is based on the disciplinary cases in Dennis's papers.

131. Dennis to Ruby Davis, May 10, 1929, box 3, Dennis Papers; Dennis to Rufus M. Jones, June 5, 1930, Purdy File; Yearly Meeting Report, 1936, box 32, Morris Papers; Landrum R. Bolling, "A Strong Man," Oct. 11, 1962, Dennis File, Earlham Presidents Collection (Friends Collection).

132. "Seventy Couples Dance at Leland," *Earlham Post*, Oct. 13, 1931, p. 1; "Dancing at Earlham," ibid., Feb. 9, 1932, p. 2; Dennis to Trueblood; Clara Comstock Memorandum, Oct. 5, 1929, box 3, Dennis Papers; Faculty to Board, Feb. 7, 1930, ibid.; Dancing Poll, 1930, ibid.; Dennis to Allee, June 22, 1933, box 1, ibid.; Dennis to "Dear Friend," Jan. 23, 1942, box 3, ibid. The last is a form letter that Dennis used to respond to critics.

133. Trueblood to Dennis, Oct. 23, 1930, box 3, ibid.; Copeland to Dennis and Walter C. Woodward, Oct. 7, 1929, ibid.; E. T. Albertson to Woodward, Feb. 5, 1930, ibid.; William W. Thornburg to Earlham College, March 21, 1929, ibid.; Dennis to Levi T. Pennington, Feb. 28, 1939, box 6, ibid.; "Summary of Answers to Questionnaire to Quaker Colleges," 1939, ibid.

134. Editorial, *Earlhamite*, 6 (April 1879), 160; Emma Thornburg to Oliver Thornburg, Aug. 2, 1865, Student Letters Collection (Archives, Earlham); Faculty Minutes, March 21, 1872; J. J. Mills to ? Sanders, Nov. 9, 1892, Mills Letterbook, Joseph John Mills Papers (Archives, Earlham); Kent S. Morse to Edwards, March 31, 1924, Edwards Papers; Edwards to Joseph A. Goddard, Dec. 4, 1925, ibid.; Edwards to E. D. Peckham, Feb. 6, 1924, ibid.; "Memorandum on Smoking," [1933], box 6, Dennis Papers.

135. Albertson to Dennis, Dec. 20, 1934, box 3, Dennis Papers; Dennis to Albertson, Oct. 18, 1939, box 6, ibid.; "Memorandum on Smoking"; Dennis to Joseph B. Rounds, July 14, 1936, Joseph B. Rounds Personnel File, Earlham Faculty Collection; Joseph and Jean Hamm Balestrieri Interview by Thomas D. Hamm, April 26, 1994, Oral History Collection.

136. "Earlham College, Democracy or Dictatorship," [1939], box 6, Dennis Papers; *Indianapolis Star* clipping, March 20, 1939, box 6, ibid.; *Palladium-Item* clipping, ibid.; Executive Committee Minutes, March 20, 1939, box 4, ibid.; Faculty Meeting Minutes, March 16, April 24, June 8, Oct. 23, 1939; Board Minutes, Oct. 7, 1939.

137. Dennis to I. E. Woodard, April 10, 1939, box 6, Dennis Papers; Dennis to Geraldine Hadley Moorman, Sept. 25, 1941, box 3, ibid.; Dennis to "Dear Friend." A poll of Earlham students in 1942 showed that 41 percent of them never smoked; 36 percent smoked occasionally; and 23 percent smoked regularly. See Smoking Poll, 1942, box 3, Dennis Papers.

138. Jim Goar, "Commons Committee Set to Submit Definite Plans," *Earlham Post*, May 6, 1941, p. 2; Dennis to Harold N. Tollefson, May 28, 1945, box 3, Dennis Papers; Orley and Edith Overman to Dennis, March 29, 1939, box 6, ibid.; Albertson to Dennis, Sept. 8, 1939, ibid.; E. T. Albertson, Albert L. Copeland, and Charles A. Reeve Statement, 1941, ibid.; *Western Yearly Meeting Minutes, 1939*, p. 127; Board Minutes, Sept. 13, 1941.

139. Dennis to Theodore Foxworthy et al., Oct. 9, 1942, box 3, Dennis Papers; Anderson Monthly Meeting Minute, 6th Mo. 17, 1942, ibid.; Van Wert Quarterly Meeting to Dennis, [1942], ibid.; Portland Quarterly Meeting to Dennis, Sept. 12, 1942, ibid.; Homer G. Biddlecum to Dennis, Nov. 26, 1941, May 8, 1942, ibid.; Dennis to Biddlecum, July 23, 1942, ibid.; Chanlis Linville

to Dennis, Aug. 13, 1942, ibid.; Sumner A. Mills to Earlham College Trustees, Aug. 17, 1943, box 3, ibid.; De Ella L. Newlin to Dennis, Jan. 30, 1942, ibid.; "Memorandum," [1943] ibid.; Dennis to Linville, Aug. 15, 1942, box 4, ibid.; Faculty Minutes, Nov. 16, 1942; "A Question for You," *Western Work,* Jan. 1, 1942, p. 2.

140. "Enrollment in Friends Colleges," 1938–1939, box 2, Dennis Papers.

141. These figures are based on the college catalogs for 1910, 1920, 1930, and 1940. I am indebted to my archival assistant, Danesha Seth, for compiling them.

142. Loren C. Petry to Search Committee, [1929], Dennis Search File, Earlham Presidents Collection.

143. "Elbert Russell Writes of Earlham's Values," *Earlham Press,* March 10, 1924, p. 4; "Westtown Head Visits College," *Earlham Post,* May 3, 1932, p. 2; Dennis to Moorman; Alson Van Wagner Interview by Thomas D. Hamm, April 19, 1994, Oral History Collection; Wayne Booth Interview by Thomas D. Hamm, Jan. 4, 1995, ibid.; Fatherley Interview.

144. Fatherley Interview; Van Wagner Interview; Calvert Interview; S. Janney Hutton to Stanley Hall, Oct. 16, 1964, Reminiscence Collection; "Honor Scholarships Are Announced," *Earlham Post,* Oct. 9, 1934, p. 1; "President Dennis Fills Interesting Series of Engagements," *Earlhamite,* 55 (April 1934), 3; Dennis to Trustees, April 10, 1933, box 6, Dennis Papers.

145. Albertson to Dennis, April 16, 1933, box 6, Dennis Papers; Biddlecum to Dennis, July 18, 1942, ibid.; W. Bruce Siler to Dennis, Feb. 15, 1942, ibid.

146. I. E. Woodard to Dennis, May 2, 1939, box 6, Dennis Papers; Allee to Dennis, Dec. 3, 1942, box 1, ibid.; F. D. Hole, "A Report on the Trip to Western Yearly Meeting," Aug. 22, 1943, box 6, ibid.; Siler to Dennis; E. Orville Johnson, "Memorandum in Regard to Conversation with Reverend Donald Spitler, Spiceland, Ind.," Feb. 29, 1936, box 3, ibid.; Charles A. Reeve to Dennis, May 25, 1938, box 5, ibid.; Morris J. Hadley to Woodward, Dec. 31, 1941, box 3, ibid.; James R. Furbay to Dennis, Dec. 9, 1940, box 4, ibid.; Lemoine Overman Memo, [1942], box 6, ibid.; Alvin T. Coate to Dennis, Sept. 7, 1943, ibid.; Frederick Wood to Dennis, Feb. 11, 1940, box 4, ibid.; Milton J. Hadley to Dennis, Aug. 28, 1939, ibid.

147. Berry to Dennis, Feb. 10, 1939, box 6, Dennis Papers; Milo S. Hinckle to Dennis, Feb. 21, 1939, ibid.; Annual Report to Yearly Meetings, 1941, ibid.; Faculty Minutes, April 8, 1940, Nov. 16, 1942; Board Minutes, Feb. 10, 1940.

148. Opal Thornburg Diary, Jan. 18, 1939; "Austrian Refugee Studies at Earlham," *Earlhamite,* 60 (April 1939), 10; Faculty Minutes, Dec. 5, 1938; Thornburg, *Earlham,* 346; Leonard S. Kenworthy, "Alice C. Shaffer: Champion of the World's Children," in *Living in the Light,* ed. Kenworthy, I, 209–10; Leonard S. Kenworthy, *Worldview: The Autobiography of a Social Studies Teacher and Quaker* (Richmond, Ind.: Friends United Press, 1977), 57–72; Opal Thornburg, *Their Exits and Their Entrances: The Story of Richmond Civic Theater* (Richmond, Ind.: Graphic Press, 1959).

149. Funston Interview; Dennis to Raymond S. Springer, July 22, 1940, Peace File, Controversial Issues Collection; Dennis to Raymond Willis, Sept. 2, 1940, ibid.; Dennis to John L. Newman, Feb. 15, 1941, box 5, Dennis Papers; Dennis to Robert E. Wood, Feb. 12, 1941, ibid.; Dennis to A. A. Eastman, Feb. 20, 1941, ibid.

150. "Earlhamites and the War," *Earlhamite,* 62 (April 1941), 16; Annual Report to Yearly Meetings, 1941; Dennis to Ray Nash, Nov. 21, 1941, box 5, Dennis Papers; "Preserve American Democracy," *Earlham Post,* Oct. 3, 1939,

p. 1; "Peace Group to Present Movie in Chapel Wednesday," Dec. 6, 1938, pp. 1, 4; "Peace Group Continues to Extend Work," ibid., Feb. 27, 1940, p. 2.

151. "Jap Hostilities Jolt E. C. Sentiment," *Earlham Post*, Dec. 9, 1941, p. 1; "All College Men Face a Vital Decision," ibid., Jan. 13, 1942, p. 2; "The College Adjusts to War," *Earlhamite*, 63 (April 1942), 7; Faculty Minutes, Jan. 8, 12, March 26, 1942; Dennis to Tollefson, May 6, 1943, box 5, Dennis Papers.

152. "Earlhamites and the Draft," *Earlhamite*, 62 (Jan. 1941), 15; "A Quaker College in War Time," ibid., 64 (Jan. 1943), 3, 13; "Militarists, Pacifists in Warm Debate," *Earlham Post*, Nov. 17, 1942, p. 1; Statement, 1948, Conscientious Objector File, Controversial Issues Collection; Annual Report to Yearly Meetings, 1942, box 6, Dennis Papers; Dennis to Eleanor W. Lippincott, March 11, 1944, box 5, ibid.; *Indianapolis Star* clipping, Aug. 20, 1943, box 6, ibid.

153. Annual Report to Yearly Meetings, 1942; Faculty Minutes, Feb. 8, 1943; Robert N. Huff to Dennis, Feb. 11, 1943, box 5, Dennis Papers.

154. Faculty Minutes, Feb. 8, 15, Sept. 23, 1943; Evans to Dennis, March 2, 1943, box 5, Dennis Papers; Kelsay to Dennis, Sept. 22, 1943, box 5.

155. "Four of College Staff Quit Post," *Earlham Post*, Jan. 21, 1941, pp. 1, 4; "Garner Tells of C. P. S. Camp Work," ibid., May 25, 1943, p. 4; Thomas E. Jones, *Light on the Horizon: The Quaker Pilgrimage of Tom Jones* (Richmond, Ind.: Friends United Press, 1973), 135–50; Wittner, *Rebels against War*, 70–84; Richard C. Anderson, *Peace Was in Their Hearts: Conscientious Objectors in World War II* (Watsonville, Calif.: Correlan Publications, 1994).

156. Faculty Minutes, Nov. 30, 1942, May 31, 1943; Paul Comly French to Pickett, July 1, 1943, box 3, Dennis Papers; Dennis to Edna Ramseyer, Jan. 22, 1943, ibid.; Dennis to Elmore Jackson, Sept. 7, 1943, ibid.; "Earlham Trains for Relief," *Earlhamite*, 64 (July 1943), 6–7; Kenworthy, *Worldview*, 81.

157. The standard account is Roger Daniels, *Concentration Camps, North America; Japanese in the United States and Canada during World War II* (Malabar, Fla.: Krieger, 1981).

158. Thornburg, *Earlham*, 225; "Locals," *Earlhamite*, 19 (March 1892), 99; "Earlhamites in Tokyo Thought To Be Safe," *Earlham Press*, Sept. 17, 1923, p. 1; "Earlham Graduate Is Principal at Tokyo," ibid., Feb. 12, 1923, p. 1; Coppelia Liebenthal, "A Bond War Could Not Break," *Earlhamite*, Spring 1996, pp. 19–20.

159. Faculty Minutes, Feb. 15, 1926; "Wilfred Jones Named," *Quaker Quill*, Jan. 17, 1927, pp. 1, 4; Thornburg, *Earlham*, 296–97. Jones's scrapbook of his stay in Japan is in the Wilfred Jones Collection (Friends Collection). For the Japanese Exclusion Act, see Roger Daniels, *The Politics of Prejudice: The Anti-Japanese Movement in California and the Struggle for Japanese Exclusion* (Berkeley: University of California Press, 1977).

160. Dennis to Floyd W. Schmoe, March 13, 1942, box 6, Dennis Papers; Dennis to Fred G. Wales, July 9, 1945, ibid.; Press Release, Sept. 4, 1942, box 5, ibid.

161. Dennis to Lura Coppock Miles, Oct. 8, 1942, box 5, Dennis Papers; Dennis to Vaughn Wise, Jan. 21, 1943, ibid.; Dennis to Virgil Binford, Aug. 3, 1943, ibid.; Dennis to Laurence Hadley, June 26, 1942, ibid.; Dennis to Donald Garrard, Sept. 10, 1942, ibid.; *Palladium-Item* clipping, April 25, 1943, ibid.

162. Petition, Oct. 1942, box 5, ibid.; Dennis to Allee, Oct. 31, 1942, ibid.; "Memorandum on Nisei Affairs," Oct. 1, 1943, ibid.; *Cincinnati Enquirer*

clipping, Sept. 30, 1942, ibid.; Dennis to Evans, Oct. 1, 1942, box 1, ibid; *Palladium-Item* clipping [ca. April 26, 1942], ibid.

163. Dennis to Gurney Binford, Oct. 1, 1943, box 5, ibid.; Deloris E. Jarress and Eldon Harzman, *History of Quaker Hill Foundation and Conference Center* (Richmond, Ind.: n.p., 1987), 14–47.

164. Lena Hiatt to Murray Kenworthy, Sept. 23, 1943, box 5, Dennis Papers.

165. "Memorandum on Conversation with Raymond Booth," Sept. 28, 1943, box 5, Dennis Papers; Dennis to Allee, Oct. 12, 1943, ibid.; Lena Hiatt letter, clipping, *Richmond Palladium-Item,* Oct. 17, 1943, ibid.; clippings, *Richmond News-Shopper,* Sept. 30, Oct. 7, Nov. 4, 1943, ibid.; Dennis to Isaac E. Woodard, Nov. 3, 1943, ibid.

166. Dennis to *Palladium-Item* Editor, April 27, 1943, box 5, Dennis Papers; Don McCullough to Dennis, [1942], ibid.; Miles to Dennis, Oct. 6, 1942, ibid.; Raymond Snyder and Eltha Thomas to Dennis, Oct. 10, 1942, ibid.; Esther Littler to Dennis, Oct. 16, 1942, ibid.; H. B. Wells to Dennis, Oct. 20, 1942, ibid.; Fremont E. Faubley to Dennis, Sept. 29, 1942, ibid.; "Win the War, or Peace?" *Earlham Post,* April 21, 1942, p. 2; "An Editorial," ibid., Oct. 6, 1942, p. 1; "Newton Wesley," *Earlhamite,* 108 (Summer 1988), 29.

167. Newton K. Uyesugi, "Chapel Talk," Jan. 22, 1943, box 5, Dennis Papers; Dennis to Herman G. Weiskotten, May 14, 1945, ibid.; "Memorandum in Regard to Charles Bishop," Dec. 6, 1944, box 2, ibid.

168. "Is This Democracy?" *Earlham Post,* May 5, 1942, p. 2, "The Gary High School Strike," ibid., Nov. 20, 1945, p. 2; "Inter-Y Lectures Designed to Help Solve Student Problems," ibid., Jan. 25, 1944, p. 1; "Race Relations Forum," ibid., Feb. 22, 1944, p. 1. For African American activism during World War II, see John Morton Blum, *V Was for Victory: Politics and American Culture during World War II* (New York: Harcourt Brace Jovanovich, 1976), 182–220.

169. "Lecturer Views Negro as Citizen," *Earlham Post,* Feb. 15, 1944, p. 1; "William J. Faulkner Earlham Speaker," ibid., Feb. 13, 1945, p. 1; Dennis to Board, Dec. 27, 1943, box 5, Dennis Papers; Dennis to Thomas E. Jones, July 7, 1944, box 6, ibid.; Dennis to Isaac E. Woodard, Sept. 15, 1944, box 6, ibid.

170. George D. Van Dyke to Dennis, April 22, 1943, box 6, Dennis Papers; Dennis to Board; Funston Interview.

171. Dennis to Board; Elbert D. Jones to Dennis, Oct. 19, 1944, box 6, Dennis Papers; Earl E. Estes to Dennis, Dec. 7, 1943, ibid.; Dennis to Estes, Dec. 9, 1943, ibid.; Camilla Flintermann to Dennis, Dec. 10, 1943, ibid.; Dennis to C. B. Mendenhall, Jan. 8, 1944, ibid.

172. Dennis to Board; Dennis to Paul Farlow, Feb. 3, 1944, box 5, Dennis Papers; Ruby Davis to Dennis, Jan. 21, 1944, ibid.; Ruth Farlow Uyesugi, *Don't Cry, Chiisai, Don't Cry* (Paoli, Ind.: Stout's Print Shop, 1977), 68–77.

173. Dennis to Jones, Jan. 17, 1944, box 6, Dennis Papers; Lilith Farlow to Dennis, Dec. 19, 1943, ibid.; Pauline S. McQuinn to Dennis, [Jan. 1944], ibid.; Dennis to Barrett, Jan. 18, 1944, ibid.; Mendenhall to Dennis, Jan. 4, 1944, ibid.

174. Wales to Dennis, Sept. 20, 1945, ibid.; Dennis to Barrett, Jan. 18, 1944, ibid.; Anna Eves to Dennis [ca. 1944], ibid.; Charles J. McCammon to Dennis, June 13, 1943, Reminiscences Collection; Thomas E. and Esther B. Jones, "Friends and Race," *Friends World News* #13 (Summer 1944), unpaged.

175. Thornburg, *Earlham,* 354–55.

176. Dennis to Charles B. Stout, March 18, 1944, box 6, Dennis Papers; Walter L. Johnson Letter, *Earlhamite,* 77 (Winter 1956), 2; Slotten Interview;

Harold and Ann Cope and Laurence and Ruth Strong Interview by Thomas D. Hamm, April 25, 1994, Oral History Collection.

5. The Creation of Modern Earlham, 1946–1958

1. Homer L. Morris to Auretta Thomas, Sept. 9, 1946, box 31, Homer L. and Edna Morris Papers (Friends Collection, Earlham College, Richmond, Ind.).

2. George M. Marsden, *The Soul of the American University: From Protestant Establishment to Established Nonbelief* (New York: Oxford University Press, 1994), 369–404.

3. Presidential Nominating Committee Minutes, 1945, box 5, William C. Dennis Presidential Papers (Friends Collection); Laurence Hadley to Charles Woodman, June 4, 1945, ibid.; Paul Furnas to Morris, July 31, 1945, ibid.

4. "President Jones Coming to Earlham College Rich in Quaker Heritage," *Earlham Post,* Oct. 4, 1946, p. 1. Thomas E. Jones's own account of his life is *Light on the Horizon: The Quaker Pilgrimage of Tom Jones* (Richmond, Ind.: Friends United Press, 1973).

5. Jones, *Light,* 63–110; Morris to Hadley, May 17, 1945, box 32, Morris Papers.

6. Isaac E. Woodard to Woodman, Aug. 26, 1945, box 5, Dennis Papers; Jones, *Light,* 151–52.

7. William M. Fuson to Lewis Hoskins, March 15, 1958, William M. Fuson Papers (Friends Collection); Fuson to "Dear Folks," Dec. 12, 1955, ibid.; William M. Fuson, "Memoirs," typescript, 1993, p. 1 (ibid.); David Telfair Interview by Thomas D. Hamm, May 9, 1995, Oral History Collection (Friends Collection); Harold and Ann Cope and Laurence and Ruth Strong Interview by Thomas D. Hamm, April 25, 1994 (ibid.).

8. Millard S. Markle to Morris, April 5, 1945, box 31, Morris Papers; Morris to Thomas E. Jones, March 15, 1946, ibid.; Jones to Morris, May 10, 1946, ibid.; Morris to Jones, May 1, 1946, W. Perry Kissick Personnel File, Earlham Faculty Collection (Friends Collection); Wildman to Morris, April 21, 1946, ibid.

9. Arthur M. Charles to Jones, March 8, 1946, Arthur M. Charles Personnel File, Earlham Faculty Collection; Dennis to Perry Kissick, March 5, May 30, 1946, Kissick File; Markle to Morris, April 23, 1946, ibid.; Morris to Wildman, May 1, 1946, ibid.; Morris to Jones, May 8, 1946, ibid.; Wildman to Morris, May 11, 1946, ibid.; Jones to Morris, May 18, 1946, ibid.

10. Joe Elmore Interview by Thomas D. Hamm, Feb. 10, 1994, Oral History Collection; *Earlham: Home of Free Men,* brochure [ca. 1947], (Friends Collection).

11. Earlham College Faculty Meeting Minutes, Sept. 18, 1946 (Friends Collection); Jones, *Light,* 160–61; Opal Thornburg, *Earlham: The Story of the College, 1847–1962* (Richmond, Ind.: Earlham College Press, 1963), 374–90.

12. Faculty Minutes, Sept. 14, 1954, Oct. 7, 1957; President's Report, Feb. 12, 1949, box 32, Morris Papers; "First Earlham Alumni Council Meeting," Oct. 1948, ibid.; Morris to Dennis, April 2, 1945, box 5, Dennis Papers; "$300 Spent on Each Student," *Earlham Post,* Jan. 17, 1957, p. 1.

13. "Davis Hired to Finance," *Earlham Post,* Oct. 26, 1954, p. 1; Jones, *Light,* 166–74; Thornburg, *Earlham,* 359–60; D. Elton Trueblood Interview by Thomas D. Hamm, April 20, 1994, Oral History Collection.

14. Faculty Minutes, Jan. 22, 1945; Jones to A. W. Kettler, Nov. 19, 1949, box

3, Thomas E. Jones Presidential Papers (Friends Collection); Jones to Paul F. Mauzy, Dec. 12, 1949, ibid.

15. Diane Ravitch, *The Troubled Crusade: American Education, 1945–1980* (New York: Basic, 1983), 10–15.

16. Jones, *Light*, 151; Thomas E. Jones, "Why I Came to Earlham," *Earlhamite*, 67 (Fall 1946), 2; "Jones, Trueblood, Address Yearly Meetings," ibid., 16; Woodman to Pauline S. McQuinn, July 23, 1945, box 5, Dennis Papers.

17. Jones to John D. Rockefeller, Dec. 30, 1947, box 20, Jones Papers; Jones to Murray C. Johnson, Nov. 21, 1946, box 14, ibid.; "Statement by the President to the Earlham Faculty at Its Meeting on February 14, 1955," box 9, ibid.

18. Jones to Moses Bailey, Feb. 27, 1952, box 3, ibid.; Jones to Rufus M. Jones, Nov. 5, 1946, box 13, ibid.

19. Earlham Faculty Interview by Thomas D. Hamm et al., Feb. 19, 1990, Oral History Collection; Jones to Sylvetta Fellow, July 2, 1953, box 9, Jones Papers; Jones to Caroline Cox, June 28, 1947, box 4, ibid.; Jones to T.T. Frankenburg, n.d., box 8, ibid.

20. "Statement by the President to the Earlham Faculty"; Jones, *Light*, 35; "Convocation Address," Sept. 23, 1948, box 1, Jones Papers; "Quakerism's Contribution to Education," ibid. For Jones's opinion of fundamentalism, see, for example, Jones to William W. Clark, April 4, 1949, box 18, Jones Papers.

21. Jones to Edgar H. Evans, Feb. 2, 1948, box 7, Jones Papers; "Convocation Speech, 1954," box 1, ibid.

22. Jones, *Light*, 17–62; "How Big Is Your God?" 1954, box 1, Jones Papers; Jones to Suzanne Lamb, Feb. 24, 1955, box 15, ibid.

23. Thomas E. Jones letter, *Earlhamite*, 68 (Spring 1947), 2.

24. James R. Newby, *Elton Trueblood: Believer, Teacher, and Friend* (San Francisco: Harper and Row, 1990), 1–77.

25. Elton Trueblood, *While It Is Day: An Autobiography* (New York: Harper and Row, 1974), 52; Dennis to Jones, Feb. 16, 1946, box 5, Dennis Papers; Dennis to Robert L. Kelly, Oct. 13, 1945, Robert L. Kelly Papers (Friends Collection); Dennis to Officers Committee, March 22, July 25, Sept. 19 1945, box 31, Morris Papers; D. Elton Trueblood to Morris, Sept. 27, 1945, ibid.

26. Opal Thornburg to Doris Eddington, July 7, 1950, D. Elton Trueblood Personnel File, Earlham Faculty Collection; D. Elton Trueblood, "Why I Chose a Small College," *Reader's Digest*, 69 (Sept. 1956), 38–42. For memories of Elton Trueblood, see Faculty Interview; Cope and Strong Interview; Earlham Students Interview by Thomas D. Hamm et al., Feb. 15, 1990, Oral History Collection; Wayne C. Booth Interview by Thomas D. Hamm, Jan. 4, 1995, ibid.; and Thomas D. S. Bassett Interview by Thomas D. Hamm, Nov. 15, 1990 (ibid.). For a typical Trueblood speaking schedule, see "New Trueblood Trek for Next Semester Is in the Making," *Earlham Post*, Jan. 20, 1953, p. 1. For Trueblood's involvement in faculty recruiting, see, for example, Jones to Trueblood, April 20, 1946, Trueblood File; Trueblood to Jones, March 24, 1946, Aug. 9, 1948, Aug. 4, 1950, ibid.

27. For American religion in this period, see Sydney E. Ahlstrom, *A Religious History of the American People* (New Haven: Yale University Press, 1972), 949–63; Robert Wuthnow, *The Restructuring of American Religion* (Princeton: Princeton University Press, 1988); and Paul Boyer, *By the Bomb's*

Early Light: American Thought and Culture at the Dawn of the Atomic Age (Chapel Hill: University of North Carolina Press, 1994), 179–240.

28. Elton Trueblood, *The Predicament of Modern Man* (New York: Harper and Row, 1944), 3; D. Elton Trueblood, *A Radical Experiment* (Philadelphia: Philadelphia Yearly Meeting, 1947), 3, 5; Elton Trueblood, *The Life We Prize* (New York: Harper and Row, 1951), 36.

29. Trueblood, *Predicament,* 20–21; D. Elton Trueblood, *Foundations for Reconstruction* (New York: Harper and Row, 1946), 39, 25–26; Trueblood, *Life We Prize,* 18–19; Trueblood, *Predicament,* 18; Elton Trueblood, *Alternative to Futility* (New York: Harper and Row, 1948), 82; Elton Trueblood, "The Idea of a College," *Earlham College Bulletin,* 32 (Dec. 1949), 5–6.

30. Trueblood, *Foundations,* 18; Trueblood, *Life We Prize,* 25; Elton Trueblood, *Declaration of Freedom* (New York: Harper and Row, 1955), 12–15, 21, 120–21.

31. D. Elton Trueblood to Albert Bailey, Jr., Feb. 10, 1947, box 3, Jones Papers; Trueblood, *Alternative,* 85–87.

32. Trueblood, *While It Is Day,* 104–24.

33. Ibid., 59; Newby, *Elton Trueblood,* 100–09, 126–29. For an appreciation of the many roles that Trueblood played at Earlham, see the comments of Hugh Barbour, William Fuson, and Warren Staebler in Earlham Faculty Interview. For the anti-intellectual fears that underlay McCarthyism, see Richard Hofstadter, *Anti-Intellectualism in American Life* (New York: Vintage, 1966), 3–4.

34. Woodard to Dennis, Jan. 28, 1946, box 6, Dennis Papers.

35. Jones to George Scherer, Oct. 14, 1955, box 10, Jones Papers; Lilith M. Farlow to Jones, March 15, 1947, box 9, ibid.; "Questionair [*sic*] on Correlation of College with Meeting," attached to William Q. Hale to Opal Thornburg, Dec. 7, 1948, box 11, ibid.; "Scherer to Do Field Work with Quakers," *Earlhamite,* 75 (Summer 1954), 12; Public Relations Report, Feb. 13, 1951, box 32, Morris Papers.

36. "The Earlham Program," n.d., box 8, Jones Papers; Jones to Robert N. Huff, May 20, 1947, box 12, ibid.; Memorandum of Meeting, May 6, 1955, box 10, ibid.; Jack Kirk to "Dear Friend," July 26, 1957, box 5, ibid.; "Choir to Tour Marion, Kokomo," *Earlham Post,* March 13, 1956, p. 1; "Students Get Key to City Meetinghouse at Webster," ibid., March 28, 1947, p. 1; Glenn Reece, "Progress Report," Jan. 1, 1958, box 2, Landrum Bolling Presidential Papers (Friends Collection).

37. Horace P. Cook to Jones, Jan. 22, 1946, Jan. 8, 1951, box 4, Jones Papers; William J. Reagan to Xen Harvey, Sept. 7, 1951, ibid.; Thornburg to Hugh Barbour, Sept. 18, 1956, box 3, ibid.; Norval Reece to Jones, Jan. 15, 1958, box 2, Bolling Papers.

38. Jones to Woodman, April 4, 1949, box 18, Jones Papers; Trueblood to Jones, Aug. 14, 1956, ibid.; "A Clear Bond between Yearly Meetings, Earlham," *American Friend,* May 5, 1955, p. 138. See also the programs in the "Pastors Conference" file, box 20, Jones Papers.

39. Jones to Carleton B. Edwards, May 24, 1956, box 7, Jones Papers; Jones to Barbour, Sept. 15, 1954, March 23, 1956, box 3, ibid.; Jones to Charles Stubbs, Dec. 1, 1947, box 23, ibid.; "Changes in Faculty Made," *Earlham Post,* March 4, 1949, p. 1; Thomas E. Jones, *Close Proving of All: Quaker Lecture Given at Western Yearly Meeting of Friends, Thursday Evening, August 21, 1958* (N.p., 1958), 8–9.

40. "Pre-Holiday Sunday at Earlham," Dec. 1954, box 5, Jones Papers; Jones to Frank Torrence, March 1, 1948, box 5, ibid.; Jones to David E. Henley, March 3, 1948, box 12, ibid.; Jones to Billy Graham, March 12, 1956, box 10, ibid.; Arthur Little to Thornburg, Feb. 23, 1954, box 15, ibid.

41. Mrs. Gerald C. Frazier to Jones, Nov. 1, 1947, box 9, Jones Papers; Vivian Edmundson to Jones, March 24, 1948, box 7, ibid.; Homer G. Biddlecum to Jones, Oct. 24, 1948, box 3, ibid.; Russell M. Ratliff to Jones, Aug. 25, 1947, box 20, ibid.; Fellow to Jones, July 2, 1953, box 9, ibid.; Jones to Fellow, Aug. 17, 1953, ibid.; William J. Reagan to Jones, Nov. 16, 1953, Race Relations Miscellaneous File, Controversial Issues Collection (Friends Collection).

42. "Meetings Are Given Quaker Student Report," *Earlhamite,* 79 (April 1958), 15; Charles A. Johnson to Mary Ruth Bridges, Aug. 15, 1951, box 14, Jones Papers; Eric G. Curtis to Jones, Sept. 5, 1956, box 5, ibid.; Jones to Barbour, Feb. 19, 1957, box 3, ibid.; Lester C. Haworth to Jones, May 18, 1953, box 11, ibid.; Registrar to President's Office, Aug. 13, 1954, Survey Collection.

43. Morris to Howard S. Mills and Catherine H. Woodward, Nov. 20, 1947, box 31, Morris Papers; Jones, *Light,* 156–60.

44. "Alumni Members of Board," 1947, box 32, Morris Papers; "Memorandum of Meeting on Nov. 8, 1947, of Joint Committee," ibid.; Morris to Jones, July 22, 1947, box 31, ibid.; "Alumni Trustee Representation," *Earlhamite,* 68 (Fall 1947), 11.

45. Morris to Jones, Dec. 13, 1946, March 10, 1947, box 31, Morris Papers; Paul H. Wolf to Jones, June 4, 1947, ibid.; Thornburg, *Earlham,* 359.

46. Jones, *Light,* 159–60; Jones to Morris, Sept. 8, 1950, box 31, Morris Papers; Lester C. Haworth to Lilly Pickett, Aug. 15, 1946, box 11, Jones Papers; Haworth to Jones, Aug. 20, 1946, ibid.; Jones to Haworth, Aug. 17, 1946, ibid.; Howard S. Mills, Sr., Interview by Thomas D. Hamm, April 6, 1990, Oral History Collection.

47. Thornburg, *Earlham,* 359–60; Mills Interview.

48. Booth Interview.

49. Ibid.

50. Charles Chatfield, *The American Peace Movement: Ideals and Activism* (New York: Twayne,1992), 83.

51. Thornburg, *Earlham,* 353.

52. Cope and Strong Interview; Faculty Interview; Little to Jones, [March 1947], box 31, Morris Papers.

53. Booth Interview; Edward Bastian Interview by Thomas D. Hamm, May 20, 1994, Oral History Collection; William K. Stephenson Interview by Thomas D. Hamm, May 23, 1995, ibid.; Jones to Morris, March 12, 1946, box 31, Morris Papers.

54. Trueblood Interview; Trueblood, *While It Is Day,* 54–55; Sara Little Interview by Thomas D. Hamm et al., Feb. 19, 1990, Oral History Collection; Fuson to Bill Clark, Sept. 10, 1950, Fuson Papers.

55. Leonard Holvik Interview by Thomas D. Hamm, Feb. 19, 1990, Oral History Collection; Booth Interview; Joseph D. Coppock Autobiography, typescript, 1983, ch. 17, pp. 9–14, Joseph D. Coppock Personnel File, Earlham Faculty Collection.

56. Kathleen Postle Interview by Thomas D. Hamm, Aug. 15, 1990, Oral History Collection; Norma Bentley Interview by Thomas D. Hamm, May 10, 1995, ibid.; Earlham Women Students Interview by Thomas D. Hamm et al., Feb. 15, 1990, ibid.; Elmore Interview. I found very helpful Erica J. Christian-

son, "The Experience of Women at Earlham College during the Tom Jones Administration," March 16, 1990, Earlham History Collection (Friends Collection). For the national situation, see Barbara Miller Solomon, *In the Company of Educated Women: A History of Women and Higher Education in America* (New Haven: Yale University Press, 1986), 189.

57. "Our Teaching Faculty," *Earlhamite,* 77 (July 1956), 13; Jones to Fuson, May 7, 1947, Fuson Papers; Fuson to Bolling, May 24, 1966, ibid.; Norman Burns and Manning M. Patillo, "Report of a Survey of Earlham College for Lilly Endowment, Inc.," 1956, pp. 3–4, Survey Collection.

58. Booth Interview; Thornburg, *Earlham,* 368–70; "Action Research at Earlham," *Earlhamite,* 68 (Fall 1947), 8–9; "'Human Engineering' at Earlham College Through Community Building," *American Friend,* June 10, 1948, p. 190; "Agricultural Science, Education New Earlham Courses," ibid., June 19, 1952, p. 209; "Earlham Projects Help Communities," *Earlham Post,* May 27, 1949, p. 4; George A. Scherer, *Ernest Atkins Wildman: A Biographical Sketch* (Dublin, Ind.: Prinit Press, 1984), 63–68; William W. Biddle, *The Community Dynamics Experiment: An Interpretation of a Process* (Richmond, Ind.: Earlham College, 1960).

59. Coppock, Autobiography, ch. 17, pp. 16–19; Booth Interview; Bassett Interview; Norman Burns and Manning M. Patillo, Jr., "Report of a Survey of Earlham College for the Lilly Endowment, Inc.," 1951, Survey Collection.

60. Earlham Student Interview, Feb. 15, 1990, Oral History Collection; Faculty Minutes, Sept. 30, 1946; Trueblood, "Idea of a College," 9; John M. Fowler letter, *Earlham Post,* Dec. 10, 1948, p. 2; Dougie Grafflin, "Chapel Speakers—the Limited View," ibid., May 16, 1957, p. 2; Ray Treadway, "Student Attitudes," ibid., April 11, 1957, p. 2; Helen G. Hole letter, April 15, 1954, box 1, Opinion Board Papers (Friends Collection).

61. Earlham College Board of Trustees Minutes, Oct. 4, 1952 (Friends Collection); Cope and Strong Interview; D. Elton Trueblood, *I Remember . . . Stout Meetinghouse* (N.p.: Earlham College, n.d.).

62. Telfair Interview; Bentley Interview; "Meetings Are Given Quaker Student Report," 5.

63. Fuson to William Clark, Sept. 10, 1950, Fuson Papers; Elizabeth Furnas to Merle Davis, n.d., attached to Jones to Elizabeth Furnas, March 23, 1948, box 10, Jones Papers; "History of Clear Creek Monthly Meeting," foreword to Clear Creek Monthly Meeting Minutes, vol. I (Friends Collection). Trueblood later transferred his membership to First Friends in Richmond, where it remained until his death.

64. Errol T. Elliott to Jones, Feb. 11, 1947, box 10, Jones Papers; Jones to Trueblood, Jan. 19, 1948, ibid.; Merle L. Davis to Jones, Feb. 12, 1948, ibid.; Markle to Jones, Feb. 12, 1948, ibid.; Telfair Interview.

65. Wildman to Jones, Sept. 22, 1946, box 1, Jones Papers; Jones to Wildman, Sept. 18, 1946, ibid.; Fuson to Jones, May 1, 1947, Fuson Papers; William Fuson, "A Remonstrance concerning the President's House," May 1950, ibid.

66. C. Wayne Carter Interview by Thomas D. Hamm, Feb. 24, 1995, Oral History Collection; James G. and Helen (Ellis) Johnson Interview by Thomas D. Hamm, Feb. 25, 1995, ibid.; Imogene (Cuffel) Holloway Interview by Thomas D. Hamm, June 24, 1994, ibid.; David E. Henley, *A Quaker Approach to Democracy, Given at Western Yearly Meeting of Friends, Tuesday Evening, August 17, 1948* (N.p., 1948), 3–4, 7, 10, 13; Thomas S. Brown, *The Flaming*

Sword: Given at Western Yearly Meeting of Friends, Tuesday Evening, August 21, 1951 (N.p., 1951); William W. Clark, *The Practice of Jesus: Given at Western Yearly Meeting of Friends, August 19, 1952* (N.p., 1952), 13–15.

67. Jones, *Close Proving of All*, 7; Chester L. Reagan to Jones, Oct., 12, 1946, box 8, Jones Papers; Jones to Jeanette Hadley, n.d., box 11, ibid.; Jones to J. Theodore Peters, Dec. 17, 1947, box 20, ibid.; Jones to David E. Henley, April 11, 1949, box 12, ibid.; William Biddle, "Summary of Jamaica Workshop," box 14, ibid.

68. McQuinn to Woodman, July 22, [1945], box 5, Dennis Papers; Woodman to McQuinn, Aug. 6, 1945, ibid.

69. Robert Goens, Jewell Spears, and Harry Leavell Interview by Thomas D. Hamm et al., Feb. 12, 1990, Oral History Collection; George Sawyer Interview by Thomas D. Hamm, May 2, 1995, ibid.; Carl and Lois (Harned) Jordan Interview by Thomas D. Hamm, May 5, 1994; R. Edd Lee, "Looking Black at Things," *Earlhamite*, 100 (Spring 1979), 2. For this section, I am greatly indebted to Ellen Swain, "Earlham in Transition: Experience of Black Students, 1946–58," Feb. 16, 1990, Earlham History Collection.

70. Elmore Interview; Goens, Leavell, Spears Interview; Sawyer Interview; Jones, *Light*, 119–24, 130–31; Faculty Interview.

71. Jones to Gertrude Bowles, March 2, 1949, box 20, Jones Papers; Jones to Charles Stout, Dec. 31, 1948, ibid.; Jones to Clarence Cunningham, Sept. 7, 1948, ibid.; Goens, Spears, Leavell Interview; R. Edward Lee Interview by Ellen D. Swain, Feb. 7, 1990 (Notes in Swain's possession); D. Elton True- blood, "Plain Speech No. 3," *American Friend*, May 31, 1956, p. 169.

72. Emma Lou Thornbrough, "Breaking Racial Barriers to Public Ac- commodations in Indiana, 1935 to 1963," *Indiana Magazine of History*, 83 (Dec. 1987), 320; A. Leon Higginbotham, *In the Matter of Color: Race and the American Legal System* (New York: Oxford University Press, 1978), vii–viii; Herman B Wells, *Being Lucky: Reminiscences and Reflections* (Bloomington: Indiana University Press, 1980), 214–21.

73. James H. Madison, *The Indiana Way: A State History* (Bloomington: Indiana University Press, 1986), 241–44; Hope Wells Farber, "The Negro Problem in Richmond Today," April 13, 1950, pp. 2–3, 6 (in Hope Farber's possession); Goens, Spears, Leavell Interview; Sawyer Interview.

74. Faculty Meeting Minutes, June 5, 1947; *Richmond Palladium-Item* clipping, June 6, 1947, Clippings Collection (Friends Collection); Robert Cohen, *When the Old Left Was Young: Student Radicals and America's First Mass Student Movement, 1929–1941* (New York: Oxford University Press, 1993), 218.

75. Goens, Spears, Leavell Interview.

76. Faculty Minutes, April 13, 1948; Morris to Jones, Nov. 23, 1948, box 31, Morris Papers; Lester Haworth Statement [1950], Race Relations File, Con- troversial Issues Collection (Friends Collection); "Review of Race Policy at Earlham College," [1950], ibid.; William J. Reagan to Ted Graves, Nov. 16, 1953, ibid.; Jones to Bowles; "Review of Race Policy at Earlham," Dec. 6, 1948, ibid.; Jack Bailey Letter, *Earlham Post*, Feb. 18, 1949, p. 2.

77. Jones to Morris, Sept. 20, 1948, box 31, Morris Papers; Jones to Mary Jane Hindman, April 16, 1947, box 20, Jones Papers; Student Interview; Goens, Spears, Leavell Interview.

78. Administrative Council Minutes, Nov. 2, 1948; Hope Farber Interview by Ellen D. Swain, Feb. 26, 1990 (Notes in Swain's possession); Veronica

Giessler to Jones, Dec. 15, 1948, box 20, Jones Papers; Wilfred Doty to Jones, Jan. 18, 1952, Race Relations File; Robert N. Huff to Edward J. Allen, June 21, 1951, with attachments, ibid.; Charlotte Carter to Jones, May 26, 1951, ibid.; Elsa Carter Littmann Interview by Thomas D. Hamm, Aug. 11, 1995, Oral History Collection.

79. Administrative Council Minutes, April 18, 19, 1952; Robert L. McAllester and Grace Cunningham letter, April 21, 1952, box 1, Opinion Board Papers (Friends Collection); Robert and Grace McAllester to Thomas D. Hamm, Jan. 4, 1996 (in Hamm's possession).

80. Faculty Minutes, April 21, 1952; Board Minutes, May 30, May 31, 1952; Guy W. Jones to Jones, June 2, 1952, Race Relations File. There is a large file of newspaper clippings about the Cunningham-McAllester case in the Race Relations File.

81. Aimee Wildman, "Critic's Corner," *Earlham Post*, Feb. 20, 1951, p. 2; "Student Attitudes on Social Relations of Races at Earlham," 1948, box 31, Morris Papers; Homer A. Jack to Jones, June 8, 1949, Conscientious Objectors File, Controversial Issues Collection; David Frazier letter, April 23, 1952, box 1, Opinion Board Papers; Jerry Hutchens letter, April 20, 1952, ibid.; Gracie Mae Regan letter, ibid.; Austin Wattles letter, ibid.; "Statement on Policy," *Earlhamite*, 73 (Spring 1952), 4; Jones to Trueblood, July 6, 1950, Trueblood Personnel File.

82. Mary James Stratton Interview by Thomas D. Hamm et al., Feb. 15, 1990, Oral History Collection; Glen Bartoo to Jones, Dec. 5, 1953, Race Relations File; Josephine Duveneck to Board, Nov. 28, [1953], ibid.; Herbert L. Wright to Jones, Nov. 27, 1953, ibid.; Jones to Russell Jorgenson, Dec. 4, 1953, ibid.; "Race Discussions Proven to Aid in Better Relations," *Earlham Post*, Jan. 20, 1953, p. 2; "Administration, Students Join Hands," ibid., Nov. 18, 1953, p. 1; "Integration in Dating," ibid., Dec. 13, 1956, p. 1; Harvey Zwick letter, Feb. 26, 1956, box 2, Opinion Board Papers; Elmore Interview.

83. McAllester to Hamm; [Signature Missing] Letter, Feb. 26, 1958, box 2, Opinion Board Papers; Jones to Ted Graves, Nov. 16, 1953, Race Relations File; Hugh Barbour and J. William Frost, *The Quakers* (Westport, Conn.: Greenwood Press, 1988), 241. Emma Lou Thornbrough of Indianapolis shared her memory of the Cunningham-McAllester case with me in February 1990.

84. "Rustin to Speak, Discuss Tour," *Earlham Post*, Nov. 11, 1952, p. 4; "Fisk University Head to Speak at Earlham College," ibid., April 29, 1949, p. 4; "Percy Julian," ibid., Feb. 17, 1953, pp. 1, 4; "Weekend Projects to Be Conducted at Townsend Center," ibid., Oct. 7, 1952, p. 2; Jones to Jorgenson; Jones to William J. Reagan, Nov. 18, 1953, Race Relations File.

85. Henry L. Anderson to Jones, Nov. 7, 1953, Race Relations File; John Sweitzer to Jones, Feb. 1, 1954, ibid.; Paul and Betty Furnas to Max Heirich, April 22, 1958, ibid.; Arthur Little to Jean Weaver, June 8, 1952, ibid.

86. Thornburg, *Earlham*, 362; William L. O'Neill, *American High: The Years of Confidence, 1945–1960* (New York: Free Press, 1986), 10; Helen Lefkowitz Horowitz, *Campus Life: Undergraduate Cultures from the End of the Eighteenth Century to the Present* (Chicago: University of Chicago Press, 1987), 184–85. In this section, I am indebted to Rebecca J. Sedam, "Peace Activism at Earlham, 1946–1958," March 1990, Earlham History Collection.

87. Sawyer Interview; Joseph and Jean (Hamm) Balestrieri Interview by Thomas D. Hamm, April 26, 1994, Oral History Collection.

88. "Jones Letter to Richmond Legion," *Earlhamite*, 70 (Winter 1949), 15; Jordan Interview; Balestrieri Interview; Fred W. Valtin to Jones, May 13,

1948, box 24, Jones Papers; "Now Is the Time," *Earlham Post*, May 7, 1946, p. 2; Jay W. and Louise M. Beede Interview by Thomas D. Hamm, June 6, 1995, Oral History Collection.

89. Zelle Andrews Larson, "An Unbroken Witness: Conscientious Objection to War, 1948–1953" (Ph.D. diss., University of Hawaii, 1975), 37–54; Lawrence S. Wittner, *Rebels against War: The American Peace Movement, 1941–1960* (New York: Columbia University Press, 1969), 162–64.

90. Jones to Morris, Jan. 2, 1948, box 31, Morris Papers; "Advices on Conscription and War," *American Friend*, Aug. 5, 1948, p. 259; "Civil Disobedience?" ibid., Sept. 2, 1948, p. 283. Formed in 1902, Friends General Conference consists of unprogrammed yearly meetings in the Hicksite tradition.

91. "Trouble Bubbles," *Earlhamite*, 70 (Winter 1949), 4; Wittner, *Rebels against War*, 156–57.

92. "Trouble Bubbles," 4–5; Ralph Cook to Jones, Sept. 16, 1948, Conscientious Objectors File; Jones to Ralph Cook, Sept. 22, 1948, ibid.; Ralph Cook letter, [Dec. 1948], ibid.; "There Must Be Grounds," *Earlham Post*, Oct. 8, 1948, p. 2.

93. "Trouble Bubbles," 5; Lorton Heusel Interview by Thomas D. Hamm et al., Jan. 25, 1990, Oral History Collection.

94. Lorton Heusel to Draft Board, Sept. 7, 1948, Conscientious Objectors File; Francis Henderson Trial Transcript, May 31, 1949, ibid.; Stephen W. Simon, "Statement Regarding Registration for the Draft," Sept. 16, 1948, ibid.; Armin L. Saeger, Jr., Statement on Conscription, [1948], ibid.; Richard H. Graves to Jones, Oct. 18, 1948, ibid.; Corona Rayle Cook letters, Feb. 15, March 15, 1949, box 1, Opinion Board Papers.

95. Jones to A. J. Muste, Sept. 30, 1948, Conscientious Objectors File; Jones to Bill and Judy Butterfield, April 9, 1949, ibid.; Opal Thornburg to Guy N. Solt, Nov. 8, 1948, ibid., Thornburg to Larry Garn, Oct. 19, 1948, ibid.; Heusel Interview.

96. "Trouble Bubbles," 4–5.

97. *Richmond News-Shopper* clipping, Nov. 12, 1943, box 5, Dennis Papers; Bernhard Knollenberg to Dennis, May 5, 1943, ibid.; Bastian Interview; Jones, *Light*, 167–68.

98. Rudolph G. Leeds to Jones, March 23, 1949, Conscientious Objectors File. See also the clippings from the *Palladium-Item* in ibid.

99. Robert N. Huff to Executive Committee, April 7, 1949, ibid.; Huff to J. Douglass Foster, March 16, 1949, ibid.; J. F. Hodge to Jones, [Feb. 14, 1949], ibid.; "Veterans of Foreign Wars Ask Violators Be Punished," *Richmond Palladium-Item* clipping, March 6, 1949, ibid.; William L. Cumback letter, Feb. 22, 1949, ibid.; Katherine Stimson letter, Nov. 3, 1950, box 1, Opinion Board Papers; K. D. Myers letter, [1949], ibid.; "Poll Results Announced by Post," *Earlham Post*, March 4, 1949, p. 1; Russell Malcolm, Jr., "Earlham Majority Suffer," ibid., p. 2.

100. Heusel Interview; Clyde Harned letter, clipping, April 19, 1949, Conscientious Objectors File; Carolyn W. Kulka letter, May 4, 1949, box 1, Opinion Board Papers; Nonregistrant Donor List, 1950, Ernest E. Mills Papers (Friends Collection).

101. T. D. S. Bassett, "Recollections," Feb. 1950, Conscientious Objectors File; William Fuson Memorandum, Aug. 3, 1949, ibid.; Faculty Minutes, Feb. 24, 1949.

102. W. C. Allee to Jones, Aug. 3, 1949, Conscientious Objectors File;

Thornburg Memorandum, March 1, 2, 1949, ibid.; William W. Clark, "Concerning the Milton Mayer Address," 1949, ibid.; Fuson Memorandum; "Trouble Bubbles," 18–19.

103. Thornburg Memorandum; Clark, "Concerning Mayer Address"; Fuson Memorandum; Huff to Allee, Aug. 6, 1949, Conscientious Objectors File; "Earlham Shows Poor Judgment," *Richmond Palladium-Item* clipping, March 3, 1949, ibid.; Ed Kaeuper, "Dead Cat Shows Up in Print," ibid., Jan. 21, 1979, ibid.

104. Thornburg, *Earlham,* 400; Jones to Bonner Fellers, March 23, 1949, Conscientious Objectors File; Furnas to Jones, March 16, 1949, ibid.

105. *Dayton Daily News* clipping, March 23, 1949, Conscientious Objectors File.

106. Ibid.; *Indianapolis News* clipping, March 22, 1949, Conscientious Objectors File; Faculty Interview.

107. Jones to Harold Ehrensberger, March 30, 1949, Conscientious Objectors File; *Cincinnati Enquirer* clipping, March 24, 1949, ibid.; Jones to Howard S. and Bernice Mills, March 25, 1949, ibid.; Jones to Howard S. Mills, April 8, 1949, ibid.; Melvin J. Maas to Howard S. Mills, March 19, 1949, ibid.; "Report of the President of Earlham College," June 10, 1949, box 32, Morris Papers.

108. Edwin E. White Interview by Thomas D. Hamm, June 29, 1995, Oral History Collection; C. J. Lapp to Jones, Feb. 16, 1949, Conscientious Objectors File; Thornburg to Jones, May 2, 1949, ibid.; Carl Welty to Jones, May 22, 1949, ibid.; Fuson to Clark, Sept. 10, 1950, Fuson Papers; "Pres. Jones States Speakers Policy," *Earlham Post,* March 11, 1949, p. 4; "2 Year Sentences Given Three COs," ibid., Oct. 25, 1951, p. 1; "Non-Violence Theme of Earlham Peace Institute," ibid., Oct. 12, 1954, p. 1.

109. Marian Sanders to Fuson, [March 1949], Conscientious Objectors File; Milton Mayer, "Earlham's Pickled Cat," *Progressive,* 13 (Aug. 1949), 13–14.

110. See, generally, Ellen W. Schrecker, *No Ivory Tower: McCarthyism and the Universities* (New York: Oxford University Press, 1986). For this section, I am indebted to Robert Micheli, "Earlham College: A Study of Community Relations in the McCarthy Era," March 12, 1990, Earlham History Collection; and Jessica Hedrick, "Earlham and McCarthyism," March 1990, ibid.

111. Schrecker, *No Ivory Tower,* 265–66; Thomas E. Jones, "The Problem of Subversives in American Colleges," n.d., box 1, Jones Papers.

112. Ralph R. Teetor to Jones, May 24, 1950, box 31, Morris Papers; Jones, *Light,* 157–58.

113. Board Minutes, Feb. 10, 1951.

114. "Discussion of Board Members concerning Earlham's Relation to the National Emergency," Aug. 12, 1950, box 1, Jones Papers.

115. Morris to Jones, Sept. 26, 1950, box 31, Morris Papers; Jones to Morris, Sept. 28, 1950, ibid.; "Crusade for Freedom Radio Address," Sept. 27, 1950, box 5, Jones Papers.

116. Faculty Minutes, Oct. 16, 1950; "About the Cover Picture," *Earlhamite,* 71 (Summer 1950), 2; Michael Deutsch letter, Oct. 21, 1950, box 1, Opinion Board Papers; Fuson to Clark; Little to Jones, Oct. 19, 1950, box 24, Jones Papers; Norma Bentley to Dean and Faculty, Oct. 16, 1950, ibid.; Bolling to Jones, Oct. 28, 1950, ibid.

117. Morris to Charles F. MacLennan, Jan. 17, 1951, box 24, Jones Papers; Jones to Haworth, Jan. 23, 1951, ibid.; Dennis to Jones, Feb. 3, 1951, ibid.; Yuan Tien to Thomas R. Fisher, Dec.8, 1950, ibid.; Bassett Interview; Tien to Thomas D. Hamm, Jan. 2, 1996 (in Hamm's possession).

118. Jones to Morris, Jan. 2, 1951, box 31, Morris Papers; *Richmond Palladium-Item* clippings, 1950–1951, box 24, Jones Papers; Jones to Richard Newby, Jan. 29, 1951, ibid.; George Mohlenhoff to Jones, Jan. 31, 1951, ibid.; Hanes W. Butterfield to Tien, Feb. 1, 1951, ibid.; Bassett Interview; Tien to Hamm.

119. Jones to Newby; J. Arthur Funston to Jones, Jan. 31, 1951, box 24, Jones Papers; Ralph Davidson to William Rahill, July 15, 1951, ibid.; Jones to Winifred Peery, Nov. 7, 1951, ibid.; Rahill to Jones, Oct. 26, 1951, March 26, 1953, ibid.; Jones to Allen C. Duvaney, Nov. 13, 1951, ibid.; Jordan Interview; MacLennan to Jones, Dec. 27, 1950, box 31, Morris Papers; Tien to Hamm. For a more critical interpretation of this incident, see Dale Rich Sorenson, "The Anticommunist Consensus in Indiana, 1945–1958" (Ph.D. diss., Indiana University, 1980), 136–59.

120. Howard E. Kershner to Trueblood, May 19, 1954, box 36, Howard E. Kershner Papers (Manuscripts Department, University of Oregon Library, Eugene, Ore.); Trueblood to Kershner, May 19, 1954, ibid.; Newby, *Elton Trueblood,* 102; Arnold Foster and Benjamin R. Epstein, *Danger on the Right* (New York: Random House, 1964), 100–14.

121. On the right in these years, especially the role played by ex leftists, see John P. Diggins, *Up from Communism: Conservative Odysseys in American Intellectual History* (New York: Harper and Row, 1975).

122. Faculty Interview; Telfair Interview; E. Merrill Root to Myriam Page, Aug. 8, 1967, box 1, E. Merrill Root Papers (Manuscripts Department, University of Oregon Library).

123. Schrecker, *No Ivory Tower,* 84–125.

124. E. Merrill Root Letter, *New York Times,* Feb. 28, 1949.

125. Edward A. Rumely to Root, March 12, 1949, E. Merrill Root Personnel File, Earlham Faculty Collection; Jones to Root, March 21, 1949, ibid.; Morris to Root, April 6, 1949, ibid.; Root to Morris, April 11, 1949, ibid.

126. E. Merrill Root, "Darkness at Noon in American Colleges," *Human Events,* July 30, 1952, pp. 275–79.

127. E. Merrill Root, "The Passive Professional Majority," ibid., Oct. 29, 1952, pp. 385–91; Root to Edmund A. Opitz, Sept. 9, 1953, box 1, Edmund A. Opitz Papers (Manuscripts Department, University of Oregon Library); Opitz to Root, Sept. 15, 1953, July 18, 1954, ibid.; Root to Mrs. M. Conan, Sept. 14, 1953, Root Personnel File; Root to Jones, June 1, 1954, ibid.; *Richmond Palladium-Item* clipping, Oct. 16, 1952, ibid.; Karl E. Mundt to Root, Nov. 28, 1952, box 1, Root Papers; William F. Buckley, Jr., to Root, Jan. 15, 1953, ibid.; Max Eastman to Root, Feb. 9, 1953, ibid.

128. Thornburg to Paul Furnas, [ca. June 2, 1953], Root Personnel File; Thornburg to Jones, June 4, 1953, ibid.; Jones to Henley, Nov. 28, 1955, ibid.; Jones to Root, June 11, 1953, box 1, Root Papers; Jack Nelson and Gene Roberts, Jr., "The Successes, Setbacks of Merrill Root, a Book Vigilante," *Chicago Sun-Times,* April 28, 1963; E. Merrill Root, *Collectivism on the Campus: The Battle for the Mind in American Colleges* (New York: Devin-Adair, 1955); E. Merrill Root, *Brainwashing in the High Schools: An Examination of Eleven American History Textbooks* (New York: Devin-Adair, 1958).

129. Nelson and Roberts, "Successes, Setbacks"; Root to Opitz, Oct. 26, 1955, box 1, Opitz Papers; Root to Kershner, Feb. 12, 1956, box 36, Kershner Papers.

130. Francis H. Horn to Jones, Dec. 5, 1952, Root Personnel File; Arthur G. Coons to Jones, Oct. 20, 1952, ibid.; Errol T. Elliott to Jones, May 19, 1953,

ibid.; Glenn and Carolyn Mallison to Jones, Nov. 19, 1953, ibid.; Root to Jones, Dec. 15, 1956, ibid.; Rachel T. Brown to Helen Johnson Garside, May 1, 1957, ibid.; Root to Kershner, May 16, 1954, box 36, Kershner Papers; William Fuson letter, May 6, 1953, box 1, Opinion Board Papers; Tom Brown letter, May 16, 1953, ibid.; Conrad Joyner letter, April 15, 1953, ibid.; Ross Smith letter, ibid.; E. Merrill Root letter, *Earlham Post*, May 19, 1956, p. 2; Trueblood Interview.

131. Jones to Coons, Oct. 27, 1952, Root Personnel File; Jones to Horn, Dec. 8, 1952, ibid.; Jones to John Swomley, April 13, 1953, ibid.; Jones to Root, Dec. 20, 1956, ibid.; Jones to Henley, July 25, 1956, ibid.; Bolling to Ralph C. Johnson, Nov. 18, 1958, ibid.; Bolling to Mrs. Alexander C. Brown, March 14, 1957, ibid.; Jones to Elliott, June 11, 1953, box 1, Root Papers.

132. Root to Kershner, Sept. 27, Dec. 9, 1955, box 15, Kershner Papers; *Richmond Palladium-Item* clipping, Oct. 16, 1952; Fuson to Root, Nov. 15, 1958, box 1, Root Papers; Booth to Bolling, Oct. 13, 1958, box 8, Bolling Papers; Faculty Interview.

133. Root to Kershner, Sept. 17, 1955, Jan. 5, 1957, box 15, Kershner Papers.

134. Bassett Interview; Jones to Stephen and Barbara Allee Angell, Aug. 12, 1949, Conscientious Objectors File.

135. Thomas D. Jones, *A Cross Between a Quaker Meetinghouse and a Scientific Laboratory* (n.p., 1946).

136. Thornburg, *Earlham*, 364–65.

137. See Aaron Parker, "Faculty Governance at Earlham College, 1917–1955," 1991 (Friends Collection); and Burns and Patillo, "Report," 1951, pp. 6–7.

138. Parker, "Faculty Governance"; Sorenson, "Anticommunist Consensus," 75–79. William Fuson shared his memories of the founding of the Earlham AAUP chapter with me in a conversation on June 23, 1995.

139. Parker, "Faculty Governance"; Board Minutes, Feb. 7–8, 1955.

140. Bentley Interview; Telfair Interview; Parker, "Faculty Governance." For an influential Earlham faculty member's view of the problem of "sense of the meeting," see Helen G. Hole, *Things Civil and Useful: A Personal View of Quaker Education* (Richmond, Ind.: Friends United Press, 1978), 91–117.

141. Parker, "Faculty Governance"; Cope and Strong Interview; Bentley Interview; Fuson Conversation.

142. "Earlham College Management Self-Study," 1956, pp. 4–10, 32, 34–37 (Friends Collection).

143. Ibid., 23–24; Jones, *Light*, 191.

144. Fuson to "Dear Folks," Dec. 12, 1955, Fuson Papers; Faculty Minutes, Nov. 14, 1955; Cope and Strong Interview.

145. "We're Losing Something," *Earlham Post*, Dec. 19, 1957, p. 2; Horowitz, *Campus Life*, 187, 220.

146. Student Interview; "Hell Night," *Earlham Post*, Oct. 25, 1951, p. 2; Millard Hunt, "Notes and Comments," ibid., March 31, 1951, p. 2; "Precedents and Hell Night Get Going Over in Senate," ibid., Oct. 31, 1951, pp. 1, 4; "Homecoming Traditions Not What They Used to Be," ibid., Oct. 24, 1957, p. 1.

147. "Senate Grown Since '44," *Earlham Post*, May 19, 1961, p. 6; Earlham College Senate Constitution, Sept. 1947, Senate Miscellaneous Papers (Friends Collection); Jones to Edward J. Allen, Feb. 7, 1950, ibid.; Burns and Patillo, "Report," 1951, pp. 12–13.

148. Faculty Minutes, Sept. 30, Dec. 6, Dec. 13, 1948; "The Honor Code of Earlham College," 1948, Senate Miscellaneous Papers; "Senate Enjoys In-

creased Authority," *Earlham Post,* Oct. 8, 1948, pp. 1, 4; Elton Trueblood, "The Meaning of Honor," ibid., Nov. 21, 1950, p. 2.

149. See the various constitutions in Senate Miscellaneous Papers. For honor systems nationwide, see Frederick Rudolph, *The American College and University: A History* (Athens: University of Georgia Press, 1990), 369–71. For Quakers and "honor," see Bertram Wyatt-Brown, *Southern Honor: Ethics and Behavior in the Old South* (New York: Oxford University Press, 1982), 75–78.

150. Jones to Allen; William Fuson, "The Honor Code—A Jeremiad," April 1957, Fuson Papers; Don Stanley letter, April 19, 1949, box 1, Opinion Board Papers; Donald Bowman letter, May 20, 1957, box 2, ibid.; Millard Hunt, "Notes and Comment," *Earlham Post,* Oct. 17, 1951, p. 2; Ted Graves, "Diverse Opinions Voiced Concerning Chapel Attendance," ibid., March 17, 1953, p. 2; "Honor System Is Not Supported," ibid., Feb. 14, 1957, p. 1; "Earlham Senate," ibid., April 17, 1951, p. 2; "New Poll Reveals Much Student Apathy on Senate," ibid., March 7, 1957, p. 1; Faculty Minutes, May 17, 1957.

151. "Too Many Onlookers," *Earlham Post,* Nov. 14, 1957, p. 2; Wayne Booth letter, Dec. 15, 1957, box 2, Opinion Board Papers. Booth's letter was the prelude to a memorable practical joke. See Thornburg, *Earlham,* 397.

152. Kitty Lambert, "Too Many Rules," *Earlham Post,* March 21, 1957, p. 3; Trueblood, "Idea of a College," 7; Trueblood to Jones, Jan. 3, 1951, Trueblood Personnel File; Faculty Minutes, May 27, 1947, Jan. 17, 1955.

153. James H. Richards, Jr., to Jones, April 6, 1950, box 31, Morris Papers; Mira Lindenmaier and Claire Zinn letter, Oct. 1957, box 2, Opinion Board Papers; D. Elton Trueblood, "Plain Speech, No. 2," *American Friend,* May 17, 1956, p. 146.

6. "The Sixties," 1958–1973

1. We still lack a definitive account of how higher education changed in the 1960s. There are provocative chapters in Helen Lefkowitz Horowitz, *Campus Life: Undergraduate Cultures from the End of the Eighteenth Century to the Present* (Chicago: University of Chicago Press, 1987), 220–44; and Diane Ravitch, *The Troubled Crusade: American Education, 1945–1980* (New York: Basic, 1983), 182–227. For an excellent study of a critical institution, see W. J. Rorabaugh, *Berkeley at War: The 1960s* (New York: Oxford University Press, 1989).

2. Frederick Rudolph, *Curriculum: A History of the American Undergraduate Course of Study since 1636* (San Francisco: Jossey-Bass, 1977), 270–74.

3. David P. Chalmers, *And the Crooked Places Made Straight: The Struggle for Social Change in the 1960s* (Baltimore: Johns Hopkins University Press, 1991), 68–87.

4. Biographical sketch in Landrum Bolling File, Earlham Presidential Miscellany (Friends Collection, Earlham College, Richmond, Ind.); D. Elton Trueblood Interview by Thomas D. Hamm, April 20, 1994, Oral History Collection (ibid.); Landrum R. Bolling to Argus Tresidder, Jan. 3, 1970, box 38, Landrum Bolling Presidential Papers (ibid.).

5. R. Dwight Young Interview by Thomas D. Hamm, May 16, 1995, Oral History Collection; Earlham College Board of Trustees Minutes, Sept. 10, 1957 (Friends Collection); William Fuson to Lewis Hoskins, March 15, 1958, William Fuson Papers (ibid.); Opal Thornburg, *Earlham: The Story of the*

College, 1847–1962 (Richmond, Ind.: Earlham College Press, 1963), 404–05; Bolling to Thomas D. Hamm, Jan. 7, 1996 (in Hamm's possession).

6. Fuson to Bolling et al., Jan. 7, 1968, Fuson Papers; William Fuson Memoirs, 1993, p. 4 (ibid.); Thornburg, Birch Bayh to Bolling, March 13, 1968, box 34, Bolling Papers; Bolling to Charles H. Harker, Oct. 4, 1968, ibid.; Bolling to Archibald Cox, Sept. 20, Oct. 13, 1960, box 8, ibid.; Arthur Settle to Bolling, Feb. 5, 1961, box 12, ibid.; Bolling to Charles Van Doren, Nov. 4, 1959, box 5, ibid.; Wayne C. Booth Interview by Thomas D. Hamm, Jan. 4, 1995, Oral History Collection; Thornburg, *Earlham*, 407; Margaret Grant Beidler, "Landrum Bolling: An Appreciation," *Earlhamite*, 94 (Winter 1973), 2.

7. Booth Interview; Joe Elmore Interview by Thomas D. Hamm, Feb. 10, 1994, Oral History Collection; Fuson to Bill Simkin, May 22, 1970, Fuson Papers.

8. Fuson Memoirs, 4, 9; Thornburg, *Earlham*, 404–05; David E. Henley to R. Dwight Young, June 1. 1959, David E. Henley Personnel File, Earlham Faculty Collection (Friends Collection). For administrative appointments, see, generally, *Alumni Directory of Earlham College, 1976* (Braintree, Mass.: Semline, 1976).

9. Elmore Interview; Paul Kortepeter, "Joe Elmore," *Earlham Post*, Nov. 13, 1980, p. 1.

10. Bolling to Hamm.

11. Elmore Interview.

12. Elmore Interview; Jerry Woolpy Interview by Thomas D. Hamm, Feb. 22, 1995 (Oral History Collection); Laurence and Ruth Strong and Harold and Ann Cope Interview by Thomas D. Hamm, April 28, 1994, Oral History Collection; Brooks Egerton, "Black Histories at Earlham," *Earlham Post*, Feb. 5, 1981, p. 1.

13. Board Minutes, Feb. 13–14, 1959; Elmore Interview; Margaret Lacey Interview by Thomas D. Hamm et al., Oct.26, 1993, Oral History Collection.

14. John E. Owen, "Entering Freshman Class Confirms Concern for Individuals," *Earlhamite*, 85 (Oct. 1964), 4; "Geographic Survey," ibid., 86 (Jan. 1965), 32; "Freshman Students Come from 29 States," ibid., 80 (Oct. 1959), 3; "Report of the Survey Committee," Jan. 30, 1947, box 3, Ernest A. Wildman Papers (Friends Collection); "Earlham's Entering Freshmen," Jan. 1972, Student Collection (ibid.).

15. Donald McKinney to Howard Mills, Oct. 29, 1962, box 15, Bolling Papers; Bolling to William B. Crist, May 31, 1961, box 11, ibid.; Edward G. Wilson to Hugh Ronald, Dec. 12, 1967, box 35, ibid.; "Quaker Students: Admissions and Financial Aid," n.d., box 6, ibid.; "Admissions Enlarge Recruiting Program in South and West," *Earlham Post*, Oct. 3, 1963, p. 1.

16. Bolling to Mrs. Clarence Gennett, March 20, 1961, box 11, Bolling Papers; Bolling to J. Victor Guthrie, June 28, 1961, ibid.; Landrum Bolling, "Who to Admit Problem for Earlham," *Earlham Post*, May 19, 1961, p. 1.

17. Fuson Memorandum, [1961], box 11, Bolling Papers; Philip R. Marshall to Bolling, Oct. 20, 1959, box 5, ibid.; Carroll Kenworthy to Bolling, June 11, 1960, box 8, ibid.; "Bolling Asks Re-Examination," *Earlham Post*, Sept. 30, 1965, p. 1; William Cadbury, "Earlham College," 1967, Joe Elmore Papers (Friends Collection); O. Theodor Benfey Interview by James J. Bohning, May 24, June 5, 1991, transcript, p. 54, Oral History Collection.

18. "Earlham Fact Book," 1979, Earlham Publications Collection (Friends Collection); John E. Owen, "Who Can Afford to Attend Earlham?" *Earlhamite*, 89 (Summer 1968), 10–11; Bolling to Hamm.

19. "Ford Foundation Grant," *Earlhamite*, 94 (Summer 1973), 33; "The Ford Matching Gift Continues to Challenge Alumni," ibid., 85 (Oct. 1964), 13; "Ford Donates $275,000 for Non-Western Studies," *Earlham Post*, April 19, 1962, p. 1; Amos Gregory to Bolling, May 24, 1960, box 8, Bolling Papers; Len Clark Interview by Thomas D. Hamm, Aug. 16, 1995, Oral History Collection.

20. See, generally, James H. Madison, *Eli Lilly: A Life, 1885–1977* (Indianapolis: Indiana Historical Society, 1989).

21. Ibid.,178, 209, 212–13; Trueblood Interview.

22. Madison, *Eli Lilly*, 190, 219.

23. Ibid., 172–77.

24. Ibid., 177–79; William K. Stephenson Interview by Thomas D. Hamm, May 23, 1995, Oral History Collection.

25. Madison, *Eli Lilly*, 179–82.

26. Ibid., 266; Earlham College Board of Trustees Minutes, June 7–8, 1973 (Friends Collection).

27. "Trustees OK Tuition Hike," *Earlham Post*, Oct. 20, 1970, p. 1; Bolling Interview.

28. John Sweitzer to Bolling et al., Sept. 12, 1964, box 23, Bolling Papers; William C. Dennis to Bolling, Sept. 24, 1959, box 2, ibid.

29. Edward Bastian Interview by Thomas D. Hamm, May 20, 1994, Oral History Collection; Benfey Interview, 29; "Intern View of Earlham: Contentions for the College," 1972, Student Development Collection (Friends Collection).

30. Booth Interview; Stephenson Interview; Earlham College Faculty Meeting Minutes, Jan. 22, 1959 (Friends Collection); Beidler, "Landrum Bolling," 3.

31. Thornburg, *Earlham*, 412–13.

32. Jackson Bailey, "The Twain Shall Meet," *Earlhamite*, 94 (Summer 1973), 2.

33. Ibid.; Stephenson Interview.

34. Bailey, "Twain Shall Meet," 2–3.

35. Ibid.

36. Ibid., 3–5; "Earlham and Antioch Professors Spend Summer in Japan," *Earlhamite*, 83 (Oct. 1962), 8.

37. Bailey, "Twain Shall Meet," 3, 6.

38. Ibid. Bailey shared a number of memories with me in a telephone conversation Dec. 12, 1995.

39. Fuson Memoirs, 11, 16.

40. Ibid.; Bolling to O. P. Kretzmann, March 31, 1961, box 11, Bolling Papers; Thornburg, *Earlham*, 423–24.

41. Bastian Interview; Strong and Cope Interview; "Earlham College Must Lead," *Earlham Post*, May 21, 1964, p. 2; "Earlham College, 11 Other Colleges Form Cooperative," ibid., April 20, 1961, p. 1.

42. Mary James, "Edinburgh Returnee Relates Experience," *Earlham Post*, Oct. 6, 1953, pp. 1, 4; *Earlham College Catalog, 1963–1965*, p. 21; "Foreign Study Program Has Increasing Impact," *Earlhamite*, 82 (Jan. 1961), 3; Mary Lane Charles, "Students Return from a Semester Abroad Full of Enthusiasm," ibid., 78 (April 1957), 8, 11; Faculty Minutes, March 5, 1956; Mary Lane Hiatt Interview by Thomas D. Hamm, April 20, 1994, Oral History Collection.

43. For this section I have drawn largely on Amity Wood, "Forging Ahead: Off-Campus Study at Earlham," Nov. 22, 1993, Earlham History Collection (Friends Collection).

44. Hiatt Interview; Paul Lacey Interview by Thomas D. Hamm et al., Oct. 14, 1993, Oral History Collection. Jackson Bailey elaborated on several of these points in a telephone conversation, Dec. 12, 1995.

45. Lewis M. Hoskins to Foreign Study Committee, Dec. 1961, box 11, Bolling Papers; Wood, "Forging Ahead," 13–14; Lacey Interview.

46. *Earlham College Catalog, 1963–1965*, p. 28.

47. Carolyn Wilbur, "Earlhamite in Japan on ICU Program," *Earlham Post*, Jan. 19, 1961, p. 3; "Earlhamite Incarcerated in Mexico," ibid., Jan. 9, 1964, p. 4; Allen Hole to Foreign Study Committee, 1961, box 11, Bolling Papers; Off-Campus Study Proposal, 1958, ibid.; Wayne Booth, "Report on First 'Term in London,'" Sept. 23, 1961, ibid.

48. Henry Merrill, "Wilderness in the Groves of Academe," ibid., 97 (Autumn 1976), 3–5; "Wilderness, Television Preterms Draw Fifty," *Earlham Post*, Sept. 28, 1971, p. 6; Margaret Lechner and Ben Foster, "Proposal for a Term-Long Wilderness Program," Dec. 1972, Curricular Policy Committee Papers (Friends Collection).

49. Thornburg, *Earlham*, 429.

50. "Earlham College Management Self-Study," 1956, p. 141 (Friends Collection). This section is based, in addition to the sources cited, on my conversations and work since 1987 with Evan Farber and Philip Shore as part of the library staff.

51. Strong and Cope Interview.

52. Information supplied by Evan Farber.

53. Thomas J. Cottle, "A Learning Place Called Earlham," *Change*, 3 (Jan.-Feb. 1971), 55; Evan Ira Farber, "Earlham's 'Considerate' Library," *Library Journal*, 88 (Dec. 1, 1963), 4561–64; Evan Ira Farber, "The Senior Art Purchase Prize," *College and Undergraduate Libraries*, 1 (1994), 23–28.

54. Evan Farber, "The Heart of Earlham: Ten Years of Life with Lilly Library," *Earlhamite*, 95 (Winter 1974), 4–5; Evan I. Farber, "Library Instruction at Earlham College," *Library Research Newsletter*, 6 (Winter and Spring 1981), 35–48.

55. Farber, "Heart of Earlham," 4–5.

56. Rudolph, *Curriculum*, 270–74.

57. Thornburg, *Earlham*, 417. Several veteran faculty have shared impressions of the Reading Program with me.

58. "A Report on Program II," *Earlhamite*, 88 (Fall 1967), 30; Clark Interview.

59. Ernest A. Wildman, "A Proposal for a Curricular Reorganization of Earlham College," Feb. 1936, box 32, Homer and Edna Morris Papers (Friends Collection); Andy Weiser, "Educational Excellence Relative," *Earlham Post*, Dec. 1, 1970, p. 12; "New System Ends Grades," ibid., Sept. 29, 1970, p. 2; Kathy Strasburgh, "Pass/Fall Relaxes Classroom, Eliminates Competition," ibid., Jan. 21, 1969, p. 6; Faculty Minutes, Oct. 9, 1967.

60. "New Grading System Evaluated," *Earlham Post*, May 25, 1971, p. 3; Sally Weeks, "New Grades Undergo Evaluation," ibid., Jan. 26, 1971, p. 1; Faculty Minutes, March 7, 1972; Stephenson Interview.

61. David Wiggins, "Earlhamites Discuss Interdisciplinary Education," *Earlham Post*, Feb. 6, 1973, p. 6; "Program to Improve Education," ibid., Oct. 12, 1971, pp. 3, 5; "PIE Debuts with 'Women and Men,'" ibid., Oct. 3, 1972, p. 8; Beverly Mills, "PIE Has Not Been a Piece of Cake," ibid., May 14, 1974, p. 2; Clark Interview.

62. Clark Interview; Benfey Interview, 54–60; Thornburg, *Earlham*, 420.

63. Susan Porter Rose Interview by Thomas D. Hamm, April 26, 1994, Oral History Collection; Carol Watkins to Gloria Watkins, Oct. 1960, Student Letters Collection (Friends Collection).

64. The articles are, respectively, in *Earlhamite*, 79 (Oct. 1958), 7; ibid., 82 (April 1961), 10; *Earlham Post*, May 13, 1964, p. 1. See also "Reputation Questioned," ibid., Feb. 19, 1959, p. 2.

65. Ed Dolan Letter, March 2, 1961, box 3, Opinion Board Papers (Friends Collection); "Earlham Goals Conflict, Say Pressure Protesters," *Earlham Post*, Jan. 24, 1967, p. 2; George Sawyer, "Tidewaters of Community Receding," ibid., Oct. 3, 1972, p. 3.

66. Booth Interview.

67. Bolling to Phil Ballard, Feb. 16, 1961, Race Relations File, Controversial Issues Collection (Friends Collection); "The Negro at Earlham," *Earlham Post*, May 13, 1965, p. 2; "Curtis Presents Dating Decision," ibid., April 26, 1962, p. 1; "Senate Approves Interracial Dating Policy," ibid., May 10, 1962, p. 1.

68. Dave Feintuch, "Speaking Out," *Earlham Post*, Sept. 26, 1963, p. 3; Richard Berliner, "Local Restaurant Refuses Service to Negroes," ibid., Feb. 17, 1966, p. 1; "Civil Rights Group Plans Local Effort," ibid., Oct. 12, 1961, p. 4; Tom Wilson Letter, Feb. 13, 1959, box 2, Opinion Board Papers.

69. Jim Breiling, "Segregation Issues Sweep E. C., Country," *Earlham Post*, April 14, 1960, p. 1; Jim Breiling, "Richmond Stores Picketed Again," ibid., April 21, 1960, pp. 1, 4; Booth Interview; Taylor Branch, *Parting the Waters: America in the King Years, 1954–63* (New York: Simon & Schuster, 1988), 272–311.

70. Bolling to Frank Drake, April 12, 1960, box 8, Bolling Papers; Jan Kem Letter, April 12, 1960, box 2, Opinion Board Papers; Malinda McCain Letter, March 21, 1960, ibid.; Larry Schunpert Letter, April 12, 1960, ibid.; Booth Interview.

71. Sally Buckley, "Townsend Dares Help," *Earlham Post*, Oct. 22, 1908, p. 10.

72. "Martin L. King to Speak Thursday," ibid., April 16, 1950, p. 1; "EERC Freedom Sing Financially Successful," ibid., Oct. 10, 1963, p. 3; Pete Klein, "Earlham Students Join in Local Social Action," ibid., May 4, 1961, p. 2; "Conference on Civil Rights Needs Friends," ibid., Jan. 21, 1965, p. 1; "Tougaloo Exchange Report," ibid., Feb. 18, 1963, pp. 2, 3; "Bevel Challenges 'Sickness,'" ibid., Oct. 31, 1963, p. 1; "Sit-In Leader to Speak at Friday Tea," ibid., Jan. 18, 1962, p. 3; "Civil Rights Bill Threat to All, Wallace Says," ibid., April 23, 1964, p. 1; Warren Staebler, "Earlham Plans Wide Range of Social Action," ibid., Nov. 19, 1964, p. 2; "A Call for Help," 1961, box 2, Opinion Board Papers; Ronald Wesner Letter, Oct. 2, 1958, ibid. See also, generally, Branch, *Parting the Waters*.

73. "Earlham College Students Join Civil Rights Drive," *Earlham Post*, Sept. 26, 1963, p. 1; "Ghetto Work Aids Insight," ibid., Oct. 8, 1968, p. 1; Mary White, "E.C. Students to Join Chicago Slum Project," ibid., April 21, 1966, pp. 1, 5; John Stevenson to Joe Elmore, Aug. 4, [1964], box 4, Elmore Papers; Seth Cagin and Philip Dray, *We Are Not Afraid: The Story of Goodman, Schwerner, and Chaney and the Civil Rights Campaign for Mississippi* (New York: Macmillan, 1988), 234–35, 410. I am grateful to my colleague Carol Hunter for drawing my attention to the last citation.

74. Bolling to Earl J. McGrath, May 7, 1964, box 22, Bolling Papers; Bolling to Will Erwin, July 31, 1963, box 17, ibid.; Nash Basom to Bolling, June 19, 1964, box 21, ibid.; Ruth Hatcher, "Upward Bound Means Change," *Earlhamite*, 91 (Fall 1970), 9–12.

75. "Upward Bound to Hit Earlham Campus," *Earlham Post*, Nov. 11, 1965,

p. 1; "Upward Bound Draws New $87,000 Allocation," ibid., April 21, 1966, p. 1; "What Is This Upward Bound?" *Earlhamite,* 88 (July 1967), 16–17; Hatcher, "Upward Bound."

76. Bolling to Vernon A. Eagle, Sept. 3, 1969, box 38, Bolling Papers; Bolling to Eleanor H. Robinson, Dec. 4, 1971, ibid.

77. Sybil Jordan Stevenson, "From Little Rock to Earlham," *Earlhamite,* 100 (Spring 1979), 5–6; Gwen Weaver Interview by Thomas D. Hamm, June 28, 1995, Oral History Collection.

78. Egerton, "Black Histories at Earlham"; Bolling to Robinson; Kathy Phelps, "College Encounters Difficulties in Recruiting Minorities," *Earlham Post,* April 25, 1972, p. 5; "Department Head Resigns," ibid., Sept. 29, 1970, p. 3.

79. Bill Marable, "Students 'Feel' Black Culture," *Earlham Post,* Nov. 5, 1968, p. 5; Faculty Minutes, Feb. 3, 1965; Peter Novick, *That Noble Dream: The "Objectivity Question" and the American Historical Profession* (New York: Cambridge University Press, 1988), 472–91.

80. "Black Studies Plan Stirs Debate," *Earlham Post,* May 6, 1969, p. 1; Faculty Minutes, May 1, May 6, 1969.

81. "Black History Enrollment Small," *Earlham Post,* April 13, 1971, p. 2; "New Black Studies Plan Needs $7,000 from Earlham," ibid., May 27, 1969, p. 2; Bolling to Vernon A. Eagle, Sept. 24, 1969, box 38, Bolling Papers.

82. Kitty Waring, "Problems Plague Urban Studies," *Earlham Post,* Nov. 16, 1971, p. 1; Melvin Cox, "The Race Problem," ibid., Oct. 21, 1976, p. 4.

83. "Negro at Earlham."

84. Barb Howarth, "Racial Gap at Earlham Produces Tension," *Earlham Post,* Feb. 25, 1969, p. 5; Mark Schlotterbeck, "Support Program Over-burdened," ibid., May 9, 1972, p. 5; John Emery, "Black Solidarity Is Essential," ibid., Feb. 2, 1971, p. 5; Simba Lewis, "Earlham College Makes Hollow Commitment," ibid., April 18, 1972, p. 3; Ralph Grant, "From a Black Friend," *Quaker Life,* 12 (Nov. 1971), pp. 38–39.

85. Bill Marable, "No Apology Offered," *Earlham Post,* April 20, 1971, p. 5; "BLAC," ibid., Oct. 1, 1968, p. 4. On Black Power, see Manning Marable, *Race, Reform, and Rebellion: The Second Reconstruction in Black America, 1945–1990* (Oxford: University Press of Mississippi, 1991), 86–148.

86. "Group Works for Black Housing Unit," *Earlham Post,* May 27, 1969, p. 1; Peter Johnson, "Black Students Seek Campus Understanding," ibid., Feb. 8, 1972, p. 5; "Community Council Seat for Minorities Urged," ibid., Nov. 16, 1971, p. 3.

87. Sawyer, "Tidewaters"; Bolling to Richard N. Hoerner, Nov. 7, 1969, box 37, Bolling Papers; Fuson to Faculty Representatives, April 27, 1968, Fuson Papers; "Community Council Gives Blacks Priority," *Earlham Post,* May 4, 1971, p. 1; "Staebler Calls for Racial Unity," ibid., Jan. 26, 1971, p. 5; Tony Bing Interview by Thomas D. Hamm, Oct. 31, 1995, Oral History Collection.

88. George Sawyer Interview by Thomas D. Hamm, May 2, 1995, Oral History Collection; "Rachel Davis Du Bois's Report of Her Residence on the Earlham College Campus, Sept. 9–Dec. 1, 1971," Race Relations File; Fuson to Sawyer, June 7, 1971, Fuson Papers; Alan Swift, "Responses Vary to Questionnaire," *Earlham Post,* May 23, 1972, p. 6; Bolling to Robinson; Bing Interview.

89. Sawyer Interview; "Richmond High School Blacks Sit In," *Earlham Post,* March 15, 1971, pp. 1–2.

90. "Richmond High Blacks Sit In"; Sawyer Interview; "Bolling Sees Dialog as Our 'Best Hope,'" *Earlham Post,* March 15, 1971, p. 4.

91. "Richmond High School Blacks Sit In"; Bolling to Paul Hardin, April 11, 1966, box 28, Bolling Papers.

92. Bernard W. Harleston, "Higher Education for the Negro: Obstacles," *Atlantic*, 216 (Nov. 1965), 139–44.

93. "100 Hear Locker at EPIC Meeting," *Earlham Post*, Oct. 5, 1961, p. 3; Michael Locker, "Forum," ibid., Oct. 15, 1964, p. 2; "Academic Achievement and Atmosphere," 1963, Survey Collection (Friends Collection).

94. Bolling to E. Raymond Wilson, Oct. 31, 1960, box 7, Bolling Papers; Bolling to Edward H. Harris, Nov. 10, 1962, box 15, ibid.; Landrum Bolling, "Quaker Non-Pacifist Writes on Recent Pacifist Action," *Earlham Post*, April 13, 1961, p. 1; Shirley Buop, "Morality of Deterrence Debated," ibid., Nov. 2, 1961, p. 2; "Professors Consider Conscientious Objection," ibid., Feb. 27, 1964, p. 1; "Letters, Letters, Lots of Letters for Landrum," ibid., April 20, 1961, p. 5.

95. "Earlham Students Protest Cuban Action," *Earlham Post*, Nov. 1, 1962, p. 1; N. Paul Harmon, "Earlham College Students Back Newport Vigil," ibid., April 6, 1961, p. 1; Bolling to Martha Peery Gwyn, April 20, 1959, box 5, Bolling Papers; Veronica G. Nicholson to Bolling, Dec. 4, 1959, ibid.; Bolling to Administrative Council, Sept. 23, 1962, box 14, ibid.; Ted Benfey to Fuson, May 17, 1963, Fuson Papers; Charles Chatfield, *The American Peace Movement: Ideals and Activism* (New York: Twayne, 1992), 100–16.

96. "Earlham Poll Favors Nixon," *Earlham Post*, Oct. 27, 1960, p. 3; Chris Clausen and Bill Dennis Letter, Oct. 1960, box 2, Opinion Board Papers; Byron F. Cranor to Bolling, March 20, 1960, box 6, Bolling Papers.

97. Kirkpatrick Sale, *SDS* (New York: Random House, 1973); Landrum R. Bolling, "From the President's Desk," *Earlhamite*, 86 (Jan. 1965), 2, 39; Lacey Interview by Hamm

98. Bolling to C. Edgar Hamilton, March 18, 1962, Speaker File, Controversial Issues Collection; Bolling to Harry J. Carman, March 22, 1963, ibid.; Bolling to David W. Dennis, May 22, May 31, 1963, ibid.

99. August Meier and Elliott Rudwick, *Black History and the Historical Profession, 1915–1980* (Urbana: University of Illinois Press, 1986), 108–09; Bolling to Harris, Nov. 24, 1963, Speaker File; Warren Staebler to Clausen, ibid.; Bruce Pearson to Bolling, Nov. 20, 1963, ibid.; D. Elton Trueblood to Fuson, Dec. 4, 1963, ibid.; Laurence Strong to Bolling, Nov. 14, 1963, ibid.; Clausen to Staebler, Dec. 23, 1963, ibid.; "The Political Double Standard," *Earlham Post*, Nov. 7, 1963, p. 2; Paul Lacey to Thomas D. Hamm, Dec. 20, 1995 (in Hamm's possession).

100. *Indianapolis News* clipping, April 7, 1964, Speaker File; *Cincinnati Enquirer* clipping, April 6, 1964, ibid.; Bolling to Mrs. Meyer Samuels, Jan. 9, 1964, ibid.; "Excerpts from Letters to President Bolling Concerning the Speakers Series," 1964, ibid.; Dave Feintuch, "Cuban Pickets Puzzle Richmond Residents," *Earlham Post*, April 9, 1964, p. 3; Robert K. Greenleaf to Bolling, May 19, 1964, box 22, Bolling Papers.

101. Mrs. C. E. Clevenger to Bolling, Jan. 2, 1964, box 27, Bolling Papers.

102. Gerald Markowitz, "U.S. Commitment Untenable Since Recent Vietnam Coup," *Earlham Post*, Nov. 14, 1963, p. 3; Tom Wells, *The War Within: America's Battle over Vietnam* (Berkeley: University of California Press, 1994), 9–65.

103. Rob Meeropol, "Tame Earlham College Students Lack Commitments," *Earlham Post*, Jan. 17, 1967, p. 2; "CSCA Plans Reform," *Earlham Post*, May 6, 1969, p. 3; Lacey Interview by Hamm; Paul Lacey to William C.

Dennis II, n.d., Paul Lacey Papers (Friends Collection). For an excellent example of the melding of older religious pacifism with ideas drawn from the New Left, see Arthur Kanegis, "The Sermon on the Mount: A 'New Left' Manual for Nonviolent Radicalism?" *Prism,* 7 (Spring 1967), 1–14.

104. Wells, *War Within,* 23–38; John Stevenson, Marilyn McNabb, Ralph Engelmann, Lewise Langston Letter, *Earlham Post,* May 13, 1965, p. 2; "Students Protest War in Vietnam," ibid., May 20, 1965, p. 1; Lewise Langston, "Peace Plea at Viet Nam Rally," ibid., April 22, 1965, p. 6; Arthur Kanegis, "Peace Movement Hits Campuses," ibid., Sept. 30, 1965, p. 1; "Peace Movement Is Now Here," ibid., Oct. 7, 1965, p. 1; Tim Zimmer, "Students Planning March on Capitol," ibid., Nov. 18, 1965, p. 1; Phil Lynes, "A Witness and a Nation," ibid., Oct. 28, 1965, p. 4; "Earlhamites Appeal in Vigil," ibid., Oct. 21, 1965, p. 1; Rob Meeropol, "Democracy," ibid., Oct. 21, 1965, p. 2.

105. Liesel Dreisbach, "Vigiler Relates Campus to Viet Crisis," *Earlham Post,* Oct. 11, 1966, p. 3; "Hostility Greets Students on Viet Peace Vigil," ibid., Nov. 29, 1966, p. 1; Paul Lacey Interview by Anthony Holtz, April 29, 1986, Oral History Collection.

106. Tony Guastini, "Tim Zimmer Receives Three Year Prison Term," ibid., May 2, 1967, p. 2; "Draft Advisor for Earlham College?" ibid., May 27, 1969, p. 2; Chris Newton, "Buddy, Can You Spare the Time?" ibid., Feb. 11, 1969, p. 4; Timothy Zimmer, "Statement of Purpose in Refusing Military Induction," *Prism,* 7 (Spring 1967), 32–34; Peter Suber Interview by Thomas D. Hamm et al., Oct. 4, 1993, ibid.; "In Memoriam," *Earlhamite,* 90 (Spring 1969), 46; *Palladium-Item* clipping, Jan. 23, 1969, Peace File, Controversial Issues Collection.

107. Bob Seeley, "As I See It," *Earlham Post,* May 20, 1965, p. 2; "PEACE Sponsors Vietnam Protest," ibid., May 19, 1966, p. 1; Emily Mills, "Study Vigil Motives," ibid., Jan. 10, 1967, p. 3; Lacey Interview by Holtz; Bastian Interview; Emily Smith, "Earlham College and Vietnam: What Happened and What Made It Different?" Nov. 23, 1993, typescript, p. 7, Earlham History Collection (Friends Collection); D. Elton Trueblood, "Prisoners of War," *Quaker Life,* 14 (May 1973), 35.

108. Smith, "Earlham College and Vietnam," 7; Lacey Interview by Holtz; Randall Shrock Interview by Thomas D. Hamm et al., Oct. 4, 1993, Oral History Collection; Bolling to J. William Fulbright, Feb. 23, 1967, box 31, Bolling Papers; Bolling to Carl and Susan Welty, June 28, 1965, box 26, ibid.; Bolling to John East, Nov. 2, 1969, box 37, ibid.; Bolling Interview.

109. Shrock Interview; "Profs Give Views on Election," *Earlham Post,* Oct. 22, 1968, p. 3.

110. Board Minutes, Nov. 1–2, 1968; Lacey Interview by Holtz; "Earlham Students to Hear Draft Director Monday," *Palladium-Item* clipping, Nov. 8, 1968, Peace File; Jim Joyner to Paul Garrison, Nov. 25, 1968, ibid.

111. "Hershey Addresses Queries on Draft Issues," clipping, [Nov. 1968], Peace File; *Palladium-Item* clipping, Nov. 10, 1968, ibid.; Byron E. Klute to Bolling, Nov. 12, 1968, ibid.; Vic Jose, "A Way to Differ," Richmond, Ind. *Graphic* clipping, Nov.14, 1968, ibid.; Lacey Interview by Holtz.

112. Wells, *War Within,* 424–37.

113. "A Statement of Concern about Arms and Demonstrations on Campus," 1970, Moratorium File, Controversial Issues Collection; Faculty Minutes, Nov. 18, 1969, May 5, 1970.

114. Elmore Interview, Feb. 17, 1994.

115. "Earlham Students Choose a Different Path," *Graphic* clipping, May

14, 1970, Kent State File; Mary Lane Hiatt Memorandum, 1970, ibid.; "Memorandum Concerning Options for the Completion of Work During Term III," May 8, 1970, ibid.; Strong and Cope Interview.

116. Bill Kates, "Students Protest Bombing," *Earlham Post*, April 25, 1972, p. 6; Cindy Maude, "Earlham Students Busted in D.C.," ibid., May 11, 1971, p. 1; clipping, May 16, 1972, Peace File; Smith, "Earlham College and Vietnam," 18; Board Minutes, Feb. 26–27, 1971.

117. Helen Lefkowitz Horowitz, *Campus Life: Undergraduate Cultures from the End of the Eighteenth Century to the Present* (Chicago: University of Chicago Press, 1987), 220–44; Sara Penhale Interview by Thomas D. Hamm et al., Oct. 4, 1993, Oral History Collection.

118. Clevenger to Bolling; Bolling to Bob Garrison, April 29, 1959, box 3, Bolling Papers; Bolling to Florence Long, Jan. 27, 1966, box 28, ibid.; Darrell Beane to Bolling, Nov. 26, 1961, box 10, ibid. On the "Beats," see Dennis McNally, *Desolate Angel: Jack Kerouac, the Beat Generation, and America* (New York: Dell, 1990).

119. "Halt Dumping," *Earlham Post*, May 19, 1966, p. 2; "Appearance Alienates Prospects," ibid., Oct. 29, 1968, pp. 1, 8; "Community Analyzed," ibid., May 26, 1966, p. 2; "Senate Views Campus Conduct," ibid., April 16, 1964, p. 1; "Senate Contests Viewbook's Wording," ibid., April 25, 1967, p. 1; Robert Parr to Bolling, March 18, 1965, box 25, Bolling Papers; Bolling to George H. Batt, March 9, 1969, box 36, ibid.; Bolling to John E. Parker, Jr., Nov. 18, 1966, box 28, ibid.; Wilson to Board, 1967, box 33, ibid.

120. Horowitz, *Campus Life*, 248–49; John E. D'Emilio and Estelle B. Freedman, *Intimate Matters: A History of Sexuality in America* (New York: Harper and Row, 1988), 301–25.

121. "No More Men," *Earlham Post*, April 19, 1962, p. 1; "Letters to the Editor," *Earlhamite*, 92 (Spring 1971), 4; Bolling Letter, 1963, box 3, Opinion Board Papers; Bolling to Murvel and Esther Garner, Nov. 16, 1963, box 18, Bolling Papers; Bolling to Paul Boren, Nov. 18, 1963, box 17, ibid.

122. "Guidelines for AWS Trial Term," Jan. 13, 1969, Senate Miscellaneous Papers, box 1 (Friends Collection). See also the Opinion Board files generally for these years.

123. "Council OK's Coed Halls," *Earlham Post*, Feb. 15, 1972, p. 2; "Trustees Receive Students' Plan for Ideal Earlham Living Situation," *Earlham Post*, April 15, 1969, p. 1; "Query and Response," *Earlhamite*, 92 (Winter 1971), 22; Gwendolyn Gosney, "Changing With the Times: Women's Experiences at Earlham College, 1958–1973," Nov. 22, 1993, typescript, p. 27, Earlham History Collection.

124. Administrative Council Memorandum, Feb. 2, 1963, box 17, Bolling Papers; Judy and Charlie Guttman Letter, June 5, 1961, box 3, Opinion Board Papers; Shrock Interview; Bob Hendricks, "Alpenfels Disappointed with Earlham Response," *Earlham Post*, May 3, 1962, p. 3.

125. James Thorp to Bolling, Feb. 8, 1963, Speaker File; "Survey," *Earlham Post*, April 1, 1969, p. 1; "The Post Box," ibid., Jan. 13, 1966, p. 2; "E. C. and Sex," ibid., Oct. 10, 1963, p. 2.

126. Steve Goodrich, "AMR Open Section Plan Vague," *Earlham Post*, May 6, 1969, p. 6; "College Asks Seven to Withdraw," ibid., Jan. 18, 1972, pp. 1–2; John Peters, "Community Council Reaches Impasse," ibid., May 23, 1972, p. 3; Tom Mullen to Joe Elmore et al., May 6, 1969, Student Development Collection; Board Minutes, Feb. 27, 1970; Faculty Minutes, Feb. 23, 1971.

127. On drug use nationally in this period, see Jay Stevens, *Storming

Heaven: LSD and the American Dream (New York: Harper and Row, 1988); and William L. O'Neill, *Coming Apart: An Informal History of America in the 1960s* (New York: Times, 1971), 233–71.

128. Jon Branstrator Interview by Thomas D. Hamm et al., Oct. 4, 1993, Oral History Collection; Charles Martin Interview by ibid., Oct. 12, 1993, ibid.; Bolling to Jeanette McKeefer, July 1, 1959, box 5, Bolling Papers; James G. Paton Letter, June 2, 1957, box 2, Opinion Board Papers; Thomas E. Jones, *Light on the Horizon: The Quaker Pilgrimage of Tom Jones* (Richmond, Ind.: Friends United Press, 1973), 164.

129. "Hello, Parents and Alumni," *Earlham Post,* May 20, 1965, p. 2; "Three Men Suspended for Drinking Violation," ibid., Feb. 11, 1965, p. 1; Bolling to J. Whittington Polk, June 22, 1965, box 25, Bolling Papers; Branstrator Interview.

130. Penhale Interview; Faculty Affairs Committee Minutes, Oct. 24, 1967, box 31, Bolling Papers; Fuson Memorandum, 1968, Fuson Papers; "'Drunks' Inconsiderate," *Earlham Post,* May 11, 1971, p. 4.

131. Suber Interview; "Student Opinion Varies," *Earlham Post,* Feb. 16, 1971, p. 6; Rob Meeropol, "Raps Drug Convo," ibid., April 4, 1967, p. 2.

132. Clyde A. Black to Faculty, March 12, 1970, Student Development Collection; Mullen to Wilson, Aug. 11, 1969, ibid.; "A Clarification," Jan. 12, 1968, ibid.; "Earlhamites Suspended for Drug Violations," *Earlham Post,* May 22, 1973, p. 2; Guy Kovner, "Administration Voices Concern on Drug Issue," ibid., March 7, 1967, pp. 1, 3; "Student Opinion Varies," ibid., Feb. 16, 1971, p. 6; "Statement on Drugs," ibid., Jan. 5, 1968, Drugs File, Controversial Issues Collection.

133. Lacey Interview by Hamm et al.

134. Shrock Interview; Penhale Interview.

135. Penhale Interview; "Homecoming Lacks New Events," *Earlham Post,* Oct. 17, 1972, p. 6; "Earlham Institutes Progressive Feeding," ibid., Sept. 27, 1966, p. 4; Barclay Howarth, "E.C. Lovely Discusses Dating Situation," ibid., April 1, 1969, p. 4; "Cast Aside Crown," ibid., Oct. 19, 1971, p. 4; "Frances Bolling Looks Back on Earlham" ibid., April 24, 1973, p. 4; Hal Cope to Administrative Council, May 17, 1967, box 30, Bolling Papers; Bolling to Guy W. Jones, May 13, 1969, box 37, ibid.

136. "The 'Guarded Well By' Begins Activities Saturday," *Earlham Post,* Jan. 16, 1964, p. 3; "Earlham Food Co-Op," *Earlhamite,* 98 (Winter 1977), 13.

137. Thornburg, *Earlham,* 421; "Harris Cites Lack of Support," *Earlham Post,* Oct. 20, 1970, p. 5; "Harris to Leave Earlham June 30," *Richmond Palladium-Item,* April 9, 1974, p. 9.

138. Gosney, "Changing with the Times," 5–12. I am also indebted to Killian Barefoot, "A Struggle for Equality: A History of Women's Education at Earlham College, 1901–1965," May 1991, Earlham History Collection.

139. Gosney, "Changing with the Times," 4–5.

140. Horowitz, *Campus Life,* 241–44, 252–53.

141. Gosney, "Changing with the Times," 11–15, 20–22.

142. Ibid., 21–22.

143. Ibid., 24–26; Brondi Topchik, "AWS Meets to Abolish Sign-Outs," *Earlham Post,* Jan. 19, 1971, p. 2.

144. Sally Wood Letter, April 9, 1964, box 4, Opinion Board Papers; "Females Face Role Conflict," *Earlham Post,* April 1, 1969, p. 5; Mary Kirby, "AMR, AWS Plan to Merge," ibid., March 2, 1971, p. 3; "Women's Center Plans

More Rap Groups," ibid., Nov. 30, 1971, p. 2; *Earlham College Catalogue for 1970*, p. 48; *Women's Center Newsletter*, Jan. 1973. To place these events in context, see William H. Chafe, *The Paradox of Change: American Women in the Twentieth Century* (New York: Oxford University Press, 1991), 194–213.

145. Gerald Bakker Interview by Thomas D. Hamm et al., Oct. 1993, Oral History Collection; Lacey Interview by Hamm et al. Margaret Grant Beidler shared her assessment of the impact of foreign study in a conversation with the author in June 1992.

146. See West Richmond Membership Records in the Friends Collection.

147. Landrum R. Bolling, "Toward Earlham's Future," Sept. 11, 1958, box 2, Bolling Papers; Landrum R. Bolling, "From the President's Office," *Earlhamite*, 92 (Summer 1971), 2.

148. Bolling to Mrs. Burton Kintner, April 29, 1966, box 28, Bolling Papers; Bolling to Harriet L. Hoyle, Nov. 12, 1964, box 22, ibid.

149. New Hope Monthly Meeting to Bolling, Oct. 9, 1958, box 2, ibid.; Bolling to Henley, Aug. 25, 1958, ibid.; Vida Wright to Bolling, Dec. 2, 1958, ibid.; Bolling to Wright, July 2, 1958, ibid.; "Notes on a Discussion at Indiana Yearly Meeting, Aug. 17, 1959," Religious Controversies File, Controversial Issues Collection.

150. "Continuation Conference," Oct. 10, 1959, box 2, Bolling Papers.

151. "Notes on a Discussion"; "Continuation Conference."

152. "Continuation Conference"; Bolling to Robert Shaffer, Feb. 5, 1060, box 9, Bolling Papers; Bolling to Miriam Cooper, Aug. 25, 1959, box 3, ibid.; "Report of the Committee to Study the Office of the Presidency," 1967, box 33, ibid.; Board Minutes, June 3, 1960.

153. Fuson Memoirs, 21; "Statistics on Friends," 1958–1959, box 1, Bolling Papers; Aldean Pitts to Bolling, May 10, 1960, box 5, ibid.; Eric G. Curtis to Bolling, June 2, 1960, box 6, ibid.; L. B. Rogers to Bolling, March 6, 1964, box 23, ibid.; Faculty Minutes, Sept. 12, 1966; Board Minutes, Feb. 9–10, 1968.

154. Board Minutes, Oct. 5, 1962; Willis H. Ratliff to Bolling, May 18, 1967, box 32, Bolling Papers; Terry Darnell to Bolling, Nov. 6, 1967, box 30, ibid.; Henry B. Bogue to Bolling, [Jan. 1968], box 34, ibid.; Eleanor Walton to Bolling, Aug. 20, 1962, box 15, ibid.; William Fuson, "Earlham's Place in an Era of Educational Change," Sept. 1971, Fuson Papers.

155. Herbert D. Pettingill to Bolling, March 4, 1964, box 23, Bolling Papers; Xen Harvey to Bolling, Nov. 18, 1959, box 4, ibid.; *Indiana Yearly Meeting Minutes, 1960*, pp. 35–36; Jay W. Beede to Bolling, Dec. 14, 1965, box 24, Bolling Papers; Wilson to Ben Carlson, Jan. 26, 1965, box 26; Bolling to Wilson, Nov. 16, 1965, ibid.

156. Bolling, "Toward Earlham's Future"; Fuson, "Earlham's Place."

157. Wilmer A. Cooper, *The Earlham School of Religion Story: A Quaker Dream Come True, 1960–1985* (Richmond, Ind.: Earlham School of Religion, 1985), 3–7; Ellison R. Purdy et al. to American Friends Board of Foreign Missions, Aug. 6, 1920, American Friends Board of Foreign Missions Papers (Friends Collection). I am indebted to Wilmer Cooper for the latter item.

158. Cooper, *Earlham School of Religion Story*, 6–8.

159. Ibid., 9; Bolling to Pettingill, Nov. 5, 1958, box 2, Bolling Papers.

160. Mooreland Monthly Meeting to Cooper, Jan. 25, 1960, box 9, Bolling Papers; Louis Harrington to Bolling, Feb. 18, 1960, box 9, ibid.; Pettingill to Bolling, Oct. 21, 1958, box 2, ibid.; Bolling to Arthur A. Rownes, Dec. 16, 1959, box 5, ibid.; "Trustees Study Religion School," *Earlham Post*, Oct. 15, 1959, p. 2.

161. Bastian Interview; Stephenson Interview; Cooper, *Earlham School of Religion Story,* 17–19; Board Minutes, Feb. 12–13, 1960; Wilson to Hugh Ronald, Dec. 12, 1967, box 30, Bolling Papers.

162. Trueblood Interview; Cooper Interview; Cooper, *Earlham School of Religion Story,* 13–25.

163. Cooper, *Earlham School of Religion Story,* 44–50.

164. Ibid., 47–48, 62–66, 149; Bolling to Alfred H. Cope, Nov. 4, 1968, box 34, Bolling Papers; Cope to Bolling, July 1, 1964, box 21, ibid.; "The Blurred Spectrum," *Friends Journal,* June 1, 1967, 291–92.

165. Cooper, *Earlham School of Religion Story,* 52–56, 64–65.

166. George M. Marsden, *The Soul of the American University: From Protestant Establishment to Established Nonbelief* (New York: Oxford University Press, 1994), 408–24.

167. Questionnaire, May 1964, box 22, Bolling Papers; Wilson to Board, Sept. 14, 1964, box 23, ibid.; "Senate Hears Policy on Faculty Hiring," *Earlham Post,* Nov. 9, 1961, p. 1; Woolpy Interview.

168. Cooper to Bolling, Aug. 8, 1961, box 13, Bolling Papers; Elmore to Bolling, Feb. 23, 1961, box 10, ibid.; Jon Smith to Bolling, March 6, 1962, box 16, ibid.; Bolling to Phil C. Becker, Aug. 13, 1959, box 5, ibid.; Elmore and Stephanie Stilwell Memorandum, Oct. 9, 1964, box 24, ibid.; Charlie Williams, "Doctrines Need Redefining," *Earlham Post,* Nov. 6, 1958, pp. 1, 3; "35 Discuss Campus Needs," ibid., May 11, 1971, p. 6; Paul Lacey Letter, March 11, 1961, box 3, Opinion Board Papers; Kathy Phelps, "Growing Campus Jesus Movement Avoids 'Watered-Down Christianity,'" ibid., Jan. 25, 1972, p. 1.

169. Faculty Minutes, Nov. 9, 1959; Bolling to Sweitzer, Jan. 28, 1963, box 19, Bolling Papers; Howard Alexander, "A Report from the Department of Mathematics," *Earlhamite,* 82 (Jan. 1961), 17; *Earlham College Catalog, 1963–1965,* pp. 11–15.

170. Landrum Bolling, "Proposals for Faculty Retreat," 1958, box 1, Bolling Papers; Wilmer A. Cooper, "Response to Hutchinson Report on School of Religion," 1964, Earlham School of Religion Collection (Friends Collection); "Earlham's Values and Standards," *Earlhamite,* 91 (Winter 1970), 7.

171. Judy Maxmin to Bolling, Aug. 23, 1969, box 38, Bolling Papers; Bob Williams, "Student Questions 'Finer Values,'" *Earlham Post,* Dec. 1, 1970, p. 10; Fuson Memoirs, 16.

172. Helen B. Hole, "Being a Provost," *Earlhamite,* 92 (Summer 1971), 6; Richard Lohaus, "Quaker Beliefs Influence Community," *Earlham Post,* May 11, 1971, p. 6; Stephenson Interview; Woolpy Interview; Board Minutes, June 4–5, 1970.

173. William Fuson, "On the Need for a Quaker President at Earlham," Nov. 1972, Fuson Papers; "Staebler Reevaluates Community," *Earlham Post,* Nov. 26, 1968, p. 3; "Community Sets Distinctive Style," ibid., Sept. 27, 1966, p. 1; Faculty Minutes, June 2, 1969.

174. William Fuson, "Notes on Community Government at Earlham," Oct. 26, 1965, Fuson Papers; Gordon Thompson, "Introductory Remarks," 1971, ibid.; Fuson to Bolling, Aug. 29, 1959, box 4, Bolling Papers; Dick Dyer, "'Community' Still Very Much Alive," *Earlham Post,* Dec. 9, 1970, p. 9; Faculty Minutes, Jan. 31, 1968; Benfey Interview, 54.

175. Faculty Minutes, Feb. 25, 1935, March 13, 1950, Nov. 3, 1952, Oct. 9, 1961; David M. Edwards to Charles T. Thwing, Jan. 30, 1928, David M. Edwards Presidential Papers (Friends Collection); Bolling to Nicholas M.

Katz, May 17, 1960, box 8, Bolling Papers; Joseph Coppock to Bolling, Feb. 17, 1961, box 12, ibid.; William Fuson, "Earlham and Phi Beta Kappa: An Open Letter," Sept. 24, 1961, Fuson Papers; Leigh Gibby Memorandum, Oct. 6, 1961, ibid.; "E. C. Given Approval by Phi Beta Kappa," *Earlham Post,* Oct. 8, 1964, p. 1.

176. Locker, "Forum"; "A Quaker Presence," *Earlham Post,* May 11, 1971, p. 4; Gordon Thompson, "Academics Aren't All," ibid., Nov. 16, 1971, p. 5; Helen G. Hole, "All Things Civil and Useful in Creation," *Earlhamite,* 97 (Winter 1976), 2–5; Bastian Interview; Gordon Thompson, "Senior Convocation Address," ibid., 91 (Winter 1970), 9; William Fuson, "Should Earlham Take a Stand?" May 5, 1972, Fuson Papers; William Fuson, "On Strengthening Quakerism at Earlham," 1967, ibid.; Thompson, "Opening Remarks"; "Intern View of Earlham."

177. Cottle, "Learning Place," pp. 52–59; Richard M. Gummere, Jr., to Bolling, April 25, 1964, box 22, ibid.; Tom Brown to Bolling, Dec. 15, 1965, box 24, ibid.

178. Bolling to Leo M. Gardner, Dec. 27, 1969, box 37, Bolling Papers; Fuson Memoirs, 26; Board Minutes, June 8–9, 1972.

7. Earlham and the Culture Wars, 1973–1996

1. The author was present at the 1991 commencement, and this description is based on his own memories and those of other faculty.
2. This description is based on comments made at the 1992 Indiana Yearly Meeting sessions, notes of which are in the author's possession.
3. James Davison Hunter, *Culture Wars: The Struggle to Define America* (New York: Basic, 1991).
4. "Earlham College Fact Book, 1995."
5. See, for example, "Zehring's New Task: Market Earlham," *Earlham Post,* April 23, 1981, pp. 1, 4; or cf. the catalogs for 1970 and 1990.
6. Tony Bing Interview by Thomas D. Hamm, Oct. 31, 1995, Oral History Collection (Friends Collection, Lilly Library, Earlham College, Richmond, Ind.).
7. Paul Lacey to Thomas D. Hamm, Jan. 2, 1990 (in Hamm's possession); Dean of Students Office Memo, April 22, 1974, Curricular Policy Committee Papers; "Report on Living/Learning Project," 1975, ibid.
8. Bing Interview; Tony Bing, "Yurt Is a Four-Letter Word," *Earlhamite,* 95 (Fall 1974), 18–21; "Board of Trustees Considered Yurts," *Earlham Post,* March 5, 1974, p. 1.
9. *Who's Who among Earlhamites: The Alumni Directory of Earlham College* (Richmond, Ind.: Earlham College, 1985), 4; Earlham College Board of Trustees Minutes, June 7, 1974 (Friends Collection).
10. Paul Kortepeter, "Joe Elmore Resigns," *Earlham Post,* Nov. 13, 1980, p. 1; "Joe Elmore to Leave Earlham after Twenty Years," *Earlhamite,* 102 (Spring 1981), 6–7.
11. "The Bolling Years: Educational Adventure," *Earlhamite,* 94 (Winter 1973), 7–8; James H. Madison, *Eli Lilly: A Life, 1885–1977* (Indianapolis: Indiana Historical Society, 1989), 219–20.
12. Board Minutes, Oct. 26, 1973.
13. "Welcome Wallins!" *Earlhamite,* 95 (Summer 1974), 5–7.
14. Earlham College Faculty Meeting Minutes, Oct. 22, 1974, Nov. 20, 1979,

Sept. 21, 1982 (Friends Collection); Board Minutes, Feb. 14, 1976, June 8, 1979; William K. Stephenson Interview by Thomas D. Hamm, May 23, 1995, Oral History Collection; "Earlham College Fact Book, 1983."

15. Len Clark Interview by Thomas D. Hamm, Aug. 16, 1995, Oral History Collection; Joe E. Elmore Interview by Thomas D. Hamm, Feb. 24, 1994, ibid.; Bing Interview; Franklin W. Wallin, "A Year of Transition," *Earlhamite*, 104 (Winter 1983), 14–15.

16. "DeWitt Baldwin to Become Earlham's President," *Earlhamite*, 103 (Summer 1983), 2.

17. Ibid; Dewitt C. Baldwin Interview by Thomas D. Hamm, June 8, 1995, Oral History Collection.

18. Stephenson Interview; Bing Interview; Baldwin Interview; "Steam Tunnel Press Letter," Fall 1984, Opinion Board Papers (Friends Collection).

19. Baldwin Interview; Clark Interview.

20. Bing Interview; Stephenson Interview; Baldwin Interview.

21. Baldwin Interview.

22. "Positively Pete," *Earlhamite*, 106 (Fall 1985), 4–5; Kara West, "Pete Leland," *Earlham Post*, Oct. 15, 1984, p. 2. Several colleagues in conversations over the years have confirmed Leland's impact on the campus.

23. Bing Interview; Faculty Minutes, Sept. 7, 1984, April 17, 1985; Board Minutes, Oct. 19, 1984.

24. Faculty Minutes, April 17, 1985.

25. Ibid.; "Students Protest, Earlham College Trustees Defend President Selection," *Richmond Palladium-Item* April 17, 1985, pp. 1, 8; "Divestment, Gay Rights Issues in Earlham College Protest," ibid., 8.

26. "Students Protest"; Faculty Minutes, April 17, 1985.

27. Richard J. Wood c.v., 1985, Presidential Search File, Controversial Issues Collection (Friends Collection).

28. Richard J. Wood Interview by Thomas D. Hamm, Dec. 18, 1995, Oral History Collection.

29. Faculty Minutes, Jan. 17, 1990, Oct. 2, 1995; Richard J. Wood, "We're in Good Shape; We Can't Go on as We Are," Sept. 15, 1993, Richard J. Wood Presidential Papers (Friends Collection).

30. "A Capital Kickoff," *Earlhamite*, 108 (Fall 1987), 4–5; "Capital Campaign Ends $3.2 Million over Goal," ibid., 110 (Spring 1991), 2; "Head of the Class," *U.S. News and World Report*, Sept. 18, 1995, p. 140.

31. "First Year Class a 'Wonderful Mix,'" *Earlhamite*, 111 (Fall 1992), 4.

32. "Time To Be Frank," *Earlham Post*, Feb. 17, 1976, p. 2; "Exit Steeples," ibid., March 1, 1979, p. 1; Faculty Minutes, May 23, 1978. Statistics come from the "Fact Book" for 1979, 1983, 1990, and 1995.

33. Statistics come from the "Fact Book" in note 32.

34. *Earlham College Catalog, 1986*, p. 2.

35. William C. Nelsen and Michael E. Siegel, eds., *Effective Approaches to Faculty Development* (Washington, D.C.: Association of American Colleges, 1980), 1.

36. Lacey to Hamm; Faculty Minutes, Feb. 18, 1975.

37. Faculty Minutes, May 14, 1974, Feb. 18, Feb. 24, April 1, May 6, 1975; Warren Staebler to faculty, May 24, 1974, bound with Faculty Minutes, May 14, 1974; Faculty Affairs Committee to Faculty, May 27, 1974, ibid.; Lacey to Hamm.

38. Gerald R. Bakker and Paul A. Lacey, "The Teaching Consultant at

Earlham," in *Effective Approaches to Faculty Development*, ed. Nelsen and Siegel, 32–37.

39. Lacey to Hamm.

40. Geoffrey Smith, "Winter Winds Blow," *Earlham Post*, Jan. 26, 1978, p. 1; "Making and Breaking a Budget," ibid., Nov. 15, 1979, p. 1; "Faculty Wages among Worst in GLCA," ibid., Nov. 18, 1979, p. 1; "No Letup to Budget Woes," ibid., Oct. 21, 1976, p. 1. Statistics are from the 1990 and 1995 "Fact Books."

41. See 1979 and 1995 "Fact Book."

42. "A Year of Transition," *Earlhamite*, 104 (Winter 1983), 14–15; "Earlham Investment Policies," *Earlham Word*, May 27, 1994, p. 5.

43. "Construction Underway on Library and Dorms," *Earlhamite*, 111 (Fall 1991), 3; *Who's Who among Earlhamites: The Alumni Directory of Earlham College* (Richmond, Ind.: Earlham College, 1985), 611.

44. "Hughes at Earlham," *Earlhamite*, 112 (Spring 1993), 21; "NEH Challenge a Success," ibid., 102 (Summer 1981), 12; "Lilly Grant to Aid Management Studies," ibid., 111 (Fall 1992), 3; "Ford Foundation Invites Earlham" ibid., 106 (Winter 1986), 2; "Ford Award to Fund Joint Research," ibid., 107 (Fall 1986), p. 3; "Lilly Awards $75,000 for Faculty Development," ibid., 107 (Spring 1987), 3; "College Receives Major Grants from Joyce, Lilly Funds," *Earlham Word*, Sept. 22, 1989, pp. 1, 3; Wood to Parents, April 6, 1988, Wood Papers; *Indiana Yearly Meeting Minutes, 1983*, pp. 84–85; Faculty Minutes, Jan. 17, 1990; Howard Lamson and Patricia O'Maley, "International Education and Liberal Learning," *Liberal Education*, 81 (Winter 1995), 27.

45. Cf. 1979 and 1990 Fact Books.

46. Board Minutes, June 7, 1974; "Fiske College Guide Appraises Earlham," *Earlhamite*, 111 (Fall 1992), 3; "Earlham Rated among Top 3% of Colleges," ibid., 108 (Fall 1987), 2; "Admissions Beats the Enrollment Slump," *Earlham Word*, Sept. 6, 1986, p. 3; Luke Clippinger, "Earlham Nabs Top Awards," ibid., Sept. 27, 1991, p. 1; Lucia Solarzano, *Barron's 300 Best Buys in College Education* (New York: Barron's, 1994), 145–46.

47. Faculty Minutes, May 20, 1986, May 16, May 30, 1990, Nov. 2, Nov. 16, 1994.

48. Faculty Minutes, April 19, 1977; Kirsten Bohl, "Professors Discuss History and Features of Humanities Program," *Earlham Word*, April 12, 1991, p. 2.

49. See, for example, the program handbook, *The Humanities Program at Earlham College, 1995–1996*.

50. Holly Harmon, "Humanities, Still Alive and Well," *Earlhamite*, 101 (Summer 1980), 2–3; "Earlham: Epitome of Reform," *New York Times*, Jan. 10, 1993, Sec. IV-A, p. 20; Elizabeth D. Kirk, "Report: Humanities Program, Earlham College," 1992 (in Hamm's possession).

51. Kirk, "Report." Much of this paragraph is based on the author's own impressions as a member of the Humanities staff since 1987.

52. "Workshop to Plan Peace Studies," *Earlham Post*, Nov. 16, 1971, p. 3; Faculty Minutes, Feb. 8, Feb. 29, 1972.

53. Faculty Minutes, April 1, 1975; Margaret Roberts, "Peace and Conflict Studies," *Earlham Post*, Nov. 12, 1974, p. 4.

54. Steve Heiny to George Lopez, April 28, 1981, Curricular Policy Committee Files; "Making Peace," *Earlhamite*, 104 (Spring 1984), 8–10; Gabrielle Horn, "Tony Bing Honored by British Embassy," *Earlham Word*, March 12, 1993, p. 1.

55. "Final Report: An Evaluation of the Program in Human Development and Social Relations," 1978, Curricular Policy Committee Files; "A Revised Proposal to the Lilly Endowment, Inc., to Establish the Center for Human Development and Social Relations," 1975, ibid.

56. 1993 North Central Association Report (Friends Collection).

57. "Proposal for a Women's Studies Major," Jan. 1987, Curricular Policy Committee Files. I am grateful to my History colleague Alice Shrock for sharing her memories of the establishment of the Women's Studies Program on several occasions. For the national context, see Sara M. Evans, *Born for Liberty: A History of Women in America* (New York: Free Press, 1989), 300–01.

58. "Proposal for a Women's Studies Major."

59. Pyke Johnson, "A Day with a College Librarian," *Earlhamite*, 99 (Spring 1978), 13–17; "Around the Heart," ibid., 105 (Fall 1985), 3; Michael Collier, "Lilly Hosts National Library Conference," *Earlham Post*, Nov. 18, 1977, p. 1.

60. Michael Harhofer Letter, *Earlham Post*, Sept. 27, 1979, p. 2; "Electronic Security Proposed for Libraries," ibid., May 10, 1979, p. 3; Johnson, "Day."

61. James Gill, "Library to Get Computerized Card Catalog," *Earlham Word*, Nov. 18, 1988, p. 1; "Earlham College Self-Study, 1993," Part II, p. 449 (Friends Collection).

62. Evan Farber, ed., *Teaching and Technology: The Impact of Unlimited Information Access on Classroom Teaching* (Ann Arbor: Pierian Press, 1991); Judith Axler Turner, "Earlham College Tests Value of Mass Use of 'Dialog' Data Base," *Chronicle of Higher Education*, Sept. 26, 1990, p. A15; "Computer Trove for Small College," *New York Times*, Nov. 4, 1990, Sec. 1, p. 58.

63. "Dedication of the Francis and Viola Anscombe Addition, Lilly Library," June 12, 1993.

64. "Earlham College Needs Computer Center Now!" *Earlham Post*, Nov. 1, 1966, p. 2; "Run Delphi?" ibid., Oct. 11, 1979, p. 2; Amy Anderson, "Computer Program Expanding," ibid., Sept. 29, 1982, pp. 1, 3; "Earlham College Self-Study," 422–24.

65. Faculty Minutes, June 1, 1976; Clark Interview; Jennifer Bruer, "Languages," *Earlham Post*, Feb. 17, 1984, p. 2.

66. Lamson and O'Maley, "International Education," 24; "Earlham Off-Campus Programs," n.d., Faculty Collection (Friends Collection); "Wood Outlines Plan for World Focus," *Richmond Palladium-Item*, April 6, 1986, p. A1; "Smashing Cultural Barriers," *Indianapolis News*, Jan. 30, 1989, pp. A 6–7; "Annual Meeting Highlights," *Perspectives*, 30 (Feb. 1992), 5.

67. See, for example, "Research Reconsidered," *Earlhamite*, 112 (Spring 1993), 19–25. The diversity of the Ford and Knight projects can be sampled in the annual reports in the Friends Collection.

68. Faculty Minutes, Oct. 9, 1984; "Do the Right Thing for Minority Students," *Earlhamite*, 110 (Spring 1991), 5; Carol Ann George, "Task Force Formed for Student Grants," *Earlham Post*, Sept. 30, 1983, p. 2; Chalis Johnson, "Earlham Replaces Loans with Grants for Indiana Black Students," *Earlham Word*, Nov. 3, 1989, p. 1.

69. Faculty Minutes, Nov. 13, 1984.

70. "Racism," *Earlham Post*, May 11, 1978, p. 2; BLAC Letter, Nov. 1986, Opinion Board Papers; Dick Wood to Earlham Community, March 14, 1989, ibid.; "Racist Graffiti Provokes Campus Unrest," *Earlham Word*, April 21, 1989, p. 1; "College Reacts to Campus Racism," ibid., April 28, 1989, p. 1; SaraAnne Acres, "Increased Racial Harassment Leads to BLAC Action," ibid., Feb. 8, 1991, p. 1.

71. "Upchurch on the Activist's Role at Earlham" *Earlham Post,* April 22, 1983, p. 6; Melvin Cox, "Or . . . A Case of Racism Revisited," ibid., Feb. 9, 1978, p. 2; Sandra Gildersleeve, "Very Few Persons Here Liberal," ibid., Oct. 21, 1976, p. 5; Roi Qualls, "Community Forum," ibid., Oct. 25, 1979, p. 2. For an instructive overview of the national situation, see "Race on Campus," *U.S. News and World Report,* April 19, 1993, pp. 52–65.

72. Bob Ubbelohde to Joe Elmore, Dec. 12, 1977, Student Development Files (Friends Collection); Office of Student Development to Students, April 12, 1977, ibid.

73. Nigel Collie Letter, *Earlham Post,* Feb. 2, 1978, p. 2; Kandi Washburn, "Facing the Reality of Race," ibid., Oct. 7, 1976, p. 2; "Lacey Clarifies Role in Tenure Case," ibid., Feb. 12, 1981, p. 2; Karen Leigh Mitchell, "The Real Earlham Experience Seen by a Black Woman," *Earlham Word,* Nov. 4, 1988, p. 4; "Professors and Students Perplexed," ibid., April 8, 1994, pp. 1–2.

74. Manning Marable, *Race, Reform, and Rebellion: The Second Reconstruction in Black America, 1945–1990* (Jackson: University Press of Mississippi, 1991), 214–15.

75. Board Minutes, Feb. 10–11, Oct. 20, 1978; Andy Leonard, "Board Meets," *Earlham Post,* Oct. 28, 1983, p. 2; "Earlham Board Refuses to Divest," ibid. There is considerable material in the Controversial Issues Collection about South African investment decisions.

76. Douglas Leith Hamilton Letter, *Earlhamite,* 107 (Fall 1986), 2; Robin Gibson, "Alumni Charge College with Censorship," *Earlham Word,* Nov. 3, 1989, p. 1; Richard Wood, "Community Must Work Together to End Apartheid," ibid., Oct. 14, 1988, p. 2; "Members of NAMED Respond to Wood's Comments on Boycott," ibid., June 3, 1988, p. 4.

77. Andy Williams, "Fabrication Detected," *Earlham Post,* Oct. 14, 1983, p. 3; Faculty Minutes, May 28, 1985.

78. Elmore Interview; Wood Interview.

79. Faculty Minutes, April 1, 1980, April 6, 1989; Cathy Flick Letter, *Earlham Post,* April 19, 1979, p. 3; Eleanor Shapiro, "Womyn's Center," ibid., Nov. 5, 1981, p. 4.

80. Evan Farber, "Off the Shelf," *Earlhamite,* 97 (Winter 1976), 18; "Women's Studies Seminar," *Earlham Post,* Oct. 26, 1978, p. 3; Barbara Welling Hall, "Electronic News Groups in the Liberal Arts Classroom," *International Studies Notes,* 20 (Winter 1995), 9.

81. Sara Payne, "Womyn's Center Busy But Struggling," *Earlham Post,* May 7, 1981, p. 3; Alice Coatney, "Womyn's Center: The 'He' in Human Debate," ibid., Oct. 8, 1981, p. 2; Sushil Narayana et al., Letter, March 7, 1988, Opinion Board Papers; Lisa Dady and Carrie Koons, ibid.; Jeni Byler, "Womyn's Center Involves Both Sexes," *Earlham Word,* Nov. 13, 1987, p. 4.

82. "Earlham Pro-Choice Group for Students," *Earlham Word,* Oct. 5, 1990, p. 2; Laurie Lehne, "Women and Work: Rhetoric and Reality," *Earlhamite,* 99 (Winter 1978), 15–16; Sarah Clarke, "Big Stick?" *Earlham Post,* Feb. 3, 1983, p. 2.

83. Jaipaul Singh Letter, *Earlham Word,* Feb. 6, 1987, pp. 2–3; Carolyn Holland and Lucinda Gatch, "Feminist View Essential to Humanities," *Earlham Post,* April 23, 1981, p. 2; "Sexism and Language: What Should Be Changed," ibid., Nov. 15, 1979, p. 2.

84. Dick Wood Letter, May 1989, Rape Controversy File, Controversial Issues Collection; Brian Nichols, "The Politics of Rape," *Earlham Word,* March 6, 1992, p. 7; Jennifer Miller, "Diversity, Criticism Are Helpful to Feminist Community," ibid., Jan. 27, 1989, p. 3; Auburn Currier Letter, ibid., Nov. 18, 1988, p. 3; "On Excluding Men," *Earlham Post,* Nov. 16, 1978, p. 3.

85. Faculty Minutes, March 26, 1985, Feb. 28, April 4, 1990; Jane Silver, "Two Couples Share Faculty Appointments," *Earlhamite*, 96 (Spring 1975), 15–17; "Joint Contracts Find Acceptance," *Earlham Post*, April 12, 1979, p. 1; Lacey to Hamm.

86. This paragraph is based on a talk given by Paul Lacey, April 3, 1991.

87. Ibid.; "Gay People's Union Seeks Recognition," *Earlham Post*, Feb. 5, 1974, p. 1; Anne Rettenberg and Lynn Fitz-Hugh, "GPU Attacks Discrimination," ibid., Jan. 28, 1982, p. 1; Barry D. Adam, *The Rise of a Gay and Lesbian Movement* (Boston: Twayne, 1987), 75–101; Lacey to Hamm.

88."GPU Still a Forgotten Minority," *Earlham Post*, March 2, 1978, p. 3; "Quaker Speaks on Sexuality at Gay Tea," ibid., May 14, 1974, p. 1; "GPU Pursues Goal," ibid., Jan. 2, 1975, p. 5; "Impotent Administrators and Non-Decision," ibid., April 2, 1974, p. 2.

89. Steven C. Munson Letter, ibid., Feb. 4, 1975, p. 2; Joan Parks, "Gay Union Is Included in Viewbook," ibid., April 20, 1984, p. 3; "Gay Alumnus Denied 'Coming Out Note,'" ibid., May 11, 1976, p. 1; "Homophobia Lurks," ibid., Oct. 9, 1980, p. 2; "GPU Discusses Affirmative Action," ibid., May 19, 1977, p. 2.

90. "GPU Provides Education, Support," ibid., Nov. 1, 1979, p. 1; "Perspectives of Gay Women," ibid., Nov. 15, 1979, p. 3; "Hate Flung," ibid., Feb. 4, 1982, p. 4; Ted Dunlap, "Earlham Intolerant," ibid., April 27, 1976, p. 2; Greg James, "Name-Calling," ibid., Nov. 4, 1976, p. 2.

91. Josh Riley, "A Blow to the Community," *Earlham Word*, Sept. 17, 1993, p. 7; Jesse Kahn Letter, Feb. 8, 1989, Opinion Board Papers; "1994 Midwest Bisexual Lesbian and Gay College Conference Brochure," Gay Conference File, Controversial Issues Collection.

92. James Jay Byler, "Moral Proselytizing Does Nothing to Fight AIDS Plague," *Earlham Word*, Feb. 2, 1990, p. 2; Michael D. Wetmore, "Homophobic Earlham Guilty of False Advertising," ibid., May 11, 1990, pp. 2–3; "Administration Ignores Systematic Harassment," ibid., Nov. 10, 1983, p. 3; Robbie Goble, "Dykes and Fags, Shut Up," ibid., Feb. 17, 1989, pp. 3–4; Queer Collective, "We're Here, We're Queer," ibid., Oct. 19, 1990, p. 7; Claudia Calhoon, "IYM and Me," ibid., Oct. 9, 1992, p. 6; Adam Thorburn, "'Objective' Scientific Research Reaffirms Prejudice," ibid., March 10, 1989, p. 3.

93. Ward Elmendorf, "Grace Cannot Abound Through Oppression," ibid., Oct. 22, 1993, p. 10; Matt Koenig, "Lesbigay Conference a Success," ibid., Feb. 25, 1994, pp. 1–2; Matt Koenig, "Where Grace Abounds Causes Stir on Campus," ibid., Oct. 29, 1993, pp. 1–2; Kirsten Bohl, "Administration Clarifies Views on Homosexual Staff," ibid., Jan. 26, 1990, pp. 1, 4; Jim Byler, "Demonstrators Protest Hiring Policy," ibid., May 20, 1988, p. 1; E. Stanley Banker, "Human Sexuality," April 3, 1991, Homosexuality File, Controversial Issues Collection.

94. The debates over multiculturalism and political correctness have generated a vast, mostly polemical literature. A good introduction is Robert Hughes, *Culture of Complaint: The Fraying of America* (New York: Oxford University Press, 1993).

95. Peter Gutkind, "Critic's Corner," *Earlham Post*, Oct. 14, 1949, p. 2; "Admissions Recruiting," ibid., Nov. 30, 1971, p. 3; Faculty Minutes, May 27, 1975; "New International Studies Program at Earlham," *Earlhamite*, 102 (Autumn 1981), 1.

96. Craig Richmond, Catherine Mehrling, and Michael Schwartzengruber,

"Liberal Solution to Sexism Touches Tip of Iceberg," *Earlham Post*, May 22, 1980, p. 2; "Legitimize Women's Work," ibid., May 8, 1980, p. 2; Harry Onwubika, "Nation Building for Whom?" ibid., Feb. 8, 1979, pp. 2–3; "Facing the Reality," ibid., Oct. 21, 1976, p. 2; Nancy Roberts, "Sexism," ibid., Oct. 28, 1976, p. 2.

97. Kirk, "Report."

98. Jim Byler, "Foreign Study Must Be More 'Foreign,'" *Earlham Word*, Feb. 17, 1989, p. 2; "National and Local Racism Stir Action," ibid., May 8, 1992, pp. 1, 3; "We Jah People Can Come Together and Make It Work," ibid., Nov. 19, 1993, p. 6; "Student Rally Concludes with Demands to Administration," ibid., May 20, 1994, pp. 1, 2; "Alliance Holds Meeting," ibid., May 6, 1994, pp. 1, 2.

99. Opal Thornburg, *Earlham: The Story of the College, 1847–1962* (Richmond, Ind.: Earlham College Press, 1963), 161–63, 223–24. For a typical early celebration, see "May Day," *Phoenixian*, 1 (June 1891), 23.

100. Thornburg, *Earlham*, 346, 391–92; Cecile Holvik, "To the Maypole Let Us On!" *Earlhamite*, 94 (Winter 1973), 12–24; "Olde English May Day at Earlham," ibid., 86 (July 1965), 22–23.

101. Faculty Minutes, June 3, 1957.

102. "Earlham Examines May Day," *Earlham Post*, April 15, 1969, p. 2; Tim Curtis, "May Day," ibid., May 19, 1977, p. 1; Jane Caleb, "May Day and Cultural Traditions," ibid., March 5, 1981, p. 6; "Fensterheim on May Day," ibid., May 22, 1973, p. 4; Charles Tinsley, "May Day 'Assimilation' Challenged," ibid., April 10, 1973, p. 4.

103. Jesse Kahn Letter, *Earlham Word*, Nov. 22, 1991, p. 6; "Big May Day Problematic, But Not Hopeless," ibid., May 19, 1989, p. 3; Priscilla Sanders and Jenn Dodson, "Selection of May Day Court Mocks Quaker Values," ibid., March 10, 1989, p. 4; Lori Southerland, "College Committee Seeks to Increase Big May Day Diversity," ibid., Oct. 23, 1992, pp. 1, 3.

104. Vicky Hunter, "Big May Day Preparations Are Coming Together," ibid., April 9, 1993, pp. 1, 5.

105. Ibid.; Andrew Hagen, "How Can May Day Happen Here?" ibid., May 28, 1993, p. 6; "Why Protest?" ibid., May 21, 1993, p. 10; Meredith Hale, "Know the Facts Before You Protest," ibid.; Gabrielle Horn, "Students to Stage Protest at Big May Day," ibid., p. 1.

106. Richard J. Wood, "A Constructive Diversity," *Friends Journal*, 41 (March 1995), 14–16; Faculty Minutes, April 6, 1989; Curricular Policy Committee Minutes, Feb. 11, Feb. 18, 1992; *Ideas That Make a Difference* (Richmond, Ind.: Earlham College, 1994), 21. See also the articles by faculty in the spring 1992 issue of the *Earlhamite*.

107. Faculty Minutes, Oct. 16, Nov. 20, 1991, April 15, 1992; *Earlham College Student Handbook, 1995–1996*, pp. 28–30. The author was one of the convenors of the group that produced the final policy.

108. Solozano, *Barrons 300 Best Buys*, 145; "The Mission of Earlham College," *Earlhamite*, 98 (Fall 1977), 1; Jeff Perkins, "Crisis and Community," *Earlham Word*, May 27, 1994, p. 15; Wood to Faculty, Sept. 7, 1995, attached to Faculty Minutes, Sept. 20, 1995.

109. Victor Chapman, "Reflection on Classroom, Community," *Earlham Post*, Jan. 23, 1985, p. 3; Clara Whitman, "Is Image Enough?" ibid., Feb. 18, 1985, p. 2; Rebecca Voelkel Speech, May 4, 1988, Community Day File, box 1, Registrar's Papers (Friends Collection); Summaries of Community Day Discussions, ibid.; Board Minutes, Feb. 8, 1985.

110. "The President's Report," *Earlhamite,* 102 (Autumn 1981), 4; "The Inauguration," ibid., 94 (Fall 1974), 9–10; Faculty Minutes, April 27, 1976; "Draft of a Report to Community Council," Nov. 15, 1973, Student Development Files.

111. Faculty Minutes, April 5, 1995.

112. Faculty Minutes, May 16, 1977, Jan. 9, 1979; Lacey to Hamm.

113. William H. Chafe, *The Unfinished Journey: America since World War II* (New York: Oxford University Press, 1991), 454.

114. Faculty Minutes, Oct. 2, 1980; Robin Stamm, "Earlham to Pay Aid Lost by Resisters," *Earlham Post,* Sept. 29, 1982, p. 1.

115. "Frisch's Concerns Sent to Trustees," *Earlham Post,* Feb. 11, 1982, p. 1; Carol Daggy, "Defense Fund Established for Draft Resister," ibid., Sept. 29, 1982, p. 1; Robin Stamm, "Pro-Registrants Speak Out," ibid., Oct. 28, 1982, p. 1; Robin Stamm, "Non-Registrant Gillis 'Goes Public,'" ibid., Oct. 14, 1982, p. 1.

116. Lynn Fitz-Hugh, "Students Trained in Civil Disobedience," ibid., Feb. 25, 1982, pp. 1, 4; Lonnie Valentine, "No More Dollars for War," ibid., Feb. 17, 1984, p. 4; Elliott Robertson, "RAD Protests," ibid., Jan. 14, 1982, p. 1; Faculty Minutes, April 6, 1988.

117. Mike Frisch, "El Salvador Demands Action," *Earlham Post,* March 5, 1981, p. 2; Siobhan H. Shea, "Mad Tea Party—No Joke," ibid., Oct. 28, 1982, p. 3; Andrew Wheat, "Peace or Justice?" ibid., Nov. 11, 1983, pp. 4–5; Clara G. Whitman, "Attitude Is Despair in 1980s," ibid., Feb. 18, 1983, p. 3.

118. John Rogers, "Bing Returns from Iraq," *Earlham Word,* Nov. 2, 1990, pp. 1, 3; "U.S.-Iraq War Begins, Sparks Debate," ibid., Jan. 18, 1990, p. 1; Michael Shellenberger, "Ideology, the War Culture, and Dick Wood," ibid., May 10, 1991, p. 6.

119. See, generally, Lois Harned Jordan, *Ramallah Teacher: The Life of Mildred White, Quaker Missionary* (N.p., 1995).

120. William Wald and Charles Fogel Letter, Feb. 26, 1957, box 2, Opinion Board Papers; "Bing and Fuchs Offer Views on Steps Toward Middle East Peace," *Earlham Word,* Jan. 25, 1991, p. 1; Daniel J. Pollin, "Anti-Semitism at Earlham," *Earlhamite,* 111 (Fall 1992), 2; Tony Bing, "One Day in Nablus," ibid., 104 (Summer 1983), 14–17; Landrum R. Bolling, "Quaker Effrontery and the Hope for Peace," ibid., 91 (Summer 1970), 6–7; Landrum Bolling Letter, *Earlham Post,* Oct. 13, 1977, p. 2; *The Search for Peace in the Middle East* (Philadelphia: American Friends Service Committee, 1970).

121. John D'Emilio and Estelle B. Freedman, *Intimate Matters: A History of Sexuality in America* (New York: Harper and Row, 1988), 304–25.

122. Jerry Woolpy Interview by Thomas D. Hamm, Feb. 22, 1995, Oral History Collection; Sara Penhale Interview by Thomas D. Hamm, June 26, 1995, ibid.; Faculty Affairs Committee, Paul Lacey, and Joe Elmore, "Report . . . Concerning the Tenure of Jerry Woolpy," Oct. 25, 1973, Paul Lacey Provost Files (Friends Collection); Lacey to Hamm.

123. Woolpy Interview.

124. Faculty Affairs Committee et al., "Report"; "Soundness of Testimony on Sexuality Questioned," *Earlham Post,* Nov. 30, 1973, p. 2; Woolpy Interview; Lacey to Hamm; "Earlham Provost Discusses Issues," *Richmond Palladium-Item,* Jan. 16, 1974, p. 23.

125. Woolpy Interview; Penhale Interview; Board Minutes, Dec. 8, 1973.

126. Woolpy Interview.

127. Board Minutes, Dec. 8, 1973; Faculty Affairs Committee et al., "Report."

128. Kimberly Painter, "Students Don't Choose Earlham College for Sex, Survey Shows," *Earlham Post,* Oct. 6, 1982, p. 2; Suzanne Kaebrick Letter, Fall 1987, Opinion Board Papers; Jonathan Hibbs, "Trueblood Decries Drop in Standards," *Earlham Post,* March 2, 1976, p. 1.

129. *Earlham College Catalog, 1973–1974,* p. 114; Larry Wichlinksi, "Sex Frustrates Task Force," *Earlham Post,* Oct. 7, 1976, p. 1; Susan Crim to Faculty, Nov. 23, 1982, Student Development Files.

130. Rob Mowry, "E.C. President's Cabinet Discusses Condoms and Nicaragua Accreditation," *Earlham Word,* Oct. 4, 1991, p. 2.

131. Beth Hayslett, "Condoms on Campus," *Earlham Word,* April 17, 1987, p. 6; Mary Kennedy, "Committee Attempts to Break Latex Barrier," ibid., May 8, 1992, pp. 1, 3; Michael Anton Dila, "The Elastic Morality of the Condom Issue," ibid., Nov. 3, 1989, p. 3; Barb Parks, "Birth Control at the Infirmary," *Earlham Post,* April 15, 1979, p. 5.

132. *Earlham College Student Handbook, 1995–1996,* pp. 28–29; "Condoms at Issue on Earlham's Campus," *Earlham Word,* April 24, 1992, pp. 1, 12.

133. John Rogers, "Wood Clarifies College Values in Convo," *Earlham Word,* Sept. 21, 1990, p. 5.

134. *Earlham College Student Handbook, 1995–1996,* p. 14; *Indiana Yearly Meeting Minutes, 1985,* p. 100; ibid., *1979,* pp. 92–93.

135. "Feeling Stabbed," *Earlham Word,* April 15, 1994, p. 13; "Openness," ibid., Oct. 9, 1987, p. 3; "Around the Heart," *Earlhamite,* 106 (Summer 1986), 2; "Continued Debate on the Future of All-College Meeting," Fall 1986, Opinion Board Papers.

136. Karla Eisin Letter, *Earlham Post,* April 20, 1984, p. 6; Faculty Meeting Minutes, May 31, 1995. Incoming Class Profiles since the 1960s are in the Friends Collection

137. Franklin Wallin Inaugural Address, Oct. 19, 1974, Franklin Wallin Presidential Papers (Friends Collection); Dewitt C. Baldwin, Jr., "Quaker Education and Earlham," *Earlhamite,* 104 (Winter 1983), 8–10; "Richard Wood Takes the Helm," ibid., 106 (Fall 1985), 7–9.

138. Tony Bing, "Remarks on Consensus," 1984, Student Development Files; Paul A. Lacey, "Decision Making in a Quaker Context," Sept. 12, 1977, ibid.; Faculty Minutes, Oct. 10, 1984; Helen G. Hole, "All Things Civil and Useful in Creation," *Earlhamite,* 97 (Winter 1976), 2–5; Paul A. Lacey, "From the Provost," ibid., 95 (Spring 1974), inside front cover; Joe Elmore, "Consensus Produces Tension at Earlham," *Earlham Post,* Nov. 4, 1976, p. 2.

139. *Earlham College Student Handbook, 1995–1996,* pp. 4–5.

140. Franklin Wallin, "What Can a Quaker College Do?" *Earlhamite,* 97 (Winter 1976), 6–7; Arthur Little, "Theater at Earlham, What It Could Become," ibid. (Spring 1976), 5; Paul A. Lacey, "All Things Sweet and Useful," ibid., 109 (Winter 1989), 12; Nelson Bingham, "Preparing Society's Servants," ibid., 104 (Summer 1983), 20–22; "Senate Panel Hears Student Volunteer Head," ibid., 109 (Spring 1989), 2.

141. "Student Government Poll Results," Sept. 21, 1984, Opinion Board Papers; "Affirmative Action at Earlham," *Earlham Post,* Oct. 25, 1979, p. 5; Joel Davis, "Hypocrisy," ibid., Feb. 27, 1984, p. 3; "EEAC: Our Statement of Purpose," *Earlham Word,* May 6, 1994, p. 7; Gertrude Ward Letter, ibid., Feb. 26, 1988, p. 3; James Jay Byler, "Clarification," ibid., April 29, 1988, pp. 2–3.

142. Elmore Interview, Feb. 17, Feb. 24, 1994; Faculty Minutes, Sept. 13, 1972; "Len Clark: More Minorities, More Quakers," *Earlham Post,* May 25,

1984, p. 5; Elmore to Bolling, Lacey, and Hole, July 5, 1972, Joe Elmore Office Files (Friends Collection).

143. "Len Clark"; Peter Burkholder, "College's Goal Is More Quakers," *Earlham Post,* May 25, 1984, pp. 1, 2; William Fuson, "The Quaker Presence at Earlham" *Earlham Faculty Newsletter,* Feb. 20, 1975.

144. "Candidly Clark," *Earlham Post,* April 23, 1981, p. 4; Faculty Minutes, Sept. 23, 1980.

145. Sandy Sweitzer, "Quaker Influence Ignored," *Earlham Post,* April 23, 1983, p. 2; Nate Terrell, "Everyone Responsible for Community Values," ibid., Oct. 21, 1976, p. 2; "Student Constitution," ibid., Jan. 18, 1977, p. 3; Josh Riley, "It's Really Not a 'Quaker Thing,'" *Earlham Word,* April 5, 1994, p. 14.

146. "On Feminism, Etc.," *Earlham Post,* Feb. 3, 1984, p. 3.

147. Wilmer A. Cooper, *The Earlham School of Religion Story: A Quaker Dream Come True, 1960–1985* (Richmond, Ind.: Earlham School of Religion, 1985), 71–72.

148. Ibid., 72–73, 149; *Indiana Yearly Meeting Minutes, 1974,* pp. 77–78.

149. Cooper, *Earlham School of Religion,* 71–92; *Indiana Yearly Meeting Minutes, 1991,* p. 57.

150. Cooper, *Earlham School of Religion,* 77–78, 153; Thomas J. Mullen, "Truth in Statistics," *Earlhamite,* 97 (Winter 1976), 12.

151. "Where Quaker Leaders Are Coming From," *Friendly Letter,* #5 (8th Mo. 1981), 3.

152. Cooper, *Earlham School of Religion,* 79; "New ESR Building Ready for Occupancy," *Earlhamite,* 109 (Fall 1989), 3.

153. *Indiana Yearly Meeting Minutes, 1994,* p. 95; "Bethany Seminary Joins Earlham Campus," *Earlham Word,* Sept. 16, 1994, p. 1; "Common Ground: Bethany Seminary and ESR," ibid., May 26, 1995, p. 4.

154. Hugh Barbour and J. William Frost, *The Quakers* (Westport, Conn.: Greenwood Press, 1988), 271–72. For Quaker universalism, see *Quaker Universalist Reader Number 1: A Collection of Essays, Addresses, and Lectures* (Landenberg, Pa.: Quaker Universalist Fellowship, 1986).

155. Barbour and Frost, *Quakers,* 242–43, 276–78. For reunited yearly meetings, see, for example, Hugh Barbour et al., *Quaker Crosscurrents: Three Hundred Years of Friends in the New York Yearly Meetings* (Syracuse: Syracuse University Press, 1995), 257–75.

156. This paragraph is based on my own contacts and experiences in a variety of Quaker groups.

157. Barbour and Frost, *Quakers,* 242–43.; Ben Richmond, "Friends United Meeting's Struggle over Sexual Ethics," in *Realignment: Nine Views among Friends* (Wallingford, Pa.: Pendle Hill, 1992), 49–60.

158. Barbour and Frost, *Quakers,* 242–43.

159. "Realignment: Destroying Quakerism in Order to Save It," *Friendly Letter,* #119 (3rd Mo. 1991), 2–3; Stephen Main, "Realignment: When Core Values Collide," in *Realignment,* 10–16; *Western Yearly Meeting Minutes, 1988,* pp. 38–40, 44–48; ibid., *1993,* 20, 35–36; ibid., *1995,* 6–12; Board Minutes, Feb. 27, 1970.

160. Evan Farber to Franklin W. Wallin et al., Oct. 20, 1976, Bookstore File, Controversial Issues Collection; Faculty Minutes, Feb. 5, 1985; Board Minutes, Oct. 14, 1977; *Indiana Yearly Meeting Minutes, 1979,* pp. 26–27; "Improving Earlham-Quaker Relations," *Earlham Word,* Jan. 16, 1987, p. 2. Ernest E. Mills, a former trustee, related the story of the problems obtaining the mailing list.

161. Mari Hughes, "ARS Proposal Bans Coed Baths," *Earlham Post,* Feb. 3, 1977, p. 1; "The Indiana Yearly Meeting and Earlham," ibid., April 2, 1981, pp. 1, 4.

162. "Mailbox," ibid., Oct. 21, 1982, p. 3; Dan Becker, "Dungeons and Dragons Banned from Bookstore as 'War Fantasy,'" ibid., Oct. 6, 1982, pp. 1, 2; Jane Cobb, "Friends' Concerns Many and Divergent," ibid., Feb. 12, 1981, pp. 1, 3.

163. This paragraph is based on my own experiences and impressions.

164. Farber to Wallin et al.; William Fuson to Wallin, July 21, 1976, William Fuson Papers (Friends Collection); *Indiana Yearly Meeting Minutes, 1975,* p. 11; ibid., *1976,* p. 53; Delonda L. Jarvis to Lymon Hall, July 12, 1976, Mooreland Monthly Meeting Minutes (Friends Collection).

165. *Indiana Yearly Meeting Minutes, 1984,* pp. 27, 63.

166. Ibid., *1985,* pp. 70–76, 99; "Wood Helps Heal Meeting-E.C. Rift," *Richmond Palladium-Item,* Aug. 17, 1985, p. B4.

167. *Indiana Yearly Meeting Minutes, 1985,* pp. 75–76; "Evaluating Earlham," *Earlhamite,* 107 (Fall 1986), 17–21; "Bias, Earlham Style," *Earlham Post,* Feb. 24, 1977, p. 2; "Report of the Earlham Quaker Relations Task Force," 1986 (Friends Collection).

168. *Indiana Yearly Meeting Minutes, 1991,* pp. 1, 13–14, 31 33; Richard J. Wood to Indiana Yearly Meeting, Aug. 5, 1991, Religious Controversies File, Controversial Issues Collection.

169. Stacy Kawamura, "IYM Proposes to Support Anderson Quaker Professor," *Earlham Word,* Oct. 25, 1991, p. 1; *Indiana Yearly Meeting Minutes, 1992,* p. 21; Indiana Yearly Meeting Executive Committee Minutes, Sept. 7, 1991 (Friends Collection).

170. Tor Lindbloom, "Conflict Arises Over Trustee Appointments," *Earlham Word,* May 22, 1992, pp. 1, 2; Martha B. Rush to Hamm, Jan. 12, 1996 (in Hamm's possession). Much of this paragraph and following comes from conversations with people at Earlham and in Indiana Yearly Meeting who were directly involved.

171. See note 174. Those involved in the "Unofficial Committee" insist that Wood's dismissal was not their goal.

172. Luke Clippinger, "Interview with Dick Wood Helps Clarify Earlham College's Position," *Earlham Word,* Feb. 8, 1991, p. 1; Daniel Becker, "Concern for Gay Rights Voiced," *Earlham Post,* Oct. 14, 1982, p. 1; Sara Beth Terrell, "Lost in Struggle," ibid., Nov. 4, 1982, p. 3. The yearly meeting reaffirmed the minute in 1993, again with some members voicing disapproval.

173. "Indiana Yearly Meeting Cannot Change Earlham College," *Earlham Word,* May 29, 1992, p. 1; Lee Chalfant et al. to Nominating Committee, April 30, 1992, 1992 Trustee Controversy, Religious Controversies File. Several members of the Nominating Committee shared impressions of the discussion with me.

174. *Indiana Yearly Meeting Minutes, 1992,* p. 17. Files of correspondence between college officials and members of the yearly meeting on this issue are in the Religious Controversies File.

175. *Indiana Yearly Meeting Minutes, 1992,* pp. 8–9, 11; Margaret Fraser, "Learning from Friends IV: The Power of Prayer and the Business Method," *Friend,* Sept. 25, 1992, pp. 1236–39. I have in my possession notes that I made during the discussion.

176. Fraser, "Learning from Friends," 1238–39; SaraAnne Acres, "Making

Friends with the Friends," *Earlham Word,* Sept. 25, 1992, p. 7; Mary Landrum, "Stormy IYM Sessions Conclude in Trustee Reappointments," ibid., pp. 1–3; *Indiana Yearly Meeting Minutes, 1992,* pp. 12–13.

177. *Indiana Yearly Meeting Minutes, 1993,* pp. 76–77.

178. Faculty Minutes, Feb. 16, 1994; "94 MBLGC" brochure.

179. David Brock to Indiana Yearly Meeting Earlham Trustees, Feb. 8, 1994, MBLGC File; Wood to Brock, Feb. 9, 1994, ibid.; Thomas D. Hamm et al. to Brock, Feb. 1994, ibid.; Faculty Minutes, Feb. 16, 1994.

180. Mike Neifert, "Allowing Conference Not Christian or Quaker," *Richmond Palladium-Item,* Feb. 19, 1994; "Quakers Blast Meeting of Conference for Gays on Earlham Campus," *Indianapolis Star,* Feb. 20, 1994, p. C3; Indiana Yearly Meeting Executive Committee Minutes, March 21, 1994.

181. *Indiana Yearly Meeting Minutes, 1995,* p. 23. I was present when Western Yearly Meeting approved the proposal in its Administrative Council, Nov. 18, 1995.

Bibliography

Archival Sources

EARLHAM COLLEGE FRIENDS COLLECTION

Earlham is blessed with abundant resources for its history. After the construction of the first library building in 1907, Harlow Lindley began to gather material from offices on campus. Thus virtually all of the college's official records, along with many others, escaped destruction when Lindley Hall burned in 1924. Thomas D.S. Bassett was the first college archivist, appointed in 1957. Opal Thornburg succeeded him in 1958, and to her must go the credit for gathering most of the material I used.

Official Records

Central to any study of Earlham are the records of the Board of Trustees and its predecessor bodies. They begin with the minutes of the Boarding School Committee in 1832, and proceed through the Board of Managers Minutes and the Board of Trustees Minutes to the present. These records include some account books of donations received before the opening of the Friends Boarding School in 1847.

The Faculty Minutes begin in 1859. Before 1900, they are concerned largely with disciplinary matters. For the twentieth century, they are the basic source for curricular change and faculty governance.

The archives include minutes of a number of faculty committees. I found those of the Curricular Policy Committee and its predecessor bodies, the Curriculum Committee and the Educational Policy Committee, especially helpful.

Presidential Papers

The Friends Collection has collections for all of Earlham's presidents. The Barnabas C. Hobbs Papers contain nothing pertaining to Earlham, relating primarily to Hobb's trip to Europe in 1878. The Joseph Moore Papers are extensive, but they consist primarily of family letters and papers relating to Moore's scientific and religious interests. There is relatively little on his administration of the college, or correspondence with colleagues or students. The Joseph John Mills Papers consist of some miscellaneous letters and an 1890s letterbook that illustrates the variety of concerns of the president at that time. The Robert L. Kelly Papers consist of a small body of letters received and a short autobiography, composed about 1940. It also includes material that Opal Thornburg gathered about 1960 concerning the controversy between Kelly and Elbert Russell. Especially valuable are photocopies of correspondence from the files of William Cullen Dennis that are among his personal papers, still privately held.

More complete holdings begin with David M. Edwards. It appears that all of his correspondence before 1924 was lost in the Lindley Hall fire, and much of that for 1926 and 1927 fell victim to rats while it was in storage. The Edwards Papers also include a small but important file of letters written to Edwards in 1929–1930, after his resignation, that are revealing of faculty attitudes toward the new president. The William Cullen Dennis and Thomas E. Jones Papers are complete. Landrum Bolling's office files are extensive, although strangely sparse for 1968. Office files from the Franklin Wallin and Dewitt C. Baldwin presidencies are still unprocessed. These files are the richest source for the history of Earlham since 1920.

Other Office Files

The deposit of other office files in the archives has been less consistent. There are no academic dean's office files before the appointment of Joe Elmore in 1963, save for a box of Harry N. Wright Papers relating to the construction of Carpenter Hall. Elmore's files are complete, as are those of Paul Lacey for the period that he was provost.

Virtually all surviving nineteenth-century materials from the offices of the treasurer and superintendent are found in dozens of ledgers. There is relatively little else from the business side of the college before 1946. The Paul Furnas Papers are extensive. Since 1958, only selected files have been deposited.

I found some crucial materials on student life in the files of the Student Development Office and its predecessor bodies. They go back to 1952 and end in 1986; holdings before 1960 are scattered.

The Alumni Development Office and its predecessor bodies have left rich holdings. They include thousands of alumni files, containing information on students since the founding of Earlham. Those for the 1940s and 1950s, created when Robert N. Huff was in charge, are rich in correspondence with alumni about a variety of matters, including considerable reminiscent material. The Alumni Association's records begin in 1871.

Two smaller but important collections are files from the Urban Studies Program, 1973–1975, and the African and African American Studies Program, 1969 to date. They concern not only the programs themselves but also blacks on campus.

The Earlham Faculty Collection consists largely of personnel files kept by the president's office, but includes biographical material, clippings, and letters from numerous sources. They often contain critical material on a variety of campus issues. Apparently all personnel files before 1924 were lost in the destruction of Lindley Hall. I have used no personnel records for faculty still living.

Student Records

About 1886, some member of the faculty, probably Eli Jay, compiled a list of all students who attended the boarding school and Earlham since 1847. The compiler used a number of registers, some of which are still in the Friends Collection.

The college archives include records of numerous student groups. The Phoenix, the Ionian, and the Anglican all left dozens of minute books. There are extensive records of student governmental organizations, such as the Senate, the dormitory councils, and the Association of Women Students. There are also scattered records of other organizations, ranging from the Press Club to the Gay People's Union. A full listing would embrace hundreds of volumes and files.

An especially rich resource for campus life are the Opinion Board files. Those saved begin in 1949, and are relatively complete until 1973, with a gap until 1984. Since then, they have been systematically preserved.

Over the years, a number of student letters, diaries, and reminiscences have been deposited in the archives. Most of the correspondence in the Student Letters Collection dates from before 1900, as do most of the extant diaries, although there are a few between 1900 and 1920. The single largest body of material in the Reminiscences Collection was solicited by Opal Thornburg between 1958 and 1960 for use in her history. It is a rich source for life on campus between 1880 and 1930.

Manuscript Collections

There are many other individual and family manuscript collections in the Friends Collection that contain valuable material on Earlham. Among the most useful were the following:

Carpenter-Wright Family Papers. This consists primarily of letters to Walter T. and Susan Carpenter and their daughter Caroline who married Henry C. Wright. It also includes diaries kept by Caroline and her sister Elizabeth while students in the 1860s. The Carpenters and Wrights were interested observers of Earlham affairs for seventy years, and much about the campus between 1860 and 1930 can be gleaned from this collection.

Naomi P. Curl Papers. This is a small but important collection of letters written mainly in the 1850s to a Quaker woman from Logan County, Ohio, who worked for a time at the Boarding School. Curl was a niece of Superintendent David Hunt, and several of the letters are from Hunt and students.

William Fuson Papers. Fuson is an archivist's delight, an important campus figure who has preserved virtually every significant memorandum and letter he received or wrote between his arrival in 1946 and his retirement in 1978. He supplemented and annotated much of this material in an extensive memoir.

Indiana Yearly Meeting Archives. I examined a few records in regard to specific events: Portland Quarterly Meeting at the time of the 1920 investigation, or Mooreland Monthly Meeting in 1976 for the bookstore controversy, for example. The large collection of West Richmond Monthly Meeting records is especially valuable for the correspondence between S. Edgar Nicholson and Charles Woodman.

Eli and Mahalah Jay Papers. This is a large collection, invaluable for numerous aspects of Quaker history between 1840 and 1910. Eli's diaries are a wonderful resource for events in the 1860s.

Thomas and Esther Jones Papers. These are personal papers, as opposed to
Tom Jones's office files. Especially valuable are the drafts of Tom Jones's
autobiography, with significant material not included in the published
version.

Ernest E. Mills Papers. This small collection contains significant material on
support for the nonregistrants in 1949–1950 and the college's relationship
with Indiana Yearly Meeting.

Homer and Edna Morris Papers. This is another large, extremely rich
collection. Like the Jays, the Morrises systematically saved correspondence and papers relating to every aspect of their lives. Morris's files from
his twenty-one years as a trustee are invaluable for the Dennis administration and the early Jones years.

Timothy Nicholson Papers. This is a small collection, but important for
anyone interested in Gurneyite Friends between 1870 and 1910. The
correspondence regarding the Dougan Clark controversy in 1894 is vital.

Elbert Russell Papers. This is a large collection that embraces Russell's entire
life. Fortunately for historians, Russell was cautious enough to make
copies of letters to theological opponents. This collection also includes
the manuscript of his autobiography, which contains valuable material
not included in the published version.

Opal Thornburg Papers. Much of this collection relates to Thornburg and
her eight sisters, all of whom were Earlham students, and their families.
It contains, however, two short diaries from 1937 and 1959 that shed
important light on campus affairs.

D. Elton Trueblood Papers. This will be one of the largest collections in the
Friends Collection, but it was received too late for me to do much more
than sample a few items.

Esther Griffin White Papers. This large collection of a former Earlham
student and leading Richmond feminist and gadfly contains material on
the Russell-Kelly controversy in 1915 and Richmond Friends and World
War I.

Ernest A. Wildman Papers. Most of the Wildman collection relates to his
scientific interests and CPS work during World War II. Wildman's draft
autobiography, however, is invaluable for student life, and there are
critical materials on the 1928 faculty survey and the controversy over the
Coffin Report in 1935.

Other Manuscript Material

Opal Thornburg created a records group that she called the "Controversial
Issues Collection." It consists of correspondence, memoranda, clippings,
and other materials relating to campus controversies since 1900. Here,
for example, are found the transcripts of the 1920 heresy hearing,
extensive materials on the draft resisters of 1948–1949, files concerning
interracial dating, and, more recently, subjects ranging from divestment
to the LBGPU to the trustee appointment controversy of 1992.

As noted in the introduction, this book is based in large part on research
done with students from 1990 to 1993. Their work included the following
papers:

Alberts, Jason. "A Study of Community Relations: Earlham College and the Greater Richmond Community." Nov. 1993.

Barefoot, Killian. "A Struggle for Equality: A History of Women's Education at Earlham College, 1901–1965." May 1991.

Carey, Kathy. "Changing Attitudes toward Temperance at Earlham College, 1847–1919." June 7, 1991.

Christianson, Erica J. "The Experience of Women at Earlham College during the Tom Jones Administration." March 16, 1990.

Gosney, Gwendolyn. "Changing with the Times: Women's Experiences at Earlham College, 1958–1973." Nov. 23, 1993.

Hedrick, Jessica. "Earlham and McCarthyism." March 1990.

Henry, Bill. "The Quaker Commitment to Gender Equality: Women Faculty at Earlham College, 1880–1940." June 11, 1991.

Micheli, Robert. "Earlham College: A Study of Community Relations in the McCarthy Era, 1946–1955." March 12, 1990.

Parker, Aaron. "Faculty Governance at Earlham College." June 1991.

Sedam, Rebecca J. "Peace Activism at Earlham, 1946–1958." March 1990.

Smith, Emily. "Earlham College and Vietnam: What Happened and What Made It Different?" Nov. 23, 1993.

Swain, Ellen. "Earlham in Transition: Experience of Black Students, 1946–58." Feb. 16, 1990.

Winternitz, Robert. "The Friendly College: Student-Faculty Relations at Earlham, 1847–1930." June 1991.

Wood, Amity. "Forging Ahead: Off-Campus Study at Earlham." Nov. 23, 1993.

I have also relied on written accounts by former students and faculty, especially the following letters to me:

Margaret Grant Beidler, Aug. 18, 1994
Landrum Bolling, Jan. 7, 1996
Francis D. Hole, Feb. 13, March 11, 1995
Kenneth Ives, Dec. 26, 1994
Paul Lacey, Dec. 18, 1995, Jan. 2, 1996
Robert and Grace (Cunningham) McAllester, Jan. 4, 1996
Esther (Winder) Nelson, Jan. 5, 1995
Marian (Binford) Sanders, Jan. 5, 1995
Yuan Tien, Jan. 2, 1996
Franklin Wallin, Jan. 15, 1996
Clifton Warren, Dec. 20, 1994

Campus Publications

The published college catalogs begin in 1858, while student handbooks were first published in 1891. I have examined almost all of them. The college archives also include thousands of ephemeral publications.

Many of the first campus literary journals were handwritten; most probably produced only one issue. The first to be put in print was the *Literary Gem* in 1853. A number of these for the 1850s and 1860s are in the archives.

As is the case with almost all college histories, campus newspapers have been my single most useful source, after the president's office files. They must be used as reflecting a certain facet of student culture, not the entire culture. Without them, however, much of Earlham's life would be lost. I examined every surviving issue of the following, virtually complete runs of all of which are in the college archives:

Earlhamite, 1873–
Phoenixian, 1891–1894
Earlham Press, 1911–1925
Quaker Quill, 1926–1931
Earlham Post, 1931–1985
Earlham Word, 1986 to date

There were other, short-lived campus journals, a few issues of which survive in the archives. In a somewhat different category are the student nonfiction magazine *Prism,* published from 1961 to 1967, and *We Speak,* published since 1984 by the Womyn's Center.

I also examined almost all years of the college yearbook, the *Sargasso.* Generally, however, I found it less illustrative of the life of the campus than the newspapers.

Oral Histories

The following were done by Thomas D. Hamm, or by him with the aid of students:

Mathew K. Amberg, April 25, 1994
Jackson H. Bailey, Oct. 14, 1993, Dec. 12, 1995
Gerald Bakker, Oct. 14, 1993
Dewitt C. Baldwin, Jr., June 8, 1995
Joseph and Jean (Hamm) Balestrieri, April 26, 1994
Thomas D. S. Bassett, Nov. 15, 1990
Edward Bastian, May 20, 1994
Jay W. and Louise (Maxwell) Beede, June 6, 1995
Norma Bentley, May 10, 1995
Tony Bing, Oct. 31, 1995
Lincoln Blake, Oct. 14, 1993
Landrum R. Bolling, Feb. 8, 1996
Wayne C. Booth, Jan. 4, 1995
Jon Branstrator, Oct. 4, 1993
Glen Bull, April 2, 1995
Mildred Henley Calvert, April 23, 1994
C. Wayne Carter, Feb. 24, 1995
Edmund C. Casey, June 26, 1994
Len Clark, Aug. 16, 1995
Wilmer Cooper, Oct. 18, 1994
Harold and Ann Cope, April 25, April 28, 1994
Joe E. Elmore, Feb. 10, Feb. 24, Feb. 27, 1994
Evan I. Farber, Oct. 14, 1993
Hope (Wells) Farber, Feb. 15, Feb. 26, 1990, Oct. 25, 1993
Robert E. Fatherley, Feb. 3, Sept. 9, 1995

J. Arthur Funston, May 20, 1994
William M. Fuson, Feb. 19, 1990
Lavona (Reece) Godsey, Feb. 15, 1990, Oct. 25, 1993
Robert Goens, Feb. 12, 1990
Lorton Heusel, Jan. 26, 1990
Mary Lane (Charles) Hiatt, April 20, 1994
Imogene (Cuffel) Holloway, June 21, 1994
Cecile Holvik, Feb. 15, 1990, Oct. 25, 1993
Leonard Holvik, Feb. 19, 1990
James G. and Helen (Ellis) Johnson, Feb. 25, 1995
Louis and Mary Ruth (Brown) Jones, May 30, 1995
Carl and Lois (Harned) Jordan, May 5, 1994
Carolyn (Carter) Kellum, June 7, 1994
Gilbert Klose, Oct. 12, 1993
Margaret (Smith) Lacey, Oct. 25, 1993
Paul Lacey, Oct. 14, 1993
Anna Langston, Dec. 5, 1994
Harry W. Leavell, Feb. 12, 1990
Sara Little, Feb. 19, 1990
Elsa (Carter) Littmann, Aug. 11, 1995
James McDowell, Feb. 19, 1990
Nancy McDowell, Feb. 15, 1990
Donald McKinney, Nov. 3, 1994
Charles Martin, Oct. 12, 1993
Howard G. Mills, Sr., April 6, 1990
Anna (Saylor) Morris, April 19, 1994
Florence L. Moyer, April 27, 1994
S. Francis Nicholson, June 7, 1996
Sara Penhale, Oct. 4, 1993, Oct. 25, 1993, June 26, 1995
Kathleen Postle, Aug. 15, 1990
Susan Porter Rose, April 26, 1994
George E. Sawyer, May 2, 1995
Roy Schuckman, Feb. 15, 1990
Randall and Alice Almond Shrock, Oct. 4, 1993
Martha (Calvert) Slotten, April 23, 1994
Jewell (King) Spears, Feb. 12, 1990
Patricia Staebler, Feb. 15, Feb. 19, 1990
Warren Staebler, Feb. 19, 1990
William K. Stephenson, May 23, 1995
Edith (Pickett) Stratton, June 27, 1994
Mary (James) Stratton, Feb. 15, 1990
Laurence and Ruth Strong, April 25, April 28, 1994
Peter Suber, Oct. 4, 1993
David Telfair, Feb. 19, 1990, May 9, 1995
D. Elton Trueblood, April 20, 1994
Alson Van Wagner, April 19, 1994
Arnold Vaught, April 25, 1994

Robert Warner, Feb. 15, 1990
Gwen Weaver, June 28, 1995
Edwin E. White, June 28, 1994
Richard J. Wood, Dec. 18, 1995
Jerry Woolpy, Feb. 22, 1995
R. Dwight Young, May 16, 1995

The following were done by other interviewers:

Margaret Grant Beidler by Patricia Staebler, Nov. 15, 1984
O. Theodor Benfey, by James J. Bohning, May 24, June 5, 1991
James Cope, by Patricia Staebler, Feb. 13, 1986
Hope Farber, by Ellen D. Swain, Feb. 26, 1990
Orville Johnson by Patricia Staebler, June 19, 1984
Paul Lacey, by Anthony Holtz, April 29, 1986
R. Edward Lee, by Ellen D. Swain, Feb. 7, 1990
Arthur Little by Patricia Staebler, June 18, 1984
James P. Mullin, by Patricia Staebler, July 13, 1986
Mary M. Mullin, by Patricia Staebler, Aug. 11, 1987

MANUSCRIPT MATERIALS FOUND ELSEWHERE

Some significant Earlham-related material is not held at Earlham. At the Friends Historical Library of Swarthmore College are three important collections. The Furnas Family Papers contain a few letters of Aaron and Margaret White, both Wayne County Friends who in the 1830s and 1840s were extremely interested in the success of the Friends Boarding School. While Earlham has a large and important collection of the papers of Charles F. and Rhoda M. Coffin, and a smaller one of papers of Elijah Coffin, it is Swarthmore's Coffin Family Collection that includes Elijah Coffin's letterbooks, with their invaluable letters to Huldah C. Hoag about her employment and to Thomas Evans in Philadelphia about purchasing books for the library. The Coffin-Baxter Collection contains useful letters for the financial problems of the 1850s as observed by Hugh Moffitt, a sympathetic Richmond Friend.

There are two useful collections in the Quaker Collection at Haverford College. The Rufus M. Jones Papers are a central resource for most aspects of twentieth-century Quaker history, and they contain significant letters from Thomas R. Kelly, Allen Jay, Elbert Russell, Amos K. Hollowell, David M. Edwards, and Robert L. Kelly, among others. There is also considerable correspondence concerning the Dougan Clark controversy in 1894. The Thomas R. Kelly Papers include several letters by Kelly and from Earlham colleagues commenting on campus affairs.

I traveled to the Manuscripts Department of the University of Oregon at Eugene to use the E. Merrill Root Papers. They contain several letters that were helpful in reconstructing Root's intellectual odyssey. I also found significant Root correspondence in the Howard E. Kershner Papers and the Edmund A. Opitz Papers. The Kershner Papers also included significant letters from Elton Trueblood, including material on his 1954 red-baiting victimization.

Published Primary Sources

QUAKER PERIODICALS

The time I devoted to Quaker periodicals was well-spent. The following all contained useful material regarding Earlham or significant articles by Earlham authors:

American Friend (Richmond, Ind.), 1867–1868
American Friend (Philadelphia and Richmond, Ind.), 1894–1960
Christian Worker (New Vienna, Ohio, and Chicago), 1871–1894
Friendly Letter (Falls Church, Va.), 1981–1994
Friends Journal (Philadelphia), 1955 to date
Friends' Review (Philadelphia), 1847–1894
Herald of Peace (Chicago), 1868–1869
Quaker Life (Richmond, Ind.), 1960 to date

OTHER PUBLISHED PRIMARY SOURCES

Baker, Jacob. *Incidents of My Life and Work of 84 Years.* Richmond, Ind.: Nicholson, 1911.
Bakker, Gerald R., and Paul A. Lacey, "The Teaching Consultant at Earlham," in *Effective Approaches to Faculty Development,* ed. William C. Nelsen and Michael E. Siegel. Washington: Association of American Colleges, 1980.
Baldwin, James. *In the Days of My Youth: An Intimate Record of Life and Manners in the Middle Ages of the Middle West.* Indianapolis: Bobbs-Merrill, 1923.
Brown, Thomas S. *The Flaming Sword: Given at Western Yearly Meeting of Friends, Tuesday Evening, August 21, 1951.* N.p., 1951.
Cadbury, Anna Moore. "Joseph Moore." *Quaker Biographies: Series II.* 5 vols. Philadelphia: Friends' Book Store, n.d.
Clark, Dougan, Jr. *Address by Dr. Dougan Clark.* N.p., 1858.
——. *The Holy Ghost Dispensation.* Chicago: Publishing Association of Friends, 1891.
——, and Joseph H. Smith. *David B. Updegraff and His Work.* Cincinnati: M. W. Knapp, 1895.
Clark, William W. *The Practice of Jesus: Given at Western Yearly Meeting of Friends, August 19, 1952.* N.p., 1952.
Coffin, Addison. *Life and Travels of Addison Coffin.* Cleveland: William G. Hubbard, 1897.
Cottle, Thomas J. "A Learning Place Called Earlham." *Change.* 3 (Jan.-Feb. 1971), 52–59.
Discipline of the Society of Friends, of Indiana Yearly Meeting. Cincinnati: A. Pugh, 1839.
Emswiler, George P. *Poems and Sketches.* Richmond, Ind.: Nicholson, 1897.
Farber, Evan I. "Library Instruction at Earlham College." *Library Research Newsletter.* 6 (Winter and Spring 1981), 35–48.

——. "The Senior Art Purchase Prize." *College and Undergraduate Libraries.* 1 (1994), 23–28.

——, ed. *Teaching and Technology: The Impact of Unlimited Information Access on Classroom Teaching.* Ann Arbor: Pierian Press, 1991.

Fosdick, Harry Emerson. *The Living of These Days.* New York: Harper and Row, 1956.

Fox, George. *Works.* 8 vols. Philadelphia: Marcus T. C. Gould, 1831.

Fraser, Margaret. "Learning from Friends IV: The Power of Prayer and the Business Method." *Friend,* Sept. 25, 1992, pp. 1236–39.

Hall, Barbara Welling. "Electronic News Groups in the Liberal Arts Classroom." *International Studies Notes.* 20 (Winter 1995), 9–15.

Heiss, Willard C., ed. *Abstracts of the Records of the Society of Friends in Indiana.* 7 vols. Indianapolis: Indiana Historical Society, 1962–1977.

Henley, David E. *A Quaker Approach to Democracy, Given at Western Yearly Meeting of Friends, Tuesday Evening, August 17, 1948.* N.p., 1948.

Hinshaw, William Wade, ed. *Encyclopedia of American Quaker Genealogy.* 6 vols. Ann Arbor: Edwards Brothers, 1936–1950.

Hoover, Henry. *Sketches and Incidents, Embracing a Period of Fifty Years.* Indianapolis: John Woolman Press, 1962.

Indiana Yearly Meeting. *Minutes.* 1821 to date.

——. *Testimony and Epistle of Advice.* N.p., 1827.

Jacob, Caroline Nicholson. *Nicholson Family History.* West Chester, Pa., 1970.

Jay, Allen. *Autobiography of Allen Jay, Born 1831, Died 1910.* Philadelphia: John C. Winston, 1910.

Johnson, Mary Coffin, ed. *Life of Elijah Coffin.* Cincinnati: E. Morgan, 1863.

Jones, Thomas E. *Close Proving of All: Quaker Lecture Given at Western Yearly Meeting of Friends, Thursday Evening, August 21, 1958.* N.p., 1958.

——. *A Fertile Cross Between a Friends Meeting House and a Scientific Laboratory.* N.p., 1946.

——. *Light on the Horizon: The Quaker Pilgrimage of Tom Jones.* Richmond, Ind.: Friends United Press, 1973.

Kenworthy, Leonard S. *Worldview: The Autobiography of a Social Studies Teacher and Quaker.* Richmond, Ind.: Friends United Press, 1977.

Mayer, Milton. "Earlham's Pickled Cat." *Progressive.* 13 (Aug. 1949), 13–14.

Minority Report on Earlham College Investigation. Knightstown, Ind., 1921.

Minutes and Proceedings of the Five Years Meeting of the American Yearly Meetings of Friends Held in Richmond, Ind., Tenth Mo. 15, to 10th Mo. 21, 1907. Philadelphia: John C. Winston, 1908.

Mott, Edward. *The Friends Church in the Light of Its Recent History.* Portland, Ore.: Loomis, n.d.

——. *Sixty Years of Gospel Ministry.* N.p., 1947.

Osborn, Charles. *Journal of That Faithful Servant of Christ, Charles Osborn, Containing an Account of Many of His Travels and Labors in the Ministry, and His Trials and Exercises in the Service of the Lord, and in Defense of the Truth, as It Is in Jesus.* Cincinnati: Achilles Pugh, 1854.

Quaker Universalist Reader Number 1: A Collection of Essays, Addresses and Lectures. Landenberg, Pa.: Quaker Universalist Fellowship, 1986.

Realignment: Nine Views among Friends. Wallingford, Pa.: Pendle Hill, 1992.

Root, E. Merrill. *Brainwashing in the High Schools: An Examination of Eleven American History Textbooks.* New York: Devin-Adair, 1958.

——. *Collectivism on the Campus: The Battle for the Mind in American Colleges.* New York: Devin-Adair, 1955.

——. "Darkness at Noon in American Colleges." *Human Events.* July 30, 1952, pp. 275–79.

——. *Dies Irae—Day of Wrath.* Richmond, Ind.: Peace Association of Friends, 1924.

——. "From Genesis to Exodus." *World Tomorrow.* (Jan. 1927), 7–9.

——. "The Passive Professional Majority." *Human Events.* Oct. 29, 1952, pp. 385–91.

Russell, Elbert. *Elbert Russell, Quaker: An Autobiography.* Jackson, Tenn.: Friendly Press, 1956.

——. *Jesus of Nazareth in the Light of Today.* Philadelphia: John C. Winston, 1909.

Search for Peace in the Middle East. Philadelphia: American Friends Service Committee, 1970.

Solorzano, Lucia. *Barron's 300 Best Buys in College Education.* New York: Barron's, 1994.

Stanton, Borden. "A Brief Account." *Friends Miscellany.* Ed. by John Comly and Isaac Comly. 12 vols. Philadelphia: J. Richards, 1831–1839.

Stenographic Report of the Funeral Services of Dr. Dougan Clark, Held in the Friends Yearly Meeting House, Richmond, Indiana, October 13th, 1896, at 2 P.M. Richmond, Ind.: J. M. Coe, 1896.

Tallack, William. *Friendly Sketches in America.* London: A. W. Bennett, 1861.

Trueblood, Elton. *Alternative to Futility.* New York: Harper and Row, 1940.

——. *Declaration of Freedom.* New York: Harper and Row, 1955.

——. *Foundations for Reconstruction.* New York: Harper and Row, 1946.

——. *The Life We Prize.* New York: Harper and Row, 1951.

——. *The Predicament of Modern Man.* New York: Harper and Row, 1944.

——. *A Radical Experiment.* Philadelphia: Philadelphia Yearly Meeting, 1947.

——. *While It Is Day: An Autobiography.* New York: Harper and Row, 1974.

——. "Why I Chose a Small College." *Reader's Digest.* 69 (Sept. 1956), 38–42.

Uyesugi, Ruth Farlow. *Don't Cry, Chiisai, Don't Cry.* Paoli, Ind.: Stout's Print Shop, 1977.

Wells, Herman B. *Being Lucky: Reminiscences and Reflections.* Bloomington: Indiana University Press, 1980.

Western Yearly Meeting. *Minutes.* 1858 to date.

Zitkala-Sa. "The School Days of an Indian Girl." *Atlantic Monthly.* 85 (Feb. 1900), 185–94.

Secondary Sources

Adam, Barry D. *The Rise of a Gay and Lesbian Movement.* Boston: Twayne, 1987.

Ahlstrom, Sydney E. *A Religious History of the American People.* New Haven: Yale University Press, 1972.

Allott, Stephen. *Lindley Murray, 1745–1826: Quaker Grammarian of New York and Old York.* York, Eng.: Sessions, 1991.

Anderson, Robert C. *Peace Was in Their Hearts: Conscientious Objectors in World War II.* Watsonville, Calif.: Correlan Publications, 1994.

Bachelder, Laura M. *Indiana Alma Maters: Student Life at Indiana Colleges, 1820–1860.* Fishers, Ind.: Conner Prairie, 1995.

Barbour, Hugh, et al., eds. *Quaker Crosscurrents: Three Hundred Years of Friends in the New York Yearly Meetings.* Syracuse: Syracuse University Press, 1995.

——, and J. William Frost. *The Quakers.* Westport: Greenwood Press, 1988.

Barnard, John. *From Evangelicalism to Progressivism at Oberlin College, 1866–1917.* Columbus: Ohio State University Press, 1969.

Beeth, Howard. "Outside Agitators in Southern History: The Society of Friends, 1656–1800." Ph.D. diss., University of Houston, 1984.

Benjamin, Philip S. *The Philadelphia Quakers in the Industrial Age, 1865–1920.* Philadelphia: Temple University Press, 1976.

Bickley, William Phillips. "Education as Reformation: An Examination of Orthodox Quakers' Formation of the Haverford School Association and Founding of Haverford School, 1815–1840." Ed.D. diss., Harvard University, 1983.

Birkel, Michael, and John W. Newman, eds. *The Lamb's War: Quaker Essays in Honor of Hugh Barbour.* Richmond, Ind.: Earlham College Press, 1992.

Bivens, Donald E. "Joseph A. Goddard: Muncie Businessman and Quaker Leader." Ph.D. diss., Ball State University, 1989.

Bledstein, Burton J. *The Culture of Professionalism: The Middle Class and the Development of Higher Education in America.* New York: Norton, 1976.

Blum, John Morton. *V Was for Victory: Politics and American Culture during World War II.* New York: Harcourt Brace Jovanovich, 1976.

Boller, Paul F. *American Thought in Transition: The Impact of Evolutionary Naturalism, 1865–1900.* Washington, D.C.: University Press of 1981.

Boone, Richard G. *A History of Education in Indiana.* New York: D. Appleton, 1892.

Boyer, Paul. *By the Bomb's Early Light: American Thought and Culture at the Dawn of the Atomic Age.* Chapel Hill: University of North Carolina Press, 1994.

Branch, Taylor. *Parting the Waters: America in the King Years, 1954–63.* New York: Simon & Schuster, 1988.

Brereton, Virginia Lieson. *Training God's Army: The American Bible School, 1880–1940.* Bloomington: Indiana University Press, 1990.

Brinton, Howard H. *Quaker Education in Theory and Practice.* Wallingford, Pa.: Pendle Hill, 1949.

——, ed. *Children of Light: In Honor of Rufus M. Jones.* New York: Macmillan, 1938.

Buys, John William. "Quakers in Indiana in the Nineteenth Century." Ph.D. diss., University of Florida, 1973.

Cadbury, Henry J. "Negro Membership in the Society of Friends." *Journal of Negro History.* 21 (April 1936), 151–213.

Cagin, Seth, and Philip Dray. *We Are Not Afraid: The Story of Goodman,*

Schwerner, and Chaney and the Civil Rights Campaign for Mississippi. New York: Macmillan, 1988.

Centennial Anniversary of West Branch Monthly Meeting of Friends, Established 1st Month 1, 1807. N.p., n.d.

Chafe, William H. *The Paradox of Change: American Women in the Twentieth Century.* New York: Oxford University Press, 1991.

———. *The Unfinished Journey: America since World War II.* New York: Oxford University Press, 1991.

Chalmers, David P. *And the Crooked Places Made Straight: The Struggle for Social Change in the 1960s.* Baltimore: Johns Hopkins University Press, 1991.

Chatfield, Charles. *The American Peace Movement: Ideals and Activism.* New York: Twayne, 1992.

———. *For Peace and Justice: Pacifism in America, 1914–1941.* Knoxville: University of Tennessee Press, 1971.

Cheek, Pauline Binkley. "A Flame Still Burning: The Story of Salem Friends Meeting." Typescript, 1992.

Clark, Minnie B. "Barnabas Coffin Hobbs." *Indiana Magazine of History.* 19 (Sept. 1923), 282–90.

Cohen, Robert. *When the Old Left Was Young: Student Radicals and America's First Mass Student Movement, 1929–1941.* New York: Oxford University Press, 1993.

Conkin, Paul K. *The Uneasy Center: Reformed Christianity in Antebellum America.* Chapel Hill: University of North Carolina Press, 1995.

Cooper, Charles W. *Whittier: Independent College in California.* Los Angeles: Ward Ritchie Press, 1967.

Cooper, William. "Joseph Moore: Quaker Evolutionist." *Indiana Magazine of History.* 72 (June 1976), 123–37.

Cooper, Wilmer A. *The Earlham School of Religion Story: A Quaker Dream Come True, 1960–1985.* Richmond, Ind.: Earlham School of Religion, 1985.

Curtis, Mark. *Enhancing Liberal Education: American Association of Colleges at 75.* Washington, D.C.: American Association of Colleges, 1988.

Daniels, Roger. *Concentration Camps, North America: Japanese in the United States and Canada during World War II.* Malabar, Fla.: Krieger, 1981.

———. *The Politics of Prejudice: The Anti-Japanese Movement in California and the Struggle for Japanese Exclusion.* Berkeley: University of California Press, 1977.

Davis, David Brion. *The Problem of Slavery in Western Culture.* Ithaca: Cornell University Press, 1966.

DeBenedetti, Charles. *An American Ordeal: The Antiwar Movement of the Vietnam Era.* Syracuse: Syracuse University Press, 1990.

D'Emilio, John, and Estelle B. Freedman. *Intimate Matters: A History of Sexuality in America.* New York: Harper and Row, 1988.

Diggins, John P. *Up from Communism: Conservative Odysseys in American Intellectual History.* New York: Harper and Row, 1975.

Drake, Thomas E. *Quakers and Slavery in America.* New Haven: Yale University Press, 1950.

Dubofsky, Melvin. *We Shall Be All: A History of the Industrial Workers of the World.* Chicago: Quadrangle, 1969.

Elliott, Errol T. *Quakers on the American Frontier: A History of the Westward Migrations, Settlements, and Developments of Friends on the American Continent.* Richmond, Ind.: Friends United Press, 1969.

Emerson, Elizabeth H. "Barnabas C. Hobbs: Midwestern Quaker Minister and Educator." *Bulletin of Friends Historical Association.* 49 (Spring 1960), 21–35.

——. *Walter C. Woodward: Friend on the Frontier.* N.p., 1952.

Epstein, Barbara Leslie. *The Politics of Domesticity: Women, Evangelism, and Temperance in Nineteenth-Century America.* Middletown, Ct.: Wesleyan University Press, 1981.

Evans, Sara M. *Born for Liberty: A History of Women in America.* New York: Free Press, 1989.

Foner, Eric, ed. *The New American History.* Philadelphia: Temple University Press, 1990.

Foster, Arnold, and Benjamin R. Epstein. *Danger on the Right.* New York: Random House, 1964.

Franer, Mickie, and Rhonda Curtis, eds. *Marcus Mote and Eli Harvey: Two Quaker Artists from Southwest Ohio.* Oxford, Ohio: Miami University, 1992.

Frost, J. William. "'Our Deeds Carry Our Message': The Early History of the American Friends Service Committee." *Quaker History.* 81 (Spring 1992), 1–51.

——. *The Quaker Family in Colonial America: A Portrait of the Society of Friends.* New York: St. Martin's, 1973.

Gilbert, Dorothy Lloyd. *Guilford: A Quaker College.* Greensboro: Guilford College, 1937.

Gordon, Lynn D. *Gender and Higher Education in the Progressive Era.* New Haven: Yale University Press, 1990.

Hamm, Thomas D. *The Transformation of American Quakerism: Orthodox Friends, 1800–1907.* Bloomington: Indiana University Press, 1988.

—— et al. "Moral Choices: Two Indiana Quaker Communities and the Antislavery Movement." *Indiana Magazine of History.* 87 (June 1991), 117–54.

Harding, Thomas S. *College Literary Societies: Their Contribution to Higher Education in the United States, 1815–1876.* New York: Pageant Press International, 1971.

Harleston, Bernard W. "Higher Education for the Negro: Obstacles." *Atlantic.* 216 (Nov. 1965), 139–44.

[Harvey, Julianna]. *Memorial of Cyrus W. Harvey.* Philadelphia: Friends' Book Store, 1920.

Hawkins, Hugh. *Banding Together: The Rise of National Associations in American Higher Education, 1887–1950.* Baltimore: Johns Hopkins University Press, 1992.

Heineman, Kenneth J. *Campus Wars: The Peace Movement at American State Universities in the Vietnam Era.* New York: New York University Press, 1993.

Higginbotham, A. Leon. *In the Matter of Color: Race and the American Legal System.* New York: Oxford University Press, 1978.

Hofstadter, Richard. *Anti-Intellectualism in American Life.* New York: Vintage, 1966.

Holbrook, Stewart H. *The Yankee Exodus: An Account of Migration from New England.* Seattle: University of Washington Press, 1950.

Hole, Helen G. *Things Civil and Useful: A Personal View of Quaker Education.* Richmond, Ind.: Friends United Press, 1978.

——. *Westtown Through the Years.* Westtown, Pa.: Westtown School, 1942.

Hoover, Dwight W. "Daisy Douglas Barr: From Quaker to Klan 'Kluckeress.'" *Indiana Magazine of History.* 87 (June 1991), 171–95.

Horowitz, Helen Lefkowitz. *Alma Mater: Design and Experience in the Women's Colleges from Their Nineteenth-Century Beginnings to the 1930s.* Boston: Beacon, 1984.

——. *Campus Life: Undergraduate Cultures from the End of the Eighteenth Century to the Present.* Chicago: University of Chicago Press, 1987.

Hutchison, William R. *The Modernist Impulse in American Protestantism.* Cambridge: Harvard University Press, 1976.

Ingle, H. Larry. *Quakers in Conflict: The Hicksite Reformation.* Knoxville: University of Tennessee Press, 1986.

James, Sydney V. *A People among Peoples: Quaker Benevolence in Eighteenth-Century America.* Cambridge: Harvard University Press, 1963.

Jarress, Deloris E., and Eldon Harzman. *History of Quaker Hill Foundation and Conference Center.* Richmond, Ind., 1987.

Johns, David L., ed. *Hope and a Future.* Richmond, Ind.: Friends United Press, 1993.

Johnson, David L., and Raymond Wilson. "Gertrude Simmons Bonnin, 1876–1938: 'Americanize the First American.'" *American Indian Quarterly.* 12 (Winter 1988), 27–40.

Johnson, Mary Coffin, and Percival Brooks Coffin, *Charles F. Coffin: A Quaker Pioneer.* Richmond, Ind.: Nicholson, 1923.

Jones, Rufus M. *Haverford College: A History and an Interpretation.* New York: Macmillan, 1933.

——. *The Later Periods of Quakerism.* 2 vols. London: Macmillan, 1921.

——. *A Service of Love in War Time: American Friends Relief Work in Europe, 1917–1919.* New York: Macmillan, 1920.

Jordan, Lois Harned. *Ramallah Teacher: The Life of Mildred White, Quaker Missionary.* N.p., 1995.

Kelly, Richard M. *Thomas Kelly: A Biography.* New York: Harper and Row, 1966.

Kelsey, Rayner Wickersham. *Centennial History of Moses Brown School, 1819–1919.* Providence, R.I.: Moses Brown School, 1919.

——. *Friends and the Indians, 1655–1917.* Philadelphia: Associated Executive Committee of Friends on Indian Affairs, 1917.

Kennedy, Thomas C. "Southland College: The Society of Friends and Black Education in Arkansas." *Arkansas Historical Quarterly.* 42 (Autumn 1983), 207–38.

Kenworthy, Leonard S. *Quaker Education: A Source Book.* Kennett Square, Pa.: Quaker Publications, [1987].

——. *Living in a Larger World: The Life of Murray S. Kenworthy.* Richmond, Ind.: Friends United Press, 1986.

——, ed. *Living in the Light: Some Quaker Pioneers of the 20th Century.* 2 vols. Kennett Square, Pa., 1984.

Kerr, K. Austin. *Organized for Prohibition: A New History of the Anti-Saloon League.* New Haven: Yale University Press, 1985.

Knollenberg, Bernhard. *Pioneer Sketches of the Upper Whitewater Valley: Quaker Stronghold of the West.* Indianapolis: Indiana Historical Society, 1945.

Larson, Zelle Andrews. "An Unbroken Witness: Conscientious Objection to War, 1948–1953." Ph.D. diss., University of Hawaii, 1975.

Leach, William R. *True Love and Perfect Union: The Feminist Reform of Sex and Society.* New York: Basic, 1980.

Leduc, Thomas. *Piety and Intellect at Amherst College, 1865–1912.* New York: Columbia University Press, 1946.

Leslie, W. Bruce. *Gentlemen and Scholars: College and Community in the "Age of the University," 1865–1917.* University Park: Pennsylvania State University Press, 1992.

McDaniel, Ethel Hittle. *The Contribution of the Society of Friends to Education in Indiana.* Indianapolis: Indiana Historical Society, 1939.

McNally, Dennis. *Desolate Angel: Jack Kerouac, The Beat Generation, and America.* New York: Dell, 1990.

Madison, James H. *Eli Lilly: A Life.* Indianapolis: Indiana Historical Society, 1989.

——. *The Indiana Way: A State History.* Bloomington: Indiana University Press, 1986.

Marable, Manning. *Race, Reform, and Rebellion: The Second Reconstruction in Black America, 1945–1991.* Oxford: University Press of Mississippi, 1991.

Marietta, Jack D. *The Reformation of American Quakerism, 1748–1783.* Philadelphia: University of Pennsylvania Press, 1984.

Marsden, George M. *Fundamentalism and American Culture: The Shaping of of Twentieth-Century Evangelicalism, 1870–1925.* New York: Oxford University Press, 1980.

——. *The Soul of the American University: From Protestant Establishment to Established Nonbelief.* New York: Oxford University Press, 1994.

——, and Bradley J. Longfield, eds. *The Secularization of the Academy.* New York: Oxford University Press, 1992.

Mather, Eleanore Price. *Anna Brinton: A Study in Quaker Character.* Wallingford, Pa.: Pendle Hill, 1971.

Meier, August, and Elliott Rudwick. *Black History and the American Historical Profession, 1915–1980.* Urbana: University of Illinois Press, 1986.

Messerli, Jonathan. *Horace Mann: A Biography.* New York: Knopf, 1972.

Metzger, Walter P. *Academic Freedom in the Age of the University.* New York: Columbia University Press, 1964.

Meyer, Donald H. *The Instructed Conscience: The Shaping of the American National Ethic.* Philadelphia: University of Pennsylvania Press, 1972.

Milner, Clyde A. II. *With Good Intentions: Quaker Work among the Pawnees,*

Otos, and Omahas in the 1870s. Lincoln: University of Nebraska Press, 1982.

Minear, Mark. *Richmond 1887: A Quaker Drama Unfolds.* Richmond, Ind.: Friends United Press, 1987.

Moore, James R. *The Post-Darwinian Controversies: A Study of the Protestant Struggle to Come to Terms with Darwin in Great Britain and America, 1870–1900.* Cambridge: Cambridge University Press, 1979.

Moore, Leonard J. *Citizen Klansmen: The Ku Klux Klan in Indiana, 1921–1928.* Chapel Hill: University of North Carolina Press, 1991.

Newby, James R. *Elton Trueblood: Believer, Teacher, and Friend.* San Francisco: Harper and Row, 1990.

Norton, James Harris. "Quakers West of the Alleghenies and in Ohio to 1861." Ph.D. diss., Case Western Reserve University, 1965.

Novick, Peter. *That Noble Dream: The "Objectivity Question" and the American Historical Profession.* Cambridge: Cambridge University Press, 1987.

O'Neall, John Belton, and John A. Chapman. *The Annals of Newberry.* Newberry, S.C.: Aull & Houseal, 1892.

O'Neill, William L. *American High: The Years of Confidence, 1945–1960.* New York: Free Press, 1986.

——. *Coming Apart: An Informal History of America in the 1960's.* New York: Times, 1971.

Peden, Creighton. *The Chicago School: Voices in Liberal Religious Thought.* Bristol, Ind.: Wyndham Press, 1987.

Peterson, H. C., and Gilbert Fite. *Opponents of War, 1917–1918.* Seattle: University of Washington Press, 1968.

Phillips, Clifton J. *Indiana in Transition: The Emergence of an Industrial Commonwealth, 1880–1920.* Indianapolis: Indiana Historical Bureau and Indiana Historical Society, 1968.

Potts, David B. *Wesleyan University, 1831–1910: Collegiate Enterprise in New England.* New Haven: Yale University Press, 1992.

Proceedings of the Celebration of the Establishment of Whitewater Monthly Meeting of the Religious Society Friends. Richmond, Ind., 1909.

"Race on Campus." *U.S. News and World Report.* April 19, 1993, pp. 52–65.

Ravitch, Diane. *The Troubled Crusade: American Education, 1945–1980.* New York: Basic, 1983.

Rawley, James A. "Joseph John Gurney's Mission to America, 1837–1840." *Mississippi Valley Historical Review.* 49 (March 1963), 653–74.

Roberts, Arthur O. *The Association of Evangelical Friends: A Story of Quaker Renewal in the Twentieth Century.* Newberg, Ore.: Barclay, 1975.

Rohrbough, Malcolm J. *The Trans-Appalachian Frontier: People, Societies, and Institutions, 1775–1850.* New York: Oxford University Press, 1978.

Rorabaugh, W. J. *Berkeley at War: The 1960s.* New York: Oxford University Press, 1989.

Rudolph, Frederick. *The American College and University: A History.* Athens: University of Georgia Press, 1990.

——. *Curriculum: A History of the American Undergraduate Course of Study since 1636.* San Francisco: Jossey-Bass, 1977.

Russell, Elbert. *The History of Quakerism.* New York: Macmillan, 1942.

Ryan, Alan. *John Dewey and the High Tide of American Liberalism.* New York: Norton, 1995.

Sale, Kirkpatrick. *SDS.* New York: Random House, 1973.

Scherer, George A. *Ernest Atkins Wildman: A Biographical Sketch.* Dublin, Ind.: Prinit Press, 1984.

Schrecker, Ellen W. *No Ivory Tower: McCarthyism and the Universities.* New York: Oxford University Press, 1986.

Sellers, Charles G., Jr. *The Market Revolution: Jacksonian America, 1815–1846.* New York: Oxford University Press, 1991.

Sellman, James Clyde. "Visions of Community in Conflict: Richmond, Indiana, 1806–1890." Ph.D. diss., Harvard University, 1993.

Smith, Simeon O., comp. *Biography of William Martin Smith and History of Union Bible Seminary, Inc.* Westfield, Ind.: Union Bible Seminary, 1982.

Soderlund, Jean R. *Quakers & Slavery: A Divided Spirit.* Princeton: Princeton University Press, 1985.

Solomon, Barbara Miller. *In the Company of Educated Women: A History of Women and Higher Education in the United States.* New Haven: Yale University Press, 1986.

Sorenson, Dale Rich. "The Anticommunist Consensus in Indiana, 1945 to 1958." Ph.D. diss., Indiana University, 1980.

Stevens, Jay. *Storming Heaven: LSD and the American Dream.* New York: Harper and Row, 1988.

Stewart, W. A. Campbell. *Quakers and Education: As Seen in Their Schools in England.* London: Epworth, 1953.

Swift, David E. *Joseph John Gurney: Banker, Reformer, Quaker.* Middletown, Ct.: Wesleyan University Press, 1962.

Szasz, Ferenc Morton. *The Divided Mind of Protestant America, 1880–1930.* University: University of Alabama Press, 1982.

Thornbrough, Emma Lou. "Breaking Racial Barriers to Public Accommodations in Indiana, 1935 to 1963." *Indiana Magazine of History.* 83 (Dec. 1987), 320.

Thornburg, Opal. *Earlham: The Story of the College, 1847–1962.* Richmond, Ind.: Earlham College Press, 1963.

———. *Their Exits and Their Entrances: The Story of Richmond Civic Theater.* Richmond, Ind.: Graphic Press, 1959.

Valentine, Steve. "Amidst the Bloody Strife: Earlham College during the Civil War Era," *Indiana Military History Journal,* 2 (Jan. 1977), 9–11.

Veysey, Laurence R. *The Emergence of the American University.* Chicago: University of Chicago Press, 1965.

Watson, S. Arthur. *Penn College: A Product and a Producer.* Oskaloosa, Iowa: William Penn College, 1971.

Weber, Timothy P. *Living in the Shadow of the Second Coming: American Premillennialism, 1875–1925.* Chicago: University of Chicago Press, 1987.

Weeks, Stephen B. *Southern Quakers and Slavery: A Study in Institutional History.* Baltimore: Johns Hopkins University Press, 1896.

Weinstein, James. *The Corporate Ideal in the Liberal State, 1900–1918.* Boston: Beacon, 1968.

Wells, Tom. *The War Within: America's Battle over Vietnam.* Berkeley: University of California Press, 1994.

White, Ronald C., Jr., and C. Howard Hopkins. *The Social Gospel: Religion and Reform in Changing America.* Philadelphia: Temple University Press, 1976.

Wiebe, Robert. *The Search for Order, 1877–1920.* New York: Hill and Wang, 1967.

Wittner, Lawrence S. *Rebels against War: The American Peace Movement, 1941–1960.* New York: Columbia University Press, 1969.

Woodward, Walter C. *Timothy Nicholson: Master Quaker.* Richmond, Ind.: Nicholson, 1927.

Woody, Thomas. *Early Quaker Education in Pennsylvania.* New York: Teachers College, Columbia University, 1920.

Wuthnow, Robert. *The Restructuring of American Religion.* Princeton: Princeton University Press, 1988.

Wyatt-Brown, Bertram. *Southern Honor: Ethics and Behavior in the Old South.* New York: Oxford University Press, 1982.

Index

Abortion, 314
Academic Freedom, 115
Academies, 53; *see also* specific institutions
Ackerman, Carl, 100
Ackworth School, 7, 20
Acres, Sara Anne, 320, 344
ACT-UP, 317
Addington, Sarah, 97
Administrative Council, 298
Admissions Office, 239–40
Agricultural Science, 244
AIDS, 317, 320
Albertson, E. T., 163–65, 167
Albrecht, Etta, 169
Alexander, Howard, 196, 333
All-Friends Conference, 125
Allee, W. C., 149–50, 158, 168, 215
Allen, Edward J., 221, 227
Allen, Mildred, 130, 132
Alumni, 51–53, 71–72, 113–14
Alumni Office, 292
Amberg, Mathew K., 155–56
American Association of University Professors (AAUP), 115, 226–27
American Council of Christian Churches, 221
American Friend, 88–89, 103, 107, 125, 129
American Friends Service Committee

(AFSC), 126, 142, 157, 158, 170–71, 185–86, 201, 207, 217, 241–42, 263, 333, 337, 342
American Legion, 155, 173, 210–11, 213–15, 217–18
American Student Union (ASU), 156 58
Anderson, Henry L, 208–09
Anderson, Paul, 333
Anderson Monthly Meeting, 165
Anderson School of Theology, 341–42
Anglican Society, 97, 153, 270, 274
Anscombe, Francis, 121
Antioch College, 32, 241, 245, 247, 263
Apgar, Lawrence, 190
Aptheker, Herbert, 264
Art, 63
Associated Colleges of Indiana, 182–83
Association of American Colleges, 99, 115, 119
Association of Men Residents (AMR), 271, 276–77
Association of Women Residents (AWR), 271, 176–77
Atherton, Charles, 16
Athletics, 58–59, 102–03, 161–62, 167, 229, 270, 275

Bailey, Jackson, 238, 245–46, 248, 267, 310
Bailey, Moses, 282

Baily, Ezra, 14, 28
Baily, Gertrude, 63
Bain, James, 55
Baker, Jacob, 105
Bakker, Gerald, 301
Baldwin, Dewitt C., Jr., 295–96, 302, 331
Baldwin, Lemuel, 28
Bales, Eleazar, 14
Bales, Elizabeth, 14
Baltimore Yearly Meeting, 139
Banker, E. Stanley, 340–41
Barbour, Hugh, 196, 283, 333, 334
Barclay, Robert, 32, 128
Barr, Daisy Douglas, 126, 152
Barr, Tom, 126, 152
Barrett, Richard Warren, 52, 94, 139
Basketball, *see* Athletics
Bassett, Thomas D. S., 196, 198–99
Bastian, Edward, 196, 243, 264, 267, 288
Beane, Darrell, 238, 270
Beidler, Margaret Grant, 238
Beit Kehillah, 330
Beittel, A. D., 145, 150, 153–54
Benfey, Theodor, 243–44, 263, 269, 287, 333
Bennett, Douglas C., 346
Bentley, Norma, 219
Berg, Eric, 267
Berry, William E., 145–46, 168
Bethany Theological Seminary, 335
Bettle, Samuel, Jr., 19
Bevel, James, 257
Bible School Institute, 87–88, 109
Biblical Department, 36, 40, 64–66, 82, 90, 103–16, 121, 130–37, 145, 190–91
Biddle, William C., 198, 244
Biddlecum, Homer G., 167
Binford, Bevan, 96
Binford, Marian, 157–59, 217
Bing, Tony, 292–93, 325–26
Biology Department, 136, 304
Birdsall, William W., 356
Blackburn, Charles G., 161
Black Leadership Action Coalition (BLAC), 260–61, 311
Black Studies, 258–59, 312, 319
Blacks: first students, 46, 151; in 1920s, 152–54; and William C. Dennis, 174–76; and Tom Jones, 202–09; in 1960s, 255–62; since 1973, 311–13
Blake, Lincoln, 258, 260
Blitz, Rudolph, 169

Bloomingdale Academy, 18
Blue River Monthly Meeting, 11
Board of Trustees: early, 14, 21–22, 25–26, 28, 33; and athletics, 58; before 1900, 70–72; and Elbert Russell, 107, 110–11, 113–14; and Survey Committee, 143–44; and William C. Dennis, 150; and dancing, 162–63; and smoking, 164–65; and interracial dating, 176, 205; expansion,192–94, 281; and Dewitt Baldwin, 295–96; and Richard Wood, 297; and divestment, 312–13; and Woolpy case, 327–28; and Community Code, 329; proposals to change, 341–45
Bohl, Kirsten, 342
Bolling Frances Morgan, 235, 275
Bolling, Landrum R.: 225, 233, 289; background, 196–97, 235–37; and governance, 237–39; and admissions, 239–40, and fund-raising, 240–41, 301; and Eli Lilly, 241–43; and calendar, 244; and Japanese Studies, 245–46; and off-campus studies, 248–49; and library, 250; and blacks, 255–56, 258, 260; and peace activism, 263; and Vietnam War, 263, 267–69; and student life, 270–74; and School of Religion, 281–84; and Indiana Yearly Meeting, 278–81; and Phi Beta Kappa, 287; resignation, 294; and Gay People's Union, 316; and Middle East, 326; and Woolpy case, 327
Books, 19–20, 30, 40
Bookstore, 339–40
Booth, Wayne C., 195, 198, 224, 231, 237, 243–44, 249, 255
Bozell, Brent, 221
Bradley, John, 61
Brainwashing the High Schools, 224
Braithwaite, William C., 88, 112
Branson, John, 40
Brinton, Anna Cox, 139–43, 145
Brinton, Howard, 139–43, 145
Brock, David, 344–45
Brown, Albert J., 88, 129–30
Brown, E. Howard, 129–30, 133–34, 136, 165
Brown, Marianna, 50
Brown, Ola, 42
Brown, Thomas, 201
Bruner, Mary L. (Binford), 52
Bryn Mawr College, 112

Bubenzer, Tillman, 241
Buckley, William F., Jr., 221
Buffum, Mary Ann, 17
Bundy, John Elwood, 63
Bundy Hall, 93, 102, 113, 160, 303
Burke, Miriam, 334
Burton, Ernest, 87, 89, 131
Butler School of Religion, 282

Cadbury, Henry J., 121, 142
Calendar, 244, 304–05
Campus Village, *see* "Vetville"
Cannon, Joseph G., 94
Capehart, Homer, 219
Carlson, Ben, 238
Carman, Harry J., 193
Carnegie, Andrew, 93
Carpenter, Susan Mabie, 48
Carpenter, Walter T., 48, 59
Carpenter Hall, 137, 144
Carter, Elsa, 206
Carter, Wayne, 191
Casey, Edmund, 177
Cave of Adullam, 150, 154
Chandlee, Florence, 63
Chapel, 125–26, 199, 275
Charles, Arthur M., 92, 138–39, 142, 145, 169, 181
Charles, Carrie, 160
Charles, Mary Lane, 239, 247–48
Charles, Matthew, 33
Chase, Cleveland K., 92, 115
Chatfield, Charles, 195
Chemical Bond Approach, 254
Chickering, Arthur, 296
Civil War, 54–55
Civilian Public Service (CPS), 171, 179, 182, 195–96, 210, 212, 227
Clark, Alida, 46
Clark, Dougan, Jr.: 35, 48, 68, 74, 82; and holiness movement, 36–37, 39–41; and Biblical Department, 49, 64–66, 86; and ordinances, 77–79, 81
Clark, Len, 253, 293, 295–96, 329, 333
Clark, Septima, 257
Clark, William W., 201, 215, 226
Clausen, Christopher, 264
Clear Creek Monthly Meeting, 200, 338
Cleveland Bible Institute, 106, 11, 128, 191
Co-Op, 275
Coeducation, 12–13, 50–51; *see also* Women

Coffin, Charles F., 12, 37–38, 73, 360
Coffin, Elijah, 12, 13, 19, 70, 73
Coffin, J. Herschel, 99, 121–23, 131, 134, 136–37, 148
Coffin, Rhoda M., 37–38, 49
Collectivism on the Campus, 223–24
Committee for Constitutional Government, 222
"Committee of Ten," 130–38
Commons, 165
Communism, 217–27
Community, 231–32, 286–88, 323–24
Community Code, 323–24, 329–30, 332, 344
Community Dynamics Program, 190, 198, 244
Computers, 309
Comstock, Clara, 161–64, 175–76
Concerned Students for Communication, 265
Congress of Racial Equality (CORE), 204, 257
Conner Prairie, 242
Conscientious Objectors, *see* Peace Activism
Consensus Process, 227–28, 286–87, 331
Conservative Club, 263–64
Convocation, *see* Chapel
Cook, Horace P., 190–91
Cook, Ralph, 211
Cooper, Wilmer, 282–83, 285, 334–35
Cope, Harold, 196, 228, 237, 281
Cope, James, 196, 242, 333
Copeland, Albert L., 137, 165, 194
Coperthwaite, Bill, 293
Coppock, Homer J., 125
Coppock, Joseph D., 197–98
Cordell, Corky, 266
Cosand, Charles, 141, 150
Cosand, Joseph, 172
Council of Church Boards of Education, 99, 119
Cousins, William, 239, 258
Crumley-Effinger, Stephanie, 342
Crusade for Freedom, 219
Cullen, Countee, 153
Cunningham, Clarence, 152, 311
Cunningham, Grace, 206–07
Cunningham Cultural Center, 311
Curriculum, 18–19, 62–69, 98–99, 145–46, 198–99, 243–54, 304–10, 321
Curtis, Eric, 192, 206, 207, 237, 273

Damascus Academy, 53

Dancing, 162–63

Danforth Foundation, 238, 241, 254

Darr, William, 246

Davis, Charlotte, 50

Davis, Clarkson, 17, 37

Davis, Paul, 182

Davis, Ruby, 138, 197

Davis, Thomas J., 259, 312

"Day Dodgers," 112, 166, 202, 220, 239

"Dead Cat" Incident, 215–16

Dennis, David Worth, 41, 57, 68, 74, 99, 121, 148, 182

Dennis, Mattie, 50–51

Dennis, William C.: 118, 159, 180, 186, 189, 227, 243; background, 144–45; political views, 145, 149; and governance, 147–48; and curriculum, 148–49; and faculty, 149–50; and campus activism, 153–59; and student life, 162–67; as Quaker, 162; and World War II, 168–77; and Japanese-Americans, 172–76; and blacks, 153–54, 175–76, 202; retires, 177, 179; and Perry Kissick, 181; and Yuan Tien, 220

Depression Era, 154–55

Development Office, 292, 302

Dewey, John, 90

Dickinson, Anna, 50

Dickinson, Joseph, 76

Diskin, Jonathan, 298

Divestment, 312–13

Doan, Joseph, 14

Doan, Eliza, 14

Doan, Wilson S., 42

Doan, Martha, 50, 92, 102

Dormitories, 270–72

Doty, Wilfred, 206

Douglas, Cornelius, 14–15

Douglas, John Henry, 37

Douglas, Phebe, 14

Douglas, Robert W., 40

Draft Resistance, 210–18, 266–67, 324–25

Drinking, 273–74

Drug Use, 273–74; *see also* Drinking

Duling, Harold, 242

Dungeons and Dragons, 339

Dunn, Undine, 239

Earlham Action against Rape, 315

Earlham Anti-War Club, 157

Earlham College: *see specific topics, such as* Religious Life; Student Origins; Student Life; Faculty; Quaker Identity

Earlham Hall, 14, 28, 34, 75, 102, 182

Earlham Political Issues Committee (EPIC), 263

Earlham Post, 323

Earlham Press, 97, 101, 127, 160–61

Earlham School of Religion, 191, 277, 281–84, 325, 333–36, 341–42

Earlham Women's Liberation Group, 277

Earlham Word, 323

Earlhamite, 57, 97, 101

East Asian Studies, 310

Eastman, Max, 221

Edgerton, Steve, 216

Education: and Quakerism, 6–9

Education Program, 244

Edwards, David M.: 118, 139, 141–42, 152, 282; background, 119; theological views, 119, 123; and 1920 investigation, 131–37; and finances, 138; resignation, 143–44; and student life, 158–62; and Press Club, 159–62; and smoking, 162, 164

Edwards, Paul K., 154

Elkinton, Joseph, 112

Elliott, Errol T., 211, 282

Elmore, Joe E., 238, 257–58, 283–85, 293–94, 300–01, 313, 327–28, 334

Endowment, *see* Finances

Engleman, Ralph, 257

English Department, 304–06, 321

Enrollment, 17–18, 44, 177, 181, 209, 294, 299

Estes, Lewis A., 16, 20, 24

Evangelical Friend, 106, 109, 128

Evangelical Friends Alliance, 335–36

Evans, Edward D., 144, 154, 171

Evans, Joseph R., 73

Evans, Thomas, 13, 19, 73

Eves, Anna, 141, 154, 197

Evolution, 66–69, 123, 130–37

Faculty: early, 15–18, 32; from 1859 to 1895, 48–50, 69–70, 75–79; and Robert L. Kelly, 92; in 1920s, 139–44; and William C. Dennis, 147–50; and Tom Jones, 182, 195–99, 226–30; in 1960s; 238–39, 243–44, 286–87; since 1973, 300–01, 313–14, 333

Faculty Affairs Committee, 228
Fager, Chuck, 335
Fairmount Academy, 44, 87
Family Relations Program, 244
Farber, Evan, 250–51, 308–09
Farlow, Lilith, 202
Farlow, Ruthanna, 176
Farnum, Elizabeth H., 65
Fatherley, Robert E., 166–67
Federal Bureau of Investigation, 213
Fellers, Bonner, 172
Fellowship of Reconciliation, 201–02, 217
Feminism, *see* Women
Finances: 11, 13, 27–29, 71–73, 75, 93–
    94, 138, 143–44, 181–82, 240–43, 301,
    301–02
Fishback, William, 296
Five Year Reviews, 300–01
Five Years Meeting, 89, 104, 108–09, 111,
    121–22, 125–26, 128–29, 133, 140, 168,
    186, 210, 282–83, 335, 336–37, 342
Fletcher, John, 143
Flirtations, 345
Football, *see* Athletics
Ford Foundation, 241, 245, 247, 300, 303
Foreign Language in the Curriculum
    (FLIC), 301, 303, 309
Forensics, 59, 102
Forward Movement, 125
Fosdick, Harry Emerson, 137
Foulke, William Dudley, 95, 99
Fowler, James, 216
Fox, George, 3, 6–7
Frame, Esther, 37, 40, 88
Frame, Nathan, 37, 40
Friends Boarding School: founding, 9–14;
    and coeducation, 12–134, 21; financial
    problems, 11, 13, 27–29; building, 13–
    14; governance, 14; faculty, 14–17; cur-
    riculum, 18–20; religious life, 20–21;
    student life, 22–27; change to Earlham
    College, 32–34
Friends Collection, 341
Friends Committee on National Legisla-
    tion, 210
Friends General Conference (FGC), 284,
    333, 335, 336
Friends Reconstruction Unit, 126–27
Friends United Meeting, *see* Five Years
    Meeting
Friends University, 53, 106, 111–12

Frisch, Michael, 325
Fuerstenberger, Albert J., 130–31, 134–36
Fulbright Scholars, 303
Fulghum, Clarkson, 26
Fund for the Improvement of Post-Sec-
    ondary Education, 301
Fundamentalism, 105–10, 115–16, 127–
    39
Funston, Arthur, 169, 177, 198, 246
Furnas, Allen, 32
Furnas, Elizabeth, 200
Furnas, Paul J., 100, 142, 161, 171, 180,
    185, 200, 206, 228, 237
Furnas, Phebe, 50
Fuson, William, 196, 201, 207, 215, 228,
    231, 237, 240, 248, 253, 260, 281, 286,
    288, 333

G.I. Bill, 181, 209
Garner, Don, 345
Garner, Murvel, 141, 150, 156, 159, 171,
    176, 190, 195
Gay People's Union, *see* Lesbian, Bisex-
    ual and Gay People's Union
General Education Board, 93–94, 138
George School, 177
Gerber, Adolph, 49
Gibby, Leigh, 287
Giessler, Veronica, 206
Gillis, Steve, 325
Glee Club, 152
Gluys, Marmaduke, 114
Goddard, Mary Hough, 70
Goddard Auditorium, 303
Godsey, Lavona, 320
Goerns, Robert, 204–06
Gordon, J. Bennett, 94
Gottschalk, Thomas, 344
Governance, 75–79, 143–44, 226–32; *see
    also* Consensus Grading System, 252–
    53
Graham, Billy, 192
Grannell, Andrew, 335
Grant, E. D., 145
Graves, Richard, 212
Gray, Corine, 220–21
Great Lakes Colleges Association (GLCA),
    246–47, 301
Greenberg, Jack, 257
Gruening, Martha, 97
"Guarded Well By," 275

Guilford College, 53, 111; *see also* New
    Garden School
Gulf War, 325–26
Gummere, Richard, 119
Gurney, Joseph John, 11–12, 34

Hadley, Chalmers, 43
Hadley, David, 88, 111
Hadley, Freda, 173
Hadley, Hiram, 24
Hadley, Josephine M., 51
Hadley, Laurence, 92, 115, 158
Hadley, Milton, 173
Hagino, Misako, 246
Hamilton, C. Edgar, 182
Hampton, Sarah Ann, 32
Hanover College, 203
Harassment Policy, 321–22
Harned, Clyde, 214
Harold, Mary M., 129–30, 135, 137
Harper, William Rainey, 85
Harris, Del, 275
Hartford Seminary, 119–21, 282
Hartley, George N., 129–30, 194
Harvey, Cyrus W., 55
Harvey, Enos, 135
Haughton, William, 17
Haverford College, 32, 88–89, 111–12, 166,
    181, 230
Haworth, Lester C., 194, 205, 220
Heavilin, Charles, 343
Hell Day, 229
Henderson, Francis, 212
Henley, David E., 179, 201, 206, 207, 225,
    237
Henley, Mildred, 123, 135
Henry, Aaron, 257
Heresy Investigation, 127–39
Hershey, Lewis B., 171, 268
Hesperian Junto, 31
Hester, Elvira, 51
Heusel, Lorton, 191, 212, 214
Hewlett Foundation, 303
Hiatt, Lena, 173–74
Hicks, Elias, 5
Higher Criticism, *see* Modernism
Highlander School, 257
Hill, Miriam Jane, 25
Hinckle, Milo, 168
Hinshaw, Cecil, 208, 217, 219
Hoag, Huldah C., 16–17, 19
Hoag, Joseph, 16

Hobbs, Barnabas C.: 41, 49, 51, 55, 64, 75,
    90; background, 15–16; as superinten-
    dent, 16, 19; as president, 40, 48, 61, 71;
    as trustee, 73
Hobbs, Grimsley, 196, 246
Hobbs, Rebecca Tatum, 15, 73
Hobbs, William, 15
Hole, Allen D., Jr., 196–97, 206, 249
Hole, Allen D., Sr., 43, 114, 121, 126, 134,
    137, 142, 168, 194
Hole, Francis D., 176
Hole, Helen G., 197, 239, 259, 260, 286–
    87, 293, 333
Holloway, Imogene, 342
Hollowell, Amos K., 113, 119, 131
Holmes, Harry N., 92, 98–99
Holvik, Leonard, 196–97, 246
Home Economics, 244
Homecoming, 274
Homosexuality, 315–18, 342–43
Honor Code, 229–31
Hook, Sidney, 264
Hopkins, Elizabeth, 16, 25
Hoskins, Lewis, 248
Hoyt, Douglas, 216
Huff, Robert N., 214, 218
Hughes Medical Foundation, 303
Human Development and Social Rela-
    tions (HDSR), 307
Humanities Program, 198, 305–06, 314–
    15, 319, 331
Hunt, David, 29
Hunt, Edith J., 51
Hunt, John, 197
Hussey, Mary I., 51
Hyman, Harold, 238

Indiana University, 203
Indiana University Center, 197
Indiana University East, 239
Indiana Yearly Meeting: 111, 119, 124,
    128, 168, 241; formation, 3; and
    Hicksite Separation, 5–6; and Friends
    Boarding School founding, 9–14; and
    Boarding School finances, 13–14, 27–
    29; membership loss, 26–27; and reviv-
    als, 36; and Civil War, 54; and Biblical
    Institute, 65; and Board, 71–72; and
    Elbert Russell, 108–110, 115; and 1920
    investigation, 117, 127–39; and Walter
    Woodward, 122; and Clarence Pickett,
    143; and blacks, 151, 205; and Ku Klux

Klan, 152; and smoking, 165; and Tom Jones, 179, 183–95; and Clear Creek Meeting, 200; and draft resistance, 210–11; 214; and 1959–1960 controversy, 278–81; and 1991 commencement, 290–91; since 1973, 336–46

Indianapolis Recorder, 207

Industrial Workers of the World (IWW), 96–97

Inman, Lydia, 130

Institute for Education on Japan, 309–10

Institute for Quaker Studies, 333

Institute of Foreign Affairs, 148

International Programs Office, 247

International Studies, 318

Interracial Dating, 174–76, 204–08, 255–56

Ionian Society, 31, 57–58, 97, 270, 274

Iowa Yearly Meeting, 71, 119–21

Ives, Kenneth, 157–58

Jackson, Arizona, 40

Jacoby, Andrea, 253

Japan, 172

Japanese-American Students, 171–76

Japanese Studies, 245–46

Jay, Allen, 37–38, 41, 73, 87, 93–94, 106–07, 109, 112

Jay, Eli, 32–33, 48, 77, 90, 108

Jay, Mahalah Pearson, 32–33, 49–50, 90, 198

Jessup, Levi, 33

Jewish Students, 326, 331

Johansen, Robert, 296

Johnson, Benjamin, 90

Johnson, Caleb, 40

Johnson, Charles, 208

Johnson, Charles A., 237

Johnson, Ira C., 108, 129–30, 135

Johnson, James G., 279

Joint Committee of Indiana and Western Yearly Meetings, 129–38

Jones, Esther Balderston, 180

Jones, Rufus M., 88, 108–09, 112, 119, 125, 128, 130, 139, 141–42, 184, 186

Jones, Thomas E. ('Tom): 113, 121, 124, 142, 171, 178–79, 195, 235, 245, 250, 270, 273, 286; and race relations, 177; background, 179–80; and fund-raising, 181–82; and federal aid, 182–83; and Quakerism, 181, 183–95, 199, 200–01; and faculty, 195–98; and blacks, 202–

09; and draft resistance, 209–17; and Cold War, 217–26; and governance, 228–32; and students, 229–32; retirement, 235, 237; and foundations, 241; and School of Religion, 282–83

Jones, Tom (Class of 1938), 157–59

Jones, Wilfred V., 172

Jordan, Sybil, 257–58

Joseph Moore Museum, 69

Joyce Foundation, 303, 311

Julian, Percy, 208

Jurasek, Richard, 301

Kaifu, Chuzo, 172

Kane, C. F., 131, 134

Kanegis, Arthur, 266

Kauper, Paul G., 142

Kelly, Cecilia, 113

Kelly, Robert L.: 83, 99, 121, 141, 152; background, 90; and professionalism, 92, 99; and foundations, 93–94; and politics, 95; and students, 100–03, and Elbert Russell, 107, 109–15; and American Association of Colleges, 115; resignation, 118–19; and World War I, 126; and 1920 investigation, 133

Kelly, Thomas R., 121–22, 141, 143, 150, 154, 159, 172

Kendall, Enos, 26

Kennedy, James, 251

Kent State University, 268–69

Kenworthy, Leonard, 7, 169

Kenworthy, Murray S., 92, 113

Kenworthy, Truman C., 109–10, 129–32, 134, 136–37

King, Martin Luther, Jr., 257

Kirk, Jack, 191

Kirk, Russell, 265

Kirk, Thomas G., 251, 209

Kissick, Perry, 141, 149–50, 159, 181

Knight Foundation, 303, 310

Knollenberg, Bernhard, 28–29, 213

Kolp, Alan, 335

Korean War, 209, 218–19

Kraft, Milton, 246

Kresge Foundation, 241, 256

Ku Klux Klan, 151–52

Lacey, Paul, 238, 258–59, 265–66, 268, 275, 293, 295, 300–01, 313, 316, 327–28, 331–32

Lawson, James, 257

Lee, Edd, 202
Leeds, Rudolph G., 174, 182, 213–14, 220
Leland, Lawrence, 283, 296
Lesbian, Bisexual, and Gay People's Union (LBGPU), 293, 297, 316–17, 344
Lewis, Simba, 260
Libby, Frederick J., 142
Library, 19–20, 92–93, 250–51, 308–09
Lilly, Eli, 182, 189, 240–43, 289, 294, 302, 313
Lilly Endowment, 182, 241–42, 246, 282–83, 294, 302–03, 308
Lindley, Alfred H., 75
Lindley, Harlow, 92, 95, 112, 114
Lindley Hall, 69, 75, 138, 141
Literary League, 31
Literary societies, 30–31; *see also* specific groups
Little, Arthur, 196, 197, 209, 216, 219, 246, 332–33
Long, Florence, 92, 197, 239
Long, Frank, 130

McAllester, Robert, 206–08
McCarthy, Joseph R., 207, 223
McDowell, James, 196
McIntyre, Carl, 221
McNabb, Marilyn, 258
McQuinn, Pauline, 202
McTaggart, Alpheus, 49, 56, 74, 76
Maas, Melvin J., 215–16
Malone, Emma, 128
Malone, J. Walter, 85, 105–08, 128, 134
Marble, Samuel, 235
Markle, Millard S., 92, 121, 131, 134, 137, 141, 150, 159, 181, 190, 200
Martin, Ken, 261
Marts and Lundy, 182
Mask and Mantle, 152
Mather, Charles, 61
Mathews, Shailer, 87, 89, 131
Matthews, J. B., 221, 223
May Day, 267, 319–21
Mayer, Milton, 215, 217
Meerepol, Robert, 266
Meerson, Dan, 305
Mendenhall, Birk, 176
Mendenhall, William O., 97, 102, 113–15, 172, 179
Midwest Bisexual Lesbian and Gay College Conference, 317, 345
Miles, Caroline, 51, 98

Miles, Walter R., 94, 96
Mills, Amos, 26
Mills, Dorothy Wildman, 299
Mills, Elden H., 124–25, 145
Mills, Emily Wanzer, 64
Mills, Eugene S., 299
Mills, Gerald, 295, 299
Mills, Howard S., Jr., 216
Mills, Howard S., Sr., 194
Mills, Joseph John: 40, 41, 60, 64, 92; as president, 48, 73–74, 79, 81; and Elbert Russell, 82–83, 85; resignation, 90
Milner, Clyde, 141, 150
Minor, Anne, 277
Modernism, 86, 103–10, 118–39
Moore, Anna M., 51
Moore, Charles T., 129–30, 135–38
Moore, Frances, 258
Moore, George H., 129–30, 135
Moore, Joseph: 17, 19, 33, 37, 40–41, 48–49, 148; background, 66; teaches evolution, 66–69, 80, 123; and Museum, 69; as president, 72–74
Mooreland Friends Church, 339–40
Moorestown Friends School, 166
Morgan, Arthur, 235
Morgan, William B., 17, 19, 33, 41, 48–49, 51, 66, 76
Morris, Edna, 172
Morris, Homer L., 100, 141–43, 145, 148, 150, 158, 160, 172, 178, 181, 193, 205, 219, 222–23, 229
Morrison, Edwin, 115, 149
Morse, Kent, 133
Mote, Marcus, 63
Mott, Edward, 106, 109
Moulton, Richard, 87
Mullen, Thomas, 191, 238, 335
Multicultural Alliance, 319
Multiculturalism, 310–22
Mundt, Karl, 223
Murray, Augustus T., 58
Music, 25, 63–64
Muste, A. J., 217

Napier, R. Aaron, 129, 132–34
National Alumni Movement for Earlham Divestment (NAMED), 313
National Association for the Advancement of Colored People (NAACP), 204, 207, 256
National Defense Education Act, 263

National Endowment for the Humanities (NEH), 241, 253–54, 301, 303, 309
National Student Association, 155–58
New England Yearly Meeting, 8–9, 139
New Garden Quarterly Meeting, 279
New Garden School, 9; *see also* Guilford College
New Student Week, 274
New York Yearly Meeting, 139, 167
Newby, Richard P., 339
Newby, Sophia, 61
Newlin, Thomas, 88
Nicholson, S. Edgar, 96, 122–24, 129–38
Nicholson, Timothy, 37, 39, 70, 75–76, 79, 107, 109–10, 136
Nicholson, Vincent, 142
Nine Partners School, 9
Noble, Elaine, 318
Non-Western Studies, 318
North Carolina Yearly Meeting, 17
North Central Association, 99
Noyd, Dale, 245, 306
Nursing Program, 198, 202, 244

Oakwood School, 166, 176–77
Oberlin College, 12, 32
Off-Campus Study, 247–49, 309
Ohio Yearly Meeting, 17, 71–72, 141
Opinion Board, 231
Osborn, Charles, 5
Owen, John, 238

Pacific College, 53, 111
Painter, Levinus K., 121
Palestinians, 326
Palladium-Item, 173–74, 213, 215, 225–26, 264, 268
Parker, Ida T., 129–30
Parry, Mordecai, 75
Parry Hall, 75
Peace Activism, 55, 126–27, 142, 155–58, 169–70, 209–18, 262–69, 324–25
Peace and Conflict Studies (PACS), 306–07, 324
Peace and Global Studies (PAGS), *see* Peace and Conflict Studies
Peace Fellowship, 169, 174, 201
Peace Studies Association, 307
Peace with Justice Week, 325
Peacemakers, 211
Pearson, Calvin W., 49, 56, 74, 76
Pearson, Morton C., 94, 109

Pearson, William L., 68
Peaslee, Dorothy Quimby, 194, 247
Penhale, Sara, 322, 327–28
Penn, William, 7
Penney, Norman, 112
Pennington, John, 78
Pennington, Levi T., 104
Pepper, Rollin, 214
Petry, Loren C., 166
Phi Beta Kappa, 287
Philadelphia Yearly Meeting, 8, 139
Philosophy Department, 254
Phoenix Society, 31, 57, 97, 270, 274
Phoenixian, 57
Pick, Martha, 197
Pickett, Clarence, 119, 140, 142–43, 145–47, 152–54, 160, 168
Pinkham, William P., 41, 73–74, 106, 109
Pitts, Lois, 130
Plainfield Academy, 44, 87
Plainness, 23–24, 54–56
Politics, 95, 155–56, 262–69
Portland Quarterly Meeting, 46, 128, 129, 137, 165
Postle, Arthur, 197
Postle, Kathleen, 197
Precedents, 159–60, 229, 274
Preparatory Department, 44–46, 62–63, 82
Press Club, 97, 101, 160–61
Prism, 264
Private Academic Library Network of Indiana (PALNI), 308
Professional Development Fund, 300
Program in Integral Education (PIE), 241, 253–54
Program II, 252
Progressive Movement, 94–99
Prohibition, 95–96
Providence School, 8–9
Provost Marshal Unit, 170–171
Pulliam, Eugene S., 218
Punshon, John, 333
Purdue University, 203
Purdy, Alexander C., 117, 119–21, 123, 130–37, 138, 140, 142, 143, 145–47, 168, 186, 194, 238, 279, 282–83
Purdy, Ellison R., 121
Pyle, H. Randolph, 145
Pyle, William L., 73

Quaker Hill, 173

Quaker Identity, 18–27, 40–43, 45, 55–56, 75–79, 110–13, 115–16, 139–50, 183–95, 199–202, 277–89, 322–46

Quaker Quill, 161

Quakers, See Society of Friends

Raisin Valley Academy, 53

Ramallah School, 326

Reading Program, 251–52

Reagan, Chester, 166

Reagan, William J., 166, 205

Realignment, 338, 341

Reece, J. R., 344

Rees, Paul S., 192

Reeve, Charles A., 165, 193

Reid Hospital, 198, 202

Religion Department, *see* Biblical Department

Religious Life, 20–21, 39–43, 107–08, 112–13, 115–16, 125–26, 33, 185–86, 199–202, 284–86, 330–31

Reller, Jean, 343–44

Richards, Howard, 306

Richardson, Henry, 154

Richmond, Ind., settlement, 1; social change in, 29–30; relations with Earlham, 20, 61, 114; and World War I, 126; and Japanese-Americans, 173–74; and blacks, 201, 203–05, 208, 256; and draft resistance, 208; and high school sit-in, 261–62; and Vietnam War, 266–69; and drugs, 274

Richmond Declaration of Faith, 128, 132–33, 137

Rife, Merle, 145

Robbins, Earl, 214

Rockefeller, John D., 94

Rockefeller Foundation, 93

Rogers, Mary H., 40

Ronald, Hugh, 237, 316

Root, E. Merrill, 141–42, 150, 155, 159, 169, 221–25

Rosenberger, Absalom, 73, 124

Ross, M. O., 145

Ross, Steve, 216

Rowntree, John Wilhelm, 87–88

Runyan Center, 287

Russell, Elbert: 43, 97–98, 121, 123, 125, 128, 130, 138–39, 143, 152, 168, 186, 194, 221, 279, 282; appointed Bible professor, 82–83; background, 82–85; becomes modernist, 85–87; Quaker activities, 87–89; opposition to, 89; at University of Chicago, 89; returns to Earlham, 89–90; and Social Gospel, 96–97; as modernist, 103–10; popularity, 107–08; at Five Years Meeting, 108–09; and Robert L. Kelly, 110–15; resignation, 113; after Earlham 114–15

Russell, Lieuetta, 88, 113

Russell, Mary, 26

Russell, William, 83

Rustin, Bayard, 208, 216–17

Saeger, Armin, 212

Sand Creek Academy, 45

Sanders, Amy, 56

Sanders, Edwin, 157–58

Sargasso, 323

Sawyer, George, 259, 261

Sayers, William J., 129, 135

Scherer, George, 190, 214

Senior Year Studies, 309

Sexuality, 272, 326–30; *see also* Homosexuality

Shaffer, Alice, 169

Shaffer, Bruce, 266

Shipley, Murray, 37

Shockley, Madison, 206

Shore, Philip, 246, 250

Shrock, Alice, 315

Shrock, Randall, 315

Silbiger, Norbert, 169

Siler, Bruce, 167

Siler, Elwood C, 40

Simkin, William E., 166–67

Simmons, Gertrude, *see* Zitkala-Sa

Simon, Steve, 212–14

Smiley, Sarah F., 21

Smith, Courtney, 237

Smith, Horace, 341–42, 344

Smith, Richard K., 298

Smith, William M., 128, 134, 137

Smoking, 163–65

Social Gospel, 96–97

Social Science Division, 198

Socialism, 155–58

Society for Religion in Higher Education, 238

Society of Friends: migration west, 1–2; and slavery, 2; Discipline and worship, 3–5; and Hicksite Separation, 5–6, 10; reformation of, 8; and Joseph John Gurney, 11–12; and social change,

26–27; and Renewal Movement, 35–37; and revivalism, 38–39; and Modernism, 103–10; and Fundamentalist controversy, 105–10, 127–39; and blacks, 151; and draft resistance, 210–11; and recent conflicts, 336–37
Soil Science, 190
Solomon Amendment, 325
South Africa, *see* Divestment
Southard, Robert, 305
Southland College, 46, 151
Speech Department, 244
Spiceland Academy, 44, 87
Spring Grove, Ind., 173
Staebler, Warren, 196, 207, 231, 247, 248, 261, 286, 333
Stanley Hall, 302
Steeples, Douglas, 305
Stephenson, William, 196, 243, 269, 276, 290
Stevens, Moses C., 17, 73
Stevenson, John, 257
Stone, Lucy, 51
Stout Meetinghouse, 199–200
Stratton, Wilmer, 238
Strong, Laurence, 196, 228, 243, 254, 264
Student Development Office, 292–93, 315
Student Government, 102; *see also* Student Senate
Student League for Industrial Democracy (SLID), 155–56, 158
Student Life, 22–27, 54–62, 97–98, 100–03, 159–68, 229–31, 269–77
Student Nonviolent Coordinating Committee (SNCC), 257
Student Origins, 17–18, 44–46, 166–67, 239–40, 299, 333, 338
Student Senate, 230, 255, 270, 286; *see also* Student Government
Student Peace Volunteers, *see* Peace Volunteers
Students for a Democratic Society (SDS), 258, 263, 265–66
Students for Choice, 314
Student Strike against War, 158
Swarthmore College, 111, 166, 181
Sweitzer, John, 196, 208, 228

Tallack, William, 21, 28–29
Tanaka, Henry, 174
Taylor, Osborn, 46, 151
Teaching Consultant, 301

Teetor, Ralph, 182, 193, 218
Telfair, David, 196
Test, Zaccheus, 17, 33–34, 66, 76–77
Thomas, Auretta, 197
Thomas, Lydia, 26
Thomas, Norman, 155, 157
Thomas, Percy, 130
Thomas, Wilbur K., 142
Thompson, Gordon, 288, 296, 305
Thornburg, Opal, 19, 31, 187, 227
Thorp, James, 196
Tokyo Friends School, 172
TIAA-CREF, 226
Tien, Hsin-Yuan, 219–21
Titleman, Pete, 257
Tougaloo College, 257
Townsend Center, 201, 208
Treber, Harry, 343–44
Trueblood, D. Elton: 172, 179, 185, 194, 196, 200, 215, 235, 241, 267, 279, 281, 286, 328, 334; considered for president, 179; background, 186–87; writings, 187–88; and US Information Agency, 188; and chapel, 188–89; as campus minister, 199; and communism, 217, 221; and Honor Code, 230; and community, 231–32; and School of Religion, 282–83
Trueblood, Edwin P., 48, 58–59
Trueblood, William N., 74, 95
Trueblood Fieldhouse, 303
Turner, James, 175

Ubbelohde, Robert, 292
Union Bible Seminary, 128
Union High School, 45
United Nations, 218–19 "Unofficial Committee," 342–44
Unthank, James B., 63
Updegraff, David B., 37–38, 40, 65, 68, 77
Upward Bound, 258
Urban Studies, 259
Uyesugi, Edward, 176

Van Wert Quarterly Meeting, 40, 105, 279, 340
Vermilion Grove Academy, 44, 87
Vernon, Sadie, 290
Veterans, 209–10
"Vetville," 209
Vietnam War, 262–69
von Jagemann, Hans, 74

Wabash College, 203
Wallace, George, 257
Wallace, Henry A., 227
Wallin, Florence, 294
Wallin, Franklin: 302; background 294; as president, 294–95; and faculty, 300; and Quaker identity, 323, 331–33; and School of Religion, 334; and Indiana Yearly Meeting, 339–40
Walnut Ridge Quarterly Meeting, 165
Warren, Clifton, 303
Washington, Booker T., 151–52
Watkins, Elizabeth Ann, 26
Weaver, Gwen, 258
Webster, Ind., 190
Weiser, Andy, 252
Wells, Herman B., 174
Welty, Carl J., 142–43
West Richmond Meeting, 111, 122, 124, 278, 338
Western Yearly Meeting: 88, 90, 125, 128, 141, 201, 241; and Biblical Institute, 65; and 1881 charter, 69–73; and Elbert Russell, 109, 115; and 1920 investigation, 127–39; and dancing, 163; and smoking, 165; and World War II, 170; and Japanese-Americans, 174; and Tom Jones, 179, 183–95, 205; in 1960s, 279–81; since 1973, 336–39, 345–46
Westtown School, 9, 166–67, 177
White, Aaron, 20
White, Edwin, 216
White, Francis T., 28, 93
White, Margaret, 20
White, Mordecai Morris, 25–26, 70, 93
White, Thomas R., 94
Whitely, Paul, 126
Whitewater Monthly Meeting, 5, 10, 20, 79, 111
Whitewater Quarterly Meeting, 10–11
Whittier College, 53, 111
"Why I Chose a Small College," 187
Wilberforce University, 153–54
Wilderness Program, 249
Wildman, Ernest A., 99, 121, 123, 141, 143, 148–50, 159, 171, 181, 195, 201, 214, 252, 299
William Penn College, 53, 106, 111–12, 119, 145, 208, 219
Wilmington College, 53, 111–12
Wilson, Edward G., 239, 281, 283–84, 302–03, 328

Winder, Esther, 158
Wolfe, J. Brandt, 139–30, 135
Women: in Boarding School, 21; as faculty, 49–50, 197; as students, 50–51; in Progressive Era, 97–98; and Press Club, 160–61; and changes in 1960s, 271, 275–77; since 1973, 313–15
Women's Center, 277, 313–14
Women's Studies, 307–08, 313
Wood, Eleanor, 59
Wood, Judy, 298
Wood, Richard J.: 246, 253, 290, 322; named president, 297; presidency, 297–99; and fund-raising, 302–03; and calendar, 304–05; multiculturalism, 310–22; and sexual issues, 329; and Quaker identity, 330–31, 333; and Indiana Yearly Meeting, 341–46; and homosexuality, 342–43
Wood, S. Adelbert, 129, 132, 135–37
Woodard, Edward, 111
Woodard, Isaac E., 167–68, 173, 189, 194
Woodard, Leander, 111
Woodard, Luke, 37, 40, 106–07, 194
Woodard, Thomas R., 130, 132, 135
Woodman, Charles M., 122, 125, 134–35, 138, 142, 158, 191, 202, 282
Woodward, Walter C., 92, 114–15, 122, 124–25, 129, 136, 138, 142, 144, 150, 163
Woolpy, Jerry, 253, 269, 317, 326–28
World War I, 126–27
World War II, 168–77
Wright, Harry N., 141, 144–45, 150
Wright, Marian, 257
Wright, Morris P., 42, 52
Wriston, Henry M., 147
Wynn, G. Richard, 295, 335

YMCA, 41, 43, 80, 97, 112–13, 125
YWCA, 41, 43, 97, 112–13
Yates, Edward, 246
Yokefellow, 189, 241
Young, Dwight, 194
Young Friends Movement, 113, 185
Yurts, 293

Zimmer, Tim, 267
Zimmerman, William W., 95
Zitkala-Sa, 47–48

THOMAS D. HAMM is College Archivist and Associate Professor of History at Earlham College, Richmond, Indiana. He is the author of *The Transformation of American Quakerism: Orthodox Friends, 1800–1907* and *God's Government Begun: The Society for Universal Inquiry and Reform, 1842–1846,* and numerous articles on Quaker History.